PENGUIN CLASSICS

WALT WHITMAN: THE COMPLETE POEMS

WALT WHITMAN, once referred to by D. H. Lawrence as the 'greatest modern poet', and 'the greatest of the Americans', was born on 31 May 1819 in West Hills, Long Island, New York, and was brought up in Brooklyn, the son of a farmer turned carpenter. At the age of fifteen he was independent of his family and working as a journalist and journey-man printer. He taught for a short time and in 1838 founded his own newspaper. He became editor of the *Brooklyn Daily Eagle* in 1846. Herman Melville once said that a whaling ship served as his Harvard College; Whitman's college was the city of Brooklyn and the island of Manhattan. He loved the opera, was a frequent visitor to galleries, and an avid reader. By the time he was thirty-five he thought of himself more and more as a poet and early in July 1855 he published *Leaves of Grass*, probably setting some of the type himself. It contained twelve un-titled poems, a preface and a now famous portrait of the unnamed author in a workman's shirt. Although some critics treated the volume as a joke and others were outraged by its bold language and themes, the book attracted the attention of some of the finest literary intelligences. Ralph Waldo Emerson greeted him 'at the beginning of a great career', and told him that he found 'incomparable things said incomparably well'.

Whitman added to, reshuffled and dropped poems in *Leaves of Grass* all his life. The great odes *Out of the Cradle Endlessly Rocking* and *As I Ebb'd with the Ocean of Life* appeared in 1860; the great poems of the Civil War – the collection called *Drum-Taps* and *When Lilacs Last in the Dooryard Bloom'd* – were published as annexes in 1867. The tenth edition, including posthumous poems, was published in Boston in 1897, five years after Whitman's death in Camden, New Jersey, on 26 March 1892. Whitman had purchased a house on Mickle Street eight years before, and it was here that he received the world's visitors.

Francis Murphy is Professor of English Emeritus at Smith College, Northampton, Massachusetts, U.S.A.

WALT WHITMAN

The Complete Poems

Edited with an Introduction and Notes by
FRANCIS MURPHY

PENGUIN BOOKS

PENGUIN BOOKS

Published by the Penguin Group
Penguin Books Ltd, 80 Strand, London WC2R ORL, England
Penguin Group (USA) Inc., 375 Hudson Street, New York, New York 10014, USA
Penguin Books Australia Ltd, 250 Camberwell Road, Camberwell, Victoria 3124, Australia
Penguin Books Canada Ltd, 10 Alcorn Avenue, Toronto, Ontario, Canada M4V 3B2
Penguin Books India (P) Ltd, 11 Community Centre, Panchsheel Park, New Delhi – 110 017, India
Penguin Books (NZ) Ltd, cnr Airborne and Rosedale Roads, Albany, Auckland, New Zealand
Penguin Books (South Africa) (Pty) Ltd, 24 Sturdee Avenue, Rosebank 2196, South Africa

Penguin Books Ltd, Registered Offices: 80 Strand, London WC2R ORL, England

www.penguin.com

First published in Penguin Education 1975
Reprinted in Penguin Books 1977
Reprinted in Penguin Classics 1986
Reprinted with revised Further Reading 1996
Reprinted with new Introduction
and Appendix 6 2004
12

Introduction copyright © Francis Murphy, 2004

Printed in England by Clays Ltd, St Ives plc
Set in Monotype Ehrhardt

ISBN-13: 978-0-140-42451-5

www.greenpenguin.co.uk

Penguin Books is committed to a sustainable future
for our business, our readers and our planet.
The book in your hands is made from paper
certified by the Forest Stewardship Council.

Contents

Drum-Taps

Autumn Rivulets

First Annex: Sands At Seventy

Appendix 2

Poems Excluded from Leaves of Grass

Appendix 3

Early Poems

Acknowledgements

I would be remiss if I did not thank Christopher Ricks once again for all his original editorial advice and Laura Barber of Penguin Classics for her continuing interest in this volume.

Table of Dates

1819   Born on 31 May at West Hills, Long Island.

1823   Whitman family moves to Brooklyn.

1825–30 Attends the public schools.

1830–34 Learns the printing trade.

1835   Works as a printer in New York.

1836–8 In the summer of 1836 Whitman begins teaching at
        East Norwich, Long Island; by the year 1838 he had
        taught at Hempstead, Babylon, Long Swamp and
        Smithtown.

1838–9 Edits the weekly *Long-Islander* in Huntington.

1840–41 Works for Van Buren in his presidential campaign;
        then returns to teaching.

1841   In May, returns to New York to work as a printer.

1842–4 Edits a daily newspaper, the *Aurora*; edits the *Evening
        Tatler*.

1845–6 Returns to Brooklyn and writes for the *Long Island
        Star*.

1846–8 Edits the *Brooklyn Daily Eagle*.

1848   In February, Whitman goes with his brother Jeff to
        New Orleans where he works on the *Crescent*; he
        leaves New Orleans on 27 May and returns via the
        Mississippi and the Great Lakes.

1848–9 Edits the *Brooklyn Freeman*.

1850–54 Operates a printing office and stationery store and
        speculates in the building trade.

1855   Early in July publishes the first edition of *Leaves of
        Grass*, printed by Rome Brothers in Brooklyn. No
        publisher's name, no author's name. It includes a
        portrait of Whitman in workman's shirt. There are
        twelve untitled poems and a preface. The typogra-
        phy is the most unorthodox of all the editions.
        Whitman's father dies 11 July.

xxiii TABLE OF DATES

Employed as a clerk in the Department of the
Interior; meets Peter Doyle; witnesses Lincoln's
second inauguration. In April, Lincoln is assassi-
nated. In May, *Drum-Taps* is published. Fired by
Secretary James Harlan who thought *Leaves of Grass*
indecent; re-employed in the Attorney General's
office. In the autumn *Sequel to Drum-Taps* is
published, including *When Lilacs Last in the
Dooryard Bloom'd*. These were added to the 1867
edition as annexes but in 1870–71 were incorporated
in the main body of *Leaves of Grass*. *Drum-Taps*
contains fifty-three new poems, dealing with the
outbreak of the Civil War and Whitman's experi-
ences in the army hospitals.

1866 William D. O'Connor's *The Good Gray Poet* appears.

1867 The fourth edition of *Leaves of Grass* is published.
Exclusive of the annexes described above, this edition
contains eight new poems. The edition is important
primarily for its extensive revisions, deletions and
rearrangements.

1868 William Michael Rossetti's selection of *Poems by Walt
Whitman* is published in London.

1870–71 The fifth edition of *Leaves of Grass* appears. A second
issue includes *Passage to India* and seventy-one other
poems, some new. *Democratic Vistas* published.

1872 Travels to Hanover, New Hampshire, for the
Dartmouth commencement. Reads *As a Strong Bird
on Pinions Free* (*Thou Mother with Thy Equal Brood*),
later published with a Preface.

1873 Partially paralysed on 23 January; Whitman's mother
dies on 23 May; stays with his brother George in
Camden, New Jersey.

1876 The sixth edition of *Leaves of Grass* appears, a two-
volume centennial edition, one volume a reprint of
the fifth edition, the other a collection (entitled *Two
Rivulets*) of prose and poetry. *Two Rivulets* contains a
Preface Whitman said was for 'all my writings'.

leaving the book complete as I left it, consecutive to
the point I left off, marking always an unmistakable,
deep down, unobliteratable division line. In the long
run the world will do as it pleases with the book. I
am determined to have the world know what I was
pleased to do.' Whitman dies on 26 March 1892 and
is buried in Harleigh Cemetery, Camden, New Jersey.
Complete Prose Works published.

1897   The tenth edition of *Leaves of Grass* is published in
Boston with the addition of *Old Age Echoes*, posthum-
ous poems.

Introduction

When it came to his poetry, the author of *Spontaneous Me* rarely did anything without forethought. And so it was that close to 4 July 1855 this most American of American poets published his *Leaves of Grass*. Charles Eliot Norton, one of Harvard's most distinguished figures, bought a copy for himself and one for the poet James Russell Lowell, mostly, Norton said, as a literary curiosity, because, as he told Lowell in a letter dated 23 September 1855, the 'external appearance of it, the covers, the portrait, the print [i.e. the typography]' are 'as odd as the inside'.[1] The cover was green and gold. Each letter in the title looked like a small growing thing, sending its roots into the ground. No author's name appeared either on the cover or the title page, but a notice of copyright appeared inside. Opposite the title page there was a handsome engraving based on a portrait of Whitman. The costume is as familiar to us as a Ralph Lauren ad, but this is no weekend carpenter, this man looks as if he could actually build something. His bearded, thirty-something face is haloed by a wide-brimmed hat placed at a rakish angle; his right hand is on his hip, his left in his pocket. He wears a cotton work shirt open at the throat and his flannel undershirt is plain to see. The look on his face is hard to define, he seems relaxed and worldly-wise, not easily fooled. In this first edition Whitman included twelve poems, all untitled. Whitman set some of the type himself and he let his lines breathe with generous ellipses (we reprint in Appendix 4 the 1855 version of the poem which came to be called *Song of Myself*). Whitman was fully aware of the boldness of his volume. He wanted to dramatize the arrival of a new voice in American poetry. His 'Preface' (reprinted here in Appendix 5) assured his reader that the old forms were dead and a vital poetry was emerging. He could confidently declare that 'the proof of a poet is that his country absorbs him as affectionately as he has absorbed it'. Whitman added to, subtracted and reshuffled the poems in his *Leaves* all his working days. When he died the poems numbered more than four hundred and his name was a household word, even if he was not read in the best households. 'There are some superbly graphic descriptions,' Norton told Lowell, 'great stretches of imagination – and then passages of intolerable coarseness.' Norton hoped that no woman would read the book, and added that it was not a volume one could leave around the house for 'chance readers'.[2] Whitman clearly had his work cut out for him before he would receive the affection of all his countrymen.

Before Whitman found his true vocation he had spent a great part of his life in the world of newspapers and he was quite savvy about ways to promote a book. He did two bold things: he published reviews of his own book anonymously, and he sent copies of his *Leaves* to some of America's most notable writers. It is part of the Whitman mythology that the Quaker poet John Greenleaf Whittier threw his copy into the fire, but the letter of appreciation he received from Ralph Waldo Emerson is a remarkably generous fact:

. . . I greet you at the beginning of a great career, which yet must have had a long foreground somewhere, for such a start . . . I did not know until I, last night, saw the book advertised in a newspaper, that I could trust the name as real and available for a post-office, and have felt much like striking my tasks and visiting New York to pay you my respects.[3]

In inquiring about Whitman's past and wondering if 'Walt Whitman' was real or a fiction, Emerson raised two questions which have engaged generations of Whitman's readers. Whitman is one of those rare figures whose historical self and fictive self became inseparable. Although Whitman suffered considerable abuse from his critics, he exaggerated in later years the negative response to the first edition. Emerson did indeed come to Brooklyn, and so did Henry David Thoreau and the Concord educator Bronson Alcott. Rather heady visitors to knock on the door of a carpenter whose formal education ended when he was eleven years old.

Whitman said that two things served as a catalyst for his *Leaves*.

The first was hearing and reading Emerson – Whitman was present in Manhattan for the essayist and poet's debut – and the second was Italian opera. Whitman instructed his biographer John Burroughs to be certain to include these words: 'It has already been told how, during the gestation of the poems, the author was saturated for years with the rendering, by the best vocalists and performers, of the best operas and oratorios.'[4] The difference between Whitman as a mere maker of verses and a true performer is dramatically apparent if we look at an early poem like *Our Future Lot* (all of Whitman's early poems are included in Appendix 3) and the opening few lines of *Song of Myself*. Everything about *Our Future Lot* is thoroughly predictable, from the shape and content of the poem's argument, to its hymn metre and rhyme scheme. The language is so traditional that it is hard to identify the century in which it was written.

> Mortal! And can thy swelling soul
>   Live with the thought that all its life
> Is centered in this earthy cage
>   Of care, and tears, and strife?
>
> Not so; that sorrowing heart of thine
>   Ere long will find a house of rest;
> Thy form, re-purified, shall rise,
>   In robes of beauty drest.

In his 1855 *Leaves* Whitman does more than abandon rhyme and conventional verse forms. We hear immediately a confident voice speaking to us as an equal, not as a preacher:

> I celebrate myself,
> And what I assume you shall assume,
> For every atom belonging to me as good belongs to you.
>
> I loafe and invite my soul,
> I lean and loafe at my ease . . . . observing a spear of
>   summer grass.

The mark of true genius in the arts is an immediately recognizable style. No one could mistake these lines for any poet other than Whitman. This is a poetry which takes its pleasure in sentence shapes, in balance and repetition rather than repeated metrical units. It is a music at once new and very old, familiar to us from the Psalms. In one sense *Song of Myself* is a conventional version of pastoral ('I will go to the bank by the wood and become undisguised and naked'), but its argument is highly unorthodox as it sets out to revise the traditional Christian hierarchy of the body and the soul (the subject of *Our Future Lot*) and deny the doctrine of original sin:

> Clear and sweet is my soul. . . . and clear and sweet is all that
>   is not my soul.

> Lack one lacks both. . . . and the unseen is proved by the seen,
> Till that becomes unseen and receives proof in its turn.

Readers of Emerson will find themselves on familiar ground in reading *Song of Myself*. The notion that we derive our abstractions from the observation of concrete particulars is central to Emerson's thought, and pastoral – 'In the wilderness, I find something more dear and connate [i.e. related] than in streets or villages'[5] – is basic to Emerson's design. No reader of Emerson, however, would ever confuse one of his lectures with a Whitman poem. Whitman's poetry is deeply sensual and erotic; human sexuality made Emerson uncomfortable. In the 1855 edition Emerson would have come across this famous passage in which the soul and the body are engaged in love-making:

> I mind how we lay in June, such a transparent summer
>   morning;
> You settled your head athwart my hips and gently turned over
>   upon me,
> And parted the shirt from my bosom-bone, and plunged your
>   tongue to my barestript heart,
> And reached till you felt my beard, and reached till you held my
>   feet.

> Swiftly arose and spread around me the peace and joy and knowl-
>   edge that pass all the art and argument of the earth;

I suspect that like most of his generation Emerson either didn't
look too closely at what he was reading or preferred to idealize this
passage. It wasn't until Whitman's gay critics began to write about
him that the act of fellatio which these lines portray was named.
We have come a long way from *Our Future Lot*, watching Whitman
subvert traditional religious language ('The peace of God which
passeth all understanding'[6]) and the conversion experience for a
personal and political vision.

When Henry Thoreau visited Whitman in 1856 he told
Harrison Blake that he 'did not get far in conversation with him'
because he told Whitman that, personally, he 'did not think much
of America, or of politics', and that this confession 'may well
have been somewhat of a damper to him'.[7] Whitman was high
on the ideals of the republic, and he inherited his enthusiasm
from his father, who named three of his eight children for his
American heroes: George Washington, Thomas Jefferson and
Andrew Jackson. At the heart of Whitman's egalitarian vision was
a world in which men and women were equal and, more daringly,
where men would share and, fearlessly accept, an affectional bond
between them. When Whitman met Emerson in 1860 the older
writer tried to dissuade him from publishing his poems about
procreation, but Whitman dug his heels in and refused. In the
third edition of *Leaves* in 1860 he included the poems now called
Children of Adam and the *Calamus* poems. Professor Betsy Erkkila
tells us that Whitman 'was the first poet to provoke among his
unsympathetic readers the deepest fear of democracy in America;
namely, that in its purest form democracy would lead to a blur-
ring of sexual bounds and thus to the breakdown of a social and
bourgeois economy grounded in the management of the body and
the polarization of the male and female spheres'.[8] Although
Whitman argues that he was not undermining the republic, he
was certainly rocking the foundations of power, because power
fades when repression retires. In 'I Hear It Was Charged against
Me' he writes:

> I hear it was charged against me that I sought to
>   destroy institutions,
> But really, I am neither for nor against institutions . . .
> Only I will establish in Manhattan and in every city of
>   these States inland and seaboard . . .
> Without edifices or rules or trustees or any argument,
> The institution of the dear love of comrades.

No more celebratory letters from Concord followed.

The ideal way to study Whitman might be in an edition which laid out the poems in their order of composition, but Whitman ruled that out and made private moments in his *Leaves* difficult to connect. (Poems Whitman excluded from his *Leaves* are here reprinted in Appendix 2 and our notes track the history of each poem as it takes its place in the final 1891–1892 edition). Emerson was right to ask if the Walt Whitman of 1855 was a fiction – most of us have never met a 'kosmos' – but it is hard not to believe that some of the poems of the third edition of 1860 are partly autobiographical. The prophetic note is gone, along with the psalm-like music; the 'you' is not some ardently pursued reader, and the 'me' is no longer a figure floating free in space, but Whitman's inner self. There were earlier moments in Whitman – I'm thinking of *Crossing Brooklyn Ferry* – where the poet confesses that he, too, has 'knitted the old knot of contrariety, /Blabb'd, blush'd, resented, lied, stole, grudg'd', but the poet too easily absolves both the reader and himself, moving on to what cannot be examined. What are we to make of the extraordinary poem *A Hand-Mirror*, with Emerson's 'I greet you at the beginning of a great career' ringing in our ears:

> Hold it up sternly – see this it sends back, (who is it? is
>   it you?)
> Outside fair costume, within ashes and filth,
> No more a flashing eye, no more a sonorous voice or springy
>   step . . .
> Such from one look in this looking-glass ere you go hence,
> Such a result so soon – and from such a beginning!

In the years between 1856 and 1860 Whitman seems to have learned that poetry can emerge from what Yeats, in *The Circus Animals' Desertion*, called 'the foul rag-and-bone shop of the heart'.[9] *A Hand-Mirror* appears late in the 1860 edition, oddly following *Kosmos*, a poem which envisions the 'most majestic lover', a man 'Who having consider'd the body finds all its organs and parts good'. *A Hand-Mirror* would not be out of place among the *Calamus* poems, love poems which strangely temper moments of happiness with unblinking realism.

> Do you suppose yourself advancing on real ground toward a
>   real heroic man?
> Have you no thought O dreamer that it may be all maya,
>   illusion?

A strange way to begin a love affair, as Whitman asks *Are You the New Person Drawn toward Me?* What one remembers most about *Calamus* is melancholy, not joy: the live-oak without a companion; the passing stranger a possible lover but never spoken to. One poem Whitman excluded from *Calamus* might provide a clue to the cause behind these poems of self-examination, *[Hours Continuing Long]*. Whitman may have excluded it not because it is erotic, far from it, but perhaps Whitman did not want to include a permanent reminder of rejection. This poem, too, is about looking in a mirror:

> Does he see himself reflected in me? In these hours, does he see
>   the face of his hours reflected?

It is as if Whitman in 1844 read Emerson's essay on 'Experience' and in 1860 was living it:

It is very unhappy, but too late to be helped, the discovery we have made that we exist. That discovery is called the Fall of Man. Ever afterwards we suspect our instruments. We have learned that we do not see directly, but mediately, and that we have no means of correcting these colored and distorting lenses which we are, or of computing the amount of their errors. . . . The great and crescive self, rooted in absolute nature, supplants all relative existence and ruins the kingdom of mortal friendship and love.[10]

Out of the dark night of Whitman's soul two of his finest poems emerged: *Out of the Cradle Endlessly Rocking* and *As I Ebb'd with the Ocean of Life*. *Out of the Cradle* is Whitman's second famous poem of childhood; the first, of course, is the 1855 poem later called *There Was a Child Went Forth*. The contrast is striking. In the earlier poem the setting is pastoral and inviting. The whole aim of the poem seems to be to create a child painter, one who delights in all sights and sounds, the lilacs, the piglets, the March lambs, the noisy hens and the blossoming apple trees. The child's response to the world is entirely an aesthetic one:

> The village on the highland seen from afar at sunset, the river
> between,
> Shadows, aureola and mist, the light falling on roofs and gables of
> white or brown two miles off . . .
> The horizon's edge, the flying sea-crow, the fragrance of salt marsh
> and shore mud,
> These became part of the child who went forth every day, and who
> now goes and always will go forth every day.

The setting of *Out of the Cradle* is the same Long Island shore, but the month is September and the time is midnight, the sands and fields 'sterile' and the shadows cast by the moonlight are frightening, snake-like, 'twining and twisting as if they were alive'. The time suggests both birth ('the Ninth month') and death. Instead of joy there are tears aplenty. This poem, too, defines an aesthetic lesson, a realization that along with the loss of innocence the artist is given a compensatory power. 'Death', as Wallace Stevens famously put it in *Sunday Morning* 'is the mother of beauty'.[11] The older poet looks back at a mythic moment when he understood who he was ('The sea whisper'd me') and discovered his subject:

> I, chanter of pains and joys, uniter of here and hereafter,
> Taking all hints to use them, but swiftly leaping beyond them,
> A reminiscence sing.

As I Ebb'd with the Ocean of Life (originally entitled *Bardic Symbols*) is a poem which has interested many late twentieth-century readers, probably because here the prophetic mode is abandoned and a hard look at the nineteenth-century poets' way of knowing – that Emersonian response to Nature Whitman described in *Out of the Cradle*: 'Taking all hints to use them, but swiftly leaping beyond them' – is scrutinized. In his essay 'The Poet' Emerson said that Nature offers all her creatures to the poet 'as a picture language. Being used as a type [i.e. an emblem], a second wonderful value appears in the object, far better than its old values.'[12] Emerson distinguished, however, between a true poet's intuited, untranslatable meanings and the allegorist's learned and fixed symbols, the icons of Christian art, for example, which depict the lamb, the pelican, or a bunch of grapes, and whose meanings never change. Whitman had always expressed full confidence in his symbol-making powers and in the worth of his symbols. *Song of Myself* began with the poet 'observing a spear of summer grass', and his promise that death is not the end grew from there; while the poet in *Crossing Brooklyn Ferry* promises his readers, present and future, that every object in the universe, those 'dumb, beautiful ministers', 'furnish your parts toward eternity, / Great or small, you furnish your parts toward the soul'. The poet in *As I Ebb'd* has none of this assurance. The contrast in the first two sections of this poem is between the past and the present. Once, he tells us, he walked the shoreline seeking the 'old thought of likenesses', that is, he looked about him and he was filled with the power of his 'electric', his creative self, and he succeeded in finding metaphors for his poetry:

> Miles walking, the sound of breaking waves the other side of me,
> Paumanok there and then as I thought the old thought of
>   likenesses,
> These you presented to me you fish-shaped island,
> As I wended the shores I know,
> As I walk'd with that electric self seeking types.

In listing these objects the poet ignores a darker meaning inherent

in the 'Scum, scales from shining rocks, leaves of salt-lettuce, left
by the tide'. These are the things which so overwhelm the poet in
the second section that he despairs of all his effort, all his earlier
blabbing, his electric self mocking him with peals of 'distant iron-
ical laughter at every word I have written':

> I perceive that I have not understood anything, not a single object,
> and that no man ever can,
> Nature here in sight of the sea taking advantage of me to dart upon
> me and sting me,
> Because I have dared to open my mouth to sing at all.

With the knowledge that revelation was never truly at hand, now
he has moved, Hamlet-like, to total despair. There must be a middle
ground somewhere between ignorant bliss and annihilating doubt,
and Whitman comes to something like a middle ground in the
difficult fourth section. Before that happens, however, he is reduced,
in the third section, to becoming a child, calling out to his father
(the earth) for some authoritative resolution, falling on his father's
breast, clinging to him, holding him 'firm till you answer me some-
thing', demanding affectionate response, a kiss, an embrace, if he
is not to be granted intellectual understanding. No answer, no
response is forthcoming, but in the space between the third and
fourth sections (this poem, like so much of Whitman, is associa-
tive in form) something has happened. The fourth section is one
of Whitman's most beautiful passages, inseparable in its meaning
from its rhythmic structure and its sentence shape. All the nega-
tives Whitman once found so devastating are repeated: we are
burdened with contradictory moods, we are capricious and
unsteady; we lack total understanding and we know neither whence
we came, nor where we are going. Yet the world seems partly made
for us, and to deny the blossoms and sunsets, to see only waste is,
for Whitman, as it was for Emerson, too negative a view.

> Just as much for us that sobbing dirge of Nature,
> Just as much whence we come that blare of the cloud-trumpets,
> We, capricious, brought hither we know not whence, spread out
> before you,

You up there walking or sitting,
Whoever you are, we too lie in drifts at your feet.

Reviewing himself anonymously, Whitman assumed, in one
instance, the role of an admiring and somewhat puzzled critic.
Whitman differs, his critic observes, in not being content with old
forms: 'He never presents for perusal a poem ready-made on the
old models, and ending when you come to the end of it; but every
sentence and every passage tells us of an interior not always
seen . . .'[13] In 1855 Whitman as critic is describing a world of endless
possibility, but his observation fits uncannily well *As I Ebb'd*, a poem
of dissolution. 'In his finding aesthetic images and rhetorical gestures
for dispersion', the critic Helen Vendler observed on the occasion
of the poet's centennial, 'Whitman is at his most original and most
instructive. He is the originator of the modern poem with an incon-
clusive ending, at odds with the teleological poem deriving from
classical and Christian metaphysics.'[14] Had Whitman continued in
this vein he would have explored the modern poem of experience,
a poetry content with what Robert Frost has called a 'momentary
stay against confusion'.[15] It is our loss that he did not. The Civil
War (1861–5) changed Whitman's life and art for ever.

Whitman had great hopes for the financial and literary success of
Drum-Taps when it appeared as a separate volume in May 1865. (It
was included in *Leaves of Grass* in 1867.) Sales of the 1860 edition
of his *Leaves* were encouraging, but *Drum-Taps* was hardly noticed
and when it was – by a generation of younger critics like Henry James
and William Dean Howells – it was treated shabbily. James thought
the world should be protected from this fraud called Whitman.

To sing aright our battles and our glories it is not enough to have served
in a hospital . . . to be aggressively careless, inelegant, and ignorant and
to be constantly preoccupied with yourself . . . You must also be serious.
You must forget yourself in your ideas.[16]

One has the feeling that James isn't responding to Whitman's little
book, but to some past Whitman literary horror, some distasteful
Whitman advertisement for himself. It wasn't until the translator
William Michael Rossetti published in England in 1868 a selected

Whitman (expurgated) that he began to receive the audience he deserved. Algernon Charles Swinburne, John Addington Symonds, Gerard Manley Hopkins and Robert Louis Stevenson were among Whitman's enthusiastic English admirers. James seems not to have recognized that the Walt Whitman speaking in *Drum-Taps* is as much a fiction as the speaker of *Song of Myself*; the 'old man' bending over the wounded was only forty-six years old in 1865. If anything, it could be argued that *Drum-Taps* is too removed from its subject matter. Whitman's letters home attest that he could describe the hospital wards he visited every afternoon and evening for years with the eye of a fine French naturalist. But Whitman always thought of his *Leaves* as above the fray of either battle or politics. He told his biographer William O'Connor that he thought *Drum-Taps* a more 'perfect work of art' than anything he had written previously: 'I have only [now] succeeded to my satisfaction in removing all superfluity from it, verbal superfluity, I mean. I delight to make a poem where I feel clear that not a word but is indispensable part thereof and of my meaning.'[17] With the exception of *Beat! Beat! Drums!* the cry to battle is quickly hushed and neither side is seen as more valorous than the other. The most memorable of the poems are word pictures and take a long, impersonal view of the battlefield, seeing it as if it were a kind of medieval tournament:

> A line in long array where they wind betwixt green islands,
> They take a serpentine course, their arms flash in the sun . . .

Like *Cavalry Crossing a Ford*, *Bivouac on a Mountain Side* and *An Army Corps on the March* also present a painter's view of the war. How could James have read *Come up from the Fields Father* as the work of a writer with a tin ear? Not even good prose was James's final judgement. This is a poem that D. H. Lawrence, one of Whitman's most astute critics, might have treasured: the contrasting sumptuous landscape, the lives of ordinary people changed for ever, the daring presence of the all-knowing, all-sympathetic poet who reveals everything in simple words of feeling like 'Ah' and 'O' and 'Lo'. James said that Whitman's 'primary purpose' in writing *Drum-Taps* was to 'celebrate the greatness of our armies'.[18] It is not the army celebrated here; what is celebrated is that fraternal love which Whitman longed for so ardently when younger. The poet who has celebrated the present in *Song of Myself* is now becoming the poet of the past; for in the midst of writing *Drum-Taps* Whitman also seems to have become aware that this great defining national and personal moment is passing. It is the poet's task to become a vessel of memory, most famously in his pastoral elegy *When Lilacs Last in the Dooryard Bloom'd*, but also in *The Wound-Dresser*, where Whitman imagines himself in future years answering the questions of children about the war, reminding himself that what stayed with him were not 'curious panics' or 'hard-fought engagements'; it was the dying young, who return to him in 'dreams' projections':

> I sit by the restless all the dark night, some are so young,
> Some suffer so much, I recall the experience sweet and sad,
> (Many a soldier's loving arms about this neck have cross'd and
>   rested,
> Many a soldier's kiss dwells on these bearded lips.)

Whitman's later revisions of his *Leaves* made a greater place for the war in his book. He liked to think of himself as a 'veteran' and could declare in *To Thee Old Cause*: 'My book and the war are one'.

Partly to rebut the criticism of adversaries like James and Howells,[19] and to direct attention away from persistent charges of obscenity (the district attorney of Boston threatened to prosecute Whitman's publisher James R. Osgood in 1881, and, so that we may have some perspective on these charges, put *The Dalliance of the Eagles* on an obscene literature list in 1882), Whitman supporters like William O'Connor rallied to his cause, and with Whitman's active involvement created a new image of the poet. Henceforth Whitman would no longer be one of the 'roughs', but *The Good Gray Poet*, the title of O'Connor's 1866 hagiography. Whitman wanted to be loved. There would be no more poems of self-examination, explorations of guilt, or the dark side of American life. As a newspaper reporter Whitman was fully aware of the difference between his vision of America and the actual world around him. In *Democratic Vistas* (1871) he lashed out at a greedy nation whose enemy was itself:

Society in these States is canker'd, crude, superstitious, and rotten. Political, or law-made society is, and private, or voluntary society, is also. In any vigor [i.e. exercise of power], the element of the moral conscience, the most important, the verteber to State or man seems to me either entirely lacking, or seriously enfeebled or ungrown.[20]

Whitman reserved his invective, however, for his prose. He always wanted his *Leaves* to be affirmative. When he addressed the Dartmouth College graduates of the class of 1872 he shared none of this outrage. Instead, in the poem we know as *Thou Mother with Thy Equal Brood* he took as his subject neither the sordid present nor the fading past, but a vision of a future America with which no one could argue, 'tolerating all, accepting all'. Whitman saw no irony in envisioning a 'Land in the realms of God to be a realm unto thyself, /Under the rule of God to be a rule unto thyself'. It is his *Leaves* which became Whitman's final subject, and, as the critic M. Wynn Thomas puts it, there is something madly audacious about Whitman's declaration in *Thou Mother* that his book will become the centre of an American mythology, replacing both the War of Independence and the Civil War:[21]

(Thy soaring course thee formulating, not in thy two great wars,
    nor in thy century's visible growth,
But far more in these leaves and chants, thy chants, great Mother!)

What this separation between the America Whitman knew and the America he envisioned suggests is that after *Drum-Taps* Whitman's best poems are shorter poems like *Give Me the Splendid Silent Sun* (included in *Drum-Taps* but not about the war), *When I Heard the Learn'd Astronomer*, *A Farm Picture*, *Warble for Lilac-Time*, *Sparkles from the Wheel*, *As Consequent, Etc.*, *The Dalliance of the Eagles*, and *Good-bye My Fancy!*, the concluding poem and one of the most moving poems in all of *Leaves of Grass*.

Just as biographers like O'Connor responded to critics like James and Howells with a saint-like caricature of their subject, modern biographers have made certain that we see Whitman warts and all, a bundle of contradictions: part Bohemian, part working man; a poet of the city who longs for old agrarian values; a Northerner who sentimentalized the South; a man who called for honesty in all things but who created outrageous fictions about himself; a man who was not above taking charity but built himself a tomb fit for a prince. Whitman had his weaknesses. Nevertheless, there is something heroic in his lifelong dedication to his *Leaves* and something miraculous in its success. It seems fitting that the last poem in Whitman's book should address his imagination, his 'Fancy', and that he should attempt to say farewell to the great love affair of his life. The poem, however, takes a wonderful turn as he realizes that the human imagination conceived of the idea of heaven and no farewell may be needed after all:

> Yet let me not be too hasty,
> Long indeed have we lived, slept, filter'd, become really blended
>   into one;
> Then if we die we die together, (yes, we'll remain one,)
> If we go anywhere we'll go together to meet what happens,
> May-be we'll be better off and blither, and learn something,
> May-be it is yourself now really ushering me to the true songs,
>   (who knows?)
> May-be it is you the mortal knob really undoing, turning – so now
>   finally,
> Good-bye – and hail! My Fancy.

As the 1992 centennial of Whitman's death proved, his poetry still exerts an enormous appeal worldwide. Thousands attended readings and lectures, museum and library exhibitions and concerts to celebrate his art. If, in our more tolerant age, his work does not change lives as dramatically as it did for novelists and poets like D. H. Lawrence and Hart Crane, or dancers like Isadora Duncan and Ted Shawn, or architects and painters like Frank Lloyd Wright and Marsden Hartley, Whitman remains for all his readers, as Emerson said a true poet will, a liberating god.

Notes

1. *The Letters of Charles Eliot Norton*, eds. Sara Norton and M. A. DeWolfe Howe (Houghton, 1913), p. 135.

2. Ibid., p. 135.

3. Emerson's letter, dated 21 July 1855, is reprinted in *Walt Whitman: A Critical Anthology*, ed. Francis Murphy (Penguin Books, 1969), p. 29.

4. From a manuscript page in the New York Public Library, reproduced in Gary Schmidgall's *Walt Whitman: A Gay Life* (E. P. Dutton, 1997), p. 27.

5. 'Nature, Part I', *The Selected Writings of Ralph Waldo Emerson*, ed. Stephen E. Whicher (Houghton Mifflin, 1957), p. 24.

6. Phillipians 4:7.

7. *The Correspondence of Henry David Thoreau*, eds. Walter Harding and Carl Bode (New York University Press, 1958), p. 445. Thoreau's letter is dated 7 December 1856.

8. 'The Political Whitman', *Democracy's Poet* (The Museum of the City of New York, 1992), p. 5.

9. *Last Poems* (Macmillan, 1939).

10. *The Selected Writings of Ralph Waldo Emerson*, p. 269.

11. *Harmonium* (Alfred A. Knopf, 1923).

12. *The Selected Writings of Ralph Waldo Emerson*, p. 227.

13. 'An English and an American Poet', *Walt Whitman: A Critical Anthology*, p. 41. Whitman's review first appeared in the *American Phrenological Journal* in October 1855.

14. 'Whitman and the Aesthetic Life', *Democracy's Poet*, p. 19.

15. 'The Figure a Poem Makes', *Selected Prose of Robert Frost*, eds. Hyde Cox and Edward Connery Latham (Holt, Rinehart & Winston, 1966), p. 18.

16. 'Mr Walt Whitman', *Walt Whitman: A Critical Anthology*, pp. 84–5. James's review originally appeared in *The Nation*, November 1865.

17. *The Correspondence of Walt Whitman*, vol. 1, ed. Edwin

Haviland Miller (New York University Press, 1961), p. 246. Whitman's letter is dated 6 January 1865.

18.   'Mr. Walt Whitman', *Walt Whitman: A Critical Anthology*, p. 82.

19.   'Mr. Walt Whitman', *Walt Whitman: A Critical Anthology*, pp. 85–8. Howell's review originally appeared in *The Round Table* for November 1865.

20.   *The Collected Prose of Walt Whitman*, vol. 2, ed. Malcolm Cowley (Farrar, Straus and Giroux, 1969), p. 214.

21.   *The Lunar Light of Whitman's Poetry* (Harvard University Press, 1987), p. 166.

Further Reading

EDITIONS

The Collected Writings of Walt Whitman, Gay Wilson Allen and Sculley Bradley, general editors, New York University Press, consists of the following:

Harold Blodgett and Sculley Bradley (eds.), *Leaves of Grass: Comprehensive Reader's Edition*, 1965; paperback edition (W. W. Norton, 1968).

Sculley Bradley, Harold W. Blodgett, Arthur Golden (eds.), *Leaves of Grass: A Variorum Edition*, 3 vols., 1980.

Thomas L. Brasher (ed.), *Early Poems and Fiction*, 1963.

Edward F. Grier (ed.), *Notebooks and Unpublished Manuscripts*, 6 vols., 1989.

Edwin Haviland Miller (ed.), *The Correspondence of Walt Whitman*: vol. 1, 1842–1867 (1961); vol. 2, 1868–1875 (1961); vol. 3, 1876–1885 (1964); vol. 4, 1886–1889 (1969); vol. 5, 1890–1892 (1969); vol. 6, a supplement (1977).

William White (ed.), *Daybooks and Notebooks*, vol. 1, 1876–1881; vol. 2, 1881–1891, (1977).

William White (ed.), *Diary in Canada* [1880], *Notebooks, Index*, 1977.

BIBLIOGRAPHY

Joel Myerson, *Walt Whitman: A Descriptive Bibliography of His Work* (University of Pittsburgh Press, 1993).

BIOGRAPHY

Gay Wilson Allen, *The Solitary Singer*, revised edition (New York University Press, 1967).

Justin Kaplan, *Walt Whitman: A Life* (Simon and Schuster, 1980).

Jerome Loving, *Walt Whitman: The Song of Himself* (University of California Press, 1999).

David S. Reynolds, *Walt Whitman's America* (Alfred A. Knopf, 1995).

Gary Schmidgall, *Walt Whitman: A Gay Life* (E. P. Dutton, 1997).

Horace Traubel, *Conversations with Walt Whitman in Camden*, vols. 1 and 2 (D. Appleton, 1908); vol. 3 (M. Kinnerley, 1914); vol. 4 (University of Pennsylvania Press, 1953); vol. 5 (Southern Illinois University Press, 1964); vol. 6 (Southern Illinois University Press, 1982); vol. 7 (Southern Illinois University Press, 1992); vols. 8 and 9 (William Bentley, 1996).

SELECTED CRITICISM

Gay Wilson Allen, *The New Walt Whitman Handbook* (New York University Press, 1986).

Newton Arvin, *Walt Whitman* (Macmillan, 1938).

Harold Aspiz, *Walt Whitman and the Body Beautiful* (University of Illinois Press, 1989).

Roger Asselineau, *The Evolution of Walt Whitman* (Harvard University Press, vol. 1, 1960, vol. 2, 1962). A translation of *L'évolution de Walt Whitman après la première édition des 'Feuilles d'Herbe'*, 1954.

Harold Bloom (ed.), *Modern Critical Views: Walt Whitman* (Chelsea House, 1985).

John Burroughs, *Whitman* (Houghton Mifflin, 1896).

Richard Chase, *Walt Whitman Reconsidered* (Gollancz Sloan, 1955).

David Cavitch, *My Soul and I* (Beacon Press, 1985).

Betsy Erkkila, *Whitman the Political Poet* (Oxford University Press, 1989).

Ed Folsom (ed.), *Walt Whitman: The Centennial Essays* (University of Iowa Press, 1994).

M. Jimmie Killingsworth, *Whitman's Poetry of the Body* (University of North Carolina Press, 1989).

D. H. Lawrence, 'Whitman', in *Studies in Classic American Literature* (Secker, 1924); reprinted (Doubleday, 1955).

Michael Lynch, '"Here is Adhesiveness": From Friendship to

Homosexuality', *Victorian Studies*, vol. 29, number 1, Autumn 1985, pp. 67–96.

Robert K. Martin, *The Homosexual Tradition in American Poetry* (University of Texas Press, 1979).

F. O. Matthiessen, *American Renaissance* (Oxford University Press, 1941).

Edwin H. Miller, *Walt Whitman's Poetry: A Psychological Journey* (New York University Press), 1968.

Michael Moon, *Disseminating Walt Whitman* (Harvard University Press, 1991).

Francis Murphy (ed.), *Walt Whitman: Penguin Critical Anthology* (Penguin, 1969).

Roy Harvey Pearce (ed.), *Whitman* (Prentice-Hall, 1962).

Kenneth M. Price and Ed Folsom, *The Walt Whitman Hypertext Archive*, University of Iowa, ongoing, at http://www.whitman archive.org/archive1/index.html

Joseph Jay Rubin, *The Historic Whitman* (Pennsylvania State University Press, 1973).

M. Wynn Thomas, *The Lunar Light of Whitman's Poetry* (Harvard University Press, 1987).

Helen Vendler, 'Whitman's Placing of the Aesthetic in two Early Poems: "There Was a Child Went Forth" and "The Sleepers"', *Delta*, vol. 16, May 1983, pp. 19–32.

Helen Vendler, 'Whitman's "When Lilacs Last in the Dooryard Bloom'd"', Mary Ann Caws (ed.), *Textual Analysis: Some Reader's Reading*, Modern Language Association, 1986, pp. 132–43.

Paul Zweig, *Walt Whitman: The Making of a Poet* (Basic Books, 1984).

A Note on the Text

The text used in this edition of *Leaves of Grass* is that published by David McKay in Philadelphia in 1891–2, and now popularly referred to as the 'death-bed' edition, although the actual copy of *Leaves of Grass* presented to Whitman in his final hours by close friends was something else. *Leaves of Grass* 1891–2 was the ninth edition that Whitman prepared for publication, the tenth if you wish to count *The Complete Poems and Prose* of 1888 and most editors do not. With the exception of the annexes, the ninth edition reprints the edition of 1881 and it is in that edition that the poems received their final arrangement. Whitman's revisions of *Leaves of Grass* were so numerous that their study has almost become an American form of small business. Whitman changed his titles, added poems, and then deleted others, revised his diction and regrouped his 'leaves' tirelessly, but by 1891 he had settled on the final shape of his book and provided future editors with a note of instruction:

I place upon you the injunction that whatever may be added to the *Leaves* be supplementary, avowed as such, leaving the book complete as I left it, consecutive to the point I left off, marking always an unmistakable, deep down, unobliterable division line. In the long run the world will do as it pleases with the book. I am determined to have the world know what I was pleased to do.

Current admirers often prefer the first edition of 1855 or the edition of 1860 as 'more imaginative, more spontaneous, more vital'; no one, however, has seriously suggested publishing either the edition of 1855 or 1860 as a substitute for the last. The edition of 1891–2 is the indispensable one, and the student interested in Whitman's earlier editions will find both readily available in paperback. I am not certain but that for polish the final edition of *Leaves of Grass* is not better both for *Song of Myself* and *Out of the Cradle Endlessly Rocking*, but I have included in an appendix all of the

1855 version of *Song of Myself* and, when useful, provided early versions of some revised poems in the Notes to this edition. Students who would like to check all of Whitman's revisions and changes in text from the earliest edition to the last should use the Variorum Edition of *Leaves of Grass* edited by Harold Blodgett and Sculley Bradley for the New York University Press. Emory Holloway's 'Inclusive Edition' of *Leaves of Grass* (New York, 1931) is accessible in most libraries and provides many variorum readings. Unfortunately, this book is now out of print.

Notes to this edition provide date of first publication and first appearance in *Leaves of Grass*. I have provided annotations whenever I could identify names and historical references and have given some assistance with place-names. Whitman's book is so large and his references so numerous that a complete identification of place-names would have turned my Notes into an elementary geography. In addition to all of Whitman's prose 'Prefaces', I have provided in the appendixes all of the poems Whitman excluded from *Leaves of Grass* 1891–2, and his early poetry. With the exception of the poem *Pictures* I have not included in this edition any of the manuscript fragments which Whitman left on his death. The interested student will find these now easily available in the New York University 'Comprehensive Reader's Edition' of *Leaves of Grass*, in *The Collected Writings of Walt Whitman* (1964), edited by Harold W. Blodgett and Sculley Bradley.

Ever since Emerson's witty remark to Sanborn that *Leaves of Grass* was a 'combination of the *Bhagavad-Gita* and the *New York Herald*' editors have taken pleasure in calling attention to Whitman's 'polyglot vocabulary'. In a famous article on 'Walt Whitman and the French Language' (*American Speech*, vol. 1, 1925–6, pp. 421–30), Louise Pound called attention, for example, to Whitman's French and made some large claims for a poet who 'was not a direct student of the language and who had never been in France'. Miss Pound thought that Whitman's predilection for things French could be attributed to his New Orleans visit in 1848. Some of the words to which she chose to call particular attention were: feuillage, ensemble, accoucheur, trottoir, rendezvous, embouchure, nonchalance, rondure, rapport. Most of these words may be found in

Noah Webster's revised *An American Dictionary of the English Language* (New Haven, 1841) or in the *Oxford English Dictionary*. Most have been a part of the English language for some time. I have tried to designate as 'foreign' only those words which were not in common English use. Whitman's voice is his own and his diction unmistakably his. There is no necessity to make it seem more peculiar than it is.

Leaves of Grass

Including

SANDS AT SEVENTY... *1st Annex*,

GOOD-BYE MY FANCY... *2d Annex*,

A BACKWARD GLANCE O'ER TRAVEL'D ROADS,

and Portrait from Life.

COME, said my Soul,
Such verses for my Body let us write, (for we are one,)
That should I after death invisibly return,
Or, long, long hence, in other spheres,
There to some group of mates the chants resuming,
(Tallying Earth's soil, trees, winds, tumultuous waves,)
Ever with pleas'd smile I may keep on,
Ever and ever yet the verses owning—as, first, I here and now,
Signing for Soul and Body, set to them my name,

Walt Whitman

PHILADELPHIA

DAVID McKAY, PUBLISHER

23 SOUTH NINTH STREET

1891-2

COPYRIGHTS, &c.

———

1st ed'n 1855, Brooklyn (N. Y., South District)—renew'd (1883) 14 yrs.

2d ed'n 1856, Brooklyn—renew'd (1884) 14 yrs.

3d ed'n 1860, Boston, Thayer & Eldridge Pub'rs.

4th ed'n 1867, N. Y., So. Dist.: Pub'd New York.

5th ed'n 1871, Washington, D. C.

6th ed'n 1876—Centennial issue—inc'd'g Two RIVULETS: two vols.

7th ed'n 1881, Boston, Mass.: Osgood Pub.: [This includes in the present vol. pages 1 to 382.]

8th ed'n 1882, Philadelphia: McKay Pub'r.

Sands at Seventy: Annex, 1888—November Boughs—Philadelphia.

A Backward Glance, &c.: November Boughs, 1888—Philadelphia.

Good-Bye my Fancy: 2d Annex, 1891—Philadelphia.

Library of Congress . . . . . Copyright Office, Washington.

No. 18382 W.
To wit: Be it remembered . . . That on the 19th day of May, *anno Domini*, 1891, Walt Whitman, of Camden, N. J., has deposited in this office the title of a Book, the title or description of which is in the following words, to wit:
GOOD-BYE MY FANCY,
2d Annex to Leaves of Grass.
Philadelphia . .˙. David McKay . . . 1891.
The right whereof he claims as author, in conformity with the laws of the United States respecting copyrights.

A. R. SPOFFORD,
Librarian of Congress.

[Which last-named copyright (holding good to 1919—then, on application, continued 14 years further) expires May 19, 1933.]

——

☞ As there are now several editions of L. of G., different texts and dates, I wish to say that I prefer and recommend this present one, complete, for future printing, if there should be any; a copy and fac-simile, indeed, of the text of these 438 pages. The subsequent adjusting interval which is so important to form'd and launch'd work, books especially, has pass'd; and waiting till fully after that, I have given (pages 423-438) my concluding words.   W. W.

A facsimile reproduction of the copyright page
for the 1891-2 edition of *Leaves of Grass*

INSCRIPTIONS

One's-Self I Sing

One's-Self I sing, a simple separate person,
Yet utter the word Democratic, the word En-Masse.

Of physiology from top to toe I sing,
Not physiognomy alone nor brain alone is worthy for the
    Muse, I say the Form complete is worthier far,
The Female equally with the Male I sing.

Of Life immense in passion, pulse, and power,
Cheerful, for freest action form'd under the laws divine,
The Modern Man I sing.

As I Ponder'd in Silence

As I ponder'd in silence,
Returning upon my poems, considering, lingering long,
A Phantom arose before me with distrustful aspect,
Terrible in beauty, age, and power,
The genius of poets of old lands,
As to me directing like flame its eyes,
With finger pointing to many immortal songs,
And menacing voice, *What singest thou?* it said,
Know'st thou not there is but one theme for ever-enduring
    bards?
10 *And that is the theme of War, the fortune of battles,*
The making of perfect soldiers.

Be it so, then I answer'd,
I too haughty Shade also sing war, and a longer and greater
    one than any,
Waged in my book with varying fortune, with flight, advance
    and retreat, victory deferr'd and wavering,
(Yet methinks certain, or as good as certain, at the last,)
    the field the world,
For life and death, for the Body and for the eternal Soul,

Lo, I too am come, chanting the chant of battles,
I above all promote brave soldiers.

In Cabin'd Ships at Sea

In cabin'd ships at sea,
The boundless blue on every side expanding,
With whistling winds and music of the waves, the large
    imperious waves,
Or some lone bark buoy'd on the dense marine,
Where joyous full of faith, spreading white sails,
She cleaves the ether mid the sparkle and the foam of day,
    or under many a star at night,
By sailors young and old haply will I, a reminiscence of
    the land, be read,
In full rapport at last.

Here are our thoughts, voyagers' thoughts,
10 *Here not the land, firm land, alone appears,* may then by them
    be said,
The sky o'erarches here, we feel the undulating deck beneath
    our feet,
We feel the long pulsation, ebb and flow of endless motion,
The tones of unseen mystery, the vague and vast suggestions of
    the briny world, the liquid-flowing syllables,
The perfume, the faint creaking of the cordage, the
    melancholy rhythm,
The boundless vista and the horizon far and dim are all here,
And this is ocean's poem.

Then falter not O book, fulfil your destiny,
You not a reminiscence of the land alone,
You too as a lone bark cleaving the ether, purpos'd I know
    not whither, yet ever full of faith,
20 Consort to every ship that sails, sail you!
Bear forth to them folded my love, (dear mariners, for you
    I fold it here in every leaf;)
Speed on my book! spread your white sails my little bark
    athwart the imperious waves,

Chant on, sail on, bear o'er the boundless blue from me to
  every sea,
This song for mariners and all their ships.

To Foreign Lands

I heard that you ask'd for something to prove this puzzle
  the New World,
And to define America, her athletic Democracy,
Therefore I send you my poems that you behold in them
  what you wanted.

To a Historian

You who celebrate bygones,
Who have explored the outward, the surfaces of the races,
  the life that has exhibited itself,
Who have treated of man as the creature of politics,
  aggregates, rulers and priests,
I, habitan of the Alleghanies, treating of him as he is in
  himself in his own rights,
Pressing the pulse of the life that has seldom exhibited itself,
  (the great pride of man in himself,)
Chanter of Personality, outlining what is yet to be,
I project the history of the future.

To Thee Old Cause

To thee old cause!
Thou peerless, passionate, good cause,
Thou stern, remorseless, sweet idea,
Deathless throughout the ages, races, lands,
After a strange sad war, great war for thee,

(I think all war through time was really fought, and ever
     will be really fought, for thee,)
These chants for thee, the eternal march of thee.

(A war O soldier not for itself alone,
Far, far more stood silently waiting behind, now to advance
     in this book.)

10   Thou orb of many orbs!
Thou seething principle! thou well-kept, latent germ!
     thou centre!
Around the idea of thee the war revolving,
With all its angry and vehement play of causes,
(With vast results to come for thrice a thousand years,)
These recitatives for thee, – my book and the war are one,
Merged in its spirit I and mine, as the contest hinged on
     thee,
As a wheel on its axis turns, this book unwitting to itself,
Around the idea of thee.

Eidólons

     I met a seer,
Passing the hues and objects of the world,
The fields of art and learning, pleasure, sense,
     To glean eidólons.

     Put in thy chants said he,
No more the puzzling hour nor day, nor segments, parts,
     put in,
Put first before the rest as light for all and entrance-song
     of all,
     That of eidólons.

     Ever the dim beginning,
10   Ever the growth, the rounding of the circle,
Ever the summit and the merge at last, (to surely start
     again,)
     Eidólons! eidólons!

Ever the mutable,
Ever materials, changing, crumbling, re-cohering,
Ever the ateliers, the factories divine,
        Issuing eidólons.

Lo, I or you,
Or woman, man, or state, known or unknown,
We seeming solid wealth, strength, beauty build,
20   But really build eidólons.

The ostent evanescent,
The substance of an artist's mood or savan's studies long,
Or warrior's, martyr's, hero's toils,
        To fashion his eidólon.

Of every human life,
(The units gather'd, posted, not a thought, emotion, deed,
        left out,)
The whole or large or small summ'd, added up,
        In its eidólon.

The old, old urge,
30 Based on the ancient pinnacles, lo, newer, higher
        pinnacles,
From science and the modern still impell'd,
        The old, old urge, eidólons.

The present now and here,
America's busy, teeming, intricate whirl,
Of aggregate and segregate for only thence releasing,
        Today's eidólons.

These with the past,
Of vanish'd lands, of all the reigns of kings across the sea,
Old conquerors, old campaigns, old sailors' voyages,
40   Joining eidólons.

Densities, growth, façades,
Strata of mountains, soils, rocks, giant trees,
Far-born, far-dying, living long, to leave,
        Eidólons everlasting.

Exaltè, rapt, ecstatic,
The visible but their womb of birth,
Of orbic tendencies to shape and shape and shape,
        The mighty earth-eidólon.

All space, all time,
50 (The stars, the terrible perturbations of the suns,
Swelling, collapsing, ending, serving their longer, shorter
        use,)
        Fill'd with eidólons only.

The noiseless myriads,
The infinite oceans where the rivers empty,
The separate countless free identities, like eyesight,
        The true realities, eidólons.

Not this the world,
Nor these the universes, they the universes,
Purport and end, ever the permanent life of life,
60   Eidólons, eidólons.

Beyond thy lectures learn'd professor,
Beyond thy telescope or spectroscope observer keen,
        beyond all mathematics,
Beyond the doctor's surgery, anatomy, beyond the chemist
        with his chemistry,
        The entities of entities, eidólons.

Unfix'd yet fix'd,
Ever shall be, ever have been and are,
Sweeping the present to the infinite future,
        Eidólons, eidólons, eidólons.

The prophet and the bard,
70 Shall yet maintain themselves, in higher stages yet,
Shall mediate to the Modern, to Democracy, interpret yet
        to them,
        God and eidólons.

And thee my soul,
Joys, ceaseless exercises, exaltations,
Thy yearning amply fed at last, prepared to meet,
    Thy mates, eidólons.

Thy body permanent,
The body lurking there within thy body,
The only purport of the form thou art, the real I myself,
80   An image, an eidólon.

Thy very songs not in thy songs,
No special strains to sing, none for itself,
But from the whole resulting, rising at last and floating,
    A round full-orb'd eidólon.

For Him I Sing

For him I sing,
I raise the present on the past,
(As some perennial tree out of its roots, the present on
   the past,)
With time and space I him dilate and fuse the immortal laws,
To make himself by them the law unto himself.

When I Read the Book

When I read the book, the biography famous,
And is this then (said I) what the author calls a man's life?
And so will some one when I am dead and gone write my
   life?
(As if any man really knew aught of my life,
Why even I myself I often think know little or nothing of
   my real life,
Only a few hints, a few diffused faint clews and indirections
I seek for my own use to trace out here.)

Beginning My Studies

Beginning my studies the first step pleas'd me so much,
The mere fact consciousness, these forms, the power of
    motion,
The least insect or animal, the senses, eyesight, love,
The first step I say awed me and pleas'd me so much,
I have hardly gone and hardly wish'd to go any farther,
But stop and loiter all the time to sing it in ecstatic songs.

Beginners

How they are provided for upon the earth, (appearing at
    intervals,)
How dear and dreadful they are to the earth,
How they inure to themselves as much as to any – what a
    paradox appears their age,
How people respond to them, yet know them not,
How there is something relentless in their fate all times,
How all times mischoose the objects of their adulation and
    reward,
And how the same inexorable price must still be paid for
    the same great purchase.

To the States

To the States or any one of them, or any city of the States,
    Resist much, obey little,
Once unquestioning obedience, once fully enslaved,
Once fully enslaved, no nation, state, city of this earth,
    ever afterward resumes its liberty.

On Journeys through the States

On journeys through the States we start,
(Ay through the world, urged by these songs,
Sailing henceforth to every land, to every sea,)
We willing learners of all, teachers of all, and lovers of all.

We have watch'd the seasons dispensing themselves and
passing on,
And have said, Why should not a man or woman do as much
as the seasons, and effuse as much?

We dwell a while in every city and town,
We pass through Kanada, the North-east, the vast valley of
the Mississippi, and the Southern States,
We confer on equal terms with each of the States,
10 We make trial of ourselves and invite men and women to
hear,
We say to ourselves, Remember, fear not, be candid,
promulge the body and the soul,
Dwell a while and pass on, be copious, temperate, chaste,
magnetic,
And what you effuse may then return as the seasons return,
And may be just as much as the seasons.

To a Certain Cantatrice

Here, take this gift,
I was reserving it for some hero, speaker, or general,
One who should serve the good old cause, the great idea,
the progress and freedom of the race,
Some brave confronter of despots, some daring rebel;
But I see that what I was reserving belongs to you just as
much as to any.

Me Imperturbe

Me imperturbe, standing at ease in Nature,
Master of all or mistress of all, aplomb in the midst of
    irrational things,
Imbued as they, passive, receptive, silent as they,
Finding my occupation, poverty, notoriety, foibles, crimes,
    less important than I thought,
Me toward the Mexican sea, or in the Mannahatta or the
    Tennessee, or far north or inland,
A river man, or a man of the woods or of any farm-life of
    these States or of the coast, or the lakes of Kanada,
Me wherever my life is lived, O to be self-balanced for
    contingencies,
To confront night, storms, hunger, ridicule, accidents,
    rebuffs, as the trees and animals do.

Savantism

Thither as I look I see each result and glory retracing itself
    and nestling close, always obligated,
Thither hours, months, years – thither trades, compacts,
    establishments, even the most minute,
Thither every-day life, speech, utensils, politics, persons,
    estates;
Thither we also, I with my leaves and songs, trustful,
    admirant,
As a father to his father going takes his children along
    with him.

The Ship Starting

Lo, the unbounded sea,
On its breast a ship starting, spreading all sails, carrying
    even her moonsails,
The pennant is flying aloft as she speeds she speeds so

stately – below emulous waves press forward,
They surround the ship with shining curving motions and
   foam.

I Hear America Singing

I hear America singing, the varied carols I hear,
Those of mechanics, each one singing his as it should be
   blithe and strong,
The carpenter singing his as he measures his plank or beam,
The mason singing his as he makes ready for work, or
   leaves off work,
The boatman singing what belongs to him in his boat, the
   deckhand singing on the steamboat dèck,
The shoemaker singing as he sits on his bench, the hatter
   singing as he stands,
The wood-cutter's song, the ploughboy's on his way in the
   morning, or at noon intermission or at sundown,
The delicious singing of the mother, or of the young wife
   at work, or of the girl sewing or washing,
Each singing what belongs to him or her and to none else,
10 The day what belongs to the day – at night the party of
   young fellows, robust, friendly,
Singing with open mouths their strong melodious songs.

What Place is Besieged?

What place is besieged, and vainly tries to raise the siege?
Lo, I send to that place a commander, swift, brave, immortal,
And with him horse and foot, and parks of artillery,
And artillery-men, the deadliest that ever fired gun.

Still though the One I Sing

Still though the one I sing,
(One, yet of contradictions made,) I dedicate to Nationality,
I leave in him revolt, (O latent right of insurrection! O
  quenchless, indispensable fire!)

Shut not Your Doors

Shut not your doors to me proud libraries,
For that which was lacking on all your well-fill'd shelves, yet
  needed most, I bring,
Forth from the war emerging, a book I have made,
The words of my book nothing, the drift of it every thing,
A book separate, not link'd with the rest nor felt by the
  intellect,
But you ye untold latencies will thrill to every page.

Poets to Come

Poets to come! orators, singers, musicians to come!
Not to-day is to justify me and answer what I am for,
But you, a new brood, native, athletic, continental, greater
  than before known,
Arouse! for you must justify me.

I myself but write one or two indicative words for the future,
I but advance a moment only to wheel and hurry back in the
  darkness.

I am a man who, sauntering along without fully stopping,
  turns a casual look upon you and then averts his face,
Leaving it to you to prove and define it,
Expecting the main things from you.

49

To You

Stranger, if you passing meet me and desire to speak to me,
    why should you not speak to me?
And why should I not speak to you?

Thou Reader

Thou reader throbbest life and pride and love the same as I,
Therefore for thee the following chants.

Starting from Paumanok

1

Starting from fish-shape Paumanok where I was born,
Well-begotten, and rais'd by a perfect mother,
After roaming many lands, lover of populous pavements,
Dweller in Mannahatta my city, or on southern savannas,
Or a soldier camp'd or carrying my knapsack and gun, or a
    miner in California,
Or rude in my home in Dakota's woods, my diet meat, my
    drink from the spring,
Or withdrawn to muse and meditate in some deep recess,
Far from the clank of crowds intervals passing rapt and
    happy,
Aware of the fresh free giver the flowing Missouri, aware of
    mighty Niagara,
10 Aware of the buffalo herds grazing the plains, the hirsute and
    strong-breasted bull,
Of earth, rocks, Fifth-month flowers experienced, stars,
    rain, snow, my amaze,
Having studied the mocking-bird's tones and the flight of
    the mountain-hawk,
And heard at dawn the unrivall'd one, the hermit thrush
    from the swamp-cedars,
Solitary, singing in the West, I strike up for a New World.

2

Victory, union, faith, identity, time,
The indissoluble compacts, riches, mystery,
Eternal progress, the kosmos, and the modern reports.

This then is life,
Here is what has come to the surface after so many throes
    and convulsions.

20 How curious! how real!
Underfoot the divine soil, overhead the sun.

See revolving the globe,
The ancestor-continents away group'd together,
The present and future continents north and south, with the
    isthmus between.

See, vast trackless spaces,
As in a dream they change, they swiftly fill,
Countless masses debouch upon them,
They are now cover'd with the foremost people, arts,
    institutions, known.

See, projected through time,
30 For me an audience interminable.

With firm and regular step they wend, they never stop,
Successions of men, Americanos, a hundred millions,
One generation playing its part and passing on,
Another generation playing its part and passing on in its
    turn,
With faces turn'd sideways or backward towards me
    to listen,
With eyes retrospective towards me.

3
Americanos! conquerors! marches humanitarian!
Foremost! century marches! Libertad! masses!
For you a programme of chants.

40 Chants of the prairies,
Chants of the long-running Mississippi, and down to
    the Mexican sea,
Chants of Ohio, Indiana, Illinois, Iowa, Wisconsin and
    Minnesota,
Chants going forth from the centre from Kansas, and
    thence equidistant,
Shooting in pulses of fire ceaseless to vivify all.

4
Take my leaves America, take them South and take them
    North,
Make welcome for them everywhere, for they are your
    own offspring,
Surround them East and West, for they would surround you,
And you precedents, connect lovingly with them, for they
    connect lovingly with you.

    I conn'd old times,
50 I sat studying at the feet of the great masters,
    Now if eligible O that the great masters might return and
        study me.

In the name of these States shall I scorn the antique?
Why these are the children of the antique to justify it.

5
Dead poets, philosophs, priests,
Martyrs, artists, inventors, governments long since,
Language-shapers on other shores,
Nations once powerful, now reduced, withdrawn, or
    desolate,
I dare not proceed till I respectfully credit what you have
    left wafted hither,
I have perused it, own it is admirable, (moving awhile
    among it,)
60 Think nothing can ever be greater, nothing can ever
    deserve more than it deserves,
Regarding it all intently a long while, then dismissing it,
I stand in my place with my own day here.

Here lands female and male,
Here the heir-ship and heiress-ship of the world, here the
    flame of materials,
Here spirituality the translatress, the openly-avow'd,
The ever-tending, the finalè of visible forms,
The satisfier, after due long-waiting now advancing,
Yes here comes my mistress the soul.

6

The soul,

70　Forever and forever – longer than soil is brown and solid –
　　longer than water ebbs and flows.

I will make the poems of materials, for I think they are to be
　　the most spiritual poems,
And I will make the poems of my body and of mortality,
For I think I shall then supply myself with the poems of my
　　soul and of immortality.

I will make a song for these States that no one State may
　　under any circumstances be subjected to another State,
And I will make a song that there shall be comity by day and
　　by night between all the States, and between any two of
　　them,
And I will make a song for the ears of the President, full of
　　weapons with menacing points,
And behind the weapons countless dissatisfied faces;
And a song make I of the One form'd out of all,
The fang'd and glittering One whose head is over all,
80　Resolute warlike One including and over all,
(However high the head of any else that head is over all.)

I will acknowledge contemporary lands,
I will trail the whole geography of the globe and salute
　　courteously every city large and small,
And employments! I will put in my poems that with you is
　　heroism upon land and sea,
And I will report all heroism from an American point of
　　view.

I will sing the song of companionship,
I will show what alone must finally compact these,
I believe these are to found their own ideal of manly love,
　　indicating it in me,
I will therefore let flame from me the burning fires that
　　were threatening to consume me,

90 I will lift what has too long kept down those smouldering
        fires,
    I will give them complete abandonment,
    I will write the evangel-poem of comrades and of love,
    For who but I should understand love with all its sorrow and
        joy?
    And who but I should be the poet of comrades?

7

I am the credulous man of qualities, ages, races,
I advance from the people in their own spirit,
Here is what sings unrestricted faith.

Omnes! omnes! let others ignore what they may,
I make the poem of evil also, I commemorate that part also,
100 I am myself just as much evil as good, and my nation is –
        and I say there is in fact no evil,
    (Or if there is I say it is just as important to you, to the land
        or to me, as any thing else.)

I too, following many and follow'd by many, inaugurate a
    religion, I descend into the arena,
(It may be I am destin'd to utter the loudest cries there, the
    winner's pealing shouts,
Who knows? they may rise from me yet, and soar above
    every thing.)

Each is not for its own sake,
I say the whole earth and all the stars in the sky are for
    religion's sake.

I say no man has ever yet been half devout enough,
None has ever yet adored or worship'd half enough,
None has begun to think how divine he himself is, and how
    certain the future is.

110 I say that the real and permanent grandeur of these States
        must be their religion,
    Otherwise there is no real and permanent grandeur;
    (Nor character nor life worthy the name without religion,
    Nor land nor man or woman without religion.)

8

What are you doing young man?
Are you so earnest, so given up to literature, science, art,
    amours?
These ostensible realities, politics, points?
Your ambition or business whatever it may be?

It is well – against such I say not a word, I am their poet
    also,
But behold! such swiftly subside, burnt up for religion's
    sake,
120 For not all matter is fuel to heat, impalpable flame, the
    essential life of the earth,
Any more than such are to religion.

9

What do you seek so pensive and silent?
What do you need camerado?
Dear son do you think it is love?

Listen dear son – listen America, daughter or son,
It is a painful thing to love a man or woman to excess, and
    yet it satisfies, it is great,
But there is something else very great, it makes the whole
    coincide,
It, magnificent, beyond materials, with continuous hands
    sweeps and provides for all.

10

Know you, solely to drop in the earth the germs of a greater
    religion,
130 The following chants each for its kind I sing.

My comrade!
For you to share with me two greatnesses, and a third one
    rising inclusive and more resplendent,
The greatness of Love and Democracy, and the greatness of
    Religion.

Melange mine own, the unseen and the seen,
Mysterious ocean where the streams empty,
Prophetic spirit of materials shifting and flickering around
    me,
Living beings, identities now doubtless near us in the air
    that we know not of,
Contact daily and hourly that will not release me,
These selecting, these in hints demanded of me.

140   Not he with a daily kiss onward from childhood kissing me,
Has winded and twisted around me that which holds me to
    him,
Any more than I am held to the heavens and all the spiritual
    world,
After what they have done to me, suggesting themes.

O such themes – equalities! O divine average!
Warblings under the sun, usher'd as now, or at noon, or
    setting,
Strains musical flowing through ages, now reaching hither,
I take to your reckless and composite chords, add to them,
    and cheerfully pass them forward.

11
As I have walk'd in Alabama my morning walk,
I have seen where the she-bird the mocking-bird sat on her
    nest in the briers hatching her brood.

150   I have seen the he-bird also,
I have paus'd to hear him near at hand inflating his throat
    and joyfully singing.

And while I paus'd it came to me that what he really sang
    for was not there only,
Nor for his mate nor himself only, nor all sent back by the
    echoes,

But subtle, clandestine, away beyond,
A charge transmitted and gift occult for those being born.

12

Democracy! near at hand to you a throat is now inflating
    itself and joyfully singing.

Ma femme! for the brood beyond us and of us,
For those who belong here and those to come,
I exultant to be ready for them will now shake out carols
    stronger and haughtier than have ever yet been heard
    upon earth.

160   I will make the songs of passion to give them their way,
And your songs outlaw'd offenders, for I scan you with
    kindred eyes, and carry you with me the same as any.

I will make the true poem of riches,
To earn for the body and the mind whatever adheres and
    goes forward and is not dropt by death;
I will effuse egotism and show it underlying all, and I will be
    the bard of personality,
And I will show of male and female that either is but the
    equal of the other.
And sexual organs and acts! do you concentrate in me, for I
    am determin'd to tell you with courageous clear voice to
    prove you illustrious,
And I will show that there is no imperfection in the present,
    and can be none in the future,
And I will show that whatever happens to anybody it may
    be turn'd to beautiful results,
And I will show that nothing can happen more beautiful
    than death,
170   And I will thread a thread through my poems that time and
    events are compact,
And that all the things of the universe are perfect miracles,
    each as profound as any.

I will not make poems with reference to parts,
But I will make poems, songs, thoughts, with reference to
    ensemble,
And I will not sing with reference to a day, but with
    reference to all days,
And I will not make a poem nor the least part of a poem but
    has reference to the soul,
Because having look'd at the objects of the universe, I find
    there is no one nor any particle of one but has reference
    to the soul.

13
Was somebody asking to see the soul?
See, your own shape and countenance, persons, substances,
    beasts, the trees, the running rivers, the rocks and sands.

All hold spiritual joys and afterwards loosen them;
180   How can the real body ever die and be buried?

Of your real body and any man's or woman's real body,
Item for item it will elude the hands of the corpse-cleaners
    and pass to fitting spheres,
Carrying what has accrued to it from the moment of birth
    to the moment of death.

Not the types set up by the printer return their impression,
    the meaning, the main concern,
Any more than a man's substance and life or a woman's
    substance and life return in the body and the soul,
Indifferently before death and after death.

Behold, the body includes and is the meaning, the main
    concern, and includes and is the soul;
Whoever you are, how superb and how divine is your body,
    or any part of it!

14
Whoever you are, to you endless announcements!

190   Daughter of the lands did you wait for your poet?
Did you wait for one with a flowing mouth and indicative
hand?
Toward the male of the States, and toward the female of the
States,
Exulting words, words to Democracy's lands.

Interlink'd, food-yielding lands!
Land of coal and iron! land of gold! land of cotton, sugar,
rice!
Land of wheat, beef, pork! land of wool and hemp! land of
the apple and the grape!
Land of the pastoral plains, the grass-fields of the world!
land of those sweet-air'd interminable plateaus!
Land of the herd, the garden, the healthy house of adobie!
Lands where the north-west Columbia winds, and where the
south-west Colorado winds!
200   Land of the eastern Chesapeake! land of the Delaware!
Land of Ontario, Erie, Huron, Michigan!
Land of the Old Thirteen! Massachusetts land! land of
Vermont and Connecticut!
Land of the ocean shores! land of sierras and peaks!
Land of boatmen and sailors! fishermen's land!
Inextricable lands! the clutch'd together! the passionate
ones!
The side by side! the elder and younger brothers! the
bony-limb'd!
The great women's land! the feminine! the experienced
sisters and the inexperienced sisters!
Far breath'd land! Arctic braced! Mexican breez'd! the
diverse! the compact!
The Pennsylvanian! the Virginian! the double Carolinian!
210   O all and each well-loved by me! my intrepid nations! O I
at any rate include you all with perfect love!
I cannot be discharged from you! not from one any sooner
than another!

O death! O for all that, I am yet of you unseen this hour
 with irrepressible love,
Walking New England, a friend, a traveler,
Splashing my bare feet in the edge of the summer ripples
 on Paumanok's sands,
Crossing the prairies, dwelling again in Chicago, dwelling
 in every town,
Observing shows, births, improvements, structures, arts,
Listening to orators and oratresses in public halls,
Of and through the States as during life, each man and
 woman my neighbor,
The Louisianian, the Georgian, as near to me, and I as near
 to him and her,
220 The Mississippian and Arkansian yet with me, and I yet
 with any of them,
Yet upon the plains west of the spinal river, yet in my house
 of adobie,
Yet returning eastward, yet in the Seaside State or in
 Maryland,
Yet Kanadian cheerily braving the winter, the snow and ice
 welcome to me,
Yet a true son either of Maine or of the Granite State, or the
 Narragansett Bay State, or the Empire State,
Yet sailing to other shores to annex the same, yet welcoming
 every new brother,
Hereby applying these leaves to the new ones from the hour
 they unite with the old ones,
Coming among the new ones myself to be their companion
 and equal, coming personally to you now,
Enjoining you to acts, characters, spectacles, with me.

15
With me with firm holding, yet haste, haste on.

230 For your life adhere to me,
 (I may have to be persuaded many times before I consent to
 give myself really to you, but what of that?
 Must not Nature be persuaded many times?)

No dainty dolce affettuoso I,
Bearded, sun-burnt, gray-neck'd, forbidding, I have
    arrived,
To be wrestled with as I pass for the solid prizes of the
    universe,
For such I afford whoever can persevere to win them.

16

On my way a moment I pause,
Here for you! and here for America!
Still the present I raise aloft, still the future of the States I
    harbinge glad and sublime,
240 And for the past I pronounce what the air holds of the red
    aborigines.

The red aborigines,
Leaving natural breaths, sounds of rain and winds, calls as
    of birds and animals in the woods, syllabled to us for
    names,
Okonee, Koosa, Ottawa, Monongahela, Sauk, Natchez,
    Chattahoochee, Kaqueta, Oronoco,
Wabash, Miami, Saginaw, Chippewa, Oshkosh,
    Walla-Walla,
Leaving such to the States they melt, they depart, charging
    the water and the land with names.

17

Expanding and swift, henceforth,
Elements, breeds, adjustments, turbulent, quick and
    audacious,
A world primal again, vistas of glory incessant and
    branching,
A new race dominating previous ones and grander far, with
    new contests,
250 New politics, new literatures and religions, new inventions
    and arts.

These, my voice announcing – I will sleep no more but
    arise,

You oceans that have been calm within me! how I feel you,
   fathomless, stirring, preparing unprecedented waves and
   storms.

18
See, steamers steaming through my poems,
See, in my poems immigrants continually coming and
   landing,
See, in arriere, the wigwam, the trail, the hunter's hut, the
   flat-boat, the maize-leaf, the claim, the rude fence, and
   the backwoods village,
See, on the one side the Western Sea and on the other the
   Eastern Sea, how they advance and retreat upon my poems
   as upon their own shores,
See, pastures and forests in my poems – see, animals wild
   and tame – see, beyond the Kaw, countless herds of
   buffalo feeding on short curly grass,
See, in my poems, cities, solid, vast, inland, with paved
   streets, with iron and stone edifices, ceaseless vehicles,
   and commerce,
See, the many-cylinder'd steam printing-press – see, the
   electric telegraph stretching across the continent,
260 See, through Atlantica's depths pulses American Europe
   reaching, pulses of Europe duly return'd,
See, the strong and quick locomotive as it departs, panting,
   blowing the steam-whistle,
See, ploughmen ploughing farms – see, miners digging
   mines – see, the numberless factories,
See, mechanics busy at their benches with tools – see from
   among them superior judges, philosophs, Presidents,
   emerge, drest in working dresses,
See, lounging through the shops and fields of the States,
   me well-belov'd, close-held by day and night,
Hear the loud echoes of my songs there – read the hints
   come at last.

19
O camerado close! O you and me at last, and us two only.
O a word to clear one's path ahead endlessly!
O something ecstatic and undemonstrable! O music wild!
O now I triumph – and you shall also;
270 O hand in hand – O wholesome pleasure – O one more
      desirer and lover!
O to haste firm holding – to haste, haste on with me.

Song of Myself

1
I celebrate myself, and sing myself,
And what I assume you shall assume,
For every atom belonging to me as good belongs to you.

I loafe and invite my soul,
I lean and loafe at my ease observing a spear of summer
      grass.

My tongue, every atom of my blood, form'd from this soil,
      this air,
Born here of parents born here from parents the same, and
      their parents the same,
I, now thirty-seven years old in perfect health begin,
Hoping to cease not till death.

10 Creeds and schools in abeyance,
Retiring back a while sufficed at what they are, but never
      forgotten,
I harbor for good or bad, I permit to speak at every hazard,
Nature without check with original energy.

2
Houses and rooms are full of perfumes, the shelves are
      crowded with perfumes,
I breathe the fragrance myself and know it and like it,
The distillation would intoxicate me also, but I shall not
      let it.

The atmosphere is not a perfume, it has no taste of
    distillation, it is odorless,
It is for my mouth forever, I am in love with it,
I will go to the bank by the wood and become undisguised
    and naked,
20   I am mad for it to be in contact with me.

The smoke of my own breath,
Echoes, ripples, buzz'd whispers, love-root, silk-thread,
    crotch and vine,
My respiration and inspiration, the beating of my heart,
    the passing of blood and air through my lungs,
The sniff of green leaves and dry leaves, and of the shore
    and dark-color'd sea-rocks, and of hay in the barn,
The sound of the belch'd words of my voice loos'd to the
    eddies of the wind,
A few light kisses, a few embraces, a reaching around of
    arms,
The play of shine and shade on the trees as the supple
    boughs wag,
The delight alone or in the rush of the streets, or along
    the fields and hill-sides,
The feeling of health, the full-noon trill, the song of me
    rising from bed and meeting the sun.

30   Have you reckon'd a thousand acres much? have you
    reckon'd the earth much?
Have you practis'd so long to learn to read?
Have you felt so proud to get at the meaning of poems?

Stop this day and night with me and you shall possess the
    origin of all poems,
You shall possess the good of the earth and sun, (there are
    millions of suns left,)
You shall no longer take things at second or third hand,
    nor look through the eyes of the dead, nor feed on the
    spectres in books,

You shall not look through my eyes either, nor take things
    from me,
You shall listen to all sides and filter them from your self.

3
I have heard what the talkers were talking, the talk of the
    beginning and the end,
But I do not talk of the beginning or the end.

40   There was never any more inception than there is now,
Nor any more youth or age than there is now,
And will never be any more perfection than there is now,
Nor any more heaven or hell than there is now.

Urge and urge and urge,
Always the procreant urge of the world.
Out of the dimness opposite equals advance, always
    substance and increase, always sex,
Always a knit of identity, always disjunction, always a
    breed of life.

To elaborate is no avail, learn'd and unlearn'd feel that
    it is so.

Sure as the most certain sure, plumb in the uprights,
    well entretied, braced in the beams,
50   Stout as a horse, affectionate, haughty, electrical,
I and this mystery here we stand.

Clear and sweet is my soul, and clear and sweet is all that
    is not my soul.

Lack one lacks both, and the unseen is proved by the seen,
Till that becomes unseen and receives proof in its turn.

Showing the best and dividing it from the worst age
    vexes age,   *evenness of mind; stressfree*
Knowing the perfect fitness and equanimity of things,
    while they discuss I am silent, and go bathe and
    admire myself.

Welcome is every organ and attribute of me, and of any man
    hearty and clean,
Not an inch nor a particle of an inch is vile, and none shall
    be less familiar than the rest.

I am satisfied – I see, dance, laugh, sing;
60 As the hugging and loving bed-fellow sleeps at my side
    through the night, and withdraws at the peep of the day
    with stealthy tread,
Leaving me baskets cover'd with white towels swelling the
    house with their plenty,
Shall I postpone my acceptation and realization and scream
    at my eyes,
That they turn from gazing after and down the road,
And forthwith cipher and show me to a cent,
Exactly the value of one and exactly the value of two, and
    which is ahead?

4
Trippers and askers surround me,
People I meet, the effect upon me of my early life or the
    ward and city I live in, or the nation,
The latest dates, discoveries, inventions, societies, authors
    old and new,
My dinner, dress, associates, looks, compliments, dues,
70 The real or fancied indifference of some man or woman I
    love,
The sickness of one of my folks or of myself, or ill-doing
    or loss or lack of money, or depressions or exaltations,
Battles, the horrors of fratricidal war, the fever of doubtful
    news, the fitful events;
These come to me days and nights and go from me again,
But they are not the Me myself.

Apart from the pulling and hauling stands what I am,
Stands amused, complacent, compassionating, idle, unitary,
Looks down, is erect, or bends an arm on an impalpable
    certain rest,

Looking with side-curved head curious what will come
   next,
Both in and out of the game and watching and wondering
   at it.

80   Backward I see in my own days where I sweated through
      fog with linguists and contenders,
   I have no mockings or arguments, I witness and wait.

   5
   I believe in you my soul, the other I am must not abase
      itself to you,

   degrade

   And you must not be abased to the other.

   Loafe with me on the grass, loose the stop from your
      throat,
   Not words, not music or rhyme I want, not custom or
      lecture, not even the best,
   Only the lull I like, the hum of your valvèd voice.

   I mind how once we lay such a transparent summer
      morning,
   How you settled your head athwart my hips and gently
      turn'd over upon me,
   And parted the shirt from my bosom-bone, and plunged
      your tongue to my bare-stript heart,
90   And reach'd till you felt my beard, and reach'd till you held
      my feet.

   Swiftly arose and spread around me the peace and
      knowledge that pass all the argument of the earth,
   And I know that the hand of God is the promise of my own,
   And I know that the spirit of God is the brother of my own,
   And that all the men ever born are also my brothers,
      and the women my sisters and lovers,
   And that a kelson of the creation is love,
   And limitless are leaves stiff or drooping in the fields,
   And brown ants in the little wells beneath them,
   And mossy scabs of the worm fence, heap'd stones, elder,
      mullein and poke-weed.

6

A child said *What is the grass?* fetching it to me with full
    hands;
100 How could I answer the child? I do not know what it is
    any more than he.

I guess it must be the flag of my disposition, out of hopeful
    green stuff woven.

Or I guess it is the handkerchief of the Lord,
A scented gift and remembrancer designedly dropt,
Bearing the owner's name someway in the corners, that we
    may see and remark, and say *Whose?*

Or I guess the grass is itself a child, the produced babe
    of the vegetation.

Or I guess it is a uniform hieroglyphic,
And it means, Sprouting alike in broad zones and narrow
    zones,
Growing among black folks as among white,
Kanuck, Tuckahoe, Congressman, Cuff, I give them the
    same, I receive them the same.

110 And now it seems to me the beautiful uncut hair of graves.

Tenderly will I use you curling grass,
It may be you transpire from the breasts of young men,
It may be if I had known them I would have loved them,
It may be you are from old people, or from offspring taken
    soon out of their mothers' laps,
And here you are the mothers' laps.

This grass is very dark to be from the white heads of old
    mothers,
Darker than the colorless beards of old men,
Dark to come from under the faint red roofs of mouths.

O I perceive after all so many uttering tongues,
120 And I perceive they do not come from the roofs of mouths
    for nothing.

I wish I could translate the hints about the dead young men
    and women,
And the hints about old men and mothers, and the offspring
    taken soon out of their laps.

What do you think has become of the young and old men?
And what do you think has become of the women and
    children?

They are alive and well somewhere,
The smallest sprout shows there is really no death,
And if ever there was it led forward life, and does not wait
    at the end to arrest it,
And ceas'd the moment life appear'd.

All goes onward and outward, nothing collapses,
130 And to die is different from what any one supposed, and
    luckier.

7
Has any one supposed it lucky to be born?
I hasten to inform him or her it is just as lucky to die, and
    I know it.

I pass death with the dying and birth with the new-wash'd
    babe, and am not contain'd between my hat and boots,
And peruse manifold objects, no two alike and every one
    good,
The earth good and the stars good, and their adjuncts all
    good.

I am not an earth nor an adjunct of an earth,
I am the mate and companion of people, all just as
    immortal and fathomless as myself,
(They do not know how immortal, but I know.)

Every kind for itself and its own, for me mine male and
    female,
140 For me those that have been boys and that love women,
For me the man that is proud and feels how it stings to be
    slighted,

For me the sweet-heart and the old maid, for me mothers
    and the mothers of mothers,
For me lips that have smiled, eyes that have shed tears,
For me children and the begetters of children.

Undrape! you are not guilty to me, nor stale nor discarded,
I see through the broadcloth and gingham whether or no,
And am around, tenacious, acquisitive, tireless, and cannot
    be shaken away.

8
The little one sleeps in its cradle,
I lift the gauze and look a long time, and silently brush
    away flies with my hand.

150   The youngster and the red-faced girl turn aside up the
        bushy hill,
    I peeringly view them from the top.

The suicide sprawls on the bloody floor of the bedroom,
I witness the corpse with its dabbled hair, I note where the
    pistol has fallen.

The blab of the pave, tires of carts, sluff of boot-soles, talk
    of the promenaders,
The heavy omnibus, the driver with his interrogating
    thumb, the clank of the shod horses on the granite floor,
The snow-sleighs, clinking, shouted jokes, pelts of
    snow-balls,
The hurrahs for popular favorites, the fury of rous'd mobs,
The flap of the curtain'd litter, a sick man inside borne to
    the hospital,
The meeting of enemies, the sudden oath, the blows and
    fall,
160   The excited crowd, the policeman with his star quickly
        working his passage to the centre of the crowd,
    The impassive stones that receive and return so many
        echoes,
    What groans of over-fed or half-starv'd who fall sunstruck
        or in fits,

What exclamations of women taken suddenly who hurry
    home and give birth to babes,
What living and buried speech is always vibrating here,
    what howls restrain'd by decorum,
Arrests of criminals, slights, adulterous offers made,
    acceptances, rejections with convex lips,
I mind them or the show or resonance of them – I come and
    I depart.

9

The big doors of the country barn stand open and ready,
The dried grass of the harvest-time loads the slow-drawn
    wagon,
The clear light plays on the brown gray and green
    intertinged,
170 The armfuls are pack'd to the sagging mow.

I am there, I help, I came stretch'd atop of the load,
I felt its soft jolts, one leg reclined on the other,
I jump from the cross-beams and seize the clover and
    timothy,
And roll head over heels and tangle my hair full of wisps.

10

Alone far in the wilds and mountains I hunt,
Wandering amazed at my own lightness and glee,
In the late afternoon choosing a safe spot to pass the night,
Kindling a fire and broiling the fresh-kill'd game,
Falling asleep on the gather'd leaves with my dog and gun
    by my side.

180 The Yankee clipper is under her sky-sails, she cuts the
    sparkle and scud,
My eyes settle the land, I bend at her prow or shout
    joyously from the deck.

The boatmen and clam-diggers arose early and stopt for me,
I tuck'd my trowser-ends in my boots and went and had a
  good time;
You should have been with us that day round the
  chowder-kettle.

I saw the marriage of the trapper in the open air in the far
  west, the bride was a red girl,
Her father and his friends sat near cross-legged and dumbly
  smoking, they had moccasins to their feet and large thick
  blankets hanging from their shoulders,
On a bank lounged the trapper, he was drest mostly in skins,
  his luxuriant beard and curls protected his neck, he held
  his bride by the hand,
She had long eyelashes, her head was bare, her coarse
  straight locks descended upon her voluptuous limbs and
  reach'd to her feet.

The runaway slave came to my house and stopt outside,
190 I heard his motions crackling the twigs of the woodpile,
Through the swung half-door of the kitchen I saw him
  limpsy and weak,
And went where he sat on a log and led him in and assured
  him,
And brought water and fill'd a tub for his sweated body and
  bruis'd feet,
And gave him a room that enter'd from my own, and gave
  him some coarse clean clothes,
And remember perfectly well his revolving eyes and his
  awkwardness,
And remember putting plasters on the galls of his neck
  and ankles;
He staid with me a week before he was recuperated and
  pass'd north,
I had him sit next me at table, my fire-lock lean'd in the
  corner.

11

Twenty-eight young men bathe by the shore,
200 Twenty-eight young men and all so friendly;
Twenty-eight years of womanly life and all so lonesome.

She owns the fine house by the rise of the bank,
She hides handsome and richly drest aft the blinds of
   the window.

Which of the young men does she like the best?
Ah the homeliest of them is beautiful to her.

Where are you off to, lady? for I see you,
You splash in the water there, yet stay stock still in your
   room.

Dancing and laughing along the beach came the
   twenty-ninth bather,
The rest did not see her, but she saw them and loved them.

210 The beards of the young men glisten'd with wet, it ran from
   their long hair,
Little streams pass'd all over their bodies.

An unseen hand also pass'd over their bodies,
It descended tremblingly from their temples and ribs.

The young men float on their backs, their white bellies
   bulge to the sun, they do not ask who seizes fast to them,
They do not know who puffs and declines with pendant
   and bending arch,
They do not think whom they souse with spray.

12

The butcher-boy puts off his killing-clothes, or sharpens
   his knife at the stall in the market,
I loiter enjoying his repartee and his shuffle and break-down.

Blacksmiths with grimed and hairy chests environ the anvil,
220 Each has his main-sledge, they are all out, there is a great
   heat in the fire.

From the cinder-strew'd threshold I follow their
    movements,
The lithe sheer of their waists plays even with their massive
    arms,
Overhand the hammers swing, overhand so slow, overhand
    so sure,
They do not hasten, each man hits in his place.

13

The negro holds firmly the reins of his four horses, the
    block swags underneath on its tied-over chain,
The negro that drives the long dray of the stone-yard,
    steady and tall he stands pois'd on one leg on the
    string-piece,
His blue shirt exposes his ample neck and breast and
    loosens over his hip-band,
His glance is calm and commanding, he tosses the slouch
    of his hat away from his forehead,
The sun falls on his crispy hair and mustache, falls on the
    black of his polish'd and perfect limbs.

230 I behold the picturesque giant and love him, and I do not
    stop there,
I go with the team also.

In me the caresser of life wherever moving, backward as
    well as forward sluing,
To niches aside and junior bending, not a person or object
    missing,
Absorbing all to myself and for this song.

Oxen that rattle the yoke and chain or halt in the leafy
    shade, what is that you express in your eyes?
It seems to me more than all the print I have read in my life.

My tread scares the wood-drake and wood-duck on my
    distant and day-long ramble,
They rise together, they slowly circle around.

I believe in those wing'd purposes,
240 And acknowledge red, yellow, white, playing within me,

And consider green and violet and the tufted crown
    intentional,
And do not call the tortoise unworthy because she is not
    something else,
And the jay in the woods never studied the gamut, yet trills
    pretty well to me,
And the look of the bay mare shames silliness out of me.

14
The wild gander leads his flock through the cool night,
Ya-honk he says, and sounds it down to me like an invitation,
The pert may suppose it meaningless, but I listening close,
Find its purpose and place up there toward the wintry sky.

The sharp-hoof'd moose of the north, the cat on the
    house-sill, the chickadee, the prairie-dog,
250   The litter of the grunting sow as they tug at her teats,
The brood of the turkey-hen and she with her half-spread
    wings,
I see in them and myself the same old law.

The press of my foot to the earth springs a hundred
    affections,
They scorn the best I can do to relate them.

I am enamour'd of growing out-doors,
Of men that live among cattle or taste of the ocean or
    woods,
Of the builders and steerers of ships and the wielders of
    axes and mauls, and the drivers of horses,
I can eat and sleep with them week in and week out.

What is commonest, cheapest, nearest, easiest, is Me,
260   Me going in for my chances, spending for vast returns,
Adorning myself to bestow myself on the first that will
    take me,
Not asking the sky to come down to my good will,
Scattering it freely forever.

15

The pure contralto sings in the organ loft,

The carpenter dresses his plank, the tongue of his foreplane
    whistles its wild ascending lisp,

The married and unmarried children ride home to their
    Thanksgiving dinner,

The pilot seizes the king-pin, he heaves down with a strong
    arm,

The mate stands braced in the whale-boat, lance and
    harpoon are ready.

The duck-shooter walks by silent and cautious stretches,

270   The deacons are ordain'd with cross'd hands at the altar,

The spinning-girl retreats and advances to the hum of the
    big wheel,

The farmer stops by the bars as he walks on a First-day
    loafe and looks at the oats and rye,

The lunatic is carried at last to the asylum a confirm'd case,

(He will never sleep any more as he did in the cot in his
    mother's bedroom;)

The jour printer with gray head and gaunt jaws works at
    his case,

He turns his quid of tobacco while his eyes blurr with the
    manuscript;

The malform'd limbs are tied to the surgeon's table,

What is removed drops horribly in a pail;

The quadroon girl is sold at the auction-stand, the drunkard
    nods by the bar-room stove,

280   The machinist rolls up his sleeves, the policeman travels
    his beat, the gate-keeper marks who pass,

The young fellow drives the express-wagon, (I love him,
    though I do not know him;)

The half-breed straps on his light boots to compete in the
    race,

The western turkey-shooting draws old and young, some
    lean on their rifles, some sit on logs,

Out from the crowd steps the marksman, takes his position,
    levels his piece;

The groups of newly-come immigrants cover the wharf or
    levee,
As the woolly-pates hoe in the sugar-field, the overseer
    views them from his saddle,
The bugle calls in the ball-room, the gentlemen run for
    their partners, the dancers bow to each other,
The youth lies awake in the cedar-roof'd garret and harks
    to the musical rain,
The Wolverine sets traps on the creek that helps fill the
    Huron,
290   The squaw wrapt in her yellow-hemm'd cloth is offering
    moccasins and bead-bags for sale,
The connoisseur peers along the exhibition-gallery with
    half-shut eyes bent sideways,
As the deck-hands make fast the steamboat the plank is
    thrown for the shore-going passengers,
The young sister holds out the skein while the elder sister
    winds it off in a ball, and stops now and then for the knots,
The one-year wife is recovering and happy having a week
    ago borne her first child,
The clean-hair'd Yankee girl works with her sewing-machine
    or in the factory or mill,
The paving-man leans on his two-handed rammer, the
    reporter's lead flies swiftly over the note-book, the
    sign-painter is lettering with blue and gold,
The canal boy trots on the tow-path, the book-keeper
    counts at his desk, the shoemaker waxes his thread,
The conductor beats time for the band and all the performers
    follow him,
The child is baptized, the convert is making his first
    professions,
300   The regatta is spread on the bay, the race is begun, (how the
    white sails sparkle!)
The drover watching his drove sings out to them that would
    stray,
The pedler sweats with his pack on his back, (the purchaser
    higgling about the odd cent;)

The bride unrumples her white dress, the minute-hand of
    the clock moves slowly,
The opium-eater reclines with rigid head and just-open'd
    lips,
The prostitute draggles her shawl, her bonnet bobs on her
    tipsy and pimpled neck,
The crowd laugh at her blackguard oaths, the men jeer and
    wink to each other,
(Miserable! I do not laugh at your oaths nor jeer you;)
The President holding a cabinet council is surrounded by
    the great Secretaries,
On the piazza walk three matrons stately and friendly with
    twined arms,
310 The crew of the fish-smack pack repeated layers of halibut
    in the hold,
The Missourian crosses the plains toting his wares and his
    cattle,
As the fare-collector goes through the train he gives notice
    by the jingling of loose change,
The floor-men are laying the floor, the tinners are tinning
    the roof, the masons are calling for mortar,
In single file each shouldering his hod pass onward the
    laborers;
Seasons pursuing each other the indescribable crowd is
    gather'd, it is the fourth of Seventh-month, (what salutes
    of cannon and small arms!)
Seasons pursuing each other the plougher ploughs, the
    mower mows, and the winter-grain falls in the ground;
Off on the lakes the pike-fisher watches and waits by the
    hole in the frozen surface,
The stumps stand thick round the clearing, the squatter
    strikes deep with his axe,
Flatboatmen make fast towards dusk near the cotton-wood
    or pecan-trees,
320 Coon-seekers go through the regions of the Red river or
    through those drain'd by the Tennessee, or through those
    of the Arkansas,

Torches shine in the dark that hangs on the Chattahooche
    or Altamahaw,
Patriarchs sit at supper with sons and grandsons and
    great-grandsons around them,
In walls of adobie, in canvas tents, rest hunters and trappers
    after their day's sport,
The city sleeps and the country sleeps,
The living sleep for their time, the dead sleep for their time,
The old husband sleeps by his wife and the young husband
    sleeps by his wife;
And these tend inward to me, and I tend outward to them,
And such as it is to be of these more or less I am,
And of these one and all I weave the song of myself.

16

330   I am of old and young, of the foolish as much as the wise,
Regardless of others, ever regardful of others,
Maternal as well as paternal, a child as well as a man,
Stuff'd with the stuff that is coarse and stuff'd with the stuff
    that is fine,
One of the Nation of many nations, the smallest the same
    and the largest the same,
A Southerner soon as a Northerner, a planter nonchalant
    and hospitable down by the Oconee I live,
A Yankee bound my own way ready for trade, my joints the
    limberest joints on earth and the sternest joints on earth,
A Kentuckian walking the vale of the Elkhorn in my
    deer-skin leggings, a Louisianian or Georgian,
A boatman over lakes or bays or along coasts, a Hoosier,
    Badger, Buckeye;
At home on Kanadian snow-shoes or up in the bush, or
    with fishermen off Newfoundland,
340   At home in the fleet of ice-boats, sailing with the rest and
    tracking,
At home on the hills of Vermont or in the woods of Maine,
    or the Texan ranch,
Comrade of Californians, comrade of free North-Westerners
    (loving their big proportions,)

Comrade of raftsmen and coalmen, comrade of all who
    shake hands and welcome to drink and meat,
A learner with the simplest, a teacher of the thoughtfullest,
A novice beginning yet experient of myriads of seasons,
Of every hue and caste am I, of every rank and religion,
A farmer, mechanic, artist, gentleman, sailor, quaker,
Prisoner, fancy-man, rowdy, lawyer, physician, priest.

I resist any thing better than my own diversity,
350 Breathe the air but leave plenty after me,
And am not stuck up, and am in my place.

(The moth and the fish-eggs are in their place,
The bright suns I see and the dark suns I cannot see are in
    their place,
The palpable is in its place and the impalpable is in its
    place.)

17
These are really the thoughts of all men in all ages and
    lands, they are not original with me,
If they are not yours as much as mine they are nothing, or
    next to nothing,
If they are not the riddle and the untying of the riddle they
    are nothing,
If they are not just as close as they are distant they are
    nothing.

This is the grass that grows wherever the land is and the
    water is,
360 This the common air that bathes the globe.

18
With music strong I come, with my cornets and my drums,
I play not marches for accepted victors only, I play marches
    for conquer'd and slain persons.

Have you heard that it was good to gain the day?
I also say it is good to fall, battles are lost in the same spirit
    in which they are won.

I beat and pound for the dead,
I blow through my embouchures my loudest and gayest
    for them.

Vivas to those who have fail'd!
And to those whose war-vessels sank in the sea!
And to those themselves who sank in the sea!
370 And to all generals that lost engagements, and all overcome
        heroes!
And the numberless unknown heroes equal to the greatest
    heroes known!

19

This is the meal equally set, this the meat for natural hunger,
It is for the wicked just the same as the righteous, I make
    appointments with all,
I will not have a single person slighted or left away,
The kept-woman, sponger, thief, are hereby invited,
The heavy-lipp'd slave is invited, the venerealee is invited;
There shall be no difference between them and the rest.

This is the press of a bashful hand, this the float and odor of
    hair,
This the touch of my lips to yours, this the murmur of
    yearning,
380 This the far-off depth and height reflecting my own face,
This the thoughtful merge of myself, and the outlet again.

Do you guess I have some intricate purpose?
Well I have, for the Fourth-month showers have, and the
    mica on the side of a rock has.

Do you take it I would astonish?
Does the daylight astonish? does the early redstart twittering
    through the woods?
Do I astonish more than they?

This hour I tell things in confidence,
I might not tell everybody, but I will tell you.

20

Who goes there? hankering, gross, mystical, nude;
390 How is it I extract strength from the beef I eat?

What is a man anyhow? what am I? what are you?

All I mark as my own you shall offset it with your own,
Else it were time lost listening to me.

I do not snivel that snivel the world over,
That months are vacuums and the ground but wallow and
    filth.

Whimpering and truckling fold with powders for invalids,
    conformity goes to the fourth-remov'd,
I wear my hat as I please indoors or out.

Why should I pray? why should I venerate and be
    ceremonious?

Having pried through the strata, analyzed to a hair,
    counsel'd with doctors and calculated close,
400 I find no sweeter fat than sticks to my own bones.

In all people I see myself, none more and not one a
    barley-corn less,
And the good or bad I say of myself I say of them.

I know I am solid and sound,
To me the converging objects of the universe perpetually
    flow,
All are written to me, and I must get what the writing means.

I know I am deathless,
I know this orbit of mine cannot be swept by a carpenter's
    compass,
I know I shall not pass like a child's carlacue cut with a burnt
    stick at night.

I know I am august,
410 I do not trouble my spirit to vindicate itself or be understood,
I see that the elementary laws never apologize,
(I reckon I behave no prouder than the level I plant my
    house by, after all.)

I exist as I am, that is enough,
If no other in the world be aware I sit content,
And if each and all be aware I sit content.

One world is aware and by far the largest to me, and that is
    myself,
And whether I come to my own to-day or on ten thousand
    or ten million years,
I can cheerfully take it now, or with equal cheerfulness I
    can wait.

My foothold is tenon'd and mortis'd in granite,
420 I laugh at what you call dissolution,
And I know the amplitude of time.

21

I am the poet of the Body and I am the poet of the Soul,
The pleasures of heaven are with me and the pains of hell
    are with me,
The first I graft and increase upon myself, the latter I
    translate into a new tongue.

I am the poet of the woman the same as the man,
And I say it is as great to be a woman as to be a man,
And I say there is nothing greater than the mother of men.

I chant the chant of dilation or pride,
We have had ducking and deprecating about enough,
430 I show that size is only development.

Have you outstript the rest? are you the President?
It is a trifle, they will more than arrive there every one, and
    still pass on.

I am he that walks with the tender and growing night,
I call to the earth and sea half-held by the night.

Press close bare-bosom'd night – press close magnetic
    nourishing night!
Night of south winds – night of the large few stars!
Still nodding night – mad naked summer night.

Smile O voluptuous cool-breath'd earth!
Earth of the slumbering and liquid trees!
440 Earth of departed sunset – earth of the mountains
    misty-topt!
Earth of the vitreous pour of the full moon just tinged
    with blue!
Earth of shine and dark mottling the tide of the river!
Earth of the limpid gray of clouds brighter and clearer for
    my sake!
Far-swooping elbow'd earth – rich apple-blossom'd earth!
Smile, for your lover comes.

Prodigal, you have given me love – therefore I to you
    give love!
O unspeakable passionate love.

22

You sea! I resign myself to you also – I guess what you
    mean,
I behold from the beach your crooked inviting fingers,
450 I believe you refuse to go back without feeling of me,
We must have a turn together, I undress, hurry me out of
    sight of the land,
Cushion me soft, rock me in billowy drowse,
Dash me with amorous wet, I can repay you.

Sea of stretch'd ground-swells,
Sea breathing broad and convulsive breaths,
Sea of the brine of life and of unshovell'd yet
    always-ready graves,
Howler and scooper of storms, capricious and dainty sea,
I am integral with you, I too am of one phase and of all
    phases.

Partaker of influx and efflux I, extoller of hate and
    conciliation,
460 Extoller of amies and those that sleep in each others' arms.

I am he attesting sympathy,
(Shall I make my list of things in the house and skip the
    house that supports them?)

I am not the poet of goodness only, I do not decline to be
    the poet of wickedness also.

What blurt is this about virtue and about vice?
Evil propels me and reform of evil propels me, I stand
    indifferent,
My gait is no fault-finder's or rejecter's gait,
I moisten the roots of all that has grown.

Did you fear some scrofula out of the unflagging
    pregnancy?
Did you guess the celestial laws are yet to be work'd over
    and rectified?

470 I find one side a balance and the antipodal side a balance,
Soft doctrine as steady help as stable doctrine,
Thoughts and deeds of the present our rouse and early start.

This minute that comes to me over the past decillions,
There is no better than it and now.

What behaved well in the past or behaves well to-day is
    not such a wonder,
The wonder is always and always how there can be a mean
    man or an infidel.

23
Endless unfolding of words of ages!
And mine a word of the modern, the word En-Masse.

A word of the faith that never balks,
480 Here or henceforward it is all the same to me, I accept
    Time absolutely.

It alone is without flaw, it alone rounds and completes all,
That mystic baffling wonder alone completes all.

I accept Reality and dare not question it,
Materialism first and last imbuing.

Hurrah for positive science! long live exact demonstration!
Fetch stonecrop mixt with cedar and branches of lilac,
This is the lexicographer, this the chemist, this made a
    grammar of the old cartouches,
These mariners put the ship through dangerous unknown
    seas.
This is the geologist, this works with the scalpel, and this
    is a mathematician.

490   Gentlemen, to you the first honors always!
Your facts are useful and yet they are not my dwelling,
I but enter by them to an area of my dwelling.

Less the reminders of properties told my words,
And more the reminders they of life untold, and of
    freedom and extrication,
And make short account of neuters and geldings, and favor
    men and women fully equipt,
And beat the gong of revolt, and stop with fugitives and
    them that plot and conspire.

24
Walt Whitman, a kosmos, of Manhattan the son,
Turbulent, fleshy, sensual, eating, drinking and breeding,
No sentimentalist, no stander above men and women or
    apart from them,
500   No more modest than immodest.

Unscrew the locks from the doors!
Unscrew the doors themselves from their jambs!

Whoever degrades another degrades me,
And whatever is done or said returns at last to me.

Through me the afflatus surging and surging, through me
    the current and index.

I speak the pass-word primeval, I give the sign of democracy,
By God! I will accept nothing which all cannot have their
  counterpart of on the same terms.

Through me many long dumb voices,
Voices of the interminable generations of prisoners and
  slaves,
510 Voices of the diseas'd and despairing and of thieves and
  dwarfs,
Voices of cycles of preparation and accretion,
And of the threads that connect the stars, and of wombs and
  of the father-stuff,
And of the rights of them the others are down upon,
Of the deform'd, trivial, flat, foolish, despised,
Fog in the air, beetles rolling balls of dung.

Through me forbidden voices,
Voices of sexes and lusts, voices veil'd and I remove the
  veil,
Voices indecent by me clarified and transfigur'd.

I do not press my fingers across my mouth,
520 I keep as delicate around the bowels as around the head
  and heart,
Copulation is no more rank to me than death is.

I believe in the flesh and the appetites,
Seeing, hearing, feeling, are miracles, and each part and
  tag of me is a miracle.

Divine am I inside and out, and I make holy whatever I
  touch or am touch'd from,
The scent of these arm-pits aroma finer than prayer,
This head more than churches, bibles, and all the creeds.

If I worship one thing more than another it shall be the
  spread of my own body, or any part of it,
Translucent mould of me it shall be you!
Shaded ledges and rests it shall be you!
530 Firm masculine colter it shall be you!
Whatever goes to the tilth of me it shall be you!

You my rich blood! your milky stream pale strippings of
    my life!
Breast that presses against other breasts it shall be you!
My brain it shall be your occult convolutions!
Root of wash'd sweet-flag! timorous pond-snipe! nest of
    guarded duplicate eggs! it shall be you!
Mix'd tussled hay of head, beard, brawn, it shall be you!
Trickling sap of maple, fibre of manly wheat, it shall be you!
Sun so generous it shall be you!
Vapors lighting and shading my face it shall be you!
540   You sweaty brooks and dews it shall be you!
Winds whose soft-tickling genitals rub against me it shall
    be you!
Broad muscular fields, branches of live oak, loving lounger
    in my winding paths, it shall be you!
Hands I have taken, face I have kiss'd, mortal I have ever
    touch'd, it shall be you.

I dote on myself, there is that lot of me and all so luscious,
Each moment and whatever happens thrills me with joy,
I cannot tell how my ankles bend, nor whence the cause of
    my faintest wish,
Nor the cause of the friendship I emit, nor the cause of the
    friendship I take again.

That I walk up my stoop, I pause to consider if it really be,
A morning-glory at my windows satisfies me more than the
    metaphysics of books.

550   To behold the day-break!
The little light fades the immense and diaphanous shadows,
The air tastes good to my palate.

Hefts of the moving world at innocent gambols silently
    rising freshly exuding,
Scooting obliquely high and low.

Something I cannot see puts upward libidinous prongs,
Seas of bright juice suffuse heaven.

The earth by the sky staid with, the daily close of their
    junction,
The heav'd challenge from the east that moment over my
    head,
The mocking taunt, See then whether you shall be master!

25

560   Dazzling and tremendous how quick the sun-rise would
    kill me,
If I could not now and always send sun-rise out of me.

We also ascend dazzling and tremendous as the sun,
We found our own O my soul in the calm and cool of the
    day-break.

My voice goes after what my eyes cannot reach,
With the twirl of my tongue I encompass words and
    volumes of worlds.

Speech is the twin of my vision, it is unequal to measure
    itself,
It provokes me forever, it says sarcastically,
Walt you contain enough, why don't you let it out then?

Come now I will not be tantalized, you conceive too much
    of articulation,
570   Do you know O speech how the buds beneath you are
    folded?
Waiting in gloom, protected by frost,
The dirt receding before my prophetical screams,
I underlying causes to balance them at last,
My knowledge my live parts, it keeping tally with the
    meaning of all things,
Happiness, (which whoever hears me let him or her set
    out in search of this day.)

My final merit I refuse you, I refuse putting from me what
    I really am,
Encompass worlds, but never try to encompass me,
I crowd your sleekest and best by simply looking toward
    you.

Writing and talk do not prove me,
580 I carry the plenum of proof and everything else in my face,
With the hush of my lips I wholly confound the skeptic.

26
Now I will do nothing but listen,
To accrue what I hear into this song, to let sounds
   contribute toward it.

I hear bravuras of birds, bustle of growing wheat, gossip of
   flames, clack of sticks cooking my meals,
I hear the sound I love, the sound of the human voice,
I hear all sounds running together, combined, fused or
   following,
Sounds of the city and sounds out of the city, sounds of
   the day and night,
Talkative young ones to those that like them, the loud
   laugh of work-people at their meals,
The angry base of disjointed friendship, the faint tones of
   the sick,
590 The judge with hands tight to the desk, his pallid lips
   pronouncing a death-sentence,
The heave'e'yo of stevedores unlading ships by the wharves,
   the refrain of the anchor-lifters,
The ring of alarm-bells, the cry of fire, the whirr of
   swift-streaking engines and hose-carts with premonitory
   tinkles and color'd lights,
The steam-whistle, the solid roll of the train of approaching
   cars,
The slow march play'd at the head of the association
   marching two and two,
(They go to guard some corpse, the flag-tops are draped
   with black muslin.)

I hear the violoncello, ('tis the young man's heart's
   complaint,)
I hear the key'd cornet, it glides quickly in through my ears,
It shakes mad-sweet pangs through my belly and breast.

I hear the chorus, it is a grand opera,
600   Ah this indeed is music – this suits me.

A tenor large and fresh as the creation fills me,
The orbic flex of his mouth is pouring and filling me full.

I hear the train'd soprano (what work with hers is this?)
The orchestra whirls me wider than Uranus flies,
It wrenches such ardors from me I did not know I
    possess'd them,
It sails me, I dab with bare feet, they are lick'd by the
    indolent waves,
I am cut by bitter and angry hail, I lose my breath,
Steep'd amid honey'd morphine, my windpipe throttled in
    fakes of death,
At length let up again to feel the puzzle of puzzles,
610   And that we call Being.

27

To be in any form, what is that?
(Round and round we go, all of us, and ever come back
    thither,)
If nothing lay more develop'd the quahaug in its callous
    shell were enough.

Mine is no callous shell,
I have instant conductors all over me whether I pass or
    stop,
They seize every object and lead it harmlessly through me.

I merely stir, press, feel with my fingers, and am happy,
To touch my person to some one else's is about as much as
    I can stand.

28

Is this then a touch? quivering me to a new identity,
620   Flames and ether making a rush for my veins,
Treacherous tip of me reaching and crowding to help them,
My flesh and blood playing out lightning to strike what is
    hardly different from myself,
On all sides prurient provokers stiffening my limbs,

Straining the udder of my heart for its withheld drip,
Behaving licentious toward me, taking no denial,
Depriving me of my best as for a purpose,
Unbuttoning my clothes, holding me by the bare waist,
Deluding my confusion with the calm of the sunlight and
    pasture-fields,
Immodestly sliding the fellow-senses away,
630   They bribed to swap off with touch and go and graze at the
    edges of me,
No consideration, no regard for my draining strength or
    my anger,
Fetching the rest of the herd around to enjoy them a while,
Then all uniting to stand on a headland and worry me.

The sentries desert every other part of me,
They have left me helpless to a red marauder,
They all come to the headland to witness and assist against
    me.

I am given up by traitors,
I talk wildly, I have lost my wits, I and nobody else am the
    greatest traitor,
I went myself first to the headland, my own hands carried
    me there.

640   You villain touch! what are you doing? my breath is tight
    in its throat,
Unclench your floodgates, you are too much for me.

29

Blind loving wrestling touch, sheath'd hooded sharp-tooth'd
    touch!
Did it make you ache so, leaving me?

Parting track'd by arriving, perpetual payment of perpetual
    loan,
Rich showering rain, and recompense richer afterward.

Sprouts take and accumulate, stand by the curb prolific
    and vital,
Landscapes projected masculine, full-sized and golden.

30

All truths wait in all things,
They neither hasten their own delivery nor resist it,
650 They do not need the obstetric forceps of the surgeon,
The insignificant is as big to me as any,
(What is less or more than a touch?)

Logic and sermons never convince,
The damp of the night drives deeper into my soul.

(Only what proves itself to every man and woman is so,
Only what nobody denies is so.)

A minute and a drop of me settle my brain,
I believe the soggy clods shall become lovers and lamps,
And a compend of compends is the meat of a man or
    woman,
660 And a summit and flower there is the feeling they have for
    each other,
And they are to branch boundlessly out of that lesson until
    it becomes omnific,
And until one and all shall delight us, and we them.

31

I believe a leaf of grass is no less than the journey-work of
    the stars,
And the pismire is equally perfect, and a grain of sand,
    and the egg of the wren,
And the tree-toad is a chef-d'œuvre for the highest,
And the running blackberry would adorn the parlors of
    heaven,
And the narrowest hinge in my hand puts to scorn all
    machinery,
And the cow crunching with depress'd head surpasses any
    statue,
And a mouse is miracle enough to stagger sextillions of
    infidels.

670   I find I incorporate gneiss, coal, long-threaded moss, fruits,
            grains, esculent roots,
       And am stucco'd with quadrupeds and birds all over,
       And have distanced what is behind me for good reasons,
       But call any thing back again when I desire it.

       In vain the speeding or shyness,
       In vain the plutonic rocks send their old heat against my
            approach,
       In vain the mastodon retreats beneath its own powder'd
            bones,
       In vain objects stand leagues off and assume manifold
            shapes,
       In vain the ocean settling in hollows and the great monsters
            lying low,
       In vain the buzzard houses herself with the sky,
680   In vain the snake slides through the creepers and logs,
       In vain the elk takes to the inner passes of the woods,
       In vain the razor-bill'd auk sails far north to Labrador,
       I follow quickly, I ascend to the nest in the fissure of the
            cliff.

       32
       I think I could turn and live with animals, they are so placid
            and self-contain'd,
       I stand and look at them long and long.

       They do not sweat and whine about their condition,
       They do not lie awake in the dark and weep for their sins,
       They do not make me sick discussing their duty to God,
       Not one is dissatisfied, not one is demented with the mania
            of owning things,
690   Not one kneels to another, nor to his kind that lived
            thousands of years ago,
       Not one is respectable or unhappy over the whole earth.

       So they show their relations to me and I accept them,
       They bring me tokens of myself, they evince them plainly in
            their possession.

I wonder where they get those tokens,
Did I pass that way huge times ago and negligently drop
   them?

Myself moving forward then and now and forever,
Gathering and showing more always and with velocity,
Infinite and omnigenous, and the like of these among them,
Not too exclusive toward the reachers of my remembrancers,
700   Picking out here one that I love, and now go with him on
   brotherly terms.

A gigantic beauty of a stallion, fresh and responsive to my
   caresses,
Head high in the forehead, wide between the ears,
Limbs glossy and supple, tail dusting the ground,
Eyes full of sparkling wickedness, ears finely cut, flexibly
   moving.

His nostrils dilate as my heels embrace him,
His well-built limbs tremble with pleasure as we race
   around and return.

I but use you a minute, then I resign you, stallion,
Why do I need your paces when I myself out-gallop them?
Even as I stand or sit passing faster than you.

33
710   Space and Time! now I see it is true, what I guess'd at,
What I guess'd when I loaf'd on the grass,
What I guess'd while I lay alone in my bed,
And again as I walk'd the beach under the paling stars of
   the morning.

My ties and ballasts leave me, my elbows rest in sea-gaps,
I skirt sierras, my palms cover continents,
I am afoot with my vision.

By the city's quadrangular houses – in log huts, camping
   with lumbermen,
Along the ruts of the turnpike, along the dry gulch and
   rivulet bed,

Weeding my onion-patch or hoeing rows of carrots and
    parsnips, crossing savannas, trailing in forests,
720 Prospecting, gold-digging, girdling the trees of a new
    purchase,
Scorch'd ankle-deep by the hot sand, hauling my boat
    down the shallow river,
Where the panther walks to and fro on a limb overhead,
    where the buck turns furiously at the hunter,
Where the rattlesnake suns his flabby length on a rock,
    where the otter is feeding on fish,
Where the alligator in his tough pimples sleeps by the bayou,
Where the black bear is searching for roots or honey, where
    the beaver pats the mud with his paddle-shaped tail;
Over the growing sugar, over the yellow-flower'd cotton
    plant, over the rice in its low moist field,
Over the sharp-peak'd farm house, with its scallop'd scum
    and slender shoots from the gutters,
Over the western persimmon, over the long-leav'd corn,
    over the delicate blue-flower flax,
Over the white and brown buckwheat, a hummer and buzzer
    there with the rest,
730 Over the dusky green of the rye as it ripples and shades in
    the breeze;
Scaling mountains, pulling myself cautiously up, holding
    on by low scragged limbs,
Walking the path worn in the grass and beat through the
    leaves of the brush,
Where the quail is whistling betwixt the woods and the
    wheat-lot,
Where the bat flies in the Seventh-month eve, where the
    great goldbug drops through the dark,
Where the brook puts out of the roots of the old tree and
    flows to the meadow,
Where cattle stand and shake away flies with the tremulous
    shuddering of their hides,
Where the cheese-cloth hangs in the kitchen, where andirons
    straddle the hearth-slab, where cobwebs fall in festoons
    from the rafters;

Where trip-hammers crash, where the press is whirling its
    cylinders,
Wherever the human heart beats with terrible throes under
    its ribs,
740 Where the pear-shaped balloon is floating aloft, (floating
    in it myself and looking composedly down,)
Where the life-car is drawn on the slip-noose, where the
    heat hatches pale-green eggs in the dented sand,
Where the she-whale swims with her calf and never forsakes
    it,
Where the steam-ship trails hind-ways its long pennant of
    smoke,
Where the fin of the shark cuts like a black chip out of the
    water,
Where the half-burn'd brig is riding on unknown currents,
Where shells grow to her slimy deck, where the dead are
    corrupting below;
Where the dense-starr'd flag is borne at the head of the
    regiments,
Approaching Manhattan up by the long-stretching island,
Under Niagara, the cataract falling like a veil over my
    countenance,
750 Upon a door-step, upon the horse-block of hard wood
    outside,
Upon the race-course, or enjoying picnics or jigs or a good
    game of base-ball,
At he-festivals, with blackguard gibes, ironical license,
    bull-dances, drinking, laughter,
At the cider-mill tasting the sweets of the brown mash,
    sucking the juice through a straw,
At apple-peelings wanting kisses for all the red fruit I find,
At musters, beach-parties, friendly bees, huskings,
    house-raisings;
Where the mocking-bird sounds his delicious gurgles,
    cackles, screams, weeps,
Where the hay-rick stands in the barn-yard, where the
    dry-stalks are scatter'd, where the brood-cow waits in
    the hovel,

Where the bull advances to do his masculine work, where
    the stud to the mare, where the cock is treading the hen,
Where the heifers browse, where geese nip their food with
    short jerks,
760 Where sun-down shadows lengthen over the limitless and
    lonesome prairie,
Where herds of buffalo make a crawling spread of the
    square miles far and near,
Where the humming-bird shimmers, where the neck of the
    long-lived swan is curving and winding,
Where the laughing-gull scoots by the shore, where she
    laughs her near-human laugh,
Where bee-hives range on a gray bench in the garden half
    hid by the high weeds,
Where band-neck'd partridges roost in a ring on the ground
    with their heads out,
Where burial coaches enter the arch'd gates of a cemetery,
Where winter wolves bark amid wastes of snow and icicled
    trees,
Where the yellow-crown'd heron comes to the edge of the
    marsh at night and feeds upon small crabs,
Where the splash of swimmers and divers cools the warm
    noon,
770 Where the katy-did works her chromatic reed on the
    walnut-tree over the well,
Through patches of citrons and cucumbers with
    silver-wired leaves,
Through the salt-lick or orange glade, or under conical firs,
Through the gymnasium, through the curtain'd saloon,
    through the office or public hall;
Pleas'd with the native and pleas'd with the foreign,
    pleas'd with the new and old,
Pleas'd with the homely woman as well as the handsome,
Pleas'd with the quakeress as she puts off her bonnet and
    talks melodiously,
Pleas'd with the tune of the choir of the whitewash'd church,
Pleas'd with the earnest words of the sweating Methodist
    preacher, impress'd seriously at the camp-meeting;

Looking in at the shop-windows of Broadway the whole
    forenoon, flatting the flesh of my nose on the thick
    plate glass,
780 Wandering the same afternoon with my face turn'd up to
    the clouds, or down a lane or along the beach,
My right and left arms round the sides of two friends,
    and I in the middle;
Coming home with the silent and dark-cheek'd bush-boy,
    (behind me he rides at the drape of the day,)
Far from the settlements studying the print of animals'
    feet, or the moccasin print,
By the cot in the hospital reaching lemonade to a feverish
    patient,
Nigh the coffin'd corpse when all is still, examining with a
    candle;
Voyaging to every port to dicker and adventure,
Hurrying with the modern crowd as eager and fickle as any,
Hot toward one I hate, ready in my madness to knife him,
Solitary at midnight in my back yard, my thoughts gone
    from me a long while,
790 Walking the old hills of Judaea with the beautiful gentle
    God by my side,
Speeding through space, speeding through heaven and
    the stars,
Speeding amid the seven satellites and the broad ring,
    and the diameter of eighty thousand miles,
Speeding with tail'd meteors, throwing fire-balls like the
    rest,
Carrying the crescent child that carries its own full mother
    in its belly,
Storming, enjoying, planning, loving, cautioning,
Backing and filling, appearing and disappearing,
I tread day and night such roads.

I visit the orchards of spheres and look at the product,
And look at quintillions ripen'd and look at quintillions
    green.

800 I fly those flights of a fluid and swallowing soul,
My course runs below the soundings of plummets.

I help myself to material and immaterial,
No guard can shut me off, no law prevent me.

I anchor my ship for a little while only,
My messengers continually cruise away or bring their
    returns to me.

I go hunting polar furs and the seal, leaping chasms with a
    pike-pointed staff, clinging to topples of brittle and blue.

I ascend to the foretruck,
I take my place late at night in the crow's-nest,
We sail the arctic sea, it is plenty light enough,
810 Through the clear atmosphere I stretch around on the
    wonderful beauty,
The enormous masses of ice pass me and I pass them,
    the scenery is plain in all directions,
The white-topt mountains show in the distance, I fling out
    my fancies toward them,
We are approaching some great battle-field in which we are
    soon to be engaged,
We pass colossal outposts of the encampment, we pass with
    still feet and caution,
Or we are entering by the suburbs some vast and ruin'd city,
The blocks and fallen architecture more than all the living
    cities of the globe.

I am a free companion, I bivouac by invading watchfires,
I turn the bridegroom out of bed and stay with the bride
    myself,
I tighten her all night to my thighs and lips.

820 My voice is the wife's voice, the screech by the rail of
    the stairs,
They fetch my man's body up dripping and drown'd.

I understand the large hearts of heroes,
The courage of present times and all times,

How the skipper saw the crowded and rudderless wreck of
the steam-ship, and Death chasing it up and down the
storm,
How he knuckled tight and gave not back an inch, and was
faithful of days and faithful of nights,
And chalk'd in large letters on a board, *Be of good cheer,
we will not desert you*;
How he follow'd with them and tack'd with them three days
and would not give it up,
How he saved the drifting company at last,
How the lank loose-gown'd women look'd when boated
from the side of their prepared graves,
830 How the silent old-faced infants and the lifted sick, and the
sharp-lipp'd unshaved men;
All this I swallow, it tastes good, I like it well, it becomes
mine,
I am the man, I suffer'd, I was there.

The disdain and calmness of martyrs,
The mother of old, condemn'd for a witch, burnt with
dry wood, her children gazing on,
The hounded slave that flags in the race, leans by the fence,
blowing, cover'd with sweat,
The twinges that sting like needles his legs and neck,
the murderous buckshot and the bullets,
All these I feel or am.

I am the hounded slave, I wince at the bite of the dogs,
Hell and despair are upon me, crack and again crack the
marksmen,
840 I clutch the rails of the fence, my gore dribs, thinn'd with
the ooze of my skin,
I fall on the weeds and stones,
The riders spur their unwilling horses, haul close,
Taunt my dizzy ears and beat me violently over the head
with whip-stocks.

Agonies are one of my changes of garments,
I do not ask the wounded person how he feels, I myself
    become the wounded person,
My hurts turn livid upon me as I lean on a cane and observe.

I am the mash'd fireman with breast-bone broken,
Tumbling walls buried me in their debris,
Heat and smoke I inspired, I heard the yelling shouts of my
    comrades,
850   I heard the distant click of their picks and shovels,
They have clear'd the beams away, they tenderly lift me
    forth.

I lie in the night air in my red shirt, the pervading hush is
    for my sake,
Painless after all I lie exhausted but not so unhappy,
White and beautiful are the faces around me, the heads are
    bared of their fire-caps,
The kneeling crowd fades with the light of the torches.

Distant and dead resuscitate,
They show as the dial or move as the hands of me, I am
    the clock myself.

I am an old artillerist, I tell of my fort's bombardment,
I am there again.

860   Again the long roll of the drummers,
Again the attacking cannon, mortars,
Again to my listening ears the cannon responsive.

I take part, I see and hear the whole,
The cries, curses, roar, the plaudits for well-aim'd shots,
The ambulanza slowly passing trailing its red drip,
Workmen searching after damages, making indispensable
    repairs,
The fall of grenades through the rent roof, the fan-shaped
    explosion,
The whizz of limbs, heads, stone, wood, iron, high in the air.

Again gurgles the mouth of my dying general, he furiously
waves with his hand,
870 He gasps through the clot *Mind not me – mind – the
entrenchments.*

34

Now I tell what I knew in Texas in my early youth,
(I tell not the fall of Alamo,
Not one escaped to tell the fall of Alamo,
The hundred and fifty are dumb yet at Alamo,)
'Tis the tale of the murder in cold blood of four hundred and
twelve young men.

Retreating they had form'd in a hollow square with their
baggage for breastworks,
Nine hundred lives out of the surrounding enemy's, nine
times their number, was the price they took in advance,
Their colonel was wounded and their ammunition gone,
They treated for an honorable capitulation, receiv'd writing
and seal, gave up their arms and march'd back
prisoners of war.

880 They were the glory of the race of rangers,
Matchless with horse, rifle, song, supper, courtship,
Large, turbulent, generous, handsome, proud, and
affectionate,
Bearded, sunburnt, drest in the free costume of hunters,
Not a single one over thirty years of age.

The second First-day morning they were brought out in
squads and massacred, it was beautiful early summer,
The work commenced about five o'clock and was over by
eight.

None obey'd the command to kneel,
Some made a mad and helpless rush, some stood stark and
straight,
A few fell at once, shot in the temple or heart, the living and
dead lay together,

890 The maim'd and mangled dug in the dirt, the new-comers
   saw them there,
Some half-kill'd attempted to crawl away,
These were despatch'd with bayonets or batter'd with the
   blunts of muskets,
A youth not seventeen years old seiz'd his assassin till two
   more came to release him,
The three were all torn and cover'd with the boy's blood.

At eleven o'clock began the burning of the bodies;
That is the tale of the murder of the four hundred and twelve
   young men.

35
Would you hear of an old-time sea-fight?
Would you learn who won by the light of the moon and stars?
List to the yarn, as my grandmother's father the sailor told
   it to me.

900 Our foe was no skulk in his ship I tell you, (said he,)
His was the surly English pluck, and there is no tougher or
   truer, and never was, and never will be;
Along the lower'd eve he came horribly raking us.

We closed with him, the yards entangled, the cannon
   touch'd,
My captain lash'd fast with his own hands.

We had receiv'd some eighteen pound shots under the
   water,
On our lower-gun-deck two large pieces had burst at the
   first fire, killing all around and blowing up overhead.

Fighting at sun-down, fighting at dark,
Ten o'clock at night, the full moon well up, our leaks on the
   gain, and five feet of water reported,
The master-at-arms loosing the prisoners confined in the
   after-hold to give them a chance for themselves.

910   The transit to and from the magazine is now stopt by the
            sentinels,
      They see so many strange faces they do not know whom to
            trust.

      Our frigate takes fire,
      The other asks if we demand quarter?
      If our colors are struck and the fighting done?

      Now I laugh content, for I hear the voice of my little
            captain,
      We have not struck, he composedly cries, *we have just begun
            our part of the fighting.*

      Only three guns are in use,
      One is directed by the captain himself against the enemy's
            main-mast,
      Two well serv'd with grape and canister silence his musketry
            and clear his decks.

920   The tops alone second the fire of this little battery,
            especially the main-top,
      They hold out bravely during the whole of the action.

      Not a moment's cease,
      The leaks gain fast on the pumps, the fire eats toward the
            powder-magazine.

      One of the pumps has been shot away, it is generally thought
            we are sinking.

      Serene stands the little captain,
      He is not hurried, his voice is neither high nor low,
      His eyes give more light to us than our battle-lanterns.

      Toward twelve there in the beams of the moon they
            surrender to us.

      36
      Stretch'd and still lies the midnight,
930   Two great hulls motionless on the breast of the darkness,

Our vessel riddled and slowly sinking, preparations to pass
    to the one we have conquer'd,
The captain on the quarter-deck coldly giving his orders
    through a countenance white as a sheet,
Near by the corpse of the child that serv'd in the cabin,
The dead face of an old salt with long white hair and
    carefully curl'd whiskers,
The flames spite of all that can be done flickering aloft and
    below,
The husky voices of the two or three officers yet fit for duty,
Formless stacks of bodies and bodies by themselves, dabs of
    flesh upon the masts and spars,
Cut of cordage, dangle of rigging, slight shock of the soothe
    of waves,
Black and impassive guns, litter of powder-parcels,
    strong scent,
940 A few large stars overhead, silent and mournful shining,
Delicate sniffs of sea-breeze, smells of sedgy grass and fields
    by the shore, death-messages given in charge to
    survivors,
The hiss of the surgeon's knife, the gnawing teeth of his saw,
Wheeze, cluck, swash of falling blood, short wild scream,
    and long, dull, tapering groan,
These so, these irretrievable.

37
You laggards there on guard! look to your arms!
In at the conquer'd doors they crowd! I am possess'd!
Embody all presences outlaw'd or suffering,
See myself in prison shaped like another man,
And feel the dull unintermitted pain.

950 For me the keepers of convicts shoulder their carbines and
    keep watch,
It is I let out in the morning and barr'd at night.

Not a mutineer walks handcuff'd to jail but I am
    handcuff'd to him and walk by his side,
(I am less the jolly one there, and more the silent one with
    sweat on my twitching lips.)

Not a youngster is taken for larceny but I go up too, and am
    tried and sentenced.

Not a cholera patient lies at the last gasp but I also lie at the
    last gasp,
My face is ash-color'd, my sinews gnarl, away from me
    people retreat.

Askers embody themselves in me and I am embodied in
    them,
I project my hat, sit shame-faced, and beg.

38
Enough! enough! enough!
960 Somehow I have been stunn'd. Stand back!
Give me a little time beyond my cuff'd head, slumbers,
    dreams, gaping,
I discover myself on the verge of a usual mistake.

That I could forget the mockers and insults!
That I could forget the trickling tears and the blows of the
    bludgeons and hammers!
That I could look with a separate look on my own crucifixion
    and bloody crowning.

I remember now,
I resume the overstaid fraction,
The grave of rock multiplies what has been confided to it,
    or to any graves,
Corpses rise, gashes heal, fastenings roll from me.

970 I troop forth replenish'd with supreme power, one of an
    average unending procession,
Inland and sea-coast we go, and pass all boundary lines,
Our swift ordinances on their way over the whole earth,

The blossoms we wear in our hats the growth of thousands
   of years.

Eleves, I salute you! come forward!
Continue your annotations, continue your questionings.

39
The friendly and flowing savage, who is he?
Is he waiting for civilization, or past it and mastering it?

Is he some Southwesterner rais'd out-doors? is he
   Kanadian?
Is he from the Mississippi country? Iowa, Oregon,
   California?
980   The mountains? prairie-life, bush-life? or sailor from the
   sea?

Wherever he goes men and women accept and desire him,
They desire he should like them, touch them, speak to them,
   stay with them.

Behavior lawless as snow-flakes, words simple as grass,
   uncomb'd head, laughter, and naivetè,
Slow-stepping feet, common features, common modes and
   emanations,
They descend in new forms from the tips of his fingers,
They are wafted with the odor of his body or breath, they
   fly out of the glance of his eyes.

40
Flaunt of the sunshine I need not your bask – lie over!
You light surfaces only, I force surfaces and depths also.

Earth! you seem to look for something at my hands,
990   Say, old top-knot, what do you want?

Man or woman, I might tell how I like you, but cannot,
And might tell what it is in me and what it is in you,
   but cannot,
And might tell that pining I have, that pulse of my nights
   and days.

Behold, I do not give lectures or a little charity,
When I give I give myself.

You there, impotent, loose in the knees,
Open your scarf'd chops till I blow grit within you,
Spread your palms and lift the flaps of your pockets,
I am not to be denied, I compel, I have stores plenty and
     to spare,
1000 And any thing I have I bestow.

I do not ask who you are, that is not important to me,
You can do nothing and be nothing but what I will infold
     you.

To cotton-field drudge or cleaner of privies I lean,
On his right cheek I put the family kiss,
And in my soul I swear I never will deny him.

On women fit for conception I start bigger and nimbler
     babes,
(This day I am jetting the stuff of far more arrogant
     republics.)

To any one dying, thither I speed and twist the knob of
     the door,
Turn the bed-clothes toward the foot of the bed,
1010 Let the physician and the priest go home.

I seize the descending man and raise him with resistless will,
O despairer, here is my neck,
By God, you shall not go down! hang your whole weight
     upon me.
I dilate you with tremendous breath, I buoy you up,
Every room of the house do I fill with an arm'd force,
Lovers of me, bafflers of graves.

Sleep – I and they keep guard all night,
Not doubt, not decrease shall dare to lay finger upon you,
I have embraced you, and henceforth possess you to myself,
1020 And when you rise in the morning you will find what I tell
     you is so.

41

I am he bringing help for the sick as they pant on their backs,
And for strong upright men I bring yet more needed help.
I heard what was said of the universe,
Heard it and heard it of several thousand years;
It is middling well as far as it goes – but is that all?

Magnifying and applying come I,
Outbidding at the start the old cautious hucksters,
Taking myself the exact dimensions of Jehovah,
Lithographing Kronos, Zeus his son, and Hercules his
  grandson,
1030 Buying drafts of Osiris, Isis, Belus, Brahma, Buddha,
In my portfolio placing Manito loose, Allah on a leaf, the
  crucifix engraved,
With Odin and the hideous-faced Mexitli and every idol and
  image,
Taking them all for what they are worth and not a cent more,
Admitting they were alive and did the work of their days,
(They bore mites as for unfledg'd birds who have now to
  rise and fly and sing for themselves,)
Accepting the rough deific sketches to fill out better in
  myself, bestowing them freely on each man and woman
  I see,
Discovering as much or more in a framer framing a house,
Putting higher claims for him there with his roll'd-up
  sleeves driving the mallet and chisel,
Not objecting to special revelations, considering a curl of
  smoke or a hair on the back of my hand just as curious as
  any revelation,
1040 Lads ahold of fire-engines and hook-and-ladder ropes no
  less to me than the gods of the antique wars,
Minding their voices peal through the crash of destruction,
Their brawny limbs passing safe over charr'd laths, their
  white foreheads whole and unhurt out of the flames;
By the mechanic's wife with her babe at her nipple
  interceding for every person born,
Three scythes at harvest whizzing in a row from three lusty

angels with shirts bagg'd out at their waists,
The snag-tooth'd hostler with red hair redeeming sins past and to come,
Selling all he possesses, traveling on foot to fee lawyers for his brother and sit by him while he is tried for forgery;
What was strewn in the amplest strewing the square rod about me, and not filling the square rod then,
The bull and the bug never worshipp'd half enough,
Dung and dirt more admirable than was dream'd,
1050 The supernatural of no account, myself waiting my time to be one of the supremes,
The day getting ready for me when I shall do as much good as the best, and be as prodigious;
By my life-lumps! becoming already a creator,
Putting myself here and now to the ambush'd womb of the shadows.

42
A call in the midst of the crowd,
My own voice, orotund sweeping and final.

Come my children,
Come my boys and girls, my women, household and intimates,
Now the performer launches his nerve, he has pass'd his prelude on the reeds within.

Easily written loose-finger'd chords – I feel the thrum of your climax and close.

1060 My head slues round on my neck,
Music rolls but not from the organ,
Folks are around me, but they are no household of mine.

Ever the hard unsunk ground,
Ever the eaters and drinkers, ever the upward and downward sun, ever the air and the ceaseless tides,
Ever myself and my neighbors, refreshing, wicked, real,
Ever the old inexplicable query, ever that thorn'd thumb, that breath of itches and thirsts,

Ever the vexer's *hoot! hoot!* till we find where the sly one
    hides and bring him forth,
Ever love, ever the sobbing liquid of life,
Ever the bandage under the chin, ever the trestles of death.

1070 Here and there with dimes on the eyes walking,
    To feed the greed of the belly the brains liberally spooning,
    Tickets buying, taking, selling, but in to the feast never once
      going,
    Many sweating, ploughing, thrashing, and then the chaff for
      payment receiving,
    A few idly owning, and they the wheat continually claiming.

This is the city and I am one of the citizens,
Whatever interests the rest interests me, politics, wars,
    markets, newspapers, schools,
The mayor and councils, banks, tariffs, steamships, factories,
    stocks, stores, real estate and personal estate.

The little plentiful manikins skipping around in collars and
    tail'd coats,
I am aware who they are, (they are positively not worms
    or fleas,)
1080 I acknowledge the duplicates of myself, the weakest and
    shallowest is deathless with me,
    What I do and say the same waits for them,
    Every thought that flounders in me the same flounders in
      them.

I know perfectly well my own egotism,
Know my omnivorous lines and must not write any less,
And would fetch you whoever you are flush with myself.

Not words of routine this song of mine,
But abruptly to question, to leap beyond yet nearer bring;
This printed and bound book – but the printer and the
    printing-office boy?
The well-taken photographs – but your wife or friend close
    and solid in your arms?
1090 The black ship mail'd with iron, her mighty guns in her

turrets – but the pluck of the captain and engineers?
In the houses the dishes and fare and furniture – but the
   host and hostess, and the look out of their eyes?
The sky up there – yet here or next door, or across the way?
The saints and sages in history – but you yourself?
Sermons, creeds, theology – but the fathomless human
   brain,
And what is reason? and what is love? and what is life?

43

I do not despise you priests, all time, the world over,
My faith is the greatest of faiths and the least of faiths,
Enclosing worship ancient and modern and all between
   ancient and modern,
Believing I shall come again upon the earth after five
   thousand years,
1100 Waiting responses from oracles, honoring the gods, saluting
   the sun,
Making a fetich of the first rock or stump, powowing with
   sticks in the circle of obis,
Helping the llama or brahmin as he trims the lamps of the
   idols,
Dancing yet through the streets in a phallic procession, rapt
   and austere in the woods a gymnosophist,
Drinking mead from the skull-cup, to Shastas and Vedas
   admirant, minding the Koran,
Walking the teokallis, spotted with gore from the stone and
   knife, beating the serpent-skin drum,
Accepting the Gospels, accepting him that was crucified,
   knowing assuredly that he is divine,
To the mass kneeling or the puritan's prayer rising, or
   sitting patiently in a pew,
Ranting and frothing in my insane crisis, or waiting
   dead-like till my spirit arouses me,
Looking forth on pavement and land, or outside of
   pavement and land,
1110 Belonging to the winders of the circuit of circuits.

One of that centripetal and centrifugal gang I turn and talk
    like a man leaving charges before a journey.

Down-hearted doubters dull and excluded,
Frivolous, sullen, moping, angry, affected, dishearten'd,
    atheistical,
I know every one of you, I know the sea of torment, doubt,
    despair and unbelief.

How the flukes splash!
How they contort rapid as lightning, with spasms and
    spouts of blood!

Be at peace bloody flukes of doubters and sullen mopers,
I take my place among you as much as among any,
The past is the push of you, me, all, precisely the same,
1120 And what is yet untried and afterward is for you, me, all,
    precisely the same.

I do not know what is untried and afterward,
But I know it will in its turn prove sufficient, and cannot
    fail.

Each who passes is consider'd, each who stops is consider'd,
    not a single one can it fail.

It cannot fail the young man who died and was buried,
Nor the young woman who died and was put by his side,
Nor the little child that peep'd in at the door, and then drew
    back and was never seen again,
Nor the old man who has lived without purpose, and feels
    it with bitterness worse than gall,
Nor him in the poor house tubercled by rum and the bad
    disorder,
Nor the numberless slaughter'd and wreck'd, nor the brutish
    koboo call'd the ordure of humanity,
1130 Nor the sacs merely floating with open mouths for food to
    slip in,
Nor any thing in the earth, or down in the oldest graves of
    the earth,

Nor any thing in the myriads of spheres, nor the myriads of
   myriads that inhabit them,
Nor the present, nor the least wisp that is known.

44
It is time to explain myself – let us stand up.

What is known I strip away,
I launch all men and women forward with me into the
   Unknown.

The clock indicates the moment – but what does eternity
   indicate?

We have thus far exhausted trillions of winters and summers,
There are trillions ahead, and trillions ahead of them.

1140 Births have brought us richness and variety,
And other births will bring us richness and variety.

I do not call one greater and one smaller,
That which fills its period and place is equal to any.

Were mankind murderous or jealous upon you, my brother,
   my sister?
I am sorry for you, they are not murderous or jealous upon
   me,
All has been gentle with me, I keep no account with
   lamentation,
(What have I to do with lamentation?)

I am an acme of things accomplish'd, and I an encloser of
   things to be.

My feet strike an apex of the apices of the stairs,
1150 On every step bunches of ages, and larger bunches between
   the steps,
All below duly travel'd, and still I mount and mount.

Rise after rise bow the phantoms behind me,
Afar down I see the huge first Nothing, I know I was even
   there,

I waited unseen and always, and slept through the lethargic
   mist,
And took my time, and took no hurt from the fetid carbon.

Long I was hugg'd close – long and long.

Immense have been the preparations for me,
Faithful and friendly the arms that have help'd me.

Cycles ferried my cradle, rowing and rowing like cheerful
   boatmen,
1160 For room to me stars kept aside in their own rings,
They sent influences to look after what was to hold me.

Before I was born out of my mother generations guided me,
My embryo has never been torpid, nothing could overlay it.

For it the nebula cohered to an orb,
The long slow strata piled to rest it on,
Vast vegetables gave it sustenance,
Monstrous sauroids transported it in their mouths and
   deposited it with care.

All forces have been steadily employ'd to complete and
   delight me,
Now on this spot I stand with my robust soul.

45
1170 O span of youth! ever-push'd elasticity!
O manhood, balanced, florid and full.

My lovers suffocate me,
Crowding my lips, thick in the pores of my skin,
Jostling me through streets and public halls, coming naked
   to me at night,
Crying by day *Ahoy!* from the rocks of the river, swinging
   and chirping over my head,
Calling my name from flower-beds, vines, tangled
   underbrush,
Lighting on every moment of my life,
Bussing my body with soft balsamic busses,

Noiselessly passing handfuls out of their hearts and giving
    them to be mine.

1180 Old age superbly rising! O welcome, ineffable grace of dying
    days!

Every condition promulges not only itself, it promulges
    what grows after and out of itself,
And the dark hush promulges as much as any.

I open my scuttle at night and see the far-sprinkled systems,
And all I see multiplied as high as I can cipher edge but the
    rim of the farther systems.

Wider and wider they spread, expanding, always expanding,
Outward and outward and forever outward.

My sun has his sun and round him obediently wheels,
He joins with his partners a group of superior circuit,
And greater sets follow, making specks of the greatest inside
    them.

1190 There is no stoppage and never can be stoppage,
If I, you, and the worlds, and all beneath or upon their
    surfaces, were this moment reduced back to a pallid float,
    it would not avail in the long run,
We should surely bring up again where we now stand,
And surely go as much farther, and then farther and farther.

A few quadrillions of eras, a few octillions of cubic leagues,
    do not hazard the span or make it impatient,
They are but parts, any thing is but a part.

See ever so far, there is limitless space outside of that,
Count ever so much, there is limitless time around that.

My rendezvous is appointed, it is certain,
The Lord will be there and wait till I come on perfect terms,
1200 The great Camerado, the lover true for whom I pine will
    be there.

46

I know I have the best of time and space, and was never
    measured and never will be measured.

I tramp a perpetual journey, (come listen all!)
My signs are a rain-proof coat, good shoes, and a staff cut
    from the woods,
No friend of mine takes his ease in my chair,
I have no chair, no church, no philosophy,
I lead no man to a dinner-table, library, exchange,
But each man and each woman of you I lead upon a knoll,
My left hand hooking you round the waist,
My right hand pointing to landscapes of continents and the
    public road.

1210 Not I, not any one else can travel that road for you,
You must travel it for yourself.

It is not far, it is within reach,
Perhaps you have been on it since you were born and did not
    know,
Perhaps it is everywhere on water and on land.

Shoulder your duds dear son, and I will mine, and let us
    hasten forth,
Wonderful cities and free nations we shall fetch as we go.

If you tire, give me both burdens, and rest the chuff of your
    hand on my hip,
And in due time you shall repay the same service to me,
For after we start we never lie by again.

1220 This day before dawn I ascended a hill and look'd at the
    crowded heaven,
And I said to my spirit *When we become the enfolders of those
orbs, and the pleasure and knowledge of every thing in them,
shall we be fill'd and satisfied then?*
And my spirit said *No, we but level that lift to pass and
continue beyond.*

You are also asking me questions and I hear you,
I answer that I cannot answer, you must find out for
yourself.

Sit a while dear son,
Here are biscuits to eat and here is milk to drink,
But as soon as you sleep and renew yourself in sweet clothes,
    I kiss you with a good-by kiss and open the gate for your
    egress hence.

Long enough have you dream'd contemptible dreams,
Now I wash the gum from your eyes,
1230 You must habit yourself to the dazzle of the light and of
    every moment of your life.

Long have you timidly waded holding a plank by the shore,
Now I will you to be a bold swimmer,
To jump off in the midst of the sea, rise again, nod to me,
    shout, and laughingly dash with your hair.

47
I am the teacher of athletes,
He that by me spreads a wider breast than my own proves
    the width of my own,
He most honors my style who learns under it to destroy the
    teacher.

The boy I love, the same becomes a man not through
    derived power, but in his own right,
Wicked rather than virtuous out of conformity or fear,
Fond of his sweetheart, relishing well his steak,
1240 Unrequited love or a slight cutting him worse than sharp
    steel cuts,
First-rate to ride, to fight, to hit the bull's eye, to sail a
    skiff, to sing a song or play on the banjo,
Preferring scars and the beard and faces pitted with
    small-pox over all latherers,
And those well-tann'd to those that keep out of the sun.

I teach straying from me, yet who can stray from me?
I follow you whoever you are from the present hour,
My words itch at your ears till you understand them.

I do not say these things for a dollar or to fill up the time
    while I wait for a boat,
(It is you talking just as much as myself, I act as the tongue
    of you,
Tied in your mouth, in mine it begins to be loosen'd.)

1250 I swear I will never again mention love or death inside a
    house,
And I swear I will never translate myself at all, only to him
    or her who privately stays with me in the open air.

If you would understand me go to the heights or water-shore,
The nearest gnat is an explanation, and a drop or motion of
    waves a key,
The maul, the oar, the hand-saw, second my words.

No shutter'd room or school can commune with me,
But roughs and little children better than they.

The young mechanic is closest to me, he knows me well,
The woodman that takes his axe and jug with him shall take
    me with him all day,
The farm-boy ploughing in the field feels good at the sound
    of my voice,
1260 In vessels that sail my words sail, I go with fishermen and
    seamen and love them.

The soldier camp'd or upon the march is mine,
On the night ere the pending battle many seek me, and I
    do not fail them,
On that solemn night (it may be their last) those that
    know me seek me.

My face rubs to the hunter's face when he lies down alone in
    his blanket,
The driver thinking of me does not mind the jolt of his
    wagon,

The young mother and old mother comprehend me,
The girl and the wife rest the needle a moment and forget
    where they are,
They and all would resume what I have told them.

48
I have said that the soul is not more than the body,
1270 And I have said that the body is not more than the soul,
And nothing, not God, is greater to one than one's self is,
And whoever walks a furlong without sympathy walks to
    his own funeral drest in his shroud,
And I or you pocketless of a dime may purchase the pick of
    the earth,
And to glance with an eye or show a bean in its pod
    confounds the learning of all times,
And there is no trade or employment but the young man
    following it may become a hero,
And there is no object so soft but it makes a hub for the
    wheel'd universe,
And I say to any man or woman, Let your soul stand cool
    and composed before a million universes.

And I say to mankind, Be not curious about God,
For I who am curious about each am not curious about God,
1280 (No array of terms can say how much I am at peace about
    God and about death.)

I hear and behold God in every object, yet understand God
    not in the least,
Nor do I understand who there can be more wonderful than
    myself.

Why should I wish to see God better than this day?
I see something of God each hour of the twenty-four, and
    each moment then,
In the faces of men and women I see God, and in my own
    face in the glass,
I find letters from God dropt in the street, and every one is
    sign'd by God's name,

And I leave them where they are, for I know that
    wheresoe'er I go,
Others will punctually come for ever and ever.

49
And as to you Death, and you bitter hug of mortality, it is
    idle to try to alarm me.

1290 To his work without flinching the accoucheur comes,
I see the elder-hand pressing receiving supporting,
I recline by the sills of the exquisite flexible doors,
And mark the outlet, and mark the relief and escape.

And as to you Corpse I think you are good manure, but
    that does not offend me,
I smell the white roses sweet-scented and growing,
I reach to the leafy lips, I reach to the polish'd breasts of
    melons.

And as to you Life I reckon you are the leavings of many
    deaths,
(No doubt I have died myself ten thousand times before.)

I hear you whispering there O stars of heaven,
1300 O suns – O grass of graves – O perpetual transfers and
    promotions,
If you do not say any thing how can I say any thing?

Of the turbid pool that lies in the autumn forest,
Of the moon that descends the steeps of the soughing
    twilight,
Toss, sparkles of day and dusk – toss on the black stems that
    decay in the muck,
Toss to the moaning gibberish of the dry limbs.

I ascend from the moon, I ascend from the night,
I perceive that the ghastly glimmer is noonday sunbeams
    reflected,
And debouch to the steady and central from the offspring
    great or small.

50

There is that in me – I do not know what it is – but I know
    it is in me.

1310 Wrench'd and sweaty – calm and cool then my body
    becomes,
I sleep – I sleep long.

I do not know it – it is without name – it is a word unsaid,
It is not in any dictionary, utterance, symbol.

Something it swings on more than the earth I swing on,
To it the creation is the friend whose embracing awakes me.

Perhaps I might tell more. Outlines! I plead for my brothers
    and sisters.

Do you see O my brothers and sisters?
It is not chaos or death – it is form, union, plan – it is
    eternal life – it is Happiness.

51

The past and present wilt – I have fill'd them, emptied
    them.
1320 And proceed to fill my next fold of the future.

Listener up there! what have you to confide to me?
Look in my face while I snuff the sidle of evening,
(Talk honestly, no one else hears you, and I stay only a
    minute longer.)

Do I contradict myself?
Very well then I contradict myself,
(I am large, I contain multitudes.)

I concentrate toward them that are nigh, I wait on the
    door-slab.

Who has done his day's work? who will soonest be through
    with his supper?
Who wishes to walk with me?

1330 Will you speak before I am gone? will you prove already
      too late?

52

The spotted hawk swoops by and accuses me, he
   complains of my gab and my loitering.

I too am not a bit tamed, I too am untranslatable,
I sound my barbaric yawp over the roofs of the world.

The last scud of day holds back for me,
It flings my likeness after the rest and true as any on the
   shadow'd wilds,
It coaxes me to the vapor and the dusk.

I depart as air, I shake my white locks at the runaway sun,
I effuse my flesh in eddies, and drift it in lacy jags.

I bequeath myself to the dirt to grow from the grass I love,
1340 If you want me again look for me under your boot-soles.

You will hardly know who I am or what I mean,
But I shall be good health to you nevertheless,
And filter and fibre your blood.

Failing to fetch me at first keep encouraged,
Missing me one place search another,
I stop somewhere waiting for you.

CHILDREN OF ADAM

To the Garden the World

To the garden the world anew ascending,
Potent mates, daughters, sons, preluding,
The love, the life of their bodies, meaning and being,
Curious here behold my resurrection after slumber,
The revolving cycles in their wide sweep having brought
     me again,
Amorous, mature, all beautiful to me, all wondrous,
My limbs and the quivering fire that ever plays through
     them, for reasons, most wondrous,
Existing I peer and penetrate still,
Content with the present, content with the past,
10 By my side or back of me Eve following,
Or in front, and I following her just the same.

From Pent-up Aching Rivers

From pent-up aching rivers,
From that of myself without which I were nothing,
From what I am determin'd to make illustrious, even if I
     stand sole among men,
From my own voice resonant, singing the phallus,
Singing the song of procreation,
Singing the need of superb children and therein superb
     grown people,
Singing the muscular urge and the blending,
Singing the bedfellow's song, (O resistless yearning!
O for any and each the body correlative attracting!
10 O for you whoever you are your correlative body! O it,
     more than all else, you delighting!)
From the hungry gnaw that eats me night and day,
From native moments, from bashful pains, singing them,
Seeking something yet unfound though I have diligently
     sought it many a long year,

Singing the true song of the soul fitful at random,
Renascent with grossest Nature or among animals,
Of that, of them and what goes with them my poems
      informing,
Of the smell of apples and lemons, of the pairing of birds,
Of the wet of woods, of the lapping of waves,
Of the mad pushes of waves upon the land, I them chanting,
20   The overture lightly sounding, the strain anticipating,
The welcome nearness, the sight of the perfect body,
The swimmer swimming naked in the bath, or motionless
      on his back lying and floating,
The female form approaching, I pensive, love-flesh
      tremulous aching,
The divine list for myself or you or for any one making,
The face, the limbs, the index from head to foot, and what it
      arouses,
The mystic deliria, the madness amorous, the utter
      abandonment,
(Hark close and still what I now whisper to you,
I love you, O you entirely possess me,
O that you and I escape from the rest and go utterly off, free
      and lawless,
30   Two hawks in the air, two fishes swimming in the sea not
      more lawless than we;)
The furious storm through me careering, I passionately
      trembling.
The oath of the inseparableness of two together, of the
      woman that loves me and whom I love more than my
      life, that oath swearing,
(O I willingly stake all for you,
O let me be lost if it must be so!
O you and I! what is to it us what the rest do or think?
What is all else to us? only that we enjoy each other and
      exhaust each other if it must be so;)
From the master, the pilot I yield the vessel to,
The general commanding me, commanding all, from him
      permission taking,

From time the programme hastening, (I have loiter'd too
    long as it is.)
40 From sex, from the warp and from the woof,
From privacy, from frequent repinings alone,
From plenty of persons near and yet the right person
    not near,
From the soft sliding of hands over me and thrusting of
    fingers through my hair and beard,
From the long sustain'd kiss upon the mouth or bosom,
From the close pressure that makes me or any man drunk,
    fainting with excess,
From what the divine husband knows, from the work of
    fatherhood,
From exultation, victory and relief, from the bedfellow's
    embrace in the night,
From the act-poems of eyes, hands, hips and bosoms,
From the cling of the trembling arm,
50 From the bending curve and the clinch,
From side by side the pliant coverlet off-throwing,
From the one so unwilling to have me leave, and me just
    as unwilling to leave,
(Yet a moment O tender waiter, and I return,)
From the hour of shining stars and dropping dews,
From the night a moment I emerging flitting out,
Celebrate you act divine and you children prepared for,
And you stalwart loins.

I Sing the Body Electric

1

I sing the body electric,
The armies of those I love <u>engirth</u> me and I <u>engirth</u> them,
They will not let me off till I go with them, respond to them,
And discorrupt them, and charge them full with the charge
    of the soul.

Was it doubted that those who corrupt their own bodies
    conceal themselves?

corrupt

And if those who defile the living are as bad as they who
    defile the dead?
And if the body does not do fully as much as the soul?
And if the body were not the soul, what is the soul?

2

The love of the body of man or woman balks account,
    the body itself balks account,
10   That of the male is perfect, and that of the female is perfect.

The expression of the face balks account,
But the expression of a well-made man appears not only
    in his face,
It is in his limbs and joints also, it is curiously in the joints
    of his hips and wrists,
It is in his walk, the carriage of his neck, the flex of his
    waist and knees, dress does not hide him,
The strong sweet quality he has strikes through the cotton
    and broadcloth,
To see him pass conveys as much as the best poem, perhaps
    more,
You linger to see his back, and the back of his neck and
    shoulder-side.

The sprawl and fulness of babes, the bosoms and heads of
    women, the folds of their dress, their style as we pass in
    the street, the contour of their shape downwards,
The swimmer naked in the swimming-bath, seen as he swims
    through the transparent green-shine, or lies with his face
    up and rolls silently to and fro in the heave of the water,
20   The bending forward and backward of rowers in row-boats,
    the horseman in his saddle,
Girls, mothers, house-keepers, in all their performances,
The group of laborers seated at noon-time with their open
    dinner-kettles, and their wives waiting,
The female soothing a child, the farmer's daughter in the
    garden or cow-yard,
The young fellow hoeing corn, the sleigh-driver driving his
    six horses through the crowd,

The wrestle of wrestlers, two apprentice-boys, quite grown,
    lusty, good-natured, native-born, out on the vacant lot at
    sundown after work,
The coats and caps thrown down, the embrace of love and
    resistance,
The upper-hold and under-hold, the hair rumpled over and
    blinding the eyes;
The march of firemen in their own costumes, the play of
    masculine muscle through clean-setting trowsers and
    waist-straps,
The slow return from the fire, the pause when the bell
    strikes suddenly again, and the listening on the alert,
30 The natural, perfect, varied attitudes, the bent head, the
    curv'd neck and the counting;
Such-like I love – I loosen myself, pass freely, am at the
    mother's breast with the little child,
Swim with the swimmers, wrestle with wrestlers, march in
    line with the firemen, and pause, listen, count.

3
I knew a man, a common farmer, the father of five sons,
And in them the fathers of sons, and in them the fathers of
    sons.

This man was of wonderful vigor, calmness, beauty of
    person,
The shape of his head, the pale yellow and white of his hair
    and beard, the immeasurable meaning of his black eyes,
    the richness and breadth of his manners,
These I used to go and visit him to see, he was wise also,
He was six feet tall, he was over eighty years old, his sons
    were massive, clean, bearded, tan-faced, handsome,
They and his daughters loved him, all who saw him loved
    him,
40 They did not love him by allowance, they loved him with
    personal love,
He drank water only, the blood show'd like scarlet through
    the clear-brown skin of his face,
He was a frequent gunner and fisher, he sail'd his boat

himself, he had a fine one presented to him by a
     ship-joiner, he had fowling-pieces presented to him by
     men that loved him,
When he went with his five sons and many grand-sons to
     hunt or fish, you would pick him out as the most
     beautiful and vigorous of the gang,
You would wish long and long to be with him, you would
     wish to sit by him in the boat that you and he might
     touch each other.

4

I have perceiv'd that to be with those I like is enough,
To stop in company with the rest at evening is enough,
To be surrounded by beautiful, curious, breathing,
     laughing flesh is enough,
To pass among them or touch any one, or rest my arm ever
     so lightly round his or her neck for a moment, what is this
     then?
I do not ask any more delight, I swim in it as in a sea.

50   There is something in staying close to men and women and
        looking on them, and in the contact and odor of them, that
        pleases the soul well,
All things please the soul, but these please the soul well.

5

This is the female form, *a radiant light surrounding a*
A divine nimbus exhales from it from head to foot, *deity*
It attracts with fierce undeniable attraction,
I am drawn by its breath as if I were no more than a
     helpless vapor, all falls aside but myself and it,
Books, art, religion, time, the visible and solid earth, and
     what was expected of heaven or fear'd of hell, are now
     consumed,
Mad filaments, ungovernable shoots play out of it, the
     response likewise ungovernable,
Hair, bosom, hips, bend of legs, negligent falling hands all
     diffused, mine too diffused,

Ebb stung by the flow and flow stung by the ebb, love-flesh
    swelling and deliciously aching,
60   Limitless limpid jets of love hot and enormous, quivering
    jelly of love, whi*e-blow and delirious juice,
Bridegroom night of love working surely and softly into
    the prostrate dawn,
Undulating into the willing and yielding day,
Lost in the cleave of the clasping and sweet-flesh'd day.

This the nucleus – after the child is born of woman, man is
    born of woman,
This the bath of birth, this the merge of small and large,
    and the outlet again.

Be not ashamed women, your privilege encloses the rest,
    and is the exit of the rest,
You are the gates of the body, and you are the gates of the
    soul.

The female contains all qualities and tempers them,
She is in her place and moves with perfect balance,
70   She is all things duly veil'd, she is both passive and active,
She is to conceive daughters as well as sons, and sons as
    well as daughters.

As I see my soul reflected in Nature,
As I see through a mist, One with inexpressible
    completeness, sanity, beauty,
See the bent head and arms folded over the breast, the
    Female I see.

6

The male is not less the soul nor more, he too is in his place,
He too is all qualities, he is action and power,
The flush of the known universe is in him,
Scorn becomes him well, and appetite and defiance become
    him well,
The wildest largest passions, bliss that is utmost, sorrow
    that is utmost become him well, pride is for him,

80   The full-spread pride of man is calming and excellent to
          the soul,
      Knowledge becomes him, he likes it always, he brings every
          thing to the test of himself,
      Whatever the survey, whatever the sea and the sail he strikes
          soundings at last only here,
      (Where else does he strike soundings except here?)

      The man's body is sacred and the woman's body is sacred,
      No matter who it is, it is sacred – is it the meanest one in
          the laborers' gang?
      Is it one of the dull-faced immigrants just landed on the
          wharf?
      Each belongs here or anywhere just as much as the well-off,
          just as much as you,
      Each has his or her place in the procession.

      (All is a procession,
90   The universe is a procession with measured and perfect
          motion.)

      Do you know so much yourself that you call the meanest
          ignorant?
      Do you suppose you have a right to a good sight, and he or
          she has no right to a sight?
      Do you think matter has cohered together from its diffuse
          float, and the soil is on the surface, and water runs and
          vegetation sprouts,
      For you only, and not for him and her?

      7
      A man's body at auction,
      (For before the war I often go to the slave-mart and watch
          the sale,)
      I help the auctioneer, the sloven does not half know his
          business.   one mat is habitually negligent
                             of hygiene

      Gentlemen look on this wonder,
      Whatever the bids of the bidders they cannot be high
          enough for it,

100   For it the globe lay preparing quintillions of years without
         one animal or plant,
       For it the revolving cycles truly and steadily roll'd.

       In this head the all-baffling brain,
       In it and below it the makings of heroes.

       Examine these limbs, red, black, or white, they are cunning
         in tendon and nerve,
       They shall be stript that you may see them.

       Exquisite senses, life-lit eyes, pluck, volition,
       Flakes of breast-muscle, pliant backbone and neck, flesh
         not flabby, good-sized arms and legs,
       And wonders within there yet.

       Within there runs blood,
110   The same old blood! the same red-running blood!
       There swells and jets a heart, there all passions, desires,
         reachings, aspirations,
       (Do you think they are not there because they are not
         express'd in parlors and lecture-rooms?)

       This is not only one man, this the father of those who shall
         be fathers in their turns,
       In him the start of populous states and rich republics,
       Of him countless immortal lives with countless
         embodiments and enjoyments.

       How do you know who shall come from the offspring of
         his offspring through the centuries?
       (Who might you find you have come from yourself, if you
         could trace back through the centuries?)

       8
       A woman's body at auction,
       She too is not only herself, she is the teeming mother of
         mothers,
120   She is the bearer of them that shall grow and be mates to
         the mothers.

Have you ever loved the body of a woman?
Have you ever loved the body of a man?
Do you not see that these are exactly the same to all in all
    nations and times all over the earth?

If any thing is sacred the human body is sacred,
And the glory and sweet of a man is the token of manhood
    untainted,
And in man or woman a clean, strong, firm-fibred body, is
    more beautiful than the most beautiful face.

Have you seen the fool that corrupted his own live body?
    or the fool that corrupted her own live body?
For they do not conceal themselves, and cannot conceal
    themselves.

9
O my body! I dare not desert the likes of you in other men
    and women, nor the likes of the parts of you,
130 I believe the likes of you are to stand or fall with the likes
    of the soul, (and that they are the soul,)
I believe the likes of you shall stand or fall with my poems,
    and that they are my poems,
Man's, woman's, child's, youth's, wife's, husband's,
    mother's, father's, young man's, young woman's poems,
Head, neck, hair, ears, drop and tympan of the ears,
Eyes, eye-fringes, iris of the eye, eyebrows, and the waking
    or sleeping of the lids,
Mouth, tongue, lips, teeth, roof of the mouth, jaws,
    and the jaw-hinges,
Nose, nostrils of the nose, and the partition,
Cheeks, temples, forehead, chin, throat, back of the neck,
    neck-slue,
Strong shoulders, manly beard, scapula, hind-shoulders,
    and the ample side-round of the chest,
Upper-arm, armpit, elbow-socket, lower-arm, arm-sinews,
    armbones,
140 Wrist and wrist-joints, hand, palm, knuckles, thumb,
    forefinger, finger-joints, finger-nails,

Broad breast-front, curling hair of the breast, breast-bone,
    breast-side,
Ribs, belly, backbone, joints of the backbone,
Hips, hip-sockets, hip-strength, inward and outward round,
    man-balls, man-root,
Strong set of thighs, well carrying the trunk above,
Leg-fibres, knee, knee-pan, upper-leg, under-leg,
Ankles, instep, foot-ball, toes, toe-joints, the heel;
All attitudes, all the shapeliness, all the belongings of my or
    your body or of any one's body, male or female,
The lung-sponges, the stomach-sac, the bowels sweet
    and clean,
The brain in its folds inside the skull-frame,
150 Sympathies, heart-valves, palate-valves, sexuality,
    maternity,
Womanhood, and all that is a woman, and the man that
    comes from woman,
The womb, the teats, nipples, breast-milk, tears, laughter,
    weeping, love-looks, love-perturbations and risings,
The voice, articulation, language, whispering, shouting
    aloud,
Food, drink, pulse, digestion, sweat, sleep, walking,
    swimming,
Poise on the hips, leaping, reclining, embracing, arm-curving
    and tightening,
The continual changes of the flex of the mouth, and around
    the eyes,
The skin, the sunburnt shade, freckles, hair,
The curious sympathy one feels when feeling with the hand
    the naked meat of the body,
The circling rivers the breath, the breathing it in and out,
160 The beauty of the waist, and thence of the hips, and thence
    downward toward the knees,
The thin red jellies within you or within me, the bones and
    the marrow in the bones,
The exquisite realization of health;

O I say these are not the parts and poems of the body only,
    but of the soul,
O I say now these are the soul!

A Woman Waits for Me

A woman waits for me, she contains all, nothing is lacking,
Yet all were lacking if sex were lacking, or if the moisture
    of the right man were lacking.

Sex contains all, bodies, souls,
Meanings, proofs, purities, delicacies, results, promulgations,
Songs, commands, health, pride, and maternal mystery,
    the seminal milk,
All hopes, benefactions, bestowals, all the passions, loves,
    beauties, delights of the earth,
All the governments, judges, gods, follow'd persons of the
    earth,
These are contain'd in sex as parts of itself and
    justifications of itself.

Without shame the man I like knows and avows the
    deliciousness of his sex,
Without shame the woman I like knows and avows hers.

Now I will dismiss myself from impassive women,
I will go stay with her who waits for me, and with those
    women that are warm-blooded and sufficient for me,
I see that they understand me and do not deny me,
I see that they are worthy of me, I will be the robust husband
    of those women.

They are not one jot less than I am,
They are tann'd in the face by shining suns and blowing
    winds,
Their flesh has the old divine suppleness and strength,
They know how to swim, row, ride, wrestle, shoot, run,
    strike, retreat, advance, resist, defend themselves,

They are ultimate in their own right – they are calm, clear,
    well-possess'd of themselves.

20 I draw you close to me, you women,
    I cannot let you go, I would do you good,
    I am for you, and you are for me, not only for our own
        sake, but for others' sakes,
    Envelop'd in you sleep greater heroes and bards,
    They refuse to awake at the touch of any man but me.

    It is I, you women, I make my way,
    I am stern, acrid, large, undissuadable, but I love you,
    I do not hurt you any more than is necessary for you,
    I pour the stuff to start sons and daughters fit for these
        States, I press with slow rude muscle,
    I brace myself effectually, I listen to no entreaties,
30 I dare not withdraw till I deposit what has so long
        accumulated within me.

    Through you I drain the pent-up rivers of myself,
    In you I wrap a thousand onward years,
    On you I graft the grafts of the best-beloved of me and
        America,
    The drops I distil upon you shall grow fierce and athletic
        girls, new artists, musicians, and singers,
    The babes I beget upon you are to beget babes in their turn,
    I shall demand perfect men and women out of my
        love-spendings,
    I shall expect them to interpenetrate with others, as I and
        you interpenetrate now,
    I shall count on the fruits of the gushing showers of them,
        as I count on the fruits of the gushing showers I give now,
    I shall look for loving crops from the birth, life, death,
        immortality, I plant so lovingly now.

Spontaneous Me

Spontaneous me, Nature,
The loving day, the mounting sun, the friend I am happy
 with,
The arm of my friend hanging idly over my shoulder,
The hillside whiten'd with blossoms of the mountain ash,
The same late in autumn, the hues of red, yellow, drab,
 purple, and light and dark green,
The rich coverlet of the grass, animals and birds, the
 private untrimm'd bank, the primitive apples, the
 pebble-stones,
Beautiful dripping fragments, the negligent list of one after
 another as I happen to call them to me or think of them,
The real poems, (what we call poems being merely pictures,)
The poems of the privacy of the night, and of men like me,
10 This poem drooping shy and unseen that I always carry, and
 that all men carry,
(Know once for all, avow'd on purpose, wherever are men
 like me, are our lusty lurking masculine poems,)
Love-thoughts, love-juice, love-odor, love-yielding,
 love-climbers, and the climbing sap,
Arms and hands of love, lips of love, phallic thumb of love,
 breasts of love, bellies press'd and glued together with
 love,
Earth of chaste love, life that is only life after love,
The body of my love, the body of the woman I love, the
 body of the man, the body of the earth,
Soft forenoon airs that blow from the south-west,
The hairy wild-bee that murmurs and hankers up and down,
 that gripes the full-grown lady-flower, curves upon her
 with amorous firm legs, takes his will of her, and holds
 himself tremulous and tight till he is satisfied;
The wet of woods through the early hours,
Two sleepers at night lying close together as they sleep, one
 with an arm slanting down across and below the waist of
 the other,

20   The smell of apples, aromas from crush'd sage-plant, mint,
      birch-bark,
      The boy's longings, the glow and pressure as he confides to
      me what he was dreaming,
      The dead leaf whirling its spiral whirl and falling still and
      content to the ground,
      The no-form'd stings that sights, people, objects, sting me
      with,
      The hubb'd sting of myself, stinging me as much as it ever
      can any one,
      The sensitive, orbic, underlapp'd brothers, that only
      privileged feelers may be intimate where they are,
      The curious roamer the hand roaming all over the body, the
      bashful withdrawing of flesh where the fingers soothingly
      pause and edge themselves,
      The limpid liquid within the young man,
      The vex'd corrosion so pensive and so painful,
      The torment, the irritable tide that will not be at rest,
30   The like of the same I feel, the like of the same in others,
      The young man that flushes and flushes, and the young
      woman that flushes and flushes,
      The young man that wakes deep at night, the hot hand
      seeking to repress what would master him,
      The mystic amorous night, the strange half-welcome pangs,
      visions, sweats,
      The pulse pounding through palms and trembling
      encircling fingers, the young man all color'd, red,
      ashamed, angry;
      The souse upon me of my lover the sea, as I lie willing and
      naked,
      The merriment of the twin babes that crawl over the grass
      in the sun, the mother never turning her vigilant eyes
      from them,
      The walnut-trunk, the walnut-husks, and the ripening or
      ripen'd long-round walnuts,
      The continence of vegetables, birds, animals,
      The consequent meanness of me should I skulk or find

myself indecent, while birds and animals never once skulk
or find themselves indecent,

40   The great chastity of paternity, to match the great chastity
of maternity,
The oath of procreation I have sworn, my Adamic and fresh
daughters,
The greed that eats me day and night with hungry gnaw,
till I saturate what shall produce boys to fill my place
when I am through,
The wholesome relief, repose, content,
And this bunch pluck'd at random from myself,
It has done its work – I toss it carelessly to fall where it may.

One Hour to Madness and Joy

One hour to madness and joy! O furious! O confine me not!
(What is this that frees me so in storms?
What do my shouts amid lightnings and raging winds
mean?)

O to drink the mystic deliria deeper than any other man!
O savage and tender achings! (I bequeath them to you my
children,
I tell them to you, for reasons, O bridegroom and bride.)

O to be yielded to you whoever you are, and you to be
yielded to me in defiance of the world!
O to return to Paradise! O bashful and feminine!
O to draw you to me, to plant on you for the first time the
lips of a determin'd man.

10   O the puzzle, the thrice-tied knot, the deep and dark pool,
all untied and illumin'd!
O to speed where there is space enough and air enough at last!
To be absolv'd from previous ties and conventions, I from
mine and you from yours!
To find a new unthought-of nonchalance with the best of
Nature!

To have the gag remov'd from one's mouth!
To have the feeling to-day or any day I am sufficient as I am.

O something unprov'd! something in a trance!
To escape utterly from others' anchors and holds!
To drive free! to love free! to dash reckless and dangerous!
To court destruction with taunts, with invitations!
20 To ascend, to leap to the heavens of the love indicated to me!
To rise thither with my inebriate soul!
To be lost if it must be so!
To feed the remainder of life with one hour of fulness and
    freedom!
With one brief hour of madness and joy.

Out of the Rolling Ocean the Crowd

Out of the rolling ocean the crowd came a drop gently to me,
Whispering *I love you, before long I die,*
I have travel'd a long way merely to look on you to touch you,
For I could not die till I once look'd on you,
For I fear'd I might afterward lose you.

Now we have met, we have look'd, we are safe,
Return in peace to the ocean my love,
I too am part of that ocean my love, we are not so much
    separated,
Behold the great rondure, the cohesion of all, how perfect!
10 But as for me, for you, the irresistible sea is to separate us,
As for an hour carrying us diverse, yet cannot carry us
    diverse forever;
Be not impatient – a little space – know you I salute the air,
    the ocean and the land,
Every day at sundown for your dear sake my love.

Ages and Ages Returning at Intervals

Ages and ages returning at intervals,
Undestroy'd, wandering immortal,
Lusty, phallic, with the potent original loins, perfectly
    sweet,
I, chanter of Adamic songs,
Through the new garden the West, the great cities calling,
Deliriate, thus prelude what is generated, offering these,
    offering myself,
Bathing myself, bathing my songs in Sex,
Offspring of my loins.

We Two, How Long We Were Fool'd

We two, how long we were fool'd,
Now transmuted, we swiftly escape as Nature escapes,
We are Nature, long have we been absent, but now we
    return,
We become plants, trunks, foliage, roots, bark,
We are bedded in the ground, we are rocks,
We are oaks, we grow in the openings side by side,
We browse, we are two among the wild herds spontaneous
    as any,
We are two fishes swimming in the sea together,
We are what locust blossoms are, we drop scent around
    lanes mornings and evenings,
10 We are also the coarse smut of beasts, vegetables, minerals,
We are two predatory hawks, we soar above and look down,
We are two resplendent suns, we it is who balance ourselves
    orbic and stellar, we are as two comets,
We prowl fang'd and four-footed in the woods, we spring on
    prey,
We are two clouds forenoons and afternoons driving
    overhead,
We are seas mingling, we are two of those cheerful waves
    rolling over each other and interwetting each other,

We are what the atmosphere is, transparent, receptive,
    previous, impervious,
We are snow, rain, cold, darkness, we are each product and
    influence of the globe,
We have circled and circled till we have arrived home again,
    we two,
We have voided all but freedom and all but our own joy.

O Hymen! O Hymenee!

O hymen! O hymenee! why do you tantalize me thus?
O why sting me for a swift moment only?
Why can you not continue? O why do you now cease?
Is it because if you continued beyond the swift moment you
    would soon certainly kill me?

I Am He that Aches with Love

I am he that aches with amorous love;
Does the earth gravitate? does not all matter, aching,
    attract all matter?
So the body of me to all I meet or know.

Native Moments

Native moments – when you come upon me – ah you are
    here now,
Give me now libidinous joys only,
Give me the drench of my passions, give me life coarse and
    rank,
To-day I go consort with Nature's darlings, to-night too,
I am for those who believe in loose delights, I share the
    midnight orgies of young men,
I dance with the dancers and drink with the drinkers,

The echoes ring with our indecent calls, I pick out some low
   person for my dearest friend,
He shall be lawless, rude, illiterate, he shall be one
   condemn'd by others for deeds done,
I will play a part no longer, why should I exile myself from
   my companions?
10 O you shunn'd persons, I at least do not shun you,
I come forthwith in your midst, I will be your poet,
I will be more to you than to any of the rest.

Once I Pass'd through a Populous City

Once I pass'd through a populous city imprinting my brain
   for future use with its shows, architecture, customs,
   traditions,
Yet now of all that city I remember only a woman I casually
   met there who detain'd me for love of me,
Day by day and night by night we were together – all else
   has long been forgotten by me,
I remember I say only that woman who passionately clung
   to me,
Again we wander, we love, we separate again,
Again she holds me by the hand, I must not go,
I see her close beside me with silent lips sad and
   tremulous.

I Heard You Solemn-Sweet Pipes of the Organ

I heard you solemn-sweet pipes of the organ as last Sunday
   morn I pass'd the church,
Winds of autumn, as I walk'd the woods at dusk I heard
   your long-stretch'd sighs up above so mournful,
I heard the perfect Italian tenor singing at the opera, I heard
   the soprano in the midst of the quartet singing;
Heart of my love! you too I heard murmuring low through
   one of the wrists around my head,

Heard the pulse of you when all was still ringing little bells
  last night under my ear.

Facing West from California's Shores

Facing west from California's shores,
Inquiring, tireless, seeking what is yet unfound,
I, a child, very old, over waves, towards the house of
  maternity, the land of migrations, look afar,
Look off the shores of my Western sea, the circle almost
  circled;
For starting westward from Hindustan, from the vales of
  Kashmere,
From Asia, from the north, from the God, the sage, and the
  hero,
From the south, from the flowery peninsulas and the spice
  islands,
Long having wander'd since, round the earth having
  wander'd,
Now I face home again, very pleas'd and joyous,
10 (But where is what I started for so long ago?
And why is it yet unfound?)

As Adam Early in the Morning

As Adam early in the morning,
Walking forth from the bower refresh'd with sleep,
Behold me where I pass, hear my voice, approach,
Touch me, touch the palm of your hand to my body as I pass,
Be not afraid of my body.

CALAMUS

In Paths Untrodden

In paths untrodden,
In the growth by margins of pond-waters,
Escaped from the life that exhibits itself,
From all the standards hitherto publish'd, from the
    pleasures, profits, conformities,
Which too long I was offering to feed my soul,
Clear to me now standards not yet publish'd, clear to me
    that my soul,
That the soul of the man I speak for rejoices in comrades,
Here by myself away from the clank of the world,
Tallying and talk'd to here by tongues aromatic,
10 No longer abash'd, (for in this secluded spot I can respond
    as I would not dare elsewhere,)
Strong upon me the life that does not exhibit itself, yet
    contains all the rest,
Resolv'd to sing no songs to-day but those of manly
    attachment,
Projecting them along that substantial life,
Bequeathing hence types of athletic love,
Afternoon this delicious Ninth-month in my forty-first
    year,
I proceed for all who are or have been young men,
To tell the secret of my nights and days,
To celebrate the need of comrades.

Scented Herbage of My Breast

Scented herbage of my breast,
Leaves from you I glean, I write, to be perused best
    afterwards,
Tomb-leaves, body-leaves growing up above me above
    death,

Perennial roots, tall leaves, O the winter shall not freeze you
    delicate leaves,
Every year shall you bloom again, out from where you
    retired you shall emerge again;
O I do not know whether many passing by will discover you
    or inhale your faint odor, but I believe a few will;
O slender leaves! O blossoms of my blood! I permit you to
    tell in your own way of the heart that is under you,
O I do not know what you mean there underneath
    yourselves, you are not happiness,
You are often more bitter than I can bear, you burn and
    sting me,
10 Yet you are beautiful to me you faint tinged roots, you
    make me think of death,
Death is beautiful from you, (what indeed is finally
    beautiful except death and love?)
O I think it is not for life I am chanting here my chant of
    lovers, I think it must be for death,
For how calm, how solemn it grows to ascend to the
    atmosphere of lovers,
Death or life I am then indifferent, my soul declines to
    prefer,
(I am not sure but the high soul of lovers welcomes death
    most,)
Indeed O death, I think now these leaves mean precisely
    the same as you mean,
Grow up taller sweet leaves that I may see! grow up out of
    my breast!
Spring away from the conceal'd heart there!
Do not fold yourself so in your pink-tinged roots timid
    leaves!
20 Do not remain down there so ashamed, herbage of my
    breast!
Come I am determin'd to unbare this broad breast of mine, I
    have long enough stifled and choked;
Emblematic and capricious blades I leave you, now you
    serve me not,
I will say what I have to say by itself,

I will sound myself and comrades only, I will never again
   utter a call only their call,
I will raise with it immortal reverberations through the
   States,
I will give an example to lovers to take permanent shape and
   will through the States,
Through me shall the words be said to make death
   exhilarating,
Give me your tone therefore O death, that I may accord
   with it,
Give me yourself, for I see that you belong to me now above
   all, and are folded inseparably together, you love and
   death are,
30   Nor will I allow you to balk me any more with what I was
   calling life,
For now it is convey'd to me that you are the purports
   essential,
That you hide in these shifting forms of life, for reasons,
   and that they are mainly for you,
That you beyond them come forth to remain, the real
   reality,
That behind the mask of materials you patiently wait, no
   matter how long,
That you will one day perhaps take control of all,
That you will perhaps dissipate this entire show of
   appearance,
That may-be you are what it is all for, but it does not last
   so very long,
But you will last very long.

Whoever You Are Holding Me Now in Hand

Whoever you are holding me now in hand,
Without one thing all will be useless,
I give you fair warning before you attempt me further,
I am not what you supposed, but far different.

Who is he that would become my follower?
Who would sign himself a candidate for my affections?

The way is suspicious, the result uncertain, perhaps
    destructive,
You would have to give up all else, I alone would expect to
    be your sole and exclusive standard,
Your novitiate would even then be long and exhausting,
The whole past theory of your life and all conformity to the
    lives around you would have to be abandon'd,
Therefore release me now before troubling yourself any
    further, let go your hand from my shoulders,
Put me down and depart on your way.

Or else by stealth in some wood for trial,
Or back of a rock in the open air,
(For in any roof'd room of a house I emerge not, nor in
    company,
And in libraries I lie as one dumb, a gawk, or unborn, or
    dead,)
But just possibly with you on a high hill, first watching lest
    any person for miles around approach unawares,
Or possibly with you sailing at sea, or on the beach of the
    sea or some quiet island,
Here to put your lips upon mine I permit you,
With the comrade's long-dwelling kiss or the new
    husband's kiss,
For I am the new husband and I am the comrade.

Or if you will, thrusting me beneath your clothing,
Where I may feel the throbs of your heart or rest upon your
    hip,
Carry me when you go forth over land or sea;
For thus merely touching you is enough, is best,
And thus touching you would I silently sleep and be carried
    eternally.

But these leaves conning you con at peril,
For these leaves and me you will not understand,

They will elude you at first and still more afterward, I will
    certainly elude you,
30 Even while you should think you had unquestionably
    caught me, behold!
Already you see I have escaped from you.

For it is not for what I have put into it that I have written
    this book,
Nor is it by reading it you will acquire it,
Nor do those know me best who admire me and vauntingly
    praise me,
Nor will the candidates for my love (unless at most a very
    few) prove victorious,
Nor will my poems do good only, they will do just as much
    evil, perhaps more,
For all is useless without that which you may guess at many
    times and not hit, that which I hinted at;
Therefore release me and depart on your way.

For You O Democracy

Come, I will make the continent indissoluble,
I will make the most splendid race the sun ever shone upon,
I will make divine magnetic lands,
    With the love of comrades,
      With the life-long love of comrades.

I will plant companionship thick as trees along all the rivers
    of America, and along the shores of the great lakes, and
    all over the prairies,
I will make inseparable cities with their arms about each
    other's necks,
    By the love of comrades,
      By the manly love of comrades.

For you these from me, O Democracy, to serve you
    ma femme!
For you, for you I am trilling these songs.

These I Singing in Spring

These I singing in spring collect for lovers,
(For who but I should understand lovers and all their
    sorrow and joy?
And who but I should be the poet of comrades?)
Collecting I traverse the garden the world, but soon I pass
    the gates,
Now along the pond-side, now wading in a little, fearing not
    the wet,
Now by the post-and-rail fences where the old stones
    thrown there, pick'd from the fields, have accumulated,
(Wild-flowers and vines and weeds come up through the
    stones and partly cover them, beyond these I pass,)
Far, far in the forest, or sauntering later in summer, before
    I think where I go,
Solitary, smelling the earthy smell, stopping now and then
    in the silence,
Alone I had thought, yet soon a troop gathers around me,
Some walk by my side and some behind, and some embrace
    my arms or neck,
They the spirits of dear friends dead or alive, thicker they
    come, a great crowd, and I in the middle,
Collecting, dispensing, singing, there I wander with them,
Plucking something for tokens, tossing toward whoever is
    near me,
Here, lilac, with a branch of pine,
Here, out of my pocket, some moss which I pull'd off a
    live-oak in Florida as it hung trailing down,
Here, some pinks and laurel leaves, and a handful of sage,
And here what I now draw from the water, wading in the
    pond-side,
(O here I last saw him that tenderly loves me, and returns
    again never to separate from me,
And this, O this shall henceforth be the token of comrades,
    this calamus-root shall,
Interchange it youths with each other! let none render it
    back!)

And twigs of maple and a bunch of wild orange and chestnut,
And stems of currants and plum-blows, and the aromatic
    cedar,
These I compass'd around by a thick cloud of spirits,
Wandering, point to or touch as I pass, or throw them
    loosely from me,
Indicating to each one what he shall have, giving something
    to each;
But what I drew from the water by the pond-side, that I
    reserve,
I will give of it, but only to them that love as I myself am
    capable of loving.

Not Heaving from my Ribb'd Breast Only

Not heaving from my ribb'd breast only,
Not in sighs at night in rage dissatisfied with myself,
Not in those long-drawn, ill-supprest sighs,
Not in many an oath and promise broken,
Not in my wilful and savage soul's volition,
Not in the subtle nourishment of the air,
Not in this beating and pounding at my temples and wrists,
Not in the curious systole and diastole within which will one
    day cease,
Not in many a hungry wish told to the skies only,
10 Not in cries, laughter, defiances, thrown from me when alone
    far in the wilds,
Not in husky pantings through clinch'd teeth,
Not in sounded and resounded words, chattering words,
    echoes, dead words,
Not in the murmurs of my dreams while I sleep,
Nor the other murmurs of these incredible dreams of every
    day,
Nor in the limbs and senses of my body that take you and
    dismiss you continually – not there,
Not in any or all of them O adhesiveness! O pulse of my life!

Need I that you exist and show yourself any more than in
these songs.

Of the Terrible Doubt of Appearances

Of the terrible doubt of appearances,
Of the uncertainty after all, that we may be deluded,
That may-be reliance and hope are but speculations after all,
That may-be identity beyond the grave is a beautiful fable
only,
May-be the things I perceive, the animals, plants, men, hills,
shining and flowing waters,
The skies of day and night, colors, densities, forms, may-be
these are (as doubtless they are) only apparitions, and the
real something has yet to be known,
(How often they dart out of themselves as if to confound me
and mock me!
How often I think neither I know, nor any man knows,
aught of them,)
May-be seeming to me what they are (as doubtless they
indeed but seem) as from my present point of view, and
might prove (as of course they would) nought of what they
appear, or nought anyhow, from entirely changed points
of view;
10 To me these and the like of these are curiously answer'd by
my lovers, my dear friends,
When he whom I love travels with me or sits a long while
holding me by the hand,
When the subtle air, the impalpable, the sense that words
and reason hold not, surround us and pervade us,
Then I am charged with untold and untellable wisdom, I am
silent, I require nothing further,
I cannot answer the question of appearances or that of
identity beyond the grave,
But I walk or sit indifferent, I am satisfied,
He ahold of my hand has completely satisfied me.

The Base of All Metaphysics

And now gentlemen,
A word I give to remain in your memories and minds,
As base and finalè too for all metaphysics.

(So to the students the old professor,
At the close of his crowded course.)

Having studied the new and antique, the Greek and
    Germanic systems,
Kant having studied and stated, Fichte and Schelling and
    Hegel,
Stated the lore of Plato, and Socrates greater than Plato,
And greater than Socrates sought and stated, Christ divine
    having studied long,
10   I see reminiscent to-day those Greek and Germanic
    systems,
See the philosophies all, Christian churches and tenets see,
Yet underneath Socrates clearly see, and underneath Christ
    the divine I see,
The dear love of man for his comrade, the attraction of
    friend to friend,
Of the well-married husband and wife, of children and
    parents,
Of city for city and land for land.

Recorders Ages Hence

Recorders ages hence,
Come, I will take you down underneath this impassive
    exterior, I will tell you what to say to me,
Publish my name and hang up my picture as that of the
    tenderest lover,
The friend the lover's portrait, of whom his friend his
    lover was fondest,
Who was not proud of his songs, but of the measureless
    ocean of love within him, and freely pour'd it forth,

Who often walk'd lonesome walks thinking of his dear
    friends, his lovers,

Who pensive away from one he lov'd often lay sleepless and
    dissatisfied at night,

Who knew too well the sick, sick dread lest the one he lov'd
    might secretly be indifferent to him,

Whose happiest days were far away through fields, in woods,
    on hills, he and another wandering hand in hand, they
    twain apart from other men,

10 Who oft as he saunter'd the streets curv'd with his arm the
    shoulder of his friend, while the arm of his friend rested
    upon him also.

When I Heard at the Close of the Day

When I heard at the close of the day how my name had been
    receiv'd with plaudits in the capitol, still it was not a
    happy night for me that follow'd,

And else when I carous'd, or when my plans were
    accomplish'd, still I was not happy,

But the day when I rose at dawn from the bed of perfect
    health, refresh'd, singing, inhaling the ripe breath of
    autumn,

When I saw the full moon in the west grow pale and
    disappear in the morning light,

When I wander'd alone over the beach, and undressing
    bathed, laughing with the cool waters, and saw the sun
    rise,

And when I thought how my dear friend my lover was on
    his way coming, O then I was happy,

O then each breath tasted sweeter, and all that day my food
    nourish'd me more, and the beautiful day pass'd well,

And the next came with equal joy, and with the next at
    evening came my friend,

And that night while all was still I heard the waters roll
    slowly continually up the shores,

10 I heard the hissing rustle of the liquid and sands as directed
   to me whispering to congratulate me,
  For the one I love most lay sleeping by me under the same
   cover in the cool night,
  In the stillness in the autumn moonbeams his face was
   inclined toward me,
  And his arm lay lightly around my breast – and that night
   I was happy.

Are You the New Person Drawn toward Me?

Are you the new person drawn toward me?
To begin with take warning, I am surely far different from
  what you suppose;
Do you suppose you will find in me your ideal?
Do you think it so easy to have me become your lover?
Do you think the friendship of me would be unalloy'd
  satisfaction?
Do you think I am trusty and faithful?
Do you see no further than this façade, this smooth and
  tolerant manner of me?
Do you suppose yourself advancing on real ground toward a
  real heroic man?
Have you no thought O dreamer that it may be all maya,
  illusion?

Roots and Leaves Themselves Alone

Roots and leaves themselves alone are these,
Scents brought to men and women from the wild woods and
  pond-side,
Breast-sorrel and pinks of love, fingers that wind around
  tighter than vines,
Gushes from the throats of birds hid in the foliage of trees
  as the sun is risen,

Breezes of land and love set from living shores to you on the
    living sea, to you O sailors!
Frost-mellow'd berries and Third-month twigs offer'd
    fresh to young persons wandering out in the fields when
    the winter breaks up,
Love-buds put before you and within you whoever you are,
Buds to be unfolded on the old terms,
If you bring the warmth of the sun to them they will open
    and bring form, color, perfume, to you,
10 If you become the aliment and the wet they will become
    flowers, fruits, tall branches and trees.

Not Heat Flames up and Consumes

Not heat flames up and consumes,
Not sea-waves hurry in and out,
Not the air delicious and dry, the air of ripe summer, bears
    lightly along white down-balls of myriads of seeds,
Wafted, sailing gracefully, to drop where they may;
Not these, O none of these more than the flames of me,
    consuming, burning for his love whom I love,
O none more than I hurrying in and out;
Does the tide hurry, seeking something, and never give up?
    O I the same,
O nor down-balls nor perfumes, nor the high rain-emitting
    clouds, are borne through the open air,
Any more than my soul is borne through the open air,
10 Wafted in all directions O love, for friendship, for you.

Trickle Drops

Trickle drops! my blue veins leaving!
O drops of me! trickle, slow drops,
Candid from me falling, drip, bleeding drops,
From wounds made to free you whence you were prison'd,
From my face, from my forehead and lips,

From my breast, from within where I was conceal'd, press
    forth red drops, confession drops,
Stain every page, stain every song I sing, every word I say,
    bloody drops,
Let them know your scarlet heat, let them glisten,
Saturate them with yourself all ashamed and wet,
10   Glow upon all I have written or shall write, bleeding drops,
Let it all be seen in your light, blushing drops.

City of Orgies

City of orgies, walks and joys,
City whom that I have lived and sung in your midst will one
    day make you illustrious,
Not the pageants of you, not your shifting tableaus, your
    spectacles, repay me,
Not the interminable rows of your houses, nor the ships
    at the wharves,
Nor the processions in the streets, nor the bright windows
    with goods in them,
Nor to converse with learn'd persons, or bear my share in
    the soiree or feast;
Not those, but as I pass O Manhattan, your frequent and
    swift flash of eyes offering me love,
Offering response to my own – these repay me,
Lovers, continual lovers, only repay me.

Behold This Swarthy Face

Behold this swarthy face, these gray eyes,
This beard, the white wool unclipt upon my neck,
My brown hands and the silent manner of me without
    charm;
Yet comes one a Manhattanese and ever at parting kisses me
    lightly on the lips with robust love,

And I on the crossing of the street or on the ship's deck give
    a kiss in return,
We observe that salute of American comrades land and sea,
We are those two natural and nonchalant persons.

I Saw in Louisiana a Live-Oak Growing

I saw in Louisiana a live-oak growing,
All alone stood it and the moss hung down from the
    branches,
Without any companion it grew there uttering joyous leaves
    of dark green,
And its look, rude, unbending, lusty, made me think of
    myself,
But I wonder'd how it could utter joyous leaves standing
    alone there without its friend near, for I knew I could not,
And I broke off a twig with a certain number of leaves upon
    it, and twined around it a little moss,
And brought it away, and I have placed it in sight in my
    room,
It is not needed to remind me as of my own dear friends,
(For I believe lately I think of little else than of them,)
10 Yet it remains to me a curious token, it makes me think of
    manly love;
For all that, and though the live-oak glistens there in
    Louisiana solitary in a wide flat space,
Uttering joyous leaves all its life without a friend a lover
    near,
I know very well I could not.

To a Stranger

Passing stranger! you do not know how longingly I look
    upon you,
You must be he I was seeking, or she I was seeking, (it
    comes to me as of a dream,)

I have somewhere surely lived a life of joy with you,
All is recall'd as we flit by each other, fluid, affectionate,
    chaste, matured,
You grew up with me, were a boy with me or a girl with me,
I ate with you and slept with you, your body has become not
    yours only nor left my body mine only,
You give me the pleasure of your eyes, face, flesh, as we pass,
    you take of my beard, breast, hands, in return,
I am not to speak to you, I am to think of you when I sit
    alone or wake at night alone,
I am to wait, I do not doubt I am to meet you again,
10 I am to see to it that I do not lose you.

This Moment Yearning and Thoughtful

This moment yearning and thoughtful sitting alone,
It seems to me there are other men in other lands yearning
    and thoughtful,
It seems to me I can look over and behold them in Germany,
    Italy, France, Spain,
Or far, far away, in China, or in Russia or Japan, talking
    other dialects,
And it seems to me if I could know those men I should
    become attached to them as I do to men in my own lands,
O I know we should be brethren and lovers,
I know I should be happy with them.

I Hear It was Charged against Me

I hear it was charged against me that I sought to destroy
    institutions,
But really I am neither for nor against institutions,
(What indeed have I in common with them? or what with
    the destruction of them?)
Only I will establish in the Mannahatta and in every city of
    these States inland and seaboard,

And in the fields and woods, and above every keel little or
    large that dents the water,
Without edifices or rules or trustees or any argument,
The institution of the dear love of comrades.

The Prairie-grass Dividing

The prairie-grass dividing, its special odor breathing,
I demand of it the spiritual corresponding,
Demand the most copious and close companionship of men,
Demand the blades to rise of words, acts, beings,
Those of the open atmosphere, coarse, sunlit, fresh,
    nutritious,
Those that go their own gait, erect, stepping with freedom
    and command, leading not following,
Those with a never-quell'd audacity, those with sweet and
    lusty flesh clear of taint,
Those that look carelessly in the faces of Presidents and
    governors, as to say *Who are you?*
Those of earth-born passion, simple, never constrain'd,
    never obedient,
10   Those of inland America.

When I Peruse the Conquer'd Fame

When I peruse the conquer'd fame of heroes and the
    victories of mighty generals, I do not envy the generals,
Nor the President in his Presidency, nor the rich in his great
    house,
But when I hear of the brotherhood of lovers, how it was
    with them,
How together through life, through dangers, odium,
    unchanging, long and long,
Through youth and through middle and old age, how
    unfaltering, how affectionate and faithful they were,

Then I am pensive – I hastily walk away fill'd with the
    bitterest envy.

We Two Boys together Clinging

We two boys together clinging,
One the other never leaving,
Up and down the roads going, North and South
    excursions making,
Power enjoying, elbows stretching, fingers clutching,
Arm'd and fearless, eating, drinking, sleeping, loving,
No law less than ourselves owning, sailing, soldiering,
    thieving, threatening,
Misers, menials, priests alarming, air breathing, water
    drinking, on the turf or the sea-beach dancing,
Cities wrenching, ease scorning, statutes mocking, feebleness
    chasing,
Fulfilling our foray.

A Promise to California

A promise to California,
Or inland to the great pastoral Plains, and on to Puget
    sound and Oregon;
Sojourning east a while longer, soon I travel toward you, to
    remain, to teach robust American love,
For I know very well that I and robust love belong among
    you, inland, and along the Western sea;
For these States tend inland and toward the Western sea,
    and I will also.

Here the Frailest Leaves of Me

Here the frailest leaves of me and yet my strongest lasting,
Here I shade and hide my thoughts, I myself do not expose
    them,
And yet they expose me more than all my other poems.

No Labor-Saving Machine

No labor-saving machine,
Nor discovery have I made,
Nor will I be able to leave behind me any wealthy bequest
    to found a hospital or library,
Nor reminiscence of any deed of courage for America,
Nor literary success nor intellect, nor book for the
    book-shelf,
But a few carols vibrating through the air I leave,
For comrades and lovers.

A Glimpse

A glimpse through an interstice caught,
Of a crowd of workmen and drivers in a bar-room around
    the stove late of a winter night, and I unremark'd seated
    in a corner,
Of a youth who loves me and whom I love, silently
    approaching and seating himself near, that he may hold
    me by the hand,
A long while amid the noises of coming and going, of
    drinking and oath and smutty jest,
There we two, content, happy in being together, speaking
    little, perhaps not a word.

A Leaf for Hand in Hand

A leaf for hand in hand;
You natural persons old and young!
You on the Mississippi and on all the branches and bayous
 of the Mississippi!
You friendly boatmen and mechanics! you roughs!
You twain! and all processions moving along the streets!
I wish to infuse myself among you till I see it common for
 you to walk hand in hand.

Earth, My Likeness

Earth, my likeness,
Though you look so impassive, ample and spheric there,
I now suspect that is not all;
I now suspect there is something fierce in you eligible to
 burst forth,
For an athlete is enamour'd of me, and I of him,
But toward him there is something fierce and terrible in me
 eligible to burst forth,
I dare not tell it in words, not even in these songs.

I Dream'd in a Dream

I dream'd in a dream I saw a city invincible to the attacks
 of the whole of the rest of the earth,
I dream'd that was the new city of Friends,
Nothing was greater there than the quality of robust love, it
 led the rest,
It was seen every hour in the actions of the men of that city,
And in all their looks and words.

What Think You I Take My Pen in Hand?

What think you I take my pen in hand to record?
The battle-ship, perfect-model'd, majestic, that I saw pass
    the offing to-day under full sail?
The splendors of the past day? or the splendor of the night
    that envelops me?
Or the vaunted glory and growth of the great city spread
    around me? – no;
But merely of two simple men I saw to-day on the pier in
    the midst of the crowd, parting the parting of dear friends,
The one to remain hung on the other's neck and
    passionately kiss'd him,
While the one to depart tightly prest the one to remain in
    his arms.

To the East and to the West

To the East and to the West,
To the man of the Seaside State and of Pennsylvania,
To the Kanadian of the north, to the Southerner I love,
These with perfect trust to depict you as myself, the germs
    are in all men,
I believe the main purport of these States is to found a
    superb friendship, exaltè, previously unknown,
Because I perceive it waits, and has been always waiting,
    latent in all men.

Sometimes with One I Love

Sometimes with one I love I fill myself with rage for fear I
    effuse unreturn'd love,
But now I think there is no unreturn'd love, the pay is
    certain one way or another,
(I loved a certain person ardently and my love was not
    return'd,
Yet out of that I have written these songs.)

166

To a Western Boy

Many things to absorb I teach to help you become eleve
  of mine;
Yet if blood like mine circle not in your veins,
If you be not silently selected by lovers and do not silently
    select lovers,
Of what use is it that you seek to become eleve of mine?

Fast-Anchor'd Eternal O Love!

Fast-anchor'd eternal O love! O woman I love!
O bride! O wife! more resistless than I can tell, the
    thought of you!
Then separate, as disembodied or another born,
Ethereal, the last athletic reality, my consolation,
I ascend, I float in the regions of your love O man,
O sharer of my roving life.

Among the Multitude

Among the men and women the multitude,
I perceive one picking me out by secret and divine signs,
Acknowledging none else, not parent, wife, husband,
    brother, child, any nearer than I am,
Some are baffled, but that one is not – that one knows me.

Ah lover and perfect equal,
I meant that you should discover me so by faint
    indirections,
And I when I meet you mean to discover you by the like
    in you.

O You whom I Often and Silently Come

O you whom I often and silently come where you are that
    I may be with you,
As I walk by your side or sit near, or remain in the same
    room with you,
Little you know the subtle electric fire that for your sake
    is playing within me.

That Shadow My Likeness

That shadow my likeness that goes to and fro seeking a
    livelihood, chattering, chaffering,
How often I find myself standing and looking at it where it
    flits,
How often I question and doubt whether that is really me;
But among my lovers and caroling these songs,
O I never doubt whether that is really me.

Full of Life Now

Full of life now, compact, visible,
I, forty years old the eighty-third year of the States,
To one a century hence or any number of centuries hence,
To you yet unborn these, seeking you.

When you read these I that was visible am become
    invisible,
Now it is you, compact, visible, realizing my poems,
    seeking me,
Fancying how happy you were if I could be with you and
    become your comrade;
Be it as if I were with you. (Be not too certain but I am now
    with you.)

Salut au Monde!

1

O take my hand Walt Whitman!
Such gliding wonders! such sights and sounds!
Such join'd unended links, each hook'd to the next,
Each answering all, each sharing the earth with all.

What widens within you Walt Whitman?
What waves and soils exuding?
What climes? what persons and cities are here?
Who are the infants, some playing, some slumbering?
Who are the girls? who are the married women?
10 Who are the groups of old men going slowly with their arms
        about each other's necks?
What rivers are these? what forests and fruits are these?
What are the mountains call'd that rise so high in the mists?
What myriads of dwellings are they fill'd with dwellers?

2

Within me latitude widens, longitude lengthens,
Asia, Africa, Europe, are to the east – America is provided
    for in the west,
Banding the bulge of the earth winds the hot equator,
Curiously north and south turn the axis-ends,
Within me is the longest day, the sun wheels in slanting
    rings, it does not set for months,
Stretch'd in due time within me the midnight sun just rises
    above the horizon and sinks again,
20 Within me zones, seas, cataracts, forests, volcanoes,
        groups,
Malaysia, Polynesia, and the great West Indian islands.

3

What do you hear Walt Whitman?

I hear the workman singing and the farmer's wife singing,
I hear in the distance the sounds of children and of animals
early in the day,
I hear emulous shouts of Australians pursuing the wild
horse,
I hear the Spanish dance with castanets in the chestnut
shade, to the rebeck and guitar,
I hear continual echoes from the Thames,
I hear fierce French liberty songs,
I hear of the Italian boat-sculler the musical recitative of old
poems,
30 I hear the locusts in Syria as they strike the grain and grass
with the showers of their terrible clouds,
I hear the Coptic refrain toward sundown, pensively falling
on the breast of the black venerable vast mother the Nile,
I hear the chirp of the Mexican muleteer, and the bells of the
mule,
I hear the Arab muezzin calling from the top of the mosque,
I hear the Christian priests at the altars of their churches, I
hear the responsive base and soprano,
I hear the cry of the Cossack, and the sailor's voice putting
to sea at Okotsk,
I hear the wheeze of the slave-coffle as the slaves march on,
as the husky gangs pass on by twos and threes, fasten'd
together with wrist-chains and ankle-chains,
I hear the Hebrew reading his records and psalms,
I hear the rhythmic myths of the Greeks, and the strong
legends of the Romans,
I hear the tale of the divine life and bloody death of the
beautiful God the Christ,
40 I hear the Hindoo teaching his favorite pupil the loves,
wars, adages, transmitted safely to this day from poets
who wrote three thousand years ago.

4

What do you see Walt Whitman?
Who are they you salute, and that one after another salute
    you?

I see a great round wonder rolling through space,
I see diminute farms, hamlets, ruins, graveyards, jails,
    factories, palaces, hovels, huts of barbarians, tents of
    nomads upon the surface,
I see the shaded part on one side where the sleepers are
    sleeping, and the sunlit part on the other side,
I see the curious rapid change of the light and shade,
I see distant lands, as real and near to the inhabitants of
    them as my land is to me.

I see plenteous waters,
I see mountain peaks, I see the sierras of Andes where they
    range,
50 I see plainly the Himalayas, Chian Shahs, Altays, Ghauts,
I see the giant pinnacles of Elbruz, Kazbek, Bazardjusi,
I see the Styrian Alps, and the Karnac Alps,
I see the Pyrenees, Balks, Carpathians, and to the north the
    Dofrafields, and off at sea mount Hecla,
I see Vesuvius and Etna, the mountains of the Moon, and
    the Red mountains of Madagascar,
I see the Lybian, Arabian, and Asiatic deserts,
I see huge dreadful Arctic and Antarctic icebergs,
I see the superior oceans and the inferior ones, the Atlantic
    and Pacific, the sea of Mexico, the Brazilian sea, and the
    sea of Peru,
The waters of Hindustan, the China sea, and the gulf of
    Guinea,
The Japan waters, the beautiful bay of Nagasaki land-lock'd
    in its mountains,
60 The spread of the Baltic, Caspian, Bothnia, the British
    shores, and the bay of Biscay,
The clear-sunn'd Mediterranean, and from one to another
    of its islands,
The White sea, and the sea around Greenland.

I behold the mariners of the world,
Some are in storms, some in the night with the watch on
	the lookout,
Some drifting helplessly, some with contagious diseases.

I behold the sail and steamships of the world, some in
	clusters in port, some on their voyages,
Some double the cape of Storms, some cape Verde, others
	capes Guardafui, Bon, or Bajadore,
Others Dondra head, others pass the straits of Sunda,
	others cape Lopatka, others Behring's straits,
Others cape Horn, others sail the gulf of Mexico or along
	Cuba or Hayti, others Hudson's bay or Baffin's bay,
70	Others pass the straits of Dover, others enter the Wash,
	others the firth of Solway, others round cape Clear,
	others the Land's End,
Others traverse the Zuyder Zee or the Scheld,
Others as comers and goers at Gibraltar or the
	Dardanelles,
Others sternly push their way through the northern
	winter-packs,
Others descend or ascend the Obi or the Lena,
Others the Niger or the Congo, others the Indus, the
	Burampooter and Cambodia,
Others wait steam'd up ready to start in the ports of
	Australia,
Wait at Liverpool, Glasgow, Dublin, Marseilles, Lisbon,
	Naples, Hamburg, Bremen, Bordeaux, the Hague,
	Copenhagen,
Wait at Valparaiso, Rio Janeiro, Panama.

5
I see the tracks of the railroads of the earth,
80	I see them in Great Britain, I see them in Europe,
I see them in Asia and in Africa.

I see the electric telegraphs of the earth,
I see the filaments of the news of the wars, deaths, losses,
	gains, passions, of my race.

I see the long river-stripes of the earth,
I see the Amazon and the Paraguay,
I see the four great rivers of China, the Amour, the Yellow
    River, the Yiang-tse, and the Pearl,
I see where the Seine flows, and where the Danube, the
    Loire, the Rhone, and the Guadalquiver flow,
I see the windings of the Volga, the Dnieper, the Oder,
I see the Tuscan going down the Arno, and the Venetian
    along the Po,
90 I see the Greek seaman sailing out of Egina bay.

6

I see the site of the old empire of Assyria, and that of Persia,
    and that of India,
I see the falling of the Ganges over the high rim of Saukara.

I see the place of the idea of the Deity incarnated by avatars
    in human forms,
I see the spots of the successions of priests on the earth,
    oracles, sacrificers, brahmins, sabians, llamas, monks,
    muftis, exhorters,
I see where druids walk'd the groves of Mona, I see the
    mistletoe and vervain,
I see the temples of the deaths of the bodies of Gods, I see
    the old signifiers.

I see Christ eating the bread of his last supper in the midst of
    youths and old persons,
I see where the strong divine young man the Hercules toil'd
    faithfully and long and then died,
I see the place of the innocent rich life and hapless fate of the
    beautiful nocturnal son, the full-limb'd Bacchus,
100 I see Kneph, blooming, drest in blue, with the crown of
    feathers on his head,
I see Hermes, unsuspected, dying, well-belov'd, saying to the
    people *Do not weep for me,*
This is not my true country, I have lived banish'd from my true
    country, I now go back there,
I return to the celestial sphere where every one goes in his turn.

7
I see the battle-fields of the earth, grass grows upon them
    and blossoms and corn,
I see the tracks of ancient and modern expeditions.

I see the nameless masonries, venerable messages of the
    unknown events, heroes, records of the earth.

I see the places of the sagas,
I see pine-trees and fir-trees torn by northern blasts,
I see granite bowlders and cliffs, I see green meadows and
    lakes,
110 I see the burial-cairns of Scandinavian warriors,
I see them raised high with stones by the marge of restless
    oceans, that the dead men's spirits when they wearied of
    their quiet graves might rise up through the mounds and
    gaze on the tossing billows, and be refresh'd by storms,
    immensity, liberty, action.

I see the steppes of Asia,
I see the tumuli of Mongolia, I see the tents of Kalmucks
    and Baskirs,
I see the nomadic tribes with herds of oxen and cows,
I see the table-lands notch'd with ravines, I see the jungles
    and deserts,
I see the camel, the wild steed, the bustard, the fat-tail'd
    sheep, the antelope, and the burrowing wolf.

I see the highlands of Abyssinia,
I see flocks of goats feeding, and see the fig-tree, tamarind,
    date,
And see fields of teff-wheat and places of verdure and gold.

120 I see the Brazilian vaquero,
I see the Bolivian ascending mount Sorata,
I see the Wacho crossing the plains, I see the incomparable
    rider of horses with his lasso on his arm,
I see over the pampas the pursuit of wild cattle for their
    hides.

8, [9]

I see the regions of snow and ice,
I see the sharp-eyed Samoiede and the Finn,
I see the seal-seeker in his boat poising his lance,
I see the Siberian on his slight-built sledge drawn by dogs,
I see the porpoise-hunters, I see the whale-crews of the
    south Pacific and the north Atlantic,
I see the cliffs, glaciers, torrents, valleys, of Switzerland – I
    mark the long winters and the isolation.

130 I see the cities of the earth and make myself at random a part
    of them,
I am a real Parisian,
I am a habitan of Vienna, St Petersburg, Berlin,
    Constantinople,
I am of Adelaide, Sidney, Melbourne,
I am of London, Manchester, Bristol, Edinburgh, Limerick,
I am of Madrid, Cadiz, Barcelona, Oporto, Lyons, Brussels,
    Berne, Frankfort, Stuttgart, Turin, Florence,
I belong in Moscow, Cracow, Warsaw, or northward in
    Christiania or Stockholm, or in Siberian Irkutsk, or in
    some street in Iceland,
I descend upon all those cities, and rise from them again.

10

I see vapors exhaling from unexplored countries,
I see the savage types, the bow and arrow, the poison'd
    splint, the fetich, and the obi.

140 I see African and Asiatic towns,
I see Algiers, Tripoli, Derne, Mogadore, Timbuctoo,
    Monrovia,
I see the swarms of Pekin, Canton, Benares, Delhi,
    Calcutta, Tokio,
I see the Kruman in his hut, and the Dahoman and
    Ashantee-man in their huts,
I see the Turk smoking opium in Aleppo,
I see the picturesque crowds at the fairs of Khiva and those
    of Herat,

I see Teheran, I see Muscat and Medina and the
 intervening sands, I see the caravans toiling onward,
I see Egypt and the Egyptians, I see the pyramids and
 obelisks,
I look on chisell'd histories, records of conquering kings,
 dynasties, cut in slabs of sand-stone, or on granite-blocks,
I see at Memphis mummy-pits containing mummies
 embalm'd, swathed in linen cloth, lying there many
 centuries,
150 I look on the fall'n Theban, the large-ball'd eyes, the
 side-drooping neck, the hands folded across the breast.

I see all the menials of the earth, laboring,
I see all the prisoners in the prisons,
I see the defective human bodies of the earth,
The blind, the deaf and dumb, idiots, hunchbacks,
 lunatics,
The pirates, thieves, betrayers, murderers, slave-makers of
 the earth,
The helpless infants, and the helpless old men and women.

I see male and female everywhere,
I see the serene brotherhood of philosophs,
I see the constructiveness of my race,
160 I see the results of the perseverance and industry of my
 race,
I see ranks, colors, barbarisms, civilizations, I go among
 them, I mix indiscriminately,
And I salute all the inhabitants of the earth.

11
You whoever you are!
You daughter or son of England!
You of the mighty Slavic tribes and empires! you Russ in
 Russia!
You dim-descended, black, divine-soul'd African, large,
 fine-headed, nobly-form'd, superbly destin'd, on equal
 terms with me!
You Norwegian! Swede! Dane! Icelander! you Prussian!

You Spaniard of Spain! you Portuguese!
You Frenchwoman and Frenchman of France!

170 You Belge! you liberty-lover of the Netherlands! (you stock
 whence I myself have descended;)
You sturdy Austrian! you Lombard! Hun! Bohemian!
 farmer of Styria!
You neighbor of the Danube!
You working-man of the Rhine, the Elbe, or the Weser!
 you working-woman too!
You Sardinian! you Bavarian! Swabian! Saxon! Wallachian!
 Bulgarian!
You Roman! Neapolitan! you Greek!
You lithe matador in the arena at Seville!
You mountaineer living lawlessly on the Taurus or
 Caucasus!
You Bokh horse-herd watching your mares and stallions
 feeding!
You beautiful-bodied Persian at full speed in the saddle
 shooting arrows to the mark!
180 You Chinaman and Chinawoman of China! you Tartar of
 Tartary!
You women of the earth subordinated at your tasks!
You Jew journeying in your old age through every risk to
 stand once on Syrian ground!
You other Jews waiting in all lands for your Messiah!
You thoughtful Armenian pondering by some stream of the
 Euphrates! you peering amid the ruins of Nineveh! you
 ascending mount Ararat!
You foot-worn pilgrim welcoming the far-away sparkle of
 the minarets of Mecca!
You sheiks along the stretch from Suez to Bab-el-mandeb
 ruling your families and tribes!
You olive-grower tending your fruit on fields of Nazareth,
 Damascus, or lake Tiberias!
You Thibet trader on the wide inland or bargaining in the
 shops of Lassa!
You Japanese man or woman! you liver in Madagascar,
 Ceylon, Sumatra, Borneo!

190   All you continentals of Asia, Africa, Europe, Australia,
indifferent of place!

All you on the numberless islands of the archipelagoes of
the sea!

And you of centuries hence when you listen to me!

And you each and everywhere whom I specify not, but
include just the same!

Health to you! good will to you all, from me and America
sent!

Each of us inevitable,

Each of us limitless – each of us with his or her right upon
the earth,

Each of us allow'd the eternal purports of the earth,

Each of us here as divinely as any is here.

12

You Hottentot with clicking palate! you woolly-hair'd
hordes!

200   You own'd persons dropping sweat-drops or blood-drops!

You human forms with the fathomless ever-impressive
countenances of brutes!

You poor koboo whom the meanest of the rest look down
upon for all your glimmering language and spirituality!

You dwarf'd Kamtschatkan, Greenlander, Lapp!

You Austral negro, naked, red, sooty, with protrusive lip,
groveling, seeking your food!

You Caffre, Berber, Soudanese!

You haggard, uncouth, untutor'd Bedowee!

You plague-swarms in Madras, Nankin, Kaubul, Cairo!

You benighted roamer of Amazonia! you Patagonian! you
Feejeeman!

I do not prefer others so very much before you either,

210   I do not say one word against you, away back there where
you stand,

(You will come forward in due time to my side.)

13

My spirit has pass'd in compassion and determination
    around the whole earth,
I have look'd for equals and lovers and found them ready for
    me in all lands,
I think some divine rapport has equalized me with them.

You vapors, I think I have risen with you, moved away to
    distant continents, and falled down there, for reasons,
I think I have blown with you you winds;
You waters I have finger'd every shore with you,
I have run through what any river or strait of the globe has
    run through,
I have taken my stand on the bases of peninsulas and on
    the high embedded rocks, to cry thence:

220 *Salut au monde!*
What cities the light or warmth penetrates I penetrate those
    cities myself,
All islands to which birds wing their way I wing my way
    myself.

Toward you all, in America's name,
I raise high the perpendicular hand, I make the signal,
To remain after me in sight forever,
For all the haunts and homes of men.

Song of the Open Road

I

Afoot and light-hearted I take to the open road,
Healthy, free, the world before me,
The long brown path before me leading wherever I choose.

Henceforth I ask not good-fortune, I myself am
    good-fortune,
Henceforth I whimper no more, postpone no more, need
    nothing,

Done with indoor complaints, libraries, querulous
    criticisms,
Strong and content I travel the open road.

The earth, that is sufficient,
I do not want the constellations any nearer,
10 I know they are very well where they are,
I know they suffice for those who belong to them.

(Still here I carry my old delicious burdens,
I carry them, men and women, I carry them with me
    wherever I go,
I swear it is impossible for me to get rid of them,
I am fill'd with them, and I will fill them in return.)

2
You road I enter upon and look around, I believe you are
    not all that is here,
I believe that much unseen is also here.

Here the profound lesson of reception, nor preference nor
    denial,
The black with his woolly head, the felon, the diseas'd, the
    illiterate person, are not denied;
20 The birth, the hasting after the physician, the beggar's
    tramp, the drunkard's stagger, the laughing party of
    mechanics,
The escaped youth, the rich person's carriage, the fop, the
    eloping couple,
The early market-man, the hearse, the moving of furniture
    into the town, the return back from the town,
They pass, I also pass, any thing passes, none can be
    interdicted,
None but are accepted, none but shall be dear to me.

3
You air that serves me with breath to speak!
You objects that call from diffusion my meanings and give
    them shape!

You light that wraps me and all things in delicate equable
    showers!
You paths worn in the irregular hollows by the roadsides!
I believe you are latent with unseen existences, you are so
    dear to me.

30 You flagg'd walks of the cities! you strong curbs at the
    edges!
You ferries! you planks and posts of wharves! you
    timber-lined sides! you distant ships!
You rows of houses! you window-pierc'd façades! you
    roofs!
You porches and entrances! you copings and iron guards!
You windows whose transparent shells might expose so
    much!
You doors and ascending steps! you arches!
You gray stones of interminable pavements! you trodden
    crossings!
From all that has touch'd you I believe you have imparted
    to yourselves, and now would impart the same secretly
    to me,
From the living and the dead you have peopled your
    impassive surface, and the spirits thereof would be
    evident and amicable with me.

4
The earth expanding right hand and left hand,
40 The picture alive, every part in its best light,
The music falling in where it is wanted, and stopping where
    it is not wanted,
The cheerful voice of the public road, the gay fresh
    sentiment of the road.

O highway I travel, do you say to me *Do not leave me?*
Do you say *Venture not – if you leave me you are lost?*
Do you say *I am already prepared, I am well-beaten and
undenied, adhere to me?*

O public road, I say back I am not afraid to leave you, yet
    I love you,
You express me better than I can express myself,
You shall be more to me than my poem.

I think heroic deeds were all conceiv'd in the open air, and
    all free poems also,
50 I think I could stop here myself and do miracles,
I think whatever I shall meet on the road I shall like, and
    whoever beholds me shall like me,
I think whoever I see must be happy.

5
From this hour I ordain myself loos'd of limits and
    imaginary lines,
Going where I list, my own master total and absolute,
Listening to others, considering well what they say,
Pausing, searching, receiving, contemplating,
Gently, but with undeniable will, divesting myself of the
    holds that would hold me.

I inhale great draughts of space,
The east and the west are mine, and the north and the
    south are mine.

60 I am larger, better than I thought,
I did not know I held so much goodness.

All seems beautiful to me,
I can repeat over to men and women You have done such
    good to me I would do the same to you,
I will recruit for myself and you as I go,
I will scatter myself among men and women as I go,
I will toss a new gladness and roughness among them,
Whoever denies me it shall not trouble me,
Whoever accepts me he or she shall be blessed and shall
    bless me.

6

Now if a thousand perfect men were to appear it would not
   amaze me,
70   Now if a thousand beautiful forms of women appear'd it
      would not astonish me.

Now I see the secret of the making of the best persons,
It is to grow in the open air and to eat and sleep with the
   earth.

Here a great personal deed has room,
(Such a deed seizes upon the hearts of the whole race of
   men,
Its effusion of strength and will overwhelms law and mocks
   all authority and all argument against it.)

Here is the test of wisdom,
Wisdom is not finally tested in schools,
Wisdom cannot be pass'd from one having it to another not
   having it,
Wisdom is of the soul, is not susceptible of proof, is its own
   proof,
80   Applies to all stages and objects and qualities and is content,
Is the certainty of the reality and immortality of things, and
   the excellence of things;
Something there is in the float of the sight of things that
   provokes it out of the soul.

Now I re-examine philosophies and religions,
They may prove well in lecture-rooms, yet not prove at all
   under the spacious clouds and along the landscape and
   flowing currents.

Here is realization,
Here is a man tallied – he realizes here what he has in him,
The past, the future, majesty, love – if they are vacant of
   you, you are vacant of them.

Only the kernel of every object nourishes;
Where is he who tears off the husks for you and me?
90   Where is he that undoes stratagems and envelopes for you
    and me?

Here is adhesiveness, it is not previously fashion'd, it is
    apropos;
Do you know what it is as you pass to be loved by strangers?
Do you know the talk of those turning eye-balls?

7
Here is the efflux of the soul,
The efflux of the soul comes from within through
    embower'd gates, ever provoking questions,
These yearnings why are they? these thoughts in the
    darkness why are they?
Why are there men and women that while they are nigh me
    the sunlight expands my blood?
Why when they leave me do my pennants of joy sink flat and
    lank?
Why are there trees I never walk under but large and
    melodious thoughts descend upon me?
100 (I think they hang there winter and summer on those trees
    and always drop fruit as I pass;)
What is it I interchange so suddenly with strangers?
What with some driver as I ride on the seat by his side?
What with some fisherman drawing his seine by the shore
    as I walk by and pause?
What gives me to be free to a woman's and man's
    good-will? what gives them to be free to mine?

8
The efflux of the soul is happiness, here is happiness,
I think it pervades the open air, waiting at all times,
Now it flows unto us, we are rightly charged.

Here rises the fluid and attaching character,
The fluid and attaching character is the freshness and
    sweetness of man and woman,

110 (The herbs of the morning sprout no fresher and sweeter
        every day out of the roots of themselves, than it sprouts
        fresh and sweet continually out of itself.)
Toward the fluid and attaching character exudes the sweat
    of the love of young and old,
From it falls distill'd the charm that mocks beauty and
    attainments,
Toward it heaves the shuddering longing ache of contact.

9

Allons! whoever you are come travel with me!
Traveling with me you find what never tires.

The earth never tires,
The earth is rude, silent, incomprehensible at first, Nature
    is rude and incomprehensible at first,
Be not discouraged, keep on, there are divine things well
    envelop'd,
I swear to you there are divine things more beautiful than
    words can tell.

120 Allons! we must not stop here,
However sweet these laid-up stores, however convenient
    this dwelling we cannot remain here,
However shelter'd this port and however calm these waters
    we must not anchor here,
However welcome the hospitality that surrounds us we are
    permitted to receive it but a little while.

10

Allons! the inducements shall be greater,
We will sail pathless and wild seas,
We will go where winds blow, waves dash, and the Yankee
    clipper speeds by under full sail.

Allons! with power, liberty, the earth, the elements,
Health, defiance, gayety, self-esteem, curiosity;
Allons! from all formules!
130 From your formules, O bat-eyed and materialistic priests.

The stale cadaver blocks up the passage – the burial waits no
    longer.

Allons! yet take warning!
He traveling with me needs the best blood, thews,
    endurance,
None may come to the trial till he or she bring courage and
    health,
Come not here if you have already spent the best of yourself,
Only those may come who come in sweet and determin'd
    bodies,
No diseas'd person, no rum-drinker or venereal taint is
    permitted here.

(I and mine do not convince by arguments, similes, rhymes,
We convince by our presence.)

11
140   Listen! I will be honest with you,
I do not offer the old smooth prizes, but offer rough new
    prizes,
These are the days that must happen to you:
You shall not heap up what is call'd riches,
You shall scatter with lavish hand all that you earn or
    achieve,
You but arrive at the city to which you were destin'd, you
    hardly settle yourself to satisfaction before you are call'd
    by an irresistible call to depart,
You shall be treated to the ironical smiles and mockings of
    those who remain behind you,
What beckonings of love you receive you shall only answer
    with passionate kisses of parting,
You shall not allow the hold of those who spread their
    reach'd hands toward you.

12
Allons! after the great Companions, and to belong to them!
150   They too are on the road – they are the swift and majestic
    men – they are the greatest women,
Enjoyers of calms of seas and storms of seas,

Sailors of many a ship, walkers of many a mile of land,
Habituès of many distant countries, habituès of far-distant
    dwellings,
Trusters of men and women, observers of cities, solitary
    toilers,
Pausers and contemplators of tufts, blossoms, shells of the
    shore,
Dancers at wedding-dances, kissers of brides, tender
    helpers of children, bearers of children,
Soldiers of revolts, standers by gaping graves, lowerers-down
    of coffins,
Journeyers over consecutive seasons, over the years, the
    curious years each emerging from that which preceded it,
Journeyers as with companions, namely their own diverse
    phases,
160 Forth-steppers from the latent unrealized baby-days,
Journeyers gayly with their own youth, journeyers with
    their bearded and well-grain'd manhood,
Journeyers with their womanhood, ample, unsurpass'd,
    content,
Journeyers with their own sublime old age of manhood or
    womanhood,
Old age, calm, expanded, broad with the haughty breadth
    of the universe,
Old age, flowing free with the delicious near-by freedom
    of death.

13
Allons! to that which is endless as it was beginningless,
To undergo much, tramps of days, rests of nights,
To merge all in the travel they tend to, and the days and
    nights they tend to,
Again to merge them in the start of superior journeys,
170 To see nothing anywhere but what you may reach it and
    pass it,
To conceive no time, however distant, but what you may
    reach it and pass it,

To look up or down no road but it stretches and waits for
    you, however long but it stretches and waits for you,
To see no being, not God's or any, but you also go thither,
To see no possession but you may possess it, enjoying all
    without labor or purchase, abstracting the feast yet not
    abstracting one particle of it,
To take the best of the farmer's farm and the rich man's
    elegant villa, and the chaste blessings of the well-married
    couple, and the fruits of orchards and flowers of gardens,
To take to your use out of the compact cities as you pass
    through,
To carry buildings and streets with you afterward wherever
    you go,
To gather the minds of men out of their brains as you
    encounter them, to gather the love out of their hearts,
To take your lovers on the road with you, for all that you
    leave them behind you,
180 To know the universe itself as a road, as many roads,
    as roads for traveling souls.

All parts away for the progress of souls,
All religion, all solid things, arts, governments – all that was
    or is apparent upon this globe or any globe, falls into
    niches and corners before the procession of souls along
    the grand roads of the universe.

Of the progress of the souls of men and women along the
    grand roads of the universe, all other progress is the
    needed emblem and sustenance.

Forever alive, forever forward,
Stately, solemn, sad, withdrawn, baffled, mad, turbulent,
    feeble, dissatisfied,
Desperate, proud, fond, sick, accepted by men, rejected by
    men,
They go! they go! I know that they go, but I know not
    where they go,
But I know that they go toward the best – toward something
    great.

Whoever you are, come forth! or man or woman come
    forth!
190 You must not stay sleeping and dallying there in the house,
    though you built it, or though it has been built for you.

Out of the dark confinement! out from behind the screen!
It is useless to protest, I know all and expose it.

Behold through you as bad as the rest,
Through the laughter, dancing, dining, supping, of people,
Inside of dresses and ornaments, inside of those wash'd and
    trimm'd faces,
Behold a secret silent loathing and despair.

No husband, no wife, no friend, trusting to hear the
    confession,
Another self, a duplicate of every one, skulking and hiding
    it goes,
Formless and wordless through the streets of the cities,
    polite and bland in the parlors,
200 In the cars of railroads, in steamboats, in the public
    assembly,
Home to the houses of men and women, at the table, in the
    bedroom, everywhere,
Smartly attired, countenance smiling, form upright, death
    under the breast-bones, hell under the skull-bones,
Under the broadcloth and gloves, under the ribbons and
    artificial flowers,
Keeping fair with the customs, speaking not a syllable of
    itself,
Speaking of any thing else but never of itself.

14
Allons! through struggles and wars!
The goal that was named cannot be countermanded.

Have the past struggles succeeded?
What has succeeded? yourself? your nation? Nature?
210 Now understand me well – it is provided in the essence of
things that from any fruition of success, no matter what,
shall come forth something to make a greater struggle
necessary.

My call is the call of battle, I nourish active rebellion,
He going with me must go well arm'd,
He going with me goes often with spare diet, poverty, angry
enemies, desertions.

15
Allons! the road is before us!
It is safe – I have tried it – my own feet have tried it well – be
not detain'd!

Let the paper remain on the desk unwritten, and the book
on the shelf unopen'd!
Let the tools remain in the workshop! let the money remain
unearn'd!
Let the school stand! mind not the cry of the teacher!
Let the preacher preach in his pulpit! let the lawyer plead
in the court, and the judge expound the law.

220 Camerado, I give you my hand!
I give you my love more precious than money,
I give you myself before preaching or law;
Will you give me yourself? will you come travel with me?
Shall we stick by each other as long as we live?

Crossing Brooklyn Ferry

1
Flood-tide below me! I see you face to face!
Clouds of the west – sun there half an hour high – I see you
also face to face.

Crowds of men and women attired in the usual costumes,
how curious you are to me!

On the ferry-boats the hundreds and hundreds that cross,
    returning home, are more curious to me than you
    suppose,
And you that shall cross from shore to shore years hence are
    more to me, and more in my meditations, than you might
    suppose.

2

The impalpable sustenance of me from all things at all
    hours of the day,
The simple, compact, well-join'd scheme, myself
    disintegrated, every one disintegrated yet part of the
    scheme,
The similitudes of the past and those of the future,
The glories strung like beads on my smallest sights and
    hearings, on the walk in the street and the passage over
    the river,
10 The current rushing so swiftly and swimming with me far
    away,
The others that are to follow me, the ties between me and
    them,
The certainty of others, the life, love, sight, hearing of
    others.

Others will enter the gates of the ferry and cross from shore
    to shore,
Others will watch the run of the flood-tide,
Others will see the shipping of Manhattan north and west,
    and the heights of Brooklyn to the south and east,
Others will see the islands large and small;
Fifty years hence, others will see them as they cross, the
    sun half an hour high,
A hundred years hence, or ever so many hundred years
    hence, others will see them,
Will enjoy the sunset, the pouring-in of the flood-tide, the
    falling-back to the sea of the ebb-tide.

3

20 It avails not, time nor place – distance avails not,
I am with you, you men and women of a generation, or
ever so many generations hence,
Just as you feel when you look on the river and sky, so I
felt,
Just as any of you is one of a living crowd, I was one of a
crowd,
Just as you are refresh'd by the gladness of the river and the
bright flow, I was refresh'd,
Just as you stand and lean on the rail, yet hurry with the
swift current, I stood yet was hurried,
Just as you look on the numberless masts of ships and the
thick-stemm'd pipes of steamboats, I look'd.

I too many and many a time cross'd the river of old,
Watched the Twelfth-month sea-gulls, saw them high in the
air floating with motionless wings, oscillating their bodies,
Saw how the glistening yellow lit up parts of their bodies
and left the rest in strong shadow,
30 Saw the slow-wheeling circles and the gradual edging
toward the south,
Saw the reflection of the summer sky in the water,
Had my eyes dazzled by the shimmering track of beams,
Look'd at the fine centrifugal spokes of light round the
shape of my head in the sunlit water,
Look'd on the haze on the hills southward and
south-westward,
Look'd on the vapor as it flew in fleeces tinged with violet,
Look'd toward the lower bay to notice the vessels arriving,
Saw their approach, saw aboard those that were near me,
Saw the white sails of schooners and sloops, saw the ships
at anchor,
The sailors at work in the rigging or out astride the spars,
40 The round masts, the swinging motion of the hulls, the
slender serpentine pennants,
The large and small steamers in motion, the pilots in their
pilot-houses,

The white wake left by the passage, the quick tremulous
  whirl of the wheels,
The flags of all nations, the falling of them at sunset,
The scallop-edged waves in the twilight, the ladled cups, the
  frolicsome crests and glistening,
The stretch afar growing dimmer and dimmer, the gray
  walls of the granite storehouses by the docks,
On the river the shadowy group, the big steam-tug closely
  flank'd on each side by the barges, the hay-boat, the
  belated lighter,
On the neighboring shore the fires from the foundry
  chimneys burning high and glaringly into the night,
Casting their flicker of black contrasted with wild red and
  yellow light over the tops of houses and down into the
  clefts of streets.

4
These and all else were to me the same as they are to you,
50   I loved well those cities, loved well the stately and rapid
  river,
The men and women I saw were all near to me,
Others the same – others who look back on me because I
  look'd forward to them,
(The time will come, though I stop here to-day and
  to-night.)

5
What is it then between us?
What is the count of the scores or hundreds of years
  between us?

Whatever it is, it avails not – distance avails not, and place
  avails not,
I too lived, Brooklyn of ample hills was mine,
I too walk'd the streets of Manhattan island, and bathed
  in the waters around it,
I too felt the curious abrupt questionings stir within me,
60   In the day among crowds of people sometimes they came
  upon me,

In my walks home late at night or as I lay in my bed they
    came upon me,
I too had been struck from the float forever held in solution,
I too had receiv'd identity by my body,
That I was I knew was of my body, and what I should be I
    knew I should be of my body.

6

It is not upon you alone the dark patches fall,
The dark threw its patches down upon me also,
The best I had done seem'd to me blank and suspicious,
My great thoughts as I supposed them, were they not in
    reality meagre?
Nor is it you alone who know what it is to be evil,
70   I am he who knew what it was to be evil,
I too knitted the old knot of contrariety,
Blabb'd, blush'd, resented, lied, stole, grudg'd,
Had guile, anger, lust, hot wishes I dared not speak,
Was wayward, vain, greedy, shallow, sly, cowardly,
    malignant,
The wolf, the snake, the hog, not wanting in me,
The cheating look, the frivolous word, the adulterous wish,
    not wanting,
Refusals, hates, postponements, meanness, laziness, none
    of these wanting,
Was one with the rest, the days and haps of the rest,
Was call'd by my nighest name by clear loud voices of
    young men as they saw me approaching or passing,
80   Felt their arms on my neck as I stood, or the negligent
    leaning of their flesh against me as I sat,
Saw many I loved in the street or ferry-boat or public
    assembly, yet never told them a word,
Lived the same life with the rest, the same old laughing,
    gnawing, sleeping,
Play'd the part that still looks back on the actor or actress,
The same old role, the role that is what we make it, as great
    as we like,
Or as small as we like, or both great and small.

7
Closer yet I approach you,
What thought you have of me now, I had as much of you –
    I laid in my stores in advance,
I consider'd long and seriously of you before you were born.

Who was to know what should come home to me?
90 Who knows but I am enjoying this?
Who knows, for all the distance, but I am as good as looking
    at you now, for all you cannot see me?

8
Ah, what can ever be more stately and admirable to me than
    mast-hemm'd Manhattan?
River and sunset and scallop-edg'd waves of flood-tide?
The sea-gulls oscillating their bodies, the hay-boat in the
    twilight, and the belated lighter?
What gods can exceed these that clasp me by the hand,
    and with voices I love call me promptly and loudly by
    my nighest name as I approach?
What is more subtle than this which ties me to the woman
    or man that looks in my face?
Which fuses me into you now, and pours my meaning into
    you?

We understand then do we not?
What I promis'd without mentioning it, have you not
    accepted?
100 What the study could not teach – what the preaching could
    not accomplish is accomplish'd, is it not?

9
Flow on, river! flow with the flood-tide, and ebb with the
    ebb-tide!
Frolic on, crested and scallop-edg'd waves!
Gorgeous clouds of the sunset! drench with your splendor
    me, or the men and women generations after me!
Cross from shore to shore, countless crowds of passengers!
Stand up, tall masts of Mannahatta! stand up, beautiful
    hills of Brooklyn!

Throb, baffled and curious brain! throw out questions and
    answers!
Suspend here and everywhere, eternal float of solution!
Gaze, loving and thirsty eyes, in the house or street or public
    assembly!
Sound out, voices of young men! loudly and musically call
    me by my nighest name!
110 Live, old life! play the part that looks back on the actor or
    actress!
Play the old role, the role that is great or small according as
    one makes it!
Consider, you who peruse me, whether I may not in
    unknown ways be looking upon you;
Be firm, rail over the river, to support those who lean idly,
    yet haste with the hasting current;
Fly on, sea-birds! fly sideways, or wheel in large circles high
    in the air;
Receive the summer sky, you water, and faithfully hold it
    till all downcast eyes have time to take it from you!
Diverge, fine spokes of light, from the shape of my head, or
    any one's head, in the sunlit water!
Come on, ships from the lower bay! pass up or down,
    white-sail'd schooners, sloops, lighters!
Flaunt away, flags of all nations! be duly lower'd at sunset!
Burn high your fires, foundry chimneys! cast black
    shadows at nightfall! cast red and yellow light over the
    tops of the houses!
120 Appearances, now or henceforth, indicate what you are,
You necessary film, continue to envelop the soul,
About my body for me, and your body for you, be hung out
    divinest aromas,
Thrive, cities – bring your freight, bring your shows, ample
    and sufficient rivers,
Expand, being than which none else is perhaps more
    spiritual,
Keep your places, objects than which none else is more
    lasting.

You have waited, you always wait, you dumb, beautiful
    ministers,
We receive you with free sense at last, and are insatiate
    henceforward,
Not you any more shall be able to foil us, or withhold
    yourselves from us,
We use you, and do not cast you aside – we plant you
    permanently within us,
130 We fathom you not – we love you – there is perfection in
    you also,
You furnish your parts toward eternity,
Great or small, you furnish your parts toward the soul.

Song of the Answerer

1

Now list to my morning's romanza, I tell the signs of the
    Answerer,
To the cities and farms I sing as they spread in the sunshine
    before me.

A young man comes to me bearing a message from his
    brother,
How shall the young man know the whether and when of his
    brother?
Tell him to send me the signs.

And I stand before the young man face to face, and take his
    right hand in my left hand and his left hand in my right
    hand,
And I answer for his brother and for men, and I answer for
    him that answers for all, and send these signs.

Him all wait for, him all yield up to, his word is decisive and
    final,
Him they accept, in him lave, in him perceive themselves as
    amid light,
10 Him they immerse and he immerses them.

Beautiful women, the haughtiest nations, laws, the
    landscape, people, animals,
The profound earth and its attributes and the unquiet
    ocean, (so tell I my morning's romanza,)
All enjoyments and properties and money, and whatever
    money will buy,
The best farms, others toiling and planting and he
    unavoidably reaps,
The noblest and costliest cities, others grading and building
    and he domiciles there,
Nothing for any one but what is for him, near and far are
    for him, the ships in the offing,
The perpetual shows and marches on land are for him if
    they are for anybody.

He puts things in their attitudes,
He puts to-day out of himself with plasticity and love,
20 He places his own times, reminiscences, parents, brothers
    and sisters, associations, employment, politics, so that the
    rest never shame them afterward, nor assume to command
    them.

He is the Answerer,
What can be answer'd he answers, and what cannot be
    answer'd he shows how it cannot be answer'd.

A man is a summons and challenge,
(It is vain to skulk – do you hear that mocking and laughter?
    do you hear the ironical echoes?)

Books, friendships, philosophers, priests, action, pleasure,
    pride, beat up and down seeking to give satisfaction,
He indicates the satisfaction, and indicates them that beat
    up and down also.

Whichever the sex, whatever the season or place, he may go
    freshly and gently and safely by day or by night,
He has the pass-key of hearts, to him the response of the
    prying of hands on the knobs.

His welcome is universal, the flow of beauty is not more
    welcome or universal than he is,
30 The person he favors by day or sleeps with at night is
    blessed.

Every existence has its idiom, every thing has an idiom and
    tongue,
He resolves all tongues into his own and bestows it upon
    men, and any man translates, and any man translates
    himself also,
One part does not counteract another part, he is the joiner,
    he sees how they join.

He says indifferently and alike *How are you friend?* to the
    President at his levee,
And he says *Good-day my brother*, to Cudge that hoes in the
    sugar-field,
And both understand him and know that his speech is right.

He walks with perfect ease in the capitol,
He walks among the Congress, and one Representative
    says to another, *Here is our equal appearing and new.*

Then the mechanics take him for a mechanic,
40 And the soldiers suppose him to be a soldier, and the sailors
    that he has follow'd the sea,
And the authors take him for an author, and the artists for
    an artist,
And the laborers perceive he could labor with them and
    love them,
No matter what the work is, that he is the one to follow it
    or has follow'd it,
No matter what the nation, that he might find his brothers
    and sisters there.

The English believe he comes of their English stock,
A Jew to the Jew he seems, a Russ to the Russ, usual and
    near, removed from none.

Whoever he looks at in the traveler's coffee-house claims
    him,

The Italian or Frenchman is sure, the German is sure, the
    Spaniard is sure, and the island Cuban is sure,
The engineer, the deck-hand on the great lakes, or on the
    Mississippi or St Lawrence or Sacramento, or Hudson or
    Paumanok sound, claims him.

50   The gentleman of perfect blood acknowledges his perfect
    blood,
The insulter, the prostitute, the angry person, the beggar,
    see themselves in the ways of him, he strangely transmutes
    them,
They are not vile any more, they hardly know themselves
    they are so grown.

2

The indications and tally of time,
Perfect sanity shows the master among philosophs,
Time, always without break, indicates itself in parts,
What always indicates the poet is the crowd of the pleasant
    company of singers, and their words,
The words of the singers are the hours or minutes of the
    light or dark, but the words of the maker of poems are the
    general light and dark,
The maker of poems settles justice, reality, immortality,
His insight and power encircle things and the human race,
60   He is the glory and extract thus far of things and of the
    human race.

The singers do not beget, only the Poet begets,
The singers are welcom'd, understood, appear often enough,
    but rare has the day been, likewise the spot, of the birth
    of the maker of poems, the Answerer,
(Not every century nor every five centuries has contain'd
    such a day, for all its names.)

The singers of successive hours of centuries may have
    ostensible names, but the name of each of them is one of
    the singers,

The name of each is, eye-singer, ear-singer, head-singer,
    sweet-singer, night-singer, parlor-singer, love-singer,
    weird-singer, or something else.

All this time and at all times wait the words of true poems,
The words of true poems do not merely please,
The true poets are not followers of beauty but the august
    masters of beauty;
The greatness of sons is the exuding of the greatness of
    mothers and fathers,
70 The words of true poems are the tuft and final applause of
    science.

Divine instinct, breadth of vision, the law of reason, health,
    rudeness of body, withdrawnness,
Gayety, sun-tan, air-sweetness, such are some of the words
    of poems.

The sailor and traveler underlie the maker of poems, the
    Answerer,
The builder, geometer, chemist, anatomist, phrenologist,
    artist, all these underlie the maker of poems, the
    Answerer.

The words of the true poems give you more than poems,
They give you to form for yourself poems, religions, politics,
    war, peace, behaviour, histories, essays, daily life, and
    every thing else,
They balance ranks, colors, races, creeds, and the sexes,
They do not seek beauty, they are sought,
Forever touching them or close upon them follows beauty,
    longing, fain, love-sick.

80 They prepare for death, yet are they not the finish, but
    rather the outset,
They bring none to his or her terminus or to be content
    and full,
Whom they take they take into space to behold the birth of
    stars, to learn one of the meanings,

To launch off with absolute faith, to sweep through the
 ceaseless rings and never be quiet again.

Our Old Feuillage

Always our old feuillage!
Always Florida's green peninsula – always the priceless
 delta of Louisiana – always the cotton-fields of Alabama
 and Texas,
Always California's golden hills and hollows, and the silver
 mountains of New Mexico – always soft-breath'd Cuba,
Always the vast slope drain'd by the Southern sea,
 inseparable with the slopes drain'd by the Eastern and
 Western seas,
The area the eighty-third year of these States, the three
 and a half millions of square miles,
The eighteen thousand miles of sea-coast and bay-coast on
 the main, the thirty thousand miles of river navigation,
The seven millions of distinct families and the same number
 of dwellings – always these, and more, branching forth
 into numberless branches,
Always the free range and diversity – always the continent
 of Democracy;
Always the prairies, pastures, forests, vast cities, travelers,
 Kanada, the snows;
10 Always these compact lands tied at the hips with the belt
 stringing the huge oval lakes;
Always the West with strong native persons, the increasing
 density there, the habitans, friendly, threatening,
 ironical, scorning invaders;
All sights, South, North, East – all deeds, promiscuously
 done at all times,
All characters, movements, growths, a few noticed, myriads
 unnoticed,
Through Mannahatta's streets I walking, these things
 gathering,

On interior rivers by night in the glare of pine knots,
steamboats wooding up,

Sunlight by day on the valley of the Susquehanna, and on
the valleys of the Potomac and Rappahannock, and the
valleys of the Roanoke and Delaware,

In their northerly wilds beasts of prey haunting the
Adirondacks the hills, or lapping the Saginaw waters to
drink,

In a lonesome inlet a sheldrake lost from the flock, sitting
on the water rocking silently,

In farmers' barns oxen in the stable, their harvest labor
done, they rest standing, they are too tired,

20   Afar on arctic ice the she-walrus lying drowsily while her
cubs play around,

The hawk sailing where men have not yet sail'd, the
farthest polar sea, ripply, crystalline, open, beyond the
floes,

White drift spooning ahead where the ship in the tempest
dashes,

On solid land what is done in cities as the bells strike
midnight together,

In primitive woods the sounds there also sounding, the howl
of the wolf, the scream of the panther, and the hoarse
bellow of the elk,

In winter beneath the hard blue ice of Moosehead lake, in
summer visible through the clear waters, the great trout
swimming,

In lower latitudes in warmer air in the Carolinas the large
black buzzard floating slowly high beyond the tree tops,

Below, the red cedar festoon'd with tylandria, the pines and
cypresses growing out of the white sand that spreads far
and flat,

Rude boats descending the big Pedee, climbing plants,
parasites with color'd flowers and berries enveloping
huge trees,

The waving drapery on the live-oak trailing long and low,
noiselessly waved by the wind,

30   The camp of Georgia wagoners just after dark, the

supper-fires and the cooking and eating by whites and
negroes,

Thirty or forty great wagons, the mules, cattle, horses,
feeding from troughs,

The shadows, gleams, up under the leaves of the old
sycamore-trees, the flames with the black smoke from the
pitch-pine curling and rising;

Southern fishermen fishing, the sounds and inlets of North
Carolina's coast, the shad-fishery and the herring-fishery,
the large sweep-seines, the windlasses on shore work'd by
horses, the clearing, curing and packing-houses;

Deep in the forest in piney woods turpentine dropping from
the incisions in the trees, there are the turpentine works,

There are the negroes at work in good health, the ground in
all directions is cover'd with pine straw;

In Tennessee and Kentucky slaves busy in the coalings, at
the forge, by the furnace-blaze, or at the corn-shucking,

In Virginia, the planter's son returning after a long
absence, joyfully welcom'd and kiss'd by the aged mulatto
nurse,

On rivers boatmen safely moor'd at nightfall in their boats
under shelter of high banks,

Some of the younger men dance to the sound of the banjo or
fiddle, others sit on the gunwale smoking and talking;

40   Late in the afternoon the mocking-bird, the American
mimic, singing in the Great Dismal Swamp,

There are the greenish waters, the resinous odor, the
plenteous moss, the cypress-tree, and the juniper-tree;

Northward, young men of Mannahatta, the target company
from an excursion returning home at evening, the
musket-muzzles all bear bunches of flowers presented by
women;

Children at play, or on his father's lap a young boy fallen
asleep, (how his lips move! how he smiles in his sleep!)

The scout riding on horseback over the plains west of the
Mississippi, he ascends a knoll and sweeps his eyes
around;

California life, the miner, bearded, dress'd in his rude

costume, the stanch California friendship, the sweet air,
the graves one in passing meets solitary just aside the
horse-path;
Down in Texas the cotton-field, the negro-cabins, drivers
driving mules or oxen before rude carts, cotton bales piled
on banks and wharves;
Encircling all, vast-darting up and wide, the American Soul,
with equal hemispheres, one Love, one Dilation or Pride;
In arriere the peace-talk with the Iroquois the aborigines,
the calumet, the pipe of good-will, arbitration, and
indorsement,
The sachem blowing the smoke first toward the sun and then
toward the earth,
50 The drama of the scalp-dance enacted with painted faces
and guttural exclamations,
The setting out of the war-party, the long and stealthy
march,
The single file, the swinging hatchets, the surprise and
slaughter of enemies;
All the acts, scenes, ways, persons, attitudes of these States,
reminiscences, institutions,
All these States compact, every square mile of these States
without excepting a particle;
Me pleas'd, rambling in lanes and country fields,
Paumanok's fields,
Observing the spiral flight of two little yellow butterflies
shuffling between each other, ascending high in the air,
The darting swallow, the destroyer of insects, the fall
traveler southward but returning northward early in the
spring,
The country boy at the close of the day driving the herd of
cows and shouting to them as they loiter to browse by
the roadside,
The city wharf, Boston, Philadelphia, Baltimore, Charleston,
New Orleans, San Francisco,
60 The departing ships when the sailors heave at the capstan;
Evening – me in my room – the setting sun,
The setting summer sun shining in my widow, showing the

swarm of flies, suspended, balancing in the air in the
centre of the room, darting athwart, up and down, casting
swift shadows in specks on the opposite wall where the
shine is;
The athletic America matron speaking in public to crowds
of listeners,
Males, females, immigrants, combinations, the copiousness,
the individuality of the States, each for itself – the
money-makers,
Factories, machinery, the mechanical forces, the windlass,
lever, pulley, all certainties,
The certainty of space, increase, freedom, futurity,
In space the sporades, the scatter'd islands, the stars – on the
firm earth, the lands, my lands,
O lands! all so dear to me – what you are, (whatever it is,) I
putting it at random in these songs, become a part of that,
whatever it is,
Southward there, I screaming, with wings slow flapping,
with the myriads of gulls wintering along the coasts of
Florida,
70   Otherways there atwixt the banks of the Arkansaw, the Rio
Grande, the Nueces, the Brazos, the Tombigbee, the Red
River, the Saskatchawan or the Osage, I with the spring
waters laughing and skipping and running,
Northward, on the sands, on some shallow bay of Paumanok,
I with parties of snowy herons, wading in the wet to seek
worms and aquatic plants,
Retreating, triumphantly twittering, the king-bird, from
piercing the crow with its bill, for amusement – and I
triumphantly twittering,
The migrating flock of wild geese alighting in autumn to
refresh themselves, the body of the flock feed, the
sentinels outside move around with erect heads watching,
and are from time to time reliev'd by other sentinels – and
I feeding and taking turns with the rest,
In Kanadian forests the moose, large as an ox, corner'd by
hunters, rising desperately on his hind-feet, and plunging
with his fore-feet, the hoofs as sharp as knives – and I,

plunging at the hunters, corner'd and desperate,
In the Mannahatta, streets, piers, shipping, store-houses,
  and the countless workmen working in the shops,
And I too of the Mannahatta, singing thereof – and no less in
  myself than the whole of the Mannahatta in itself,
Singing the song of These, my ever-united lands – my body
  no more inevitably united, part to part, and made out of a
  thousand diverse contributions one identity, any more
  than my lands are inevitably united and made ONE
  IDENTITY;
Nativities, climates, the grass of the great pastoral Plains,
Cities, labors, death, animals, products, war, good and evil –
  these me,
80 These affording, in all their particulars, the old feuillage to
  me and to America, how can I do less than pass the clew of
  the union of them, to afford the like to you?
Whoever you are! how can I but offer you divine leaves, that
  you also be eligible as I am?
How can I but as here chanting, invite you for yourself to
  collect bouquets of the incomparable feuillage of these
  States?

A Song of Joys

O to make the most jubilant song!
Full of music – full of manhood, womanhood, infancy!
Full of common employments – full of grain and trees.

O for the voices of animals – O for the swiftness and
  balance of fishes!
O for the dropping of raindrops in a song!
O for the sunshine and motion of waves in a song!

O the joy of my spirit – it is uncaged – it darts like
  lightning!
It is not enough to have this globe or a certain time,
I will have thousands of globes and all time.

10 O the engineer's joys! to go with a locomotive!
To hear the hiss of steam, the merry shriek, the
    steam-whistle, the laughing locomotive!
To push with resistless way and speed off in the distance.

O the gleesome saunter over fields and hillsides!
The leaves and flowers of the commonest weeds, the moist
    fresh stillness of the woods,
The exquisite smell of the earth at daybreak, and all
    through the forenoon.

O the horseman's and horsewoman's joys!
The saddle, the gallop, the pressure upon the seat, the cool
    gurgling by the ears and hair.

O the fireman's joys!
I hear the alarm at dead of night,
20 I hear bells, shouts! I pass the crowd, I run!
The sight of the flames maddens me with pleasure.

O the joy of the strong-brawn'd fighter, towering in the
    arena in perfect condition, conscious of power, thirsting
    to meet his opponent.

O the joy of that vast elemental sympathy which only the
    human soul is capable of generating and emitting in
    steady and limitless floods.

O the mother's joys!
The watching, the endurance, the precious love, the
    anguish, the patiently yielded life.

O the joy of increase, growth, recuperation,
The joy of soothing and pacifying, the joy of concord and
    harmony.

O to go back to the place where I was born,
To hear the birds sing once more,
30 To ramble about the house and barn and over the fields
    once more,
And through the orchard and along the old lanes once more.

O to have been brought up on bays, lagoons, creeks, or
    along the coast,
To continue and be employ'd there all my life,
The briny and damp smell, the shore, the salt weeds
    exposed at low water,
The work of fishermen, the work of the eel-fisher and
    clam-fisher;
I come with my clam-rake and spade, I come with my
    eel-spear,
Is the tide out? I join the group of clam-diggers on the flats,
I laugh and work with them, I joke at my work like a
    mettlesome young man;
In winter I take my eel-basket and eel-spear and travel out
    on foot on the ice – I have a small axe to cut holes in
    the ice,
40 Behold me well-clothed going gayly or returning in the
    afternoon, my brood of tough boys accompanying me,
My brood of grown and part-grown boys, who love to be
    with no one else so well as they love to be with me,
By day to work with me, and by night to sleep with me.

Another time in warm weather out in a boat, to lift the
    lobster-pots where they are sunk with heavy stones, (I
    know the buoys,)
O the sweetness of the Fifth-month morning upon the water
    as I row just before sunrise toward the buoys,
I pull the wicker pots up slantingly, the dark green lobsters
    are desperate with their claws as I take them out, I insert
    wooden pegs in the joints of their pincers,
I go to all the places one after another, and then row back
    to the shore,
There in a huge kettle of boiling water the lobsters shall be
    boil'd till their color becomes scarlet.

Another time mackerel-taking,
Voracious, mad for the hook, near the surface, they seem to
    fill the water for miles;
50 Another time fishing for rock-fish in Chesapeake bay, I one
    of the brown-faced crew;

Another time trailing for blue-fish off Paumanok, I stand
    with braced body,
My left foot is on the gunwale, my right arm throws far out
    the coils of slender rope,
In sight around me the quick veering and darting of fifty
    skiffs, my companions.

O boating on the rivers,
The voyage down the St Lawrence, the superb scenery, the
    steamers,
The ships sailing, the Thousand Islands, the occasional
    timber-raft and the raftsmen with long-reaching
    sweep-oars,
The little huts on the rafts, and the stream of smoke when
    they cook supper at evening.

(O something pernicious and dread!
Something far away from a puny and pious life!
60   Something unproved! something in a trance!
Something escaped from the anchorage and driving free.)

O to work in mines, or forging iron,
Foundry casting, the foundry itself, the rude high roof, the
    ample and shadow'd space;
The furnace, the hot liquid pour'd out and running.

O to resume the joys of the soldier!
To feel the presence of a brave commanding officer – to feel
    his sympathy!
To behold his calmness – to be warm'd in the rays of his
    smile!
To go to battle – to hear the bugles play and the drums beat!
To hear the crash of artillery – to see the glittering of the
    bayonets and musket-barrels in the sun!
70   To see men fall and die and not complain!
To taste the savage taste of blood – to be so devilish!
To gloat so over the wounds and deaths of the enemy.

O the whaleman's joys! O I cruise my old cruise again!
I feel the ship's motion under me, I feel the Atlantic breezes
fanning me,
I hear the cry again sent down from the mast-head, *There –
she blows!*
Again I spring up the rigging to look with the rest – we
descend, wild with excitement,
I leap in the lower'd boat, we row toward our prey where he
lies,
We approach stealthy and silent, I see the mountainous mass,
lethargic, basking,
I see the harpooneer standing up, I see the weapon dart from
his vigorous arm;
80 O swift again far out in the ocean the wounded whale,
settling, running to windward, tows me,
Again I see him rise to breathe, we row close again,
I see a lance driven through his side, press'd deep, turn'd in
the wound,
Again we back off, I see him settle again, the life is leaving
him fast,
As he rises he spouts blood, I see him swim in circles
narrower and narrower, swiftly cutting the water – I see
him die,
He gives one convulsive leap in the centre of the circle, and
then falls flat and still in the bloody foam.

O the old manhood of me, my noblest joy of all!
My children and grand-children, my white hair and beard,
My largeness, calmness, majesty, out of the long stretch of
my life.

O ripen'd joy of womanhood! O happiness at last!
90 I am more than eighty years of age, I am the most venerable
mother,
How clear is my mind – how all people draw nigh to me!
What attractions are these beyond any before? what bloom
more than the bloom of youth?
What beauty is this that descends upon me and rises out
of me?

O the orator's joys!
To inflate the chest, to roll the thunder of the voice out from
  the ribs and throat,
To make the people rage, weep, hate, desire, with yourself,
To lead America – to quell America with a great tongue.

O the joy of my soul leaning pois'd on itself, receiving
  identity through materials and loving them, observing
  characters and absorbing them,
My soul vibrated back to me from them, from sight,
  hearing, touch, reason, articulation, comparison, memory,
  and the like,
100   The real life of my senses and flesh transcending my senses
  and flesh,
My body done with materials, my sight done with my
  material eyes,
Proved to me this day beyond cavil that it is not my material
  eyes which finally see,
Nor my material body which finally loves, walks, laughs,
  shouts, embraces, procreates.

O the farmer's joys!
Ohioan's, Illinoisian's, Wisconsinese', Kanadian's, Iowan's,
  Kansian's, Missourian's, Oregonese' joys!
To rise at peep of day and pass forth nimbly to work,
To plough land in the fall for winter-sown crops,
To plough land in the spring for maize,
To train orchards, to graft the trees, to gather apples in
  the fall.

110   O to bathe in the swimming-bath, or in a good place along
  shore,
To splash the water! to walk ankle-deep, or race naked
  along the shore.

O to realize space!
The plenteousness of all, that there are no bounds,
To emerge and be of the sky, of the sun and moon and
  flying clouds, as one with them.

O the joy of a manly self-hood!

To be servile to none, to defer to none, not to any tyrant
    known or unknown,
To walk with erect carriage, a step springy and elastic,
To look with calm gaze or with a flashing eye,
To speak with a full and sonorous voice out of a broad chest,
120   To confront with your personality all the other
    personalities of the earth.

Know'st thou the excellent joys of youth?
Joys of the dear companions and of the merry word and
    laughing face?
Joy of the glad light-beaming day, joy of the
    wide-breath'd games?
Joy of sweet music, joy of the lighted ball-room and the
    dancers?
Joy of the plenteous dinner, strong carouse and drinking?

Yet O my soul supreme!
Know'st thou the joys of pensive thought?
Joys of the free and lonesome heart, the tender, gloomy
    heart?
Joys of the solitary walk, the spirit bow'd yet proud, the
    suffering and the struggle?
130   The agonistic throes, the ecstasies, joys of the solemn
    musings day or night?
Joys of the thought of Death, the great spheres Time and
    Space?
Prophetic joys of better, loftier love's ideals, the divine wife,
    the sweet, eternal, perfect comrade?
Joys all thine own undying one, joys worthy thee O soul.

O while I live to be the ruler of life, not a slave,
To meet life as a powerful conqueror,
No fumes, no ennui, no more complaints or scornful
    criticisms,
To these proud laws of the air, the water and the ground,
    proving my interior soul impregnable,
And nothing exterior shall ever take command of me.

For not life's joys alone I sing, repeating – the joy of death!
140 The beautiful touch of Death, soothing and benumbing a
       few moments, for reasons,
Myself discharging my excrementitious body to be burn'd,
       or render'd to powder, or buried,
My real body doubtless left to me for other spheres,
My voided body nothing more to me, returning to the
       purifications, further offices, eternal uses of the earth.

O to attract by more than attraction!
How it is I know not – yet behold! the something which
       obeys none of the rest,
It is offensive, never defensive – yet how magnetic it draws.

O to struggle against great odds, to meet enemies
       undaunted!
To be entirely alone with them, to find how much one can
       stand!
To look strife, torture, prison, popular odium, face to face!
150 To mount the scaffold, to advance to the muzzles of guns
       with perfect nonchalance!
To be indeed a God!

O to sail to sea in a ship!
To leave this steady unendurable land,
To leave the tiresome sameness of the streets, the sidewalks
       and the houses,
To leave you O you solid motionless land, and entering a
       ship,
To sail and sail and sail!

O to have life henceforth a poem of new joys!
To dance, clap hands, exult, shout, skip, leap, roll on,
       float on!
To be a sailor of the world bound for all ports,
160 A ship itself, (see indeed these sails I spread to the sun and
       air,)
A swift and swelling ship full of rich words, full of joys.

Song of the Broad-Axe

1

Weapon shapely, naked, wan,
Head from the mother's bowels drawn,
Wooded flesh and metal bone, limb only one and lip only
one,
Gray-blue leaf by red-heat grown, helve produced from a
little seed sown,
Resting the grass amid and upon,
To be lean'd and to lean on.

Strong shapes and attributes of strong shapes, masculine
trades, sights and sounds,
Long varied train of an emblem, dabs of music,
Fingers of the organist skipping staccato over the keys of
the great organ.

2

10 Welcome are all earth's lands, each for its kind,
Welcome are lands of pine and oak,
Welcome are lands of the lemon and fig,
Welcome are lands of gold,
Welcome are lands of wheat and maize, welcome those of the
grape,
Welcome are lands of sugar and rice,
Welcome the cotton-lands, welcome those of the white
potato and sweet potato,
Welcome are mountains, flats, sands, forests, prairies,
Welcome the rich borders of rivers, table-lands, openings,
Welcome the measureless grazing-lands, welcome the
teeming soil of orchards, flax, honey, hemp;
20 Welcome just as much the other more hard-faced lands,
Lands rich as lands of gold or wheat and fruit lands,
Lands of mines, lands of the manly and rugged ores,
Lands of coal, copper, lead, tin, zinc,
Lands of iron – lands of the make of the axe.

3

The log at the wood-pile, the axe supported by it,
The sylvan hut, the vine over the doorway, the space
    clear'd for a garden,
The irregular tapping of rain down on the leaves after the
    storm is lull'd,
The wailing and moaning at intervals, the thought of the
    sea,
The thought of ships struck in the storm and put on their
    beam ends, and the cutting away of masts,
30   The sentiment of the huge timbers of old-fashion'd houses
    and barns,
The remember'd print or narrative, the voyage at a venture
    of men, families, goods,
The disembarkation, the founding of a new city,
The voyage of those who sought a New England and found
    it, the outset anywhere,
The settlements of the Arkansas, Colorado, Ottawa,
    Willamette,
The slow progress, the scant fare, the axe, rifle,
    saddle-bags;
The beauty of all adventurous and daring persons,
The beauty of wood-boys and wood-men with their clear
    untrimm'd faces,
The beauty of independence, departure, actions that rely on
    themselves,
The American contempt for statutes and ceremonies, the
    boundless impatience of restraint,
40   The loose drift of character, the inkling through random
    types, the solidification;
The butcher in the slaughter-house, the hands aboard
    schooners and sloops, the raftsman, the pioneer,
Lumbermen in their winter camp, daybreak in the woods,
    stripes of snow on the limbs of trees, the occasional
    snapping,
The glad clear sound of one's own voice, the merry song, the
    natural life of the woods, the strong day's work,
The blazing fire at night, the sweet taste of supper, the talk,

the bed of hemlock-boughs and the bear-skin;
The house-builder at work in cities or anywhere,
The preparatory jointing, squaring, sawing, mortising,
The hoist-up of beams, the push of them in their places,
    laying them regular,
Setting the studs by their tenons in the mortises according as
    they were prepared,
The blows of mallets and hammers, the attitudes of the men,
    their curv'd limbs,
50 Bending, standing, astride the beams, driving in pins,
    holding on by posts and braces,
The hook'd arm over the plate, the other arm wielding the
    axe,
The floor-men forcing the planks close to be nail'd,
Their postures bringing their weapons downward on the
    bearers,
The echoes resounding through the vacant building;
The huge storehouse carried up in the city well under way,
The six framing-men, two in the middle and two at each
    end, carefully bearing on their shoulders a heavy stick
    for a cross-beam,
The crowded line of masons with trowels in their right
    hands rapidly laying the long side-wall, two hundred feet
    from front to rear,
The flexible rise and fall of backs, the continual click of the
    trowels striking the bricks,
The bricks one after another each laid so workmanlike in its
    place, and set with a knock of the trowel-handle,
60 The piles of materials, the mortar on the mortar-boards, and
    the steady replenishing by the hod-men;
Spar-makers in the spar-yard, the swarming row of
    well-grown apprentices,
The swing of their axes on the square-hew'd log shaping it
    toward the shape of a mast,
The brisk short crackle of the steel driven slantingly into the
    pine,
The butter-color'd chips flying off in great flakes and slivers,

The limber motion of brawny young arms and hips in easy
costumes,
The constructor of wharves, bridges, piers, bulk-heads,
floats, stays against the sea;
The city fireman, the fire that suddenly bursts forth in the
close-pack'd square,
The arriving engines, the hoarse shouts, the nimble stepping
and daring,
The strong command through the fire-trumpets, the falling
in line, the rise and fall of the arms forcing the water,
70   The slender, spasmic, blue-white jets, the bringing to bear
of the hooks and ladders and their execution,
The crash and cut away of connecting wood-work, or
through floors if the fire smoulders under them,
The crowd with their lit faces watching, the glare and dense
shadows;
The forger at his forge-furnace and the user of iron after
him,
The maker of the axe large and small, and the welder and
temperer,
The chooser breathing his breath on the cold steel and
trying the edge with his thumb,
The one who clean-shapes the handle and sets it firmly in
the socket;
The shadowy processions of the portraits of the past users
also,
The primal patient mechanics, the architects and engineers,
The far-off Assyrian edifice and Mizra edifice,
80   The Roman lictors preceding the consuls,
The antique European warrior with his axe in combat,
The uplifted arm, the clatter of blows on the helmeted head,
The death-howl, the limpsy tumbling body, the rush of
friend and foe thither,
The siege of revolted lieges determin'd for liberty,
The summons to surrender, the battering at castle gates, the
truce and parley,
The sack of an old city in its time,

The bursting in of mercenaries and bigots tumultuously and
    disorderly,
Roar, flames, blood, drunkenness, madness,
Goods freely rifled from houses and temples, screams of
    women in the gripe of brigands,
90 Craft and thievery of camp-followers, men running, old
    persons despairing,
The hell of war, the cruelties of creeds,
The list of all executive deeds and words just or unjust,
The power of personality just or unjust.

4

Muscle and pluck forever!
What invigorates life invigorates death,
And the dead advance as much as the living advance,
And the future is no more uncertain than the present,
For the roughness of the earth and of man encloses as much
    as the delicatesse of the earth and of man,
And nothing endures but personal qualities.

100 What do you think endures?
Do you think a great city endures?
Or a teeming manufacturing state? or a prepared
    constitution? or the best built steamships?
Or hotels of granite and iron? or any chef-d'oeuvres of
    engineering, forts, armaments?

Away! these are not to be cherish'd for themselves,
They fill their hour, the dancers dance, the musicians play
    for them,
The show passes, all does well enough of course,
All does very well till one flash of defiance.

A great city is that which has the greatest men and women,
If it be a few ragged huts it is still the greatest city in the
    whole world.

5

110 The place where a great city stands is not the place of
    stretch'd wharves, docks, manufactures, deposits of
    produce merely,

Nor the place of ceaseless salutes of new-comers or the
anchor-lifters of the departing,
Nor the place of the tallest and costliest buildings or shops
selling goods from the rest of the earth,
Nor the place of the best libraries and schools, nor the
place where money is plentiest,
Nor the place of the most numerous population.

Where the city stands with the brawniest breed of orators
and bards,
Where the city stands that is belov'd by these, and loves
them in return and understands them,
Where no monuments exist to heroes but in the common
words and deeds,
Where thrift is in its place, and prejudice is in its place,
Where the men and women think lightly of the laws,
120   Where the slave ceases and the master of slaves ceases,
Where the populace rise at once against the never-ending
audacity of elected persons,
Where fierce men and women pour forth as the sea to the
whistle of death pours its sweeping and unript waves,
Where outside authority enters always after the precedence
of inside authority,
Where the citizen is always the head and ideal, and
President, Mayor, Governor and what not, are agents for
pay,
Where children are taught to be laws to themselves, and to
depend on themselves,
Where equanimity is illustrated in affairs,
Where speculations on the soul are encouraged,
Where women walk in public processions in the streets
the same as the men,
Where they enter the public assembly and take places the
same as the men;
130   Where the city of the faithfulest friends stands,
Where the city of the cleanliness of the sexes stands,
Where the city of the healthiest fathers stands,

Where the city of the best-bodied mothers stands,
There the great city stands.

6

How beggarly appear arguments before a defiant deed!
How the floridness of the materials of cities shrivels before
    a man's or woman's look!

All waits or goes by default till a strong being appears;
A strong being is the proof of the race and of the ability of
    the universe,
When he or she appears materials are overaw'd,
140 The dispute on the soul stops,
The old customs and phrases are confronted, turn'd back, or
    laid away.

What is your money-making now? what can it do now?
What is your respectability now?
What are your theology, tuition, society, traditions,
    statute-books, now?
Where are your jibes of being now?
Where are your cavils about the soul now?

7

A sterile landscape covers the ore, there is as good as the best
    for all the forbidding appearance,
There is the mine, there are the miners,
The forge-furnace is there, the melt is accomplish'd, the
    hammersmen are at hand with their tongs and hammers,
150 What always served and always serves is at hand.

Than this nothing has better served, it has served all,
Served the fluent-tongued and subtle-sensed Greek, and
    long ere the Greek,
Served in building the buildings that last longer than any,
Served the Hebrew, the Persian, the most ancient
    Hindustanee,
Served the mound-raiser on the Mississippi, served those
    whose relics remain in Central America,

Served Albic temples in woods or on plains, with unhewn
    pillars and the druids,
Served the artificial clefts, vast, high, silent, on the
    snow-cover'd hills of Scandinavia,
Served those who time out of mind made on the granite
    walls rough sketches of the sun, moon, stars, ships, ocean
    waves,
Served the paths of the irruptions of the Goths, served the
    pastoral tribes and nomads,
160   Served the long distant Kelt, served the hardy pirates of the
    Baltic,
Served before any of those the venerable and harmless men
    of Ethiopia,
Served the making of helms for the galleys of pleasure and
    the making of those for war,
Served all great works on land and all great works on the
    sea,
For the mediaeval ages and before the mediaeval ages,
Served not the living only then as now, but served the dead.

8
I see the European headsman,
He stands mask'd, clothed in red, with huge legs and strong
    naked arms,
And leans on a ponderous axe.

(Whom have you slaughter'd lately European headsman?
170   Whose is that blood upon you so wet and sticky?)

I see the clear sunsets of the martyrs,
I see from the scaffolds the descending ghosts,
Ghosts of dead lords, uncrown'd ladies, impeach'd
    ministers, rejected kings,
Rivals, traitors, prisoners, disgraced chieftains and the rest.

I see those who in any land have died for the good cause,
The seed is spare, nevertheless the crop shall never run out,
(Mind you O foreign kings, O priests, the crop shall never
    run out.)

I see the blood wash'd entirely away from the axe,
Both blade and helve are clean,
180   They spirt no more the blood of European nobles, they clasp
     no more the necks of queens.

I see the headsman withdraw and become useless,
I see the scaffold untrodden and mouldy, I see no longer any
     axe upon it,
I see the mighty and friendly emblem of the power of my
     own race, the newest, largest race.

9
(America! I do not vaunt my love for you,
I have what I have.)

The axe leaps!
The solid forest gives fluid utterances,
They tumble forth, they rise and form,
Hut, tent, landing, survey,
190   Flail, plough, pick, crowbar, spade,
Shingle, rail, prop, wainscot, jamb, lath, panel, gable,
Citadel, ceiling, saloon, academy, organ, exhibition-house,
     library,
Cornice, trellis, pilaster, balcony, window, turret, porch,
Hoe, rake, pitchfork, pencil, wagon, staff, saw, jack-plane,
     mallet, wedge, rounce,
Chair, tub, hoop, table, wicket, vane, sash, floor,
Work-box, chest, string'd instrument, boat, frame, and what
     not,
Capitols of States, and capitol of the nation of States,
Long stately rows in avenues, hospitals for orphans or for
     the poor or sick,
Manhattan steamboats and clippers taking the measure of
     all seas.

200   The shapes arise!
Shapes of the using of axes anyhow, and the users and all
     that neighbors them,
Cutters down of wood and haulers of it to the Penobscot or
     Kennebec,

Dwellers in cabins among the Californian mountains or by
the little lakes, or on the Columbia,
Dwellers south on the banks of the Gila or Rio Grande,
friendly gatherings, the characters and fun,
Dwellers along the St Lawrence, or north in Kanada, or
down by the Yellowstone, dwellers on coasts and off
coasts,
Seal-fishers, whalers, arctic seamen breaking passages
through the ice.

The shapes arise!
Shapes of factories, arsenals, foundries, markets,
Shapes of the two-threaded tracks of railroads,
210   Shapes of the sleepers of bridges, vast frameworks, girders,
arches,
Shapes of the fleets of barges, tows, lake and canal craft,
river craft,
Ship-yards and dry-docks along the Eastern and Western
seas, and in many a bay and by-place,
The live-oak kelsons, the pine planks, the spars, the
hackmatack-roots for knees,
The ships themselves on their ways, the tiers of scaffolds,
the workmen busy outside and inside,
The tools lying around, the great auger and little auger, the
adze, bolt, line, square, gouge, and bead-plane.

10
The shapes arise!
The shape measur'd, saw'd, jack'd, join'd, stain'd,
The coffin-shape for the dead to lie within in his shroud,
The shape got out in posts, in the bedstead posts, in the
posts of the bride's bed,
220   The shape of the little trough, the shape of the rockers
beneath, the shape of the babe's cradle,
The shape of the floor-planks, the floor-planks for dancers'
feet,
The shape of the planks of the family home, the home of the
friendly parents and children,
The shape of the roof of the home of the happy young man

and woman, the roof over the well-married young man
and woman,
The roof over the supper joyously cook'd by the chaste
wife, and joyously eaten by the chaste husband, content
after his day's work.

The shapes arise!
The shape of the prisoner's place in the court-room, and of
him or her seated in the place,
The shape of the liquor-bar lean'd against by the young
rum-drinker and the old rum-drinker,
The shape of the shamed and angry stairs trod by sneaking
footsteps,
The shape of the sly settee, and the adulterous
unwholesome couple,
230   The shape of the gambling-board with its devilish winnings
and losings,
The shape of the step-ladder for the convicted and
sentenced murderer, the murderer with haggard face and
pinion'd arms,
The sheriff at hand with his deputies, the silent and
white-lipp'd crowd, the dangling of the rope.

The shapes arise!
Shapes of doors giving many exits and entrances,
The door passing the dissever'd friend flush'd and in haste,
The door that admits good news and bad news,
The door whence the son left home confident and puff'd up,
The door he enter'd again from a long and scandalous
absence, diseas'd, broken down, without innocence,
without means.

11
Her shape arises,
240   She less guarded than ever, yet more guarded than ever,
The gross and soil'd she moves among do not make her
gross and soil'd,
She knows the thoughts as she passes, nothing is conceal'd
from her,

She is none the less considerate or friendly therefor,
She is the best belov'd, it is without exception, she has no
    reason to fear and she does not fear,
Oaths, quarrels, hiccupp'd songs, smutty expressions, are
    idle to her as she passes,
She is silent, she is possess'd of herself, they do not offend
    her,
She receives them as the laws of Nature receive them, she is
    strong,
She too is a law of Nature – there is no law stronger than
    she is.

12
The main shapes arise!
250 Shapes of Democracy total, result of centuries,
Shapes ever projecting other shapes,
Shapes of turbulent manly cities,
Shapes of the friends and home-givers of the whole earth,
Shapes bracing the earth and braced with the whole earth.

Song of the Exposition

1
(Ah little recks the laborer,
How near his work is holding him to God,
The loving Laborer through space and time.)

After all not to create only, or found only,
But to bring perhaps from afar what is already founded,
To give it our own identity, average, limitless, free,
To fill the gross the torpid bulk with vital religious fire,
Not to repel or destroy so much as accept, fuse,
    rehabilitate,
To obey as well as command, to follow more than to lead,
10 These also are the lessons of our New World;
While how little the New after all, how much the Old,
    Old World!

Long and long has the grass been growing,
Long and long has the rain been falling,
Long has the globe been rolling round.

2
Come Muse migrate from Greece and Ionia,
Cross out please those immensely overpaid accounts,
That matter of Troy and Achilles' wrath, and Aeneas',
    Odysseus' wanderings,
Placard 'Removed' and 'To let' on the rocks of your snowy
    Parnassus,
Repeat at Jerusalem, place the notice high on Jaffa's gate
    and on Mount Moriah,
20 The same on the walls of your German, French and Spanish
    castles, and Italian collections,
For know a better, fresher, busier sphere, a wide, untried
    domain awaits, demands you.

3
Responsive to our summons,
Or rather to her long-nurs'd inclination,
Join'd with an irresistible, natural gravitation,
She comes! I hear the rustling of her gown,
I scent the odor of her breath's delicious fragrance,
I mark her step divine, her curious eyes a-turning, rolling,
Upon this very scene.

The dame of dames! can I believe then,
30 Those ancient temples, sculptures classic, could none of
    them retain her?
Nor shades of Virgil and Dante, nor myriad memories,
    poems, old associations, magnetize and hold on to her?
But that she's left them all – and here?

Yes, if you will allow me to say so,
I, my friends, if you do not, can plainly see her,
The same undying soul of earth's, activity's, beauty's,
    heroism's expression,
Out from her evolutions hither come, ended the strata of her
    former themes,

Hidden and cover'd by to-day's, foundation of to-day's,
Ended, deceas'd through time, her voice by Castaly's
    fountain,
Silent the broken-lipp'd Sphynx in Egypt, silent all those
    century-baffling tombs,
40 Ended for aye the epics of Asia's, Europe's helmeted
    warriors, ended the primitive call of the muses,
Calliope's call forever closed, Clio, Melpomene, Thalia
    dead,
Ended the stately rhythmus of Una and Oriana, ended the
    quest of the holy Graal,
Jerusalem a handful of ashes blown by the wind, extinct,
The Crusaders' streams of shadowy midnight troops sped
    with the sunrise,
Amadis, Tancred, utterly gone, Charlemagne, Roland,
    Oliver gone,
Palmerin, ogre, departed, vanish'd the turrets that Usk
    from its waters reflected,
Arthur vanish'd with all his knights, Merlin and Lancelot
    and Galahad, all gone, dissolv'd utterly like an exhalation;
Pass'd! pass'd! for us, forever pass'd, that once so mighty
    world, now void, inanimate, phantom world,
Embroider'd, dazzling, foreign world, with all its gorgeous
    legends, myths,
50 Its kings and castles proud, its priests and warlike lords and
    courtly dames,
Pass'd to its charnel vault, coffin'd with crown and armor
    on,
Blazon'd with Shakspere's purple page,
And dirged by Tennyson's sweet sad rhyme.

I say I see, my friends, if you do not, the illustrious emigré,
    (having it is true in her day, although the same, changed,
    journey'd considerable,)
Making directly for this rendezvous, vigorously clearing a
    path for herself, striding through the confusion,
By thud of machinery and shrill steam-whistle undismay'd,

Bluff'd not a bit by drain-pipe, gasometers, artificial
   fertilizers,
Smiling and pleas'd with palpable intent to stay,
She's here, install'd amid the kitchen ware!

4

60 But hold – don't I forget my manners?
To introduce the stranger, (what else indeed do I live to
   chant for?) to thee Columbia;
In liberty's name welcome immortal! clasp hands,
And ever henceforth sisters dear be both.

Fear not O Muse! truly new ways and days receive,
   surround you,
I candidly confess a queer, queer race, of novel fashion,
And yet the same old human race, the same within, without,
Faces and hearts the same, feelings the same, yearnings
  the same,
The same old love, beauty and use the same.

5

We do not blame thee elder World, nor really separate
   ourselves from thee,
70 (Would the son separate himself from the father?)
Looking back on thee, seeing thee to thy duties,
   grandeurs, through past ages bending, building,
We build to ours to-day.

Mightier than Egypt's tombs,
Fairer than Grecia's, Roma's temples,
Prouder than Milan's statued, spired cathedral,
More picturesque than Rhenish castle-keeps,
We plan even now to raise, beyond them all,
Thy great cathedral sacred industry, no tomb,
A keep for life for practical invention.

80 As in a waking vision,
E'en while I chant I see it rise, I scan and prophesy outside
   and in,
Its manifold ensemble.

Around a palace, loftier, fairer, ampler than any yet,
Earth's modern wonder, history's seven outstripping,
High rising tier on tier with glass and iron façades,
Gladdening the sun and sky, enhued in cheerfulest hues,
Bronze, lilac, robin's-egg, marine and crimson,
Over whose golden roof shall flaunt, beneath thy banner
    Freedom,
The banners of the States and flags of every land,
90 A brood of lofty, fair, but lesser palaces shall cluster.

Somewhere within their walls shall all that forwards perfect
    human life be started,
Tried, taught, advanced, visibly exhibited.

Not only all the world of works, trade, products,
But all the workmen of the world here to be represented.
Here shall you trace in flowing operation,
In every state of practical, busy movement, the rills of
    civilization,
Materials here under your eye shall change their shape as if
    by magic,
The cotton shall be pick'd almost in the very field,
Shall be dried, clean'd, ginn'd, baled, spun into thread and
    cloth before you,
100 You shall see hands at work at all the old processes and all
    the new ones,
You shall see the various grains and how flour is made and
    then bread baked by the bakers,
You shall see the crude ores of California and Nevada
    passing on and on till they become bullion,
You shall watch how the printer sets type and learn what
    a composing-stick is,
You shall mark in amazement the Hoe press whirling its
    cylinders, shedding the printed leaves steady and fast,
The photograph, model, watch, pin, nail, shall be created
    before you.

In large calm halls, a stately museum shall teach you the
    infinite lessons of minerals,
In another, woods, plants, vegetation shall be illustrated – in
    another animals, animal life and development.

One stately house shall be the music house,
Others for other arts – learning, the sciences, shall all be
    here,
110 None shall be slighted, none but shall here be honor'd,
    help'd, exampled.

6

(This, this and these, America, shall be *your* pyramids and
    obelisks,
Your Alexandrian Pharos, gardens of Babylon,
Your temple at Olympia.)

The male and female many laboring not,
Shall ever here confront the laboring many,
With precious benefits to both, glory to all,
To thee America, and thee eternal Muse.

And here shall ye inhabit powerful Matrons!
In your vast state vaster than all the old,
120 Echoed through long, long centuries to come,
To sound of different, prouder songs, with stronger themes,
Practical, peaceful life, the people's life, the People
    themselves,
Lifted, illumin'd, bathed in peace – elate, secure in peace.

7

Away with themes of war! away with war itself!
Hence from my shuddering sight to never more return that
    show of blacken'd, mutilated corpses!
That hell unpent and raid of blood, fit for wild tigers or for
    lop-tongued wolves, not reasoning men,
And in its stead speed industry's campaigns,
With thy undaunted armies, engineering,
Thy pennants labor, loosen'd to the breeze,
130 Thy bugles sounding loud and clear.

Away with old romance!
Away with novels, plots and plays of foreign courts,
Away with love-verses sugar'd in rhyme, the intrigues,
    amours of idlers,
Fitted for only banquets of the night where dancers to late
    music slide,
The unhealthy pleasures, extravagant dissipations of the
    few,
With perfumes, heat and wine, beneath the dazzling
    chandeliers.

To you ye reverent sane sisters,
I raise a voice for far superber themes for poets and for art,
To exalt the present and the real,
140 To teach the average man the glory of his daily walk and
    trade,
To sing in songs how exercise and chemical life are never
    to be baffled,
To manual work for each and all, to plough, hoe, dig,
To plant and tend the tree, the berry, vegetables, flowers,
For every man to see to it that he really do something, for
    every woman too;
To use the hammer and the saw, (rip, or cross-cut,)
To cultivate a turn for carpentering, plastering, painting,
To work as tailor, tailoress, nurse, hostler, porter,
To invent a little, something ingenious, to aid the washing,
    cooking, cleaning,
And hold it no disgrace to take a hand at them themselves.

150 I say, I bring thee Muse to-day and here,
All occupations, duties broad and close,
Toil, healthy toil and sweat, endless, without cessation,
The old, old practical burdens, interests, joys,
The family, parentage, childhood, husband and wife,
The house-comforts, the house itself and all its belongings,
Food and its preservation, chemistry applied to it,
Whatever forms the average, strong, complete,
    sweet-blooded man or woman, the perfect longeve
    personality,

And helps its present life to health and happiness, and
    shapes its soul,
For the eternal real life to come.

160 With latest connections, works, the inter-transportation of
    the world,
Steam-power, the great express lines, gas, petroleum,
These triumphs of our time, the Atlantic's delicate cable,
The Pacific railroad, the Suez canal, the Mont Cenis and
    Gothard and Hoosac tunnels, the Brooklyn bridge,
This earth all spann'd with iron rails, with lines of
    steamships threading every sea,
Our own rondure, the current globe I bring.

8

And thou America,
Thy offspring towering e'er so high, yet higher Thee above
    all towering,
With Victory on thy left, and at thy right hand Law;
Thou Union holding all, fusing, absorbing, tolerating all,
170 Thee, ever thee, I sing.

Thou, also thou, a World,
With all thy wide geographies, manifold, different, distant,
Rounded by thee in one – one common orbic language,
One common indivisible destiny for All.

And by the spells which ye vouchsafe to those your ministers
    in earnest,
I here personify and call my themes, to make them pass
    before ye.

Behold, America! (and thou, ineffable guest and sister!)
For thee come trooping up thy waters and thy lands;
Behold! thy fields and farms, thy far-off woods and
    mountains,
180 As in procession coming.

Behold, the sea itself,
And on its limitless, heaving breast, the ships;

See, where their white sails, bellying in the wind, speckle
    the green and blue,
See, the steamers coming and going, steaming in or out of
    port,
See, dusky and undulating, the long pennants of smoke.

Behold, in Oregon, far in the north and west,
Or in Maine, far in the north and east, thy cheerful
    axemen,
Wielding all day their axes.

Behold, on the lakes, thy pilots at their wheels, thy
    oarsmen,
190   How the ash writhes under those muscular arms!

There by the furnace, and there by the anvil,
Behold thy sturdy blacksmiths swinging their sledges,
Overhand so steady, overhand they turn and fall with
    joyous clank,
Like a tumult of laughter.

Mark the spirit of invention everywhere, thy rapid patents,
Thy continual workshops, foundries, risen or rising,
See, from their chimneys how the tall flame-fires stream.

Mark, thy interminable farms, North, South,
Thy wealthy daughter-states, Eastern and Western,
200   The varied products of Ohio, Pennsylvania, Missouri,
    Georgia, Texas, and the rest,
Thy limitless crops, grass, wheat, sugar, oil, corn, rice,
    hemp, hops,
Thy barns all fill'd, the endless freight-train and the
    bulging storehouse,
The grapes that ripen on thy vines, the apples in thy
    orchards,
Thy incalculable lumber, beef, pork, potatoes, thy coal, thy
    gold and silver,
The inexhaustible iron in thy mines.

All thine O sacred Union!
Ships, farms, shops, barns, factories, mines,
City and State, North, South, item and aggregate,
We dedicate, dread Mother, all to thee!

210 Protectress absolute, thou! bulwark of all!
For well we know that while thou givest each and all,
      (generous as God,)
Without thee neither all nor each, nor land, home,
Nor ship, nor mine, nor any here this day secure,
Nor aught, nor any day secure.

9
And thou, the Emblem waving over all!
Delicate beauty, a word to thee, (it may be salutary,)
Remember thou hast not always been as here to-day so
      comfortably ensovereign'd,
In other scenes than these have I observ'd thee flag,
Not quite so trim and whole and freshly blooming in folds
      of stainless silk,
220 But I have seen thee bunting, to tatters torn upon thy
      splinter'd staff,
Or clutch'd to some young color-bearer's breast with
      desperate hands,
Savagely struggled for, for life or death, fought over long,
'Mid cannons' thunder-crash and many a curse and groan
      and yell, and rifle-volleys cracking sharp,
And moving masses as wild demons surging, and lives as
      nothing risk'd,
For thy mere remnant grimed with dirt and smoke and
      sopp'd in blood,
For sake of that, my beauty, and that thou might'st dally as
      now secure up there,
Many a good man have I seen go under.

Now here and these and hence in peace, all thine O Flag!
And here and hence for thee, O universal Muse! and thou
      for them!

230   And here and hence O Union, all the work and workmen
         thine!
       None separate from thee – henceforth One only, we and
         thou,
       (For the blood of the children, what is it, only the blood
         maternal?
       And lives and works, what are they all at last, except the
         roads to faith and death?)

       While we rehearse our measureless wealth, it is for thee,
         dear Mother,
       We own it all and several to-day indissoluble in thee;
       Think not our chant, our show, merely for products gross
         or lucre – it is for thee, the soul in thee, electric, spiritual!
       Our farms, inventions, crops, we own in thee! cities and
         States in thee!
       Our freedom all in thee! our very lives in thee!

Song of the Redwood-Tree

1

A California song,
A prophecy and indirection, a thought impalpable to
  breathe as air,
A chorus of dryads, fading, departing, or hamadryads
  departing,
A murmuring, fateful, giant voice, out of the earth and sky,
Voice of a mighty dying tree in the redwood forest dense.

Farewell my brethren,
Farewell O earth and sky, farewell ye neighboring waters,
My time has ended, my term has come.

       Along the northern coast,
10   Just back from the rock-bound shore and the caves,
       In the saline air from the sea in the Mendocino country,
       With the surge for base and accompaniment low and
         hoarse,

With crackling blows of axes sounding musically driven by
    strong arms,
Riven deep by the sharp tongues of the axes, there in the
    redwood forest dense,
I heard the mighty tree its death-chant chanting.

The choppers heard not, the camp shanties echoed not,
The quick-ear'd teamsters and chain and jack-screw men
    heard not,
As the wood-spirits came from their haunts of a thousand
    years to join the refrain,
But in my soul I plainly heard.

20   Murmuring out of its myriad leaves,
Down from its lofty top rising two hundred feet high,
Out of its stalwart trunk and limbs, out of its foot-thick bark,
That chant of the seasons and time, chant not of the past
    only but the future.

You untold life of me,
And all you venerable and innocent joys,
Perennial hardy life of me with joys 'mid rain and many a
    summer sun,
And the white snows and night and the wild winds;
O the great patient rugged joys, my soul's strong joys
    unreck'd by man,
(For know I bear the soul befitting me, I too have
    consciousness, identity,
30   *And all the rocks and mountains have, and all the earth,)*
Joys of the life befitting me and brothers mine,
Our time, our term has come.

Nor yield we mournfully majestic brothers,
We who have grandly fill'd our time;
With Nature's calm content, with tacit huge delight,
We welcome what we wrought for through the past,
And leave the field for them.
For them predicted long,
For a superber race, they too to grandly fill their time,

40 *For them we abdicate, in them ourselves ye forest kings!*
In them these skies and airs, these mountain peaks, Shasta,
Nevadas,
These huge precipitous cliffs, this amplitude, these valleys, far
Yosemite,
To be in them absorb'd, assimilated.

Then to a loftier strain,
Still prouder, more ecstatic rose the chant,
As if the heirs, the deities of the West,
Joining with master-tongue bore part.

Not wan from Asia's fetiches,
Nor red from Europe's old dynastic slaughter-house,
50 *(Area of murder-plots of thrones, with scent left yet of wars and*
scaffolds everywhere,)
But come from Nature's long and harmless throes, peacefully
builded thence,
These virgin lands, lands of the Western shore,
To the new culminating man, to you, the empire new,
You promis'd long, we pledge, we dedicate.

You occult deep volitions,
You average spiritual manhood, purpose of all, pois'd on
yourself, giving not taking law,
You womanhood divine, mistress and source of all, whence life
and love and aught that comes from life and love,
You unseen moral essence of all the vast materials of America,
(age upon age working in death the same as life,)
You that, sometimes known, oftener unknown, really shape and
mould the New World, adjusting it to Time and Space,
60 *You hidden national will lying in your abysms, conceal'd but*
ever alert,
You past and present purposes tenaciously pursued, may-be
unconsious of yourselves,
Unswerv'd by all the passing errors, perturbations of the
surface ;
You vital, universal, deathless germs, beneath all creeds, arts,
statutes, literatures,

*Here build your homes for good, establish here, these areas
  entire, lands of the Western shore,*
We pledge, we dedicate to you.

For man of you, your characteristic race,
*Here may he hardy, sweet, gigantic grow, here tower
  proportionate to Nature,*
*Here climb the vast pure spaces unconfined, uncheck'd by wall
  or roof,*
Here laugh with storm or sun, here joy, here patiently inure,
70   *Here heed himself, unfold himself, (not others' formulas heed,)
  here fill his time,*
To duly fall, to aid, unreck'd at last,
To disappear, to serve.

Thus on the northern coast,
In the echo of teamsters' calls and the clinking chains,
  and the music of choppers' axes,
The falling trunk and limbs, the crash, the muffled shriek,
  the groan,
Such words combined from the redwood-tree, as of voices
  ecstatic, ancient and rustling,
The century-lasting, unseen dryads, singing, withdrawing,
All their recesses of forests and mountains leaving,
From the Cascade range to the Wahsatch, or Idaho far, or
  Utah,
80   To the deities of the modern henceforth yielding,
The chorus and indications, the vistas of coming humanity,
  the settlements, features all,
In the Mendocino woods I caught.

2

The flashing and golden pageant of California,
The sudden and gorgeous drama, the sunny and ample
  lands,
The long and varied stretch from Puget sound to Colorado
  south,
Lands bathed in sweeter, rarer, healthier air, valleys and
  mountain cliffs,

The fields of Nature long prepared and fallow, the silent,
    cyclic chemistry,
The slow and steady ages plodding, the unoccupied surface
    ripening, the rich ores forming beneath;
At last the New arriving, assuming, taking possession,
90 A swarming and busy race settling and organizing
        everywhere,
Ships coming in from the whole round world, and going
    out to the whole world,
To India and China and Australia and the thousand island
    paradises of the Pacific,
Populous cities, the latest inventions, the steamers on the
    rivers, the railroads, with many a thrifty farm, with
    machinery,
And wool and wheat and the grape, and diggings of yellow
    gold.

3
But more in you than these, lands of the Western shore,
(These but the means, the implements, the
    standing-ground,)
I see in you, certain to come, the promise of thousands of
    years, till now deferr'd,
Promis'd to be fulfill'd, our common kind, the race.

The new society at last, proportionate to Nature,
100 In man of you, more than your mountain peaks or stalwart
        trees imperial,
In woman more, far more, than all your gold or vines, or
    even vital air.

Fresh come, to a new world indeed, yet long prepared,
I see the genius of the modern, child of the real and ideal,
Clearing the ground for broad humanity, the true America,
    heir of the past so grand,
To build a grander future.

240

A Song for Occupations

1
A song for occupations!
In the labor of engines and trades and the labor of fields I
    find the developments,
And find the eternal meanings.

Workmen and Workwomen!
Were all educations practical and ornamental well display'd
    out of me, what would it amount to?
Were I as the head teacher, charitable proprietor, wise
    statesman, what would it amount to?
Were I to you as the boss employing and paying you, would
    that satisfy you?

The learn'd, virtuous, benevolent, and the usual terms,
A man like me and never the usual terms.

10 Neither a servant nor a master I,
I take no sooner a large price than a small price, I will
    have my own whoever enjoys me,
I will be even with you and you shall be even with me.

If you stand at work in a shop I stand as nigh as the nighest
    in the same shop,
If you bestow gifts on your brother or dearest friend·I
    demand as good as your brother or dearest friend,
If your lover, husband, wife, is welcome by day or night, I
    must be personally as welcome,
If you become degraded, criminal, ill, then I become so for
    your sake,
If you remember your foolish and outlaw'd deeds, do you
    think I cannot remember my own foolish and outlaw'd
    deeds?
If you carouse at the table I carouse at the opposite side of
    the table,
If you meet some stranger in the streets and love him or her,
    why I often meet strangers in the street and love them.

20 Why what have you thought of yourself?
Is it you then that thought yourself less?
Is it you that thought the President greater than you?
Or the rich better off than you? or the educated wiser than
  you?

(Because you are greasy or pimpled, or were once drunk, or a
  thief,
Or that you are diseas'd, or rheumatic, or a prostitute,
Or from frivolity or impotence, or that you are no scholar
  and never saw your name in print,
Do you give in that you are any less immortal?)

2
Souls of men and women! it is not you I call unseen,
  unheard, untouchable and untouching,
It is not you I go argue pro and con about, and to settle
  whether you are alive or no,
30 I own publicly who you are, if nobody else owns.

Grown, half-grown and babe, of this country and every
  country, in-doors and out-doors, one just as much as the
  other, I see,
And all else behind or through them.

The wife, and she is not one jot less than the husband,
The daughter, and she is just as good as the son,
The mother, and she is every bit as much as the father.

Offspring of ignorant and poor, boys apprenticed to trades,
Young fellows working on farms and old fellows working on
  farms,
Sailor-men, merchant-men, coasters, immigrants,
All these I see, but nigher and farther the same I see,
40 None shall escape me and none shall wish to escape me.

I bring what you much need yet always have,
Not money, amours, dress, eating, erudition, but as good,
I send no agent or medium, offer no representative of
  value, but offer the value itself.

There is something that comes to one now and perpetually,
It is not what is printed, preach'd, discussed, it eludes
    discussion and print,
It is not to be put in a book, it is not in this book,
It is for you whoever you are, it is no farther from you than
    your hearing and sight are from you,
It is hinted by nearest, commonest, readiest, it is ever
    provoked by them.

You may read in many languages, yet read nothing about it,
50 You may read the President's message and read nothing
    about it there,
Nothing in the reports from the State department or
    Treasury department, or in the daily papers or weekly
    papers,
Or in the census or revenue returns, prices current, or any
    accounts of stock.

3
The sun and stars that float in the open air,
The apple-shaped earth and we upon it, surely the drift of
    them is something grand,
I do not know what it is except that it is grand, and that it is
    happiness,
And that the enclosing purport of us here is not a speculation
    or bon-mot or reconnoissance,
And that it is not something which by luck may turn out
    well for us, and without luck must be a failure for us,
And not something which may yet be retracted in a certain
    contingency.

The light and shade, the curious sense of body and identity,
    the greed that with perfect complaisance devours all
    things,
60 The endless pride and outstretching of man, unspeakable
    joys and sorrows,
The wonder every one sees in every one else he sees, and the
    wonders that fill each minute of time forever,
What have you reckon'd them for, camerado?

Have you reckon'd them for your trade or farm-work?
or for the profits of your store?
Or to achieve yourself a position? or to fill a gentleman's
leisure, or a lady's leisure?

Have you reckon'd that the landscape took substance and
form that it might be painted in a picture?
Or men and women that they might be written of, and songs
sung?
Or the attraction of gravity, and the great laws and
harmonious combinations and the fluids of the air,
as subjects for the savans?
Or the brown land and the blue sea for maps and charts?
Or the stars to be put in constellations and named fancy
names?
70 Or that the growth of seeds is for agricultural tables, or
agriculture itself?

Old institutions, these arts, libraries, legends, collections,
and the practice handed along in manufactures, will we
rate them so high?
Will we rate our cash and business high? I have no objection,
I rate them as high as the highest – then a child born of a
woman and man I rate beyond all rate.

We thought our Union grand, and our Constitution grand,
I do not say they are not grand and good, for they are,
I am this day just as much in love with them as you,
Then I am in love with You, and with all my fellows upon
the earth.

We consider bibles and religions divine – I do not say they
are not divine,
I say they have all grown out of you, and may grow out
of you still,
80 It is not they who give the life, it is you who give the life,
Leaves are not more shed from the trees, or trees from the
earth, than they are shed out of you.

4

The sum of all known reverence I add up in you whoever
you are,

The President is there in the White House for you, it is not
you who are here for him,

The Secretaries act in their bureaus for you, not you here
for them,

The Congress convenes every Twelfth-month for you,

Laws, courts, the forming of States, the charters of cities,
the going and coming of commerce and mails, are all
for you.

List close my scholars dear,

Doctrines, politics, and civilization exurge from you,

Sculpture and monuments and any thing inscribed anywhere
are tallied in you,

90 The gist of histories and statistics as far back as the records
reach is in you this hour, and myths and tales the same,

If you were not breathing and walking here, where would
they all be?

The most renown'd poems would be ashes, orations and
plays would be vacuums.

All architecture is what you do to it when you look upon it,

(Did you think it was in the white or gray stone? or the lines
of the arches and cornices?)

All music is what awakes from you when you are reminded
by the instruments,

It is not the violins and the cornets, it is not the oboe nor
the beating drums, nor the score of the baritone singer
singing his sweet romanza, nor that of the men's chorus,
nor that of the women's chorus,

It is nearer and farther than they.

5

Will the whole come back then?

Can each see signs of the best by a look in the looking-glass?
is there nothing greater or more?

100 Does all sit there with you, with the mystic unseen soul?

Strange and hard that paradox true I give,
Objects gross and the unseen soul are one.

House-building, measuring, sawing the boards,
Blacksmithing, glass-blowing, nail-making, coopering,
   tin-roofing, shingle-dressing,
Ship-joining, dock-building, fish-curing, flagging of
   sidewalks by flaggers,
The pump, the pile-driver, the great derrick, the coal-kiln
   and brick-kiln,
Coal-mines and all that is down there, the lamps in the
   darkness, echoes, songs, what meditations, what vast
   native thoughts looking through smutch'd faces,
Iron-works, forge-fires in the mountains or by river-banks,
   men around feeling the melt with huge crowbars, lumps
   of ore, the due combining of ore, limestone, coal,
The blast-furnace and the pudding-furnace, the loup-lump
   at the bottom of the melt at last, the rolling-mill, the
   stumpy bars of pig-iron, the strong clean-shaped T-rail
   for rail-roads,
110   Oil-works, silk-works, white-lead-works, the sugar-house,
   steam-saws, the great mills and factories,
Stone-cutting, shapely trimmings for façades or window or
   door-lintels, the mallet, the tooth-chisel, the jib to
   protect the thumb,
The calking-iron, the kettle of boiling vault-cement, and
   the fire under the kettle,
The cotton-bale, the stevedore's hook, the saw and buck of
   the sawyer, the mould of the moulder, the
   working-knife of the butcher, the ice-saw, and all the
   work with ice,
The work and tools of the rigger, grappler, sail-maker,
   block-maker,
Goods of gutta-percha, papier-maché, colors, brushes,
   brush-making, glazier's implements,
The veneer and glue-pot, the confectioner's ornaments, the
   decanter and glasses, the shears and flat-iron,
The awl and knee-strap, the pint measure and quart

measure, the counter and stool, the writing-pen of quill
   or metal, the making of all sorts of edged tools,
The brewery, brewing, the malt, the vats, every thing that
   is done by brewers, wine-makers, vinegar-makers,
Leather-dressing, coach-making, boiler-making,
   rope-twisting, distilling, sign-painting, lime-burning,
   cotton-picking, electroplating, electrotyping,
   stereotyping,
120   Stave-machines, planing-machines, reaping-machines,
   ploughing-machines, thrashing-machines, steam wagons,
The cart of the carman, the omnibus, the ponderous dray,
Pyrotechny, letting off color'd fireworks at night, fancy
   figures and jets;
Beef on the butcher's stall, the slaughter-house of the
   butcher, the butcher in his killing-clothes,
The pens of live pork, the killing-hammer, the hog-hook, the
   scalder's tub, gutting, the cutter's cleaver, the packer's
   maul, and the plenteous winterwork of pork-packing,
Flour-works, grinding of wheat, rye, maize, rice, the
   barrels and the half and quarter barrels, the loaded barges,
   the high piles on wharves and levees,
The men and the work of the men on ferries, railroads,
   coasters, fish-boats, canals;
The hourly routine of your own or any man's life, the shop,
   yard, store, or factory,
These shows all near you by day and night – workman!
   whoever you are, your daily life!
In that and them the heft of the heaviest – in that and them
   far more than you estimated, (and far less also,)
130   In them realities for you and me, in them poems for you
   and me,
In them, not yourself – you and your soul enclose all things,
   regardless of estimation,
In them the development good – in them all themes, hints,
   possibilities.

I do not affirm that what you see beyond is futile, I do not
    advise you to stop,
I do not say leadings you thought great are not great,
But I say that none lead to greater than these lead to.

6

Will you seek afar off? you surely come back at last,
In things best known to you finding the best, or as good as
    the best,
In folks nearest to you finding the sweetest, strongest,
    lovingest,
Happiness, knowledge, not in another place but this place,
    not for another hour but this hour,
140 Man in the first you see or touch, always in friend, brother,
    nighest neighbor – woman in mother, sister, wife,
The popular tastes and employments taking precedence in
    poems or anywhere,
You workwomen and workmen of these States having your
    own divine and strong life,
And all else giving place to men and women like you.

When the psalm sings instead of the singer,
When the script preaches instead of the preacher,
When the pulpit descends and goes instead of the carver
    that carved the supporting desk,
When I can touch the body of books by night or by day,
    and when they touch my body back again,
When a university course convinces like a slumbering
    woman and child convince,
When the minted gold in the vault smiles like the
    night-watchman's daughter,
150 When warrantee deeds loafe in chairs opposite and are my
    friendly companions,
I intend to reach them my hand, and make as much of them
    as I do of men and women like you.

A Song of the Rolling Earth

I

A song of the rolling earth, and of words according,
Were you thinking that those were the words, those
    upright lines? those curves, angles, dots?
No, those are not the words, the substantial words are in the
    ground and sea,
They are in the air, they are in you.

Were you thinking that those were the words, those
    delicious sounds out of your friends' mouths?
No, the real words are more delicious than they.

Human bodies are words, myriads of words,
(In the best poems re-appears the body, man's or woman's,
    well-shaped, natural, gay,
Every part able, active, receptive, without shame or the
    need of shame.)

10 Air, soil, water, fire – those are words,
I myself am a word with them – my qualities interpenetrate
    with theirs – my name is nothing to them,
Though it were told in the three thousand languages, what
    would air, soil, water, fire, know of my name?

A healthy presence, a friendly or commanding gesture,
    are words, sayings, meanings,
The charms that go with the mere looks of some men and
    women, are sayings and meanings also.

The workmanship of souls is by those inaudible words of
    the earth,
The masters know the earth's words and use them more than
    audible words.

Amelioration is one of the earth's words,
The earth neither lags nor hastens,
It has all attributes, growths, effects, latent in itself from
    the jump,

20   It is not half beautiful only, defects and excrescences show
       just as much as perfections show.

The earth does not withhold, it is generous enough,
The truths of the earth continually wait, they are not so
     conceal'd either,
They are calm, subtle, untransmissible by print,
They are imbued through all things conveying themselves
     willingly,
Conveying a sentiment and invitation, I utter and utter,
I speak not, yet if you hear me not of what avail am I to you?
To bear, to better, lacking these of what avail am I?

(Accouche! accouchez!
Will you rot your own fruit in yourself there?
30   Will you squat and stifle there?)

The earth does not argue,
Is not pathetic, has no arrangements,
Does not scream, haste, persuade, threaten, promise,
Makes no discriminations, has no conceivable failures,
Closes nothing, refuses nothing, shuts none out,
Of all the powers, objects, states, it notifies, shuts none out.

The earth does not exhibit itself nor refuse to exhibit itself,
     possesses still underneath,
Underneath the ostensible sounds, the august chorus of
     heroes, the wail of slaves,
Persuasions of lovers, curses, gasps of the dying, laughter of
     young people, accents of bargainers,
40   Underneath these possessing words that never fail.

To her children the words of the eloquent dumb great
     mother never fail,
The true words do not fail, for motion does not fail and
     reflection does not fail,
Also the day and night do not fail, and the voyage we
     pursue does not fail.

Of the interminable sisters,
Of the ceaseless cotillons of sisters,
Of the centripetal and centrifugal sisters, the elder and
  younger sisters,
The beautiful sister we know dances on with the rest.

With her ample back towards every beholder,
With the fascinations of youth and the equal fascinations
  of age,
50 Sits she whom I too love like the rest, sits undisturb'd,
Holding up in her hand what has the character of a mirror,
  while her eyes glance back from it,
Glance as she sits, inviting none, denying none,
Holding a mirror day and night tirelessly before her own
  face.

Seen at hand or seen at a distance,
Duly the twenty-four appear in public every day,
Duly approach and pass with their companions or a
  companion,
Looking from no countenances of their own, but from the
  countenances of those who are with them,
From the countenances of children or women or the manly
  countenance,
From the open countenances of animals or from inanimate
  things,
60 From the landscape or waters or from the exquisite
  apparition of the sky,
From our countenances, mine and yours, faithfully
  returning them,
Every day in public appearing without fail, but never twice
  with the same companions.

Embracing man, embracing all, proceed the three hundred
  and sixty-five resistlessly round the sun;
Embracing all, soothing, supporting, follow close three
  hundred and sixty-five offsets of the first, sure and
  necessary as they.

Tumbling on steadily, nothing dreading,
Sunshine, storm, cold, heat, forever withstanding, passing,
    carrying,
The soul's realization and determination still inheriting,
The fluid vacuum around and ahead still entering and
    dividing,
No balk retarding, no anchor anchoring, on no rock
    striking,
70   Swift, glad, content, unbereav'd, nothing losing,
Of all able and ready at any time to give strict account,
The divine ship sails the divine sea.

2

Whoever you are! motion and reflection are especially
    for you,
The divine ship sails the divine sea for you.

Whoever you are! you are he or she for whom the earth is
    solid and liquid,
You are he or she for whom the sun and moon hang in
    the sky,
For none more than you are the present and the past,
For none more than you is immortality.

Each man to himself and each woman to herself, is the
    word of the past and present, and the true word of
    immortality;
80   No one can acquire for another – not one,
Not one can grow for another – not one.

The song is to the singer, and comes back most to him,
The teaching is to the teacher, and comes back most to him,
The murder is to the murderer, and comes back most to
    him,
The theft is to the thief, and comes back most to him,
The love is to the lover, and comes back most to him,
The gift is to the giver, and comes back most to him – it
    cannot fail,
The oration is to the orator, the acting is to the actor and
    actress not to the audience,

And no man understands any greatness or goodness but his own, or the indication of his own.

3

90 I swear the earth shall surely be complete to him or her who shall be complete,
The earth remains jagged and broken only to him or her who remains jagged and broken.

I swear there is no greatness or power that does not emulate those of the earth,
There can be no theory of any account unless it corroborate the theory of the earth,
No politics, song, religion, behavior, or what not, is of account, unless it compare with the amplitude of the earth,
Unless it face the exactness, vitality, impartiality, rectitude of the earth.

I swear I begin to see love with sweeter spasms than that which responds love,
It is that which contains itself, which never invites and never refuses.

I swear I begin to see little or nothing in audible words,
All merges toward the presentation of the unspoken meanings of the earth,
100 Toward him who sings the songs of the body and of the truths of the earth,
Toward him who makes the dictionaries of words that print cannot touch.

I swear I see what is better than to tell the best,
It is always to leave the best untold.

When I undertake to tell the best I find I cannot,
My tongue is ineffectual on its pivots,
My breath will not be obedient to its organs,
I become a dumb man.

The best of the earth cannot be told anyhow, all or any is best,

It is not what you anticipated, it is cheaper, easier, nearer,
110   Things are not dismiss'd from the places they held before,
The earth is just as positive and direct as it was before,
Facts, religions, improvements, politics, trades, are as real
   as before,
But the soul is also real, it too is positive and direct,
No reasoning, no proof has establish'd it,
Undeniable growth has establish'd it.

4
These to echo the tones of souls and the phrases of souls,
(If they did not echo the phrases of souls what were they
   then?
If they had not reference to you in especial what were they
   then?)

I swear I will never henceforth have to do with the faith that
   tells the best,
120   I will have to do only with that faith that leaves the best
   untold.

Say on, sayers! sing on, singers!
Delve! mould! pile the words of the earth!
Work on, age after age, nothing is to be lost,
It may have to wait long, but it will certainly come in use,
When the materials are all prepared and ready, the
   architects shall appear.

I swear to you the architects shall appear without fail,
I swear to you they will understand you and justify you,
The greatest among them shall be he who best knows you,
   and encloses all and is faithful to all,
He and the rest shall not forget you, they shall perceive
   that you are not an iota less than they,
130   You shall be fully glorified in them.

Youth, Day, Old Age and Night

Youth, large, lusty, loving – youth full of grace, force,
    fascination,
Do you know that Old Age may come after you with equal
    grace, force, fascination?

Day full-blown and splendid – day of the immense sun,
    action, ambition, laughter,
The Night follows close with millions of suns, and sleep and
    restoring darkness.

BIRDS OF PASSAGE

Song of the Universal

1

Come said the Muse,
Sing me a song no poet yet has chanted,
Sing me the universal.

In this broad earth of ours,
Amid the measureless grossness and the slag,
Enclosed and safe within its central heart,
Nestles the seed perfection.

By every life a share or more or less,
None born but it is born, conceal'd or unconceal'd the seed
    is waiting.

2

Lo! keen-eyed towering science,
As from tall peaks the modern overlooking,
Successive absolute fiats issuing.

Yet again, lo! the soul, above all science,
For it has history gather'd like husks around the globe,
For it the entire star-myriads roll through the sky.

In spiral routes by long detours,
(As a much-tacking ship upon the sea,)
For it the partial to the permanent flowing;
For it the real to the ideal tends.

For it the mystic evolution,
Not the right only justified, what we call evil also justified.

Forth from their masks, no matter what,
From the huge festering trunk, from craft and guile and
    tears,
Health to emerge and joy, joy universal.

Out of the bulk, the morbid and the shallow,
Out of the bad majority, the varied countless frauds of men
    and states,
Electric, antiseptic yet, cleaving, suffusing all,
Only the good is universal.

3
Over the mountain-growths disease and sorrow,
30 An uncaught bird is ever hovering, hovering,
High in the purer, happier air.

From imperfection's murkiest cloud,
Darts always forth one ray of perfect light,
One flash of heaven's glory.

To fashion's, custom's discord,
To the mad Babel-din, the deafening orgies,
Soothing each lull a strain is heard, just heard,
From some far shore the final chorus sounding.

O the blest eyes, the happy hearts,
40 That see, that know the guiding thread so fine,
Along the mighty labyrinth.

4
And thou America,
For the scheme's culmination, its thought and its reality,
For these (not for thyself) thou has arrived.

Thou too surroundest all,
Embracing carrying welcoming all, thou too by pathways
    broad and new,
To the ideal tendest.

The measur'd faiths of other lands, the grandeurs of the
    past,
Are not for thee, but grandeurs of thine own,
50 Deific faiths and amplitudes, absorbing, comprehending all,
All eligible to all.

All, all for immortality,
Love like the light silently wrapping all,

Nature's amelioration blessing all,
The blossoms, fruits of ages, orchards divine and certain,
Forms, objects, growths, humanities, to spirtual images
    ripening.

Give me O God to sing that thought,
Give me, give him or her I love this quenchless faith,
In Thy ensemble, whatever else withheld withhold not
    from us,
60 Belief in plan of Thee enclosed in Time and Space,
Health, peace, salvation universal.

Is it a dream?
Nay but the lack of it the dream,
And failing it life's lore and wealth a dream,
And all the world a dream.

Pioneers! O Pioneers!

    Come my tan-faced children,
Follow well in order, get your weapons ready,
Have you your pistols? have you your sharp-edged axes?
    Pioneers! O pioneers!

    For we cannot tarry here,
We must march my darlings, we must bear the brunt of
    danger,
We the youthful sinewy races, all the rest on us depend,
    Pioneers! O pioneers!

    O you youths, Western youths,
10 So impatient, full of action, full of manly pride and
    friendship,
Plain I see you Western youths, see you tramping with the
    foremost,
    Pioneers! O pioneers!

Have the elder races halted?
Do they droop and end their lesson, wearied over there
    beyond the seas?
We take up the task eternal, and the burden and the lesson,
    Pioneers! O pioneers!

All the past we leave behind,
We debouch upon a newer mightier world, varied world,
Fresh and strong the world we seize, world of labor and
    the march,
20   Pioneers! O pioneers!

We detachments steady throwing,
Down the edges, through the passes, up the mountains
    steep,
Conquering, holding, daring, venturing as we go the
    unknown ways,
    Pioneers! O pioneers!

We primeval forests felling,
We the rivers stemming, vexing we and piercing deep the
    mines within,
We the surface broad surveying, we the virgin soil
    upheaving,
    Pioneers! O pioneers!

Colorado men are we,
30 From the peaks gigantic, from the giant sierras and the high
    plateaus,
From the mine and from the gully, from the hunting trail
    we come,
    Pioneers! O pioneers!

From Nebraska, from Arkansas,
Central inland race are we, from Missouri, with the
    continental blood intervein'd,
All the hands of comrades clasping, all the Southern, all the
    Northern,
    Pioneers! O pioneers!

O resistless restless race!
O beloved race in all!·O my breast aches with tender love
for all!
O I mourn and yet exult, I am rapt with love for all,
40   Pioneers! O pioneers!

Raise the mighty mother mistress,
Waving high the delicate mistress, over all the starry
mistress, (bend your heads all,)
Raise the fang'd and warlike mistress, stern, impassive,
weapon'd mistress,
      Pioneers! O pioneers!

See my children, resolute children,
By those swarms upon our rear we must never yield or falter,
Ages back in ghostly millions frowning there behind us
urging,
      Pioneers! O pioneers!

On and on the compact ranks,
50   With accessions ever waiting, with the places of the dead
quickly fill'd,
Through the battle, through defeat, moving yet and never
stopping,
      Pioneers! O pioneers!

O to die advancing on!
Are there some of us to droop and die? has the hour come?
Then upon the march we fittest die, soon and sure the
gap is fill'd,
      Pioneers! O pioneers!

All the pulses of the world,
Falling in they beat for us, with the Western movement
beat,
Holding single or together, steady moving to the front,
all for us,
60   Pioneers! O pioneers!

Life's involv'd and varied pageants,
All the forms and shows, all the workmen at their work,
All the seamen and the landsmen, all the masters with their
 slaves,
 Pioneers! O pioneers!

All the hapless silent lovers,
All the prisoners in the prisons, all the righteous and the
 wicked,
All the joyous, all the sorrowing, all the living, all the dying,
 Pioneers! O pioneers!

I too with my soul and body,
70 We, a curious trio, picking, wandering on our way,
Through these shores amid the shadows, with the
 apparitions pressing,
 Pioneers! O pioneers!

Lo, the darting bowling orb!
Lo, the brother orbs around, all the clustering suns and
 planets,
All the dazzling days, all the mystic nights with dreams,
 Pioneers! O pioneers!

These are of us, they are with us,
All for primal needed work, while the followers there in
 embryo wait behind,
We to-day's procession heading, we the route for travel
 clearing,
80 Pioneers! O pioneers!

O you daughters of the West!
O you young and elder daughters! O you mothers and
 you wives!
Never must you be divided, in our ranks you move united,
 Pioneers! O pioneers!

Minstrels latent on the prairies!
(Shrouded bards of other lands, you may rest, you have
   done your work,)
Soon I hear you coming warbling, soon you rise and tramp
   amid us,
   Pioneers! O pioneers!

Not for delectations sweet,
90 Not the cushion and the slipper, not the peaceful and the
   studious,
Not the riches safe and palling, not for us the tame
   enjoyment,
   Pioneers! O pioneers!

Do the feasters gluttonous feast?
Do the corpulent sleepers sleep? have they lock'd and
   bolted doors?
Still be ours the diet hard, and the blanket on the ground,
   Pioneers! O pioneers!

Has the night descended?
Was the road of late so toilsome? did we stop
   discouraged nodding on our way?
Yet a passing hour I yield you in your tracks to pause
   oblivious,
100   Pioneers! O pioneers!

Till with sound of trumpet,
Far, far off the daybreak call – hark! how loud and clear I
   hear it wind,
Swift! to the head of the army! – swift! spring to your
   places,
   Pioneers! O pioneers!

To You

Whoever you are, I fear you are walking the walks of dreams,
I fear these supposed realities are to melt from under your
   feet and hands,

Even now your features, joys, speech, house, trade, manners,
 troubles, follies, costume, crimes, dissipate away from
 you,
Your true soul and body appear before me,
They stand forth out of affairs, out of commerce, shops,
 work, farms, clothes, the house, buying, selling, eating,
 drinking, suffering, dying.

Whoever you are, now I place my hand upon you, that you
 be my poem,
I whisper with my lips close to your ear,
I have loved many women and men, but I love none better
 than you.

O I have been dilatory and dumb,
10 I should have made my way straight to you long ago,
I should have blabb'd nothing but you, I should have
 chanted nothing but you.

I will leave all and come and make the hymns of you,
None has understood you, but I understand you,
None has done justice to you, you have not done justice to
 yourself,
None but has found you imperfect, I only find no
 imperfection in you,
None but would subordinate you, I only am he who will
 never consent to subordinate you,
I only am he who places over you no master, owner, better,
 God, beyond what waits intrinsically in yourself.

Painters have painted their swarming groups and the
 centre-figure of all,
From the head of the centre-figure spreading a nimbus of
 gold-color'd light,
20 But I paint myriads of heads, but paint no head without its
 nimbus of gold-color'd light,
From my hand from the brain of every man and woman it
 streams, effulgently flowing forever.

O I could sing such grandeurs and glories about you!
You have not known what you are, you have slumber'd upon
yourself all your life,
Your eyelids have been the same as closed most of the time,
What you have done returns already in mockeries,
(Your thrift, knowledge, prayers, if they do not return in
mockeries, what is their return?)

The mockeries are not you,
Underneath them and within them I see you lurk,
I pursue you where none else has pursued you,
30 Silence, the desk, the flippant expression, the night, the
accustom'd routine, if these conceal you from others or
from yourself, they do not conceal you from me,
The shaved face, the unsteady eye, the impure complexion,
if these balk others they do not balk me,
The pert apparel, the deform'd attitude, drunkenness,
greed, premature death, all these I part aside.

There is no endowment in man or woman that is not tallied
in you,
There is no virtue, no beauty in man or woman, but as
good is in you,
No pluck, no endurance in others, but as good is in you,
No pleasure waiting for others, but an equal pleasure waits
for you.

As for me, I give nothing to any one except I give the like
carefully to you,
I sing the songs of the glory of none, not God, sooner than I
sing the songs of the glory of you.

Whoever you are! claim your own at any hazard!
40 These shows of the East and West are tame compared to
you,
These immense meadows, these interminable rivers, you
are immense and interminable as they,
These furies, elements, storms, motions of Nature, throes of
apparent dissolution, you are he or she who is master or
mistress over them,

Master or mistress in your own right over Nature, elements,
    pain, passion, dissolution.

The hopples fall from your ankles, you find an unfailing
    sufficiency,
Old or young, male or female, rude, low, rejected by the
    rest, whatever you are promulges itself,
Through birth, life, death, burial, the means are provided,
    nothing is scanted,
Through angers, losses, ambition, ignorance, ennui, what
    you are picks its way.

France,
THE 18TH YEAR OF THESE STATES

A great year and place.
A harsh discordant natal scream out-sounding, to touch the
    mother's heart closer than any yet.

I walk'd the shores of my Eastern sea,
Heard over the waves the little voice,
Saw the divine infant where she woke mournfully wailing,
    amid the roar of cannon, curses, shouts, crash of falling
    buildings,
Was not so sick from the blood in the gutters running, nor
    from the single corpses, nor those in heaps, nor those
    borne away in the tumbrils,
Was not so desperate at the battues of death – was not so
    shock'd at the repeated fusillades of the guns.

Pale, silent, stern, what could I say to that long-accrued
    retribution?
Could I wish humanity different?
10   Could I wish the people made of wood and stone?
Or that there be no justice in destiny or time?

O Liberty! O mate for me!
Here too the blaze, the grape-shot and the axe, in reserve,
    to fetch them out in case of need,

Here too, though long represt, can never be destroy'd,
Here too could rise at last murdering and ecstatic,
Here too demanding full arrears of vengeance.

Hence I sign this salute over the sea,
And I do not deny that terrible red birth and baptism,
But remember the little voice that I heard wailing, and wait
    with perfect trust, no matter how long,
20   And from to-day sad and cogent I maintain the bequeath'd
    cause, as for all lands,
And I send these words to Paris with my love,
And I guess some chansonniers there will understand them,
For I guess there is latent music yet in France, floods of it,
O I hear already the bustle of instruments, they will soon be
    drowning all that would interrupt them,
O I think the east wind brings a triumphal and free march,
It reaches hither, it swells me to joyful madness,
I will run transpose it in words, to justify it,
I will yet sing a song for you ma femme.

Myself and Mine

Myself and mine gymnastic ever,
To stand the cold or heat, to take good aim with a gun, to
    sail a boat, to manage horses, to beget superb children,
To speak readily and clearly, to feel at home among
    common people,
And to hold our own in terrible positions on land and sea.

Not for an embroiderer,
(There will always be plenty of embroiderers, I welcome
    them also,)
But for the fibre of things and for inherent men and women.

Not to chisel ornaments,
But to chisel with free stroke the heads and limbs of
    plenteous supreme Gods, that the States may realize them
    walking and talking.

10   Let me have my own way,
    Let others promulge the laws, I will make no account of
       the laws,
    Let others praise eminent men and hold up peace, I hold up
       agitation and conflict,
    I praise no eminent man, I rebuke to his face the one that
       was thought most worthy.

    (Who are you? and what are you secretly guilty of all your
       life?
    Will you turn aside all your life? will you grub and chatter
       all your life?
    And who are you, blabbing by rote, years, pages, languages,
       reminiscences,
    Unwitting to-day that you do not know how to speak
       properly a single word?)

    Let others finish specimens, I never finish specimens,
    I start them by exhaustless laws as Nature does, fresh and
       modern continually.

20   I give nothing as duties,
    What others give as duties I give as living impulses,
    (Shall I give the heart's action as a duty?)

    Let others dispose of questions, I dispose of nothing, I
       arouse unanswerable questions,
    Who are they I see and touch, and what about them?
    What about these likes of myself that draw me so close by
       tender directions and indirections?

    I call to the world to distrust the accounts of my friends, but
       listen to my enemies, as I myself do,
    I charge you forever reject those who would expound me, for
       I cannot expound myself,
    I charge that there be no theory or school founded out of me,
    I charge you to leave all free, as I have left all free.

30   After me, vista!
       O I see life is not short, but immeasurably long,
       I henceforth tread the world chaste, temperate, an early
          riser, a steady grower,
       Every hour the semen of centuries, and still of centuries.

       I must follow up these continual lessons of the air, water,
          earth,
       I perceive I have no time to lose.

Year of Meteors (1859–60)

       Year of meteors! brooding year!
       I would bind in words retrospective some of your deeds and
          signs,
       I would sing your contest for the 19th Presidentiad,
       I would sing how an old man, tall, with white hair, mounted
          the scaffold in Virginia,
       (I was at hand, silent I stood with teeth shut close, I watch'd,
       I stood very near you old man when cool and indifferent,
          but trembling with age and your unheal'd wounds you
          mounted the scaffold;)
       I would sing in my copious song your census returns of the
          States,
       The tables of population and products, I would sing of
          your ships and their cargoes,
       The proud black ships of Manhattan arriving, some fill'd
          with immigrants, some from the isthmus with cargoes of
          gold,
10   Songs thereof would I sing, to all that hitherward comes
          would I welcome give,
       And you would I sing, fair stripling! welcome to you from
          me, young prince of England!
       (Remember you surging Manhattan's crowds as you pass'd
          with your cortege of nobles?
       There in the crowds stood I, and singled you out with
          attachment;)

Nor forget I to sing of the wonder, the ship as she swam up
    my bay,
Well-shaped and stately the Great Eastern swam up my bay,
    she was 600 feet long,
Her moving swiftly surrounded by myriads of small craft I
    forget not to sing;
Nor the comet that came unannounced out of the north
    flaring in heaven,
Nor the strange huge meteor-procession dazzling and clear
    shooting over our heads,
(A moment, a moment long it sail'd its balls of unearthly
    light over our heads,
20 Then departed, dropt in the night, and was gone;)
Of such, and fitful as they, I sing – with gleams from them
    would I gleam and patch these chants,
Your chants, O year all mottled with evil and good – year of
    forebodings!
Year of comets and meteors transient and strange – lo! even
    here one equally transient and strange!
As I flit through you hastily, soon to fall and be gone, what
    is this chant,
What am I myself but one of your meteors?

With Antecedents

1

With antecedents,
With my fathers and mothers and the accumulations of
    past ages,
With all which, had it not been, I would not now be here,
    as I am,
With Egypt, India, Phenicia, Greece and Rome,
With the Kelt, the Scandinavian, the Alb and the Saxon,
With antique maritime ventures, laws, artisanship, wars and
    journeys,
With the poet, the skald, the saga, the myth, and the oracle,

With the sale of slaves, with enthusiasts, with the
   troubadour, the crusader, and the monk,
With those old continents whence we have come to this
   new continent,
10   With the fading kingdoms and kings over there,
With the fading religions and priests,
With the small shores we look back to from our own large
   and present shores,
With countless years drawing themselves onward and
   arrived at these years,
You and me arrived – America arrived and making this
   year,
This year! sending itself ahead countless years to come.

2

O but it is not the years – it is I, it is You,
We touch all laws and tally all antecedents,
We are the skald, the oracle, the monk and the knight, we
   easily include them and more,
We stand amid time beginningless and endless, we stand
   amid evil and good,
20   All swings around us, there is as much darkness as light,
The very sun swings itself and its system of planets around
   us,
Its sun, and its again, all swing around us.

As for me, (torn, stormy, amid these vehement days,)
I have the idea of all, and am all and believe in all,
I believe materialism is true and spiritualism is true, I reject
   no part.

(Have I forgotten any part? any thing in the past?
Come to me whoever and whatever, till I give you
   recognition.)

I respect Assyria, China, Teutonia, and the Hebrews,
I adopt each theory, myth, god, and demi-god,
30   I see that the old accounts, bibles, genealogies, are true,
   without exception,
I assert that all past days were what they must have been,

And that they could no-how have been better than they
  were,
And that to-day is what it must be, and that America is,
And that to-day and America could no-how be better than
  they are.

3
In the name of these States and in your and my name, the
  Past,
And in the name of these States and in your and my name,
  the Present time.

I know that the past was great and the future will be great,
And I know that both curiously conjoint in the present
  time,
(For the sake of him I typify, for the common average man's
  sake, your sake if you are he,)
40 And that where I am or you are this present day, there is the
  centre of all days, all races,
And there is the meaning to us of all that has ever come of
  races and days, or ever will come.

A Broadway Pageant

1

Over the Western sea hither from Niphon come,
Courteous, the swart-cheek'd two-sworded envoys,
Leaning back in their open barouches, bare-headed,
  impassive,
Ride to-day through Manhattan.

Libertad! I do not know whether others behold what I
  behold,
In the procession along with the nobles of Niphon, the
  errand-bearers,
Bringing up the rear, hovering above, around, or in the
  ranks marching,
But I will sing you a song of what I behold Libertad.
When million-footed Manhattan unpent descends to her
  pavements,
10 When the thunder-cracking guns arouse me with the proud
  roar I love,
When the round-mouth'd guns out of the smoke and smell I
  love spit their salutes,
When the fire-flashing guns have fully alerted me, and
  heaven-clouds canopy my city with a delicate thin haze,
When gorgeous the countless straight stems, the forests at
  the wharves, thicken with colors,
When every ship richly drest carries her flag at the peak,
When pennants trail and street-festoons hang from the
  windows,
When Broadway is entirely given up to foot-passengers and
  foot-standers, when the mass is densest,
When the façades of the houses are alive with people, when
  eyes gaze riveted tens of thousands at a time,
When the guests from the islands advance, when the pageant
  moves forward visible,
When the summons is made, when the answer that waited
  thousands of years answers,
20 I too arising, answering, descend to the pavements, merge
  with the crowd, and gaze with them.

2

Superb-faced Manhattan!
Comrade Americanos! to us, then at last the Orient comes.

To us, my city,
Where our tall-topt marble and iron beauties range on
    opposite sides, to walk in the space between,
To-day our Antipodes comes.

The Originatress comes,
The nest of languages, the bequeather of poems, the race
    of eld,
Florid with blood, pensive, rapt with musings, hot with
    passion,
Sultry with perfume, with ample and flowing garments,
30 With sunburnt visage, with intense soul and glittering eyes,
The race of Brahma comes.

See my cantabile! these and more are flashing to us from
    the procession,
As it moves changing, a kaleidoscope divine it moves
    changing before us.

For not the envoys nor the tann'd Japanee from his island
    only,
Lithe and silent the Hindoo appears, the Asiatic continent
    itself appears, the past, the dead,
The murky night-morning of wonder and fable inscrutable,
The envelop'd mysteries, the old and unknown hive-bees,
The north, the sweltering south, eastern Assyria, the
    Hebrews, the ancient of ancients,
Vast desolated cities, the gliding present, all of these and
    more are in the pageant-procession.

40 Geography, the world, is in it,
The Great Sea, the brood of islands, Polynesia, the coast
    beyond,
The coast you henceforth are facing – you Libertad! from
    your Western golden shores,

The countries there with their populations, the millions
    en-masse are curiously here,
The swarming market-places, the temples with idols ranged
    along the sides or at the end, bonze, brahmin, and llama,
Mandarin, farmer, merchant, mechanic, and fisherman,
The singing-girl and the dancing-girl, the ecstatic persons,
    the secluded emperors,
Confucious himself, the great poets and heroes, the
    warriors, the castes, all,
Trooping up, crowding from all directions, from the Altay
    mountains,
From Thibet, from the four winding and far-flowing rivers
    of China,
50 From the southern peninsulas and the demi-continental
    islands, from Malaysia,
These and whatever belongs to them palpable show forth
    to me, and are seiz'd by me,
And I am seiz'd by them, and friendlily held by them,
Till as here them all I chant, Libertad! for themselves and
    for you.

For I too raising my voice join the ranks of this pageant,
I am the chanter, I chant aloud over the pageant,
I chant the world on my Western sea,
I chant copious the islands beyond, thick as stars in the sky,
I chant the new empire grander than any before, as in a
    vision it comes to me,
I chant America the mistress, I chant a greater supremacy,
60 I chant projected a thousand blooming cities yet in time on
    those groups of sea-islands,
My sail-ships and steam-ships threading the archipelagoes,
My stars and stripes fluttering in the wind,
Commerce opening, the sleep of ages having done its work,
    races reborn, refresh'd,
Lives, works resumed – the object I know not – but the old,
    the Asiatic renew'd as it must be,
Commencing from this day surrounded by the world.

3
And you Libertad of the world!
You shall sit in the middle well-pois'd thousands and
    thousands of years,
As to-day from one side the nobles of Asia come to you,
As to-morrow from the other side the queen of England
    sends her eldest son to you.

70 The sign is reversing, the orb is enclosed,
The ring is circled, the journey is done,
The box-lid is but perceptibly open'd, nevertheless the
    perfume pours copiously out of the whole box.
Young Libertad! with the venerable Asia, the all-mother,
Be considerate with her now and ever hot Libertad, for you
    are all,
Bend your proud neck to the long-off mother now sending
    messages over the archipelagoes to you,
Bend your proud neck low for once, young Libertad.

Were the children straying westward so long? so wide the
    tramping?
Were the precedent dim ages debouching westward from
    Paradise so long?
Were the centuries steadily footing it that way, all the while
    unknown, for you, for reasons?

80 They are justified, they are accomplish'd, they shall now be
    turn'd the other way also, to travel toward you thence,
They shall now also march obediently eastward for your
    sake Libertad.

SEA-DRIFT

Out of the Cradle Endlessly Rocking

Out of the cradle endlessly rocking,
Out of the mocking-bird's throat, the musical shuttle,
Out of the Ninth-month midnight,
Over the sterile sands and the fields beyond, where the child
    leaving his bed wander'd alone, bareheaded, barefoot,
Down from the shower'd halo,
Up from the mystic play of shadows twining and twisting
    as if they were alive,
Out from the patches of briers and blackberries,
From the memories of the bird that chanted to me,
From your memories sad brother, from the fitful risings and
    fallings I heard,
From under that yellow half-moon late-risen and swollen
    as if with tears,
From those beginning notes of yearning and love there in
    the mist,
From the thousand responses of my heart never to cease,
From the myriad thence-arous'd words,
From the word stronger and more delicious than any,
From such as now they start the scene revisiting,
As a flock, twittering, rising, or overhead passing,
Borne hither, ere all eludes me, hurriedly,
A man, yet by these tears a little boy again,
Throwing myself on the sand, confronting the waves,
I, chanter of pains and joys, uniter of here and hereafter,
Taking all hints to use them, but swiftly leaping beyond
    them,
A reminiscence sing.

Once Paumanok,
When the lilac-scent was in the air and Fifth-month grass
    was growing,
Up this seashore in some briers,
Two feather'd guests from Alabama, two together,

And their nest, and four light-green eggs spotted with
    brown,
And every day the he-bird to and fro near at hand,
And every day the she-bird crouch'd on her nest, silent,
    with bright eyes,
30   And every day I, a curious boy, never too close, never
    disturbing them,
Cautiously peering, absorbing, translating.

Shine! shine! shine!
Pour down your warmth, great sun!
While we bask, we two together.

Two together!
Winds blow south, or winds blow north,
Day come white, or night come black,
Home, or rivers and mountains from home,
Singing all time, minding no time,
40   *While we two keep together.*

Till of a sudden,
May-be kill'd, unknown to her mate,
One forenoon the she-bird crouch'd not on the nest,
Nor return'd that afternoon, nor the next,
Nor ever appear'd again.

And thenceforward all summer in the sound of the sea,
And at night under the full of the moon in calmer weather,
Over the hoarse surging of the sea,
Or flitting from brier to brier by day,
50   I saw, I heard at intervals the remaining one, the he-bird,
The solitary guest from Alabama.

Blow! blow! blow!
Blow up sea-winds along Paumanok's shore;
I wait and I wait till you blow my mate to me.

Yes, when the stars glisten'd,
All night long on the prong of a moss-scallop'd stake,
Down almost amid the slapping waves,
Sat the lone singer wonderful causing tears.

He call'd on his mate,
60 He pour'd forth the meanings which I of all men know.

Yes my brother I know,
The rest might not, but I have treasur'd every note,
For more than once dimly down to the beach gliding,
Silent, avoiding the moonbeams, blending myself with the
    shadows,
Recalling now the obscure shapes, the echoes, the sounds
    and sights after their sorts,
The white arms out in the breakers tirelessly tossing,
I, with bare feet, a child, the wind wafting my hair,
Listen'd long and long.

Listen'd to keep, to sing, now translating the notes,
70 Following you my brother.

Soothe! soothe! soothe!
Close on its wave soothes the wave behind,
And again another behind embracing and lapping, every one
    close,
But my love soothes not me, not me.

Low hangs the moon, it rose late,
It is lagging – O I think it is heavy with love, with love.

O madly the sea pushes upon the land,
With love, with love.

O night! do I not see my love fluttering out among the
    breakers?
80 *What is that little black thing I see there in the white?*

Loud! loud! loud!
Loud I call to you, my love!
High and clear I shoot my voice over the waves,
Surely you must know who is here, is here,
You must know who I am, my love.

Low-hanging moon!
What is that dusky spot in your brown yellow?
O it is the shape, the shape of my mate!
O moon do not keep her from me any longer.

90   Land! land! O land!
Whichever way I turn, O I think you could give me my mate
    back again if you only would,
For I am almost sure I see her dimly whichever way I look.

O rising stars!
Perhaps the one I want so much will rise, will rise with some
    of you.

O throat! O trembling throat!
Sound clearer through the atmosphere!
Pierce the woods, the earth,
Somewhere listening to catch you must be the one I want.

Shake out carols!
100   Solitary here, the night's carols!
Carols of lonesome love! death's carols!
Carols under that lagging, yellow, waning moon!
O under that moon where she droops almost down into the sea!
O reckless despairing carols.

But soft! sink low!
Soft! let me just murmur,
And do you wait a moment you husky-nois'd sea,
For somewhere I believe I heard my mate responding to me,
So faint, I must be still, be still to listen,
110   But not altogether still, for then she might not come
    immediately to me.

Hither my love!
Here I am! here!
With this just-sustain'd note I announce myself to you,
This gentle call is for you my love, for you.

Do not be decoy'd elsewhere,
That is the whistle of the wind, it is not my voice,
That is the fluttering, the fluttering of the spray,
Those are the shadows of leaves.

O darkness! O in vain!
120 *O I am very sick and sorrowful.*

O brown halo in the sky near the moon, drooping upon the sea!
O troubled reflection in the sea!
O throat! O throbbing heart!
And I singing uselessly, uselessly all the night.

O past! O happy life! O songs of joy!
In the air, in the woods, over fields,
Loved! loved! loved! loved! loved!
But my mate no more, no more with me!
We two together no more.

130 The aria sinking,
All else continuing, the stars shining,
The winds blowing, the notes of the bird continuous
    echoing,
With angry moans the fierce old mother incessantly moaning,
On the sands of Paumanok's shore gray and rustling,
The yellow half-moon enlarged, sagging down, drooping,
    the face of the sea almost touching,
The boy ecstatic, with his bare feet the waves, with his
    hair the atmosphere dallying,
The love in the heart long pent, now loose, now at last
    tumultuously bursting,
The aria's meaning, the ears, the soul, swiftly depositing,
The strange tears down the cheeks coursing,
140 The colloquy there, the trio, each uttering,
The undertone, the savage old mother incessantly crying,
To the boy's soul's questions sullenly timing, some
    drown'd secret hissing,
To the outsetting bard.

Demon or bird! (said the boy's soul,)
Is it indeed toward your mate you sing? or is it really to me?
For I, that was a child, my tongue's use sleeping, now I have
 heard you,
Now in a moment I know what I am for, I awake,
And already a thousand singers, a thousand songs, clearer,
 louder and more sorrowful than yours,
A thousand warbling echoes have started to life within me,
 never to die.

150 O you singer solitary, singing by yourself, projecting me,
O solitary me listening, never more shall I cease
 perpetuating you,
Never more shall I escape, never more the reverberations,
Never more the cries of unsatisfied love be absent from me,
Never again leave me to be the peaceful child I was before
 what there in the night,
By the sea under the yellow and sagging moon,
The messenger there arous'd, the fire, the sweet hell
 within,
The unknown want, the destiny of me.

O give me the clew! (it lurks in the night here somewhere,)
O if I am to have so much, let me have more!

160 A word then, (for I will conquer it,)
The word final, superior to all,
Subtle, sent up – what is it? – I listen;
Are you whispering it, and have been all the time, you
 sea-waves?
Is that it from your liquid rims and wet sands?

Whereto answering, the sea,
Delaying not, hurrying not,
Whisper'd me through the night, and very plainly before
 daybreak,
Lisp'd to me the low and delicious word death,
And again death, death, death, death,
170 Hissing melodious, neither like the bird nor like my
 arous'd child's heart,

But edging near as privately for me rustling at my feet,
Creeping thence steadily up to my ears and laving me softly
    all over,
Death, death, death, death, death.

Which I do not forget,
But fuse the song of my dusky demon and brother,
That he sang to me in the moonlight on Paumanok's gray
    beach,
With the thousand responsive songs at random,
My own songs awaked from that hour,
And with them the key, the word up from the waves,
180 The word of the sweetest song and all songs,
That strong and delicious word which, creeping to my feet,
(Or like some old crone rocking the cradle, swathed in sweet
    garments, bending aside,)
The sea whisper'd me.

As I Ebb'd with the Ocean of Life

1

As I ebb'd with the ocean of life,
As I wended the shores I know,
As I walk'd where the ripples continually wash you
    Paumanok,
Where they rustle up hoarse and sibilant,
Where the fierce old mother endlessly cries for her castaways,
I musing late in the autumn day, gazing off southward,
Held by this electric self out of the pride of which I utter
    poems,
Was seiz'd by the spirit that trails in the lines underfoot,
The rim, the sediment that stands for all the water and all
    the land of the globe.

10   Fascinated, my eyes reverting from the south, dropt, to
        follow those slender windrows,
Chaff, straw, splinters of wood, weeds, and the sea-gluten,

Scum, scales from shining rocks, leaves of salt-lettuce, left
    by the tide,
Miles walking, the sound of breaking waves the other side
    of me,
Paumanok there and then as I thought the old thought of
    likenesses,
These you presented to me you fish-shaped island,
As I wended the shores I know,
As I walk'd with that electric self seeking types.

2

As I wend to the shores I know not,
As I list to the dirge, the voices of men and women
    wreck'd,
20   As I inhale the impalpable breezes that set in upon me,
As the ocean so mysterious rolls toward me closer and closer,
I too but signify at the utmost a little wash'd-up drift,
A few sands and dead leaves to gather,
Gather, and merge myself as part of the sands and drift.

O baffled, balk'd, bent to the very earth,
Oppress'd with myself that I have dared to open my mouth,
Aware now that amid all that blab whose echoes recoil upon
    me I have not once had the least idea who or what I am,
But that before all my arrogant poems the real Me stands
    yet untouch'd, untold, altogether unreach'd,
Withdrawn far, mocking me with mock-congratulatory signs
    and bows,
30   With peals of distant ironical laughter at every word I have
    written,
Pointing in silence to these songs, and then to the sand
    beneath.
I perceive I have not really understood any thing, not a
    single object, and that no man ever can,
Nature here in sight of the sea taking advantage of me to dart
    upon me and sting me,
Because I have dared to open my mouth to sing at all.

3
You oceans both, I close with you,
We murmur alike reproachfully rolling sands and drift,
     knowing not why,
These little shreds indeed standing for you and me and all.

You friable shore with trails of debris,
You fish-shaped island, I take what is underfoot,
40   What is yours is mine my father.

I too Paumanok,
I too have bubbled up, floated the measureless float, and
     been wash'd on your shores,
I too am but a trail of drift and debris,
I too leave little wrecks upon you, you fish-shaped island.

I throw myself upon your breast my father,
I cling to you so that you cannot unloose me,
I hold you so firm till you answer me something.

Kiss me my father,
Touch me with your lips as I touch those I love,
50   Breathe to me while I hold you close the secret of the
     murmuring I envy.

4
Ebb, ocean of life, (the flow will return,)
Cease not your moaning you fierce old mother,
Endlessly cry for your castaways, but fear not, deny not me,
Rustle not up so hoarse and angry against my feet as I
     touch you or gather from you.

I mean tenderly by you and all,
I gather for myself and for this phantom looking down
     where we lead, and following me and mine.

Me and mine, loose windrows, little corpses,
Froth, snowy white, and bubbles,
(See, from my dead lips the ooze exuding at last,
60   See, the prismatic colors glistening and rolling,)
Tufts of straw, sands, fragments,

Buoy'd hither from many moods, one contradicting another,
From the storm, the long calm, the darkness, the swell,
Musing, pondering, a breath, a briny tear, a dab of liquid or
    soil,
Up just as much out of fathomless workings fermented and
    thrown,
A limp blossom or two, torn, just as much over waves
    floating, drifted at random,
Just as much for us that sobbing dirge of Nature,
Just as much whence we come that blare of the
    cloud-trumpets,
We, capricious, brought hither we know not whence,
    spread out before you,
70 You up there walking or sitting,
Whoever you are, we too lie in drifts at your feet.

Tears

Tears! tears! tears!
In the night, in solitude, tears,
On the white shore dripping, dripping, suck'd in by the
    sand,
Tears, not a star shining, all dark and desolate,
Moist tears from the eyes of a muffled head;
O who is that ghost? that form in the dark, with tears?
What shapeless lump is that, bent, crouch'd there on the
    sand?
Streaming tears, sobbing tears, throes, choked with wild
    cries;
O storm, embodied, rising, careering with swift steps along
    the beach!
10 O wild and dismal night storm, with wind – O belching and
    desperate!
O shade so sedate and decorous by day, with calm
    countenance and regulated pace,

But away at night as you fly, none looking – O then the
    unloosen'd ocean,
Of tears! tears! tears!

To the Man-of-War Bird

Thou who hast slept all night upon the storm,
Waking renew'd on thy prodigious pinions,
(Burst the wild storm? above it thou ascended'st,
And rested on the sky, thy slave that cradled thee,)
Now a blue point, far, far, in heaven floating,
As to the light emerging here on deck I watch thee,
(Myself a speck, a point on the world's floating vast.)

Far, far at sea,
After the night's fierce drifts have strewn the shore with
    wrecks,
10   With re-appearing day as now so happy and serene,
The rosy and elastic dawn, the flashing sun,
The limpid spread of air cerulean,
Thou also re-appearest.

Thou born to match the gale, (thou art all wings,)
To cope with heaven and earth and sea and hurricane,
Thou ship of air that never furl'st thy sails,
Days, even weeks untired and onward, through spaces,
    realms gyrating,
At dusk that look'st on Senegal, at morn America,
That sport'st amid the lightning-flash and thunder-cloud,
20   In them, in thy experiences, had'st thou my soul,
What joys! what joys were thine!

Aboard at a Ship's Helm

Aboard at a ship's helm,
A young steersman steering with care.

Through fog on a sea-coast dolefully ringing,
An ocean-bell – O a warning bell, rock'd by the waves.

O you give good notice indeed, you bell by the sea-reefs
    ringing,
Ringing, ringing, to warn the ship from its wreck-place.

For as on the alert O steersman, you mind the loud
    admonition,
The bows turn, the freighted ship tacking speeds away
    under her gray sails,
The beautiful and noble ship with all her precious wealth
    speeds away gayly and safe.

10 But O the ship, the immortal ship! O ship aboard the ship!
Ship of the body, ship of the soul, voyaging, voyaging,
    voyaging.

On the Beach at Night

On the beach at night,
Stands a child with her father,
Watching the east, the autumn sky.

Up through the darkness,
While ravening clouds, the burial clouds, in black masses
    spreading,
Lower sullen and fast athwart and down the sky,
Amid a transparent clear belt of ether yet left in the east,
Ascends large and calm the lord-star Jupiter,
And nigh at hand, only a very little above,
10 Swim the delicate sisters the Pleiades.

From the beach the child holding the hand of her father,
Those burial-clouds that lower victorious soon to devour all,
Watching, silently weeps.

Weep not, child,
Weep not, my darling,
With these kisses let me remove your tears,
The ravening clouds shall not long be victorious,
They shall not long possess the sky, they devour the stars
    only in apparition,
Jupiter shall emerge, be patient, watch again another night,
    the Pleiades shall emerge,
20 They are immortal, all those stars both silvery and golden
    shall shine out again,
The great stars and the little ones shall shine out again, they
    endure,
The vast immortal suns and the long-enduring pensive
    moons shall again shine.

Then dearest child mournest thou only for Jupiter?
Considerest thou alone the burial of the stars?

Something there is,
(With my lips soothing thee, adding I whisper,
I give thee the first suggestion, the problem and indirection,)
Something there is more immortal even than the stars,
(Many the burials, many the days and nights, passing away,)
30 Something that shall endure longer even than lustrous
    Jupiter,
Longer than sun or any revolving satellite,
Or the radiant sisters the Pleiades.

The World Below the Brine

The world below the brine,
Forests at the bottom of the sea, the branches and leaves,
Sea-lettuce, vast lichens, strange flowers and seeds, the
    thick tangle, openings, and pink turf,

Different colors, pale gray and green, purple, white, and
    gold, the play of light through the water,
Dumb swimmers there among the rocks, coral, gluten,
    grass, rushes, and the aliment of the swimmers,
Sluggish existences grazing there suspended, or slowly
    crawling close to the bottom,
The sperm-whale at the surface blowing air and spray, or
    disporting with his flukes,
The leaden-eyed shark, the walrus, the turtle, the hairy
    sea-leopard, and the sting-ray,
Passions there, wars, pursuits, tribes, sight in those
    ocean-depths, breathing that thick-breathing air, as so
    many do,
10 The change thence to the sight here, and to the subtle air
    breathed by beings like us who walk this sphere,
The change onward from ours to that of beings who walk
    other spheres.

On the Beach at Night Alone

On the beach at night alone,
As the old mother sways her to and fro singing her husky
    song,
As I watch the bright stars shining, I think a thought of the
    clef of the universes and of the future.

A vast similitude interlocks all,
All spheres, grown, ungrown, small, large, suns, moons,
    planets,
All distances of place however wide,
All distances of time, all inanimate forms,
All souls, all living bodies though they be ever so different,
    or in different worlds,
All gaseous, watery, vegetable, mineral processes, the fishes,
    the brutes,
10 All nations, colors, barbarisms, civilizations, languages,

All identities that have existed or may exist on this globe,
  or any globe,
All lives and deaths, all of the past, present, future,
This vast similitude spans them, and always has spann'd,
And shall forever span them and compactly hold and
  enclose them.

Song for All Seas, All Ships

1

To-day a rude brief recitative,
Of ships sailing the seas, each with its special flag or
  ship-signal,
Of unnamed heroes in the ships – of waves spreading and
  spreading far as the eye can reach,
Of dashing spray, and the winds piping and blowing,
And out of these a chant for the sailors of all nations,
Fitful, like a surge.

Of sea-captains young or old, and the mates, and of all
  intrepid sailors,
Of the few, very choice, taciturn, whom fate can never
  surprise nor death dismay,
Pick'd sparingly without noise by thee old ocean, chosen
  by thee,
10 Thou sea that pickest and cullest the race in time, and
  unitest nations,
Suckled by thee, old husky nurse, embodying thee,
Indomitable, untamed as thee.

(Ever the heroes on water or on land, by ones or twos
  appearing,
Ever the stock preserv'd and never lost, though rare,
  enough for seed preserv'd.)

2

Flaunt out O sea your separate flags of nations!
Flaunt out visible as ever the various ship-signals!

But do you reserve especially for yourself and for the soul
   of man one flag above all the rest,
A spiritual woven signal for all nations, emblem of man elate
   above death,
Token of all brave captains and all intrepid sailors and
   mates,
20 And all that went down doing their duty,
Reminiscent of them, twined from all intrepid captains
   young or old,
A pennant universal, subtly waving all time, o'er all brave
   sailors,
All seas, all ships.

Patroling Barnegat

Wild, wild the storm, and the sea high running,
Steady the roar of the gale, with incessant undertone
   muttering,
Shouts of demoniac laughter fitfully piercing and pealing,
Waves, air, midnight, their savagest trinity lashing,
Out in the shadows there milk-white combs careering,
On beachy slush and sand spirts of snow fierce slanting,
Where through the murk the easterly death-wind breasting,
Through cutting swirl and spray watchful and firm
   advancing,
(That in the distance! is that a wreck? is the red signal
   flaring?)
10 Slush and sand of the beach tireless till daylight wending,
Steadily, slowly, through hoarse roar never remitting,
Along the midnight edge by those milk-white combs
   careering,
A group of dim, weird forms, struggling, the night
   confronting,
That savage trinity warily watching.

After the Sea-Ship

After the sea-ship, after the whistling winds,
After the white-gray sails taut to their spars and ropes,
Below, a myriad myriad waves hastening, lifting up their
    necks,
Tending in ceaseless flow toward the track of the ship,
Waves of the ocean bubbling and gurgling, blithely prying,
Waves, undulating waves, liquid, uneven, emulous waves,
Toward that whirling current, laughing and buoyant, with
    curves,
Where the great vessel sailing and tacking displaces the
    surface,
Larger and smaller waves in the spread of the ocean
    yearnfully flowing,
10   The wake of the sea-ship after she passes, flashing and
    frolicsome under the sun,
A motley procession with many a fleck of foam and many
    fragments,
Following the stately and rapid ship, in the wake following.

BY THE ROADSIDE

A Boston Ballad (1854)

To get betimes in Boston town I rose this morning early,
Here's a good place at the corner, I must stand and see
    the show.

Clear the way there Jonathan!
Way for the President's marshal – way for the government
    cannon!
Way for the Federal foot and dragoons, (and the apparitions
    copiously tumbling.)

I love to look on the Stars and Stripes, I hope the fifes will
    play Yankee Doodle.

How bright shine the cutlasses of the foremost troops!
Every man holds his revolver, marching stiff through
    Boston town.

A fog follows, antiques of the same come limping,
10 Some appear wooden-legged, and some appear bandaged
    and bloodless.

Why this is indeed a show – it has called the dead out of the
    earth!
The old graveyards of the hills have hurried to see!
Phantoms! phantoms countless by flank and rear!
Cock'd hats of mothy mould – crutches made of mist!
Arms in slings – old men leaning on young men's shoulders.

What troubles you Yankee phantoms? what is all this
    chattering of bare gums?
Does the ague convulse your limbs? do you mistake your
    crutches for firelocks and level them?

If you blind your eyes with tears you will not see the
    President's marshal,
If you groan such groans you might balk the government
    cannon.

20   For shame old maniacs – bring down those toss'd arms, and let your white hair be,
Here gape your great grandsons, their wives gaze at them from the windows,
See how well dress'd, see how orderly they conduct themselves.

Worse and worse – can't you stand it? are you retreating?
Is this hour with the living too dead for you?

Retreat then – pell-mell!
To your graves – back – back to the hills old limpers!
I do not think you belong here anyhow.

But there is one thing that belongs here – shall I tell you what it is, gentlemen of Boston?

I will whisper it to the Mayor, he shall send a committee to England,
30   They shall get a grant from the Parliament, go with a cart to the royal vault,
Dig out King George's coffin, unwrap him quick from the grave-clothes, box up his bones for a journey,
Find a swift Yankee clipper – here is freight for you, black-bellied clipper,
Up with your anchor – shake out your sails – steer straight toward Boston bay.

Now call for the President's marshal again, bring out the government cannon,
Fetch home the roarers from Congress, make another procession, guard it with foot and dragoons.

This centre-piece for them;
Look, all orderly citizens – look from the windows, women!

The committee open the box, set up the regal ribs, glue those that will not stay,
Clap the skull on top of the ribs, and clap a crown on top of the skull.

40   You have got your revenge, old buster – the crown is come
      to its own, and more than its own.

Stick your hands in your pockets, Jonathan – you are a made
    man from this day,
You are mighty cute – and here is one of your bargains.

Europe,
THE 72D AND 73D YEARS OF THESE STATES

Suddenly out of its stale and drowsy lair, the lair of slaves,
Like lightning it le'pt forth half startled at itself,
Its feet upon the ashes and the rags, its hands tight to the
    throats of kings.

O hope and faith!
O aching close of exiled patriots' lives!
O many a sicken'd heart!
Turn back unto this day and make yourselves afresh.

And you, paid to defile the People – you liars, mark!
Not for numberless agonies, murders, lusts,
10   For court thieving in its manifold mean forms, worming
    from his simplicity the poor man's wages,
For many a promise sworn by royal lips and broken and
    laugh'd at in the breaking,
Then in their power not for all these did the blows strike
    revenge, or the heads of the nobles fall;
The People scorn'd the ferocity of kings.

But the sweetness of mercy brew'd bitter destruction, and
    the frighten'd monarchs come back,
Each comes in state with his train, hangman, priest,
    tax-gatherer,
Soldier, lawyer, lord, jailer, and sycophant.

Yet behind all lowering stealing, lo, a shape,
Vague as the night, draped interminably, head, front and
    form, in scarlet folds,

Whose face and eyes none may see,
20 Out of its robes only this, the red robes lifted by the arm,
One finger crook'd pointed high over the top, like the head
of a snake appears.

Meanwhile corpses lie in new-made graves, bloody corpses
of young men,
The rope of the gibbet hangs heavily, the bullets of princes
are flying, the creatures of power laugh aloud,
And all these things bear fruits, and they are good.

Those corpses of young men,
Those martyrs that hang from the gibbets, those hearts
pierc'd by the gray lead,
Cold and motionless as they seem live elsewhere with
unslaughter'd vitality.

They live in other young men O kings!
They live in brothers again ready to defy you,
30 They were purified by death, they were taught and exalted.

Not a grave of the murder'd for freedom but grows seed for
freedom, in its turn to bear seed,
Which the winds carry afar and re-sow, and the rains and
the snows nourish.

Not a disembodied spirit can the weapons of tyrants let
loose,
But it stalks invisibly over the earth, whispering, counseling,
cautioning.

Liberty, let others despair of you – I never despair of you.

Is the house shut? is the master away?
Nevertheless, be ready, be not weary of watching,
He will soon return, his messengers come anon.

A Hand-Mirror

Hold it up sternly – see this it sends back, (who is it? is it
    you?)
Outside fair costume, within ashes and filth,
No more a flashing eye, no more a sonorous voice or
    springy step,
Now some slave's eye, voice, hands, step,
A drunkard's breath, unwholesome eater's face,
    venerealee's flesh,
Lungs rotting away piecemeal, stomach sour and cankerous,
Joints rheumatic, bowels clogged with abomination,
Blood circulating dark and poisonous streams,
Words babble, hearing and touch callous,
10 No brain, no heart left, no magnetism of sex;
Such from one look in this looking-glass ere you go hence,
Such a result so soon – and from such a beginning!

Gods

Lover divine and perfect Comrade,
Waiting content, invisible yet, but certain,
Be thou my God.

Thou, thou, the Ideal Man,
Fair, able, beautiful, content, and loving,
Complete in body and dilate in spirit,
Be thou my God.

O Death, (for Life has served its turn,)
Opener and usher to the heavenly mansion,
10 Be thou my God.

Aught, aught of mightiest, best I see, conceive, or know,
(To break the stagnant tie – thee, thee to free, O soul,)
Be thou my God.

All great ideas, the races' aspirations,
All heroisms, deeds of rapt enthusiasts,
Be ye my Gods.

Or Time and Space,
Or shape of Earth divine and wondrous,
Or some fair shape I viewing, worship,
20   Or lustrous orb of sun or star by night,
Be ye my Gods.

Germs

Forms, qualities, lives, humanity, language, thoughts,
The ones known, and the ones unknown, the ones on the
    stars,
The stars themselves, some shaped, others unshaped,
Wonders as of those countries, the soil, trees, cities,
    inhabitants, whatever they may be,
Splendid suns, the moons and rings, the countless
    combinations and effects,
Such-like, and as good as such-like, visible here or
    anywhere, stand provided for in a handful of space, which
    I extend my arm and half enclose with my hand,
That containing the start of each and all, the virtue, the
    germs of all.

Thoughts

Of ownership – as if one fit to own things could not at
    pleasure enter upon all, and incorporate them into
    himself or herself;
Of vista – suppose some sight in arriere through the
    formative chaos, presuming the growth, fulness, life, now
    attain'd on the journey,
(But I see the road continued, and the journey ever
    continued;)

Of what was once lacking on earth, and in due time has
　　become supplied – and of what will yet be supplied,
Because all I see and know I believe to have its main purport
　　in what will yet be supplied.

When I Heard the Learn'd Astronomer

When I heard the learn'd astronomer,
When the proofs, the figures, were ranged in columns before
　　me,
When I was shown the charts and diagrams, to add, divide,
　　and measure them,
When I sitting heard the astronomer where he lectured with
　　much applause in the lecture-room,
How soon unaccountable I became tired and sick,
Till rising and gliding out I wander'd off by myself,
In the mystical moist night-air, and from time to time,
Look'd up in perfect silence at the stars.

Perfections

Only themselves understand themselves and the like of
　　themselves,
As souls only understand souls.

O Me! O Life!

O me! O life! of the questions of these recurring,
Of the endless trains of the faithless, of cities fill'd with the
　　foolish,
Of myself forever reproaching myself, (for who more
　　foolish than I, and who more faithless?)
Of eyes that vainly crave the light, of the objects mean, of
　　the struggle ever renew'd,

Of the poor results of all, of the plodding and sordid
    crowds I see around me,
Of the empty and useless years of the rest, with the rest me
    intertwined,
The question, O me! so sad, recurring – What good amid
    these, O me, O life?

Answer
That you are here – that life exists and identity,
That the powerful play goes on, and you may
    contribute a verse.

To a President

All you are doing and saying is to America dangled mirages,
You have not learn'd of Nature – of the politics of Nature
    you have not learn'd the great amplitude, rectitude,
    impartiality,
You have not seen that only such as they are for these States,
And that what is less than they must sooner or later lift off
    from these States.

I Sit and Look Out

I sit and look out upon all the sorrows of the world, and
    upon all oppression and shame,
I hear secret convulsive sobs from young men at anguish
    with themselves, remorseful after deeds done,
I see in low life the mother misused by her children, dying,
    neglected, gaunt, desperate,
I see the wife misused by her husband, I see the
    treacherous seducer of young women,
I mark the ranklings of jealousy and unrequited love
    attempted to be hid, I see these sights on the earth,
I see the workings of battle, pestilence, tyranny, I see
    martyrs and prisoners,

I observe a famine at sea, I observe the sailors casting lots
 who shall be kill'd to preserve the lives of the rest,
I observe the slights and degradations cast by arrogant
 persons upon laborers, the poor, and upon negroes, and
 the like;
All these – all the meanness and agony without end I sitting
 look out upon,
10 See, hear, and am silent.

To Rich Givers

What you give me I cheerfully accept,
A little sustenance, a hut and garden, a little money, as I
 rendezvous with my poems,
A traveler's lodging and breakfast as I journey through the
 States, – why should I be ashamed to own such gifts? why
 to advertise for them?
For I myself am not one who bestows nothing upon man
 and woman,
For I bestow upon any man or woman the entrance to all
 the gifts of the universe.

The Dalliance of the Eagles

Skirting the river road, (my forenoon walk, my rest,)
Skyward in air a sudden muffled sound, the dalliance of the
 eagles,
The rushing amorous contact high in space together,
The clinching interlocking claws, a living, fierce, gyrating
 wheel,
Four beating wings, two beaks, a swirling mass tight
 grappling,
In tumbling turning clustering loops, straight downward
 falling,
Till o'er the river pois'd, the twain yet one, a moment's lull,

A motionless still balance in the air, then parting, talons
    loosing,
Upward again on slow-firm pinions slanting, their separate
    diverse flight,
10 She hers, he his, pursuing.

Roaming in Thought
(AFTER READING HEGEL)

Roaming in thought over the Universe, I saw the little that is
    Good steadily hastening towards immortality,
And the vast all that is call'd Evil I saw hastening to merge
    itself and become lost and dead.

A Farm Picture

Through the ample open door of the peaceful country barn,
A sunlit pasture field with cattle and horses feeding,
And haze and vista, and the far horizon fading away.

A Child's Amaze

Silent and amazed even when a little boy,
I remember I heard the preacher every Sunday put God in
    his statements,
As contending against some being or influence.

The Runner

On a flat road runs the well-train'd runner,
He is lean and sinewy with muscular legs,
He is thinly clothed, he leans forward as he runs,
With lightly closed fists and arms partially rais'd.

Beautiful Women

Women sit or move to and fro, some old, some young,
The young are beautiful – but the old are more beautiful
    than the young.

Mother and Babe

I see the sleeping babe nestling the breast of its mother,
The sleeping mother and babe – hush'd, I study them long
    and long.

Thought

Of obedience, faith, adhesiveness;
As I stand aloof and look there is to me something
    profoundly affecting in large masses of men following the
    lead of those who do not believe in men.

Visor'd

A mask, a perpetual natural disguiser of herself,
Concealing her face, concealing her form,
Changes and transformations every hour, every moment,
Falling upon her even when she sleeps.

Thought

Of Justice – as if Justice could be any thing but the same
    ample law, expounded by natural judges and saviors,
As if it might be this thing or that thing, according to
    decisions.

Gliding o'er All

Gliding o'er all, through all,
Through Nature, Time, and Space,
As a ship on the waters advancing,
The voyage of the soul – not life alone,
Death, many deaths I'll sing.

Hast Never Come to Thee an Hour

Hast never come to thee an hour,
A sudden gleam divine, precipitating, bursting all these
    bubbles, fashions, wealth?
These eager business aims – books, politics, art, amours,
To utter nothingness?

Thought

Of Equality – as if it harm'd me, giving others the same
    chances and rights as myself – as if it were not
    indispensable to my own rights that others possess the
    same.

To Old Age

I see in you the estuary that enlarges and spreads itself
    grandly as it pours in the great sea.

Locations and Times

Locations and times – what is it in me that meets them all,
    whenever and wherever, and makes me at home?
Forms, colors, densities, odors – what is it in me that
    corresponds with them?

Offerings

A thousand perfect men and women appear,
Around each gathers a cluster of friends, and gay children
    and youths, with offerings.

To the States,
TO IDENTIFY THE 16TH, 17TH, OR 18TH
PRESENTIAD

Why reclining, interrogating? why myself and all drowsing?
What deepening twilight – scum floating atop of the waters,
Who are they as bats and night-dogs askant in the capitol?
What a filthy Presidentiad! (O South, your torrid suns! O
    North, your arctic freezings!)
Are those really Congressmen? are those the great Judges?
    is that the President?
Then I will sleep awhile yet, for I see that these States sleep,
    for reasons;
(With gathering murk, with muttering thunder and lambent
    shoots we all duly awake,
South, North, East, West, inland and seaboard, we will
    surely awake.)

DRUM-TAPS

First O Songs for a Prelude

First O songs for a prelude,
Lightly strike on the stretch'd tympanum pride and joy in
    my city,
How she led the rest to arms, how she gave the cue,
How at once with lithe limbs unwaiting a moment she
    sprang,
(O superb! O Manhattan, my own, my peerless!
O strongest you in the hour of danger, in crisis! O truer
    than steel!)
How you sprang – how you threw off the costumes of peace
    with indifferent hand,
How your soft opera-music changed, and the drum and
    fife were heard in their stead,
How you led to the war, (that shall serve for our prelude,
    songs of soldiers,)
10 How Manhattan drum-taps led.

Forty years had I in my city seen soldiers parading,
Forty years as a pageant, till unawares the lady of this
    teeming and turbulent city,
Sleepless amid her ships, her houses, her incalculable
    wealth,
With her million children around her, suddenly,
At dead of night, at news from the south,
Incens'd struck with clinch'd hand the pavement.

A shock electric, the night sustain'd it,
Till with ominous hum our hive at daybreak pour'd out its
    myriads.

From the houses then and the workshops, and through all
    the doorways,
20 Leapt they tumultuous, and lo! Manhattan arming.

To the drum-taps prompt,
The young men falling in and arming,

The mechanics arming, (the trowel, the jack-plane, the
    blacksmith's hammer, tost aside with precipitation,)
The lawyer leaving his office and arming, the judge leaving
    the court,
The driver deserting his wagon in the street, jumping down,
    throwing the reins abruptly down on the horses' backs,
The salesman leaving the store, the boss, book-keeper,
    porter, all leaving;
Squads gather everywhere by common consent and arm,
The new recruits, even boys, the old men show them how
    to wear their accoutrements, they buckle the straps
    carefully,
Outdoors arming, indoors arming, the flash of the
    musket-barrels,
30   The white tents cluster in camps, the arm'd sentries around,
    the sunrise cannon and again at sunset,
Arm'd regiments arrive every day, pass through the city, and
    embark from the wharves,
(How good they look as they tramp down to the river,
    sweaty, with their guns on their shoulders!
How I love them! how I could hug them, with their brown
    faces and their clothes and knapsacks cover'd with dust!)
The blood of the city up – arm'd! arm'd! the cry
    everywhere,
The flags flung out from the steeples of churches and from
    all the public buildings and stores,
The tearful parting, the mother kisses her son, the son kisses
    his mother,
(Loth is the mother to part, yet not a word does she speak to
    detain him,)
The tumultuous escort, the ranks of policemen preceding,
    clearing the way,
The unpent enthusiasm, the wild cheers of the crowd for
    their favorites,
40   The artillery, the silent cannons bright as gold, drawn along,
    rumble lightly over the stones,
(Silent cannons, soon to cease your silence,
Soon unlimber'd to begin the red business;)

All the mutter of preparation, all the determin'd arming,
The hospital service, the lint, bandages and medicines,
The women volunteering for nurses, the work begun for in
earnest, no mere parade now;
War! an arm'd race is advancing! the welcome for battle, no
turning away;
War! be it weeks, months, or years, an arm'd race is
advancing to welcome it.

Mannahatta a-march – and it's O to sing it well!
It's O for a manly life in the camp.

50 And the sturdy artillery,
The guns bright as gold, the work for giants, to serve well
the guns,
Unlimber them! (no more as the past forty years for salutes
for courtesies merely,
Put in something now besides powder and wadding.)

And you lady of ships, you Mannahatta,
Old matron of this proud, friendly, turbulent city,
Often in peace and wealth you were pensive or covertly
frown'd amid all your children,
But now you smile with joy exulting old Mannahatta.

Eighteen Sixty-One

Arm'd year – year of the struggle,
No dainty rhymes or sentimental love verses for you terrible
year,
Not you as some pale poetling seated at a desk lisping
cadenzas piano,
But as a strong man erect, clothed in blue clothes,
advancing, carrying a rifle on your shoulder,
With well-gristled body and sunburnt face and hands, with
a knife in the belt at your side,
As I heard you shouting loud, your sonorous voice ringing
across the continent,

Your masculine voice O year, as rising amid the great cities,
Amid the men of Manhattan I saw you as one of the
    workmen, the dwellers in Manhattan,
Or with large steps crossing the prairies out of Illinois and
    Indiana,
10   Rapidly crossing the West with springy gait, and descending
    the Alleghanies,
Or down from the great lakes or in Pennsylvania, or on deck
    along the Ohio river,
Or southward along the Tennessee or Cumberland rivers,
    or at Chattanooga on the mountain top,
Saw I your gait and saw I your sinewy limbs clothed in blue,
    bearing weapons, robust year,
Heard your determin'd voice launch'd forth again and
    again,
Year that suddenly sang by the mouths of the round-lipp'd
    cannon,
I repeat you, hurrying, crashing, sad, distracted year.

Beat! Beat! Drums!

Beat! beat! drums! – blow! bugles! blow!
Through the windows – through doors – burst like a
    ruthless force,
Into the solemn church, and scatter the congregation,
Into the school where the scholar is studying;
Leave not the bridegroom quiet – no happiness must he have
    now with his bride,
Nor the peaceful farmer any peace, ploughing his field or
    gathering his grain,
So fierce you whirr and pound you drums – so shrill you
    bugles blow.

Beat! beat! drums! – blow! bugles! blow!
Over the traffic of cities – over the rumble of wheels in the
    streets;

10 Are beds prepared for sleepers at night in the houses? no
      sleepers must sleep in those beds,
    No bargainers' bargains by day – no brokers or
      speculators – would they continue?
    Would the talkers be talking? would the singer attempt to
      sing?
    Would the lawyer rise in the court to state his case before the
      judge?
    Then rattle quicker, heavier drums – you bugles wilder
      blow.

    Beat! beat! drums! – blow! bugles! blow!
    Make no parley – stop for no expostulation,
    Mind not the timid – mind not the weeper or prayer,
    Mind not the old man beseeching the young man,
    Let not the child's voice be heard, nor the mother's
      entreaties,
20 Make even the trestles to shake the dead where they lie
      awaiting the hearses,
    So strong you thump O terrible drums – so loud you bugles
      blow.

From Paumanok Starting I Fly Like a Bird

From Paumanok starting I fly like a bird,
Around and around to soar to sing the idea of all,
To the north betaking myself to sing there arctic songs,
To Kanada till I absorb Kanada in myself, to Michigan
  then,
To Wisconsin, Iowa, Minnesota, to sing their songs, (they
  are inimitable;)
Then to Ohio and Indiana to sing theirs, to Missouri and
  Kansas and Arkansas to sing theirs,
To Tennessee and Kentucky, to the Carolinas and Georgia
  to sing theirs,
To Texas and so along up toward California, to roam
  accepted everywhere;

To sing first, (to the tap of the war-drum if need be,)
10 The idea of all, of the Western world one and inseparable,
And then the song of each member of these States.

Song of the Banner at Daybreak

POET
O a new song, a free song,
Flapping, flapping, flapping, flapping, by sounds, by voices
    clearer,
By the wind's voice and that of the drum,
By the banner's voice and child's voice and sea's voice and
    father's voice,
Low on the ground and high in the air,
On the ground where father and child stand,
In the upward air where their eyes turn,
Where the banner at daybreak is flapping.

Words! book-words! what are you?
10 Words no more, for hearken and see,
My song is there in the open air, and I must sing,
With the banner and pennant a-flapping.

I'll weave the chord and twine in,
Man's desire and babe's desire, I'll twine them in, I'll put
    in life,
I'll put the bayonet's flashing point, I'll let bullets and
    slugs whizz,
(As one carrying a symbol and menace far into the future,
Crying with trumpet voice, *Arouse and beware! Beware and
    arouse!*)
I'll pour the verse with streams of blood, full of volition,
    full of joy,
Then loosen, launch forth, to go and compete,
20 With the banner and pennant a-flapping.

PENNANT

Come up here, bard, bard,
Come up here, soul, soul,
Come up here, dear little child,
To fly in the clouds and winds with me, and play with the
    measureless light.

CHILD

Father what is that in the sky beckoning to me with long
    finger?
And what does it say to me all the while?

FATHER

Nothing my babe you see in the sky,
And nothing at all to you it says – but look you my babe,
Look at these dazzling things in the houses, and see you the
    money-shops opening,
30   And see you the vehicles preparing to crawl along the streets
    with goods;
These, ah these, how valued and toil'd for these!
How envied by all the earth.

POET

Fresh and rosy red the sun is mounting high,
On floats the sea in distant blue careering through its
    channels,
On floats the wind over the breast of the sea setting in
    toward land,
The great steady wind from west or west-by-south,
Floating so buoyant with milk-white foam on the waters.

But I am not the sea nor the red sun,
I am not the wind with girlish laughter,
40   Not the immense wind which strengthens, not the wind
    which lashes,
Not the spirit that ever lashes its own body to terror and
    death,
But I am that which unseen comes and sings, sings, sings,
Which babbles in brooks and scoots in showers on the land,
Which the birds know in the woods mornings and evenings,

And the shore-sands know and the hissing wave, and that
    banner and pennant,
Aloft there flapping and flapping.

CHILD
O father it is alive – it is full of people – it has children,
O now it seems to me it is talking to its children,
I hear it – it talks to me – O it is wonderful!
50 O it stretches – it spreads and runs so fast – O my father,
It is so broad it covers the whole sky.

FATHER
Cease, cease, my foolish babe,
What you are saying is sorrowful to me, much it displeases
    me;
Behold with the rest again I say, behold not banners and
    pennants aloft,
But the well-prepared pavements behold, and mark the
    solid-wall'd houses.

BANNER AND PENNANT
Speak to the child O bard out of Manhattan,
To our children all, or north or south of Manhattan,
Point this day, leaving all the rest, to us over all – and yet we
    know not why,
For what are we, mere strips of cloth profiting nothing,
60 Only flapping in the wind?

POET
I hear and see not strips of cloth alone,
I hear the tramp of armies, I hear the challenging sentry,
I hear the jubilant shouts of millions of men, I hear
    Liberty!
I hear the drums beat and the trumpets blowing,
I myself move abroad swift-rising flying then,
I use the wings of the land-bird and use the wings of the
    sea-bird, and look down as from a height,
I do not deny the precious results of peace, I see populous
    cities with wealth incalculable,

I see numberless farms, I see the farmers working in their
    fields or barns,
I see mechanics working, I see buildings everywhere
    founded, going up, or finish'd,
70   I see trains of cars swiftly speeding along railroad tracks
    drawn by the locomotives,
I see the stores, depots, of Boston, Baltimore, Charleston,
    New Orleans,
I see far in the West the immense area of grain, I dwell
    awhile hovering,
I pass to the lumber forests of the North, and again to the
    Southern plantation, and again to California;
Sweeping the whole I see the countless profit, the busy
    gatherings, earn'd wages,
See the Identity formed out of thirty-eight spacious and
    haughty States, (and many more to come,)
See forts on the shores of harbors, see ships sailing in and
    out;
Then over all, (aye! aye!) my little and lengthen'd pennant
    shaped like a sword,
Runs swiftly up indicating war and defiance – and now the
    halyards have rais'd it,
Side of my banner broad and blue, side of my starry
    banner,
80   Discarding peace over all the sea and land.

BANNER AND PENNANT

Yet louder, higher, stronger, bard! yet farther, wider cleave!
No longer let our children deem us riches and peace alone,
We may be terror and carnage, and are so now,
Not now are we any one of these spacious and haughty
    States, (nor any five, nor ten,)
Nor market nor depot we, nor money-bank in the city,
But these and all, and the brown and spreading land, and the
    mines below, are ours,
And the shores of the sea are ours, and the rivers great and
    small,

And the fields they moisten, and the crops and the fruits
    are ours,
Bays and channels and ships sailing in and out are ours –
    while we over all,
90   Over the area spread below, the three or four millions of
    square miles, the capitals,
The forty millions of people, – O bard! in life and death
    supreme,
We, even we, henceforth flaunt out masterful, high up
    above,
Not for the present alone, for a thousand years chanting
    through you,
This song to the soul of one poor little child.

CHILD
O my father I like not the houses,
They will never to me be any thing, nor do I like money,
But to mount up there I would like, O father dear, that
    banner I like,
That pennant I would be and must be.

FATHER
Child of mine you fill me with anguish,
100 To be that pennant would be too fearful,
Little you know what it is this day, and after this day,
    forever,
It is to gain nothing, but risk and defy every thing,
Forward to stand in front of wars – and O, such wars! –
    what have you to do with them?
With passions of demons, slaughter, premature death?

BANNER
Demons and death then I sing,
Put in all, aye all will I, sword-shaped pennant for war,
And a pleasure new and ecstatic, and the prattled yearning
    of children,
Blent with the sounds of the peaceful land and the liquid
    wash of the sea,
And the black ships fighting on the sea envelop'd in smoke,

110 And the icy cool of the far, far north, with rustling cedars
    and pines,
And the whirr of drums and the sound of soldiers marching,
    and the hot sun shining south,
And the beach-waves combing over the beach on my
    Eastern shore, and my Western shore the same,
And all between those shores, and my ever running
    Mississippi with bends and chutes,
And my Illinois fields, and my Kansas fields, and my fields
    of Missouri,
The Continent, devoting the whole identity without
    reserving an atom,
Pour in! whelm that which asks, which sings, with all and
    the yield of all,
Fusing and holding, claiming, devouring the whole,
No more with tender lip, nor musical labial sound,
But out of the night emerging for good, our voice persuasive
    no more,
120 Croaking like crows here in the wind.

POET
My limbs, my veins dilate, my theme is clear at last,
Banner so broad advancing out of the night, I sing you
    haughty and resolute,
I burst through where I waited long, too long, deafen'd and
    blinded,
My hearing and tongue are come to me, (a little child
    taught me,)
I hear from above O pennant of war your ironical call and
    demand,
Insensate! insensate! (yet I at any rate chant you,) O
    banner!
Not houses of peace indeed are you, nor any nor all their
    prosperity, (if need be, you shall again have every one of
    those houses to destroy them,
You thought not to destroy those valuable houses, standing
    fast, full of comfort, built with money,

May they stand fast, then? not an hour except you above
    them and all stand fast;)
130 O banner, not money so precious are you, not farm produce
    you, nor the material good nutriment,
Nor excellent stores, nor landed on wharves from the ships,
Not the superb ships with sail-power or steam-power,
    fetching and carrying cargoes,
Nor machinery, vehicles, trade, nor revenues – but you as
    henceforth I see you,
Running up out of the night, bringing your cluster of stars,
    (ever-enlarging stars,)
Divider of daybreak you, cutting the air, touch'd by the sun,
    measuring the sky,
(Passionately seen and yearn'd for by one poor little child,
While others remain busy or smartly talking, forever
    teaching thrift, thrift;)
O you up there! O pennant! where you undulate like a
    snake hissing so curious,
Out of reach, an idea only, yet furiously fought for, risking
    bloody death, loved by me,
140 So loved – O you banner leading the day with stars brought
    from the night!
Valueless, object of eyes, over all and demanding all –
    (absolute owner of all) – O banner and pennant!
I too leave the rest – great as it is, it is nothing – houses,
    machines are nothing – I see them not,
I see but you, O warlike pennant! O banner so broad, with
    stripes, I sing you only,
Flapping up there in the wind.

Rise O Days from Your Fathomless Deeps

1
Rise O days from your fathomless deeps, till you loftier,
    fiercer sweep,
Long for my soul hungering gymnastic I devour'd what the
    earth gave me,

Long I roam'd the woods of the north, long I watch'd
   Niagara pouring,
I travel'd the prairies over and slept on their breast, I
   cross'd the Nevadas, I cross'd the plateaus,
I ascended the towering rocks along the Pacific, I sail'd out
   to sea,
I sail'd through the storm, I was refresh'd by the storm,
I watch'd with joy the threatening maws of the waves,
I mark'd the white combs where they career'd so high,
   curling over,
I heard the wind piping, I saw the black clouds,
10   Saw from below what arose and mounted, (O superb! O
   wild as my heart, and powerful!)
Heard the continuous thunder as it bellow'd after the
   lightning,
Noted the slender and jagged threads of lightning as sudden
   and fast amid the din they chased each other across
   the sky;
These, and such as these, I, elate, saw – saw with wonder,
   yet pensive and masterful,
All the menacing might of the globe uprisen around me,
Yet there with my soul I fed, I fed content, supercilious.

2
'Twas well, O soul – 'twas a good preparation you gave me,
Now we advance our latent and ampler hunger to fill,
Now we go forth to receive what the earth and the sea never
   gave us,
Not through the mighty woods we go, but through the
   mightier cities,
20   Something for us is pouring now more than Niagara
   pouring,
Torrents of men, (sources and rills of the Northwest are you
   indeed inexhaustible?)
What, to pavements and homesteads here, what were those
   storms of the mountains and sea?
What, to passions I witness around me to-day? was the
   sea risen?

Was the wind piping the pipe of death under the black
    clouds?
Lo! from deeps more unfathomable, something more deadly
    and savage,
Manhattan rising, advancing with menacing front –
    Cincinnati, Chicago, unchain'd;
What was that swell I saw on the ocean? behold what comes
    here,
How it climbs with daring feet and hands – how it dashes!
How the true thunder bellows after the lightning – how
    bright the flashes of lightning!
30 How Democracy with desperate vengeful port strides on,
    shown through the dark by those flashes of lightning!
(Yet a mournful wail and low sob I fancied I heard through
    the dark,
In a lull of the deafening confusion.)

3
Thunder on! stride on, Democracy! strike with vengeful
    stroke!
And do you rise higher than ever yet O days, O cities!
Crash heavier, heavier yet O storms! you have done me
    good,
My soul prepared in the mountains absorbs your immortal
    strong nutriment,
Long had I walk'd my cities, my country roads through
    farms, only half satisfied,
One doubt nauseous undulating like a snake, crawl'd on the
    ground before me,
Continually preceding my steps, turning upon me oft,
    ironically hissing low;
40 The cities I loved so well I abandon'd and left, I sped to the
    certainties suitable to me,
Hungering, hungering, hungering, for primal energies and
    Nature's dauntlessness,
I refresh'd myself with it only, I could relish it only,
I waited the bursting forth of the pent fire – on the water and
    air I waited long;

But now I no longer wait, I am fully satisfied, I am glutted,
I have witness'd the true lightning, I have witness'd my
    cities electric,
I have lived to behold man burst forth and warlike America
    rise,
Hence I will seek no more the food of the northern solitary
    wilds,
No more the mountains roam or sail the stormy sea.

Virginia – the West

The noble sire fallen on evil days,
I saw with hand uplifted, menacing, brandishing,
(Memories of old in abeyance, love and faith in abeyance,)
The insane knife towards the Mother of All.

The noble son on sinewy feet advancing,
I saw, out of the land of prairies, land of Ohio's waters and
    of Indiana,
To the rescue the stalwart giant hurry his plenteous
    offspring,
Drest in blue, bearing their trusty rifles on their shoulders.

Then the Mother of All with calm voice speaking,
10 As to you Rebellious, (I seemed to hear her say,) why strive
    against me, and why seek my life?
When you yourself forever provide to defend me?
For you provided me Washington – and now these also.

City of Ships

City of ships!
(O the black ships! O the fierce ships!
O the beautiful sharp-bow'd steam-ships and sail-ships!)
City of the world! (for all races are here,
All the lands of the earth make contributions here;)
City of the sea! city of hurried and glittering tides!

City whose gleeful tides continually rush or recede, whirling
    in and out with eddies and foam!
City of wharves and stores – city of tall façades of marble and
    iron!
Proud and passionate city – mettlesome, mad, extravagant
    city!
10 Spring up O city – not for peace alone, but be indeed
    yourself, warlike!
Fear not – submit to no models but your own O city!
Behold me – incarnate me as I have incarnated you!
I have rejected nothing you offer'd me – whom you adopted
    I have adopted,
Good or bad I never question you – I love all – I do not
    condemn any thing,
I chant and celebrate all that is yours – yet peace no more,
In peace I chanted peace, but now the drum of war is mine,
War, red war is my song through your streets, O city!

The Centenarian's Story
VOLUNTEER OF 1861–2 (AT WASHINGTON PARK,
BROOKLYN, ASSISTING THE CENTENARIAN)

Give me your hand old Revolutionary,
The hill-top is nigh, but a few steps, (make room
    gentlemen,)
Up the path you have follow'd me well, spite of your
    hundred and extra years,
You can walk old man, though your eyes are almost done,
Your faculties serve you, and presently I must have them
    serve me.

Rest, while I tell what the crowd around us means,
On the plain below recruits are drilling and exercising,
There is the camp, one regiment departs to-morrow,
Do you hear the officers giving their orders?
10 Do you hear the clank of the muskets?

Why what comes over you now old man?
Why do you tremble and clutch my hand so convulsively?
The troops are but drilling, they are yet surrounded with
     smiles,
Around them at hand the well-drest friends and the women,
While splendid and warm the afternoon sun shines down,
Green the midsummer verdure and fresh blows the
     dallying breeze,
O'er proud and peaceful cities and arm of the sea between.

But drill and parade are over, they march back to quarters,
Only hear that approval of hands! hear what a clapping!

20 As wending the crowds now part and disperse – but we old
     man,
Not for nothing have I brought you hither – we must
     remain,
You to speak in your turn, and I to listen and tell.

THE CENTENARIAN
When I clutch'd your hand it was not with terror,
But suddenly pouring about me here on every side,
And below there where the boys were drilling, and up the
     slopes they ran,
And where tents are pitch'd, and wherever you see south and
     south-east and south-west,
Over hills, across lowlands, and in the skirts of woods,
And along the shores, in mire (now fill'd over) came again
     and suddenly raged,
As eighty-five years a-gone no mere parade receiv'd with
     applause of friends,
30 But a battle which I took part in myself – aye, long ago as it
     is, I took part in it,
Walking then this hilltop, this same ground.

Aye, this is the ground,
My blind eyes even as I speak behold it re-peopled from
     graves,
The years recede, pavements and stately houses disappear,
Rude forts appear again, the old hoop'd guns are mounted,

I see the lines of rais'd earth stretching from river to bay,
I mark the vista of waters, I mark the uplands and slopes;
Here we lay encamp'd, it was this time in summer also.

As I talk I remember all, I remember the Declaration,
40   It was read here, the whole army paraded, it was read to us
     here,
By his staff surrounded the General stood in the middle, he
     held up his unsheath'd sword,
It glitter'd in the sun in full sight of the army.

'Twas a bold act then – the English war-ships had just
     arrived,
We could watch down the lower bay where they lay at
     anchor,
And the transports swarming with soldiers.

A few days more and they landed, and then the battle.

Twenty thousand were brought against us,
A veteran force furnish'd with good artillery.

I tell not now the whole of the battle,
50   But one brigade early in the forenoon order'd forward to
     engage the red-coats,
Of that brigade I tell, and how steadily it march'd,
And how long and well it stood confronting death.

Who do you think that was marching steadily sternly
     confronting death?
It was the brigade of the youngest men, two thousand
     strong,
Rais'd in Virginia and Maryland, and most of them known
     personally to the General.

Jauntily forward they went with quick step toward
     Gowanus' waters,
Till of a sudden unlook'd for by defiles through the woods,
     gain'd at night,
The British advancing, rounding in from the east, fiercely
     playing their guns,

That brigade of the youngest was cut off and at the
enemy's mercy.

60 The General watch'd them from this hill,
They made repeated desperate attempts to burst their
environment,
Then drew close together, very compact, their flag flying in
the middle,
But O from the hills how the cannon were thinning and
thinning them!

It sickens me yet, that slaughter!
I saw the moisture gather in drops on the face of the
General.
I saw how he wrung his hands in anguish.

Meanwhile the British manoeuvr'd to draw us out for a
pitch'd battle,
But we dared not trust the chances of a pitch'd battle.

We fought the fight in detachments,
70 Sallying forth we fought at several points, but in each the
luck was against us,
Our foe advancing, steadily getting the best of it, push'd us
back to the works on this hill,
Till we turn'd menacing here, and then he left us.

That was the going out of the brigade of the youngest men,
two thousand strong,
Few return'd, nearly all remain in Brooklyn.

That and here my General's first battle,
No women looking on nor sunshine to bask in, it did not
conclude with applause,
Nobody clapp'd hands here then.

But in darkness in mist on the ground under a chill rain,
Wearied that night we lay foil'd and sullen,
80 While scornfully laugh'd many an arrogant lord off against
us encamp'd,

Quite within hearing, feasting, clinking wineglasses
  together over their victory.

So dull and damp and another day,
But the night of that, mist lifting, rain ceasing,
Silent as a ghost while they thought they were sure of him,
  my General retreated.

I saw him at the river-side,
Down by the ferry lit by torches, hastening the embarcation;
My General waited till the soldiers and wounded were all
  pass'd over,
And then, (it was just ere sunrise,) these eyes rested on him
  for the last time.

Every one else seem'd fill'd with gloom,
90 Many no doubt thought of capitulation.

But when my General pass'd me,
As he stood in his boat and look'd toward the coming sun,
I saw something different from capitulation.

TERMINUS
Enough, the Centenarian's story ends,
The two, the past and present, have interchanged,
I myself as connecter, as chansonnier of a great future,
  am now speaking.

And is this the ground Washington trod?
And these waters I listlessly daily cross, are these the waters
  he cross'd,
As resolute in defeat as other generals in their proudest
  triumphs?

100 I must copy the story, and send it eastward and westward,
I must preserve that look as it beam'd on you rivers of
  Brooklyn.

See – as the annual round returns the phantoms return,
It is the 27th of August and the British have landed,
The battle begins and goes against us, behold through the
  smoke Washington's face,

The brigade of Virginia and Maryland have march'd forth
    to intercept the enemy,
They are cut off, murderous artillery from the hills plays
    upon them,
Rank after rank falls, while over them silently droops the
    flag,
Baptized that day in many a young man's bloody wounds,
In death, defeat, and sisters', mothers' tears.

110 Ah, hills and slopes of Brooklyn! I perceive you are more
    valuable than your owners supposed;
In the midst of you stands an encampment very old,
Stands forever the camp of that dead brigade.

Cavalry Crossing a Ford

A line in long array where they wind betwixt green islands,
They take a serpentine course, their arms flash in the sun –
    hark to the musical clank,
Behold the silvery river, in it the splashing horses loitering
    stop to drink,
Behold the brown-faced men, each group, each person a
    picture, the negligent rest on the saddles,
Some emerge on the opposite bank, others are just entering
    the ford – while,
Scarlet and blue and snowy white,
The guidon flags flutter gayly in the wind.

Bivouac on a Mountain Side

I see before me now a traveling army halting,
Below a fertile valley spread, with barns and the orchards of
    summer,
Behind, the terraced sides of a mountain, abrupt, in places
    rising high,

Broken, with rocks, with clinging cedars, with tall shapes
   dingily seen,
The numerous camp-fires scatter'd near and far, some away
   up on the mountain,
The shadowy forms of men and horses, looming, large-sized,
   flickering,
And over all the sky – the sky! far, far out of reach, studded,
   breaking out, the eternal stars.

An Army Corps on the March

With its cloud of skirmishers in advance,
With now the sound of a single shot snapping like a whip,
   and now an irregular volley,
The swarming ranks press on and on, the dense brigades
   press on,
Glittering dimly, toiling under the sun – the dust-cover'd
   men,
In columns rise and fall to the undulations of the ground,
With artillery interspers'd – the wheels rumble, the horses
   sweat,
As the army corps advances.

By the Bivouac's Fitful Flame

By the bivouac's fitful flame,
A procession winding around me, solemn and sweet and
   slow – but first I note,
The tents of the sleeping army, the fields' and woods' dim
   outline,
The darkness lit by spots of kindled fire, the silence,
Like a phantom far or near an occasional figure moving,
The shrubs and trees, (as I lift my eyes they seem to be
   stealthily watching me,)
While wind in procession thoughts, O tender and wondrous
   thoughts,

Of life and death, of home and the past and loved, and of
 those that are far away;
A solemn and slow procession there as I sit on the ground,
10 By the bivouac's fitful flame.

Come up from the Fields Father

Come up from the fields father, here's a letter from our
 Pete,
And come to the front door mother, here's a letter from thy
 dear son.

Lo, 'tis autumn,
Lo, where the trees, deeper green, yellower and redder,
Cool and sweeten Ohio's villages with leaves fluttering in
 the moderate wind,
Where apples ripe in the orchard hang and grapes on the
 trellis'd vines,
(Smell you the smell of the grapes on the vines?
Smell you the buckwheat where the bees were lately
 buzzing?)

Above all, lo, the sky so calm, so transparent after the rain,
 and with wondrous clouds,
10 Below too, all calm, all vital and beautiful, and the farm
 prospers well.

Down in the fields all prospers well,
But now from the fields come father, come at the daughter's
 call,
And come to the entry mother, to the front door come right
 away.

Fast as she can she hurries, something ominous, her steps
 trembling,
She does not tarry to smooth her hair nor adjust her cap.

Open the envelope quickly,
O this is not our son's writing, yet his name is sign'd,

O a strange hand writes for our dear son, O stricken
    mother's soul!
All swims before her eyes, flashes with black, she catches the
    main words only,
20 Sentences broken, *gunshot wound in the breast, cavalry
    skirmish, taken to hospital,*
At present low, but will soon be better.

Ah now the single figure to me,
Amid all teeming and wealthy Ohio with all its cities and
    farms,
Sickly white in the face and dull in the head, very faint,
By the jamb of a door leans.

Grieve not so, dear mother, (the just-grown daughter speaks
    through her sobs,
The little sisters huddle around speechless and dismay'd,)
See, dearest mother, the letter says Pete will soon be better.

Alas poor boy, he will never be better, (nor may-be needs
    to be better, that brave and simple soul,)
30 While they stand at home at the door he is dead already,
The only son is dead.

But the mother needs to be better,
She with thin form presently drest in black,
By day her meals untouch'd, then at night fitfully sleeping,
    often waking,
In the midnight waking, weeping, longing with one deep
    longing,
O that she might withdraw unnoticed, silent from life escape
    and withdraw,
To follow, to seek, to be with her dear dead son.

Vigil Strange I Kept on the Field One Night

Vigil strange I kept on the field one night;
When you my son and my comrade dropt at my side that
    day,

One look I but gave which your dear eyes return'd with a
    look I shall never forget,
One touch of your hand to mine O boy, reach'd up as you
    lay on the ground,
Then onward I sped in the battle, the even-contested battle,
Till late in the night reliev'd to the place at last again I made
    my way,
Found you in death so cold, dear comrade, found your body
    son of responding kisses, (never again on earth
    responding,)
Bared your face in the starlight, curious the scene, cool blew
    the moderate night-wind,
Long there and then in vigil I stood, dimly around me the
    battlefield spreading,
10 Vigil wondrous and vigil sweet there in the fragrant silent
    night,
But not a tear fell, not even a long-drawn sigh, long, long I
    gazed,
Then on the earth partially reclining sat by your side leaning
    my chin in my hands,
Passing sweet hours, immortal and mystic hours with you
    dearest comrade – not a tear, not a word,
Vigil of silence, love and death, vigil for you my son and my
    soldier,
As onward silently stars aloft, eastward new ones upward
    stole,
Vigil final for you brave boy, (I could not save you, swift was
    your death,
I faithfully loved you and cared for you living, I think we
    shall surely meet again,)
Till at latest lingering of the night, indeed just as the dawn
    appear'd,
My comrade I wrapt in his blanket, envelop'd well his form,
20 Folded the blanket well, tucking it carefully over head and
    carefully under feet,
And there and then and bathed by the rising sun, my son in
    his grave, in his rude-dug grave I deposited,

Ending my vigil strange with that, vigil of night and
    battle-field dim,
Vigil for boy of responding kisses, (never again on earth
    responding,)
Vigil for comrade swiftly slain, vigil I never forget, how as
    day brighten'd,
I rose from the chill ground and folded my soldier well in
    his blanket,
And buried him where he fell.

A March in the Ranks Hard-Prest,
and the Road Unknown

A march in the ranks hard-prest, and the road unknown,
A route through a heavy wood with muffled steps in the
    darkness,
Our army foil'd with loss severe, and the sullen remnant
    retreating,
Till after midnight glimmer upon us the lights of a
    dim-lighted building,
We come to an open space in the woods, and halt by the
    dim-lighted building,
'Tis a large old church at the crossing roads, now an
    impromptu hospital,
Entering but for a minute I see a sight beyond all the
    pictures and poems ever made,
Shadows of deepest, deepest black, just lit by moving
    candles and lamps,
And by one great pitchy torch stationary with wild red flame
    and clouds of smoke,
10 By these, crowds, groups of forms vaguely I see on the floor,
    some in the pews laid down,
At my feet more distinctly a soldier, a mere lad, in danger of
    bleeding to death, (he is shot in the abdomen,)
I stanch the blood temporarily, (the youngster's face is white
    as a lily,)
Then before I depart I sweep my eyes o'er the scene fain to
    absorb it all,

Faces, varieties, postures beyond description, most in
  obscurity, some of them dead,
Surgeons operating, attendants holding lights, the smell of
  ether, the odor of blood,
The crowd, O the crowd of the bloody forms, the yard
  outside also fill'd,
Some on the bare ground, some on planks or stretchers,
  some in the death-spasm sweating,
An occasional scream or cry, the doctor's shouted orders or
  calls,
The glisten of the little steel instruments catching the glint
  of the torches,
20 These I resume as I chant, I see again the forms, I smell
  the odor,
Then hear outside the orders given, *Fall in, my men, fall in*;
But first I bend to the dying lad, his eyes open, a half-smile
  gives he me,
Then the eyes close, calmly close, and I speed forth to the
  darkness,
Resuming, marching, ever in darkness marching, on in the
  ranks,
The unknown road still marching.

A Sight in Camp in the Daybreak Gray and Dim

A sight in camp in the daybreak gray and dim,
As from my tent I emerge so early sleepless,
As slow I walk in the cool fresh air the path near by the
  hospital tent,
Three forms I see on stretchers lying, brought out there
  untended lying,
Over each the blanket spread, ample brownish woolen
  blanket,
Gray and heavy blanket, folding, covering all.

Curious I halt and silent stand,
Then with light fingers I from the face of the nearest the
    first just lift the blanket;
Who are you elderly man so gaunt and grim, with
    well-gray'd hair, and flesh all sunken about the eyes?
10 Who are you my dear comrade?

Then to the second I step – and who are you my child and
    darling?
Who are you sweet boy with cheeks yet blooming?

Then to the third – a face nor child nor old, very calm, as of
    beautiful yellow-white ivory;
Young man I think I know you – I think this face is the face
    of the Christ himself,
Dead and divine and brother of all, and here again he lies.

As Toilsome I Wander'd Virginia's Woods

As toilsome I wander'd Virginia's woods,
To the music of rustling leaves kick'd by my feet, (for 'twas
    autumn,)
I mark'd at the foot of a tree the grave of a soldier;
Mortally wounded he and buried on the retreat, (easily all
    could I understand,)
The halt of a mid-day hour, when up! no time to lose – yet
    this sign left,
On a tablet scrawl'd and nail'd on the tree by the grave,
Bold, cautious, true, and my loving comrade.

Long, long I muse, then on my way go wandering,
Many a changeful season to follow, and many a scene of life,
10 Yet at times through changeful season and scene, abrupt,
    alone, or in the crowded street,
Comes before me the unknown soldier's grave, comes the
    inscription rude in Virginia's woods,
Bold, cautious, true, and my loving comrade.

Not the Pilot

Not the pilot has charged himself to bring his ship into port,
  though beaten back and many times baffled;
Not the pathfinder penetrating inland weary and long,
By deserts parch'd, snows chill'd, rivers wet, perseveres till
  he reaches his destination,
More than I have charged myself, heeded or unheeded, to
  compose a march for these States,
For a battle-call, rousing to arms if need be, years,
  centuries hence.

Year that Trembled and Reel'd beneath Me

Year that trembled and reel'd beneath me!
Your summer wind was warm enough, yet the air I breathed
  froze me,
A thick gloom fell through the sunshine and darken'd me,
Must I change my triumphant songs? said I to myself,
Must I indeed learn to chant the cold dirges of the baffled?
And sullen hymns of defeat?

The Wound-Dresser

1

An old man bending I come among new faces,
Years looking backward resuming in answer to children,
Come tell us old man, as from young men and maidens that
  love me,
(Arous'd and angry, I'd thought to beat the alarum, and urge
  relentless war,
But soon my fingers fail'd me, my face droop'd and I
  resign'd myself,
To sit by the wounded and soothe them, or silently watch
  the dead;)

Years hence of these scenes, of these furious passions, these
   chances,
Of unsurpass'd heroes, (was one side so brave? the other was
   equally brave;)
Now be witness again, paint the mightiest armies of earth,
10 Of those armies so rapid so wondrous that saw you to tell us?
What stays with you latest and deepest? of curious panics,
Of hard-fought engagements or sieges tremendous what
   deepest remains?

2

O maidens and young men I love and that love me,
What you ask of my days those the strangest and sudden
   your talking recalls,
Soldier alert I arrive after a long march cover'd with sweat
   and dust,
In the nick of time I come, plunge in the fight, loudly shout
   in the rush of successful charge,
Enter the captur'd works – yet lo, like a swift-running river
   they fade,
Pass and are gone they fade – I dwell not on soldiers' perils
   or soldiers' joys,
(Both I remember well – many the hardships, few the joys,
   yet I was content.)

20 But in silence, in dreams' projections,
While the world of gain and appearance and mirth goes on,
So soon what is over forgotten, and waves wash the
   imprints off the sand,
With hinged knees returning I enter the doors, (while for
   you up there,
Whoever you are, follow without noise and be of strong
   heart.)

Bearing the bandages, water and sponge,
Straight and swift to my wounded I go,
Where they lie on the ground after the battle brought in,
Where their priceless blood reddens the grass the ground,

Or to the rows of the hospital tent, or under the roof'd
    hospital,
30 To the long rows of cots up and down each side I return,
To each and all one after another I draw near, not one do I
    miss,
An attendant follows holding a tray, he carries a refuse pail,
Soon to be fill'd with clotted rags and blood, emptied,
    and fill'd again.

I onward go, I stop,
With hinged knees and steady hand to dress wounds,
I am firm with each, the pangs are sharp yet unavoidable,
One turns to me his appealing eyes – poor boy! I never
    knew you,
Yet I think I could not refuse this moment to die for you, if
    that would save you.

3
On, on I go, (open doors of time! open hospital doors!)
40 The crush'd head I dress, (poor crazed hand tear not the
    bandage away,)
The neck of the cavalry-man with the bullet through and
    through I examine,
Hard the breathing rattles, quite glazed already the eye, yet
    life struggles hard,
(Come sweet death! be persuaded O beautiful death!
In mercy come quickly.)

From the stump of the arm, the amputated hand,
I undo the clotted lint, remove the slough, wash off the
    matter and blood,
Back on his pillow the soldier bends with curv'd neck and
    side-falling head,
His eyes are closed, his face is pale, he dares not look on the
    bloody stump,
And has not yet look'd on it.

50   I dress a wound in the side, deep, deep,
But a day or two more, for see the frame all wasted and
    sinking,
And the yellow-blue countenance see.

I dress the perforated shoulder, the foot with the
    bullet-wound,
Cleanse the one with a gnawing and putrid gangrene, so
    sickening, so offensive,
While the attendant stands behind aside me holding the tray
    and pail.

I am faithful, I do not give out,
The fractur'd thigh, the knee, the wound in the abdomen,
These and more I dress with impassive hand, (yet deep in my
    breast a fire, a burning flame.)

4
Thus in silence in dreams' projections,
60   Returning, resuming, I thread my way through the hospitals,
The hurt and wounded I pacify with soothing hand,
I sit by the restless all the dark night, some are so young,
Some suffer so much, I recall the experience sweet and sad,
(Many a soldier's loving arms about this neck have cross'd
    and rested,
Many a soldier's kiss dwells on these bearded lips.)

Long, too Long America

Long, too long America,
Traveling roads all even and peaceful you learn'd from joys
    and prosperity only,
But now, ah now, to learn from crises of anguish, advancing,
    grappling with direst fate and recoiling not,
And now to conceive and show to the world what your
    children en-masse really are,
(For who except myself has yet conceiv'd what your
    children en-masse really are?)

Give Me the Splendid Silent Sun

I

Give me the splendid silent sun with all his beams
full-dazzling,
Give me juicy autumnal fruit ripe and red from the
orchard,
Give me a field where the unmow'd grass grows,
Give me an arbor, give me the trellis'd grape,
Give me fresh corn and wheat, give me serene-moving
animals teaching content,
Give me nights perfectly quiet as on high plateaus west of
the Mississippi, and I looking up at the stars,
Give me odorous at sunrise a garden of beautiful flowers
where I can walk undisturb'd,
Give me for marriage a sweet-breath'd woman of whom I
should never tire,
Give me a perfect child, give me away aside from the noise
of the world a rural domestic life,
Give me to warble spontaneous songs recluse by myself,
for my own ears only,
Give me solitude, give me Nature, give me again O Nature
your primal sanities!

These demanding to have them, (tired with ceaseless
excitement, and rack'd by the war-strife,)
These to procure incessantly asking, rising in cries from my
heart,
While yet incessantly asking still I adhere to my city,
Day upon day and year upon year O city, walking your
streets,
Where you hold me enchain'd a certain time refusing to give
me up,
Yet giving to make me glutted, enrich'd of soul, you give me
forever faces;
(O I see what I sought to escape, confronting, reversing my
cries,
I see my own soul trampling down what it ask'd for.)

2

20   Keep your splendid silent sun,
Keep your woods O Nature, and the quiet places by the
        woods,
Keep your fields of clover and timothy, and your
        corn-fields and orchards,
Keep the blossoming buckwheat fields where the
        Ninth-month bees hum;
Give me faces and streets – give me these phantoms
        incessant and endless along the trottoirs!
Give me interminable eyes – give me women – give me
        comrades and lovers by the thousand!
Let me see new ones every day – let me hold new ones by
        the hand every day!
Give me such shows – give me the streets of Manhattan!
Give me Broadway, with the soldiers marching – give me
        the sound of the trumpets and drums!
(The soldiers in companies or regiments – some starting
        away, flush'd and reckless,
30   Some, their time up, returning with thinn'd ranks, young,
        yet very old, worn, marching, noticing nothing;)
Give me the shores and wharves heavy-fringed with black
        ships!
O such for me! O an intense life, full to repletion and
        varied!
The life of the theatre, bar-room, huge hotel, for me!
The saloon of the steamer! the crowded excursion for me!
        the torchlight procession!
The dense brigade bound for the war, with high piled
        military wagons following;
People, endless, streaming, with strong voices, passions,
        pageants,
Manhattan streets with their powerful throbs, with beating
        drums as now,
The endless and noisy chorus, the rustle and clank of
        muskets, (even the sight of the wounded,)
Manhattan crowds, with their turbulent musical chorus!
40   Manhattan faces and eyes forever for me.

Dirge for Two Veterans

The last sunbeam
Lightly falls from the finish'd Sabbath,
On the pavement here, and there beyond it is looking,
    Down a new-made double grave.

Lo, the moon ascending,
Up from the east the silvery round moon,
Beautiful over the house-tops, ghastly, phantom moon,
    Immense and silent moon.

I see a sad procession,
10 And I hear the sound of coming full-key'd bugles,
All the channels of the city streets they're flooding,
    As with voices and with tears.

I hear the great drums pounding,
And the small drums steady whirring,
And every blow of the great convulsive drums,
    Strikes me through and through.

For the son is brought with the father,
(In the foremost ranks of the fierce assault they fell,
Two veterans son and father dropt together,
20   And the double grave awaits them.)

Now nearer blow the bugles,
And the drums strike more convulsive,
And the daylight o'er the pavement quite has faded,
    And the strong dead-march enwraps me.

In the eastern sky up-buoying,
The sorrowful vast phantom moves illumin'd,
('Tis some mother's large transparent face,
    In heaven brighter growing.)

O strong dead-march you please me!
30 O moon immense with your silvery face you soothe me!
O my soldiers twain! O my veterans passing to burial!
    What I have I also give you.

The moon gives you light,
And the bugles and the drums give you music,
And my heart, O my soldiers, my veterans,
    My heart gives you love.

Over the Carnage Rose Prophetic a Voice

Over the carnage rose prophetic a voice,
Be not dishearten'd, affection shall solve the problems of
   freedom yet,
Those who love each other shall become invincible,
They shall yet make Columbia victorious.

Sons of the Mother of All, you shall yet be victorious,
You shall yet laugh to scorn the attacks of all the remainder
   of the earth.

No danger shall balk Columbia's lovers,
If need be a thousand shall sternly immolate themselves
   for one.

One from Massachusetts shall be a Missourian's comrade,
From Maine and from hot Carolina, and another an
   Oregonese, shall be friends triune,
More precious to each other than all the riches of the earth.

To Michigan, Florida perfumes shall tenderly come,
Not the perfumes of flowers, but sweeter, and wafted
   beyond death.

It shall be customary in the houses and streets to see manly
   affection,
The most dauntless and rude shall touch face to face lightly,
The dependence of Liberty shall be lovers,
The continuance of Equality shall be comrades.

These shall tie you and band you stronger than hoops of
   iron,
I, ecstatic, O partners! O lands! with the love of lovers
   tie you.

20   (Were you looking to be held together by lawyers?
Or by an agreement on a paper? or by arms?
Nay, nor the world, nor any living thing, will so cohere.)

I Saw Old General at Bay

I saw old General at bay,
(Old as he was, his gray eyes yet shone out in battle like
    stars,)
His small force was now completely hemm'd in, in his works,
He call'd for volunteers to run the enemy's lines, a desperate
    emergency,
I saw a hundred and more step forth from the ranks, but
    two or three were selected,
I saw them receive their orders aside, they listen'd with
    care, the adjutant was very grave,
I saw them depart with cheerfulness, freely risking their
    lives.

The Artilleryman's Vision

While my wife at my side lies slumbering, and the wars are
    over long,
And my head on the pillow rests at home, and the vacant
    midnight passes,
And through the stillness, through the dark, I hear, just
    hear, the breath of my infant,
There in the room as I wake from sleep this vision presses
    upon me;
The engagement opens there and then in fantasy unreal,
The skirmishers begin, they crawl cautiously ahead, I hear
    the irregular snap! snap!
I hear the sounds of the different missiles, the short *t-h-t!
t-h-t!* of the rifle-balls,
I see the shells exploding leaving small white clouds, I hear
    the great shells shrieking as they pass,

The grape like the hum and whirr of wind through the trees,
(tumultuous now the contest rages,)

10 All the scenes at the batteries rise in detail before me again,

The crashing and smoking, the pride of the men in their
pieces,

The chief-gunner ranges and sights his piece and selects a
fuse of the right time,

After firing I see him lean aside and look eagerly off to note
the effect;

Elsewhere I hear the cry of a regiment charging, (the young
colonel leads himself this time with brandish'd sword,)

I see the gaps cut by the enemy's volleys, (quickly fill'd up,
no delay,)

I breathe the suffocating smoke, then the flat clouds hover
low concealing all;

Now a strange lull for a few seconds, not a shot fired on
either side,

Then resumed the chaos louder than ever, with eager calls
and orders of officers,

While from some distant part of the field the wind wafts to
my ears a shout of applause, (some special success,)

20 And ever the sound of the cannon far or near, (rousing even
in dreams a devilish exultation and all the old mad joy in
the depths of my soul,)

And ever the hastening of infantry shifting positions,
batteries, cavalry, moving hither and thither,

(The falling, dying, I heed not, the wounded dripping and
red I heed not, some to the rear are hobbling,)

Grime, heat, rush, aide-de-camps galloping by or on a full
run,

With the patter of small arms, the warning s-s-t of the rifles,
(these in my vision I hear or see,)

And bombs bursting in air, and at night the vari-color'd
rockets.

Ethiopia Saluting the Colors

Who are you dusky woman, so ancient hardly human,
With your woolly-white and turban'd head, and bare bony
    feet?
Why rising by the roadside here, do you the colors greet?

('Tis while our army lines Carolina's sands and pines,
Forth from thy hovel door thou Ethiopia com'st to me,
As under doughty Sherman I march toward the sea.)

Me master years a hundred since from my parents sunder'd,
A little child, they caught me as the savage beast is caught,
Then hither me across the sea the cruel slaver brought.

10 No further does she say, but lingering all the day,
Her high-borne turban'd head she wags, and rolls her
    darkling eye,
And courtesies to the regiments, the guidons moving by.

What is it fateful woman, so blear, hardly human?
Why wag your head with turban bound, yellow, red and
    green?
Are the things so strange and marvelous you see or have
    seen?

Not Youth Pertains to Me

Not youth pertains to me,
Nor delicatesse, I cannot beguile the time with talk,
Awkward in the parlor, neither a dancer nor elegant,
In the learn'd coterie sitting constrain'd and still, for
    learning inures not to me,
Beauty, knowledge, inure not to me – yet there are two or
    three things inure to me,
I have nourish'd the wounded and sooth'd many a dying
    soldier,
And at intervals waiting or in the midst of camp,
Composed these songs.

Race of Veterans

Race of veterans – race of victors!
Race of the soil, ready for conflict – race of the conquering
    march!
(No more credulity's race, abiding-temper'd race,)
Race henceforth owning no law but the law of itself,
Race of passion and the storm.

World Take Good Notice

World take good notice, silver stars fading,
Milky hue ript, weft of white detaching,
Coals thirty-eight, baleful and burning,
Scarlet, significant, hands off warning,
Now and henceforth flaunt from these shores.

O Tan-Faced Prairie-Boy

O tan-faced prairie-boy,
Before you came to camp came many a welcome gift,
Praises and presents came and nourishing food, till at last
    among the recruits,
You came, taciturn, with nothing to give – we but look'd on
    each other,
When lo! more than all the gifts of the world you gave me.

Look Down Fair Moon

Look down fair moon and bathe this scene,
Pour softly down night's nimbus floods on faces ghastly,
    swollen, purple,
On the dead on their backs with arms toss'd wide,
Pour down your unstinted nimbus sacred moon.

Reconciliation

Word over all, beautiful as the sky,
Beautiful that war and all its deeds of carnage must in time
    be utterly lost,
That the hands of the sisters Death and Night incessantly
    softly wash again, and ever again, this soil'd world;
For my enemy is dead, a man divine as myself is dead,
I look where he lies white-faced and still in the coffin – I
    draw near,
Bend down and touch lightly with my lips the white face
    in the coffin.

How Solemn as One by One
(WASHINGTON CITY, 1865)

How solemn as one by one,
As the ranks returning worn and sweaty, as the men file by
    where I stand,
As the faces the masks appear, as I glance at the faces
    studying the masks,
(As I glance upward out of this page studying you, dear
    friend, whoever you are,)
How solemn the thought of my whispering soul to each in
    the ranks, and to you,
I see behind each mask that wonder a kindred soul,
O the bullet could never kill what you really are, dear
    friend,
Nor the bayonet stab what you really are;
The soul! yourself I see, great as any, good as the best,
10   Waiting secure and content, which the bullet could never
    kill,
Nor the bayonet stab O friend.

As I Lay with my Head in Your Lap Camerado

As I lay with my head in your lap camerado,
The confession I made I resume, what I said to you and the
    open air I resume,
I know I am restless and make others so,
I know my words are weapons full of danger, full of death,
For I confront peace, security, and all the settled laws, to
    unsettle them,
I am more resolute because all have denied me than I could
    ever have been had all accepted me,
I heed not and have never heeded either experience,
    cautions, majorities, nor ridicule,
And the threat of what is call'd hell is little or nothing to me,
And the lure of what is call'd heaven is little or nothing
    to me;
10   Dear camerado! I confess I have urged you onward with
    me, and still urge you, without the least idea what is our
    destination,
Or whether we shall be victorious, or utterly quell'd and
    defeated.

Delicate Cluster

Delicate cluster! flag of teeming life!
Covering all my lands – all my seashores lining!
Flag of death! (how I watch'd you through the smoke of
    battle pressing!
How I heard you flap and rustle, cloth defiant!)
Flag cerulean – sunny flag, with the orbs of night dappled!
Ah my silvery beauty – ah my woolly white and crimson!
Ah to sing the song of you, my matron mighty!
My sacred one, my mother.

To a Certain Civilian

Did you ask dulcet rhymes from me?
Did you seek the civilian's peaceful and languishing
    rhymes?
Did you find what I sang erewhile so hard to follow?
Why I was not singing erewhile for you to follow, to
    understand – nor am I now;
(I have been born of the same as the war was born,
The drum-corps' rattle is ever to me sweet music, I love
    well the martial dirge,
With slow wail and convulsive throb leading the officer's
    funeral;)
What to such as you anyhow such a poet as I? therefore
    leave my works,
And go lull yourself with what you can understand, and
    with piano-tunes,
10 For I lull nobody, and you will never understand me.

Lo, Victress on the Peaks

Lo, Victress on the peaks,
Where thou with mighty brow regarding the world,
(The world O Libertad, that vainly conspired against thee,)
Out of its countless beleaguering toils, after thwarting them
    all,
Dominant, with the dazzling sun around thee,
Flauntest now unharm'd in immortal soundness and bloom
    – lo, in these hours supreme,
No poem proud, I chanting bring to thee, nor mastery's
    rapturous verse,
But a cluster containing night's darkness and
    blood-dripping wounds,
And psalms of the dead.

Spirit Whose Work is Done
(WASHINGTON CITY, 1865)

Spirit whose work is done – spirit of dreadful hours!
Ere departing fade from my eyes your forests of bayonets;
Spirit of gloomiest fears and doubts, (yet onward ever
    unfaltering pressing,)
Spirit of many a solemn day and many a savage scene –
    electric spirit,
That with muttering voice through the war now closed, like
    a tireless phantom flitted,
Rousing the land with breath of flame, while you beat and
    beat the drum,
Now as the sound of the drum, hollow and harsh to the last,
    reverberates round me,
As your ranks, your immortal ranks, return, return from the
    battles,
As the muskets of the young men yet lean over their
    shoulders,
10 As I look on the bayonets bristling over their shoulders,
As those slanted bayonets, whole forests of them appearing
    in the distance, approach and pass on, returning
    homeward,
Moving with steady motion, swaying to and fro to the right
    and left,
Evenly lightly rising and falling while the steps keep time;
Spirit of hours I knew, all hectic red one day, but pale as
    death next day,
Touch my mouth ere you depart, press my lips close,
Leave me your pulses of rage – bequeath them to me – fill me
    with currents convulsive,
Let them scorch and blister out of my chants when you are
    gone,
Let them identify you to the future in these songs.

Adieu to a Soldier

Adieu O soldier,
You of the rude campaigning, (which we shared,)
The rapid march, the life of the camp,
The hot contention of opposing fronts, the long
    manoeuvre,
Red battles with their slaughter, the stimulus, the strong
    terrific game,
Spell of all brave and manly hearts, the trains of time
    through you and like of you all fill'd,
With war and war's expression.

Adieu dear comrade,
Your mission is fulfill'd – but I, more warlike,
10 Myself and this contentious soul of mine,
Still on our own campaigning bound,
Through untried roads with ambushes opponents lined,
Through many a sharp defeat and many a crisis, often
    baffled,
Here marching, ever marching on, a war fight out – aye here,
To fiercer, weightier battles give expression.

Turn O Libertad

Turn O Libertad, for the war is over,
From it and all henceforth expanding, doubting no more,
    resolute, sweeping the world,
Turn from lands retrospective recording proofs of the past,
From the singers that sing the trailing glories of the past,
From the chants of the feudal world, the triumphs of kings,
    slavery, caste,
Turn to the world, the triumphs reserv'd and to come – give
    up that backward world,
Leave to the singers of hitherto, give them the trailing past,
But what remains remains for singers for you – wars to come
    are for you,

(Lo, how the wars of the past have duly inured to you, and
  the wars of the present also inure;)
10 Then turn, and be not alarm'd O Libertad – turn your
  undying face,
To where the future, greater than all the past,
Is swiftly, surely preparing for you.

To the Leaven'd Soil They Trod

To the leaven'd soil they trod calling I sing for the last,
(Forth from my tent emerging for good, loosing, untying
  the tent-ropes,)
In the freshness the forenoon air, in the far-stretching
  circuits and vistas again to peace restored,
To the fiery fields emanative and the endless vistas beyond,
  to the South and the North,
To the leaven'd soil of the general Western world to attest
  my songs,
To the Alleghanian hills and the tireless Mississippi,
To the rocks I calling sing, and all the trees in the woods,
To the plains of the poems of heroes, to the prairies
  spreading wide,
To the far-off sea and the unseen winds, and the sane
  impalpable air;
10 And responding they answer all, (but not in words,)
The average earth, the witness of war and peace,
  acknowledges mutely,
The prairie draws me close, as the father to bosom broad
  the son,
The Northern ice and rain that began me nourish me to the
  end,
But the hot sun of the South is to fully ripen my songs.

MEMORIES OF PRESIDENT LINCOLN

When Lilacs Last in the Dooryard Bloom'd

1

When lilacs last in the dooryard bloom'd,
And the great star early droop'd in the western sky in the
    night,
I mourn'd, and yet shall mourn with ever-returning spring.

Ever-returning spring, trinity sure to me you bring,
Lilac blooming perennial and drooping star in the west,
And thought of him I love.

2

O powerful western fallen star!
O shades of night – O moody, tearful night!
O great star disappear'd – O the black murk that hides the
    star!
O cruel hands that hold me powerless – O helpless soul of
    me!
O harsh surrounding cloud that will not free my soul.

3

In the dooryard fronting an old farm-house near the
    white-wash'd palings,
Stands the lilac-bush tall-growing with heart-shaped leaves
    of rich green,
With many a pointed blossom rising delicate, with the
    perfume strong I love,
With every leaf a miracle – and from this bush in the
    dooryard,
With delicate-color'd blossoms and heart-shaped leaves of
    rich green,
A sprig with its flower I break.

4

In the swamp in secluded recesses,
A shy and hidden bird is warbling a song.

20 Solitary the thrush,
The hermit withdrawn to himself, avoiding the settlements,
Sings by himself a song.

Song of the bleeding throat,
Death's outlet song of life, (for well dear brother I know,
If thou wast not granted to sing thou would'st surely die.)

5
Over the breast of the spring, the land, amid cities,
Amid lanes and through old woods, where lately the violets
    peep'd from the ground, spotting the gray debris,
Amid the grass in the fields each side of the lanes, passing
    the endless grass,
Passing the yellow-spear'd wheat, every grain from its
    shroud in the dark-brown fields uprisen,
30 Passing the apple-tree blows of white and pink in the
    orchards,
Carrying a corpse to where it shall rest in the grave,
Night and day journeys a coffin.

6
Coffin that passes through lanes and streets,
Through day and night with the great cloud darkening the
    land,
With the pomp of the inloop'd flags with the cities draped
    in black,
With the show of the States themselves as of crape-veil'd
    women standing,
With processions long and winding and the flambeaus of the
    night,
With the countless torches lit, with the silent sea of faces
    and the unbared heads,
With the waiting depot, the arriving coffin, and the sombre
    faces,
40 With dirges through the night, with the thousand voices
    rising strong and solemn,
With all the mournful voices of the dirges pour'd around the
    coffin,

The dim-lit churches and the shuddering organs – where
    amid these you journey,
With the tolling tolling bells' perpetual clang,
Here, coffin that slowly passes,
I give you my sprig of lilac.

7
(Nor for you, for one alone,
Blossoms and branches green to coffins all I bring,
For fresh as the morning, thus would I chant a song for you
    O sane and sacred death.

All over bouquets of roses,
50 O death, I cover you over with roses and early lilies,
But mostly and now the lilac that blooms the first,
Copious I break, I break the sprigs from the bushes,
With loaded arms I come, pouring for you,
For you and the coffins all of you O death.)

8
O western orb sailing the heaven,
Now I know what you must have meant as a month since I
    walk'd,
As I walk'd in silence the transparent shadowy night,
As I saw you had something to tell as you bent to me night
    after night,
As you droop'd from the sky low down as if to my side,
    (while the other stars all look'd on,)
60 As we wander'd together the solemn night, (for something I
    know not what kept me from sleep,)
As the night advanced, and I saw on the rim of the west how
    full you were of woe,
As I stood on the rising ground in the breeze in the cool
    transparent night,
As I watch'd where you pass'd and was lost in the
    netherward black of the night,
As my soul in its trouble dissatisfied sank, as where you sad
    orb,
Concluded, dropt in the night, and was gone.

9
Sing on there in the swamp,
O singer bashful and tender, I hear your notes, I hear your
    call,
I hear, I come presently, I understand you,
But a moment I linger, for the lustrous star has detain'd me,
70 The star my departing comrade holds and detains me.

10
O how shall I warble myself for the dead one there I loved?
And how shall I deck my song for the large sweet soul that
    has gone?
And what shall my perfume be for the grave of him I love?

Sea-winds blown from east and west,
Blown from the Eastern sea and blown from the Western
    sea, till there on the prairies meeting,
These and with these and the breath of my chant,
I'll perfume the grave of him I love.

11
O what shall I hang on the chamber walls?
And what shall the pictures be that I hang on the walls,
80 To adorn the burial-house of him I love?

Pictures of growing spring and farms and homes,
With the Fourth-month eve at sundown, and the gray smoke
    lucid and bright,
With floods of the yellow gold of the gorgeous, indolent,
    sinking sun, burning, expanding the air,
With the fresh sweet herbage under foot, and the pale
    green leaves of the trees prolific,
In the distance the flowing glaze, the breast of the river, with
    a wind-dapple here and there,
With ranging hills on the banks, with many a line against the
    the sky, and shadows,
And the city at hand with dwellings so dense, and stacks of
    chimneys,
And all the scenes of life and the workshops, and the
    workmen homeward returning.

12

Lo, body and soul – this land,
90 My own Manhattan with spires, and the sparkling and
      hurrying tides, and the ships,
The varied and ample land, the South and the North in the
      light, Ohio's shores and flashing Missouri,
And ever the far-spreading prairies cover'd with grass and
      corn.

Lo, the most excellent sun so calm and haughty,
The violet and purple morn with just-felt breezes,
The gentle soft-born measureless light,
The miracle spreading bathing all, the fulfill'd noon,
The coming eve delicious, the welcome night and the stars,
Over my cities shining all, enveloping man and land.

13

Sing on, sing on you gray-brown bird,
100 Sing from the swamps, the recesses, pour your chant from
      the bushes,
Limitless out of the dusk, out of the cedars and pines.

Sing on dearest brother, warble your reedy song,
Loud human song, with voice of uttermost woe.

O liquid and free and tender!
O wild and loose to my soul – O wondrous singer!
You only I hear – yet the star holds me, (but will soon
      depart,)
Yet the lilac with mastering odor holds me.

14

Now while I sat in the day and look'd forth,
In the close of the day with its light and the fields of spring,
      and the farmers preparing their crops,
110 In the large unconscious scenery of my land with its lakes
      and forests,
In the heavenly aerial beauty, (after the perturb'd winds and
      the storms,)

Under the arching heavens of the afternoon swift passing,
and the voices of children and women,
The many-moving sea-tides, and I saw the ships how they
sail'd,
And the summer approaching with richness, and the fields
all busy with labor,
And the infinite separate houses, how they all went on, each
with its meals and minutia of daily usages,
And the streets how their throbbings throbb'd, and the
cities pent – lo, then and there,
Falling upon them all and among them all, enveloping me
with the rest,
Appear'd the cloud, appear'd the long black trail,
And I knew death, its thought, and the sacred knowledge of
death.

120   Then with the knowledge of death as walking one side of me,
And the thought of death close-walking the other side of me,
And I in the middle as with companions, and as holding the
hands of companions,
I fled forth to the hiding receiving night that talks not,
Down to the shores of the water, the path by the swamp in
the dimness,
To the solemn shadowy cedars and ghostly pines so still.

And the singer so shy to the rest receiv'd me,
The gray-brown bird I know receiv'd us comrades three,
And he sang the carol of death, and a verse for him I love.

From deep secluded recesses,
130   From the fragrant cedars and the ghostly pines so still,
Came the carol of the bird.

And the charm of the carol rapt me,
As I held as if by their hands my comrades in the night,
And the voice of my spirit tallied the song of the bird.

Come lovely and soothing death,
Undulate round the world, serenely arriving, arriving,
In the day, in the night, to all, to each,
Sooner or later delicate death.

Prais'd be the fathomless universe,
140 For life and joy, and for objects and knowledge curious,
And for love, sweet love – but praise! praise! praise!
For the sure-enwinding arms of cool-enfolding death.

Dark mother always gliding near with soft feet,
Have none chanted for thee a chant of fullest welcome?
Then I chant it for thee, I glorify thee above all,
I bring thee a song that when thou must indeed come, come
    unfalteringly.

Approach strong deliveress,
When it is so, when thou hast taken them I joyously sing the
    dead,
Lost in the loving floating ocean of thee,
150 Laved in the flood of thy bliss O death.

From me to thee glad serenades,
Dances for thee I propose saluting thee, adornments and
    feastings for thee,
And the sights of the open landscape and the high-spread sky
    are fitting,
And life and the fields, and the huge and thoughtful night.

The night in silence under many a star,
The ocean shore and the husky whispering wave whose voice I
    know,
And the soul turning to thee O vast and well-veil'd death,
And the body gratefully nestling close to thee.

Over the tree-tops I float thee a song,
160 Over the rising and sinking waves, over the myriad fields and
    the prairies wide,
Over the dense-pack'd cities all and the teeming wharves and
    ways,
I float this carol with joy, with joy to thee O death.

15

To the tally of my soul,
Loud and strong kept up the gray-brown bird,
With pure deliberate notes spreading filling the night.

Loud in the pines and cedars dim,
Clear in the freshness moist and the swamp-perfume,
And I with my comrades there in the night.

While my sight that was bound in my eyes unclosed,
170 As to long panoramas of visions.

And I saw askant the armies,
I saw as in noiseless dreams hundreds of battle-flags,
Borne through the smoke of the battles and pierc'd with
     missiles I saw them,
And carried hither and yon through the smoke, and torn
     and bloody,
And at last but a few shreds left on the staffs, (and all in
     silence,)
And the staffs all splinter'd and broken.

I saw battle-corpses, myriads of them,
And the white skeletons of young men, I saw them,
I saw the debris and debris of all the slain soldiers of the
     war,
180 But I saw they were not as was thought,
They themselves were fully at rest, they suffer'd not,
The living remain'd and suffer'd, the mother suffer'd,
And the wife and the child and the musing comrade suffer'd,
And the armies that remain'd suffer'd.

16

Passing the visions, passing the night,
Passing, unloosing the hold of my comrades' hands,
Passing the song of the hermit bird and the tallying song of
     my soul,
Victorious song, death's outlet song, yet varying
     ever-altering song,

As low and wailing, yet clear the notes, rising and falling,
    flooding the night,
190 Sadly sinking and fainting, as warning and warning, and yet
    again bursting with joy,
Covering the earth and filling the spread of the heaven,
As that powerful psalm in the night I heard from recesses,
Passing, I leave thee lilac with heart-shaped leaves,
I leave thee there in the door-yard, blooming, returning
    with spring.

I cease from my song for thee,
From my gaze on thee in the west, fronting the west,
    communing with thee,
O comrade lustrous with silver face in the night.

Yet each to keep and all, retrievements out of the night,
The song, the wondrous chant of the gray-brown bird,
200 And the tallying chant, the echo arous'd in my soul,
With the lustrous and drooping star with the countenance
    full of woe,
With the holders holding my hand nearing the call of the
    bird,
Comrades mine and I in the midst, and their memory ever
    to keep, for the dead I loved so well,
For the sweetest, wisest soul of all my days and lands – and
    this for his dear sake,
Lilac and star and bird twined with the chant of my soul,
There in the fragrant pines and the cedars dusk and dim.

O Captain! My Captain!

O Captain! my Captain! our fearful trip is done,
The ship has weather'd every rack, the prize we sought is
    won,
The port is near, the bells I hear, the people all exulting,
While follow eyes the steady keel, the vessel grim and
    daring:
    But O heart! heart! heart!

O the bleeding drops of red,
   Where on the deck my Captain lies,
      Fallen cold and dead.

O Captain! my Captain! rise up and hear the bells;
10 Rise up – for you the flag is flung – for you the bugle trills,
For you bouquets and ribbon'd wreaths – for you the shores
   a-crowding,
For you they call, the swaying mass, their eager faces
   turning;
   Here Captain! dear father!
     This arm beneath your head!
      It is some dream that on the deck,
        You've fallen cold and dead.

My Captain does not answer, his lips are pale and still,
My father does not feel my arm, he has no pulse nor will,
The ship is anchor'd safe and sound, its voyage closed and
   done,
20 From fearful trip the victor ship comes in with object won;
   Exult O shores, and ring O bells!
     But I with mournful tread,
      Walk the deck my Captain lies,
        Fallen cold and dead.

Hush'd Be the Camps To-day
(MAY 4, 1865)

Hush'd be the camps to-day,
And soldiers let us drape our war-worn weapons,
And each with musing soul retire to celebrate,
Our dear commander's death.

No more for him life's stormy conflicts,
Nor victory, nor defeat – no more time's dark events,
Charging like ceaseless clouds across the sky.

But sing poet in our name,
Sing of the love we bore him – because you, dweller in
    camps, know it truly.

10   As they invault the coffin there,
Sing – as they close the doors of earth upon him – one verse,
For the heavy hearts of soldiers.

This Dust Was Once the Man

This dust was once the man,
Gentle, plain, just and resolute, under whose cautious hand,
Against the foulest crime in history known in any land or
    age,
Was saved the Union of these States.

By Blue Ontario's Shore

1

By blue Ontario's shore,
As I mused of these warlike days and of peace return'd, and
    the dead that return no more,
A Phantom gigantic superb, with stern visage accosted me,
Chant me the poem, it said, *that comes from the soul of America,*
    chant me the carol of victory,
And strike up the marches of Libertad, marches more
    powerful yet,
And sing me before you go the song of the throes of
    Democracy.

(Democracy, the destin'd conqueror, yet treacherous
    lip-smiles everywhere,
And death and infidelity at every step.)

2

A Nation announcing itself,
10 I myself make the only growth by which I can be appreciated,
I reject none, accept all, then reproduce all in my own
    forms.

A breed whose proof is in time and deeds,
What we are we are, nativity is answer enough to
    objections,
We wield ourselves as a weapon is wielded,
We are powerful and tremendous in ourselves,
We are executive in ourselves, we are sufficient in the variety
    of ourselves,
We are the most beautiful to ourselves and in ourselves,
We stand self-pois'd in the middle, branching thence over
    the world,
From Missouri, Nebraska, or Kansas, laughing attacks to
    scorn.

20 Nothing is sinful to us outside of ourselves,
Whatever appears, whatever does not appear, we are
    beautiful or sinful in ourselves only.

(O Mother – O Sisters dear!
If we are lost, no victor else has destroy'd us,
It is by ourselves we go down to eternal night.)

3
Have you thought there could be but a single supreme?
There can be any number of supremes – one does not
    countervail another any more than one eyesight
    countervails another, or one life countervails another.

All is eligible to all,
All is for individuals, all is for you,
No condition is prohibited, not God's or any.

30   All comes by the body, only health puts you rapport with
    the universe.

Produce great Persons, the rest follows.

4
Piety and conformity to them that like,
Peace, obesity, allegiance, to them that like,
I am he who tauntingly compels men, women, nations,
Crying, Leap from your seats and contend for your lives!

I am he who walks the States with a barb'd tongue,
    questioning every one I meet,
Who are you that wanted only to be told what you knew
    before?
Who are you that wanted only a book to join you in your
    nonsense?

(With pangs and cries as thine own O bearer of many
    children,
40   These clamors wild to a race of pride I give.)

O lands, would you be freer than all that has ever been
    before?
If you would be freer than all that has been before, come
    listen to me.

Fear grace, elegance, civilization, delicatesse,
Fear the mellow sweet, the sucking of honey-juice,
Beware the advancing mortal ripening of Nature,
Beware what precedes the decay of the ruggedness of states
and men.

5
Ages, precedents, have long been accumulating undirected
materials,
America brings builders, and brings its own styles.

The immortal poets of Asia and Europe have done their
work and pass'd to other spheres,
50   A work remains, the work of surpassing all they have done.

America, curious toward foreign characters, stands by its
own at all hazards,
Stands removed, spacious, composite, sound, initiates the
true use of precedents,
Does not repel them or the past or what they have
produced under their forms,
Takes the lesson with calmness, perceives the corpse slowly
borne from the house,
Perceives that it waits a little while in the door, that it was
fittest for its days,
That its life has descended to the stalwart and well-shaped
heir who approaches,
And that he shall be fittest for his days.

Any period one nation must lead,
One land must be the promise and reliance of the future.

60   These States are the amplest poem,
Here is not merely a nation but a teeming Nation of nations,
Here the doings of men correspond with the broadest doings
of the day and night,
Here is what moves in magnificent masses careless of
particulars,
Here are the roughs, beards, friendliness, combativeness,
the soul loves,

Here the flowing trains, here the crowds, equality,
    diversity, the soul loves.

6

Land of lands and bards to corroborate!
Of them standing among them, one lifts to the light a
    west-bred face,
To him the hereditary countenance bequeath'd both
    mother's and father's,
His first parts substances, earth, water, animals, trees,
70 Built of the common stock, having room for far and near,
Used to dispense with other lands, incarnating this land,
Attracting it body and soul to himself, hanging on its neck
    with incomparable love,
Plunging his seminal muscle into its merits and demerits,
Making its cities, beginnings, events, diversities, wars,
    vocal in him,
Making its rivers, lakes, bays, embouchure in him,
Mississippi with yearly freshets and changing chutes,
    Columbia, Niagara, Hudson, spending themselves
    lovingly in him,
In the Atlantic coast stretch or the Pacific coast stretch, he
    stretching with them North or South,
Spanning between them East and West, and touching
    whatever is between them,
Growths growing from him to offset the growths of pine,
    cedar, hemlock, live-oak, locust, chestnut, hickory,
    cottonwood, orange, magnolia,
80 Tangles as tangled in him as any canebrake or swamp,
He likening sides and peaks of mountains, forests coated
    with northern transparent ice,
Off him pasturage sweet and natural as savanna, upland,
    prairie,
Through him flights, whirls, screams, answering those of
    the fish-hawk, mocking-bird, night-heron and eagle,
His spirit surrounding his country's spirit, unclosed to good
    and evil,

Surrounding the essences of real things, old times and
 present times,
Surrounding just found shores, islands, tribes of red
 aborigines,
Weather-beaten vessels, landings, settlements, embryo
 stature and muscle,
The haughty defiance of the Year One, war, peace, the
 formation of the Constitution,
The separate States, the simple elastic scheme, the
 immigrants,
90 The Union always swarming with blatherers and always
 sure and impregnable,
The unsurvey'd interior, log-houses, clearings, wild
 animals, hunters, trappers,
Surrounding the multiform agriculture, mines, temperature,
 the gestation of new States,
Congress convening every Twelfth-month, the members
 duly coming up from the uttermost parts,
Surrounding the noble character of mechanics and farmers,
 especially the young men,
Responding their manners, speech, dress, friendships, the
 gait they have of persons who never knew how it felt to
 stand in the presence of superiors,
The freshness and candor of their physiognomy, the
 copiousness and decision of their phrenology,
The picturesque looseness of their carriage, their fierceness
 when wrong'd,
The fluency of their speech, their delight in music, their
 curiosity, good temper and open-handedness, the whole
 composite make,
The prevailing ardor and enterprise, the large amativeness,
100 The perfect equality of the female with the male, the fluid
 movement of the population,
The superior marine, free commerce, fisheries, whaling,
 gold-digging,
Wharf-hemm'd cities, railroad and steamboat lines
 intersecting all points,

Factories, mercantile life, labor-saving machinery, the
    Northeast, Northwest, Southwest,
Manhattan firemen, the Yankee swap, southern plantation
    life,
Slavery – the murderous, treacherous conspiracy to raise it
    upon the ruins of all the rest,
On and on to the grapple with it – Assassin! then your life
    or ours be the stake, and respite no more.

7
(Lo, high toward heaven, this day,
Libertad, from the conqueress' field return'd,
I mark the new aureola around your head,
110   No more of soft astral, but dazzling and fierce,
With war's flames and the lambent lightnings playing,
And your poet immovable where you stand,
With still the inextinguishable glance and the clinch'd and
    lifted fist,
And your foot on the neck of the menacing one, the scorner
    utterly crush'd beneath you,
The menacing arrogant one that strode and advanced with
    his senseless scorn, bearing the murderous knife,
The wide-swelling one, the braggart that would yesterday
    do so much,
To-day a carrion dead and damn'd, the despised of all the
    earth,
An offal rank, to the dunghill maggots spurn'd.)

8
Others take finish, but the Republic is ever constructive and
    ever keeps vista,
120   Others adorn the past, but you O days of the present, I
    adorn you,
O days of the future I believe in you – I isolate myself for
    your sake,
O America because you build for mankind I build for you,
O well-beloved stone-cutters, I lead them who plan with
    decision and science,
Lead the present with friendly hand toward the future.

(Bravas to all impulses sending sane children to the next age!
But damn that which spends itself with no thought of the
    stain, pains, dismay, feebleness, it is bequeathing.)

9

I listened to the Phantom by Ontario's shore,
I heard the voice arising demanding bards,
By them all native and grand, by them alone can these States
    be fused into the compact organism of a Nation.

130 To hold men together by paper and seal or by compulsion
    is no account,
That only holds men together which aggregates all in a
    living principle, as the hold of the limbs of the body or the
    fibres of plants.

Of all races and eras these States with veins full of poetical
    stuff most need poets, and are to have the greatest, and use
    them the greatest,
Their Presidents shall not be their common referee so much
    as their poets shall.

(Soul of love and tongue of fire!
Eye to pierce the deepest deeps and sweep the world!
Ah Mother, prolific and full in all besides, yet how long
    barren, barren?)

10

Of these States the poet is the equable man,
Not in him but off from him things are grotesque, eccentric,
    fail of their full returns,
Nothing out of its place is good, nothing in its place is bad,
140 He bestows on every object or quality its fit proportion,
    neither more nor less,
He is the arbiter of the diverse, he is the key,
He is the equalizer of his age and land,
He supplies what wants supplying, he checks what wants
    checking,
In peace out of him speaks the spirit of peace, large, rich,
    thrifty, building populous towns, encouraging

agriculture, arts, commerce, lighting the study of man,
   the soul, health, immortality, government,
In war he is the best backer of the war, he fetches artillery
   as good as the engineer's, he can make every word he
   speaks draw blood,
The years straying towards infidelity he withholds by his
   steady faith,
He is no arguer, he is judgment, (Nature accepts him
   absolutely,)
He judges not as the judge judges but as the sun falling
   round a helpless thing,
As he sees the farthest he has the most faith,
150   His thoughts are the hymns of the praise of things,
In the dispute on God and eternity he is silent,
He sees eternity less like a play with a prologue and
   denouement,
He sees eternity in men and women, he does not see men
   and women as dreams or dots.

For the great Idea, the idea of perfect and free individuals,
For that, the bard walks in advance, leader of leaders,
The attitude of him cheers up slaves and horrifies foreign
   despots.

Without extinction is Liberty, without retrograde is
   Equality,
They live in the feelings of young men and the best women,
(Not for nothing have the indomitable heads of the earth
   been always ready to fall for Liberty.)

11
160   For the great Idea,
That, O my brethren, that is the mission of poets.

Songs of stern defiance ever ready,
Songs of the rapid arming and the march,
The flag of peace quick-folded, and instead the flag we
   know,
Warlike flag of the great Idea.

(Angry cloth I saw there leaping!
I stand again in leaden rain your flapping folds saluting,
I sing you over all, flying beckoning through the fight – O
    the hard-contested fight!
The cannons ope their rosy-flashing muzzles – the hurtled
    balls scream,
170 The battle-fronts form amid the smoke – the volleys pour
    incessant from the line,
Hark, the ringing word *Charge!* – now the tussle and the
    furious maddening yells,
Now the corpses tumble curl'd upon the ground,
Cold, cold in death, for precious life of you,
Angry cloth I saw there leaping.)

12

Are you he who would assume a place to teach or be a poet
    here in the States?
The place is august, the terms obdurate.

Who would assume to teach here may well prepare himself
    body and mind,
He may well survey, ponder, arm, fortify, harden, make lithe
    himself,
He shall surely be question'd beforehand by me with many
    and stern questions.
180 Who are you indeed who would talk or sing to America?
Have you studied out the land, its idioms and men?
Have you learn'd the physiology, phrenology, politics,
    geography, pride, freedom, friendship of the land? its
    substratums and objects?
Have you consider'd the organic compact of the first day of
    the first year of Independence, sign'd by the
    Commissioners, ratified by the States, and read by
    Washington at the head of the army?
Have you possess'd yourself of the Federal Constitution?
Do you see who have left all feudal processes and poems
    behind them, and assumed the poems and processes of
    Democracy?
Are you faithful to things? do you teach what the land and

sea, the bodies of men, womanhood, amativeness, heroic
    angers, teach?
Have you sped through fleeting customs, popularities?
Can you hold your hand against all seductions, follies,
    whirls, fierce contentions? are you very strong? are you
    really of the whole People?
Are you not of some coterie? some school or mere religion?
190 Are you done with reviews and criticisms of life? animating
    now to life itself?
Have you vivified yourself from the maternity of these
    States?
Have you too the old ever-fresh forbearance and
    impartiality?
Do you hold the like love for those hardening to maturity?
    for the last-born? little and big? and for the errant?

What is this you bring my America?
Is it uniform with my country?
Is it not something that has been better told or done
    before?
Have you not imported this or the spirit of it in some ship?
Is it not a mere tale? a rhyme? a prettiness? – is the good old
    cause in it?
Has it not dangled long at the heels of the poets,
    politicians, literats, of enemies' lands?
200 Does it not assume that what is notoriously gone is still here?
Does it answer universal needs? will it improve manners?
Does it sound with trumpet-voice the proud victory of the
    Union in that secession war?
Can your performance face the open fields and the seaside?
Will it absorb into me as I absorb food, air, to appear again
    in my strength, gait, face?
Have real employments contributed to it? original makers,
    not mere amanuenses?
Does it meet modern discoveries, calibres, facts, face to
    face?
What does it mean to American persons, progresses, cities?
    Chicago, Kanada, Arkansas?

Does it see behind the apparent custodians the real
custodians standing, menacing, silent, the mechanics,
Manhattanese, Western men, Southerners, significant
alike in their apathy, and in the promptness of their love?
Does it see what finally befalls, and has always finally
befallen, each temporizer, patcher, outsider, partialist,
alarmist, infidel, who has ever ask'd any thing of
America?
210 What mocking and scornful negligence?
The track strew'd with the dust of skeletons,
By the roadside others disdainfully toss'd.

13
Rhymes and rhymers pass away, poems distill'd from poems
pass away,
The swarms of reflectors and the polite pass, and leave ashes,
Admirers, importers, obedient persons, make but the soil of
literature,
America justifies itself, give it time, no disguise can deceive
it or conceal from it, it is impassive enough,
Only toward the likes of itself will it advance to meet them,
If its poets appear it will in due time advance to meet them,
there is no fear of mistake,
(The proof of a poet shall be sternly deferr'd till his
country absorbs him as affectionately as he has absorb'd
it.)

220 He masters whose spirit masters, he tastes sweetest who
results sweetest in the long run,
The blood of the brawn beloved of time is unconstraint;
In the need of songs, philosophy, an appropriate native
grand-opera, shipcraft, any craft,
He or she is greatest who contributes the greatest original
practical example.

Already a nonchalant breed, silently emerging, appears on
the streets,
People's lips salute only doers, lovers, satisfiers, positive
knowers,

There will shortly be no more priests, I say their work is
    done,
Death is without emergencies here, but life is perpetual
    emergencies here,
Are your body, days, manners, superb? after death you shall
    be superb,
Justice, health, self-esteem, clear the way for irresistible
    power;
230 How dare you place any thing before a man?

14
Fall behind me States!
A man before all – myself, typical, before all.

Give me the pay I have served for,
Give me to sing the songs of the great Idea, take all the rest,
I have loved the earth, sun, animals, I have despised riches,
I have given alms to every one that ask'd, stood up for the
    stupid and crazy, devoted my income and labor to others,
Hated tyrants, argued not concerning God, had patience and
    indulgence toward the people, taken off my hat to nothing
    known or unknown,
Gone freely with powerful uneducated persons and with the
    young, and with the mothers of families,
Read these leaves to myself in the open air, tried them by
    trees, stars, rivers,
240 Dismiss'd whatever insulted my own soul or defiled my
    body,
Claim'd nothing to myself which I have not carefully
    claim'd for others on the same terms,
Sped to the camps, and comrades found and accepted from
    every State,
(Upon this breast has many a dying soldier lean'd to breathe
    his last,
This arm, this hand, this voice, have nourish'd, rais'd,
    restored,
To life recalling many a prostrate form;)

I am willing to wait to be understood by the growth of the
    taste of myself,
Rejecting none, permitting all.

(Say O Mother, have I not to your thought been faithful?
Have I not through life kept you and yours before me?)

15
250 I swear I begin to see the meaning of these things,
    It is not the earth, it is not America who is so great,
    It is I who am great or to be great, it is You up there, or any
        one,
    It is to walk rapidly through civilizations, governments,
        theories,
    Through poems, pageants, shows, to form individuals.

Underneath all, individuals,
I swear nothing is good to me now that ignores individuals,
The American compact is altogether with individuals,
The only government is that which makes minute of
    individuals,
The whole theory of the universe is directed unerringly to
    one single individual – namely to You.

260 (Mother! with subtle sense severe, with the naked sword in
    your hand,
    I saw you at last refuse to treat but directly with
        individuals.)

16
Underneath all, Nativity,
I swear I will stand by my own nativity, pious or impious so
    be it;
I swear I am charm'd with nothing except nativity,
Men, women, cities, nations, are only beautiful from
    nativity.

Underneath all is the Expression of love for men and
    women,
(I swear I have seen enough of mean and impotent modes
    of expressing love for men and women,

After this day I take my own modes of expressing love for
    men and women.)

I swear I will have each quality of my race in myself,
270 (Talk as you like, he only suits these States whose manners
    favor the audacity and sublime turbulence of the States.)

Underneath the lessons of things, spirits, Nature,
    governments, ownerships, I swear I perceive other
    lessons,
Underneath all to me is myself, to you yourself, (the same
    monotonous old song.)

17
O I see flashing that this America is only you and me,
Its power, weapons, testimony, are you and me,
Its crimes, lies, thefts, defections, are you and me,
Its Congress is you and me, the officers, capitols, armies,
    ships, are you and me,
Its endless gestations of new States are you and me,
The war, (that war so bloody and grim, the war I will
    henceforth forget), was you and me,
Natural and artificial are you and me,
280 Freedom, language, poems, employments, are you and me,
Past, present, future, are you and me.

I dare not shirk any part of myself,
Not any part of America good or bad,
Not to build for that which builds for mankind,
Not to balance ranks, complexions, creeds, and the sexes,
Not to justify science nor the march of equality,
Nor to feed the arrogant blood of the brawn belov'd of time.

I am for those that have never been master'd,
For men and women whose tempers have never been
    master'd,
290 For those whom laws, theories, conventions, can never
    master.

I am for those who walk abreast with the whole earth,
Who inaugurate one to inaugurate all.

I will not be outfaced by irrational things,
I will penetrate what it is in them that is sarcastic upon me,
I will make cities and civilizations defer to me,
This is what I have learnt from America – it is the amount,
    and it I teach again.

(Democracy, while weapons were everywhere aim'd at your
    breast,
I saw you serenely give birth to immortal children, saw in
    dreams your dilating form,
Saw you with spreading mantle covering the world.)

18

300 I will confront these shows of the day and night,
I will know if I am to be less than they,
I will see if I am not as majestic as they,
I will see if I am not as subtle and real as they,
I will see if I am to be less generous than they,
I will see if I have no meaning, while the houses and ships
    have meaning,
I will see if the fishes and birds are to be enough for
    themselves, and I am not to be enough for myself.

I match my spirit against yours you orbs, growths,
    mountains, brutes,
Copious as you are I absorb you all in myself, and become
    the master myself,
America isolated yet embodying all, what is it finally except
    myself?
310 These States, what are they except myself?

I know now why the earth is gross, tantalizing, wicked, it is
    for my sake,
I take you specially to be mine, you terrible, rude forms.

(Mother, bend down, bend close to me your face,
I know not what these plots and wars and deferments are for,
I know not fruition's success, but I know that through war
    and crime your work goes on, and must yet go on.)

19

Thus by blue Ontario's shore,
While the winds fann'd me and the waves came trooping
    toward me,
I thrill'd with the power's pulsations, and the charm of my
    theme was upon me,
Till the tissues that held me parted their ties upon me.

320 And I saw the free souls of poets,
The loftiest bards of past ages strode before me,
Strange large men, long unwaked, undisclosed, were
    disclosed to me.

20

O my rapt verse, my call, mock me not!
Not for the bards of the past, not to invoke them have I
    launch'd you forth,
Not to call even those lofty bards here by Ontario's shores,
Have I sung so capricious and loud my savage song.

Bards for my own land only I invoke,
(For the war the war is over, the field is clear'd,)
Till they strike up marches henceforth triumphant and
    onward,
330 To cheer O Mother your boundless expectant soul.

Bards of the great Idea! bards of the peaceful inventions!
    (for the war, the war is over!)
Yet bards of latent armies, a million soldiers waiting
    ever-ready,
Bards with songs as from burning coals or the lightning's
    fork'd stripes!
Ample Ohio's, Kanada's bards – bards of California! inland
    bards – bards of the war!
You by my charm I invoke.

Reversals

Let that which stood in front go behind,
Let that which was behind advance to the front,
Let bigots, fools, unclean persons, offer new propositions,
Let the old propositions be postponed,
Let a man seek pleasure everywhere except in himself,
Let a woman seek happiness everywhere except in herself.

AUTUMN RIVULETS

As Consequent, Etc.

As consequent from store of summer rains,
Or wayward rivulets in autumn flowing,
Or many a herb-lined brook's reticulations,
Or subterranean sea-rills making for the sea,
Songs of continued years I sing.

Life's ever-modern rapids first, (soon, soon to blend,
With the old streams of death.)

Some threading Ohio's farm-fields or the woods,
Some down Colorado's cañons from sources of perpetual
    snow,
Some half-hid in Oregon, or away southward in Texas,
Some in the north finding their way to Erie, Niagara,
    Ottawa,
Some to Atlantica's bays, and so to the great salt brine.

In you whoe'er you are my book perusing,
In I myself, in all the world, these currents flowing,
All, all toward the mystic ocean tending.

Currents for starting a continent new,
Overtures sent to the solid out of the liquid,
Fusion of ocean and land, tender and pensive waves,
(Not safe and peaceful only, waves rous'd and ominous too,
Out of the depths the storm's abysmic waves, who knows
    whence?
Raging over the vast, with many a broken spar and tatter'd
    sail.)

Or from the sea of Time, collecting vasting all, I bring,
A windrow-drift of weeds and shells.

O little shells, so curious-convolute, so limpid-cold and
    voiceless,
Will you not little shells to the tympans of temples held,

Murmurs and echoes still call up, eternity's music faint and
    far,
Wafted inland, sent from Atlantica's rim, strains for the
    soul of the prairies,
Whisper'd reverberations, chords for the ear of the West
    joyously sounding,
Your tidings old, yet ever new and untranslatable,
30 Infinitesimals out of my life, and many a life,
(For not my life and years alone I give – all, all I give,)
These waifs from the deep, cast high and dry,
Wash'd on America's shores?

The Return of the Heroes

1

For the lands and for these passionate days and for myself,
Now I awhile retire to thee O soil of autumn fields,
Reclining on thy breast, giving myself to thee,
Answering the pulses of thy sane and equable heart,
Tuning a verse for thee.

O earth that hast no voice, confide to me a voice,
O harvest of my lands – O boundless summer growths,
O lavish brown parturient earth – O infinite teeming womb,
A song to narrate thee.

2

10 Ever upon this stage,
Is acted God's calm annual drama,
Gorgeous processions, songs of birds,
Sunrise that fullest feeds and freshens most the soul,
The heaving sea, the waves upon the shore, the musical,
    strong waves,
The woods, the stalwart trees, the slender, tapering trees,
The liliput countless armies of the grass,
The heat, the showers, the measureless pasturages,
The scenery of the snows, the winds' free orchestra,

The stretching light-hung roof of clouds, the clear cerulean
and the silvery fringes,

20   The high dilating stars; the placid beckoning stars,

The moving flocks and herds, the plains and emerald
meadows,

The shows of all the varied lands and all the growths
and products.

3

Fecund America – to-day,

Thou art all over set in births and joys!

Thou groan'st with riches, thy wealth clothes thee as a
swathing-garment,

Thou laughest loud with ache of great possessions,

A myriad-twining life like interlacing vines binds all thy
vast demesne,

As some huge ship freighted to water's edge thou ridest into
port,

As rain falls from the heaven and vapors rise from earth, so
have the precious values fallen upon thee and risen out of
thee;

30   Thou envy of the globe! thou miracle!

Thou, bathed, choked, swimming in plenty,

Thou lucky Mistress of the tranquil barns,

Thou Prairie Dame that sittest in the middle and lookest out
upon thy world, and lookest East and lookest West,

Dispensatress, that by a word givest a thousand miles, a
million farms, and missest nothing,

Thou all-acceptress – thou hospitable, (thou only art
hospitable as God is hospitable.)

4

When late I sang sad was my voice,

Sad were the shows around me with deafening noises of
hatred and smoke of war;

In the midst of the conflict, the heroes, I stood,

Or pass'd with slow step through the wounded and dying.

40   But now I sing not war,
     Nor the measur'd march of soldiers, nor the tents of camps,
     Nor the regiments hastily coming up deploying in line of
        battle;
     No more the sad, unnatural shows of war.

     Ask'd room those flush'd immortal ranks, the first forth-
        stepping armies?
     Ask room alas the ghastly ranks, the armies dread that
        follow'd.

     (Pass, pass, ye proud brigades, with your tramping sinewy
        legs,
     With your shoulders young and strong, with your knapsacks
        and your muskets;
     How elate I stood and watch'd you, where starting off you
        march'd.

     Pass – then rattle drums again,
50   For an army heaves in sight, O another gathering army,
     Swarming, trailing on the rear, O you dread accruing army,
     O you regiments so piteous, with your mortal diarrhoea, with
        your fever,
     O my land's maim'd darlings, with the plenteous bloody
        bandage and the crutch,
     Lo, your pallid army follows.)

     5
     But on these days of brightness,
     On the far-stretching beauteous landscape, the roads and
        lanes, the high-piled farm-wagons, and the fruits and
        barns,
     Should the dead intrude?

     Ah the dead to me mar not, they fit well in Nature,
     They fit very well in the landscape under the trees and grass,
60   And along the edge of the sky in the horizon's far margin.

Nor do I forget you Departed,
Nor in winter or summer my lost ones,
But most in the open air as now when my soul is rapt and at
    peace, like pleasing phantoms,
Your memories rising glide silently by me.

6
I saw the day the return of the heroes,
(Yet the heroes never surpass'd shall never return,
Them that day I saw not.)

I saw the interminable corps, I saw the processions of
    armies,
I saw them approaching, defiling by with divisions,
70 Streaming northward, their work done, camping awhile in
    clusters of mighty camps.

No holiday soldiers – youthful, yet veterans,
Worn, swart, handsome, strong, of the stock of homestead
    and workshop,
Harden'd of many a long campaign and sweaty march,
Inured on many a hard-fought bloody field.

A pause – the armies wait,
A million flush'd embattled conquerors wait,
The world too waits, then soft as breaking night and sure as
    dawn,
They melt, they disappear.

Exult O lands! victorious lands!
80 Not there your victory on those red shuddering fields,
But here and hence your victory.

Melt, melt away ye armies – disperse ye blue-clad soldiers,
Resolve ye back again, give up for good your deadly arms,
Other the arms the fields henceforth for you, or South or
    North,
With saner wars, sweet wars, life-giving wars.

7
Loud O my throat, and clear O soul!
The season of thanks and the voice of full-yielding,
The chant of joy and power for boundless fertility.

All till'd and untill'd fields expand before me,
90   I see the true arenas of my race, or first or last,
Man's innocent and strong arenas.

I see the heroes at other toils,
I see well-wielded in their hands the better weapons.

I see where the Mother of All,
With full-spanning eye gazes forth, dwells long,
And counts the varied gathering of the products.

Busy the far, the sunlit panorama,
Prairie, orchard, and yellow grain of the North,
Cotton and rice of the South and Louisianian cane,
100 Open unseeded fallows, rich fields of clover and timothy,
Kine and horses feeding, and droves of sheep and swine,
And many a stately river flowing and many a jocund brook,
And healthy uplands with herby-perfumed breezes,
And the good green grass, that delicate miracle the
     ever-recurring grass.

8
Toil on heroes! harvest the products!
Not alone on those warlike fields the Mother of All,
With dilated form and lambent eyes watch'd you.

Toil on heroes! toil well! handle the weapons well!
The Mother of All, yet here as ever she watches you.

110 Well-pleased America thou beholdest,
Over the fields of the West those crawling monsters,
The human-divine inventions, the labor-saving implements;
Beholdest moving in every direction imbued as with life the
     revolving hay-rakes,
The steam-power reaping-machines and the horse-power
     machines.

The engines, thrashers of grain and cleaners of grain, well
    separating the straw, the nimble work of the patent
    pitchfork,
Beholdest the newer saw-mill, the southern cotton-gin, and
    the rice-cleanser.

Beneath thy look O Maternal,
With these and else and with their own strong hands the
    heroes harvest.

All gather and all harvest,
120 Yet but for thee O Powerful, not a scythe might swing as
    now in security,
Not a maize-stalk dangle as now its silken tassels in peace.

Under thee only they harvest, even but a wisp of hay under
    thy great face only,
Harvest the wheat of Ohio, Illinois, Wisconsin, every barbed
    spear under thee,
Harvest the maize of Missouri, Kentucky, Tennessee, each
    ear in its light-green sheath,
Gather the hay to its myriad mows in the odorous tranquil
    barns,
Oats to their bins, the white potato, the buckwheat of
    Michigan, to theirs;
Gather the cotton in Mississippi or Alabama, dig and hoard
    the golden the sweet potato of Georgia and the Carolinas,
Clip the wool of California or Pennsylvania,
Cut the flax in the Middle States, or hemp or tobacco in the
    Borders,
130 Pick the pea and the bean, or pull apples from the trees or
    bunches of grapes from the vines,
Or aught that ripens in all these States or North or South,
Under the beaming sun and under thee.

There Was a Child Went Forth

There was a child went forth every day,
And the first object he look'd upon, that object he became,
And that object became part of him for the day or a certain
part of the day,
Or for many years or stretching cycles of years.

The early lilacs became part of this child,
And grass and white and red morning-glories, and white and
red clover, and the song of the phoebe-bird,
And the Third-month lambs and the sow's pink-faint litter,
and the mare's foal and the cow's calf,
And the noisy brood of the barnyard or by the mire of the
pond-side,
And the fish suspending themselves so curiously below
there, and the beautiful curious liquid,
10   And the water-plants with their graceful flat heads, all
became part of him.

The field-sprouts of Fourth-month and Fifth-month
became part of him,
Winter-grain sprouts and those of the light-yellow corn, and
the esculent roots of the garden,
And the apple-trees cover'd with blossoms and the fruit
afterward, and wood-berries and the commonest weeds by
the road,
And the old drunkard staggering home from the outhouse of
the tavern whence he had lately risen,
And the schoolmistress that pass'd on her way to the school,
And the friendly boys that pass'd, and the quarrelsome boys,
And the tidy and fresh-cheek'd girls, and the barefoot negro
boy and girl,
And all the changes of city and country wherever he went.

His own parents, he that had father'd him and she that had
conceiv'd him in her womb and birth'd him,
20   They gave this child more of themselves than that,
They gave him afterward every day, they became part of
him.

The mother at home quietly placing the dishes on the
supper-table,
The mother with mild words, clean her cap and gown, a
wholesome odor falling off her person and clothes as she
walks by,
The father, strong, self-sufficient, manly, mean, anger'd,
unjust,
The blow, the quick loud word, the tight bargain, the crafty
lure,
The family usages, the language, the company, the furniture,
the yearning and swelling heart,
Affection that will not be gainsay'd, the sense of what is real,
the thoughts if after all it should prove unreal,
The doubts of day-time and the doubts of night-time, the
curious whether and how,
Whether that which appears so is so, or is it all flashes and
specks?
30   Men and women crowding fast in the streets, if they are not
flashes and specks what are they?
The streets themselves and the façades of houses, and goods
in the windows,
Vehicles, teams, the heavy-plank'd wharves, the huge
crossing at the ferries,
The village on the highland seen from afar at sunset, the
river between,
Shadows, aureola and mist, the light falling on roofs and
gables of white or brown two miles off,
The schooner near by sleepily dropping down the tide, the
little boat slack-tow'd astern,
The hurrying tumbling waves, quick-broken crests,
slapping,

The strata of color'd clouds, the long bar of maroon-tint
  away solitary by itself, the spread of purity it lies
  motionless in,
The horizon's edge, the flying sea-crow, the fragrance of
  salt marsh and shore mud,
These became part of that child who went forth every day,
  and who now goes, and will always go forth every day.

Old Ireland

Far hence amid an isle of wondrous beauty,
Crouching over a grave an ancient sorrowful mother,
Once a queen, now lean and tatter'd seated on the ground,
Her old white hair drooping dishevel'd round her shoulders,
At her feet fallen an unused royal harp,
Long silent, she too long silent, mourning her shrouded hope
  and heir,
Of all the earth her heart most full of sorrow because most
  full of love.

Yet a word ancient mother,
You need crouch there no longer on the cold ground with
  forehead between your knees,
10   O you need not sit there veil'd in your old white hair so
  dishevel'd,
For know you the one you mourn is not in that grave,
It was an illusion, the son you love was not really dead,
The Lord is not dead, he is risen again young and strong in
  another country,
Even while you wept there by your fallen harp by the grave,
What you wept for was translated, pass'd from the grave,
The winds favour'd and the sea sail'd it,
And now with rosy and new blood,
Moves to-day in a new country.

The City Dead-House

By the city dead-house by the gate,
As idly sauntering wending my way from the clangor,
I curious pause, for lo, an outcast form, a poor dead
   prostitute brought,
Her corpse they deposit unclaim'd, it lies on the damp brick
   pavement,
The divine woman, her body, I see the body, I look on it
   alone,
That house once full of passion and beauty, all else I notice
   not,
Nor stillness so cold, nor running water from faucet, nor
   odors morbific impress me,
But the house alone – that wondrous house – that delicate
   fair house – that ruin!
That immortal house more than all the rows of dwellings
   ever built!
10   Or white-domed capitol with majestic figure surmounted,
   or all the old high-spired cathedrals,
That little house alone more than them all – poor,
   desperate house!
Fair, fearful wreck – tenement of a soul – itself a soul,
Unclaim'd, avoided house – take one breath from my
   tremulous lips,
Take one tear dropt aside as I go for thought of you,
Dead house of love – house of madness and sin, crumbled,
   crush'd,
House of life, erewhile talking and laughing – but ah, poor
   house, dead even then,
Months, years, an echoing, garnish'd house – but dead,
   dead, dead.

This Compost

1

Something startles me where I thought I was safest,
I withdraw from the still woods I loved,
I will not go now on the pastures to walk,
I will not strip the clothes from my body to meet my lover
    the sea,
I will not touch my flesh to the earth as to other flesh to
    renew me.

O how can it be that the ground itself does not sicken?
How can you be alive you growths of spring?
How can you furnish health you blood of herbs, roots,
    orchards, grain?
Are they not continually putting distemper'd corpses
    within you?
Is not every continent work'd over and over with sour dead?

Where have you disposed of their carcasses?
Those drunkards and gluttons of so many generations?
Where have you drawn off all the foul liquid and meat?
I do not see any of it upon you to-day, or perhaps I am
    deceiv'd,
I will run a furrow with my plough, I will press my spade
    through the sod and turn it up underneath,
I am sure I shall expose some of the foul meat.

2

Behold this compost! behold it well!
Perhaps every mite has once form'd part of a sick person –
    yet behold!
The grass of spring covers the prairies,
The bean bursts noiselessly through the mould in the
    garden,
The delicate spear of the onion pierces upward,
The apple-buds cluster together on the apple-branches,
The resurrection of the wheat appears with pale visage out
    of its graves,

The tinge awakes over the willow-tree and the
    mulberry-tree,
The he-birds carol mornings and evenings while the
    she-birds sit on their nests,
The young of poultry break through the hatch'd eggs,
The new-born of animals appear, the calf is dropt from the
    cow, the colt from the mare,
Out of its little hill faithfully rise the potato's dark green
    leaves,
Out of its hill rises the yellow maize-stalk, the lilacs bloom
    in the dooryards,
30 The summer growth is innocent and disdainful above all
    those strata of sour dead.

What chemistry!
That the winds are really not infectious,
That this is no cheat, this transparent green-wash of the sea
    which is so amorous after me,
That it is safe to allow it to lick my naked body all over with
    its tongues,
That it will not endanger me with the fevers that have
    deposited themselves in it,
That all is clean forever and forever,
That the cool drink from the well tastes so good,
That blackberries are so flavorous and juicy,
That the fruits of the apple-orchard and the orange-orchard,
    that melons, grapes, peaches, plums, will none of them
    poison me,
40 That when I recline on the grass I do not catch any disease,
Though probably every spear of grass rises out of what
    was once a catching disease.

Now I am terrified at the Earth, it is that calm and patient,
It grows such sweet things out of such corruptions,
It turns harmless and stainless on its axis, with such endless
    successions of diseas'd corpses,
It distills such exquisite winds out of such infused fetor,
It renews with such unwitting looks its prodigal, annual,
    sumptuous crops,

It gives such divine materials to men, and accepts such
    leavings from them at last.

To a Foil'd European Revolutionaire

Courage yet, my brother or my sister!
Keep on – Liberty is to be subserv'd whatever occurs;
That is nothing that is quell'd by one or two failures, or any
    number of failures,
Or by the indifference or ingratitude of the people, or by any
    unfaithfulness,
Or the show of the tushes of power, soldiers, cannon, penal
    statutes.

What we believe in waits latent forever through all the
    continents,
Invites no one, promises nothing, sits in calmness and light,
    is positive, and composed, knows no discouragement,
Waiting patiently, waiting its time.

(Not songs of loyalty alone are these,
10   But songs of insurrection also,
For I am the sworn poet of every dauntless rebel the world
    over,
And he going with me leaves peace and routine behind him,
And stakes his life to be lost at any moment.)

The battle rages with many a loud alarm and frequent
    advance and retreat,
The infidel triumphs, or supposes he triumphs,
The prison, scaffold, garroté, handcuffs, iron necklace and
    lead-balls do their work,
The named and unnamed heroes pass to other spheres,
The great speakers and writers are exiled, they lie sick in
    distant lands,
The cause is asleep, the strongest throats are choked with
    their own blood,

20 The young men droop their eyelashes toward the ground
      when they meet;
   But for all this Liberty has not gone out of the place, nor
      the infidel enter'd into full possession.

   When liberty goes out of a place it is not the first to go, nor
      the second or third to go,
   It waits for all the rest to go, it is the last.

   When there are no more memories of heroes and martyrs,
   And when all life and all the souls of men and women are
      discharged from any part of the earth,
   Then only shall liberty or the idea of liberty be
      discharged from that part of the earth,
   And the infidel come into full possession.

   Then courage European revolter, revoltress!
   For till all ceases neither must you cease.

30 I do not know what you are for, (I do not know what I am
      for myself, nor what any thing is for,)
   But I will search carefully for it even in being foil'd,
   In defeat, poverty, misconception, imprisonment – for they
      too are great.

   Did we think victory great?
   So it is – but now it seems to me, when it cannot be help'd,
      that defeat is great,
   And that death and dismay are great.

Unnamed Lands

Nations ten thousand years before these States, and many
   times ten thousand years before these States,
Garner'd clusters of ages that men and women like us grew
   up and travel'd their course and pass'd on,
What vast-built cities, what orderly republics, what pastoral
   tribes and nomads,

What histories, rulers, heroes, perhaps transcending all
    others,
What laws, customs, wealth, arts, traditions,
What sort of marriage, what costumes, what physiology and
    phrenology,
What of liberty and slavery among them, what they thought
    of death and the soul,
Who were witty and wise, who beautiful and poetic, who
    brutish and undevelop'd,
Not a mark, not a record remains – and yet all remains.

10   O I know that those men and women were not for nothing,
    any more than we are for nothing,
    I know that they belong to the scheme of the world every
    bit as much as we now belong to it.

Afar they stand, yet near to me they stand,
Some with oval countenances learn'd and calm,
Some naked and savage, some like huge collections of
    insects,
Some in tents, herdsmen, patriarchs, tribes, horsemen,
Some prowling through woods, some living peaceably on
    farms, laboring, reaping, filling barns,
Some traversing paved avenues, amid temples, palaces,
    factories, libraries, shows, courts, theatres, wonderful
    monuments.

Are those billions of men really gone?
Are those women of the old experience of the earth gone?
20   Do their lives, cities, arts, rest only with us?
Did they achieve nothing for good for themselves?

I believe of all those men and women that fill'd the
    unnamed lands, every one exists this hour here or
    elsewhere, invisible to us,
In exact proportion to what he or she grew from in life, and
    out of what he or she did, felt, became, loved, sinn'd,
    in life.

I believe that was not the end of those nations or any
    person of them, any more than this shall be the end of
    my nation, or of me;
Of their languages, governments, marriage, literature,
    products, games, wars, manners, crimes, prisons, slaves,
    heroes, poets,
I suspect their results curiously await in the yet unseen
    world, counterparts of what accrued to them in the seen
    world,
I suspect I shall meet them there,
I suspect I shall there find each old particular of those
    unnamed lands.

Song of Prudence

Manhattan's streets I saunter'd pondering,
On Time, Space, Reality – on such as these, and abreast
    with them Prudence.

The last explanation always remains to be made about
    prudence,
Little and large alike drop quietly aside from the prudence
    that suits immortality.

The soul is of itself,
All verges to it, all has reference to what ensues,
All that a person does, says, thinks, is of consequence,
Not a move can a man or woman make, that affects him or
    her in a day, month, any part of the direct lifetime, or the
    hour of death,
But the same affects him or her onward afterward through
    the indirect lifetime.

10   The indirect is just as much as the direct,
The spirit receives from the body just as much as it gives to
    the body, if not more.

Not one word or deed, not venereal sore, discoloration,
    privacy of the onanist,
Putridity of gluttons or rum-drinkers, peculation, cunning,
    betrayal, murder, seduction, prostitution,
But has results beyond death as really as before death.

Charity and personal force are the only investments worth
    any thing.

No specification is necessary, all that a male or female does,
    that is vigorous, benevolent, clean, is so much profit to
    him or her,
In the unshakable order of the universe and through the
    whole scope of it forever.

Who has been wise receives interest,
Savage, felon, President, judge, farmer, sailor, mechanic,
    literat, young, old, it is the same,
20 The interest will come round – all will come round.

Singly, wholly, to affect now, affected their time, will
    forever affect all of the past and all of the present and all
    of the future,
All the brave actions of war and peace,
All help given to relatives, strangers, the poor, old,
    sorrowful, young children, widows, the sick, and to
    shunn'd persons,
All self-denial that stood steady and aloof on wrecks, and
    saw others fill the seats of the boats,
All offering of substance or life for the good old cause, or for
    a friend's sake, or opinion's sake,
All pains of enthusiasts scoff'd at by their neighbors,
All the limitless sweet love and precious suffering of mothers,
All honest men baffled in strifes recorded or unrecorded,
All the grandeur and good of ancient nations whose
    fragments we inherit,
30 All the good of the dozens of ancient nations unknown to
    us by name, date, location,
All that was ever manfully begun, whether it succeeded or
    no,

All suggestions of the divine mind of man or the divinity
    of his mouth, or the shaping of his great hands,
All that is well thought or said this day on any part of the
    globe, or on any of the wandering stars, or on any of the
    fix'd stars, by those there as we are here,
All that is henceforth to be thought or done by you whoever
    you are, or by any one,
These inure, have inured, shall inure, to the identities from
    which they sprang, or shall spring.

Did you guess any thing lived only its moment?
The world does not so exist, no parts palpable or impalpable
    so exist,
No consummation exists without being from some long
    previous consummation, and that from some other,
Without the farthest conceivable one coming a bit nearer the
    beginning than any.

40 Whatever satisfies souls is true;
Prudence entirely satisfies the craving and glut of souls,
Itself only finally satisfies the soul,
The soul has that measureless pride which revolts from
    every lesson but its own.

Now I breathe the word of the prudence that walks abreast
    with time, space, reality,
That answers the pride which refuses every lesson but its
    own.

What is prudence is indivisible,
Declines to separate one part of life from every part,
Divides not the righteous from the unrighteous or the living
    from the dead,
Matches every thought or act by its correlative,
50 Knows no possible forgiveness or deputed atonement,
Knows that the young man who composedly peril'd his life
    and lost it has done exceedingly well for himself without
    doubt,
That he who never peril'd his life, but retains it to old age in

riches and ease, has probably achiev'd nothing for himself
    worth mentioning,
Knows that only that person has really learn'd who has
    learn'd to prefer results,
Who favors body and soul the same,
Who perceives the indirect assuredly following the direct,
Who in his spirit in any emergency whatever neither
    hurries nor avoids death.

The Singer in the Prison

1

O sight of pity, shame and dole!
O fearful thought – a convict soul.

Rang the refrain along the hall, the prison,
Rose to the roof, the vaults of heaven above,
Pouring in floods of melody in tones so pensive sweet and
    strong the like whereof was never heard,
Reaching the far-off sentry and the armed guards, who
    ceas'd their pacing,
Making the hearer's pulses stop for ecstasy and awe.

2

The sun was low in the west one winter day,
When down a narrow aisle amid the thieves and outlaws of
    the land,
10 (There by the hundreds seated, sear-faced murderers, wily
    counterfeiters,
Gather'd to Sunday church in prison walls, the keepers
    round,
Plenteous, well-armed, watching with vigilant eyes,)
Calmly a lady walk'd holding a little innocent child by
    either hand,
Whom seating on their stools beside her on the platform,
She, first preluding with the instrument a low and musical
    prelude,
In voice surpassing all, sang forth a quaint old hymn.

A soul confined by bars and bands,
Cries, help! O help! and wrings her hands,
Blinded her eyes, bleeding her breast,
20 Nor pardon finds, nor balm of rest.

Ceaseless she paces to and fro,
O heart-sick days! O nights of woe!
Nor hand of friend, nor loving face,
Nor favor comes, nor word of grace.

It was not I that sinn'd the sin,
The ruthless body dragg'd me in;'
Though long I strove courageously,
The body was too much for me.

Dear prison'd soul bear up a space,
30 For soon or late the certain grace;
To set thee free and bear thee home,
The heavenly pardoner death shall come.

Convict no more, nor shame, nor dole!
Depart – a God-enfranchis'd soul!

3
The singer ceas'd,
One glance swept from her clear calm eyes o'er all those
        upturn'd faces,
Strange sea of prison faces, a thousand varied, crafty, brutal,
        seam'd and beauteous faces,
Then rising, passing back along the narrow aisle between
        them,
While her gown touch'd them rustling in the silence,
40 She vanish'd with her children in the dusk.
While upon all, convicts and armed keepers ere they stirr'd,
(Convict forgetting prison, keeper his loaded pistol,)
A hush and pause fell down a wondrous minute,
With deep half-stifled sobs and sound of bad men bow'd and
        moved to weeping,
And youth's convulsive breathings, memories of home,

The mother's voice in lullaby, the sister's care, the happy
    childhood,
The long-pent spirit rous'd to reminiscence;
A wondrous minute then – but after in the solitary night, to
    many, many there,
Years after, even in the hour of death, the sad refrain, the
    tune, the voice, the words,
50   Resumed, the large calm lady walks the narrow aisle,
The wailing melody again, the singer in the prison sings,

> *O sight of pity, shame and dole!*
> *O fearful thought – a convict soul.*

Warble for Lilac-Time

Warble me now for joy of lilac-time, (returning in
    reminiscence,)
Sort me O tongue and lips for Nature's sake, souvenirs of
    earliest summer,
Gather the welcome signs, (as children with pebbles or
    stringing shells,)
Put in April and May, the hylas croaking in the ponds, the
    elastic air,
Bees, butterflies, the sparrow with its simple notes,
Blue-bird and darting swallow, nor forget the high-hole
    flashing his golden wings,
The tranquil sunny haze, the clinging smoke, the vapor,
Shimmer of waters with fish in them, the cerulean above,
All that is jocund and sparkling, the brooks running,
10   The maple woods, the crisp February days and the
    sugar-making,
The robin where he hops, bright-eyed, brown-breasted,
With musical clear call at sunrise, and again at sunset,
Or flitting among the trees of the apple-orchard, building
    the nest of his mate,
The melted snow of March, the willow sending forth its
    yellow-green sprouts,

For spring-time is here! the summer is here! and what is
  this in it and from it?
Thou, soul, unloosen'd – the restlessness after I know not
  what;
Come, let us lag here no longer, let us be up and away!
O if one could but fly like a bird!
O to escape, to sail forth as in a ship!
20 To glide with thee O soul, o'er all, in all, as a ship o'er the
  waters;
Gathering these hints, the preludes, the blue sky, the grass,
  the morning drops of dew,
The lilac-scent, the bushes with dark green heart-shaped
  leaves,
Wood-violets, the little delicate pale blossoms called
  innocence,
Samples and sorts not for themselves alone, but for their
  atmosphere,
To grace the bush I love – to sing with the birds,
A warble for joy of lilac-time, returning in reminiscence.

Outlines for a Tomb
(G.P., BURIED 1870)

1

What may we chant, O thou within this tomb?
What tablets, outlines, hang for thee, O millionaire?
The life thou lived'st we know not,
But that thou walk'dst thy years in barter, 'mid the haunts of
  brokers,
Nor heroism thine, nor war, nor glory.

2

Silent, my soul,
With drooping lids, as waiting, ponder'd,
Turning from all the samples, monuments of heroes.

While through the interior vistas,
10   Noiseless uprose, phantasmic, (as by night Auroras of the
      north,)
Lambent tableaus, prophetic, bodiless scenes,
Spiritual projections.

In one, among the city streets a laborer's home appear'd,
After his day's work done, cleanly, sweet-air'd, the gaslight
      burning,
The carpet swept and a fire in the cheerful stove.

In one, the sacred parturition scene,
A happy painless mother birth'd a perfect child.

In one, at a bounteous morning meal,
Sat peaceful parents with contented sons.

20   In one, by twos and threes, young people,
Hundreds concentring, walk'd the paths and streets and
      roads,
Toward a tall-domed school.

In one a trio beautiful,
Grandmother, loving daughter, loving daughter's daughter,
      sat,
Chatting and sewing.

In one, along a suite of noble rooms,
'Mid plenteous books and journals, paintings on the walls,
      fine statuettes,
Were groups of friendly journeymen, mechanics young and
      old,
Reading, conversing.

30   All, all the shows of laboring life,
City and country, women's, men's and children's,
Their wants provided for, hued in the sun and tinged for
      once with joy,
Marriage, the street, the factory, farm, the house-room,
      lodging-room,

Labor and toil, the bath, gymnasium, playground, library,
    college,
The student, boy or girl, led forward to be taught,
The sick cared for, the shoeless shod, the orphan father'd
    and mother'd,
The hungry fed, the houseless housed;
(The intentions perfect and divine,
The workings, details, haply human.)

3

40 O thou within this tomb,
From thee such scenes, thou stintless, lavish giver,
Tallying the gifts of earth, large as the earth,
Thy name an earth, with mountains, fields and tides.

Nor by your streams alone, you rivers,
By you, your banks Connecticut,
By you and all your teeming life old Thames,
By you Potomac laving the ground Washington trod, by you
    Patapsco,
You Hudson, you endless Mississippi – nor you alone,
But to the high seas launch, my thought, his memory.

Out from Behind This Mask
(TO CONFRONT A PORTRAIT)

1

Out from behind this bending rough-cut mask,
These lights and shades, this drama of the whole,
This common curtain of the face contain'd in me for me, in
    you for you, in each for each,
(Tragedies, sorrows, laughter, tears – O heaven!
The passionate teeming plays this curtain hid!)
This glaze of God's serenest purest sky,
This film of Satan's seething pit,
This heart's geography's map, this limitless small continent,
    this soundless sea;
Out from the convolutions of this globe,

10   This subtler astronomic orb than sun or moon, than
        Jupiter, Venus, Mars,
     This condensation of the universe, (nay here the only
        universe,
     Here the idea, all in this mystic handful wrapt;)
     These burin'd eyes, flashing to you to pass to future time,
     To launch and spin through space revolving sideling, from
        these to emanate,
     To you whoe'er you are – a look.

     2

     A traveler of thoughts and years, of peace and war,
     Of youth long sped and middle age declining,
     (As the first volume of a tale perused and laid away, and this
        the second,
     Songs, ventures, speculations, presently to close,)
20   Lingering a moment here and now, to you I opposite turn,
     As on the road or at some crevice door by chance, or
        open'd window,
     Pausing, inclining, baring my head, you specially I greet,
     To draw and clinch your soul for once inseparably with
        mine,
     Then travel travel on.

Vocalism

1

Vocalism, measure, concentration, determination, and the
     divine power to speak words;
Are you full-lung'd and limber-lipp'd from long trial? from
     vigorous practice? from physique?
Do you move in these broad lands as broad as they?
Come duly to the divine power to speak words?
For only at last after many years, after chastity, friendship,
     procreation, prudence, and nakedness,
After treading ground and breasting river and lake,
After a loosen'd throat, after absorbing eras,
     temperaments, races, after knowledge, freedom, crimes,

After complete faith, after clarifyings, elevations, and
  removing obstructions,
After these and more, it is just possible there comes to a man,
  a woman, the divine power to speak words;
10 Then toward that man or that woman swiftly hasten all—
  none refuse, all attend,
Armies, ships, antiquities, libraries, paintings, machines,
  cities, hate, despair, amity, pain, theft, murder, aspiration,
  form in close ranks,
They debouch as they are wanted to march obediently
  through the mouth of that man or that woman.

2
O what is it in me that makes me tremble so at voices?
Surely whoever speaks to me in the right voice, him or her
  I shall follow,
As the water follows the moon, silently, with fluid steps,
  anywhere around the globe.

All waits for the right voices;
Where is the practis'd and perfect organ? where is the
  develop'd soul?
For I see every word utter'd thence has deeper, sweeter,
  new sounds, impossible on less terms.
I see brains and lips closed, tympans and temples unstuck,
20 Until that comes which has the quality to strike and to
  unclose,
Until that comes which has the quality to bring forth what
  lies slumbering forever ready in all words.

To Him That was Crucified

My spirit to yours dear brother,
Do not mind because many sounding your name do not
  understand you,
I do not sound your name, but I understand you,
I specify you with joy O my comrade to salute you, and to

salute those who are with you, before and since, and those
to come also,
That we all labor together transmitting the same charge and
succession,
We few equals indifferent of lands, indifferent of times,
We, enclosers of all continents, all castes, allowers of all
theologies,
Compassionaters, perceivers, rapport of men,
We walk silent among disputes and assertions, but reject not
the disputers nor any thing that is asserted,
10 We hear the bawling and din, we are reach'd at by divisions,
jealousies, recriminations on every side,
They close peremptorily upon us to surround us, my
comrade,
Yet we walk unheld, free, the whole earth over, journeying
up and down till we make our ineffaceable mark upon
time and the diverse eras,
Till we saturate time and eras, that the men and women of
races, ages to come, may prove brethren and lovers as
we are.

You Felons on Trial in Courts

You felons on trial in courts,
You convicts in prison-cells, you sentenced assassins chain'd
and handcuff'd with iron,
Who am I too that I am not on trial or in prison?
Me ruthless and devilish as any, that my wrists are not
chain'd with iron, or my ankles with iron?

You prostitutes flaunting over the trottoirs or obscene in
your rooms,
Who am I that I should call you more obscene than myself?

O culpable! I acknowledge – I exposé!
(O admirers, praise not me – compliment not me – you make
me wince,
I see what you do not – I know what you do not.)

10   Inside these breast-bones I lie smutch'd and choked,
Beneath this face that appears so impassive hell's tides
    continually run,
Lusts and wickedness are acceptable to me,
I walk with delinquents with passionate love,
I feel I am of them – I belong to those convicts and
    prostitutes myself,
And henceforth I will not deny them – for how can I deny
    myself?

Laws for Creations

Laws for creations,
For strong artists and leaders, for fresh broods of teachers
    and perfect literats for America,
For noble savans and coming musicians.

All must have reference to the ensemble of the world, and
    the compact truth of the world,
There shall be no subject too pronounced – all works shall
    illustrate the divine law of indirections.

What do you suppose creation is?
What do you suppose will satisfy the soul, except to walk
    free and own no superior?
What do you suppose I would intimate to you in a hundred
    ways, but that man or woman is as good as God?
And that there is no God any more divine than Yourself?
10   And that that is what the oldest and newest myths finally
    mean?
And that you or any one must approach creations through
    such laws?

To a Common Prostitute

Be composed – be at ease with me – I am Walt Whitman,
    liberal and lusty as Nature,
Not till the sun excludes you do I exclude you,
Not till the waters refuse to glisten for you and the leaves to
    rustle for you, do my words refuse to glisten and rustle
    for you.

My girl I appoint with you an appointment, and I charge
    you that you make preparation to be worthy to meet me,
And I charge you that you be patient and perfect till I come.

Till then I salute you with a significant look that you do not
    forget me.

I Was Looking a Long While

I was looking a long while for Intentions,
For a clew to the history of the past for myself, and for these
    chants – and now I have found it,
It is not in those paged fables in the libraries, (them I
    neither accept nor reject,)
It is no more in the legends than in all else,
It is in the present – it is this earth to-day,
It is in Democracy – (the purport and aim of all the past,)
It is the life of one man or one woman to-day – the average
    man of to-day,
It is in languages, social customs, literatures, arts,
It is in the broad show of artificial things, ships, machinery,
    politics, creeds, modern improvements, and the
    interchange of nations,
10   All for the modern – all for the average man of to-day.

Thought

Of persons arrived at high positions, ceremonies, wealth,
    scholarships, and the like;
(To me all that those persons have arrived at sinks away from
    them, except as it results to their bodies and souls,
So that often to me they appear gaunt and naked,
And often to me each one mocks the others, and mocks
    himself or herself,
And of each one the core of life, namely happiness, is full of
    the rotten excrement of maggots,
And often to me those men and women pass unwittingly the
    true realities of life, and go toward false realities,
And often to me they are alive after what custom has served
    them, but nothing more,
And often to me they are sad, hasty, unwaked
    sonnambules walking the dusk.)

Miracles

Why, who makes much of a miracle?
As to me I know of nothing else but miracles,
Whether I walk the streets of Manhattan,
Or dart my sight over the roofs of houses toward the sky,
Or wade with naked feet along the beach just in the edge
    of the water,
Or stand under trees in the woods,
Or talk by day with any one I love, or sleep in the bed at
    night with any one I love,
Or sit at table at dinner with the rest,
Or look at strangers opposite me riding in the car,
10   Or watch honey-bees busy around the hive of a summer
    forenoon,
Or animals feeding in the fields,
Or birds, or the wonderfulness of insects in the air,
Or the wonderfulness of the sundown, or of stars shining so
    quiet and bright,

Or the exquisite delicate thin curve of the new moon in
 spring;
These with the rest, one and all, are to me miracles,
The whole referring, yet each distinct and in its place.

To me every hour of the light and dark is a miracle,
Every cubic inch of space is a miracle,
Every square yard of the surface of the earth is spread with
 the same,
20 Every foot of the interior swarms with the same.

To me the sea is a continual miracle,
The fishes that swim – the rocks – the motion of the waves –
 the ships with men in them,
What stranger miracles are there?

Sparkles from the Wheel

Where the city's ceaseless crowd moves on the livelong day,
Withdrawn I join a group of children watching, I pause
 aside with them.

By the curb toward the edge of the flagging,
A knife-grinder works at his wheel sharpening a great knife,
Bending over he carefully holds it to the stone, by foot and
 knee,
With measur'd tread he turns rapidly, as he presses with
 light but firm hand,
Forth issue then in copious golden jets,
Sparkles from the wheel.

The scene and all its belongings, how they seize and affect
 me,
10 The sad sharp-chinn'd old man with worn clothes and
 broad shoulder-band of leather,
Myself effusing and fluid, a phantom curiously floating,
 now here absorb'd and arrested,
The group, (an unminded point set in a vast surrounding,)

The attentive, quiet children, the loud, proud, restive base
    of the streets,
The low hoarse purr of the whirling stone, the light-press'd
    blade,
Diffusing, dropping, sideways-darting, in tiny showers of
    gold,
Sparkles from the wheel.

To a Pupil

Is reform needed? is it through you?
The greater the reform needed, the greater the Personality
    you need to accomplish it.

You! do you not see how it would serve to have eyes,
    blood, complexion, clean and sweet?
Do you not see how it would serve to have such a body and
    soul that when you enter the crowd an atmosphere of
    desire and command enters with you, and every one is
    impress'd with your Personality?

O the magnet! the flesh over and over!
Go, dear friend, if need be give up all else, and commence
    to-day to inure yourself to pluck, reality, self-esteem,
    definiteness, elevatedness,
Rest not till you rivet and publish yourself of your own
    Personality.

Unfolded Out of the Folds

Unfolded out of the folds of the woman man comes unfolded,
    and is always to come unfolded,
Unfolded only out of the superbest woman of the earth is
    to come the superbest man of the earth,
Unfolded out of the friendliest woman is to come the
    friendliest man,

412   WHAT AM I AFTER ALL

Unfolded only out of the perfect body of a woman can a man
be form'd of perfect body,
Unfolded only out of the inimitable poems of woman can
come the poems of man, (only thence have my poems
come;)
Unfolded out of the strong and arrogant woman I love, only
thence can appear the strong and arrogant man I love,
Unfolded by brawny embraces from the well-muscled
woman I love, only thence come the brawny embraces of
the man,
Unfolded out of the folds of the woman's brain come all the
folds of the man's brain, duly obedient,
Unfolded out of the justice of the woman all justice is
unfolded,
10 Unfolded out of the sympathy of the woman is all
sympathy;
A man is a great thing upon the earth and through eternity,
but every jot of the greatness of man is unfolded out of
woman;
First the man is shaped in the woman, he can then be
shaped in himself.

What am I After All

What am I after all but a child, pleas'd with the sound of
my own name? repeating it over and over;
I stand apart to hear – it never tires me.

To you your name also;
Did you think there was nothing but two or three
pronunciations in the sound of your name?

Kosmos

Who includes diversity and is Nature,
Who is the amplitude of the earth and the coarseness and
    sexuality of the earth, and the great charity of the earth,
    and the equilibrium also,
Who has not look'd forth from the windows the eyes for
    nothing, or whose brain held audience with messengers
    for nothing,
Who contains believers and disbelievers, who is the most
    majestic lover,
Who holds duly his or her triune proportion of realism,
    spiritualism, and of the aesthetic or intellectual,
Who having consider'd the body finds all its organs and
    parts good,
Who, out of the theory of the earth and of his or her body,
    understands by subtle analogies all other theories,
The theory of a city, a poem, and of the large politics of
    these States;
Who believes not only in our globe with its sun and moon,
    but in other globes with their suns and moons,
10 Who, constructing the house of himself or herself, not for a
    day but for all time, sees races, eras, dates, generations,
The past, the future, dwelling there, like space,
    inseparable together.

Others May Praise What They Like

Others may praise what they like;
But I, from the banks of the running Missouri, praise
    nothing in art or aught else,
Till it has well inhaled the atmosphere of this river, also the
    western prairie-scent,
And exudes it all again.

Who Learns My Lesson Complete?

Who learns my lesson complete?
Boss, journeyman, apprentice, churchman and atheist,
The stupid and the wise thinker, parents and offspring,
    merchant, clerk, porter and customer,
Editor, author, artist, and schoolboy – draw nigh and
    commence;
It is no lesson – it lets down the bars to a good lesson,
And that to another, and every one to another still.

The great laws take and effuse without argument,
I am of the same style, for I am their friend,
I love them quits and quits, I do not halt and make salaams.

10   I lie abstracted and hear beautiful tales of things and the
    reasons of things,
They are so beautiful I nudge myself to listen.

I cannot say to any person what I hear – I cannot say it to
    myself – it is very wonderful.

It is no small matter, this round and delicious globe moving
    so exactly in its orbit for ever and ever, without one jolt
    or the untruth of a single second,
I do not think it was made in six days, nor in ten
    thousand years, nor ten billions of years,
Nor plann'd and built one thing after another as an
    architect plans and builds a house.

I do not think seventy years is the time of a man or
    woman,
Nor that seventy millions of years is the time of a man or
    woman,
Nor that years will ever stop the existence of me, or any
    one else.

Is it wonderful that I should be immortal? as every one is
    immortal;
20   I know it is wonderful, but my eyesight is equally wonderful,

and how I was conceived in my mother's womb is equally
    wonderful,
And pass'd from a babe in the creeping trance of a couple of
    summers and winters to articulate and walk – all this is
    equally wonderful.

And that my soul embraces you this hour, and we affect each
    other without ever seeing each other, and never perhaps to
    see each other, is every bit as wonderful.

And that I can think such thoughts as these is just as
    wonderful,
And that I can remind you, and you think them and know
    them to be true, is just as wonderful.

And that the moon spins round the earth and on with the
    earth, is equally wonderful,
And that they balance themselves with the sun and stars is
    equally wonderful.

Tests

All submit to them where they sit, inner, secure,
    unapproachable to analysis in the soul,
Not traditions, not the outer authorities are the judges,
They are the judges of outer authorities and of all traditions,
They corroborate as they go only whatever corroborates
    themselves, and touches themselves;
For all that, they have it forever in themselves to corroborate
    far and near without one exception.

The Torch

On my Northwest coast in the midst of the night a
    fisherman's group stands watching,
Out on the lake that expands before them, others are
    spearing salmon,

The canoe, a dim shadowy thing, moves across the black
    water,
Bearing a torch ablaze at the prow.

O Star of France (1870-71)

O star of France,
The brightness of thy hope and strength and fame,
Like some proud ship that led the fleet so long,
Beseems to-day a wreck driven by the gale, a mastless hulk,
And 'mid its teeming madden'd half-drown'd crowds,
Nor helm nor helmsman.

Dim smitten star,
Orb not of France alone, pale symbol of my soul, its
    dearest hopes,
The struggle and the daring, rage divine for liberty,
10 Of aspirations toward the far ideal, enthusiast's dreams of
    brotherhood,
Of terror to the tyrant and the priest.

Star crucified – by traitors sold,
Star panting o'er a land of death, heroic land,
Strange, passionate, mocking, frivolous land.

Miserable! yet for thy errors, vanities, sins, I will not now
    rebuke thee,
Thy unexampled woes and pangs have quell'd them all,
And left thee sacred.

In that amid thy many faults thou ever aimedst highly,
In that thou wouldst not really sell thyself however great the
    price,
20 In that thou surely wakedst weeping from thy drugg'd
    sleep,
In that alone among thy sisters thou, giantess, didst rend
    the ones that shamed thee,
In that thou couldst not, wouldst not, wear the usual chains,

This cross, thy livid face, thy pierced hands and feet,
The spear thrust in thy side.

O star! O ship of France, beat back and baffled long!
Bear up O smitten orb! O ship continue on!

Sure as the ship of all, the Earth itself,
Product of deathly fire and turbulent chaos,
Forth from its spasms of fury and its poisons,
30 Issuing at last in perfect power and beauty,
Onward beneath the sun following its course,
So thee O ship of France!

Finish'd the days, the clouds dispel'd,
The travail o'er, the long-sought extrication,
When lo! reborn high o'er the European world,
(In gladness answering thence, as face afar to face, reflecting
   ours Columbia,)
Again thy star O France, fair lustrous star,
In heavenly peace, clearer, more bright than ever,
Shall beam immortal.

The Ox-Tamer

In a far-away northern county in the placid pastoral region,
Lives my farmer friend, the theme of my recitative, a
   famous tamer of oxen,
There they bring him the three-year-olds and the
   four-year-olds to break them,
He will take the wildest steer in the world and break him and
   tame him,
He will go fearless without any whip where the young
   bullock chafes up and down the yard,
The bullock's head tosses restless high in the air with raging
   eyes,
Yet see you! how soon his rage subsides – how soon this
   tamer tames him;
See you! on the farms hereabout a hundred oxen young and
   old, and he is the man who has tamed them,

They all know him, all are affectionate to him;

10 See you! some are such beautiful animals, so lofty looking;

Some are buff-color'd, some mottled, one has a white line
running along his back, some are brindled,

Some have wide flaring horns (a good sign) – see you! the
bright hides,

See, the two with stars on their foreheads – see, the round
bodies and broad backs,

How straight and square they stand on their legs – what fine
sagacious eyes!

How they watch their tamer – they wish him near them –
how they turn to look after him!

What yearning expression! how uneasy they are when he
moves away from them;

Now I marvel what it can be he appears to them, (books,
politics, poems, depart – all else departs,)

I confess I envy only his fascination – my silent, illiterate
friend,

Whom a hundred oxen love there in his life on farms,

20 In the northern county far, in the placid pastoral region.

An Old Man's Thought of School
FOR THE INAUGURATION OF A PUBLIC SCHOOL,
CAMDEN, NEW JERSEY, 1874

An old man's thought of school,
An old man gathering youthful memories and blooms that
youth itself cannot.

Now only do I know you,
O fair auroral skies – O morning dew upon the grass!

And these I see, these sparkling eyes,
These stores of mystic meaning, these young lives,
Building, equipping like a fleet of ships, immortal ships,
Soon to sail out over the measureless seas,
On the soul's voyage.

10   Only a lot of boys and girls?
      Only the tiresome spelling, writing, ciphering classes?
      Only a public school?

      Ah more, infinitely more;
      (As George Fox rais'd his warning cry, 'Is it this pile of
          brick and mortar, these dead floors, windows, rails, you
          call the church?
      Why this is not the church at all – the church is living, ever
          living souls.')

      And you America,
      Cast you the real reckoning for your present?
      The lights and shadows of your future, good or evil?
      To girlhood, boyhood look, the teacher and the school.

Wandering at Morn

      Wandering at morn,
      Emerging from the night from gloomy thoughts, thee in my
          thoughts,
      Yearning for thee harmonious Union! thee, singing bird
          divine!
      Thee coil'd in evil times my country, with craft and black
          dismay, with every meanness, treason thrust upon thee,
      This common marvel I beheld – the parent thrush I
          watch'd feeding its young,
      The singing thrush whose tones of joy and faith ecstatic,
      Fail not to certify and cheer my soul.

      There ponder'd, felt I,
      If worms, snakes, loathsome grubs, may to sweet spiritual
          songs be turn'd,
10   If vermin so transposed, so used and bless'd may be,
      Then may I trust in you, your fortunes, days, my country;
      Who knows but these may be the lessons fit for you?
      From these your future song may rise with joyous trills,
      Destin'd to fill the world.

Italian Music in Dakota
('THE SEVENTEENTH – THE FINEST REGIMENTAL
BAND I EVER HEARD.')

Through the soft evening air enwinding all,
Rocks, woods, fort, cannon, pacing sentries, endless wilds,
In dulcet streams, in flutes' and cornets' notes,
Electric, pensive, turbulent, artificial,
(Yet strangely fitting even here, meanings unknown before,
Subtler than ever, more harmony, as if born here, related
        here,
Not to the city's fresco'd rooms, not to the audience of the
        opera house,
Sounds, echoes, wandering strains, as really here at home,
Sonnambula's innocent love, trios with *Norma's* anguish,
10 And thy ecstatic chorus *Poliuto;*)
Ray'd in the limpid yellow slanting sundown,
Music, Italian music in Dakota.

While Nature, sovereign of this gnarl'd realm,
Lurking in hidden barbaric grim recesses,
Acknowledging rapport however far remov'd,
(As some old root or soil of earth its last-born flower or
        fruit,)
Listens well pleas'd.

With All Thy Gifts

With all thy gifts America,
Standing secure, rapidly tending, overlooking the world,
Power, wealth, extent, vouchsafed to thee – with these and
        like of these vouchsafed to thee,
What if one gift thou lackest? (the ultimate human problem
        never solving,)
The gift of perfect women fit for thee – what if that gift of
        gifts thou lackest?

The towering feminine of thee? the beauty, health,
  completion, fit for thee?
The mothers fit for thee?

My Picture-Gallery

In a little house keep I pictures suspended, it is not a fix'd
  house,
It is round, it is only a few inches from one side to the
  other;
Yet behold, it has room for all the shows of the world, all
  memories!
Here the tableaus of life, and here the groupings of death;
Here, do you know this? this is cicerone himself,
With finger rais'd he points to the prodigal pictures.

The Prairie States

A newer garden of creation, no primal solitude,
Dense, joyous, modern, populous millions, cities and farms,
With iron interlaced, composite, tied, many in one,
By all the world contributed – freedom's and law's and
  thrift's society,
The crown and teeming paradise, so far, of time's
  accumulations,
To justify the past.

Proud Music of the Storm

1

Proud music of the storm,
Blast that careers so free, whistling across the prairies,
Strong hum of forest tree-tops – wind of the mountains,
Personified dim shapes – you hidden orchestras,
You serenades of phantoms, with instruments alert,
Blending with Nature's rhythmus all the tongues of
    nations;
You chords left as by vast composers – you choruses,
You formless, free, religious dances – you from the Orient,
You undertone of rivers, roar of pouring cataracts,
10 You sounds from distant guns with galloping cavalry,
Echoes of camps with all the different bugle-calls,
Trooping tumultuous, filling the midnight late, bending me
    powerless,
Entering my lonesome slumber-chamber, why have you
    seiz'd me?

2

Come forward O my soul, and let the rest retire,
Listen, lose not, it is toward thee they tend,
Parting the midnight, entering my slumber-chamber,
For thee they sing and dance O soul.

A festival song,
The duet of the bridegroom and the bride, a
    marriage-march,
20 With lips of love, and hearts of lovers fill'd to the brim with
    love,
The red-flush'd cheeks and perfumes, the cortege swarming
    full of friendly faces young and old,
To flutes' clear notes and sounding harps' cantabile.

Now loud approaching drums,
Victoria! see'st thou in powder-smoke the banners torn but
    flying? the rout of the baffled?
Hearest those shouts of a conquering army?

(Ah soul, the sobs of women, the wounded groaning in agony,
The hiss and crackle of flames, the blacken'd ruins, the
    embers of cities,
The dirge and desolation of mankind.)

Now airs antique and mediaeval fill me,
30 I see and hear old harpers with their harps at Welsh festivals,
I hear the minnesingers singing their lays of love,
I hear the minstrels, gleemen, troubadours, of the middle
    ages.

Now the great organ sounds,
Tremulous, while underneath, (as the hid footholds of the
    earth,
On which arising rest, and leaping forth depend,
All shapes of beauty, grace and strength, all hues we know,
Green blades of grass and warbling birds, children that
    gambol and play, the clouds of heaven above,)
The strong base stands, and its pulsations intermits not,
Bathing, supporting, merging all the rest, maternity of all
    the rest,
40 And with it every instrument in multitudes,
The players playing, all the world's musicians,
The solemn hymns and masses rousing adoration,
All passionate heart-chants, sorrowful appeals,
The measureless sweet vocalists of ages,
And for their solvent setting earth's own diapason,
Of winds and woods and mighty ocean waves,
A new composite orchestra, binder of years and climes,
    ten-fold renewer,
As of the far-back days the poets tell, the Paradiso,
The straying thence, the separation long, but now the
    wandering done,
50 The journey done, the journeyman come home,
And man and art with Nature fused again.

Tutti! for earth and heaven;
(The Almighty leader now for once has signal'd with his
    wand.)

The manly strophe of the husbands of the world,
And all the wives responding.

The tongues of violins,
(I think O tongues ye tell this heart, that cannot tell itself,
This brooding yearning heart, that cannot tell itself.)

3
Ah from a little child,
60 Thou knowest soul how to me all sounds became music,
My mother's voice in lullaby or hymn,
(The voice, O tender voices, memory's loving voices,
Last miracle of all, O dearest mother's, sister's, voices;)
The rain, the growing corn, the breeze among the
    long-leav'd corn,
The measur'd sea-surf beating on the sand,
The twittering bird, the hawk's sharp scream,
The wild-fowl's notes at night as flying low migrating north
    or south,
The psalm in the country church or mid the clustering
    trees, the open air camp-meeting,
The fiddler in the tavern, the glee, the long-strung
    sailor-song,
70 The lowing cattle, bleating sheep, the crowing cock at dawn.

All songs of current lands come sounding round me,
The German airs of friendship, wine and love,
Irish ballads, merry jigs and dances, English warbles,
Chansons of France, Scotch tunes, and o'er the rest,
Italia's peerless compositions.

Across the stage with pallor on her face, yet lurid passion,
Stalks Norma brandishing the dagger in her hand.

I see poor crazed Lucia's eyes' unnatural gleam,
Her hair down her back falls loose and dishevel'd.

80 I see where Ernani walking the bridal garden,
Amid the scent of night-roses, radiant, holding his bride by
    the hand,
Hears the infernal call, the death-pledge of the horn.

To crossing swords and gray hairs bared to heaven,
The clear electric base and baritone of the world,
The trombone duo, Libertad forever!
From Spanish chestnut trees' dense shade,
By old and heavy convent walls a wailing song,
Song of lost love, the torch of youth and life quench'd in
    despair,
Song of the dying swan, Fernando's heart is breaking.

90 Awaking from her woes at last retriev'd Amina sings,
Copious as stars and glad as morning light the torrents of her
    joy.

(The teeming lady comes,
The lustrious orb, Venus contralto, the blooming mother,
Sister of loftiest gods, Alboni's self I hear.)

4
I hear those odes, symphonies, operas,
I hear in the *William Tell* the music of an arous'd and angry
    people,
I hear Meyerbeer's *Huguenots*, the *Prophet*, or *Robert*,
Gounod's *Faust*, or Mozart's *Don Juan*.

I hear the dance-music of all nations,
100 The waltz, some delicious measure, lapsing, bathing me in
    bliss,
The bolero to tinkling guitars and clattering castanets.

I see religious dances old and new,
I hear the sound of the Hebrew lyre,
I see the crusaders marching bearing the cross on high, to
    the martial clang of cymbals,
I hear dervishes monotonously chanting, interspers'd with
    frantic shouts, as they spin around turning always towards
    Mecca,
I see the rapt religious dances of the Persians and the Arabs,
Again, at Eleusis, home of Ceres, I see the modern Greeks
    dancing,
I hear them clapping their hands as they bend their bodies,
I hear the metrical shuffling of their feet.

110   I see again the wild old Corybantian dance, the performers
       wounding each other,
    I see the Roman youth to the shrill sound of flageolets
       throwing and catching their weapons,
    As they fall on their knees and rise again.

    I hear from the Mussulman mosque the muezzin calling,
    I see the worshippers within, nor form nor sermon, argument
       nor word,
    But silent, strange, devout, rais'd, glowing heads, ecstatic
       faces.

    I hear the Egyptian harp of many strings,
    The primitive chants of the Nile boatmen,
    The sacred imperial hymns of China,
    To the delicate sounds of the king, (the stricken wood and
       stone,)
120   Or to Hindu flutes and the fretting twang of the vina,
    A band of bayaderes.

    5
    Now Asia, Africa leave me, Europe seizing inflates me,
    To organs huge and bands I hear as from vast concourses of
       voices,
    Luther's strong hymn *Eine feste Burg ist unser Gott*,
    Rossini's *Stabat Mater dolorosa*,
    Or floating in some high cathedral dim with gorgeous
       color'd windows,
    The passionate *Agnus Dei* or *Gloria in Excelsis*.

    Composers! mighty maestros!
    And you, sweet singers of old lands, soprani, tenori, bassi!
130   To you a new bard caroling in the West,
    Obeisant sends his love.

    (Such led to thee O soul,
    All senses, shows and objects, lead to thee,
    But now it seems to me sound leads o'er all the rest.)

I hear the annual singing of the children in St Paul's
   cathedral,
Or, under the high roof of some colossal hall, the
   symphonies, oratorios of Beethoven, Handel, or Haydn,
The *Creation* in billows of godhood laves me.

Give me to hold all sounds, (I madly struggling cry,)
Fill me with all the voices of the universe,
140   Endow me with their throbbings, Nature's also,
The tempests, waters, winds, operas and chants, marches
   and dances,
Utter, pour in, for I would take them all!

6
Then I woke softly,
And pausing, questioning awhile the music of my dream,
And questioning all those reminiscences, the tempest in its
   fury,
And all the songs of sopranos and tenors,
And those rapt oriental dances of religious fervor,
And the sweet varied instruments, and the diapason of
   organs,
And all the artless plaints of love and grief and death,
150   I said to my silent curious soul out of the bed of the
   slumber-chamber,
Come, for I have found the clew I sought so long,
Let us go forth refresh'd amid the day,
Cheerfully tallying life, walking the world, the real,
Nourish'd henceforth by our celestial dream.

And I said, moreover,
Haply what thou hast heard O soul was not the sound of
   winds,
Nor dream of raging storm, nor sea-hawk's flapping wings
   nor harsh scream,
Nor vocalism of sun-bright Italy,
Nor German organ majestic, nor vast concourse of voices,
   nor layers of harmonies,

160   Nor strophes of husbands and wives, nor sound of
      marching soldiers,
    Nor flutes, nor harps, nor the bugle-calls of camps,
    But to a new rhythmus fitted for thee,
    Poems bridging the way from Life to Death, vaguely wafted
      in night air, uncaught, unwritten,
    Which let us go forth in the bold day and write.

Passage to India

1

Singing my days,
Singing the great achievements of the present,
Singing the strong light works of engineers,
Our modern wonders, (the antique ponderous Seven
    outvied,)
In the Old World the east the Suez canal,
The New by its mighty railroad spann'd,
The seas inlaid with eloquent gentle wires;
Yet first to sound, and ever sound, the cry with thee O soul,
The Past! the Past! the Past!

10   The Past – the dark unfathom'd retrospect!
    The teeming gulf – the sleepers and the shadows!
    The past – the infinite greatness of the past!
    For what is the present after all but a growth out of the
      past?
    (As a projectile form'd, impell'd, passing a certain line, still
      keeps on,
    So the present, utterly form'd, impell'd by the past.)

2

Passage O soul to India!
Eclaircise the myths Asiatic, the primitive fables.

Not you alone proud truths of the world,
Nor you alone ye facts of modern science,
20   But myths and fables of eld, Asia's, Africa's fables,
    The far-darting beams of the spirit, the unloos'd dreams,

The deep diving bibles and legends,
The daring plots of the poets, the elder religions;
O you temples fairer than lilies pour'd over by the rising
    sun!
O you fables spurning the known, eluding the hold of the
    known, mounting to heaven!
You lofty and dazzling towers, pinnacled, red as roses,
    burnish'd with gold!
Towers of fables immortal fashion'd from mortal dreams!
You too I welcome and fully the same as the rest!
You too with joy I sing.

30   Passage to India!
Lo, soul, seest thou not God's purpose from the first?
The earth to be spann'd, connected by network,
The races, neighbors, to marry and be given in marriage,
The oceans to be cross'd, the distant brought near,
The lands to be welded together.

A worship new I sing,
You captains, voyagers, explorers, yours,
You engineers, you architects, machinists, yours,
You, not for trade or transportation only,
40   But in God's name, and for thy sake O soul.

3
Passage to India!
Lo soul for thee of tableaus twain,
I see in one the Suez canal initiated, open'd,
I see the procession of steamships, the Empress Eugenie's
    leading the van,
I mark from on deck the strange landscape, the pure sky, the
    level sand in the distance,
I pass swiftly the picturesque groups, the workmen
    gather'd,
The gigantic dredging machines.

In one again, different, (yet thine, all thine, O soul, the
    same,)

I see over my own continent the Pacific railroad
   surmounting every barrier,
50 I see continual trains of cars winding along the Platte
   carrying freight and passengers,
I hear the locomotives rushing and roaring, and the shrill
   steam-whistle,
I hear the echoes reverberate through the grandest scenery
   in the world,
I cross the Laramie plains, I note the rocks in grotesque
   shapes, the buttes,
I see the plentiful larkspur and wild onions, the barren,
   colorless, sage-deserts,
I see in glimpses afar or towering immediately above me the
   great mountains, I see the Wind river and the Wahsatch
   mountains,
I see the Monument mountain and the Eagle's Nest, I pass
   the Promontory, I ascend the Nevadas,
I scan the noble Elk mountain and wind around its base,
I see the Humboldt range, I thread the valley and cross the
   river,
I see the clear waters of lake Tahoe, I see forests of
   majestic pines,
60 Or crossing the great desert, the alkaline plains, I behold
   enchanting mirages of waters and meadows,
Marking through these and after all, in duplicate slender
   lines,
Bridging the three or four thousand miles of land travel,
Tying the Eastern to the Western sea,
The road between Europe and Asia.

(Ah Genoese thy dream! thy dream!
Centuries after thou art laid in thy grave,
The shore thou foundest verifies thy dream.)

4
Passage to India!
Struggles of many a captain, tales of many a sailor dead,
70 Over my mood stealing and spreading they come,
Like clouds and cloudlets in the unreach'd sky.

Along all history, down the slopes,
As a rivulet running, sinking now, and now again to the
surface rising,
A ceaseless thought, a varied train – lo, soul, to thee, thy
sight, they rise,
The plans, the voyages again, the expeditions;
Again Vasco de Gama sails forth,
Again the knowledge gain'd, the mariner's compass,
Lands found and nations born, thou born America,
For purpose vast, man's long probation fill'd,
80 Thou rondure of the world at last accomplish'd.

5
O vast Rondure, swimming in space,
Cover'd all over with visible power and beauty,
Alternate light and day and the teeming spiritual darkness,
Unspeakable high processions of sun and moon and countless
stars above,
Below, the manifold grass and waters, animals, mountains,
trees,
With inscrutable purpose, some hidden prophetic intention,
Now first it seems my thought begins to span thee.

Down from the gardens of Asia descending radiating,
Adam and Eve appear, then their myriad progeny after
them,
90 Wandering, yearning, curious, with restless explorations,
With questionings, baffled, formless, feverish, with
never-happy hearts,
With that sad incessant refrain, *Wherefore unsatisfied soul?*
and *Wither O mocking life?*

Ah who shall soothe these feverish children?
Who justify these restless explorations?
Who speak the secret of impassive earth?
Who bind it to us? what is this separate Nature so
unnatural?

What is this earth to our affections? (unloving earth,
    without a throb to answer ours,
Cold earth, the place of graves.)

Yet soul be sure the first intent remains, and shall be carried
    out,
100 Perhaps even now the time has arrived.

After the seas are all cross'd, (as they seem already cross'd,)
After the great captains and engineers have accomplish'd
    their work,
After the noble inventors, after the scientists, the chemist,
    the geologist, ethnologist,
Finally shall come the poet worthy that name,
The true son of God shall come singing his songs.

Then not your deeds only O voyagers, O scientists and
    inventors, shall be justified,
All these hearts as of fretted children shall be sooth'd,
All affection shall be fully responded to, the secret shall be
    told,
All these separations and gaps shall be taken up and hook'd
    and link'd together,
110 The whole earth, this cold, impassive, voiceless earth, shall
    be completely justified,
Trinitas divine shall be gloriously accomplish'd and
    compacted by the true son of God, the poet,
(He shall indeed pass the straits and conquer the
    mountains,
He shall double the cape of Good Hope to some purpose,)
Nature and Man shall be disjoin'd and diffused no more,
The true son of God shall absolutely fuse them.

6
Year at whose wide-flung door I sing!
Year of the purpose accomplish'd!
Year of the marriage of continents, climates and oceans!
(No mere doge of Venice now wedding the Adriatic,)
120 I see O year in you the vast terraqueous globe given and
    giving all,

Europe to Asia, Africa join'd, and they to the New World,
The lands, geographies, dancing before you, holding a
    festival garland,
As brides and bridegrooms hand in hand.

Passage to India!
Cooling airs from Caucasus far, soothing cradle of man,
The river Euphrates flowing, the past lit up again.

Lo soul, the retrospect brought forward,
The old, most populous, wealthiest of earth's lands,
The streams of the Indus and the Ganges and their many
    affluents,
130   (I my shores of America walking to-day behold, resuming
    all,)
The tale of Alexander on his warlike marches suddenly
    dying,
On one side China and on the other side Persia and Arabia,
To the south the great seas and the bay of Bengal,
The flowing literatures, tremendous epics, religions, castes,
Old occult Brahma interminably far back, the tender and
    junior Buddha,
Central and southern empires and all their belongings,
    possessors,
The wars of Tamerlane, the reign of Aurungzebe,
The traders, rulers, explorers, Moslems, Venetians,
    Byzantium, the Arabs, Portuguese,
The first travelers famous yet, Marco Polo, Batouta the
    Moor,
140   Doubts to be solv'd, the map incognita, blanks to be fill'd,
The foot of man unstay'd, the hands never at rest,
Thyself O soul that will not brook a challenge.

The mediaeval navigators rise before me,
The world of 1492, with its awaken'd enterprise,
Something swelling in humanity now like the sap of the
    earth in spring,
The sunset splendor of chivalry declining.

And who art thou sad shade?
Gigantic, visionary, thyself a visionary,
With majestic limbs and pious beaming eyes,
150   Spreading around with every look of thine a golden word,
Enhuing it with gorgeous hues.

As the chief histrion,
Down to the footlights walks in some great scena,
Dominating the rest I see the Admiral himself,
(History's type of courage, action, faith,)
Behold him sail from Palos leading his little fleet,
His voyage behold, his return, his great fame,
His misfortune, calumniators, behold him a prisoner,
    chain'd,
Behold his dejection, poverty, death.

160   (Curious in time I stand, noting the efforts of heroes,
Is the deferment long? bitter the slander, poverty, death?
Lies the seed unreck'd for centuries in the ground? lo, to
    God's due occasion,
Uprising in the night, it sprouts, blooms,
And fills the earth with use and beauty.)

7
Passage indeed O soul to primal thought,
Not lands and seas alone, thy own clear freshness,
The young maturity of brood and bloom,
To realms of budding bibles.

O soul, repressless, I with thee and thou with me,
170   The circumnavigation of the world begin,
Of man, the voyage of his mind's return,
To reason's early paradise,
Back, back to wisdom's birth, to innocent intuitions,
Again with fair creation.

8
O we can wait no longer,
We too take ship O soul,
Joyous we too launch out on trackless seas,

Fearless for unknown shores on waves of ecstasy to sail,
Amid the wafting winds, (thou pressing me to thee, I thee
   to me, O soul,)
180 Caroling free, singing our song of God,
Chanting our chant of pleasant exploration.

With laugh and many a kiss,
(Let others deprecate, let others weep for sin, remorse,
   humiliation,)
O soul thou pleasest me, I thee.

Ah more than any priest O soul we too believe in God,
But with the mystery of God we dare not dally.

O soul thou pleasest me, I thee,
Sailing these seas or on the hills, or waking in the night,
Thoughts, silent thoughts, of Time and Space and Death,
   like waters flowing,
190 Bear me indeed as through the regions infinite,
Whose air I breathe, whose ripples hear, lave me all over,
Bathe me O God in thee, mounting to thee,
I and my soul to range in range of thee.

O Thou transcendent,
Nameless, the fibre and the breath,
Light of the light, shedding forth universes, thou centre of
   them,
Thou mightier centre of the true, the good, the loving,
Thou moral, spiritual fountain – affection's source – thou
   reservoir,
(O pensive soul of me – O thirst unsatisfied – waitest not
   there?
200 Waitest not haply for us somewhere there the Comrade
   perfect?)
Thou pulse – thou motive of the stars, suns, systems,
That, circling, move in order, safe, harmonious,
Athwart the shapeless vastnesses of space,
How should I think, how breathe a single breath, how speak
   if, out of myself,
I could not launch, to those, superior universes?

Swiftly I shrivel at the thought of God,
At Nature and its wonders, Time and Space and Death,
But that I, turning, call to thee O soul, thou actual Me,
And lo, thou gently masterest the orbs,
210 Thou matest Time, smilest content at Death,
And fillest, swellest full the vastnesses of Space.

Greater than stars or suns,
Bounding O soul thou journeyest forth;
What love than thine and ours could wider amplify?
What aspirations, wishes, outvie thine and ours O soul?
What dreams of the ideal? what plans of purity, perfection,
    strength?
What cheerful willingness for others' sake to give up all?
For others' sake to suffer all?

Reckoning ahead O soul, when thou, the time achiev'd,
220 The seas all cross'd, weather'd the capes, the voyage done,
Surrounded, copest, frontest God, yieldest, the aim
    attain'd,
As fill'd with friendship, love complete, the Elder Brother
    found,
The Younger melts in fondness in his arms.

9
Passage to more than India!
Are thy wings plumed indeed for such far flights?
O soul, voyagest thou indeed on voyages like those?
Disportest thou on waters such as those?
Soundest below the Sanscrit and the Vedas?
Then have they bent unleash'd.

230 Passage to you, your shores, ye aged fierce enigmas!
Passage to you, to mastership of you, ye strangling problems!
You, strew'd with the wrecks of skeletons, that, living, never
    reach'd you.

Passage to more than India!
O secret of the earth and sky!
Of you O waters of the sea! O winding creeks and rivers!

Of you O woods and fields! of you strong mountains of my
    land!
Of you O prairies! of you gray rocks!
O morning red! O clouds! O rain and snows!
O day and night, passage to you!

240 O sun and moon and all you stars! Sirius and Jupiter!
Passage to you!

Passage, immediate passage! the blood burns in my veins!
Away O soul! hoist instantly the anchor!
Cut the hawsers – haul out – shake out every sail!
Have we not stood here like trees in the ground long
    enough?
Have we not grovel'd here long enough, eating and
    drinking like mere brutes?
Have we not darken'd and dazed ourselves with books long
    enough?

Sail forth – steer for the deep waters only,
Reckless O soul, exploring, I with thee, and thou with me,
250 For we are bound where mariner has not yet dared to go,
And we will risk the ship, ourselves and all.

O my brave soul!
O farther farther sail!
O daring joy, but safe! are they not all the seas of God?
O farther, farther, farther sail!

Prayer of Columbus

A batter'd, wreck'd old man,
Thrown on this savage shore, far, far from home,
Pent by the sea and dark rebellious brows, twelve dreary
    months,
Sore, stiff with many toils, sicken'd and nigh to death,
I take my way along the island's edge,
Venting a heavy heart.

I am too full of woe!
Haply I may not live another day;
I cannot rest O God, I cannot eat or drink or sleep,
10 Till I put forth myself, my prayer, once more to Thee,
Breathe, bathe myself once more in Thee, commune with
    Thee,
Report myself once more to Thee.

Thou knowest my years entire, my life,
My long and crowded life of active work, not adoration
    merely;
Thou knowest the prayers and vigils of my youth,
Thou knowest my manhood's solemn and visionary
    meditations,
Thou knowest how before I commenced I devoted all to
    come to Thee,
Thou knowest I have in age ratified all those vows and
    strictly kept them,
Thou knowest I have not once lost nor faith nor ecstasy in
    Thee,
20 In shackles, prison'd, in disgrace, repining not,
Accepting all from Thee, as duly come from Thee.

All my emprises have been fill'd with Thee,
My speculations, plans, begun and carried on in thoughts of
    Thee,
Sailing the deep or journeying the land for Thee;
Intentions, purports, aspirations mine, leaving results to
    Thee.

O I am sure they really came from Thee,
The urge, the ardor, the unconquerable will,
The potent, felt, interior command, stronger than words,
A message from the Heavens whispering to me even in sleep,
30 These sped me on.

By me and these the work so far accomplish'd,
By me earth's elder cloy'd and stifled lands uncloy'd,
  unloos'd,
By me the hemispheres rounded and tied, the unknown to
  the known.

The end I know not, it is all in Thee,
Or small or great I know not – haply what broad fields, what
  lands,
Haply the brutish measureless human undergrowth I know,
Transplanted there may rise to stature, knowledge worthy
  Thee,
Haply the swords I know may there indeed be turn'd to
  reaping-tools,
Haply the lifeless cross I know, Europe's dead cross, may
  bud and blossom there.

40   One effort more, my altar this bleak sand;
That Thou O God my life hast lighted,
With ray of light, steady, ineffable, vouchsafed of Thee,
Light rare untellable, lighting the very light,
Beyond all signs, descriptions, languages;
For that O God, be it my latest word, here on my knees,
Old, poor, and paralyzed, I thank Thee.

My terminus near,
The clouds already closing in upon me,
The voyage balk'd the course disputed, lost,
50   I yield my ships to Thee.

My hands, my limbs grow nerveless,
My brain feels rack'd, bewilder'd,
Let the old timbers part, I will not part,
I will cling fast to Thee, O God, though the waves buffet
  me,
Thee, Thee at least I know.

Is it the prophet's thought I speak, or am I raving?
What do I know of life? what of myself?
I know not even my own work past or present,

Dim ever-shifting guesses of it spread before me,
60 Of newer better worlds, their mighty paturition,
Mocking, perplexing me.

And these things I see suddenly, what mean they?
As if some miracle, some hand divine unseal'd my eyes,
Shadowy vast shapes smile through the air and sky,
And on the distant waves sail countless ships,
And anthems in new tongues I hear saluting me.

The Sleepers

1

I wander all night in my vision,
Stepping with light feet, swiftly and noiselessly stepping
    and stopping,
Bending with open eyes over the shut eyes of sleepers,
Wandering and confused, lost to myself, ill-assorted,
    contradictory,
Pausing, gazing, bending, and stopping.

How solemn they look there, stretch'd and still,
How quiet they breathe, the little children in their cradles.

The wretched features of ennuyés, the white features of
    corpses, the livid faces of drunkards, the sick-gray faces
    of onanists, self-gratification
The gash'd bodies on battle-fields, the insane in their
    strong-door'd rooms, the sacred idiots, the new-born
    emerging from gates, and the dying emerging from gates,
10 The night pervades them and infolds them.

The married couple sleep calmly in their bed, he with his
    palm on the hip of the wife, and she with her palm on the
    hip of the husband,
The sisters sleep lovingly side by side in their bed,
The men sleep lovingly side by side in theirs,
And the mother sleeps with her little child carefully wrapt.

The blind sleep, and the deaf and dumb sleep,
The prisoner sleeps well in the prison, the runaway son
    sleeps,
The murderer that is to be hung next day, how does he
    sleep?
And the murder'd person, how does he sleep?

The female that loves unrequited sleeps,
20   And the male that loves unrequited sleeps,
The head of the money-maker that plotted all day sleeps,
And the enraged and treacherous dispositions, all, all sleep.

I stand in the dark with drooping eyes by the worst-suffering
    and the most restless,
I pass my hands soothingly to and fro a few inches from
    them,
The restless sink in their beds, they fitfully sleep.

Now I pierce the darkness, new beings appear,
The earth recedes from me into the night,
I saw that it was beautiful, and I see that what is not the
    earth is beautiful.

I go from bedside to bedside, I sleep close with the other
    sleepers each in turn,
30   I dream in my dream all the dreams of the other dreamers,
And I become the other dreamers.

I am a dance – play up there! the fit is whirling me fast!

I am the ever-laughing – it is new moon and twilight,
I see the hiding of douceurs, I see nimble ghosts whichever
    way I look,
Cache and cache again deep in the ground and sea, and
    where it is neither ground nor sea.

Well do they do their jobs those journeymen divine,
Only from me can they hide nothing, and would not if they
    could,
I reckon I am their boss and they make me a pet besides,
And surround me and lead me and run ahead when I walk,

40   To lift their cunning covers to signify me with stretch'd
  arms, and resume the way;
 Onward we move, a gay gang of blackguards! with
  mirth-shouting music and wild-flapping pennants of joy!

I am the actor, the actress, the voter, the politician,
The emigrant and the exile, the criminal that stood in the
 box,
He who has been famous and he who shall be famous after
 to-day,
The stammerer, the well-form'd person, the wasted or
 feeble person.
I am she who adorn'd herself and folded her hair
 expectantly,
My truant lover has come, and it is dark.

Double yourself and receive me darkness,
Receive me and my lover too, he will not let me go
 without him.

50   I roll myself upon you as upon a bed, I resign myself to
  the dusk.

He whom I call answers me and takes the place of my lover,
He rises with me silently from the bed.

Darkness, you are gentler than my lover, his flesh was
 sweaty and panting,
I feel the hot moisture yet that he left me.

My hands are spread forth, I pass them in all directions,
I would sound up the shadowy shore to which you are
 journeying.

Be careful darkness! already what was it touch'd me?
I thought my lover had gone, else darkness and he are one,
I hear the heart-beat, I follow, I fade away.

2

60   I descend my western course, my sinews are flaccid,
 Perfume and youth course through me and I am their wake.

It is my face yellow and wrinkled instead of the old
    woman's,
I sit low in a straw-bottom chair and carefully darn my
    grandson's stockings.

It is I too, the sleepless widow looking out on the winter
    midnight,
I see the sparkles of starshine on the icy and pallid earth.

A shroud I see and I am the shroud, I wrap a body and lie
    in the coffin,
It is dark here under ground, it is not evil or pain here, it is
    blank here, for reasons.

(It seems to me that every thing in the light and air ought
    to be happy,
Whoever is not in his coffin and the dark grave let him know
    he has enough.)

3
70   I see a beautiful gigantic swimmer swimming naked through
    the eddies of the sea,
His brown hair lies close and even to his head, he strikes out
    with courageous arms, he urges himself with his legs,
I see his white body, I see his undaunted eyes,
I hate the swift-running eddies that would dash him
    head-foremost on the rocks.

What are you doing you ruffianly red-trickled waves?
Will you kill the courageous giant? will you kill him in the
    prime of his middle age?

Steady and long he struggles,
He is baffled, bang'd, bruis'd, he holds out while his strength
    holds out,
The slapping eddies are spotted with his blood, they bear
    him away, they roll him, swing him, turn him,
His beautiful body is borne in the circling eddies, it is
    continually bruis'd on rocks,
80   Swiftly and out of sight is borne the brave corpse.

4
I turn but do not extricate myself,
Confused, a past-reading, another, but with darkness yet.

The beach is cut by the razory ice-wind, the wreck-guns
    sound,
The tempest lulls, the moon comes floundering through the
    drifts.

I look where the ship helplessly heads end on, I hear the
    burst as she strikes, I hear the howls of dismay, they grow
    fainter and fainter.

I cannot aid with my wringing fingers,
I can but rush to the surf and let it drench me and freeze
    upon me.

I search with the crowd, not one of the company is wash'd
    to us alive,
In the morning I help pick up the dead and lay them in rows
    in a barn.

5
90 Now of the older war-days, the defeat at Brooklyn,
Washington stands inside the lines, he stands on the
    intrench'd hills amid a crowd of officers,
His face is cold and damp, he cannot repress the weeping
    drops,
He lifts the glass perpetually to his eyes, the color is
    blanch'd from his cheeks,
He sees the slaughter of the southern braves confided to him
    by their parents.

The same at last and at last when peace is declared,
He stands in the room of the old tavern, the well-belov'd
    soldiers all pass through,
The officers speechless and slow draw near in their turns,
The chief encircles their necks with his arm and kisses them
    on the cheek,
He kisses lightly the wet cheeks one after another, he shakes
    hands and bids good-by to the army.

6

100 Now what my mother told me one day as we sat at dinner
together,
Of when she was a nearly grown girl living home with her
parents on the old homestead.

A red squaw came one breakfast-time to the old homestead,
On her back she carried a bundle of rushes for
rush-bottoming chairs,
Her hair, straight, shiny, coarse, black, profuse,
half-envelop'd her face,
Her step was free and elastic, and her voice sounded
exquisitely as she spoke.

My mother look'd in delight and amazement at the stranger,
She look'd at the freshness of her tall-borne face and full and
pliant limbs,
The more she look'd upon her she loved her,
Never before had she seen such wonderful beauty and
purity,
110 She made her sit on a bench by the jamb of the fireplace, she
cook'd food for her,
She had no work to give her, but she gave her
remembrance and fondness.

The red squaw staid all the forenoon, and toward the middle
of the afternoon she went away,
O my mother was loth to have her go away,
All the week she thought of her, she watch'd for her many a
month,
She remember'd her many a winter and many a summer,
But the red squaw never came nor was heard of there again.

7

A show of the summer softness – a contact of something
unseen – an amour of the light and air,
I am jealous and overwhelm'd with friendliness,
And will go gallivant with the light and air myself.

120 O love and summer, you are in the dreams and in me,
    Autumn and winter are in the dreams, the farmer goes with
        his thrift,
    The droves and crops increase, the barns are well-fill'd.

    Elements merge in the night, ships make tracks in the
        dreams,
    The sailor sails, the exile returns home,
    The fugitive returns unharm'd, the immigrant is back
        beyond months and years,
    The poor Irishman lives in the simple house of his
        childhood with the well-known neighbors and faces,
    They warmly welcome him, he is barefoot again, he forgets
        he is well off,
    The Dutchman voyages home, and the Scotchman and
        Welshman voyage home, and the native of the
        Mediterranean voyages home,
    To every port of England, France, Spain, enter well-fill'd
        ships,
130 The Swiss foots it toward his hills, the Prussian goes his
        way, the Hungarian his way, and the Pole his way,
    The Swede returns, and the Dane and Norwegian return.

    The homeward bound and the outward bound,
    The beautiful lost swimmer, the ennuyé, the onanist, the
        female that loves unrequited, the money-maker,
    The actor and actress, those through with their parts and
        those waiting to commence,
    The affectionate boy, the husband and wife, the voter, the
        nominee that is chosen and the nominee that has fail'd,
    The great already known and the great any time after
        to-day,
    The stammerer, the sick, the perfect-form'd, the homely,
    The criminal that stood in the box, the judge that sat and
        sentenced him, the fluent lawyers, the jury, the
        audience,
    The laughter and weeper, the dancer, the midnight widow,
        the red squaw,

140 The consumptive, the erysipalite, the idiot, he that is
       wrong'd,
    The antipodes, and every one between this and them in the
       dark,
    I swear they are averaged now – one is no better than the
       other,
    The night and sleep have liken'd them and restored them.

    I swear they are all beautiful,
    Every one that sleeps is beautiful, every thing in the dim
       light is beautiful,
    The wildest and bloodiest is over, and all is peace.

    Peace is always beautiful,
    The myth of heaven indicates peace and night.

    The myth of heaven indicates the soul,
150 The soul is always beautiful, it appears more or it appears
       less, it comes or it lags behind,
    It comes from its embower'd garden and looks pleasantly
       on itself and encloses the world,
    Perfect and clean the genitals previously jetting, and perfect
       and clean the womb cohering,
    The head well-grown proportion'd and plumb, and the
       bowels and joints proportion'd and plumb.

    The soul is always beautiful,
    The universe is duly in order, every thing is in its place,
    What has arrived is in its place and what waits shall be in its
       place,
    The twisted skull waits, the watery or rotten blood waits,
    The child of the glutton or venerealee waits long, and the
       child of the drunkard waits long, and the drunkard
       himself waits long,
    The sleepers that lived and died wait, the far advanced are
       to go on in their turns, and the far behind are to come on
       in their turns,
160 The diverse shall be no less diverse, but they shall flow and
       unite – they unite now.

8

The sleepers are very beautiful as they lie unclothed,
They flow hand in hand over the whole earth from east to
    west as they lie unclothed,
The Asiatic and African are hand in hand, the European and
    American are hand in hand,
Learn'd and unlearn'd are hand in hand, and male and
    female are hand in hand,
The bare arm of the girl crosses the bare breast of her lover,
    they press close without lust, his lips press her neck,
The father holds his grown or ungrown son in his arms with
    measureless love, and the son holds the father in his arms
    with measureless love,
The white hair of the mother shines on the white wrist of the
    daughter,
The breath of the boy goes with the breath of the man,
    friend is inarm'd by friend,
The scholar kisses the teacher and the teacher kisses the
    scholar, the wrong'd is made right,
170   The call of the slave is one with the master's call, and the
    master salutes the slave,
The felon steps forth from the prison, the insane becomes
    sane, the suffering of sick persons is reliev'd,
The sweatings and fevers stop, the throat that was unsound
    is sound, the lungs of the consumptive are resumed, the
    poor distress'd head is free,
The joints of the rheumatic move as smoothly as ever, and
    smoother than ever,
Stiflings and passages open, the paralyzed become supple,
The swell'd and convuls'd and congested awake to
    themselves in condition,
They pass the invigoration of the night and the chemistry
    of the night, and awake.

I too pass from the night,
I stay a while away O night, but I return to you again and
    love you.

Why should I be afraid to trust myself to you?
180   I am afraid, I have been well brought forward by you,
I love the rich running day, but I do not desert her in
      whom I lay so long,
I know not how I came of you and I know not where I go
      with you, but I know I came well and shall go well.

I will stop only a time with the night, and rise betimes,
I will duly pass the day O my mother, and duly return to you.

Transpositions

Let the reformers descend from the stands where they are
      forever bawling – let an idiot or insane person appear on
      each of the stands;
Let judges and criminals be transposed – let the
      prison-keepers be put in prison – let those that were
      prisoners take the keys;
Let them that distrust birth and death lead the rest.

To Think of Time

1

To think of time – of all that retrospection,
To think of to-day, and the ages continued henceforward.

Have you guess'd you yourself would not continue?
Have you dreaded these earth-beetles?
Have you fear'd the future would be nothing to you?

Is to-day nothing? is the beginningless past nothing?
If the future is nothing they are just as surely nothing.

To think that the sun rose in the east – that men and
    women were flexible, real, alive – that every thing was
    alive,
To think that you and I did not see, feel, think, nor bear our
    part,
10 To think that we are now here and bear our part.

2
Not a day passes, not a minute or second without an
    accouchement,
Not a day passes, not a minute or second without a corpse.

The dull nights go over and the dull days also,
The soreness of lying so much in bed goes over,
The physician after long putting off gives the silent and
    terrible look for an answer,
The children come hurried and weeping, and the brothers
    and sisters are sent for,
Medicines stand unused on the shelf, (the camphor-smell
    has long pervaded the rooms,)
The faithful hand of the living does not desert the hand of
    the dying,
The twitching lips press lightly on the forehead of the dying,
20 The breath ceases and the pulse of the heart ceases,
The corpse stretches on the bed and the living look upon it,
It is palpable as the living are palpable.

The living look upon the corpse with their eyesight,
But without eyesight lingers a different living and looks
    curiously on the corpse.

3
To think the thought of death merged in the thought of
    materials,
To think of all these wonders of city and country, and others
    taking great interest in them, and we taking no interest
    in them.

To think how eager we are in building our houses,
To think others shall be just as eager, and we quite
   indifferent.

(I see one building the house that serves him a few years, or
   seventy or eighty years at most,
30   I see one building the house that serves him longer than
   that.)

Slow-moving and black lines creep over the whole earth –
   they never cease – they are the burial lines,
He that was President was buried, and he that is now
   President shall surely be buried.

4
A reminiscence of the vulgar fate,
A frequent sample of the life and death of workmen,
Each after his kind.

Cold dash of waves at the ferry-wharf, posh and ice in the
   river, half-frozen mud in the streets,
A gray discouraged sky overhead, the short last daylight of
   December,
A hearse and stages, the funeral of an old Broadway
   stage-driver, the cortege mostly drivers.

Steady the trot to the cemetery, duly rattles the death-bell,
40   The gate is pass'd, the new-dug grave is halted at, the living
   alight, the hearse uncloses,
The coffin is pass'd out, lower'd and settled, the whip is laid
   on the coffin, the earth is swiftly shovel'd in,
The mound above is flatted with the spades – silence,
A minute – no one moves or speaks – it is done,
He is decently put away – is there any thing more?

He was a good fellow, free-mouth'd, quick-temper'd, not
   bad-looking,
Ready with life or death for a friend, fond of women,
   gambled, ate hearty, drank hearty,

Had known what it was to be flush, grew low-spirited
toward the last, sicken'd, was help'd by a contribution,
Died, aged forty-one years – and that was his funeral.

Thumb extended, finger uplifted, apron, cape, gloves,
strap, wet-weather clothes, whip carefully chosen,
50   Boss, spotter, starter, hostler, somebody loafing on you, you
loafing on somebody, headway, man before and man
behind,
Good day's work, bad day's work, pet stock, mean stock,
first out, last out, turning-in at night,
To think that these are so much and so nigh to other
drivers, and he that takes no interest in them.

5
The markets, the government, the working-man's wages,
to think what account they are through our nights and
days,
To think that other working-men will make just as great
account of them, yet we make little or no account.

The vulgar and the refined, what you call sin and what you
call goodness, to think how wide a difference,
To think the difference will still continue to others, yet we
lie beyond the difference.

To think how much pleasure there is,
Do you enjoy yourself in the city? or engaged in business?
or planning a nomination and election? or with your wife
and family?
Or with your mother and sisters? or in womanly housework?
or the beautiful maternal cares?
60   These also flow onward to others, you and I flow onward,
But in due time you and I shall take less interest in them.

Your farm, profits, crops – to think how engross'd you are,
To think there will still be farms, profits, crops, yet for you
of what avail?

6

What will be will be well, for what is is well,
To take interest is well, and not to take interest shall be well.

The domestic joys, the daily housework or business, the
    building of houses, are not phantasms, they have weight,
    form, location,
Farms, profits, crops, markets, wages, government, are
    none of them phantasms,
The difference between sin and goodness is no delusion,
The earth is not an echo, man and his life and all the things
    of his life are well-consider'd.

70 You are not thrown to the winds, you gather certainly and
    safely around yourself,
Yourself! yourself! yourself, for ever and ever!

7

It is not to diffuse you that you were born of your mother
    and father, it is to identify you,
It is not that you should be undecided, but that you should
    be decided,
Something long preparing and formless is arrived and
    form'd in you,
You are henceforth secure, whatever comes or goes.

The threads that were spun are gather'd, the weft crosses the
    warp, the pattern is systematic.

The preparations have every one been justified,
The orchestra have sufficiently tuned their instruments, the
    baton has given the signal.

The guest that was coming, he waited long, he is now
    housed,
80 He is one of those who are beautiful and happy, he is one of
    those that to look upon and be with is enough.

The law of the past cannot be eluded,
The law of the present and future cannot be eluded,
The law of the living cannot be eluded, it is eternal,

The law of promotion and transformation cannot be eluded,
The law of heroes and good-doers cannot be eluded,
The law of drunkards, informers, mean persons, not one iota
    thereof can be eluded.

8

Slow moving and black lines go ceaselessly over the earth,
Northerner goes carried and Southerner goes carried, and
    they on the Atlantic side and they on the Pacific,
And they between, and all through the Mississippi
    country, and all over the earth.

90 The great masters and kosmos are well as they go, the heroes
    and good-doers are well,
The known leaders and inventors and the rich owners and
    pious and distinguish'd may be well,
But there is more account than that, there is strict account of
    all.

The interminable hordes of the ignorant and wicked are not
    nothing,
The barbarians of Africa and Asia are not nothing,
The perpetual successions of shallow people are not nothing
    as they go.

Of and in all these things,
I have dream'd that we are not to be changed so much, nor
    the law of us changed,
I have dream'd that heroes and good-doers shall be under
    the present and past law,
And that murderers, drunkards, liars, shall be under the
    present and past law,
100 For I have dream'd that the law they are under now is
    enough.

And I have dream'd that the purpose and essence of the
    known life, the transient,
Is to form and decide identity for the unknown life, the
    permanent.

If all came but to ashes of dung,
If maggots and rats ended us, then Alarum! for we are
      betray'd,
Then indeed suspicion of death.

Do you suspect death? if I were to suspect death I should
      die now,
Do you think I could walk pleasantly and well-suited
      toward annihilation?

Pleasantly and well-suited I walk,
Whither I walk I cannot define, but I know it is good,
110   The whole universe indicates that it is good,
The past and the present indicate that it is good.

How beautiful and perfect are the animals!
How perfect the earth, and the minutest thing upon it!
What is called good is perfect, and what is called bad is just
      as perfect,
The vegetables and minerals are all perfect, and the
      imponderable fluids perfect;
Slowly and surely they have pass'd on to this, and slowly and
      surely they yet pass on.

9
I swear I think now that every thing without exception has
      an eternal soul!
The trees have, rooted in the ground! the weeds of the sea
      have! the animals!

I swear I think there is nothing but immortality!
120   That the exquisite scheme is for it, and the nebulous float is
      for it, and the coh'ering is for it!
And all preparation is for it – and identity is for it – and life
      and materials are altogether for it!

WHISPERS OF HEAVENLY DEATH

Darest Thou Now O Soul

Darest thou now O soul,
Walk out with me toward the unknown region,
Where neither ground is for the feet nor any path to follow?

No map there, nor guide,
Nor voice sounding, nor touch of human hand,
Nor face with blooming flesh, nor lips, nor eyes, are in that
    land.

I know it not O soul,
Nor dost thou, all is a blank before us,
All waits undream'd of in that region, that inaccessible land.

10   Till when the ties loosen,
All but the ties eternal, Time and Space,
Nor darkness, gravitation, sense, nor any bounds bounding
    us.

Then we burst forth, we float,
In Time and Space O soul, prepared for them,
Equal, equipt at last, (O joy! O fruit of all!) them to fulfil O
    soul.

Whispers of Heavenly Death

Whispers of heavenly death murmur'd I hear,
Labial gossip of night, sibilant chorals,
Footsteps gently ascending, mystical breezes wafted soft and
    low,
Ripples of unseen rivers, tides of a current flowing, forever
    flowing,
(Or is it the plashing of tears? the measureless waters of
    human tears?)

I see, just see skyward, great cloud-masses,
Mournfully slowly they roll, silently swelling and mixing,
With at times a half-dimm'd sadden'd far-off star,
Appearing and disappearing.

10 (Some parturition rather, some solemn immortal birth;
On the frontiers to eyes impenetrable,
Some soul is passing over.)

Chanting the Square Deific

I

Chanting the square deific, out of the One advancing, out of
    the sides,
Out of the old and new, out of the square entirely divine,
Solid, four-sided, (all the sides needed,) from this side
    Jehovah am I,
Old Brahm I, and I Saturnius am;
Not Time affects me – I am Time, old, modern as any,
Unpersuadable, relentless, executing righteous judgments,
As the Earth, the Father, the brown old Kronos, with laws,
Aged beyond computation, yet ever new, ever with those
    mighty laws rolling,
Relentless I forgive no man – whoever sins dies – I will have
    that man's life;
10 Therefore let none expect mercy – have the seasons,
    gravitation, the appointed days, mercy? no more have I,
But as the seasons and gravitation, and as all the appointed
    days that forgive not,
I dispense from this side judgments inexorable without the
    least remorse.

2

Consolator most mild, the promis'd one advancing,
With gentle hand extended, the mightier God am I,
Foretold by prophets and poets in their most rapt prophecies
    and poems,

From this side, lo! the Lord Christ gazes – lo! Hermes I – lo!
    mine is Hercules' face,
All sorrow, labor, suffering, I, tallying it, absorb in myself,
Many times have I been rejected, taunted, put in prison, and
    crucified, and many times shall be again,
All the world have I given up for my dear brothers' and
    sisters' sake, for the soul's sake,
20 Wending my way through the homes of men, rich or poor,
    with the kiss of affection,
For I am affection, I am the cheer-bringing God, with hope
    and all-enclosing charity,
With indulgent words as to children, with fresh and sane
    words, mine only,
Young and strong I pass knowing well I am destin'd myself
    to an early death;
But my charity has no death – my wisdom dies not, neither
    early nor late,
And my sweet love bequeath'd here and elsewhere never
    dies.

3
Aloof, dissatisfied, plotting revolt,
Comrade of criminals, brother of slaves,
Crafty, despised, a drudge, ignorant,
With sudra face and worn brow, black, but in the depths of
    my heart, proud as any,
30 Lifted now and always against whoever scorning assumes to
    rule me,
Morose, full of guile, full of reminiscences, brooding, with
    many wiles,
(Though it was thought I was baffled and dispel'd, and my
    wiles done, but that will never be,)
Defiant, I, Satan, still live, still utter words, in new lands
    duly appearing, (and old ones also,)
Permanent here from my side, warlike, equal with any, real
    as any,
Nor time nor change shall ever change me or my words.

4

Santa Spirita, breather, life,
Beyond the light, lighter than light,
Beyond the flames of hell, joyous, leaping easily above hell,
Beyond Paradise, perfumed solely with mine own perfume,
40 Including all life on earth, touching, including God,
        including Saviour and Satan,
Ethereal, pervading all, (for without me what were all? what
        were God?)
Essence of forms, life of the real identities, permanent,
        positive, (namely the unseen,)
Life of the great round world, the sun and stars, and of man,
        I, the general soul,
Here the square finishing, the solid, I the most solid,
Breathe my breath also through these songs.

Of Him I Love Day and Night

Of him I love day and night I dream'd I heard he was dead,
And I dream'd I went where they had buried him I love,
        but he was not in that place,
And I dream'd I wander'd searching among burial-places to
        find him,
And I found that every place was a burial-place;
The houses full of life were equally full of death, (this house
        is now,)
The streets, the shipping, the places of amusement, the
        Chicago, Boston, Philadelphia, the Mannahatta, were as
        full of the dead as of the living,
And fuller, O vastly fuller of the dead than of the living;
And what I dream'd I will henceforth tell to every person
        and age,
And I stand henceforth bound to what I dream'd,
10 And now I am willing to disregard burial-places and
        dispense with them,

And if the memorials of the dead were put up indifferently
  everywhere, even in the room where I eat or sleep, I
  should be satisfied,
And if the corpse of any one I love, or if my own corpse, be
  duly render'd to powder and pour'd in the sea, I shall be
  satisfied,
Or if it be distributed to the winds I shall be satisfied.

Yet, Yet, Ye Downcast Hours

Yet, yet, ye downcast hours, I know ye also,
Weights of lead, how ye clog and cling at my ankles,
Earth to a chamber of mourning turns – I hear the
  o'erweening, mocking voice,
*Matter is conqueror – matter, triumphant only, continues
  onward.*

Despairing cries float ceaselessly toward me,
The call of my nearest lover, putting forth, alarm'd,
  uncertain,
The sea I am quickly to sail, come tell me,
Come tell me where I am speeding, tell me my destination.

I understand your anguish, but I cannot help you,
10 I approach, hear, behold, the sad mouth, the look out of the
  eyes, your mute inquiry,
Whither I go from the bed I recline on, come tell me;
Old age, alarm'd, uncertain – a young woman's voice,
  appealing to me for comfort;
A young man's voice, *Shall I not escape?*

As if a Phantom Caress'd Me

As if a phantom caress'd me,
I thought I was not alone walking here by the shore;
But the one I thought was with me as now I walk by the
shore, the one I loved that caress'd me,
As I lean and look through the glimmering light, that one
has utterly disappear'd,
And those appear that are hateful to me and mock me.

Assurances

I need no assurances, I am a man who is pre-occupied of his
own soul;
I do not doubt that from under the feet and beside the hands
and face I am cognizant of, are now looking faces I am not
cognizant of, calm and actual faces,
I do not doubt but the majesty and beauty of the world are
latent in any iota of the world,
I do not doubt I am limitless, and that the universes are
limitless, in vain I try to think how limitless,
I do not doubt that the orbs and the systems of orbs play
their swift sports through the air on purpose, and that I
shall one day be eligible to do as much as they, and more
than they,
I do not doubt that temporary affairs keep on and on millions
of years,
I do not doubt interiors have their interiors, and exteriors
have their exteriors, and that the eyesight has another
eyesight, and the hearing another hearing, and the voice
another voice,
I do not doubt that the passionately wept deaths of young
men are provided for, and that the deaths of the young
women and the deaths of little children are provided for,
(Did you think Life was so well provided for, and Death, the
purport of all Life, is not well provided for?)

10   I do not doubt that wrecks at sea, no matter what the
        horrors of them, no matter whose wife, child, husband,
        father, lover, has gone down, are provided for, to the
        minutest points,
    I do not doubt that whatever can possibly happen anywhere
        at any time, is provided for in the inherences of things,
    I do not think Life provides for all and for Time and Space,
        but I believe Heavenly Death provides for all.

Quicksand Years

Quicksand years that whirl me I know not whither,
Your schemes, politics, fail, lines give way, substances mock
    and elude me,
Only the theme I sing, the great and strong-possess'd soul,
    eludes not,
One's-self must never give way – that is the final substance –
    that out of all is sure,
Out of politics, triumphs, battles, life, what at last finally
    remains?
When shows break up what but One's-Self is sure?

That Music Always Round Me

That music always round me, unceasing, unbeginning, yet
    long untaught I did not hear,
But now the chorus I hear and am elated,
A tenor, strong, ascending with power and health, with glad
    notes of daybreak I hear,
A soprano at intervals sailing buoyantly over the tops of
    immense waves,
A transparent base shuddering lusciously under and through
    the universe,
The triumphant tutti, the funeral wailings with sweet flutes
    and violins, all these I fill myself with,

I hear not the volumes of sound merely, I am moved by the
  exquisite meanings,
I listen to the different voices winding in and out, striving,
  contending with fiery vehemence to excel each other in
  emotion;
I do not think the performers know themselves – but now I
  think I begin to know them.

What Ship Puzzled at Sea

What ship puzzled at sea, cons for the true reckoning?
Or coming in, to avoid the bars and follow the channel a
  perfect pilot needs?
Here, sailor! here, ship! take aboard the most perfect pilot,
Whom, in a little boat, putting off and rowing, I hailing you
  offer.

A Noiseless Patient Spider

A noiseless patient spider,
I mark'd where on a little promontory it stood isolated,
Mark'd how to explore the vacant vast surrounding,
It launch'd forth filament, filament, filament, out of itself,
Ever unreeling them, ever tirelessly speeding them.

And you O my soul where you stand,
Surrounded, detached, in measureless oceans of space,
Ceaselessly musing, venturing, throwing, seeking the
  spheres to connect them,
Till the bridge you will need be form'd, till the ductile
  anchor hold,
10 Till the gossamer thread you fling catch somewhere, O my
  soul.

O Living Always, Always Dying

O living always, always dying!
O the burials of me past and present,
O me while I stride ahead, material, visible, imperious as
    ever;
O me, what I was for years, now dead, (I lament not, I am
    content;)
O to disengage myself from those corpses of me, which I
    turn and look at where I cast them,
To pass on, (O living! always living!) and leave the corpses
    behind.

To One Shortly to Die

From all the rest I single out you, having a message for you,
You are to die – let others tell you what they please, I
    cannot prevaricate,
I am exact and merciless, but I love you – there is no escape
    for you.

Softly I lay my right hand upon you, you just feel it,
I do not argue, I bend my head close and half envelop it,
I sit quietly by, I remain faithful,
I am more than nurse, more than parent or neighbor,
I absolve you from all except yourself spiritual bodily, that
    is eternal, you yourself will surely escape,
The corpse you will leave will be but excrementitious.

10   The sun bursts through in unlooked-for directions,
Strong thoughts fill you and confidence, you smile,
You forget you are sick, as I forget you are sick,
You do not see the medicines, you do not mind the weeping
    friends, I am with you,
I exclude others from you, there is nothing to be
    commiserated,
I do not commiserate, I congratulate you.

465

Night on the Prairies

Night on the prairies,
The supper is over, the fire on the ground burns low,
The wearied emigrants sleep, wrapt in their blankets;
I walk by myself – I stand and look at the stars, which I
    think now I never realized before.

Now I absorb immortality and peace,
I admire death and test propositions.

How plenteous! how spiritual! how resumé!
The same old man and soul – the same old aspirations, and
    the same content.

I was thinking the day most splendid till I saw what the
    not-day exhibited,
10 I was thinking this globe enough till there sprang out so
    noiseless around me myriads of other globes.

Now while the great thoughts of space and eternity fill me I
    will measure myself by them,
And now touch'd with the lives of other globes arrived as
    far along as those of the earth,
Or waiting to arrive, or pass'd on farther than those of the
    earth,
I henceforth no more ignore them than I ignore my own life,
Or the lives of the earth arrived as far as mine, or waiting to
    arrive.

O I see now that life cannot exhibit all to me, as the day
    cannot,
I see that I am to wait for what will be exhibited by death.

Thought

As I sit with others at a great feast, suddenly while the music
    is playing,
To my mind, (whence it comes I know not,) spectral in mist
    of a wreck at sea,
Of certain ships, how they sail from port with flying
    streamers and wafted kisses, and that is the last of them,
Of the solemn and murky mystery about the fate of the
    President,
Of the flower of the marine science of fifty generations
    founder'd off the Northeast coast and going down – of the
    steamship Arctic going down,
Of the veil'd tableau – women gather'd together on deck,
    pale, heroic, waiting the moment that draws so close – O
    the moment!
A huge sob – a few bubbles – the white foam spirting up –
    and then the women gone,
Sinking there while the passionless wet flows on – and I now
    pondering, Are those women indeed gone?
Are souls drown'd and destroy'd so?
10 Is only matter triumphant?

The Last Invocation

At the last, tenderly,
From the walls of the powerful fortress'd house,
From the clasp of the knitted locks, from the keep of the
    well-closed doors,
Let me be wafted.

Let me glide noiselessly forth;
With the key of softness unlock the locks – with a whisper,
Set ope the doors O soul.

Tenderly – be not impatient,
(Strong is your hold O mortal flesh,
10 Strong is your hold O love.)

As I Watch'd the Ploughman Ploughing

As I watch'd the ploughman ploughing,
Or the sower sowing in the fields, or the harvester
  harvesting,
I saw there too, O life and death, your analogies;
(Life, life is the tillage, and Death is the harvest according.)

Pensive and Faltering

Pensive and faltering,
The words *the Dead* I write,
For living are the Dead,
(Haply the only living, only real,
And I the apparition, I the spectre.)

Thou Mother with Thy Equal Brood

1

Thou Mother with thy equal brood,
Thou varied chain of different States, yet one identity only,
A special song before I go I'd sing o'er all the rest,
For thee, the future.

I'd sow a seed for thee of endless Nationality,
I'd fashion thy ensemble including body and soul,
I'd show away ahead thy real Union, and how it may be
    accomplish'd.

The paths to the house I seek to make,
But leave to those to come the house itself.

10 Belief I sing, and preparation;
As Life and Nature are not great with reference to the
    present only,
But greater still from what is yet to come,
Out of that formula for thee I sing.

2

As a strong bird on pinions free,
Joyous, the amplest spaces heavenward cleaving,
Such be the thought I'd think of thee America,
Such be the recitative I'd bring for thee.

The conceits of the poets of other lands I'd bring thee not,
Nor the compliments that have served their turn so long,
20 Nor rhyme, nor the classics, nor perfume of foreign court or
    indoor library;
But an odor I'd bring as from forests of pine in Maine, or
    breath of an Illinois prairie,
With open airs of Virginia or Georgia or Tennessee, or from
    Texas uplands, or Florida's glades,
Or the Saguenay's black stream, or the wide blue spread of
    Huron,
With presentment of Yellowstone's scenes, or Yosemite,
And murmuring under, pervading all, I'd bring the
    rustling sea-sound,
That endlessly sounds from the two Great Seas of the world.

And for thy subtler sense subtler refrains dread Mother,
Preludes of intellect tallying these and thee, mind-formulas
　　fitted for thee, real and sane and large as these and thee,
Thou! mounting higher, diving deeper than we knew, thou
　　transcendental Union!
30　By thee fact to be justified, blended with thought,
Thought of man justified, blended with God,
Through thy idea, lo, the immortal reality!
Through thy reality, lo, the immortal idea!

3

Brain of the New World, what a task is thine,
To formulate the Modern – out of the peerless grandeur of
　　the modern,
Out of thyself, comprising science, to recast poems,
　　churches, art,
(Recast, may-be discard them, end them –
　　may-be their work is done, who knows?)
By vision, hand conception, on the background of the
　　mighty past, the dead,
To limn with absolute faith the mighty living present.

40　And yet thou living present brain, heir of the dead, the Old
　　World brain,
Thou that lay folded like an unborn babe within its folds so
　　long,
Thou carefully prepared by it so long – haply thou but
　　unfoldest it, only maturest it,
It to eventuate in thee – the essence of the by-gone time
　　contain'd in thee,
Its poems, churches, arts, unwitting to themselves,
　　destined with reference to thee;
Thou but the apples, long, long, long a-growing,
The fruit of all the Old ripening to-day in thee.

4

Sail, sail thy best, ship of Democracy,
Of value is thy freight, 'tis not the Present only,
The Past is also stored in thee,

50 Thou holdest not the venture of thyself alone, not of the
  Western continent alone,
 Earth's *résumé* entire floats on thy keel O ship, is steadied by
  thy spars,
 With thee Time voyages in trust, the antecedent nations sink
  or swim with thee,
 With all their ancient struggles, martyrs, heroes, epics,
  wars, thou bear'st the other continents,
 Theirs, theirs as much as thine, the destination-port
  triumphant;
 Steer then with good strong hand and wary eye O
  helmsman, thou carriest great companions,
 Venerable priestly Asia sails this day with thee,
 And royal feudal Europe sails with thee.

5

 Beautiful world of new superber birth that rises to my eyes,
 Like a limitless golden cloud filling the western sky,
60 Emblem of general maternity lifted above all,
 Sacred shape of the bearer of daughters and sons,
 Out of thy teeming womb thy giant babes in ceaseless
  procession issuing,
 Acceding from such gestation, taking and giving continual
  strength and life,
 World of the real – world of the twain in one,
 World of the soul, born by the world of the real alone, led to
  identity, body, by it alone,
 Yet in beginning only, incalculable masses of composite
  precious materials,
 By history's cycles forwarded, by every nation, language,
  hither sent,
 Ready, collected here, a freer, vast, electric world, to be
  constructed here,
 (The true New World, the world of orbic science, morals,
  literatures to come,)
70 Thou wonder world yet undefined, unform'd, neither do I
  define thee,
 How can I pierce the impenetrable blank of the future?
 I feel thy ominous greatness evil as well as good,

I watch thee advancing, absorbing the present, transcending
the past,
I see thy light lighting, and thy shadow shadowing, as if the
entire globe,
But I do not undertake to define thee, hardly to comprehend
thee,
I but thee name, thee prophesy, as now,
I merely thee ejaculate!

Thee in thy future,
Thee in thy only permanent life, career, thy own
unloosen'd mind, thy soaring spirit,
Thee as another equally needed sun, radiant, ablaze,
swift-moving, fructifying all,
Thee risen in potent cheerfulness and joy, in endless great
hilarity,
Scattering for good the cloud that hung so long, that
weigh'd so long upon the mind of man,
The doubt, suspicion, dread, of gradual, certain decadence
of man;
Thee in thy larger, saner brood of female, male – thee in thy
athletes, moral, spiritual, South, North, West, East,
(To thy immortal breasts, Mother of All, thy every daughter,
son, endear'd alike, forever equal,)
Thee in thy own musicians, singers, artists, unborn yet, but
certain,
Thee in thy moral wealth and civilization, (until which thy
proudest material civilization must remain in vain,)
Thee in thy all-supplying, all-enclosing worship – thee in no
single bible, saviour, merely,
Thy saviours countless, latent within thyself, thy bibles
incessant within thyself, equal to any, divine as any,
(Thy soaring course thee formulating, not in thy two great
wars, nor in thy century's visible growth,
But far more in these leaves and chants, thy chants, great
Mother!)
Thee in an education grown of thee, in teachers, studies,
students, born of thee,

Thee in thy democratic fêtes en-masse, thy high original
    festivals, operas, lecturers, preachers,
Thee in thy ultimate, (the preparations only now
    completed, the edifice on sure foundations tied,)
Thee in thy pinnacles, intellect, thought, thy topmost
    rational joys, thy love and godlike aspiration,
In thy resplendent coming literati, thy full-lung'd orators,
    thy sacerdotal bards, kosmic savans,
These! these in thee, (certain to come,) to-day I prophesy.

6

Land tolerating all, accepting all, not for the good alone, all
    good for thee,
Land in the realms of God to be a realm unto thyself,
100 Under the rule of God to be a rule unto thyself.

(Lo, where arise three peerless stars,
To be thy natal stars my country, Ensemble, Evolution,
    Freedom,
Set in the sky of Law.)

Land of unprecedented faith, God's faith,
Thy soil, thy very subsoil, all upheav'd,
The general inner earth so long so sedulously draped over,
    now hence for what it is boldly laid bare,
Open'd by thee to heaven's light for benefit or bale.

Not for success alone,
Not to fair-sail unintermitted always,
110 The storm shall dash thy face, the murk of war and worse
    than war shall cover thee all over,
(Wert capable of war, its tug and trials? be capable of peace,
    its trials,
For the tug and mortal strain of nations come at last in
    prosperous peace, not war;)
In many a smiling mask death shall approach beguiling thee,
    thou in disease shalt swelter,
The livid cancer spread its hideous claws, clinging upon thy
    breasts, seeking to strike thee deep within,
Consumption of the worst, moral consumption, shall rouge
    thy face with hectic,

But thou shalt face thy fortunes, thy diseases, and surmount
   them all,
Whatever they are to-day and whatever through time they
   may be,
They each and all shall lift and pass away and cease from
   thee,
While thou, Time's spirals rounding, out of thyself, thyself
   still extricating, fusing,
120 Equable, natural, mystical Union thou, (the mortal with
   immortal blent,)
Shalt soar toward the fulfilment of the future, the spirit of
   the body and the mind,
The soul, its destinies.
The soul, its destinies, the real real,
(Purport of all these apparitions of the real;)
In thee America, the soul, its destinies,
Thou globe of globes! thou wonder nebulous!
By many a throe of heat and cold convuls'd, (by these
   thyself solidifying,)
Thou mental, moral orb – thou New, indeed new, Spiritual
   World!
The Present holds thee not – for such vast growth as thine,
130 For such unparallel'd flight as thine, such brood as thine,
The FUTURE only holds thee and can hold thee.

A Paumanok Picture

Two boats with nets lying off the sea-beach, quite still,
Ten fishermen waiting – they discover a thick school of
   mossbonkers – they drop the join'd seine-ends in the water,
The boats separate and row off, each on its rounding course
   to the beach, enclosing the mossbonkers,
The net is drawn in by a windlass by those who stop ashore,
Some of the fishermen lounge in their boats, others stand
   ankle-deep in the water, pois'd on strong legs,
The boats partly drawn up, the water slapping against them,
Strew'd on the sand in heaps and windrows, well out from
   the water, the green-back'd spotted mossbonkers.

FROM NOON TO STARRY NIGHT
Thou Orb Aloft Full-Dazzling

Thou orb aloft full-dazzling! thou hot October noon!
Flooding with sheeny light the gray beach sand,
The sibilant near sea with vistas far and foam,
And tawny streaks and shades and spreading blue;
O sun of noon refulgent! my special word to thee.

Hear me illustrious!
Thy lover me, for always I have loved thee,
Even as basking babe, then happy boy alone by some wood
    edge, thy touching-distant beams enough,
Or man matured, or young or old, as now to thee I launch
    my invocation.

10   (Thou canst not with thy dumbness me deceive,
I know before the fitting man all Nature yields,
Though answering not in words, the skies, trees, hear his
    voice – and thou O sun,
As for thy throes, thy perturbations, sudden breaks and
    shafts of flame gigantic,
I understand them, I know those flames, those perturbations
    well.)

Thou that with fructifying heat and light,
O'er myriad farms, o'er lands and waters North and South,
O'er Mississippi's endless course, o'er Texas' grassy plains,
    Kanada's woods,
O'er all the globe that turns its face to thee shining in space,
Thou that impartially infoldest all, not only continents, seas,
20   Thou that to grapes and weeds and little wild flowers givest
    so liberally,
Shed, shed thyself on mine and me, with but a fleeting ray
    out of thy million millions,
Strike through these chants.

Nor only launch thy subtle dazzle and thy strength for these,
Prepare the later afternoon of me myself – prepare my
lengthening shadows,
Prepare my starry nights.

Faces

1

Sauntering the pavement or riding the country by-road, lo,
such faces!
Faces of friendship, precision, caution, suavity, ideality,
The spiritual-prescient face, the always welcome common
benevolent face,
The face of the singing of music, the grand faces of natural
lawyers and judges broad at the back-top,
The faces of hunters and fishers bulged at the brows, the
shaved blanch'd faces of orthodox citizens,
The pure, extravagant, yearning, questioning artist's face,
The ugly face of some beautiful soul, the handsome
detested or despised face,
The sacred faces of infants, the illuminated face of the
mother of many children,
The face of an amour, the face of veneration,
10 The face as of a dream, the face of an immobile rock,
The face withdrawn of its good and bad, a castrated face,
A wild hawk, his wings clipp'd by the clipper,
A stallion that yielded at last to the thongs and knife of the
gelder.

Sauntering the pavement thus, or crossing the ceaseless
ferry, faces and faces and faces,
I see them and complain not, and am content with all.

2

Do you suppose I could be content with all if I thought
them their own finalè?

This now is too lamentable a face for a man,
Some abject louse asking leave to be, cringing for it,
Some milk-nosed maggot blessing what lets it wrig to its
    hole.

20   This face is a dog's snout sniffing for garbage,
Snakes nest in that mouth, I hear the sibilant threat.

This face is a haze more chill than the arctic sea,
Its sleepy and wabbling icebergs crunch as they go.

This is a face of bitter herbs, this an emetic, they need no
    label,
And more of the drug-shelf, laudanum, caoutchouc, or
    hog's-lard.

This face is an epilepsy, its wordless tongue gives out the
    unearthly cry,
Its veins down the neck distend, its eyes roll till they show
    nothing but their whites,
Its teeth grit, the palms of the hands are cut by the
    turn'd-in nails,
The man falls struggling and foaming to the ground, while
    he speculates well.

30   This face is bitten by vermin and worms,
And this is some murderer's knife with a half-pull'd
    scabbard.

This face owes to the sexton his dismalest fee,
An unceasing death-bell tolls there.

3
Features of my equals would you trick me with your
    creas'd and cadaverous march?
Well, you cannot trick me.

I see your rounded never-erased flow,
I see 'neath the rims of your haggard and mean disguises.

Splay and twist as you like, poke with the tangling fores of
fishes or rats,
You'll be unmuzzled, you certainly will.

40 I saw the face of the most smear'd and slobbering idiot they
had at the asylum,
And I knew for my consolation what they knew not,
I knew of the agents that emptied and broke my brother,
The same wait to clear the rubbish from the fallen
tenement,
And I shall look again in a score or two of ages,
And I shall meet the real landlord perfect and unharm'd,
every inch as good as myself.

4
The Lord advances, and yet advances,
Always the shadow in front, always the reach'd hand
bringing up the laggards.

Out of this face emerge banners and horses – O superb! I see
what is coming,
I see the high pioneer-caps, see staves of runners clearing
the way,
50 I hear victorious drums.

This face is a life-boat,
This is the face commanding and bearded, it asks no odds of
the rest,
This face is flavor'd fruit ready for eating,
This face of a healthy honest boy is the programme of all
good.

These faces bear testimony slumbering or awake,
They show their descent from the Master himself.

Off the word I have spoken I except not one – red, white,
black, are all deific,
In each house is the ovum, it comes forth after a thousand
years.

Spots or cracks at the windows do not disturb me,
60   Tall and sufficient stand behind and make signs to me,
I read the promise and patiently wait.

This is a full-grown lily's face,
She speaks to the limber-hipp'd man near the garden
    pickets,
Come here she blushingly cries, *Come nigh to me
    limber-hipp'd man,*
Stand at my side till I lean as high as I can upon you,
Fill me with albescent honey, bend down to me,
*Rub to me with your chafing beard, rub to my breast and
    shoulders.*

5
The old face of the mother of many children,
Whist! I am fully content.

70   Lull'd and late in the smoke of the First-day morning,
It hangs low over the rows of trees by the fences,
It hangs thin by the sassafras and wild-cherry and cat-brier
    under them.

I saw the rich ladies in full dress at the soiree,
I heard what the singers were singing so long,
Heard who sprang in crimson youth from the white froth
    and the water-blue.

Behold a woman!
She looks out from her quaker cap, her face is clearer and
    more beautiful than the sky.

She sits in an armchair under the shaded porch of the
    farmhouse,
The sun just shines on her old white head.

80   Her ample gown is of cream-hued linen,
Her grandsons raised the flax, and her grand-daughters spun
    it with the distaff and the wheel.

The melodious character of the earth,
The finish beyond which philosophy cannot go and does not
     wish to go,
The justified mother of men.

The Mystic Trumpeter

1

Hark, some wild trumpeter, some strange musician,
Hovering unseen in air, vibrates capricious tunes to-night.

I hear thee trumpeter, listening alert I catch thy notes,
Now pouring, whirling like a tempest round me,
Now low, subdued, now in the distance lost.

2

Come nearer bodiless one, haply in thee resounds
Some dead composer, haply thy pensive life
Was fill'd with aspirations high, unform'd ideals,
Waves, oceans musical, chaotically surging,
10   That now ecstatic ghost, close to me bending, thy cornet
        echoing, pealing,
Gives out to no one's ears but mine, but freely gives to
        mine,
That I may thee translate.

3

Blow trumpeter free and clear, I follow thee,
While at thy liquid prelude, glad, serene,
The fretting world, the streets, the noisy hours of day
        withdraw,
A holy calm descends like dew upon me,
I walk in cool refreshing night the walks of Paradise,
I scent the grass, the moist air and the roses;
Thy song expands my numb'd imbonded spirit, thou freest,
        launchest me,
20   Floating and basking upon heaven's lake.

4

Blow again trumpeter! and for my sensuous eyes,
Bring the old pageants, show the feudal world.

What charm thy music works! thou makest pass before me,
Ladies and cavaliers long dead, barons are in their castle
    halls, the troubadours are singing,
Arm'd knights go forth to redress wrongs, some in quest of
    the holy Graal;
I see the tournament, I see the contestants incased in heavy
    armor seated on stately champing horses,
I hear the shouts, the sounds of blows and smiting steel;
I see the Crusaders' tumultuous armies – hark, how the
    cymbals clang,
Lo, where the monks walk in advance, bearing the cross
    on high.

5

30 Blow again trumpeter! and for thy theme,
Take now the enclosing theme of all, the solvent and the
    setting,
Love, that is pulse of all, the sustenance and the pang,
The heart of man and woman all for love,
No other theme but love – knitting, enclosing, all-diffusing
    love.

O how the immortal phantoms crowd around me!
I see the vast alembic ever working, I see and know the
    flames that heat the world,
The glow, the blush, the beating hearts of lovers,
So blissful happy some, and some so silent, dark, and nigh to
    death;
Love, that is all the earth to lovers – love, that mocks time
    and space,
40 Love, that is day and night – love, that is sun and moon and
    stars,
Love, that is crimson, sumptuous, sick with perfume,
No other words but words of love, no other thought but
    love.

6

Blow again trumpeter – conjure war's alarums.

Swift to thy spell a shuddering hum like distant thunder
   rolls,
Lo, where the arm'd men hasten – lo, mid the clouds of dust
   the glint of bayonets,
I see the grime-faced cannoneers, I mark the rosy flash amid
   the smoke, I hear the cracking of the guns;
Nor war alone – thy fearful music-song, wild player, brings
   every sight of fear,
The deeds of ruthless brigands, rapine, murder – I hear the
   cries for help!
I see ships foundering at sea, I behold on deck and below
   deck the terrible tableaus.

7

50 O trumpeter, methinks I am myself the instrument thou
       playest,
Thou melt'st my heart, my brain – thou movest, drawest,
   changest them at will;
And now thy sullen notes send darkness through me,
Thou takest away all cheering light, all hope,
I see the enslaved, the overthrown, the hurt, the opprest of
   the whole earth,
I feel the measureless shame and humiliation of my race, it
   becomes all mine,
Mine too the revenges of humanity, the wrongs of ages,
   baffled feuds and hatreds,
Utter defeat upon me weighs – all lost – the foe victorious,
(Yet 'mid the ruins Pride colossal stands unshaken to the
   last,
Endurance, resolution to the last.)

8

60 Now trumpeter for thy close,
Vouchsafe a higher strain than any yet,
Sing to my soul, renew its languishing faith and hope,
Rouse up my slow belief, give me some vision of the future,
Give me for once its prophecy and joy.

O glad, exulting, culminating song!
A vigor more than earth's is in thy notes,
Marches of victory – man disenthral'd – the conqueror at
   last,
Hymns to the universal God from universal man – all joy!
A reborn race appears – a perfect world, all joy!
70 Women and men in wisdom innocence and health – all joy!
Riotous laughing bacchanals fill'd with joy!
War, sorrow, suffering gone – the rank earth purged –
   nothing but joy left!
The ocean fill'd with joy – the atmosphere all joy!
Joy! joy! in freedom, worship, love! joy in the ecstasy of life!
Enough to merely be! enough to breathe!
Joy! joy! all over joy!

To a Locomotive in Winter

Thee for my recitative,
Thee in the driving storm even as now, the snow, the
   winter-day declining,
Thee in thy panoply, thy measur'd dual throbbing and thy
   beat convulsive,
Thy black cylindric body, golden brass and silvery steel,
Thy ponderous side-bars, parallel and connecting rods,
   gyrating, shuttling at thy sides,
Thy metrical, now swelling pant and roar, now tapering in
   the distance,
Thy great protruding head-light fix'd in front,
Thy long, pale, floating vapor-pennants, tinged with
   delicate purple,

The dense and murky clouds out-belching from thy
    smoke-stack,
10 Thy knitted frame, thy springs and valves, the tremulous
    twinkle of thy wheels,
Thy train of cars behind, obedient, merrily following,
Through gale or calm, now swift, now slack, yet steadily
    careering;
Type of the modern – emblem of motion and power –
    pulse of the continent,
For once come serve the Muse and merge in verse, even as
    here I see thee,
With storm and buffeting gusts of wind and falling snow,
By day thy warning ringing bell to sound its notes,
By night thy silent signal lamps to swing.

Fierce-throated beauty!
Roll through my chant with all thy lawless music, thy
    swinging lamps at night,
20 Thy madly-whistled laughter, echoing, rumbling like an
    earthquake, rousing all,
Law of thyself complete, thine own track firmly holding,
(No sweetness debonair of tearful harp or glib piano thine,)
Thy trills of shrieks by rocks and hills return'd,
Launch'd o'er the prairies wide, across the lakes,
To the free skies unpent and glad and strong.

O Magnet-South

O Magnet-South! O glistening perfumed South! my South!
O quick mettle, rich blood, impulse and love! good and evil!
    O all dear to me!
O dear to me my birth-pangs – all moving things and the
    trees where I was born – the grains, plants, rivers,
Dear to me my own slow sluggish rivers where they flow,
    distant, over flats of silvery sands or through swamps,
Dear to me the Roanoke, the Savannah, the Altamahaw,

the Pedee, the Tombigbee, the Santee, the Coosa and the
  Sabine,
O pensive, far away wandering, I return with my soul to
  haunt their banks again,
Again in Florida I float on transparent lakes, I float on the
  Okeechobee, I cross the hummock-land or through
  pleasant openings or dense forests,
I see the parrots in the woods, I see the papaw-tree and the
  blossoming titi;
Again, sailing in my coaster on deck, I coast off Georgia, I
  coast up the Carolinas,
10 I see where the live-oak is growing, I see where the
  yellow-pine, the scented bay-tree, the lemon and orange,
  the cypress, the graceful palmetto,
I pass rude sea-headlands and enter Pamlico sound through
  an inlet, and dart my vision inland;
O the cotton plant! the growing fields of rice, sugar, hemp!
The cactus guarded with thorns, the laurel-tree with large
  white flowers,
The range afar, the richness and barrenness, the old woods
  charged with mistletoe and trailing moss,
The piney odor and the gloom, the awful natural stillness,
  (here in these dense swamps the freebooter carries his gun,
  and the fugitive has his conceal'd hut;)
O the strange fascination of these half-known
  half-impassable swamps, infested by reptiles, resounding
  with the bellow of the alligator, the sad noises of the
  night-owl and the wild-cat, and the whirr of the
  rattlesnake,
The mocking-bird, the American mimic, singing all the
  forenoon, singing through the moon-lit night,
The humming-bird, the wild turkey, the raccoon, the
  opossum;
A Kentucky corn-field, the tall, graceful, long-leav'd corn,
  slender, flapping, bright green, with tassels, with
  beautiful ears each well-sheath'd in its husk;

20   O my heart! O tender and fierce pangs, I can stand them
         not, I will depart;
     O to be a Virginian where I grew up! O to be a Carolinian!
     O longings irrepressible! O I will go back to old
         Tennessee and never wander more.

Mannahatta

I was asking for something specific and perfect for my city,
Whereupon lo! upsprang the aboriginal name.

Now I see what there is in a name, a word, liquid, sane,
     unruly, musical, self-sufficient,
I see that the word of my city is that word from of old,
Because I see that word nested in nests of water-bays,
     superb,
Rich, hemm'd thick all around with sailships and
     steamships, an island sixteen miles long, solid-founded,
Numberless crowded streets, high growths of iron, slender,
     strong, light, splendidly uprising toward clear skies,
Tides swift and ample, well-loved by me, toward sundown,
The flowing sea-currents, the little islands, larger adjoining
     islands, the heights, the villas,
10   The countless masts, the white shore-steamers, the
         lighters, the ferry-boats, the black sea-steamers
         well-model'd,
     The down-town streets, the jobbers' houses of business, the
         houses of business of the ship-merchants and
         money-brokers, the river-streets,
     Immigrants arriving, fifteen or twenty thousand in a week,
     The carts hauling goods, the manly race of drivers of
         horses, the brown-faced sailors,
     The summer air, the bright sun shining, and the sailing
         clouds aloft,
     The winter snows, the sleigh-bells, the broken ice in the
         river, passing along up or down with the flood-tide or
         ebb-tide,

The mechanics of the city, the masters, well-form'd,
    beautiful-faced, looking you straight in the eyes,
Trottoirs throng'd, vehicles, Broadway, the women, the
    shops and shows,
A million people – manners free and superb – open voices –
    hospitality – the most courageous and friendly young men,
City of hurried and sparkling waters! city of spires and
    masts!
20   City nested in bays! my city!

All is Truth

O me, man of slack faith so long,
Standing aloof, denying portions so long,
Only aware to-day of compact all-diffused truth,
Discovering to-day there is no lie or form of lie, and can be
    none, but grows as inevitably upon itself as the truth does
    upon itself,
Or as any law of the earth or any natural production of the
    earth does.

(This is curious and may not be realized immediately, but
    it must be realized,
I feel in myself that I represent falsehoods equally with the
    rest,
And that the universe does.)

Where has fail'd a perfect return indifferent of lies or the
    truth?
10   Is it upon the ground, or in water or fire? or in the spirit of
    man? or in the meat and blood?

Meditating among liars and retreating sternly into myself, I
    see that there are really no liars or lies after all,
And that nothing fails its perfect return, and that what are
    called lies are perfect returns,
And that each thing exactly represents itself and what has
    preceded it,

And that the truth includes all, and is compact just as much
    as space is compact,
And that there is no flaw or vacuum in the amount of the
    truth – but that all is truth without exception;
And henceforth I will go celebrate any thing I see or am,
And sing and laugh and deny nothing.

A Riddle Song

That which eludes this verse and any verse,
Unheard by sharpest ear, unform'd in clearest eye or
    cunningest mind,
Nor lore nor fame, nor happiness nor wealth,
And yet the pulse of every heart and life throughout the
    world incessantly,
Which you and I and all pursuing ever ever miss,
Open but still a secret, the real of the real, an illusion,
Costless, vouchsafed to each, yet never man the owner,
Which poets vainly seek to put in rhyme, historians in prose,
Which sculptor never chisel'd yet, nor painter painted,
Which vocalist never sung, nor orator nor actor ever utter'd,
Invoking here and now I challenge for my song.

Indifferently, 'mid public, private haunts, in solitude,
Behind the mountain and the wood,
Companion of the city's busiest streets, through the
    assemblage,
It and its radiations constantly glide.

In looks of fair unconscious babes,
Or strangely in the coffin'd dead,
Or show of breaking dawn or stars by night,
As some dissolving delicate film of dreams,
Hiding yet lingering.

Two little breaths of words comprising it,
Two words, yet all from first to last comprised in it.

How ardently for it!

How many ships have sail'd and sunk for it!
How many travelers started from their homes and ne'er
return'd!
How much of genius boldly staked and lost for it!
What countless stores of beauty, love, ventur'd for it!
How all superbest deeds since Time began are traceable to
it – and shall be to the end!
How all heroic martyrdoms to it!
30 How, justified by it, the horrors, evils, battles of the earth!
How the bright fascinating lambent flames of it, in every age
and land, have drawn men's eyes,
Rich as a sunset on the Norway coast, the sky, the islands,
and the cliffs,
Or midnight's silent glowing northern lights unreachable.

Haply God's riddle it, so vague and yet so certain,
The soul for it, and all the visible universe for it,
And heaven at last for it.

Excelsior

Who has gone farthest? for I would go farther,
And who has been just? for I would be the most just person
of the earth,
And who most cautious? for I would be more cautious,
And who has been happiest? O I think it is I – I think no one
was ever happier than I,
And who has lavish'd all? for I lavish constantly the best I
have,
And who proudest? for I think I have reason to be the
proudest son alive – for I am the son of the brawny and
tall-topt city,
And who has been bold and true? for I would be the
boldest and truest being of the universe,
And who benevolent? for I would show more benevolence
than all the rest,

And who has receiv'd the love of the most friends? for I
    know what it is to receive the passionate love of many
    friends,
10 And who possesses a perfect and enamour'd body? for I do
    not believe any one possesses a more perfect or
    enamour'd body than mine,
And who thinks the amplest thoughts? for I would
    surround those thoughts,
And who has made hymns fit for the earth? for I am mad
    with devouring ecstasy to make joyous hymns for the
    whole earth.

Ah Poverties, Wincings, and Sulky Retreats

Ah poverties, wincings, and sulky retreats,
Ah you foes that in conflict have overcome me,
(For what is my life or any man's life but a conflict with foes,
    the old, the incessant war?)
You degradations, you tussle with passions and
    appetites,
You smarts from dissatisfied friendships, (ah wounds the
    sharpest of all!)
You toil of painful and choked articulations, you
    meannesses,
You shallow tongue-talks at tables, (my tongue the
    shallowest of any;)
You broken resolutions, you racking angers, you
    smother'd ennuis!
Ah think not you finally triumph, my real self has yet to
    come forth,
10 It shall yet march forth o'ermastering, till all lies beneath
    me,
It shall yet stand up the soldier of ultimate victory.

Thoughts

Of public opinion,

Of a calm and cool fiat sooner or later, (how impassive! how
certain and final!)

Of the President with pale face asked secretly to himself,
What will the people say at last?

Of the frivolous Judge – of the corrupt Congressman,
Governor, Mayor – of such as these standing helpless and
exposed,

Of the mumbling and screaming priest, (soon, soon
deserted,)

Of the lessening year by year of venerableness, and of the
dicta of officers, statutes, pulpits, school,

Of the rising forever taller and stronger and broader of the
intuitions of men and women, and of Self-esteem and
Personality;

Of the true New World – of the Democracies resplendent
en-masse,

Of the conformity of politics, armies, navies, to them,

10 Of the shining sun by them – of the inherent light, greater
than the rest,

Of the envelopment of all by them, and the effusion of all
from them.

Mediums

They shall arise in the States,

They shall report Nature, laws, physiology, and happiness,

They shall illustrate Democracy and the kosmos,

They shall be alimentive, amative, perceptive,

They shall be complete women and men, their pose brawny
and supple, their drink water, their blood clean and clear,

They shall fully enjoy materialism and the sight of
products, they shall enjoy the sight of the beef, lumber,
bread-stuffs, of Chicago the great city,

They shall train themselves to go in public to become
     orators and oratresses,
Strong and sweet shall their tongues be, poems and
     materials of poems shall come from their lives, they shall
     be makers and finders,
Of them and of their works shall emerge divine conveyers,
     to convey gospels,
10   Characters, events, retrospections, shall be convey'd in
     gospels, trees, animals, waters, shall be convey'd,
Death, the future, the invisible faith, shall all be convey'd.

Weave in, My Hardy Life

Weave in, weave in, my hardy life,
Weave yet a soldier strong and full for great campaigns to
     come,
Weave in red blood, weave sinews in like ropes, the senses,
     sight weave in,
Weave lasting sure, weave day and night the weft, the warp,
     incessant weave, tire not,
(We know not what the use O life, nor know the aim, the
     end, nor really aught we know,
But know the work, the need goes on and shall go on, the
     death-envelop'd march of peace as well as war goes on,)
For great campaigns of peace the same the wiry threads to
     weave,
We know not why or what, yet weave, forever weave.

Spain, 1873-74

Out of the murk of heaviest clouds,
Out of the feudal wrecks and heap'd-up skeletons of kings,
Out of that old entire European debris, the shatter'd
     mummeries,
Ruin'd cathedrals, crumble of palaces, tombs of priests,
Lo, Freedom's features fresh undimm'd look forth – the

same immortal face looks forth;
(A glimpse as of thy Mother's face Columbia,
A flash significant as of a sword,
Beaming towards thee.)

Nor think we forget thee maternal;
10 Lag'd'st thou so long? shall the clouds close again upon thee?
Ah, but thou hast thyself now appear'd to us – we know
    thee,
Thou hast given us a sure proof, the glimpse of thyself,
Thou waitest there as everywhere thy time.

By Broad Potomac's Shore

By broad Potomac's shore, again old tongue,
(Still uttering, still ejaculating, canst never cease this
    babble?)
Again old heart so gay, again to you, your sense, the full
    flush spring returning,
Again the freshness and the odors, again Virginia's summer
    sky, pellucid blue and silver,
Again the forenoon purple of the hills,
Again the deathless grass, so noiseless soft and green,
Again the blood-red roses blooming.

Perfume this book of mine O blood-red roses!
Lave subtly with your waters every line Potomac!
10 Give me of you O spring, before I close, to put between its
    pages!
O forenoon purple of the hills, before I close, of you!
O deathless grass, of you!

From Far Dakota's Cañons (June 25, 1876)

From far Dakota's cañons,
Lands of the wild ravine, the dusky Sioux, the lonesome
    stretch, the silence,
Haply to-day a mournful wail, haply a trumpet-note for
    heroes.

The battle-bulletin,
The Indian ambuscade, the craft, the fatal environment,
The cavalry companies fighting to the last in sternest
    heroism,
In the midst of their little circle, with their slaughter'd
    horses for breastworks,
The fall of Custer and all his officers and men.

Continues yet the old, old legend of our race,
10   The loftiest of life upheld by death,
The ancient banner perfectly maintain'd,
O lesson opportune, O how I welcome thee!

As sitting in dark days,
Lone, sulky, through the time's thick murk looking in vain
    for light, for hope,
From unsuspected parts a fierce and momentary proof,
(The sun there at the centre though conceal'd,
Electric life forever at the centre,)
Breaks forth a lightning flash.

Thou of the tawny flowing hair in battle,
20   I erewhile saw, with erect head, pressing ever in front,
    bearing a bright sword in thy hand,
Now ending well in death the splendid fever of thy deeds,
(I bring no dirge for it or thee, I bring a glad triumphal
    sonnet,)
Desperate and glorious, aye in defeat most desperate, most
    glorious,
After thy many battles in which never yielding up a gun or
    a color,

Leaving behind thee a memory sweet to soldiers,
Thou yieldest up thyself.

Old War-Dreams

In midnight sleep of many a face of anguish,
Of the look at first of the mortally wounded, (of that
    indescribable look,)
Of the dead on their backs with arms extended wide,
      I dream, I dream, I dream.

Of scenes of Nature, fields and mountains,
Of skies so beauteous after a storm, and at night the moon
    so unearthly bright,
Shining sweetly, shining down, where we dig the trenches
    and gather the heaps,
      I dream, I dream, I dream.

Long have they pass'd, faces and trenches and fields,
Where through the carnage I moved with a callous
    composure, or away from the fallen,
Onward I sped at the time – but now of their forms at night,
      I dream, I dream, I dream.

Thick-Sprinkled Bunting

Thick-sprinkled bunting! flag of stars!
Long yet your road, fatal flag – long yet your road, and
    lined with bloody death,
For the prize I see at issue at last is the world,
All its ships and shores I see interwoven with your threads
    greedy banner;
Dream'd again the flags of kings, highest borne, to flaunt
    unrival'd?
O hasten flag of man – O with sure and steady step, passing
    highest flags of kings,

Walk supreme to the heavens mighty symbol – run up above
    them all,
Flag of stars! thick-sprinkled bunting!

What Best I See in Thee
(TO U.S.G. RETURN'D FROM HIS WORLD'S TOUR)

What best I see in thee,
Is not that where thou mov'st down history's great
    highways,
Ever undimm'd by time shoots warlike victory's dazzle,
Or that thou sat'st where Washington sat, ruling the land in
    peace,
Or thou the man whom feudal Europe feted, venerable Asia
    swarm'd upon,
Who walk'd with kings with even pace the round world's
    promenade;
But that in foreign lands, in all thy walks with kings,
Those prairie sovereigns of the West, Kansas, Missouri,
    Illinois,
Ohio's, Indiana's millions, comrades, farmers, soldiers, all
    to the front,
10   Invisibly with thee walking with kings with even pace the
    round world's promenade,
Were all so justified.

Spirit That Form'd This Scene
(WRITTEN IN PLATTE CAÑON, COLORADO)

Spirit that form'd this scene,
These tumbled rock-piles grim and red,
These reckless heaven-ambitious peaks,
These gorges, turbulent-clear streams, this naked
    freshness,
These formless wild arrays, for reasons of their own,
I know thee, savage spirit – we have communed together,

Mine too such wild arrays, for reasons of their own;
Was't charged against my chants they had forgotten art?
To fuse within themselves its rules precise and delicatesse?
10   The lyrist's measur'd beat, the wrought-out temple's grace –
        column and polish'd arch forgot?
But thou that revelest here – spirit that form'd this scene,
They have remember'd thee.

As I Walk These Broad Majestic Days

As I walk these broad majestic days of peace,
(For the war, the struggle of blood finish'd, wherein, O
     terrific Ideal,
Against vast odds erewhile having gloriously won,
Now thou stridest on, yet perhaps in time toward denser
     wars,
Perhaps to engage in time in still more dreadful contests,
     dangers,
Longer campaigns and crises, labors beyond all others,)
Around me I hear that eclat of the world, politics, produce,
The announcements of recognized things, science,
The approved growth of cities and the spread of inventions.

10   I see the ships, (they will last a few years,)
The vast factories with their foremen and workmen,
And hear the indorsement of all, and do not object to it.

But I too announce solid things,
Science, ships, politics, cities, factories, are not nothing,
Like a grand procession to music of distant bugles pouring,
     triumphantly moving, and grander heaving in sight,
They stand for realities – all is as it should be.

Then my realities;
What else is so real as mine?
Libertad and the divine average, freedom to every slave on
     the face of the earth,

20   The rapt promises and luminè of seers, the spiritual world,
these centuries-lasting songs,
And our visions, the visions of poets, the most solid
announcements of any.

A Clear Midnight

This is thy hour O Soul, thy free flight into the wordless,
Away from books, away from art, the day erased, the lesson
done,
Thee fully forth emerging, silent, gazing, pondering the
themes thou lovest best,
Night, sleep, death and the stars.

SONGS OF PARTING

As the Time Draws Nigh

As the time draws nigh glooming a cloud,
A dread beyond of I know not what darkens me.

I shall go forth,
I shall traverse the States awhile, but I cannot tell whither or
  how long,
Perhaps soon some day or night while I am singing my voice
  will suddenly cease.

O book, O chants! must all then amount to but this?
Must we barely arrive at this beginning of us? – and yet it is
  enough, O soul;
O soul, we have positively appear'd – that is enough.

Years of the Modern

Years of the modern! years of the unperform'd!
Your horizon rises, I see it parting away for more august
  dramas,
I see not America only, not only Liberty's nation but other
  nations preparing,
I see tremendous entrances and exits, new combinations,
  the solidarity of races,
I see that force advancing with irresistible power on the
  world's stage,
(Have the old forces, the old wars, played their parts? are
  the acts suitable to them closed?)
I see Freedom, completely arm'd and victorious and very
  haughty, with Law on one side and Peace on the other,
A stupendous trio all issuing forth against the idea of caste;
What historic denouements are these we so rapidly
  approach?
10 I see men marching and countermarching by swift millions,

I see the frontiers and boundaries of the old aristocracies
    broken,
I see the landmarks of European kings removed,
I see this day the People beginning their landmarks, (all
    others give way;)
Never were such sharp questions ask'd as this day,
Never was average man, his soul, more energetic, more like
    a God,
Lo, how he urges and urges, leaving the masses no rest!
His daring foot is on land and sea everywhere, he
    colonizes the Pacific, the archipelagoes,
With the steamship, the electric telegraph, the newspaper,
    the wholesale engines of war,
With these and the world-spreading factories he interlinks
    all geography, all lands;
20 What whispers are these O lands, running ahead of you,
    passing under the seas?
Are all nations communing? is there going to be but one
    heart to the globe?
Is humanity forming en-masse? for lo, tyrants tremble,
    crowns grow dim,
The earth, restive, confronts a new era, perhaps a general
    divine war,
No one knows what will happen next, such portents fill the
    days and nights;
Years prophetical! the space ahead as I walk, as I vainly try
    to pierce it, is full of phantoms,
Unborn deeds, things soon to be, project their shapes
    around me,
This incredible rush and heat, this strange ecstatic fever of
    dreams O years!
Your dreams O years, how they penetrate through me! (I
    know not whether I sleep or wake;)
The perform'd America and Europe grow dim, retiring in
    shadow behind me,
30 The unperform'd, more gigantic than ever, advance, advance
    upon me.

Ashes of Soldiers

Ashes of soldiers South or North,
As I muse retrospective murmuring a chant in thought,
The war resumes, again to my sense your shapes,
And again the advance of the armies.

Noiseless as mists and vapors,
From their graves in the trenches ascending,
From cemeteries all through Virginia and Tennessee,
From every point of the compass out of the countless graves,
In wafted clouds, in myriads large, or squads of twos or
    threes or single ones they come,
10 And silently gather round me.

Now sound no note O trumpeters,
Not at the head of my cavalry parading on spirited horses,
With sabres drawn and glistening, and carbines by their
    thighs, (ah my brave horsemen!
My handsome tan-faced horsemen! what life, what joy and
    pride,
With all the perils were yours.)

Nor you drummers, neither at reveillé at dawn,
Nor the long roll alarming the camp, nor even the muffled
    beat for a burial,
Nothing from you this time O drummers bearing my
    warlike drums.

But aside from these and the marts of wealth and the
    crowded promenade,
20 Admitting around me comrades close unseen by the rest and
    voiceless,
The slain elate and alive again, the dust and debris alive,
I chant this chant of my silent soul in the name of all dead
    soldiers.

Faces so pale with wondrous eyes, very dear, gather closer
    yet,
Draw close, but speak not.

Phantoms of countless lost,
Invisible to the rest henceforth become my companions,
Follow me ever – desert me not while I live.

Sweet are the blooming cheeks of the living – sweet are the
    musical voices sounding,
But sweet, ah sweet, are the dead with their silent eyes.

30   Dearest comrades, all is over and long gone,
But love is not over – and what love, O comrades!
Perfume from battle-fields rising, up from the fœtor arising.

Perfume therefore my chant, O love, immortal love,
Give me to bathe the memories of all dead soldiers,
Shroud them, embalm them, cover them all over with
    tender pride.

Perfume all – make all wholesome,
Make these ashes to nourish and blossom,
O love, solve all, fructify all with the last chemistry.

Give me exhaustless, make me a fountain,
40   That I exhale love from me wherever I go like a moist
    perennial dew,
For the ashes of all dead soldiers South or North.

Thoughts

1

Of these years I sing,
How they pass and have pass'd through convuls'd pains, as
    through parturitions,
How America illustrates birth, muscular youth, the promise,
    the sure fulfilment, the absolute success, despite of
    people – illustrates evil as well as good,
The vehement struggle so fierce for unity in one's-self;
How many hold despairingly yet to the models departed,
    caste, myths, obedience, compulsion, and to infidelity,
How few see the arrived models, the athletes, the Western

States, or see freedom or spirituality, or hold any faith in
results,
(But I see the athletes, and I see the results of the war
glorious and inevitable, and they again leading to other
results.)

How the great cities appear – how the Democratic masses,
turbulent, wilful, as I love them,
How the whirl, the contest, the wrestle of evil with good, the
sounding and resounding, keep on and on,
10 How society waits unform'd, and is for a while between
things ended and things begun,
How America is the continent of glories, and of the
triumph of freedom and of the Democracies, and of the
fruits of society, and of all that is begun,
And how the States are complete in themselves – and how all
triumphs and glories are complete in themselves, to lead
onward,
And how these of mine and of the States will in their turn be
convuls'd, and serve other parturitions and transitions,
And how all people, sights, combinations, the democratic
masses too, serve – and how every fact, and war itself, with
all its horrors, serves,
And how now or at any time each serves the exquisite
transition of death.

2

Of seeds dropping into the ground, of births,
Of the steady concentration of America, inland, upward, to
impregnable and swarming places,
Of what Indiana, Kentucky, Arkansas, and the rest, are to be,
Of what a few years will show there in Nebraska, Colorado,
Nevada, and the rest,
20 (Or afar, mounting the Northern Pacific to Sitka or Aliaska,)
Of what the feuillage of America is the preparation for – and
of what all sights, North, South, East and West are,
Of this Union welded in blood, of the solemn price paid, of
the unnamed lost ever present in my mind;
Of the temporary use of materials for identity's sake,

Of the present, passing, departing – of the growth of
    completer men than any yet,
Of all sloping down there where the fresh free giver the
    mother, the Mississippi flows,
Of mighty inland cities yet unsurvey'd and unsuspected,
Of the new and good names, of the modern developments, of
    inalienable homesteads,
Of a free and original life there, of simple diet and clean and
    sweet blood,
Of litheness, majestic faces, clear eyes, and perfect
    physique there,
30 Of immense spiritual results future years far West, each side
    of the Anahuacs,
Of these songs, well understood there, (being made for that
    area,)
Of the native scorn of grossness and gain there,
(O it lurks in me night and day – what is gain after all to
    savageness and freedom?)

Song at Sunset

Splendor of ended day floating and filling me,
Hour prophetic, hour resuming the past,
Inflating my throat, you divine average,
You earth and life till the last ray gleams I sing.

Open mouth of my soul uttering gladness,
Eyes of my soul seeing perfection,
Natural life of me faithfully praising things,
Corroborating forever the triumph of things.

Illustrious every one!
10 Illustrious what we name space, sphere of unnumber'd
    spirits,
Illustrious the mystery of motion in all beings, even the
    tiniest insect,
Illustrious the attribute of speech, the senses, the body,

Illustrious the passing light – illustrious the pale reflection
    on the new moon in the western sky,
Illustrious whatever I see or hear or touch, to the last.

Good in all,
In the satisfaction and aplomb of animals,
In the annual return of the seasons,
In the hilarity of youth,
In the strength and flush of manhood,
20 In the grandeur and exquisiteness of old age,
In the superb vistas of death.

Wonderful to depart!
Wonderful to be here!
The heart, to jet the all-alike and innocent blood!
To breathe the air, how delicious!
To speak – to walk – to seize something by the hand!
To prepare for sleep, for bed, to look on my rose-color'd
    flesh!
To be conscious of my body, so satisfied, so large!
To be this incredible God I am!
30 To have gone forth among other Gods, these men and
    women I love.

Wonderful how I celebrate you and myself!
How my thoughts play subtly at the spectacles around!
How the clouds pass silently overhead!
How the earth darts on and on! and how the sun, moon,
    stars, dart on and on!
How the water sports and sings! (surely it is alive!)
How the trees rise and stand up, with strong trunks, with
    branches and leaves!
(Surely there is something more in each of the trees, some
    living soul.)

O amazement of things – even the least particle!
O spirituality of things!
40 O strain musical flowing through ages and continents, now
reaching me and America!
I take your strong chords, intersperse them, and cheerfully
pass them forward.

I too carol the sun, usher'd or at noon, or as now, setting,
I too throb to the brain and beauty of the earth and of all the
growths of the earth,
I too have felt the resistless call of myself.

As I steam'd down the Mississippi,
As I wander'd over the prairies,
As I have lived, as I have look'd through my windows my
eyes,
As I went forth in the morning, as I beheld the light breaking
in the east,
As I bathed on the beach of the Eastern Sea, and again on
the beach of the Western Sea,
50 As I roam'd the streets of inland Chicago, whatever streets
I have roam'd,
Or cities or silent woods, or even amid the sights of war,
Wherever I have been I have charged myself with
contentment and triumph.

I sing to the last the equalities modern or old,
I sing the endless finalés of things,
I say Nature continues, glory continues,
I praise with electric voice,
For I do not see one imperfection in the universe,
And I do not see one cause or result lamentable at last in the
universe.

O setting sun! though the time has come,
60 I still warble under you, if none else does, unmitigated
adoration.

As at Thy Portals Also Death

As at thy portals also death,
Entering thy sovereign, dim, illimitable grounds,
To memories of my mother, to the divine blending,
    maternity,
To her, buried and gone, yet buried not, gone not from me,
(I see again the calm benignant face fresh and beautiful
    still,
I sit by the form in the coffin,
I kiss and kiss convulsively again the sweet old lips, the
    cheeks, the closed eyes in the coffin;)
To her, the ideal woman, practical, spiritual, of all of earth,
    life, love, to me the best,
I grave a monumental line, before I go, amid these songs,
10 And set a tombstone here.

My Legacy

The business man the acquirer vast,
After assiduous years surveying results, preparing for
    departure,
Devises houses and lands to his children, bequeaths stocks,
    goods, funds for a school or hospital,
Leaves money to certain companions to buy tokens,
    souvenirs of gems and gold.

But I, my life surveying, closing,
With nothing to show to devise from its idle years,
Nor houses nor lands, nor tokens of gems or gold for my
    friends,
Yet certain remembrances of the war for you, and after you,
And little souvenirs of camps and soldiers, with my love,
10 I bind together and bequeath in this bundle of songs.

Pensive on Her Dead Gazing

Pensive on her dead gazing I heard the Mother of All,
Desperate on the torn bodies, on the forms covering the
    battlefields gazing,
(As the last gun ceased, but the scent of the powder-smoke
    linger'd,)
As she call'd to her earth with mournful voice while she
    stalk'd,
Absorb them well O my earth, she cried, I charge you lose
    not my sons, lose not an atom,
And you streams absorb them well, taking their dear blood,
And you local spots, and you airs that swim above lightly
    impalpable,
And all you essences of soil and growth, and you my rivers'
    depths,
And you mountain sides, and the woods where my dear
    children's blood trickling redden'd,
10 And you trees down in your roots to bequeath to all future
    trees,
My dead absorb or South or North – my young men's
    bodies absorb, and their precious precious blood,
Which holding in trust for me faithfully back again give me
    many a year hence,
In unseen essence and odor of surface and grass, centuries
    hence,
In blowing airs from the fields back again give me my
    darlings, give my immortal heroes,
Exhale me them centuries hence, breathe me their breath,
    let not an atom be lost,
O years and graves! O air and soil! O my dead, an aroma
    sweet!
Exhale them perennial sweet death, years, centuries hence.

Camps of Green

Not alone those camps of white, old comrades of the wars,
When as order'd forward, after a long march,
Footsore and weary, soon as the light lessens we halt for the
  night,
Some of us so fatigued carrying the gun and knapsack,
  dropping asleep in our tracks,
Others pitching the little tents, and the fires lit up begin to
  sparkle,
Outposts of pickets posted surrounding alert through the
  dark,
And a word provided for countersign, careful for safety,
Till to the call of the drummers at daybreak loudly beating
  the drums,
We rise up refresh'd, the night and sleep pass'd over, and
  resume our journey,
10 Or proceed to battle.

Lo, the camps of the tents of green,
Which the days of peace keep filling, and the days of war
  keep filling,
With a mystic army, (is it too order'd forward? is it too only
  halting awhile,
Till night and sleep pass over?)

Now in those camps of green, in their tents dotting the
  world,
In the parents, children, husbands, wives, in them, in the
  old and young,
Sleeping under the sunlight, sleeping under the moonlight,
  content and silent there at last,
Behold the mighty bivouac-field and waiting-camp of all,
Of the corps and generals all, and the President over the
  corps and generals all,
20 And of each of us O soldiers, and of each and all in the ranks
  we fought,
(Thee without hatred we all, all meet.)

For presently O soldiers, we too camp in our place in the
    bivouac-camps of green,
But we need not provide for outposts, nor word for the
    counter-sign,
Nor drummer to beat the morning drum.

The Sobbing of the Bells
(MIDNIGHT, SEPT. 19–20, 1881)

The sobbing of the bells, the sudden death-news
    everywhere,
The slumberers rouse, the rapport of the People,
(Full well they know that message in the darkness,
Full well return, respond within their breasts, their brains,
    the sad reverberations,)
The passionate toll and clang – city to city, joining,
    sounding, passing,
Those heart-beats of a Nation in the night.

As They Draw to a Close

As they draw to a close,
Of what underlies the precedent songs – of my aims in them,
Of the seed I have sought to plant in them,
Of joy, sweet joy, through many a year, in them,
(For them, for them have I lived, in them my work is done,)
Of many an aspiration fond, of many a dream and plan;
Through Space and Time fused in a chant, and the flowing
    eternal identity,
To Nature encompassing these, encompassing God – to the
    joyous, electric all,
To the sense of Death, and accepting exulting in Death in
    its turn the same as life,
10   The entrance of man to sing;
To compact you, ye parted, diverse lives,

To put rapport the mountains and rocks and streams,
And the winds of the north, and the forests of oak and pine,
With you O soul.

Joy, Shipmate, Joy!

Joy, shipmate, joy!
(Pleas'd to my soul at death I cry,)
Our life is closed, our life begins,
The long, long anchorage we leave,
The ship is clear at last, she leaps!
She swiftly courses from the shore,
Joy, shipmate, joy.

The Untold Want

The untold want by life and land ne'er granted,
Now voyager sail thou forth to seek and find.

Portals

What are those of the known but to ascend and enter the
    Unknown?
And what are those of life but for Death?

These Carols

These carols sung to cheer my passage through the world
    I see,
For completion I dedicate to the Invisible World.

Now Finalè to the Shore

Now finalè to the shore,
Now land and life finalè and farewell,
Now Voyager depart, (much, much for thee is yet in store,)
Often enough hast thou adventur'd o'er the seas,
Cautiously cruising, studying the charts,
Duly again to port and hawser's tie returning;
But now obey thy cherish'd secret wish,
Embrace thy friends, leave all in order,
To port and hawser's tie no more returning,
10 Depart upon thy endless cruise old Sailor.

So Long!

To conclude, I announce what comes after me.

I remember I said before my leaves sprang at all,
I would raise my voice jocund and strong with reference to
    consummations.

When America does what was promis'd,
When through these States walk a hundred millions of
    superb persons,
When the rest part away for superb persons and contribute
    to them,
When breeds of the most perfect mothers denote America,
Then to me and mine our due fruition.

I have press'd through in my own right,
10 I have sung the body and the soul, war and peace have I
    sung, and the songs of life and death,
And the songs of birth, and shown that there are many births.

I have offer'd my style to every one, I have journey'd with
    confident step;
While my pleasure is yet at the full I whisper *So long!*
And take the young woman's hand and the young man's
    hand for the last time.

I announce natural persons to arise,
I announce justice triumphant,
I announce uncompromising liberty and equality,
I announce the justification of candor and the justification of
    pride.

I announce that the identity of these States is a single
    identity only,
20   I announce the Union more and more compact,
    indissoluble,
I announce splendors and majesties to make all the previous
    politics of the earth insignificant.

I announce adhesiveness, I say it shall be limitless,
    unloosen'd,
I say you shall yet find the friend you were looking for.

I announce a man or woman coming, perhaps you are the
    one, (*So long!*)
I announce the great individual, fluid as Nature, chaste,
    affectionate, compassionate, fully arm'd.

I announce a life that shall be copious, vehement, spiritual,
    bold,
I announce an end that shall lightly and joyfully meet its
    translation.

I announce myriads of youths, beautiful, gigantic,
    sweet-blooded,
I announce a race of splendid and savage old men.

30   O thicker and faster – (*So long!*)
O crowding too close upon me,
I foresee too much, it means more than I thought,
It appears to me I am dying.

Hasten throat and sound your last,
Salute me – salute the days once more. Peal the old cry
    once more.

Screaming electric, the atmosphere using,
At random glancing, each as I notice absorbing,
Swiftly on, but a little while alighting,
Curious envelop'd messages delivering,
40   Sparkles hot, seed ethereal down in the dirt drooping,
Myself unknowing, my commission obeying, to question it
      never daring,
To ages and ages yet the growth of the seed leaving,
To troops out of the war arising, they the tasks I have set
      promulging,
To women certain whispers of myself bequeathing, their
      affection me more clearly explaining,
To young men my problems offering – no dallier I – I the
      muscle of their brains trying,
So I pass, a little time vocal, visible, contrary,
Afterward a melodious echo, passionately bent for, (death
      making me really undying,)
The best of me then when no longer visible, for toward that
      I have been incessantly preparing.

What is there more, that I lag and pause and crouch
      extended with unshut mouth?
50   Is there a single final farewell?

My songs cease, I abandon them,
From behind the screen where I hid I advance personally
      solely to you.

Camerado, this is no book,
Who touches this touches a man,
(Is it night? are we here together alone?)
It is I you hold and who holds you,
I spring from the pages into your arms – decease calls me
      forth.

O how your fingers drowse me,
Your breath falls around me like dew, your pulse lulls the
      tympans of my ears,
60   I feel immerged from heat to foot,
Delicious, enough.

Enough O deed impromptu and secret,
Enough O gliding present – enough O summ'd-up past.

Dear friend whoever you are take this kiss,
I give it especially to you, do not forget me,
I feel like one who has done work for the day to retire
    awhile,
I receive now again of my many translations, from my
    avataras ascending, while others doubtless await me,
An unknown sphere more real than I dream'd, more direct,
    darts awakening rays about me, *So long!*
Remember my words, I may again return,
70 I love you, I depart from materials,
I am as one disembodied, triumphant, dead.

SANDS AT SEVENTY

Mannahatta

My city's fit and noble name resumed,
Choice aboriginal name, with marvellous beauty, meaning,
A rocky founded island – shores where ever gayly dash the
  coming, going, hurrying sea waves.

Paumanok

Sea-beauty! stretch'd and basking!
One side thy inland ocean laving, broad, with copious
  commerce, steamers, sails,
And one the Atlantic's wind caressing, fierce or gentle –
  mighty hulls dark-gliding in the distance.
Isle of sweet brooks of drinking-water – healthy air and
  soil!
Isle of the salty shore and breeze and brine!

From Montauk Point

I stand as on some mighty eagle's beak,
Eastward the sea absorbing, viewing, (nothing but sea and
  sky,)
The tossing waves, the foam, the ships in the distance,
The wild unrest, the snowy, curling caps – that inbound urge
  and urge of waves,
Seeking the shores forever.

To Those Who've Fail'd

To those who've fail'd, in aspiration vast,
To unnam'd soldiers fallen in front on the lead,
To calm, devoted engineers – to over-ardent travelers – to
  pilots of their ships,

To many a lofty song and picture without recognition – I'd
    rear a laurel-cover'd monument,
High, high above the rest – To all cut off before their time,
Possess'd by some strange spirit of fire,
Quench'd by an early death.

A Carol Closing Sixty-Nine

A carol closing sixty-nine – a *résumé* – a repetition,
My lines in joy and hope continuing on the same,
Of ye, O God, Life, Nature, Freedom, Poetry;
Of you, my Land – your rivers, prairies, States – you,
    mottled Flag I love,
Your aggregate retain'd entire – Of north, south, east and
    west, your items all;
Of me myself – the jocund heart yet beating in my breast,
The body wreck'd, old, poor and paralyzed – the strange
    inertia falling pall-like round me,
The burning fires down in my sluggish blood not yet
    extinct,
The undiminish'd faith – the groups of loving friends.

The Bravest Soldiers

Brave, brave were the soldiers (high named to-day) who
    lived through the fight;
But the bravest press'd to the front and fell, unnamed,
    unknown.

A Font of Type

This latent mine – these unlaunch'd voices – passionate
    powers,
Wrath, argument, or praise, or comic leer, or prayer devout,
(Not nonpareil, brevier, bourgeois, long primer merely,)
These ocean waves arousable to fury and to death,
Or sooth'd to ease and sheeny sun and sleep,
Within the pallid slivers slumbering.

As I Sit Writing Here

As I sit writing here, sick and grown old,
Not my least burden is that dulness of the years, querilities,
Ungracious glooms, aches, lethargy, constipation,
    whimpering *ennui*,
May filter in my daily songs.

My Canary Bird

Did we count great, O soul, to penetrate the themes of
    mighty books,
Absorbing deep and full from thoughts, plays,
    speculations?
But now from thee to me, caged bird, to feel thy joyous
    warble,
Filling the air, the lonesome room, the long forenoon,
Is it not just as great, O soul?

Queries to My Seventieth Year

Approaching, nearing, curious,
Thou dim, uncertain spectre – bringest thou life or death?
Strength, weakness, blindness, more paralysis and heavier?
Or placid skies and sun? Wilt stir the waters yet?
Or haply cut me short for good? Or leave me here as now,
Dull, parrot-like and old, with crack'd voice harping,
    screeching?

The Wallabout Martyrs

(In Brooklyn, in an old vault, mark'd by no special recognition,
lie huddled at this moment the undoubtedly authentic remains
of the stanchest and earliest revolutionary patriots from the
British prison ships and prisons of the times of 1776–83, in and
around New York, and from all over Long Island; originally
buried – many thousands of them – in trenches in the Wallabout
sands.)

Greater than memory of Achilles or Ulysses,
More, more by far to thee than tomb of Alexander,
Those cart loads of old charnel ashes, scales and splints of
    mouldy bones,
Once living men – once resolute courage, aspiration,
    strength,
The stepping stones to thee to-day and here, America.

The First Dandelion

Simple and fresh and fair from winter's close emerging,
As if no artifice of fashion, business, politics, had ever been,
Forth from its sunny nook of shelter'd grass – innocent,
    golden, calm as the dawn,
The spring's first dandelion shows its trustful face.

America

Centre of equal daughters, equal sons,
All, all alike endear'd, grown, ungrown, young or old,
Strong, ample, fair, enduring, capable, rich,
Perennial with the Earth, with Freedom, Law and Love,
A grand, sane, towering, seated Mother,
Chair'd in the adamant of Time.

Memories

How sweet the silent backward tracings!
The wanderings as in dreams – the meditation of old times
    resumed – their loves, joys, persons, voyages.

To-day and Thee

The appointed winners in a long-stretch'd game;
The course of Time and nations – Egypt, India, Greece and
    Rome;
The past entire, with all its heroes, histories, arts,
    experiments,
Its store of songs, inventions, voyages, teachers, books,
Garner'd for now and thee – To think of it!
The heirdom all converged in thee!

After the Dazzle of Day

After the dazzle of day is gone,
Only the dark, dark night shows to my eyes the stars;
After the clangor of organ majestic, or chorus, or perfect
    band,
Silent, athwart my soul, moves the symphony true.

Abraham Lincoln, Born Feb. 12, 1809

To-day, from each and all, a breath of prayer – a pulse of
    thought,
To memory of Him – to birth of Him.

Published Feb. 12, 1888

Out of May's Shows Selected

Apple orchards, the trees all cover'd with blossoms;
Wheat fields carpeted far and near in vital emerald green;
The eternal, exhaustless freshness of each early morning;
The yellow, golden, transparent haze of the warm
    afternoon sun;
The aspiring lilac bushes with profuse purple or white
    flowers.

Halcyon Days

Not from successful love alone,
Nor wealth, nor honor'd middle age, nor victories of
    politics or war;
But as life wanes, and all the turbulent passions calm,
As gorgeous, vapory, silent hues cover the evening sky,
As softness, fulness, rest, suffuse the frame, like freshier,
    balmier air,
As the days take on a mellower light, and the apple at last
    hangs really finish'd and indolent-ripe on the tree,
Then for the teeming quietest, happiest days of all!
The brooding and blissful halcyon days!

Fancies at Navesink

The Pilot in the Mist

Steaming the northern rapids – (an old St Lawrence
    reminiscence,
A sudden memory-flash comes back, I know not why,
Here waiting for the sunrise, gazing from this hill;)[1]
Again 'tis just at morning – a heavy haze contends with
    day-break,
Again the trembling, laboring vessel veers me – I press
    through foam-dash'd rocks that almost touch me,
Again I mark where aft the small thin Indian helmsman
Looms in the mist, with brow elate and governing hand.

Had I the Choice

Had I the choice to tally greatest bards,
To limn their portraits, stately, beautiful, and emulate at
    will,
Homer with all his wars and warriors – Hector, Achilles,
    Ajax,
Or Shakspere's woe-entangled Hamlet, Lear, Othello –
    Tennyson's fair ladies,
Metre or wit the best, or choice conceit to wield in perfect
    rhyme, delight of singers;
These, these, O sea, all these I'd gladly barter,
Would you the undulation of one wave, its trick to me
    transfer,
Or breathe one breath of yours upon my verse,
And leave its odor there.

You Tides with Ceaseless Swell

You tides with ceaseless swell! you power that does this
    work!
You unseen force, centripetal, centrifugal, through space's
    spread,
Rapport of sun, moon, earth, and all the constellations,

1. Navesink – a sea-side mountain, lower entrance of New York Bay.

What are the messages by you from distant stars to us? what
    Sirius'? what Capella's?
What central heart – and you the pulse – vivifies all? what
    boundless aggregate of all?
What subtle indirection and significance in you? what clue
    to all in you? what fluid, vast identity,
Holding the universe with all its parts as one – as sailing
    in a ship?

Last of Ebb, and Daylight Waning

Last of ebb, and daylight waning,
Scented sea-cool landward making, smells of sedge and salt
    incoming,
With many a half-caught voice sent up from the eddies,
Many a muffled confession – many a sob and whisper'd
    word,
As of speakers far or hid.

How they sweep down and out! how they mutter!
Poets unnamed – artists greatest of any, with cherish'd lost
    designs,
Love's unresponse – a chorus of age's complaints – hope's
    last words,
Some suicide's despairing cry, *Away to the boundless waste,
and never again return.*

10 On to oblivion then!
On, on, and do your part, ye burying, ebbing tide!
On for your time, ye furious débouché!

And Yet Not You Alone

And yet not you alone, twilight and burying ebb,
Nor you, ye lost designs alone – nor failures, aspirations;
I know, divine deceitful ones, your glamour's seeming;
Duly by you, from you, the tide and light again – duly the
   hinges turning,
Duly the needed discord-parts offsetting, blending,
Weaving from you, from Sleep, Night, Death itself,
The rhythmus of Birth eternal.

Proudly the Flood Comes In

Proudly the flood comes in, shouting, foaming, advancing,
Long it holds at the high, with bosom broad outswelling,
All throbs, dilates – the farms, woods, streets of cities –
   workmen at work,
Mainsails, topsails, jibs, appear in the offing – steamers'
   pennants of smoke – and under the forenoon sun,
Freighted with human lives, gaily the outward bound, gaily
   the inward bound,
Flaunting from many a spar the flag I love.

By That Long Scan of Waves

By that long scan of waves, myself call'd back, resumed upon
   myself,
In every crest some undulating light or shade – some
   retrospect,
Joys, travels, studies, silent panoramas – scenes
   ephemeral,
The long past war, the battles, hospital sights, the wounded
   and the dead,
Myself through every by-gone phase – my idle youth – old
   age at hand,
My three-score years of life summ'd up, and more, and past,
By any grand ideal tried, intentionless, the whole a nothing,

And haply yet some drop within God's scheme's ensemble –
    some wave, or part of wave,
Like one of yours, ye multitudinous ocean.

Then Last of All

Then last of all, caught from these shores, this hill,
Of you O tides, the mystic human meaning:
Only by law of you, your swell and ebb, enclosing me the
    same,
The brain that shapes, the voice that chants this song.

Election Day, November, 1884

If I should need to name, O Western World, your
    powerfulest scene and show,
'Twould not be you, Niagara – nor you, ye limitless
    prairies – nor your huge rifts of canyons, Colorado,
Nor you, Yosemite – nor Yellowstone, with all its spasmic
    geyser-loops ascending to the skies, appearing and
    disappearing,
Nor Oregon's white cones – nor Huron's belt of mighty
    lakes – nor Mississippi's stream:
– This seething hemisphere's humanity, as now, I'd name –
    the still small voice vibrating – America's choosing day,
(The heart of it not in the chosen – the act itself the main,
    the quadriennial choosing,)
The stretch of North and South arous'd – sea-board and
    inland – Texas to Maine – the Prairie States – Vermont,
    Virginia, California,
The final ballot-shower from East to West – the paradox and
    conflict,
The countless snow-flakes falling – (a swordless conflict,
10 Yet more than all Rome's wars of old, or modern
    Napoleon's:) the peaceful choice of all,
Or good or ill humanity – welcoming the darker odds, the
    dross:

– Foams and ferments the wine? it serves to purify – while
    the heart pants, life glows:
These stormy gusts and winds waft precious ships,
Swell'd Washington's, Jefferson's, Lincoln's sails.

With Husky-Haughty Lips, O Sea!

With husky-haughty lips, O sea!
Where day and night I wend thy surf-beat shore,
Imaging to my sense thy varied strange suggestions,
(I see and plainly list thy talk and conference here,)
Thy troops of white-maned racers racing to the goal,
Thy ample, smiling face, dash'd with the sparkling dimples
    of the sun,
Thy brooding scowl and murk – thy unloos'd hurricanes,
Thy unsubduedness, caprices, wilfulness;
Great as thou art above the rest, thy many tears – a lack
    from all eternity in thy content,
10 (Naught but the greatest struggles, wrongs, defeats, could
    make thee greatest – no less could make thee,)
Thy lonely state – something thou ever seek'st and seek'st,
    yet never gain'st,
Surely some right withheld – some voice, in huge
    monotonous rage, of freedom-lover pent,
Some vast heart, like a planet's, chain'd and chafing in those
    breakers,
By lengthen'd swell, and spasm, and panting breath,
And rhythmic rasping of thy sand and waves,
And serpent hiss, and savage peals of laughter,
And undertones of distant lion roar,
(Sounding, appealing to the sky's deaf ear – but now,
    rapport for once,
A phantom in the night thy confidant for once,)
20 The first and last confession of the globe,
Outsurging, muttering from thy soul's abysms,
The tale of cosmic elemental passion,
Thou tellest to a kindred soul.

Death of General Grant

As one by one withdraw the lofty actors,
From that great play on history's stage eterne,
That lurid, partial act of war and peace – of old and new
    contending,
Fought out through wrath, fears, dark dismays, and many a
    long suspense;
All past – and since, in countless graves receding,
    mellowing,
Victor's and vanquish'd – Lincoln's and Lee's – now thou
    with them,
Man of the mighty days – and equal to the days!
Thou from the prairies! – tangled and many-vein'd and
    hard has been thy part,
To admiration has it been enacted!

Red Jacket (from Aloft)
(IMPROMPTU ON BUFFALO CITY'S MONUMENT TO,
AND RE-BURIAL OF THE OLD IROQUOIS ORATOR,
OCTOBER 9, 1884)

Upon this scene, this show,
Yielded to-day by fashion, learning, wealth,
(Nor in caprice alone – some grains of deepest meaning,)
Haply, aloft, (who knows?) from distant sky-clouds'
    blended shapes,
As some old tree, or rock or cliff, thrill'd with its soul,
Product of Nature's sun, stars, earth direct – a towering
    human form,
In hunting-shirt of film, arm'd with the rifle, a half-ironical
    smile curving its phantom lips,
Like one of Ossian's ghosts looks down.

Washington's Monument, February, 1885

Ah, not this marble, dead and cold:
Far from its base and shaft expanding – the round zones
    circling, comprehending,
Thou, Washington, art all the world's, the continents'
    entire – not yours alone, America,
Europe's as well, in every part, castle of lord or laborer's cot,
Or frozen North, or sultry South – the African's – the
    Arab's in his tent,
Old Asia's there with venerable smile, seated amid her
    ruins;
(Greets the antique the hero new? 'tis but the same – the
    heir legitimate, continued ever,
The indomitable heart and arm – proofs of the
    never-broken line,
Courage, alertness, patience, faith, the same – e'en in
    defeat defeated not, the same:)
10 Wherever sails a ship, or house is built on land, or day or
    night,
Through teeming cities' streets, indoors or out, factories or
    farms,
Now, or to come, or past – where patriot wills existed or
    exist,
Wherever Freedom, pois'd by Toleration, sway'd by Law,
Stands or is rising thy true monument.

Of That Blithe Throat of Thine

(MORE THAN EIGHTY-THREE DEGREES NORTH —
ABOUT A GOOD DAY'S STEAMING DISTANCE TO
THE POLE BY ONE OF OUR FAST OCEANERS IN
CLEAR WATER — GREELY THE EXPLORER HEARD THE
SONG OF A SINGLE SNOW-BIRD MERRILY SOUNDING
OVER THE DESOLATION)

Of that blithe throat of thine from arctic bleak and blank,
I'll mind the lesson, solitary bird – let me too welcome
    chilling drifts,
E'en the profoundest chill, as now – a torpid pulse, a brain
    unnerv'd,
Old age land-lock'd within its winter bay – (cold, cold, O
    cold!)
These snowy hairs, my feeble arm, my frozen feet,
For them thy faith, thy rule I take, and grave it to the last;
Not summer's zones alone – not chants of youth, or
    south's warm tides alone,
But held by sluggish floes, pack'd in the northern ice, the
    cumulus of years,
These with gay heart I also sing.

Broadway

What hurrying human tides, or day or night!
What passions, winnings, losses, ardours, swim thy waters!
What whirls of evil, bliss and sorrow, stem thee!
What curious questioning glances – glints of love!
Leer, envy, scorn, contempt, hope, aspiration!
Thou portal – thou arena – thou of the myriad long-drawn
    lines and groups!
(Could but thy flagstones, curbs, façades, tell their
    inimitable tales;
Thy windows rich, and huge hotels – thy side-walks wide;)
Thou of the endless sliding, mincing, shuffling feet!

10   Thou, like the parti-colored world itself – like infinite,
        teeming, mocking life!
      Thou visor'd, vast, unspeakable show and lesson!

To Get the Final Lilt of Songs

To get the final lilt of songs,
To penetrate the inmost lore of poets – to know the mighty
    ones,
Job, Homer, Eschylus, Dante, Shakspere, Tennyson,
    Emerson;
To diagnose the shifting-delicate tints of love and pride and
    doubt – to truly understand,
To encompass these, the last keen faculty and
    entrance-price,
Old age, and what it brings from all its past experiences.

Old Salt Kossabone

Far back, related on my mother's side,
Old Salt Kossabone, I'll tell you how he died:
(Had been a sailor all his life – was nearly 90 – lived with his
    married grandchild, Jenny;
House on a hill, with view of bay at hand, and distant cape,
    and stretch to open sea;)
The last of afternoons, the evening hours, for many a year
    his regular custom,
In his great arm chair by the window seated,
(Sometimes, indeed, through half the day,)
Watching the coming, going of the vessels, he mutters to
    himself – And now the close of all:
One struggling outbound brig, one day, baffled for long –
    cross-tides and much wrong going,
10   At last at nightfall strikes the breeze aright, her whole luck
        veering,

And swiftly bending round the cape, the darkness proudly
  entering, cleaving, as he watches,
'She's free – she's on.her destination' – these the last
  words – when Jenny came, he sat there dead,
Dutch Kossabone, Old Salt, related on my mother's side,
  far back.

The Dead Tenor

As down the stage again,
With Spanish hat and plumes, and gait inimitable,
Back from the fading lessons of the past, I'd call, I'd tell and
  own,
How much from thee! the revelation of the singing voice
  from thee!
(So firm – so liquid-soft – again that tremulous, manly
  timbre!
The perfect singing voice – deepest of all to me the lesson –
  trial and test of all:)
How through those strains distill'd – how the rapt ears, the
  soul of me, absorbing
Fernando's heart, *Manrico*'s passionate call, *Ernani*'s, sweet
  Gennaro's,
I fold thenceforth, or seek to fold, within my chants
  transmuting,
10   Freedom's and Love's and Faith's unloos'd cantabile,
(As perfume's, color's, sunlight's correlation:)
From these, for these, with these, a hurried line, dead tenor,
A wafted autumn leaf, dropt in the closing grave, the
  shovel'd earth,
To memory of thee.

Continuities
(FROM A TALK I HAD LATELY WITH A
GERMAN SPIRITUALIST)

Nothing is ever really lost, or can be lost,
No birth, identity, form – no object of the world.
Nor life, nor force, nor any visible thing;
Appearance must not foil, nor shifted sphere confuse thy
    brain.
Ample are time and space – ample the fields of Nature.
The body, sluggish, aged, cold – the embers left from earlier
    fires,
The light in the eye grown dim, shall duly flame again;
The sun now low in the west rises for mornings and for
    noons continual;
To frozen clods ever the spring's invisible law returns,
10   With grass and flowers and summer fruits and corn.

Yonnondio
(THE SENSE OF THE WORD IS *lament for the aborigines.*
IT IS AN IROQUOIS TERM; AND HAS BEEN USED FOR
A PERSONAL NAME)

A song, a poem of itself – the word itself a dirge,
Amid the wilds, the rocks, the storm and wintry night,
To me such misty, strange tableaux the syllables calling up;
Yonnondio – I see, far in the west or north, a limitless ravine,
    with plains and mountains dark,
I see swarms of stalwart chieftains, medicine-men, and
    warriors,
As flitting by like clouds of ghosts, they pass and are gone
    in the twilight,
(Race of the woods, the landscapes free, and the falls!
No picture, poem, statement, passing them to the future:)
Yonnondio! Yonnondio! – unlimn'd they disappear;

10   To-day gives place, and fades – the cities, farms, factories
fade;
A muffled sonorous sound, a wailing word is borne through
the air for a moment,
Then blank and gone and still, and utterly lost.

Life

Ever the undiscouraged, resolute, struggling soul of man;
(Have former armies fail'd? then we send fresh armies – and
fresh again;)
Ever the grappled mystery of all earth's ages old or new;
Ever the eager eyes, hurrahs, the welcome-clapping hands,
the loud applause;
Ever the soul dissatisfied, curious, unconvinced at last;
Struggling to-day the same – battling the same.

'Going Somewhere'

My science-friend, my noblest woman-friend,
(Now buried in an English grave – and this a memory-leaf
for her dear sake,)
Ended our talk – 'The sum, concluding all we know of old or
modern learning, intuitions deep,
Of all Geologies – Histories – of all Astronomy – of
Evolution, Metaphysics all,
Is, that we all are onward, onward, speeding slowly, surely
bettering,
Life, life an endless march, an endless army, (no halt, but
it is duly over,)
The world, the race, the soul – in space and time the
universes,
All bound as is befitting each – all surely going somewhere.'

535

Small the Theme of My Chant
(FROM THE 1867 EDITION OF *Leaves of Grass*)

Small the theme of my Chant, yet the greatest – namely,
  One's-Self – a simple, separate person. That, for the use
  of the New World, I sing.
Man's physiology complete, from top to toe, I sing. Not
  physiognomy alone, nor brain alone, is worthy for the
  Muse; – I say the Form complete is worthier far. The
  Female equally with the Male, I sing.
Nor cease at the theme of One's-Self. I speak the word of
  the modern, the word En-Masse.
My Days I sing, and the Lands – with interstice I knew of
  hapless War.
(O friend, whoe'er you are, at last arriving hither to
  commence, I feel through every leaf the pressure of your
  hand, which I return.
And thus upon our journey, footing the road, and more than
  once, and link'd together let us go.)

True Conquerors

Old farmers, travelers, workmen (no matter how crippled or
  bent,)
Old sailors, out of many a perilous voyage, storm and
  wreck,
Old soldiers from campaigns, with all their wounds,
  defeats and scars;
Enough that they've survived at all – long life's unflinching
  ones?
Forth from their struggles, trials, fights, to have emerged
  at all – in that alone,
True conquerors o'er all the rest.

The United States to Old World Critics

Here first the duties of to-day, the lessons of the concrete,
Wealth, order, travel, shelter, products, plenty;
As of the building of some varied, vast, perpetual edifice,
Whence to arise inevitable in time, the towering roofs, the
    lamps,
The solid-planted spires tall shooting to the stars.

The Calming Thought of All

That coursing on, whate'er men's speculations,
Amid the changing schools, theologies, philosophies,
Amid the bawling presentations new and old,
The round earth's silent vital laws, facts, modes continue.

Thanks in Old Age

Thanks in old age – thanks ere I go,
For health, the midday sun, the impalpable air – for life,
    mere life,
For precious ever-lingering memories, (of you my mother
    dear – you, father – you, brothers, sisters, friends,)
For all my days – not those of peace alone – the days of war
    the same,
For gentle words, caresses, gifts from foreign lands,
For shelter, wine and meat – for sweet appreciation,
(You distant, dim unknown – or young or old – countless,
    unspecified, readers belov'd,
We never met, and ne'er shall meet – and yet our souls
    embrace, long, close and long;)
For beings, groups, love, deeds, words, books – for colors,
    forms,

10   For all the brave strong men – devoted, hardy men –
         who've forward sprung in freedom's help, all years, all
         lands,
      For braver, stronger, more devoted men – (a special laurel
         ere I go, to life's war's chosen ones,
      The cannoneers of song and thought – the great artillerists –
         the foremost leaders, captains of the soul:)
      As soldier from an ended war return'd – As traveler out of
         myriads, to the long procession retrospective,
      Thanks – joyful thanks! – a soldier's, traveler's thanks.

Life and Death

The two old, simple problems ever intertwined,
Close home, elusive, present, baffled, grappled.
By each successive age insoluble, pass'd on,
To ours to-day – and we pass on the same.

The Voice of the Rain

And who art thou? said I to the soft-falling shower,
Which, strange to tell, gave me an answer, as here
   translated:
I am the Poem of Earth, said the voice of the rain,
Eternal I rise impalpable out of the land and the bottomless
   sea,
Upward to heaven, whence, vaguely form'd, altogether
   changed, and yet the same,
I descend to lave the drouths, atomies, dust-layers of the
   globe,
And all that in them without me were seeds only, latent,
   unborn;
And forever, by day and night, I give back life to my own
   origin, and make pure and beautify it;

(For song, issuing from its birth-place, after fulfilment,
     wandering,
10 Reck'd or unreck'd, duly with love returns.)

Soon Shall the Winter's Foil Be Here

Soon shall the winter's foil be here;
Soon shall these icy ligatures unbind and melt – A little
     while,
And air, soil, wave, suffused shall be in softness, bloom and
     growth – a thousand forms shall rise
From these dead clods and chills as from low burial graves.
Thine eyes, ears – all thy best attributes – all that takes
     cognizance of natural beauty,
Shall wake and fill. Thou shalt perceive the simple shows,
     the delicate miracles of earth,
Dandelions, clover, the emerald grass, the early scents and
     flowers,
The arbutus under foot, the willow's yellow-green, the
     blossoming plum and cherry;
With these the robin, lark and thrush, singing their songs –
     the flitting bluebird;
10 For such the scenes the annual play brings on.

While Not the Past Forgetting
(PUBLISH'D MAY 30, 1888)

While not the past forgetting,
To-day, at least, contention sunk entire – peace,
     brotherhood uprisen;
For sign reciprocal our Northern, Southern hands,
Lay on the graves of all dead soldiers, North or South,
(Nor for the past alone – for meanings to the future,)
Wreaths of roses and branches of palm.

539

The Dying Veteran

(A LONG ISLAND INCIDENT –
EARLY PART OF THE PRESENT CENTURY)

Amid these days of order, ease, prosperity,
Amid the current songs of beauty, peace, decorum,
I cast a reminiscence – (likely 'twill offend you,
I heard it in my boyhood;) – More than a generation since,
A queer old savage man, a fighter under Washington
    himself,
(Large, brave, cleanly, hot-blooded, no talker, rather
    spiritualistic,
Had fought in the ranks – fought well – had been all
    through the Revolutionary war,)
Lay dying – sons, daughters, church-deacons, lovingly
    tending him,
Sharping their sense, their ears, towards his murmuring,
    half-caught words:
10 'Let me return again to my war-days,
To the sights and scenes – to forming the line of battle,
To the scouts ahead reconnoitering,
To the cannons, the grim artillery,
To the galloping aids, carrying orders,
To the wounded, the fallen, the heat, the suspense,
The perfume strong, the smoke, the deafening noise;
Away with your life of peace! – your joys of peace!
Give me my old wild battle-life again!'

Stronger Lessons

Have you learn'd lessons only of those who admired you,
and were tender with you, and stood aside for you?
Have you not learn'd great lessons from those who reject
you, and brace themselves against you? or who treat you
with contempt, or dispute the passage with you?

A Prairie Sunset

Shot gold, maroon and violet, dazzling silver, emerald, fawn,
The earth's whole amplitude and Nature's multiform power
consign'd for once to colors;
The light, the general air possess'd by them – colors till
now unknown,
No limit, confine – not the Western sky alone – the high
meridian – North, South, all,
Pure luminous color fighting the silent shadows to the last.

Twenty Years

Down on the ancient wharf, the sand, I sit, with a
new-comer chatting:
He shipp'd as green-hand boy, and sail'd away, (took some
sudden, vehement notion;)
Since, twenty years and more have circled round and round,
While he the globe was circling round and round, – and now
returns:
How changed the place – all the old land-marks gone – the
parents dead;
(Yes, he comes back *to lay in port for good – to settle* – has a
well-fill'd purse – no spot will do but this;)
The little boat that scull'd him from the sloop, now held in
leash I see,

I hear the slapping waves, the restless keel, the rocking in
    the sand,
I see the sailor kit, the canvas bag, the great box bound with
    brass,
10 I scan the face all berry-brown and bearded – the
    stout-strong frame,
Dress'd in its russet suit of good Scotch cloth:
(Then what the told-out story of those twenty years? What
    of the future?)

Orange Buds by Mail from Florida
(VOLTAIRE CLOSED A FAMOUS ARGUMENT BY
CLAIMING THAT A SHIP OF WAR AND THE
GRAND OPERA WERE PROOFS ENOUGH OF
CIVILIZATION'S AND FRANCE'S PROGRESS, IN
HIS DAY)

A lesser proof than old Voltaire's, yet greater,
Proof of this present time, and thee, thy broad expanse,
    America,
To my plain Northern hut, in outside clouds and snow,
Brought safely for a thousand miles o'er land and tide,
Some three days since on their own soil live-sprouting,
Now here their sweetness through my room unfolding,
A bunch of orange buds by mail from Florida.

Twilight

The soft voluptuous opiate shades,
The sun just gone, the eager light dispell'd – (I too will soon
    be gone, dispell'd,)
A haze – nirwana – rest and night – oblivion.

542

You Lingering Sparse Leaves of Me

You lingering sparse leaves of me on winter-nearing boughs,
And I some well-shorn tree of field or orchard-row;
You tokens diminute and lorn – (not now the flush of May,
    or July clover-bloom – no grain of August now;)
You pallid banner-staves – you pennants valueless – you
    over-stay'd of time,
Yet my soul-dearest leaves confirming all the rest,
The faithfulest – hardiest – last.

Not Meagre, Latent Boughs Alone

Not meagre, latent boughs alone, O songs! (scaly and bare,
    like eagles' talons,)
But haply for some sunny day (who knows?) some future
    spring, some summer – bursting forth,
To verdant leaves, or sheltering shade – to nourishing fruit,
Apples and grapes – the stalwart limbs of trees emerging –
    the fresh, free, open air,
And love and faith, like scented roses blooming.

The Dead Emperor

To-day, with bending head and eyes, thou, too, Columbia,
Less for the mighty crown laid low in sorrow – less for the
    Emperor,
Thy true condolence breathest, sendest out o'er many a salt
    sea mile,
Mourning a good old man – a faithful shepherd, patriot.

Published March 10, 1888

543

As the Greek's Signal Flame
(FOR WHITTIER'S EIGHTIETH BIRTHDAY,
DECEMBER 17, 1887)

As the Greek's signal flame, by antique records told,
Rose from the hill-top, like applause and glory,
Welcoming in fame some special veteran, hero,
With rosy tinge reddening the land he'd served,
So I aloft from Mannahatta's ship-fringed shore,
Lift high a kindled brand for thee, Old Poet.

The Dismantled Ship

In some unused lagoon, some nameless bay,
On sluggish, lonesome waters, anchor'd near the shore,
An old, dismasted, gray and batter'd ship, disabled, done,
After free voyages to all the seas of earth, haul'd up at last
    and hawser'd tight,
Lies rusting, mouldering.

Now Precedent Songs, Farewell

Now precedent songs, farewell – by every name farewell,
(Trains of a staggering line in many a strange procession,
    waggons,
From ups and downs – with intervals – from elder years,
    mid-age, or youth,)
'In Cabin'd Ships', or 'Thee Old Cause' or 'Poets to
    Come'
Or 'Paumanok', 'Song of Myself', 'Calamus', or 'Adam',
Or 'Beat! Beat! Drums!' or 'To the Leaven'd Soil they
    Trod',
Or 'Captain! My Captain!' 'Kosmos', 'Quicksand Years',
    or 'Thoughts',

'Thou Mother with thy Equal Brood', and many, many
    more unspecified,
From fibre heart of mine – from throat and tongue – (My
    life's hot pulsing blood,
10 The personal urge and form for me – not merely paper,
    automatic type and ink,)
Each song of mine – each utterance in the past – having its
    long, long history,
Of life or death, or soldier's wound, of country's loss or
    safety,
(O heaven! what flash and started endless train of all!
    compared indeed to that!
What wretched shred e'en at the best of all!)

An Evening Lull

After a week of physical anguish,
Unrest and pain, and feverish heat,
Toward the ending day a calm and lull comes on,
Three hours of peace and soothing rest of brain.[1]

Old Age's Lambent Peaks

The touch of flame – the illuminating fire – the loftiest look
    at last,
O'er city, passion, sea – o'er prairie, mountain, wood – the
    earth itself;
The airy, different, changing hues of all, in falling twilight,
Objects and groups, bearings, faces, reminiscences;
The calmer sight – the golden setting, clear and broad:

1. The two songs [*Now Precedent Songs, Farewell* and *An Evening Lull*] on this [and the preceding] page are eked out during an afternoon, June 1888, in my seventieth year, at a critical spell of illness. Of course no reader and probably no human being at any time will ever have such phases of emotional and solemn action as these involve to me. I feel in them an end and close of all.

So much i' the atmosphere, the points of view, the
    situations whence we scan,
Bro't out by them alone – so much (perhaps the best)
    unreck'd before;
The lights indeed from them – old age's lambent peaks.

After the Supper and Talk

After the supper and talk – after the day is done,
As a friend from friends his final withdrawal prolonging,
Good-bye and Good-bye with emotional lips repeating,
(So hard for his hand to release those hands – no more will
    they meet,
No more for communion of sorrow and joy, of old and
    young,
A far-stretching journey awaits him, to return no more,)
Shunning, postponing severance – seeking to ward off the
    last word ever so little,
E'en at the exit-door turning – charges superfluous calling
    back – e'en as he descends the steps,
Something to eke out a minute additional – shadows of
    nightfall deepening,
10   Farewells, messages lessening – dimmer the forthgoer's
    visage and form,
Soon to be lost for aye in the darkness – loth, O so loth to
    depart!
Garrulous to the very last.

GOOD-BYE MY FANCY

Preface Note to Second Annex

concluding L. of G. – 1891

Had I not better withhold (in this old age and paralysis of me) such little tags and fringe-dots (maybe specks, stains,) as follow a long dusty journey, and witness it afterward? I have probably not been enough afraid of careless touches, from the first – and am not now – nor of parrot-like repetitions – nor platitudes and the commonplace. Perhaps I am too democratic for such avoidances. Besides, is not the verse-field, as originally plann'd by my theory, now sufficiently illustrated – and full time for me to silently retire? – (indeed amid no loud call or market for my sort of poetic utterance.)

In answer, or rather defiance, to that kind of well-put interrogation, here comes this little cluster, and conclusion of my preceding clusters. Though not at all clear that, as here collated, it is worth printing (certainly I have nothing fresh to write) – I while away the hours of my 72nd year – hours of forced confinement in my den – by putting in shape this small old age collation:

Last droplets of and after spontaneous rain,
From many limpid distillations and past showers;
(Will they germinate anything? mere exhalations as they all are –
    the land's and sea's – America's;
Will they filter to any deep emotion? any heart and brain?)

However that may be, I feel like improving to-day's opportunity and wind up. During the last two years I have sent out, in the lulls of illness and exhaustion, certain chirps – lingering-dying ones probably (undoubtedly) – which now I may as well gather and put in fair type while able to see correctly – (for my eyes plainly warn me they are dimming, and my brain more and more palpably neglects or refuses, month after month, even slight tasks or revisions.)

In fact, here I am these current years 1890 and 1891, (each successive fortnight getting stiffer and stuck deeper) much like some hard-cased dilapidated grim ancient shell-fish or time-bang'd conch (no legs, utterly non-locomotive) cast up high and dry on the shore-sands, helpless to move anywhere – nothing left but behave myself quiet, and while away the days yet assign'd, and discover if there is anything for the said grim and time-bang'd conch to be got at last out of inherited good spirits and primal buoyant centre-pulses down there deep somewhere within his gray-blurr'd old shell. . . . (Reader, you must allow a little fun here – for one reason there are too many of the following poemets about death, etc., and for another the passing hours (July 5, 1890) are so sunny-fine. And old as I am I feel to-day almost a part of some frolicsome wave, or for sporting yet like a kid or kitten – probably a streak of physical adjustment and perfection here and now. I believe I have it in me perennially anyhow.)

Then behind all, the deep-down consolation (it is a glum one, but I dare not be sorry for the fact of it in the past, nor refrain from dwelling, even vaunting here at the end) that this late-years palsied old shorn and shell-fish condition of me is the indubitable outcome and growth, now near for twenty years along, of too over-zealous, over-continued bodily and emotional excitement and action through the times of 1862, 63, 64 and 65, visiting and waiting on wounded and sick army volunteers, both sides, in campaigns or contests, or after them, or in hospitals or fields south of Washington City, or in that place and elsewhere – those hot, sad, wrenching times – the army volunteers, all States, – or North or South – the wounded, suffering, dying – the exhausting, sweat-ing summers, marches, battles, carnage – those trenches hurriedly heap'd by the corpse-thousands, mainly unknown – Will the America of the future – will this vast rich Union ever realize what itself cost, back there after all? – those hecatombs of battle-deaths – Those times of which, O far-off reader, this whole book is in-deed finally but a reminiscent memorial from thence by me to you?

Sail Out for Good, Eidólon Yacht!

Heave the anchor short!
Raise main-sail and jib – steer forth,
O little white-hull'd sloop, now speed on really deep
    waters,
(I will not call it our concluding voyage,
But outset and sure entrance to the truest, best, maturest;)
Depart, depart from solid earth – no more returning to these
    shores,
Now on for aye our infinite free venture wending,
Spurning all yet tried ports, seas, hawsers, densities,
    gravitation,
Sail out for good, eidólon yacht of me!

Lingering Last Drops

And whence and why come you?

We know not whence, (was the answer,)
We only know that we drift here with the rest,
That we linger'd and lagg'd – but were wafted at last, and
    are now here,
To make the passing shower's concluding drops.

Good-Bye My Fancy

Good-bye[1] my fancy – (I had a word to say,
But 'tis not quite the time – The best of any man's word
    or say,
Is when its proper place arrives – and for its meaning,
I keep mine till the last.)

1. Behind a Good-bye there lurks much of the salutation of another beginning – to me, Development, Continuity, Immortality, Transformation, are the chiefest life-meanings of Nature and Humanity, and are the *sine qua non* of all facts, and each fact.
    Why do folks dwell so fondly on the last words, advice, appearance,

On, on the Same, Ye Jocund Twain!

On, on the same, ye jocund twain!
My life and recitative, containing birth, youth, mid-age
    years,
Fitful as motley-tongues of flame, inseparably twined and
    merged in one – combining all,
My single soul – aims, confirmations, failures, joys – Nor
    single soul alone,
I chant my nation's crucial stage, (America's, haply
    humanity's) – the trial great, the victory great,
A strange *eclaircissement* of all the masses past, the eastern
    world, the ancient, medieval,
Here, here from wanderings, strayings, lessons, wars,
    defeats – here at the west a voice triumphant – justifying
    all,
A gladsome pealing cry – a song for once of utmost pride and
    satisfaction;
I chant from it the common bulk, the general average horde,
    (the best no sooner than the worst) – And now I chant old
    age,
10 (My verses, written first for forenoon life, and for the
    summer's, autumn's spread,
I pass to snow-white hairs the same, and give to pulses
    winter-cool'd the same;)
As here in careless trill, I and my recitatives, with faith and
    love,
Wafting to other work, to unknown songs, conditions,
On, on, ye jocund twain! continue on the same!

---

of the departing? Those last words are not samples of the best, which
involve vitality at its full, and balance, and perfect control and scope.
But they are valuable beyond measure to confirm and endorse the
varied train, facts, theories and faith of the whole preceding life.

553

My 71st Year

After surmounting three-score and ten,
With all their chances, changes, losses, sorrows,
My parents' deaths, the vagaries of my life, the many tearing
. passions of me, the war of '63 and '64,
As some old broken soldier, after a long, hot, wearying
  march, or haply after battle,
To-day at twilight, hobbling, answering company roll-call,
  Here, with vital voice,
Reporting yet, saluting yet the Officer over all.

Apparitions

A vague mist hanging 'round half the pages:
(Sometimes how strange and clear to the soul,
That all these solid things are indeed but apparitions,
  concepts, non-realities.)

The Pallid Wreath

Somehow I cannot let it go yet, funeral though it is,
Let it remain back there on its nail suspended,
With pink, blue, yellow, all blanch'd, and the white now
  gray and ashy,
One wither'd rose put years ago for thee, dear friend;
But I do not forget thee. Hast thou then faded?
Is the odor exhaled? Are the colors, vitalities, dead?
No, while memories subtly play – the past vivid as ever;
For but last night I woke, and in that spectral ring saw thee,
Thy smile, eyes, face, calm, silent, loving as ever:
10 So let the wreath hang still awhile within my eye-reach,
It is not yet dead to me, nor even pallid.

An Ended Day

The soothing sanity and blitheness of completion,
The pomp and hurried contest-glare and rush are done;
Now triumph! transformation! jubilate![1]

Old Age's Ship & Crafty Death's

From east and west across the horizon's edge,
Two mighty masterful vessels sailers steal upon us:
But we'll make race a-time upon the seas – a battle-contest
    yet! bear lively there!
(Our joys of strife and derring-do to the last!)

1. NOTE – *Summer country life – Several years* – In my rambles and explorations I found a woody place near the creek, where for some reason the birds in happy mood seem'd to resort in unusual numbers. Especially at the beginning of the day, and again at the ending, I was sure to get there the most copious bird-concerts. I repair'd there frequently at sunrise – and also at sunset, or just before . . . . Once the question arose in me: Which is the best singing, the first or the lattermost? The first always exhilarated, and perhaps seem'd more joyous and stronger; but I always felt the sunset or late afternoon sounds more penetrating and sweeter – seem'd to touch the soul – often the evening thrushes, two or three of them, responding and perhaps blending. Though I miss'd some of the mornings, I found myself getting to be quite strictly punctual at the evening utterances.
ANOTHER NOTE – 'He went out with the tide and the sunset' was a phrase I heard from a surgeon describing an old sailor's death under peculiarly gentle conditions.

During the Secession War, 1863 and 1864, visiting the Army Hospitals around Washington, I form'd the habit, and continued it to the end, whenever the ebb or flood tide began the latter part of day, of punctually visiting those at that time populous wards of suffering men. Somehow (or I thought so) the effect of the hour was palpable. The badly wounded would get some ease, and would like to talk a little, or be talk'd to. Intellectual and emotional natures would be at their best: Deaths were always easier; medicines seem'd to have better effect when given then, and a lulling atmosphere would pervade the wards.

Similar influences, similar circumstances and hours, day-close, after great battles, even with all their horrors. I had more than once the same experience on the fields cover'd with fallen or dead.

Put on the old ship all her power to-day!
Crowd top-sail, top-gallant and royal studding-sails,
Out challenge and defiance – flags and flaunting pennants
    added,
As we take to the open – take to the deepest, freest waters.

To the Pending Year

Have I no weapon-word for thee – some message brief and
    fierce?
(Have I fought out and done indeed the battle?) Is there no
    shot left,
For all thy affectations, lisps, scorns, manifold silliness?
Nor for myself – my own rebellious self in thee?

Down, down, proud gorge! – though choking thee;
Thy bearded throat and high-borne forehead to the gutter;
Crouch low thy neck to eleemosynary gifts.

Shakspere–Bacon's Cipher

I doubt it not – then more, far more;
In each old song bequeath'd – in every noble page or text,
(Different – something unreck'd before – some unsuspected
    author,)
In every object, mountain, tree, and star – in every birth and
    life,
As part of each – evolv'd from each – meaning, behind the
    ostent,
A mystic cipher waits infolded.

Long, Long Hence

After a long, long course, hundreds of years, denials,
Accumulations, rous'd love and joy and thought,
Hopes, wishes, aspirations, ponderings, victories, myriads
    of readers,
Coating, compassing, covering – after ages' and ages'
    encrustations,
Then only may these songs reach fruition.

Bravo, Paris Exposition!

Add to your show, before you close it, France,
With all the rest, visible, concrete, temples, towers, goods,
    machines and ores,
Our sentiment wafted from many million heart-throbs,
    ethereal but solid,
(We grand-sons and great-grand-sons do not forget your
    grand-sires,)
From fifty Nations and nebulous Nations, compacted, sent
    oversea to-day,
America's applause, love, memories and good-will.

Interpolation Sounds
(GENERAL PHILIP SHERIDAN WAS BURIED AT THE
CATHEDRAL, WASHINGTON, DC, AUGUST, 1888,
WITH ALL THE POMP, MUSIC AND CEREMONIES
OF THE ROMAN CATHOLIC SERVICE)

Over and through the burial chant,
Organ and solemn service, sermon, bending priests,
To me come interpolation sounds not in the show – plainly
    to me, crowding up the aisle and from the window,
Of sudden battle's hurry and harsh noises – war's grim game
    to sight and ear in earnest;

The scout call'd up and forward – the general mounted and
　　his aids around him – the new-brought word – the
　　instantaneous order issued;
The rifle crack – the cannon thud – the rushing forth of men
　　from their tents;
The clank of cavalry – the strange celerity of forming ranks –
　　the slender bugle note;
The sound of horses' hoofs departing – saddles, arms,
　　accoutrements.

NOTE: CAMDEN, N J, August 7, 1888. – Walt Whitman asks the
New York Herald 'to add his tribute to Sheridan':
　'In the grand constellation of five or six names, under Lincoln's
Presidency, that history will bear for ages in her firmament as marking
the last life-throbs of secession, and beaming on its dying gasps,
Sheridan's will be bright. One consideration rising out of the now dead
soldier's example as it passes my mind, is worth taking notice of. If
the war had continued any long time these States, in my opinion,
would have shown and proved the most conclusive military talents
ever evinced by any nation on earth. That they posess'd a rank and file
ahead of all other known in points of quality and limitlessness of
number are easily admitted. But we have, too, the eligibility of
organizing, handling and officering equal to the other. These two, with
modern arms, transportation, and inventive American genius, would
make the United States, with earnestness, not only able to stand the
whole world, but conquer that world united against us.'

To the Sun-set Breeze

Ah, whispering, something again, unseen,
Where late this heated day thou enterest at my window,
　　door,
Thou, laving, tempering all, cool-freshing, gently
　　vitalizing
Me, old, alone, sick, weak-down, melted-worn with sweat;
Thou, nestling, folding close and firm yet soft, companion
　　better than talk, book, art,
(Thou hast, O Nature! elements! utterance to my heart
　　beyond the rest – and this is of them,)

So sweet thy primitive taste to breathe within – thy soothing
    fingers on my face and hands,
Thou, messenger-magical strange bringer to body and spirit
    of me,
(Distances balk'd – occult medicines penetrating me from
    head to foot,)
10 I feel the sky, the prairies vast – I feel the mighty northern
    lakes,
I feel the ocean and the forest – somehow I feel the globe
    itself swift-swimming in space;
Thou blown from lips so loved, now gone – haply from
    endless store, God-sent,
(For thou art spiritual, Godly, most of all known to my
    sense,)
Minister to speak to me, here and now, what word has never
    told, and cannot tell,
Art thou not universal concrete's distillation? Law's, all
    Astronomy's last refinement?
Hast thou no soul? Can I not know, identify thee?

Old Chants

An ancient song, reciting, ending,
Once gazing toward thee, Mother of All,
Musing, seeking themes fitted for thee,
Accept for me, thou saidst, *the elder ballads*,
And name for me before thou goest each ancient poet.

(Of many debts incalculable,
Haply our New World's chiefest debt is to old poems.)

Ever so far back, preluding thee, America,
Old chants, Egyptian priests, and those of Ethiopia,
10 The Hindu epics, the Grecian, Chinese, Persian,
The Biblic books and prophets, and deep idyls of the
    Nazarene,
The Iliad, Odyssey, plots, doings, wanderings of Eneas,
Hesiod, Eschylus, Sophocles, Merlin, Arthur,

The Cid, Roland at Roncesvalles, the Nibelungen,
The troubadours, minstrels, minnesingers, skalds,
Chaucer, Dante, flocks of singing birds,
The Border Minstrelsy, the bye-gone ballads, feudal tales,
    essays, plays,
Shakspere, Schiller, Walter Scott, Tennyson,
As some vast wondrous weird dream-presences,
20 The great shadowy groups gathering around,
Darting their mighty masterful eyes forward at thee,
Thou! with as now thy bending neck and head, with
    courteous hand and word, ascending,
Thou! pausing a moment, drooping thine eyes upon them,
    blent with their music,
Well pleased, accepting all, curiously prepared for by them,
Thou enterest at thy entrance porch.

A Christmas Greeting
(FROM A NORTHERN STAR-GROUP TO A
SOUTHERN. 1889–90)

Welcome, Brazilian brother – thy ample place is ready;
A loving hand – a smile from the north – a sunny instant
    hail!
(Let the future care for itself, where it reveals its troubles,
    impedimentas,
Ours, ours the present throe, the democratic aim, the
    acceptance and the faith;)
To thee to-day our reaching arm, our turning neck – to thee
    from us the expectant eye,
Thou cluster free! thou brilliant lustrous one! thou,
    learning well,
The true lesson of a nation's light in the sky,
(More shining than the Cross, more than the Crown,)
The height to be superb humanity.

Sounds of the Winter

Sounds of the winter too,
Sunshine upon the mountains – many a distant strain
From cheery railroad train – from nearer field, barn, house,
The whispering air – even the mute crops, garner'd apples,
   corn,
Children's and women's tones – rhythm of many a farmer
   and of flail,
An old man's garrulous lips among the rest, *Think not we*
   give out yet,
Forth from these snowy hairs we keep up yet the lilt.

A Twilight Song

As I sit in twilight late alone by the flickering oak-flame,
Musing on long-pass'd war-scenes – of the countless buried
   unknown soldiers,
Of the vacant names, as unindented air's and sea's – the
   unreturn'd,
The brief truce after battle, with grim burial-squads, and
   the deep-fill'd trenches
Of gather'd dead from all America, North, South, East,
   West, whence they came up,
From wooded Maine, New-England's farms, from fertile
   Pennsylvania, Illinois, Ohio,
From the measureless West, Virginia, the South, the
   Carolinas, Texas,
(Even here in my room-shadows and half-lights in the
   noiseless flickering flames,
Again I see the stalwart ranks on-filing, rising – I hear the
   rhythmic tramp of the armies;)
You million unwrit names all, all – you dark bequest from
   all the war,
A special verse for you – a flash of duty long neglected –
   your mystic roll strangely gather'd here,

Each name recall'd by me from out the darkness and death's
    ashes,
Henceforth to be, deep, deep within my heart recording, for
    many a future year,
Your mystic roll entire of unknown names, or North or
    South,
Embalm'd with love in this twilight song.

When the Full-Grown Poet Came

When the full-grown poet came,
Out spake pleased Nature (the round impassive globe, with
    all its shows of day and night,) saying, *He is mine*;
But out spake too the Soul of man, proud, jealous and
    unreconciled, *Nay, he is mine alone*;
– Then the full-grown poet stood between the two, and took
    each by the hand;
And to-day and ever so stands, as blender, uniter, tightly
    holding hands,
Which he will never release until he reconciles the two,
And wholly and joyously blends them.

Osceola

(When I was nearly grown to manhood in Brooklyn, New York
(middle of 1838) I met one of the return'd US Marines from Fort
Moultrie, S. C., and had long talks with him – learn'd the occurrence
below described – death of Osceola. The latter was a young, brave,
leading Seminole in the Florida war of that time – was surrender'd to
our troops, imprison'd and literally died of 'a broken heart', at Fort
Moultrie. He sicken'd of his confinement – the doctor and officers
made every allowance and kindness possible for him; then the close:)

When his hour for death had come,
He slowly rais'd himself from the bed on the floor,
Drew on his war-dress, shirt, leggings, and girdled the belt
    around his waist,

Call'd for vermilion paint (his looking-glass was held before
  him,)
Painted half his face and neck, his wrists, and back-hands.
Put the scalp-knife carefully in his belt – then lying down,
  resting a moment,
Rose again, half sitting, smiled, gave in silence his extended
  hand to each and all,
Sank faintly low to the floor (tightly grasping the tomahawk
  handle,)
Fix'd his look on wife and little children – the last:
10   (And here a line in memory of his name and death.)

A Voice From Death
(THE JOHNSTOWN, PENN., CATACLYSM,
MAY 31, 1889)

A voice from Death, solemn and strange, in all his sweep and
  power,
With sudden, indescribable blow – towns drown'd –
  humanity by thousands slain,
The vaunted work of thrift, goods, dwellings, forge, street,
  iron bridge,
Dash'd pell-mell by the blow – yet usher'd life continuing
  on,
(Amid the rest, amid the rushing, whirling, wild debris,
A suffering woman saved – a baby safely born!)

Although I come and unannounc'd, in horror and in pang,
In pouring flood and fire, and wholesale elemental crash,
  (this voice so solemn, strange,)
I too a minister of Deity.

10   Yea, Death, we bow our faces, veil our eyes to thee,
We mourn the old, the young untimely drawn to thee,
The fair, the strong, the good, the capable,
The household wreck'd, the husband and the wife, the
  engulf'd forger in his forge,
The corpses in the whelming waters and the mud,

The gather'd thousands to their funeral mounds, and
    thousands never found or gather'd.

Then after burying, mourning the dead,
(Faithful to them found or unfound, forgetting not, bearing
    the past, here new musing,)
A day – a passing moment or an hour – America itself bends
    low,
Silent, resign'd, submissive.

20   War, death, cataclysm like this, America,
Take deep to thy proud prosperous heart.

E'en as I chant, lo! out of death, and out of ooze and slime,
The blossoms rapidly blooming, sympathy, help, love,
From West and East, from South and North and over sea,
Its hot-spurr'd hearts and hands humanity to human aid
    moves on;
And from within a thought and lesson yet.

Thou ever-darting Globe! through Space and Air!
Thou waters that encompass us!
Thou that in all the life and death of us, in action or in
    sleep!
30   Thou laws invisible that permeate them and all,
Thou that in all, and over all, and through and under all,
    incessant!
Thou! thou! the vital, universal, giant force resistless,
    sleepless, calm,
Holding Humanity as in thy open hand, as some ephemeral
    toy,
How ill to e'er forget thee!

For I too have forgotten,
(Wrapt in these little potencies of progress, politics,
    culture, wealth, inventions, civilization,)
Have lost my recognition of your silent ever-swaying power,
    ye mighty, elemental throes,
In which and upon which we float, and every one of us is
    buoy'd.

A Persian Lesson

For his o'erarching and last lesson the greybeard sufi,
In the fresh scent of the morning in the open air,
On the slope of a teeming Persian rose-garden,
Under an ancient chestnut-tree wide spreading its branches,
Spoke to the young priests and students.

'Finally my children, to envelop each word, each part of the
    rest,
Allah is all, all, all – is immanent in every life and object,
May-be at many and many-a-more removes – yet Allah,
    Allah, Allah is there.

'Has the estray wander'd far? Is the reason-why strangely
    hidden?
10 Would you sound below the restless ocean of the entire
    world?
Would you know the dissatisfaction? the urge and spur of
    every life;
The something never still'd – never entirely gone? the
    invisible need of every seed?

'It is the central urge in every atom,
(Often unconscious, often evil, downfallen,)
To return to its divine source and origin, however distant,
Latent the same in subject and in object, without one
    exception.'

The Commonplace

The commonplace I sing;
How cheap is health! how cheap nobility!
Abstinence, no falsehood, no gluttony, lust;
The open air I sing, freedom, toleration,
(Take here the mainest lesson – less from books – less from
    the schools,)

The common day and night – the common earth and waters,
Your farm – your work, trade, occupation,
The democratic wisdom underneath, like solid ground for all.

'The Rounded Catalogue Divine Complete'

(Sunday, —. – Went this forenoon to church. A college
professor, Rev. Dr —, gave us a fine sermon, during which I
caught the above words; but the minister included in his 'rounded
catalogue' letter and spirit, only the esthetic things, and entirely
ignored what I name in the following:)

The devilish and the dark, the dying and diseas'd,
The countless (nineteen-twentieths) low and evil, crude and
    savage,
The crazed, prisoners in jail, the horrible, rank, malignant,
Venom and filth, serpents, the ravenous sharks, liars, the
    dissolute;
(What is the part the wicked and the loathesome bear
    within earth's orbic scheme?)
Newts, crawling things in slime and mud, poisons,
The barren soil, the evil men, the slag and hideous rot.

Mirages

(NOTED VERBATIM AFTER A SUPPER-TALK OUT DOORS
IN NEVADA WITH TWO OLD MINERS)

More experiences and sights, stranger, than you'd think for;
Times again, now mostly just after sunrise or before sunset,
Sometimes in spring, oftener in autumn, perfectly clear
    weather, in plain sight,
Camps far or near, the crowded streets of cities and the
    shopfronts,
(Account for it or not – credit or not – it is all true,
And my mate there could tell you the like – we have often
    confab'd about it,)

People and scenes, animals, trees, colors and lines, plain as
could be,
Farms and dooryards of home, paths border'd with box,
lilacs in corners,
Weddings in churches, thanksgiving dinners, returns of
long-absent sons,
10   Glum funerals, the crape-veil'd mother and the daughters,
Trials in courts, jury and judge, the accused in the box,
Contestants, battles, crowds, bridges, wharves,
Now and then mark'd faces of sorrow or joy,
(I could pick them out this moment if I saw them again,)
Show'd to me just aloft to the right in the sky-edge,
Or plainly there to the left on the hill-tops.

L. of G.'s Purport

Not to exclude or demarcate, or pick out evils from their
formidable masses (even to expose them,)
But add, fuse, complete, extend – and celebrate the
immortal and the good.

Haughty this song, its words and scope,
To span vast realms of space and time,
Evolution – the cumulative – growths and generations.

Begun in ripen'd youth and steadily pursued,
Wandering, peering, dallying with all – war, peace, day and
night absorbing,
Never even for one brief hour abandoning my task,
I end it here in sickness, poverty, and old age.

10   I sing of life, yet mind we well of death:
To-day shadowy Death dogs my steps, my seated shape, and
has for years –
Draws sometimes close to me, as face to face.

The Unexpress'd

How dare one say it?
After the cycles, poems, singers, plays,
Vaunted Ionia's, India's – Homer, Shakspere – the long,
    long times' thick dotted roads, areas,
The shining clusters and the Milky Ways of stars – Nature's
    pulses reap'd,
All retrospective passions, heroes, war, love, adoration,
All ages' plummets dropt to their utmost depths,
All human lives, throats, wishes, brains – all experiences'
    utterance;
After the countless songs, or long or short, all tongues, all
    lands,
Still something not yet told in poesy's voice or print –
    something lacking,
10 (Who knows? the best yet unexpress'd and lacking.)

Grand Is the Seen

Grand is the seen, the light, to me – grand are the sky and
    stars,
Grand is the earth, and grand are lasting time and space,
And grand their laws, so multiform, puzzling,
    evolutionary;
But grander far the unseen soul of me, comprehending,
    endowing all those,
Lighting the light, the sky and stars, delving the earth,
    sailing the sea,
(What were all those, indeed, without thee, unseen soul? of
    what amount without thee?)
More evolutionary, vast, puzzling, O my soul!
More multiform far – more lasting thou than they.

Unseen Buds

Unseen buds, infinite, hidden well,
Under the snow and ice, under the darkness, in every square
    or cubic inch,
Germinal, exquisite, in delicate lace, microscopic, unborn,
Like babes in wombs, latent, folded, compact, sleeping;
Billions of billions, and trillions of trillions of them waiting,
(On earth and in the sea – the universe – the stars there in the
    heavens,)
Urging slowly, surely forward, forming endless,
And waiting ever more, forever more behind.

Good-Bye My Fancy!

Good-bye my Fancy!
Farewell dear mate, dear love!
I'm going away, I know not where,
Or to what fortune, or whether I may ever see you again,
So Good-bye my Fancy.

Now for my last – let me look back a moment;
The slower fainter ticking of the clock is in me,
Exit, nightfall, and soon the heart-thud stopping.

Long have we lived, joy'd, caress'd together;
Delightful! – now separation – Good-bye my Fancy.

Yet let me not be too hasty,
Long indeed have we lived, slept, filter'd, become really
    blended into one;
Then if we die we die together, (yes, we'll remain one,)
If we go anywhere we'll go together to meet what happens,
May-be we'll be better off and blither, and learn something,
May-be it is yourself now really ushering me to the true
    songs, (who knows?)
May-be it is you the mortal knob really undoing, turning –
    so now finally,
Good-bye – and hail! my Fancy.

A BACKWARD GLANCE O'ER
TRAVEL'D ROADS

Perhaps the best of songs heard, or of any and all true love, or life's fairest episodes, or sailors', soldiers' trying scenes on land or sea, is the *résumé* of them, or any of them, long afterwards, looking at the actualities away back past, with all their practical excitations gone. How the soul loves to float amid such reminiscences!

So here I sit gossiping in the early candle-light of old age – I and my book – casting backward glances over our travel'd road. After completing, as it were, the journey – (a varied jaunt of years, with many halts and gaps of intervals – or some lengthen'd ship-voyage, wherein more than once the last hour had apparently arrived, and we seem'd certainly going down – yet reaching port in a sufficient way through all discomfitures at last) – After completing my poems, I am curious to review them in the light of their own (at the time unconscious, or mostly unconscious) intentions, with certain unfoldings of the thirty years they seek to embody. These lines, therefore, will probably blend the weft of first purposes and speculations, with the warp of that experience afterwards, always bringing strange developments.

Result of seven or eight stages and struggles extending through nearly thirty years, (as I nigh my three-score-and-ten I live largely on memory,) I look upon *Leaves of Grass* now finish'd to the end of its opportunities and powers, as my definitive *carte visite* to the coming generations of the New World,[1] if I may assume to say so. That I have not gain'd the acceptance of my own time, but have fallen back on fond dreams of the future – anticipations – ('still lives the song, though Regnar dies') – That from a worldly and business point of view *Leaves of Grass* has been worse than a failure – that public criticism on the book and myself as author of it yet shows mark'd anger and contempt more than anything else – ('I find a solid line of enemies to you everywhere,' – letter from W. S. K., Boston, 28 May 1884) – And that solely for publishing it I have been the object of two or three pretty serious special official

1. When Champollion, on his death-bed, handed to the printer the revised proof of his *Egyptian Grammar*, he said gayly, 'Be careful of this – it is my *carte de visite* to posterity.'

buffetings – is all probably no more than I ought to have expected.
I had my choice when I commenc'd. I bid neither for soft eulogies,
big money returns, nor the approbation of existing schools and
conventions. As fulfill'd, or partially fulfill'd, the best comfort of
the whole business (after a small band of the dearest friends and
upholders ever vouchsafed to man or cause – doubtless all the
more faithful and uncompromising – this little phalanx! – for being
so few) is that, unstopp'd and unwarp'd by any influence outside
the soul within me, I have had my say entirely my own way, and
put it unerringly on record – the value thereof to be decided by
time.

In calculating that decision, William O'Connor and Dr Bucke
are far more peremptory than I am. Behind all else that can be
said, I consider *Leaves of Grass* and its theory experimental – as,
in the deepest sense, I consider our American republic itself to be,
with its theory. (I think I have at least enough philosophy not to
be too absolutely certain of any thing, or any results.) In the
second place, the volume is a *sortie* – whether to prove triumphant,
and conquer its field of aim and escape and construction, nothing
less than a hundred years from now can fully answer. I consider
the point that I have positively gain'd a hearing, to far more than
make up any and all other lacks and withholdings. Essentially, *that*
was from the first, and has remain'd throughout, the main object.
Now it seems to be achiev'd, I am certainly contented to waive any
otherwise momentous drawbacks, as of little account. Candidly and
dispassionately reviewing all my intentions, I feel that they were
creditable – and I accept the result, whatever it may be.

After continued personal ambition and effort, as a young fellow,
to enter with the rest into competition for the usual rewards,
business, political, literary, etc. – to take part in the great *mêlée*,
both for victory's prize itself and to do some good – After years of
those aims and pursuits, I found myself remaining possess'd, at
the age of thirty-one to thirty-three, with a special desire and con-
viction. Or rather, to be quite exact, a desire that had been flitting
through my previous life, or hovering on the flanks, mostly indefi-
nite hitherto, had steadily advanced to the front, defined itself,
and finally dominated everything else. This was a feeling or ambi-
tion to articulate and faithfully express in literary or poetic form,

and uncompromisingly, my own physical, emotional, moral, intellectual, and aesthetic Personality, in the midst of, and tallying, the momentous spirit and facts of its immediate days, and of current America – and to exploit that Personality, identified with place and date, in a far more candid and comprehensive sense than any hitherto poem or book.

Perhaps this is in brief, or suggests, all I have sought to do. Given the Nineteenth Century, with the United States, and what they furnish as area and points of view, *Leaves of Grass* is, or seeks to be, simply a faithful and doubtless self-will'd record. In the midst of all, it gives one man's – the author's – identity, ardors, observations, faiths, and thoughts, color'd hardly at all with any deciding coloring from other faiths or other identities. Plenty of songs had been sung – beautiful, matchless songs – adjusted to other lands than these – another spirit and stage of evolution; but I would sing, and leave out or put in, quite solely with reference to America and to-day. Modern science and democracy seem'd to be throwing out their challenge to poetry to put them in its statements in contradistinction to the songs and myths of the past. As I see it now (perhaps too late,) I have unwittingly taken up that challenge and made an attempt at such statements – which I certainly would not assume to do now, knowing more clearly what it means.

For grounds for *Leaves of Grass*, as a poem, I abandon'd the conventional themes, which do not appear in it: none of the stock ornamentation, or choice plots of love or war, or high, exceptional personages of Old-World song; nothing, as I may say, for beauty's sake – no legend, or myth, or romance, nor euphemism, nor rhyme. But the broadest average of humanity and its identities in the now ripening Nineteenth Century, and especially in each of their countless examples and practical occupations in the United States to-day.

One main contrast of the ideas behind every page of my verses, compared with establish'd poems, is their different relative attitude towards God, towards the objective universe, and still more (by reflection, confession, assumption, etc.) the quite changed attitude of the ego, the one chanting or talking, towards himself and towards his fellow-humanity. It is certainly time for America, above all, to begin this readjustment in the scope and basic point of view of verse; for everything else has changed. As I write, I see in an article on Wordsworth, in one of the current English magazines, the lines, 'A few weeks ago an eminent French critic said that, owing to the special tendency to science and to its all-devouring force, poetry would cease to be read in fifty years.' But I anticipate the very contrary. Only a firmer, vastly broader, new area begins to exist – nay, is already form'd – to which the poetic genius must emigrate. Whatever may have been the case in years gone by, the true use for the imaginative faculty of modern times is to give ultimate vivification to facts, to science, and to common lives, endowing them with the glows and glories and final illustriousness which belong to every real thing, and to real things only. Without that ultimate vivification – which the poet or other artist alone can give – reality would seem incomplete, and science, democracy, and life itself, finally in vain.

Few appreciate the moral revolutions, our age, which have been profounder far than the material or inventive or war-produced ones. The Nineteenth Century, now well towards its close (and ripening into fruit the seeds of the two preceding centuries[1]) – the uprisings of national masses and shiftings of boundary-lines – the historical and other prominent facts of the United States – the war of attempted Secession – the stormy rush and haste of nebulous forces – never can future years witness more excitement and din of action – never completer change of army front along the whole line, the whole civilized world. For all these new and evolutionary facts, meanings, purposes, new poetic messages, new forms and expressions, are inevitable.

My Book and I – what a period we have presumed to span! those thirty years from 1850 to '80 – and America in them! Proud, proud indeed may we be, if we have cull'd enough of that period in its own spirit to worthily waft a few live breaths of it to the future!

Let me not dare, here or anywhere, for my own purposes, or

1. The ferment and germination even of the United States to-day, dating back to, and in my opinion mainly founded on, the Elizabethan age in English history, the age of Francis Bacon and Shakspere. Indeed, when we pursue it, what growth or advent is there that does not date back, back, until lost – perhaps its most tantalizing clues lost – in the receded horizons of the past?

any purposes, to attempt the definition of Poetry, nor answer the question what it is. Like Religion, Love, Nature, while those terms are indispensable, and we all give a sufficiently accurate meaning to them, in my opinion no definition that has ever been made sufficiently encloses the name Poetry; nor can any rule or convention ever so absolutely obtain but some great exception may arise and disregard and overturn it.

Also it must be carefully remember'd that first-class literature does not shine by any luminosity of its own; nor do its poems. They grow of circumstances, and are evolutionary. The actual living light is always curiously from elsewhere – follows unaccountable sources, and is lunar and relative at the best. There are, I know, certain controling themes that seem endlessly appropriated to the poets – as war, in the past – in the Bible, religious rapture and adoration – always love, beauty, some fine plot, or pensive or other emotion. But, strange as it may sound at first, I will say there is something striking far deeper and towering far higher than those themes for the best elements of modern song.

Just as all the old imaginative works rest, after their kind, on long trains of presuppositions, often entirely unmention'd by themselves, yet supplying the most important bases of them, and without which they could have had no reason for being, so *Leaves of Grass*, before a line was written, presupposed something different from any other, and, as it stands, is the result of such presupposition. I should say, indeed, it were useless to attempt reading the book without first carefully tallying that preparatory background and quality in the mind. Think of the United States to-day – the facts of these thirty-eight or forty empires solder'd in one – sixty or seventy millions of equals, with their lives, their passions, their future – these incalculable, modern, American, seething multitudes around us, of which we are inseparable parts! Think, in comparison, of the petty environage and limited area of the poets of past or present Europe, no matter how great their genius. Think of the absence and ignorance, in all cases hitherto, of the multitudinousness, vitality, and the unprecedented stimulants of to-day and here. It almost seems as if a poetry with cosmic and dynamic features of magnitude and limitlessness suitable to the human soul, were never possible before. It is certain that a poetry

of absolute faith and equality for the use of the democratic masses
never was.

In estimating first-class song, a sufficient Nationality, or, on the
other hand, what may be call'd the negative and lack of it, (as in
Goethe's case, it sometimes seems to me,) is often, if not always,
the first element. One needs only a little penetration to see, at
more or less removes, the material facts of their country and
radius, with the coloring of the moods of humanity at the time,
and its gloomy or hopeful prospects, behind all poets and each
poet, and forming their birth-marks. I know very well that my
Leaves could not possibly have emerged or been fashion'd or com-
pleted, from any other era than the latter half of the Nineteenth
Century, nor any other land than democratic America, and from
the absolute triumph of the National Union arms.

And whether my friends claim it for me or not, I know well
enough, too, that in respect to pictorial talent, dramatic situations,
and especially in verbal melody and all the conventional technique
of poetry, not only the divine works that to-day stand ahead in the
world's reading, but dozens more, transcend (some of them im-
measurably transcend) all I have done, or could do. But it seem'd
to me, as the objects in Nature, the themes of aestheticism, and all
special exploitations of the mind and soul, involve not only their
own inherent quality, but the quality, just as inherent and im-
portant, of *their point of view*,[1] the time had come to reflect all
themes and things, old and new, in the lights thrown on them by
the advent of America and democracy – to chant those themes
through the utterance of one, not only the grateful and reverent
legatee of the past, but the born child of the New World – to
illustrate all through the genesis and ensemble of to-day; and that
such illustration and ensemble are the chief demands of America's
prospective imaginative literature. Not to carry out, in the ap-
proved style, some choice plot of fortune or misfortune, or fancy,
or fine thoughts, or incidents, or courtesies – all of which has been
done overwhelmingly and well, probably never to be excell'd – but
that while in such aesthetic presentation of objects, passions, plots,
thoughts, etc., our lands and days do not want, and probably will

1. According to Immanuel Kant, the last essential reality, giving shape and
significance to all the rest.

never have, anything better than they already possess from the bequests of the past, it still remains to be said that there is even towards all those a subjective and contemporary point of view appropriate to ourselves alone, and to our new genius and environments, different from anything hitherto; and that such conception of current or gone-by life and art is for us the only means of their assimilation consistent with the Western world.

Indeed, and anyhow, to put it specifically, has not the time arrived when, (if it must be plainly said, for democratic America's sake, if for no other) there must imperatively come a readjustment of the whole theory and nature of Poetry? The question is important, and I may turn the argument over and repeat it: does not the best thought of our day and Republic conceive of a birth and spirit of song superior to anything past or present? To the effectual and moral consolidation of our lands (already, as materially establish'd, the greatest factors in known history, and far, far greater through what they prelude and necessitate, and are to be in future) – to conform with and build on the concrete realities and theories of the universe furnish'd by science, and henceforth the only irrefragable basis for anything, verse included – to root both influences in the emotional and imaginative action of the modern time, and dominate all that precedes or opposes them – is not either a radical advance and step forward, or a new verteber of the best song indispensable?

The New World receives with joy the poems of the antique, with European feudalism's rich fund of epics, plays, ballads – seeks not in the least to deaden or displace those voices from our ear and area – holds them indeed as indispensable studies, influences, records, comparisons. But though the dawn-dazzle of the sun of literature is in those poems for us of to-day – though perhaps the best parts of current character in nations, social groups, or any man's or woman's individuality, Old World or New, are from them – and though if I were ask'd to name the most precious bequest to current American civilization from all the hitherto ages, I am not sure but I would name those old and less old songs ferried hither from east and west – some serious words and debits remain; some acrid considerations demand a hearing. Of the great poems receiv'd from abroad and from the ages, and to-day enveloping and

penetrating America, is there one that is consistent with these
United States, or essentially applicable to them as they are and are
to be? Is there one whose underlying basis is not a denial and insult
to democracy? What a comment it forms, anyhow, on this era of
literary fulfilment, with the splendid day-rise of science and resus-
citation of history, that our chief religious and poetical works are
not our own, nor adapted to our light, but have been furnish'd by
far-back ages out of their arriere and darkness, or, at most, twilight
dimness! What is there in those works that so imperiously and
scornfully dominates all our advanced civilization, and culture?

Even Shakspere, who so suffuses current letters and art (which
indeed have in most degrees grown out of him,) belongs essentially
to the buried past. Only he holds the proud distinction for certain
important phases of that past, of being the loftiest of the singers
life has yet given voice to. All, however, relate to and rest upon
conditions, standards, politics, sociologies, ranges of belief, that
have been quite eliminated from the Eastern hemisphere, and
never existed at all in the Western. As authoritative types of song
they belong in America just about as much as the persons and
institutes they depict. True, it may be said, the emotional, moral
and aesthetic natures of humanity have not radically changed –
that in these the old poems apply to our times and all times,
irrespective of date; and that they are of incalculable value as
pictures of the past. I willingly make those admissions, and to their
fullest extent; then advance the points herewith as of serious, even
paramount importance.

I have indeed put on record elsewhere my reverence and eulogy
for those never-to-be-excell'd poetic bequests, and their indescrib-
able preciousness as heirlooms for America. Another and separate
point must now be candidly stated. If I had not stood before those
poems with uncover'd head, fully aware of their colossal grandeur
and beauty of form and spirit, I could not have written *Leaves of
Grass*. My verdict and conclusions as illustrated in its pages are
arrived at through the temper and inculcation of the old works as
much as through anything else – perhaps more than through any-
thing else. As America fully and fairly construed is the legitimate
result and evolutionary outcome of the past, so I would dare to
claim for my verse. Without stopping to qualify the averment,

the Old World has had the poems of myths, fictions, feudalism, conquest, caste, dynastic wars, and splendid exceptional characters and affairs, which have been great; but the New World needs the poems of realities and science and of the democratic average and basic equality, which shall be greater. In the centre of all, and object of all, stands the Human Being, towards whose heroic and spiritual evolution poems and everything directly or indirectly tend, Old World or New.

Continuing the subject, my friends have more than once suggested – or may be the garrulity of advancing age is possessing me – some further embryonic facts of *Leaves of Grass*, and especially how I enter'd upon them. Dr Bucke has, in his volume, already fully and fairly described the preparation of my poetic field, with the particular and general plowing, planting, seeding and occupation of the ground, till everything was fertilized, rooted and ready to start its own way for good or bad. Not till after all this, did I attempt any serious acquaintance with poetic literature. Along in my sixteenth year I had become possessor of a stout, well-cramm'd one thousand page octavo volume (I have it yet,) containing Walter Scott's poetry entire – an inexhaustible mine and treasury of poetic forage (especially the endless forests and jungles of notes) – has been so to me for fifty years, and remains so to this day.[1]

Later, at intervals, summers and falls, I used to go off, sometimes for a week at a stretch, down in the country, or to Long Island's seashores – there, in the presence of outdoor influences, I went over thoroughly the Old and New Testaments, and absorb'd (probably to better advantage for me than in any library or indoor room – it makes such difference *where* you read) Shakspere, Ossian, the best translated versions I could get of Homer, Eschylus, Sophocles, the old German Nibelungen, the ancient

1. Sir Walter Scott's *Complete Poems*; especially including *Border Minstrelsy*; then *Sir Tristrem*; *Lay of the last Minstrel*; *Ballads from the German*; *Marmion*; *Lady of the Lake*; *Vision of Don Roderick*; *Lord of the Isles*; *Rokeby*; *Bridal of Triermain*; *Field of Waterloo*; *Harold the Dauntless*; all the Dramas; various Introductions, endless interesting Notes, and Essays on Poetry, Romance, etc.

Lockhart's 1833 (or '34) edition with Scott's latest and copious revisions and annotations. (All the poems were thoroughly read by me, but the ballads of the *Border Minstrelsy* over and over again.)

Hindoo poems, and one or two other masterpieces, Dante's among them. As it happen'd, I read the latter mostly in an old wood. The *Iliad* (Buckley's prose version) I read first thoroughly on the peninsula of Orient, north-east end of Long Island, in a shelter'd hollow of rocks and sand, with the sea on each side. (I have wonder'd since why I was not overwhelm'd by those mighty masters. Likely because I read them, as described, in the full presence of Nature, under the sun, with the far-spreading landscape and vistas, or the sea rolling in.)

Toward the last I had among much else look'd over Edgar Poe's poems – of which I was not an admirer, tho' I always saw that beyond their limited range of melody (like perpetual chimes of music bells, ringing from lower *b* flat up to *g*) they were melodious expressions, and perhaps never excell'd ones, of certain pronounc'd phases of human morbidity. (The Poetic area is very spacious – has room for all – has so many mansions!) But I was repaid in Poe's prose by the idea that (at any rate for our occasions, our day) there can be no such thing as a long poem. The same thought had been haunting my mind before, but Poe's argument, though short, work'd the sum out and proved it to me.

Another point had an early settlement, clearing the ground greatly. I saw, from the time my enterprise and questionings positively shaped themselves (how best can I express my own distinctive era and surroundings, America, Democracy?) that the trunk and centre whence the answer was to radiate, and to which all should return from straying however far a distance, must be an identical body and soul, a personality – which personality, after many considerations and ponderings I deliberately settled should be myself – indeed could not be any other. I also felt strongly (whether I have shown it or not) that to the true and full estimate of the Present both the Past and the Future are main considerations.

These, however, and much more might have gone on and come to naught (almost positively would have come to naught,) if a sudden, vast, terrible, direct and indirect stimulus for new and national declamatory expression had not been given to me. It is certain, I say, that, although I had made a start before, only from the occurrence of the Secession War, and what it show'd me as by flashes of lightning, with the emotional depths it sounded and arous'd (of course, I don't mean in my own heart only, I saw it just as plainly in others, in millions) – that only from the strong flare and provocation of that war's sights and scenes the final reasons-for-being of an autochthonic and passionate song definitely came forth.

I went down to the war fields in Virginia (end of 1862), lived thenceforward in camp – saw great battles and the days and nights afterward – partook of all the fluctuations, gloom, despair, hopes again arous'd, courage evoked – death readily risk'd – *the cause*, too – along and filling those agonistic and lurid following years, 1863-'64-'65 – the real parturition years (more than 1776-'83) of this henceforth homogeneous Union. Without those three or four years and the experiences they gave, *Leaves of Grass* would not now be existing.

But I set out with the intention also of indicating or hinting some point-characteristics which I since see (though I did not then, at least not definitely) were bases and object-urgings toward those *Leaves* from the first. The word I myself put primarily for the description of them as they stand at last, is the word Suggestiveness. I round and finish little, if anything; and could not, consistently with my scheme. The reader will always have his or her part to do, just as much as I have had mine. I seek less to state or display any theme or thought, and more to bring you, reader, into the atmosphere of the theme or thought – there to pursue your own flight. Another impetus-word is Comradeship as for all lands, and in a more commanding and acknowledg'd sense than hitherto. Other word-signs would be Good Cheer, Content and Hope.

The chief trait of any given poet is always the spirit he brings to the observation of Humanity and Nature – the mood out of which he contemplates his subjects. What kind of temper and what amount of faith report these things? Up to how recent a date is the song carried? What the equipment, and special raciness of the singer – what his tinge of coloring? The last value of artistic expressers, past and present – Greek aesthetes, Shakspere – or in our own day Tennyson, Victor Hugo, Carlyle, Emerson – is certainly involv'd in such questions. I say the profoundest service that poems or any other writings can do for their reader is not merely to satisfy the intellect, or supply something polish'd and interesting, nor even to depict great passions, or persons or events, but to fill him with vigorous and clean manliness, religiousness, and give him *good heart* as a radical possession and habit. The educated world seems to have been growing more and more ennuyed for ages, leaving to our time the inheritance of it all. Fortunately there is the original inexhaustible fund of buoyancy, normally resident in the race, forever eligible to be appeal'd to and relied on.

As for native American individuality, though certain to come, and on a large scale, the distinctive and ideal type of Western character (as consistent with the operative political and even money-making features of United States' humanity in the Nineteenth Century as chosen knights, gentlemen and warriors were the ideals of the centuries of European feudalism) it has not yet appear'd. I have allow'd the stress of my poems from beginning to end to bear upon American individuality and assist it – not only because that is a great lesson in Nature, amid all her generalizing laws, but as counterpoise to the leveling tendencies of Democracy – and for other reasons. Defiant of ostensible literary and other conventions, I avowedly chant 'the great pride of man in himself', and permit it to be more or less a *motif* of nearly all my verse. I think this pride indispensable to an American. I think it not inconsistent with obedience, humility, deference and self-questioning.

Democracy has been so retarded and jeopardized by powerful personalities, that its first instincts are fain to clip, conform, bring in stragglers, and reduce everything to a dead level. While the ambitious thought of my song is to help the forming of a great aggregate Nation, it is, perhaps, altogether through the forming of myriads of fully develop'd and enclosing individuals. Welcome as are equality's and fraternity's doctrines and popular education, a certain liability accompanies them all, as we see. That primal and interior something in man, in his soul's abysms, coloring all, and, by exceptional fruitions, giving the last majesty to him – something continually touch'd upon and attain'd by the old poems and ballads of feudalism, and often the principal foundation of them – modern science and democracy appear to be endangering, perhaps eliminating. But that forms an appearance only; the reality is quite different. The new influences, upon the whole, are surely preparing the way for grander individualities than ever. To-day and here personal force is behind everything, just the same. The times and depictions from the *Iliad* to Shakspere inclusive can happily never again be realized – but the elements of courageous and lofty manhood are unchanged.

Without yielding an inch the working-man and working-woman were to be in my pages from first to last. The ranges of heroism and loftiness with which Greek and feudal poets endow'd their god-like or lordly born characters – indeed prouder and better based and with fuller ranges than those – I was to endow the democratic averages of America. I was to show that we, here and to-day, are eligible to the grandest and the best – more eligible now than any times of old were. I will also want my utterances (I said to myself before beginning) to be in spirit the poems of the morning. (They have been founded and mainly written in the sunny forenoon and early midday of my life.) I will want them to be the poems of women entirely as much as men. I have wish'd to put the complete Union of the States in my songs without any preference or partiality whatever. Henceforth, if they live and are read, it must be just as much South as North – just as much along the Pacific as Atlantic – in the valley of the Mississippi, in Canada, up in Maine, down in Texas, and on the shores of Puget Sound.

From another point of view *Leaves of Grass* is avowedly the song of Sex and Amativeness, and even Animality – though meanings that do not usually go along with those words are behind all, and will duly emerge; and all are sought to be lifted into a different light and atmosphere. Of this feature, intentionally palpable in a few lines, I shall only say the espousing principle of those lines so gives breath of life to my whole scheme that the bulk of the pieces might as well have been left unwritten were those lines omitted. Difficult as it will be, it has become, in my opinion, imperative to achieve a shifted attitude from superior men and women towards the thought and fact of sexuality, as an element in character, personality, the emotions, and a theme in literature. I am not going to argue the question by itself; it does not stand by itself. The vitality of it is altogether in its relations, bearings, significance – like the clef of a symphony. At last analogy the lines I allude to, and the spirit in which they are spoken, permeate all *Leaves of Grass*, and the work must stand or fall with them, as the human body and soul must remain as an entirety.

Universal as are certain facts and symptoms of communities or individuals all times, there is nothing so rare in modern conventions and poetry as their normal recognizance. Literature is always calling in the doctor for consultation and confession, and always giving evasions and swathing suppressions in place of that 'heroic nudity'[1] on which only a genuine diagnosis of serious cases can be built. And in respect to editions of *Leaves of Grass* in time to come (if there should be such) I take occasion now to confirm those lines with the settled convictions and deliberate renewals of thirty years, and to hereby prohibit, as far as word of mine can do so, any elision of them.

Then still a purpose enclosing all, and over and beneath all. Ever since what might be call'd thought, or the budding of thought, fairly began in my youthful mind, I had had a desire to attempt some worthy record of that entire faith and acceptance ('to justify the ways of God to man' is Milton's well-known and ambitious phrase) which is the foundation of moral America. I felt it all as positively then in my young days as I do now in my old ones; to formulate a poem whose every thought or fact should directly or indirectly be or connive at an implicit belief in the wisdom, health, mystery, beauty of every process, every concrete object, every human or other existence, not only consider'd from the point of view of all, but of each.

While I can not understand it or argue it out, I fully believe in a clue and purpose in Nature, entire and several; and that invisible spiritual results, just as real and definite as the visible, eventuate all concrete life and all materialism, through Time. My book ought to emanate buoyancy and gladness legitimately enough, for it was grown out of those elements, and has been the comfort of my life since it was originally commenced.

One main genesis-motive of the *Leaves* was my conviction (just as strong to-day as ever) that the crowning growth of the United

1. *Nineteenth Century*, July, 1883.

States is to be spiritual and heroic. To help start and favor that growth – or even to call attention to it, or the need of it – is the beginning, middle and final purpose of the poems. (In fact, when really cipher'd out and summ'd to the last, plowing up in earnest the interminable average fallows of humanity – not 'good government' merely, in the common sense – is the justification and main purpose of these United States.)

Isolated advantages in any rank or grace or fortune – the direct or indirect threads of all the poetry of the past – are in my opinion distasteful to the republican genius, and offer no foundation for its fitting verse. Establish'd poems, I know, have the very great advantage of chanting the already perform'd, so full of glories, reminiscences dear to the minds of men. But my volume is a candidate for the future. 'All original art,' says Taine, anyhow, 'is self-regulated, and no original art can be regulated from without; it carries its own counterpoise, and does not receive it from elsewhere – lives on its own blood' – a solace to my frequent bruises and sulky vanity.

As the present is perhaps mainly an attempt at personal statement or illustration, I will allow myself as further help to extract the following anecdote from a book, *Annals of Old Painters*, conn'd by me in youth. Rubens, the Flemish painter, in one of his wanderings through the galleries of old convents, came across a singular work. After looking at it thoughtfully for a good while, and listening to the criticisms of his suite of students, he said to the latter, in answer to their questions (as to what school the work implied or belong'd,) 'I do not believe the artist, unknown and perhaps no longer living, who has given the world this legacy, ever belong'd to any school, or ever painted anything but this one picture, which is a personal affair – a piece out of a man's life.'

Leaves of Grass indeed (I cannot too often reiterate) has mainly been the outcropping of my own emotional and other personal nature – an attempt, from first to last, to put *a Person*, a human being (myself, in the latter half of the Nineteenth Century, in America,) freely, fully and truly on record. I could not find any similar personal record in current literature that satisfied me. But it is not on *Leaves of Grass* distinctively as *literature*, or a specimen thereof, that I feel to dwell, or advance claims. No one will get at my verses who insists upon viewing them as a literary per-formance, or attempt at such performance, or as aiming mainly toward art or aestheticism.

I say no land or people or circumstances ever existed so needing a race of singers and poems differing from all others, and rigidly their own, as the land and people and circumstances of our United States need such singers and poems to-day, and for the future. Still further, as long as the States continue to absorb and be dominated by the poetry of the Old World, and remain unsupplied with autochthonous song, to express, vitalize and give color to and define their material and political success, and minister to them distinctively, so long will they stop short of first-class Nationality and remain defective.

In the free evening of my day I give to you, reader, the foregoing garrulous talk, thoughts, reminiscences,

As idly drifting down the ebb,
Such ripples, half-caught voices, echo from the shore.

Concluding with two items for the imaginative genius of the West, when it worthily rises – First, what Herder taught to the young Goethe, that really great poetry is always (like the Homeric or Biblical canticles) the result of a national spirit, and not the privilege of a polish'd and select few; Second, that the strongest and sweetest songs yet remain to be sung.

APPENDIX I

Old Age Echoes

An Executor's Diary Note, 1891

I said to W. W. today: 'Though you have put the finishing touches on the *Leaves*, closed them with your good-by, you will go on living a year or two longer and writing more poems. The question is, what will you do with these poems when the time comes to fix their place in the volume?' 'Do with them? I am not unprepared – I have even contemplated that emergency – I have a title in reserve: Old Age Echoes – applying not so much to things as to echoes of things, reverberant, an aftermath.' 'You have dropt enough by the roadside, as you went along, from different editions, to make a volume. Some day the world will demand to have that put together somewhere.' 'Do you think it?' 'Certainly. Should you put it under ban?' 'Why should I – how could I? So far as you may have anything to do with it I place upon you the injunction that whatever may be added to the *Leaves* shall be supplementary, avowed as such, leaving the book complete as I left it, consecutive to the point I left off, marking always an unmistakable, deep down, unobliteratable division line. In the long run the world will do as it pleases with the book. I am determined to have the world know what I was pleased to do.'

Here is a late personal note from W. W.: 'My tho't is to collect a lot of prose and poetry pieces – small or smallish mostly, but a few larger – appealing to the good will, the heart – sorrowful ones not rejected – but no morbid ones given.'

There is no reason for doubt that *A Thought of Columbus*, closing *Old Age Echoes*, was W. W.'s last deliberate composition, dating December, 1891.

To Soar in Freedom and in Fullness of Power

I have not so much emulated the birds that musically sing,
I have abandon'd myself to flights, broad circles.
The hawk, the seagull, have far more possess'd me than the
    canary or mocking-bird,
I have not felt to warble and trill, however sweetly,
I have felt to soar in freedom and in the fullness of power,
    joy, volition.

Then Shall Perceive

In softness, languor, bloom, and growth,
Thine eyes, ears, all thy sense – thy loftiest attribute – all
    that takes cognizance of beauty,
Shall rouse and fill – then shall perceive!

The Few Drops Known

Of heroes, history, grand events, premises, myths, poems,
The few drops known must stand for oceans of the unknown,
On this beautiful and thick peopl'd earth, here and there a
    little specimen put on record.
A little of Greeks and Romans, a few Hebrew canticles, a few
    death odors as from graves, from Egypt –
What are they to the long and copious retrospect of
    antiquity?

One Thought Ever at the Fore

One thought ever at the fore –
That in the Divine Ship, the World, breasting Time and
    Space,
All Peoples of the globe together sail, sail the same voyage,
    are bound to the same destination.

While Behind All, Firm and Erect

While behind all, firm and erect as ever,
Undismay'd amid the rapids – amid the irresistible and
    deadly urge,
Stands a helmsman, with brow elate and strong hand.

A Kiss to the Bride
(MARRIAGE OF NELLY GRANT, MAY 21, 1874)

Sacred, blithesome, undenied,
With benisons from East and West,
And salutations North and South,
Through me indeed to-day a million hearts and hands,
Wafting a million loves, a million soul felt prayers;
– Tender and true remain the arm that shields thee!
Fair winds always fill the ship's sails that sail thee!
Clear sun by day, and light stars at night, beam on thee!
Dear girl – through me the ancient privilege too,
10 For the New World, through me, the old, old wedding
    greeting:
O youth and health! O sweet Missouri rose! O bonny bride!
Yield thy red cheeks, thy lips, to-day,
Unto a Nation's loving kiss.

Nay, Tell Me Not To-day the Publish'd Shame
(WINTER OF 1873, CONGRESS IN SESSION)

Nay, tell me not to-day the publish'd shame,
Read not to-day the journal's crowded page,
The merciless reports still branding forehead after
    forehead,
The guilty column following guilty column.

To-day to me the tale refusing,
Turning from it – from the white capitol turning,
Far from these swelling domes, topt with statues,
More endless, jubilant, vital visions rise
Unpublish'd, unreported.

10   Through all your quiet ways, or North or South, you Equal
       States, you honest farms,
     Your million untold manly healthy lives, or East or West,
       city or country,
     Your noiseless mothers, sisters, wives, unconscious of their
       good,
     Your mass of homes nor poor nor rich, in visions rise – (even
       your excellent poverties,)
     Your self-distilling, never-ceasing virtues, self-denials,
       graces,
     Your endless base of deep integrities within, timid but
       certain,
     Your blessings steadily bestow'd, sure as the light, and still,
     (Plunging to these as a determin'd diver down the deep
       hidden waters,)
     These, these to-day I brood upon – all else refusing, these
       will I con,
     To-day to these give audience.

Supplement Hours

Sane, random, negligent hours,
Sane, easy, culminating hours,
After the flush, the Indian summer, of my life,
Away from Books – away from Art – the lesson learn'd,
  pass'd o'er,
Soothing, bathing, merging all – the sane, magnetic,
Now for the day and night themselves – the open air,
Now for the fields, the seasons, insects, trees – the rain and
  snow,
Where wild bees flitting hum,

    Or August mulleins grow, or winter's snowflakes fall,
10 Or stars in the skies roll round –
    The silent sun and stars.

Of Many a Smutch'd Deed Reminiscent

Full of wickedness, I – of many a smutch'd deed
    reminiscent – of worse deeds capable,
Yet I look composedly upon nature, drink day and night the
    joys of life, and await death with perfect equanimity,
Because of my tender and boundless love for him I love and
    because of his boundless love for me.

To Be at All
(CF. STANZA 27, *Song of Myself*)

To be at all – what is better than that?
I think if there were nothing more developed, the clam in its
    callous shell in the sand were august enough.
I am not in any callous shell;
I am cased with supple conductors, all over,
They take every object by the hand, and lead it within me;
They are thousands, each one with his entry to himself;
They are always watching with their little eyes, from my
    head to my feet;
One no more than a point lets in and out of me such bliss
    and magnitude,
I think I could lift the girder of the house away if it lay
    between me and whatever I wanted.

Death's Valley
(TO ACCOMPANY A PICTURE; BY REQUEST.
The Valley of the Shadow of Death,
FROM THE PAINTING BY GEORGE INNESS)

Nay, do not dream, designer dark,
Thou hast portray'd or hit thy theme entire;
I, hoverer of late by this dark valley, by its confines, having
    glimpses of it,
Here enter lists with thee, claiming my right to make a
    symbol too.
For I have seen many wounded soldiers die,
And dread suffering – have seen their lives pass off with
    smiles;
And I have watch'd the death-hours of the old; and seen
    the infant die;
The rich, with all his nurses and his doctors;
And then the poor, in meagerness and poverty;
10 And I myself for long, O Death, have breath'd my every
    breath
Amid the nearness and the silent thought of thee.
And out of these and thee,
I make a scene, a song (not fear of thee,
Nor gloom's ravines, nor bleak, nor dark – for I do not fear
    thee,
Nor celebrate the struggle, or contortion, or hard-tied knot),
Of the broad blessed light and perfect air, with meadows,
    rippling tides, and trees and flowers and grass,
And the low hum of living breeze – and in the midst God's
    beautiful eternal right hand,
Thee, holiest minister of Heaven – thee, envoy, usherer,
    guide at last of all,
Rich, florid, loosener of the stricture-knot call'd life,
20 Sweet, peaceful, welcome Death.

593

On the Same Picture

(INTENDED FOR FIRST STANZA OF *Death's Valley*)

Aye, well I know 'tis ghastly to descend that valley:
Preachers, musicians, poets, painters, always render it,
Philosophs exploit – the battlefield, the ship at sea, the
    myriad beds, all lands,
All, all the past have enter'd, the ancientest humanity we
    know,
Syria's, India's, Egypt's, Greece's, Rome's;
Till now for us under our very eyes spreading the same
    to-day,
Grim, ready, the same to-day, for entrance, yours and mine,
Here, here 'tis limn'd.

A Thought of Columbus

The mystery of mysteries, the crude and hurried ceaseless
    flame, spontaneous, bearing on itself.
The bubble and the huge, round, concrete orb!
A breath of Deity, as thence the bulging universe unfolding!
The many issuing cycles from their precedent minute!
The eras of the soul incepting in an hour,
Haply the widest, farthest evolutions of the world and man.

Thousands and thousands of miles hence, and now four
    centuries back,
A mortal impulse thrilling its brain cell,
Reck'd or unreck'd, the birth can no longer be postpon'd:
10   A phantom of the moment, mystic, stalking, sudden,
Only a silent thought, yet toppling down of more than walls
    of brass or stone.
(A flutter at the darkness' edge as if old Time's and Space's
    secret near revealing.)
A thought! a definite thought works out in shape.
Four hundred years roll on.

The rapid cumulus – trade, navigation, war, peace,
    democracy, roll on;
The restless armies and the fleets of time following their
    leader – the old camps of ages pitch'd in newer, larger
    areas,
The tangl'd, long-deferr'd eclaircissement of human life and
    hopes boldly begins untying,
As here to-day up-grows the Western World.

(An added word yet to my song, far Discoverer, as ne'er
    before sent back to son of earth –
20 If still thou hearest, hear me,
Voicing as now – lands, races, arts, bravas to thee,
O'er the long backward path to thee – one vast consensus,
    north, south, east, west,
Soul plaudits! acclamation! reverent echoes!
One manifold, huge memory to thee! oceans and lands!
The modern world to thee and thought of thee!)

Poems Excluded from Leaves of Grass

Great Are the Myths

Great are the myths – I too delight in them,
Great are Adam and Eve – I too look back and accept them,
Great the risen and fallen nations, and their poets, women,
    sages, inventors, rulers, warriors, and priests.

Great is Liberty! great is Equality! I am their follower,
Helmsmen of nations, choose your craft! where you sail, I
    sail,
Yours is the muscle of life or death – yours is the
    perfect science – in you I have absolute faith.

Great is To-day, and beautiful,
It is good to live in this age – there never was any better.

Great are the plunges, throes, triumphs, downfalls of
    Democracy,
10 Great the reformers, with their lapses and screams,
Great the daring and venture of sailors, on new explorations.

Great are Yourself and Myself,
We are just as good and bad as the oldest and youngest
    or any,
What the best and worst did, we could do,
What they felt, do not we feel it in ourselves?
What they wished, do we not wish the same?

Great is Youth – equally great is Old Age – great are the
    Day and Night,
Great is Wealth – great is Poverty – great is Expression –
    great is Silence.

Youth, large, lusty, loving – Youth, full of grace, force,
    fascination,
20 Do you know that Old Age may come after you,
    with equal grace, force, fascination?

Day, full-blown and splendid – Day of the immense sun,
   action, ambition, laughter,
The Night follows close, with millions of suns, and sleep,
   and restoring darkness.

Wealth with the flush hand, fine clothes, hospitality,
But then the Soul's wealth, which is candor, knowledge,
   pride, enfolding love;
(Who goes for men and women showing Poverty richer
   than wealth?)

Expression of speech! in what is written or said, forget not
   that Silence is also expressive,
That anguish as hot as the hottest, and contempt as cold
   as the coldest, may be without words,
That the true adoration is likewise without words, and
   without kneeling.

Great is the greatest Nation – the nation of clusters of
   equal nations.

30   Great is the Earth, and the way it became what it is;
Do you imagine it is stopped at this? the increase
   abandoned?
Understand then that it goes as far onward from this, as
   this is from the times when it lay in covering waters and
   gases, before man had appeared.

Great is the quality of Truth in man,
The quality of truth in man supports itself through all
   changes,
It is inevitably in the man – he and it are in love, and never·
   leave each other.

The truth in man is no dictum, it is vital as eyesight,
If there be any Soul, there is truth – if there be man or
   woman, there is truth – if there be physical or moral,
   there is truth,
If there be equilibrium or volition, there is truth – if there be
   things at all upon the earth, there is truth.

O truth of the earth! O truth of things! I am determined
   to press my way toward you,
40   Sound your voice! I scale mountains, or dive in the sea
   after you.

Great is Language – it is the mightiest of the sciences,
It is the fulness, color, form, diversity of the earth, and of
   men and women, and of all qualities and processes,
It is greater than wealth – it is greater than buildings, ships,
   religions, paintings, music.

Great is the English speech – what speech is so great as
   the English?
Great is the English brood – what brood has so vast a
   destiny as the English?
It is the mother of the brood that must rule the earth with
   the new rule,
The new rule shall rule as the Soul rules, and as the love,
   justice, equality in the Soul, rule.

Great is Law – great are the old few landmarks of the law,
They are the same in all times, and shall not be disturbed.

50   Great are commerce, newspapers, books, free-trade,
   railroads, steamers, international mails, telegraphs,
   exchanges.

Great is Justice!
Justice is not settled by legislators and laws – it is in the
   Soul,
It cannot be varied by statutes, any more than love, pride,
   the attraction of gravity, can,
It is immutable – it does not depend on majorities –
   majorities or what not come at last before the same
   passionless and exact tribunal.

For justice are the grand natural lawyers and perfect
    judges – it is in their Souls,
It is well assorted – they have not studied for
    nothing – the great includes the less,
They rule on the highest grounds – they oversee all eras,
    states, administrations.

The perfect judge fears nothing – he could go front to front
    before God,
Before the perfect judge all shall stand back – life and death
    shall stand back – heaven and hell shall stand back.

60   Great is Goodness!
I do not know what it is, any more than I know what
    health is – but I know it is great.

Great is Wickedness – I find I often admire it, just as
    much as I admire goodness,
Do you call that a paradox? It certainly is a paradox.

The eternal equilibrium of things is great, and the eternal
    overthrow of things is great,
And there is another paradox.

Great is Life, real and mystical, wherever and whoever,
Great is Death – sure as Life holds all parts together,
    Death holds all parts together,
Death has just as much purport as Life has,
Do you enjoy what Life confers? you shall enjoy what
    Death confers,
70   I do not understand the realities of Death, but I know they
    are great,
I do not understand the least reality of Life – how then
    can I understand the realities of Death?

Poem of Remembrances
for a Girl or a Boy of These States

You just maturing youth! You male or female!
Remember the organic compact of These States,
Remember the pledge of the Old Thirteen thenceforward
  to the rights, life, liberty, equality of man,
Remember what was promulged by the founders, ratified
  by The States, signed in black and white by the
  Commissioners, and read by Washington at the head
  of the army,
Remember the purposes of the founders, – Remember
  Washington;
Remember the copious humanity streaming from every
  direction toward America;
Remember the hospitality that belongs to nations and men;
  (Cursed be nation, woman, man, without hospitality!)
Remember, government is to subserve individuals,
Not any, not the President, is to have one jot more than you
  or me,
Not any habitan of America is to have one jot less than
  you or me.

Anticipate when the thirty or fifty millions, are to become
  the hundred, or two hundred millions, of equal freemen
  and freewomen, amicably joined.

Recall ages – One age is but a part – ages are but a part;
Recall the angers, bickerings, delusions, superstitions, of
  the idea of caste,
Recall the bloody cruelties and crimes.

Anticipate the best women;
I say an unnumbered new race of hardy and well-defined
  women are to spread through all These States,
I say a girl fit for These States must be free, capable,
  dauntless, just the same as a boy.

Anticipate your own life – retract with merciless power,
Shirk nothing – retract in time – Do you see those errors,
    diseases, weaknesses, lies, thefts?
20 Do you see that lost character? – Do you see decay,
    consumption, rum-drinking, dropsy, fever, mortal cancer
    or inflammation?
Do you see death, and the approach of death?

Think of the Soul

Think of the Soul;
I swear to you that body of yours gives proportions to
    your Soul somehow to live in other spheres;
I do not know how, but I know it is so.

Think of loving and being loved;
I swear to you, whoever you are, you can interfuse yourself
    with such things that everybody that sees you shall look
    longingly upon you.

Think of the past;
I warn you that in a little while others will find their
    past in you and your times.

The race is never separated – nor man nor woman escapes;
All is inextricable – things, spirits, Nature, nations, you
    too – from precedents you come.

10 Recall the ever-welcome defiers, (The mothers precede
    them;)
Recall the sages, poets, saviors, inventors, lawgivers,
    of the earth;
Recall Christ, brother of rejected persons -- brother of slaves,
    felons, idiots, and of insane and diseas'd persons.

Think of the time when you were not yet born;
Think of times you stood at the side of the dying;
Think of the time when your own body will be dying.

Think of spiritual results,
Sure as the earth swims through the heavens, does every
  one of its objects pass into spiritual results.

Think of manhood, and you to be a man;
Do you count manhood, and the sweet of manhood,
  nothing?

20   Think of womanhood, and you to be a woman;
The creation is womanhood;
Have I not said that womanhood involves all?
Have I not told how the universe has nothing better
  than the best womanhood?

Respondez!

Respondez! Respondez!
(The war is completed – the price is paid – the title is
  settled beyond recall;)
Let every one answer! let those who sleep be waked!
  let none evade!
Must we still go on with our affectations and sneaking?
Let me bring this to a close – I pronounce openly for a new
  distribution of roles;
Let that which stood in front go behind! and let that which
  was behind advance to the front and speak;
Let murderers, bigots, fools, unclean persons, offer new
  propositions!
Let the old propositions be postponed!
Let faces and theories be turn'd inside out! let meanings be
  freely criminal, as well as results!
10   Let there be no suggestion above the suggestion of
  drudgery!
Let none be pointed toward his destination! (Say! do you
  know your destination?)
Let men and women be mock'd with bodies and mock'd
  with Souls!
Let the love that waits in them, wait! let it die, or pass
  still-born to other spheres!

Let the sympathy that waits in every man, wait! or let
    it also pass, a dwarf, to other spheres!
Let contradictions prevail! let one thing contradict another!
    and let one line of my poems contradict another!
Let the people sprawl with yearning, aimless hands! let
    their tongues be broken! let their eyes be discouraged!
    let none descend into their hearts with the fresh
    lusciousness of love!
(Stifled, O days! O lands! in every public and private
    corruption!
Smother'd in thievery, impotence, shamelessness,
    mountain-high;
Brazen effrontery, scheming, rolling like ocean's waves
    around and upon you, O my days! my lands!
20   For not even those thunderstorms, nor fiercest lightnings
    of the war, have purified the atmosphere;)
– Let the theory of America still be management, caste,
    comparison! (Say! what other theory would you?)
Let them that distrust birth and death still lead the rest!
    (Say! why shall they not lead you?)
Let the crust of hell be neared and trod on! let the days be
    darker than the nights! let slumber bring less slumber
    than waking time brings!
Let the world never appear to him or her for whom it was
    all made!
Let the heart of the young man still exile itself from the
    heart of the old man! and let the heart of the old man be
    exiled from that of the young man!
Let the sun and moon go! let scenery take the applause of
    the audience! let there be apathy under the stars!
Let freedom prove no man's inalienable right! every one
    who can tyrannize, let him tyrannize to his satisfaction!
Let none but infidels be countenanced!
Let the eminence of meanness, treachery, sarcasm, hate,
    greed, indecency, impotence, lust, be taken for granted
    above all! let writers, judges, governments, households,
    religions, philosophies, take such for granted above all!

30   Let the worst men beget children out of the worst women!

Let the priest still play at immortality!

Let death be inaugurated!

Let nothing remain but the ashes of teachers, artists,
    moralists, lawyers, and learn'd and polite persons!

Let him who is without my poems be assassinated!

Let the cow, the horse, the camel, the garden-bee – let the
    mud-fish, the lobster, the mussel, eel, the sting-ray, and
    the grunting pig-fish – let these, and the like of these, be
    put on a perfect equality with man and woman!

Let churches accommodate serpents, vermin, and the
    corpses of those who have died of the most filthy of
    diseases!

Let marriage slip down among fools, and be for none but
    fools!

Let men among themselves talk and think forever obscenely
    of women! and let women among themselves talk and
    think obscenely of men!

Let us all, without missing one, be exposed in public, naked,
    monthly, at the peril of our lives! let our bodies be freely
    handled and examined by whoever chooses!

40   Let nothing but copies at second hand be permitted to exist
    upon the earth!

Let the earth desert God, nor let there ever henceforth be
    mention'd the name of God!

Let there be no God!

Let there be money, business, imports, exports, custom,
    authority, precedents, pallor, dyspepsia, smut,
    ignorance, unbelief!

Let judges and criminals be transposed! let the
    prison-keepers be put in prison! let those that were
    prisoners take the keys! (Say! why might they not just
    as well be transposed?)

Let the slaves be masters! let the masters become slaves!

Let the reformers descend from the stands where they are
    forever bawling! let an idiot or insane person appear on
    each of the stands!

Let the Asiatic, the African, the European, the American,

and the Australian, go armed against the murderous
    stealthiness of each other! let them sleep armed! let none
    believe in good will!
Let there be no unfashionable wisdom! let such be scorn'd
    and derided off from the earth!
Let a floating cloud in the sky – let a wave of the sea – let
    growing mint, spinach, onions, tomatoes – let these be
    exhibited as shows, at a great price for admission!
50 Let all the men of These States stand aside for a few
    smouchers! let the few seize on what they choose! let the
    rest gawk, giggle, starve, obey!
Let shadows be furnish'd with genitals! let substances be
    deprived of their genitals!
Let there be wealthy and immense cities – but still through
    any of them, not a single poet, savior, knower, lover!
Let the infidels of These States laugh all faith away!
If one man be found who has faith, let the rest set upon him!
Let them affright faith! let them destroy the power of
    breeding faith!
Let the she-harlots and the he-harlots be prudent!
    let them dance on, while seeming lasts!
    (O seeming! seeming! seeming!)
Let the preachers recite creeds! let them still teach
    only what they have been taught!
Let insanity still have charge of sanity!
Let books take the place of trees, animals, rivers, clouds!
60 Let the daub'd portraits of heroes supersede heroes!
Let the manhood of man never take steps after itself!
Let it take steps after eunuchs, and after consumptive and
    genteel persons!
Let the white person again tread the black person under his
    heel! (Say! which is trodden under heel, after all?)
Let the reflections of the things of the world be studied in
    mirrors! let the things themselves still continue
    unstudied!
Let a man seek pleasure everywhere except in himself!
Let a woman seek happiness everywhere except in herself!

(What real happiness have you had one single hour through
    your whole life?)
Let the limited years of life do nothing for the limitless years
    of death! (What do you suppose death will do, then?)

[In the New Garden]

In the new garden, in all the parts,
In cities now, modern, I wander,
Through the second or third result, or still further,
    primitive yet,
Days, places, indifferent – though various, the same,
Time, Paradise, the Mannahatta, the prairies, finding me
    unchanged,
Death indifferent – Is it that I lived long since?
    Was I buried very long ago?
For all that, I may now be watching you here, this moment;
For the future, with determined will, I seek – the woman of
    the future,
You, born years, centuries after me, I seek.

[Who Is Now Reading This?]

Who is now reading this?

May-be one is now reading this who knows some
    wrong-doing of my past life,
Or may-be a stranger is reading this who has secretly loved
    me,
Or may-be one who meets all my grand assumptions
    and egotisms with derision,
Or may-be one who is puzzled at me.

As if I were not puzzled at myself!
Or as if I never deride myself! (O conscience-struck!
    O self-convicted!)

Or as if I do not secretly love strangers! (O tenderly,
a long time, and never avow it;)
Or as if I did not see, perfectly well, interior in myself,
the stuff of wrong-doing,
10 Or as if it could cease transpiring from me until it must
cease.

[I Thought That Knowledge Alone Would Suffice]

Long I thought that knowledge alone would suffice me – O
if I could but obtain knowledge!
Then my lands engrossed me – Lands of the prairies, Ohio's
land, the southern savannas, engrossed me – For them I
would live – I would be their orator;
Then I met the examples of old and new heroes – I heard of
warriors, sailors, and all dauntless persons – And it seemed
to me that I too had it in me to be as dauntless as any – and
would be so;
And then, to enclose all, it came to me to strike up the songs
of the New World – And then I believed my life must be
spent in singing;
But now take notice, land of the prairies, land of
the south savannas, Ohio's land,
Take notice, you Kanuck woods – and you Lake Huron –
and all that with you roll toward Niagara – and you
Niagara also,
And you, Californian mountains – That you each and all
find somebody else to be your singer of songs,
For I can be your singer of songs no longer – One who loves
me is jealous of me, and withdraws me from all but love,
With the rest I dispense – I sever from what I thought would
suffice me, for it does not – it is now empty and tasteless
to me,
10 I heed knowledge, and the grandeur of The States,
and the example of heroes, no more,

I am indifferent to my own songs – I will go with him I love,
It is to be enough for us that we are together – We never
separate again.

[Hours Continuing Long]

Hours continuing long, sore and heavy-hearted,
Hours of the dusk, when I withdraw to a lonesome and
unfrequented spot, seating myself, leaning my face in my
hands;
Hours sleepless, deep in the night, when I go forth,
speeding swiftly the country roads, or through the city
streets, or pacing miles and miles, stifling plaintive cries;
Hours discouraged. distracted – for the one I cannot content
myself without, soon I saw him content himself without
me;
Hours when I am forgotten, (O weeks and months are
passing, but I believe I am never to forget!)
Sullen and suffering hours! (I am ashamed – but it
is useless – I am what I am;)
Hours of my torment – I wonder if other men ever
have the like, out of the like feelings?
Is there even one other like me – distracted – his
friend, his lover, lost to him?
Is he too as I am now? Does he still rise in the morning,
dejected, thinking who is lost to him? and at night,
awaking, think who is lost?
10 Does he too harbor his friendship silent and endless?
harbor his anguish and passion?
Does some stray reminder, or the casual mention of a name,
bring the fit back upon him, taciturn and deprest?
Does he see himself reflected in me? In these hours,
does he see the face of his hours reflected?

[So Far, and So Far, and On Toward the End]

So far, and so far, and on toward the end,
Singing what is sung in this book, from the irresistible
    impulses of me;
But whether I continue beyond this book, to maturity,
Whether I shall dart forth the true rays, the ones that wait
    unfired,
(Did you think the sun was shining its brightest?
No – it has not yet fully risen;)
Whether I shall complete what is here started,
Whether I shall attain my own height, to justify these,
    yet unfinished,
Whether I shall make THE POEM OF THE NEW WORLD,
    transcending all others – depends, rich persons,
    upon you,
10   Depends, whoever you are now filling the current
    Presidentiad, upon you,
Upon you, Governor, Mayor, Congressman,
And you, contemporary America.

Thoughts – 1: Visages

Of the visages of things – And of piercing through
    to the accepted hells beneath;
Of ugliness – To me there is just as much in it as there is in
    beauty – And now the ugliness of human beings is
    acceptable to me;
Of detected persons – To me, detected persons are not, in
    any respect, worse than undetected persons – and are not
    in any respect worse than I am myself;
Of criminals – To me, any judge, or any juror, is equally
    criminal – and any reputable person is also – and the
    President is also.

Leaflets

What General has a good army in himself, has a good army;
He happy in himself, or she happy in herself, is happy.

Thoughts – 6: 'Of What I Write'

Of what I write from myself – As if that were not the
    resumé;
Of Histories – As if such, however complete, were
    not less complete than the preceding poems;
As if those shreds, the records of nations, could possibly
    be as lasting as the preceding poems;
As if here were not the amount of all nations, and of all the
    lives of heroes.

Says

1
I say whatever tastes sweet to the most perfect person, that
    is finally right.

2
I say nourish a great intellect, a great brain;
If I have said anything to the contrary, I hereby retract it.

3
I say man shall not hold property in man;
I say the least developed person on earth is just as important
    and sacred to himself or herself, as the most developed
    person is to himself or herself.

4
I say where liberty draws not the blood out of
    slavery, there slavery draws the blood out of liberty,
I say the word of the good old cause in These States,
    and resound it hence over the world.

5

I say the human shape or face is so great, it must never be
made ridiculous;
I say for ornaments nothing outre can be allowed,
10 And that anything is most beautiful without ornament,
And that exaggerations will be sternly revenged in your own
physiology, and in other persons' physiology also;
And I say that clean-shaped children can be jetted and
conceived only where natural forms pervail in public, and
the human face and form are never caricatured;
And I say that genius need never more be turned to
romances,
(For facts properly told, how mean appear all romances.)

6

I say the word of lands fearing nothing – I will have no other
land;
I say discuss all and expose all – I am for every topic openly;
I say there can be no salvation for These States without
innovators – without free tongues, and ears willing to hear
the tongues;
And I announce as a glory of These States, that they
respectfully listen to propositions, reforms, fresh views
and doctrines, from successions of men and women,
Each age with its own growth.

7

20 I have said many times that materials and the Soul
are great, and that all depends on physique;
Now I reverse what I said, and affirm that all depends
on the aesthetic or intellectual,
And that criticism is great – and that refinement is greatest
of all;
And I affirm now that the mind governs – and that
all depends on the mind.

8

With one man or woman – (no matter which one – I
   even pick out the lowest,)
With him or her I now illustrate the whole law;
I say that every right, in politics or what-not, shall be
   eligible to that one man or woman, on the same terms
   as any.

Apostroph

O mater! O fils!
O brood continental!
O flowers of the prairies!
O space boundless! O hum of mighty products!
O you teeming cities! O so invincible, turbulent, proud!
O race of the future! O women!
O fathers! O you men of passion and the storm!
O native power only! O beauty!
O yourself! O God! O divine average!
10 O you bearded roughs! O bards! O all those slumberers!
O arouse! the dawn-bird's throat sounds shrill!
   Do you not hear the cock crowing?
O, as I walk'd the beach, I heard the mournful notes
   foreboding a tempest – the low, oft-repeated shriek of the
   diver, the long-lived loon;
O I heard, and yet hear, angry thunder; – O you sailors!
   O ships! make quick preparation!
O from his masterful sweep, the warning cry of the eagle!
(Give way there, all! It is useless! Give up your spoils;)
O sarcasms! Propositions! (O if the whole world
   should prove indeed a sham, a sell!)
O I believe there is nothing real but America and freedom!
O to sternly reject all except Democracy!
O imperator! O who dare confront you and me?
20 O to promulgate our own! O to build for that which builds
   for mankind!

O feuillage! O North! O the slope drained by the Mexican
    sea!
O all, all inseparable – ages, ages, ages!
O a curse on him that would dissever this Union for any
    reason whatever!
O climates, labors! O good and evil! O death!
O you strong with iron and wood! O Personality!
O the village or place which has the greatest man or
    woman! even if it be only a few ragged huts;
O the city where women walk in public processions in
    the streets, the same as the men;
O a wan and terrible emblem, by me adopted!
O shapes arising! shapes of the future centuries!
30 O muscle and pluck forever for me!
O workmen and workwomen forever for me!
O farmers and sailors! O drivers of horses forever for me!
O I will make the new bardic list of trades and tools!
O you coarse and wilful! I love you!
O South! O longings for my dear home! O soft and sunny
    airs!
O pensive! O I must return where the palm grows and the
    mocking-bird sings, or else I die!
O equality! O organic compacts! I am come to be your born
    poet!
O whirl, contest, sounding and resounding! I am your poet,
    because I am part of you;
O days by-gone! Enthusiasts! Antecedents!
40 O vast preparations for These States! O years!
O what is now being sent forward thousands of years to
    come!
O mediums! O to teach! to convey the invisible faith!
To promulge real things! to journey through all The States!
O creation! O to-day! O laws! O unmitigated adoration!
O for mightier broods of orators, artists, and singers!
O for native songs! carpenter's, boatman's,
    ploughman's songs! shoemaker's songs!
O haughtiest growth of time! O free and extatic!
O what I, here, preparing, warble for!

O you hastening light! O the sun of the world will ascend,
    dazzling, and take his height – and you too will ascend;
50 O so amazing and so broad! up there resplendent, darting
    and burning;
O prophetic! O vision staggered with weight of light!
    with pouring glories!
O copious! O hitherto unequalled!
O Libertad! O compact! O union impossible to dissever!
O my Soul! O lips becoming tremulous, powerless!
O centuries, centuries yet ahead!
O voices of greater orators! I pause – I listen for you!
O you States! Cities! defiant of all outside authority! I
    spring at once into your arms! you I most love!
O you grand Presidentiads! I wait for you!
New history! New heroes! I project you!
60 Visions of poets! only you really last! O sweep on! sweep on!
O Death! O you striding there! O I cannot yet!
O heights! O infinitely too swift and dizzy yet!
O purged lumine! you threaten me more than I can stand!
O present! I return while yet I may to you!
O poets to come, I depend upon you!

O Sun of Real Peace

O sun of real peace! O hastening light!
O free and extatic! O what I here, preparing, warble for!
O the sun of the world will ascend, dazzling, and take his
    height – and you too, O my Ideal, will surely ascend!
O so amazing and broad – up there resplendent, darting and
    burning!
O vision prophetic, stagger'd with weight of light! with
    pouring glories!
O lips of my soul, already becoming powerless!
O ample and grand Presidentiads! Now the war, the war
    is over!
New history! new heroes! I project you!
Visions of poets! only you really last! sweep on! sweep on!

10 O heights too swift and dizzy yet!
  O purged and luminous! you threaten me more than I can
   stand!
  (I must not venture – the ground under my feet menaces
   me – it will not support me:
  O future too immense,) – O present, I return, while yet
   I may, to you.

To You

Let us twain walk aside from the rest;
Now we are together privately, do you discard ceremony;
Come! vouchsafe to me what has yet been vouchsafed to
 none – Tell me the whole story,
Let us talk of death – unbosom all freely,
Tell me what you would not tell your brother, wife,
 husband, or physician.

Now Lift Me Close

Now lift me close to your face till I whisper,
What you are holding is in reality no book, nor part of
 a book;
It is a man, flush'd and full-blooded – it is I – *So long!* –
We must separate awhile – Here! take from my lips this kiss;
Whoever you are, I give it especially to you;
So long! – And I hope we shall meet again.

To the Reader at Parting

Now, dearest comrade, lift me to your face,
We must separate awhile – Here! take from my lips this kiss;
Whoever you are, I give it especially to you;
So long! – And I hope we shall meet again.

Debris

*

He is wisest who has the most caution,
He only wins who goes far enough.

*

Any thing is as good as established, when that is
    established that will produce it and continue it.

*

What General has a good army in himself, has a good army;
He happy in himself, or she happy in herself, is happy,
But I tell you you cannot be happy by others, any more than
    you can beget or conceive a child by others.

*

Have you learned lessons only of those who admired you,
    and were tender with you, and stood aside for you?
Have you not learned the great lessons of those who
    rejected you, and braced themselves against you? or who
    treated you with contempt, or disputed the passage
    with you?
Have you had no practice to receive opponents when they
    come?

*

10   Despairing cries float ceaselessly toward me, day and night,
The sad voice of Death – the call of my nearest lover,
    putting forth, alarmed, uncertain,
This sea I am quickly to sail, come tell me,
Come tell me where I am speeding – tell me my destination.

*

I understand your anguish, but I cannot help you,
I approach, hear, behold – the sad mouth, the look
    out of the eyes, your mute inquiry,
Whither I go from the bed I now recline on, come tell me;

Old age, alarmed, uncertain – A young woman's voice
  appealing to me, for comfort,
A young man's voice, *Shall I not escape?*

*

A thousand perfect men and women appear,
20 Around each gathers a cluster of friends, and gay
      children and youths, with offerings.

*

A mask – a perpetual natural disguiser of herself,
Concealing her face, concealing her form,
Changes and transformations every hour, every moment,
Falling upon her even when she sleeps.

*

One sweeps by, attended by an immense train,
All emblematic of peace – not a soldier or menial among
  them.

*

One sweeps by, old, with black eyes, and profuse white hair,
He has the simple magnificence of health and strength,
His face strikes as with flashes of lightning whoever it turns
  toward.

*

30 Three old men slowly pass, followed by three others, and
      they by three others,
They are beautiful – the one in the middle of each
  group holds his companions by the hand,
As they walk, they give out perfume wherever they walk.

*

Women sit, or move to and fro – some old, some young,
The young are beautiful – but the old are more beautiful
  than the young.

*

What weeping face is that looking from the window?
Why does it stream those sorrowful tears?
Is it for some burial place, vast and dry?
Is it to wet the soil of graves?

*

I will take an egg out of the robin's nest in the orchard,
40   I will take a branch of gooseberries from the old bush
        in the garden, and go and preach to the world;
You shall see I will not meet a single heretic or scorner,
You shall see how I stump clergymen, and confound them,
You shall see me showing a scarlet tomato, and a
        white pebble from the beach.

*

Behaviour – fresh, native, copious, each one for himself or
        herself,
Nature and the Soul expressed – America and freedom
        expressed – In it the finest art,
In it pride, cleanliness, sympathy, to have their chance,
In it physique, intellect, faith – in it just as much as to
        manage an army or a city, or to write a book – perhaps
        more,
The youth, the laboring person, the poor person, rivalling
        all the rest – perhaps outdoing the rest,
The effects of the universe no greater than its;
50   For there is nothing in the whole universe that can be more
        effective than a man's or woman's daily behaviour can be,
In any position, in any one of These States.

*

Not the pilot has charged himself to bring his ship into
        port, though beaten back, and many times baffled,
Not the path-finder, penetrating inland, weary and long,
By deserts parched, snows chilled, rivers wet, perseveres till
        he reaches his destination,

More than I have charged myself, heeded or unheeded, to
    compose a free march for These States,
To be exhilarating music to them, years, centuries hence.

        *

I thought I was not alone, walking here by the shore,
But the one I thought was with me, as now I walk by the
    shore,
As I lean and look through the glimmering light –
    that one has utterly disappeared,
60   And those appear that perplex me.

[States!]

States!
Were you looking to be held together by the lawyers?
By an agreement on paper? Or by arms?

Away!
I arrive, bringing these, beyond all the forces of courts and
    arms,
These! to hold you together as firmly as the earth itself is
    held together.

The old breath of life, ever new,
Here! I pass it by contact to you, America.

O mother! have you done much for me?
10   Behold, there shall from me be much done for you.

There shall from me be a new friendship – It shall be called
    after my name,
It shall circulate through The States, indifferent of place,
It shall twist and intertwist them through and around each
    other – Compact shall they be, showing new signs,
Affection shall solve every one of the problems of freedom,
Those who love each other shall be invincible,
They shall finally make America completely victorious,
    in my name.

One from Massachusetts shall be a comrade to a Missourian,
One from Maine or Vermont, and a Carolinian and an
    Oregonese, shall be friends triune, more precious to each
    other than all the riches of the earth.
To Michigan shall be wafted perfume from Florida,
20 To the Mannahatta from Cuba or Mexico,
Not the perfume of flowers, but sweeter, and wafted
    beyond death.

No danger shall balk Columbia's lovers,
If need be, a thousand shall sternly immolate themselves
    for one,
The Kanuck shall be willing to lay down his life for the
    Kansian, and the Kansian for the Kanuck, on due need.

It shall be customary in all directions, in the houses and
    streets, to see manly affection,
The departing brother or friend shall salute the remaining
    brother or friend with a kiss.

There shall be innovations,
There shall be countless linked hands – namely, the
    Northeasterner's, and the Northwesterner's, and the
    Southwesterners', and those of the interior, and all their
    brood,
These shall be masters of the world under a new power,
30 They shall laugh to scorn the attacks of all the remainder
    of the world.

The most dauntless and rude shall touch face to face
    lightly,
The dependence of Liberty shall be lovers,
The continuance of Equality shall be comrades.

These shall tie and band stronger than hoops of iron,
I, extatic, O partners! O lands! henceforth with the love of
    lovers tie you.

I will make the continent indissoluble,
I will make the most splendid race the sun ever yet shone
    upon,
I will make divine magnetic lands.

I will plant companionship thick as trees along all the rivers
    of America, and along the shores of the great lakes, and
    all over the prairies,
40 I will make inseparable cities, with their arms about each
    other's necks.

For you these, from me, O Democracy, to serve you,
    ma femme!
For you! for you, I am trilling these songs.

Bathed In War's Perfume

Bathed in war's perfume – delicate flag!
(Should the days needing armies, needing fleets, come
    again,)
O to hear you call the sailors and the soldiers! flag like a
    beautiful woman!
O to hear the tramp, tramp, of a million answering men!
    O the ships they arm with joy!
O to see you leap and beckon from the tall masts of ships!
O to see you peering down on the sailors on the decks!
Flag like the eyes of women.

Solid, Ironical, Rolling Orb

Solid, ironical, rolling orb!
Master of all, the matter of fact! – at last I accept your
    terms;
Bringing to practical, vulgar tests, of all my ideal dreams,
And of me, as lover and hero.

Not My Enemies Ever Invade Me

Not my enemies ever invade me – no harm to my pride from
  them I fear;
But the lovers I recklessly love – lo! how they master me!
Lo! me, ever open and helpless, bereft of my strength!
Utterly abject, grovelling on the ground before them.

This Day, O Soul

This day, O Soul, I give you a wondrous mirror;
Long in the dark, in tarnish and cloud it lay – But the
  cloud has pass'd, and the tarnish gone;
... Behold, O Soul! it is now a clean and bright mirror,
Faithfully showing you all the things of the world.

Ashes of Soldiers: Epigraph

Again a verse for sake of you,
You soldiers in the ranks – you Volunteers,
Who bravely fighting, silent fell,
To fill unmention'd graves.

One Song, America, Before I Go

One song, America, before I go,
I'd sing, o'er all the rest, with trumpet sound,
For thee – the Future.

I'd sow a seed for thee of endless Nationality;
I'd fashion thy Ensemble, including Body and Soul;
I'd show, away ahead, thy real Union, and how it may be
  accomplish'd.

(The paths to the House I seek to make,
But leave to those to come, the House itself.)

Belief I sing – and Preparation;
10 As Life and Nature are not great with reference to the
      Present only,
   But greater still from what is yet to come,
   Out of that formula for Thee I sing.

Souvenirs of Democracy

The business man, the acquirer vast,
After assiduous years, surveying results, preparing for
   departure,
Devises houses and lands to his children – bequeaths
   stocks, goods – funds for a school or hospital,
Leaves money to certain companions to buy tokens,
   souvenirs of gems and gold;
Parceling out with care – And then, to prevent all cavil,
His name to his testament formally signs.

But I, my life surveying,
With nothing to show, to devise, from its idle years,
Nor houses, nor lands – nor tokens of gems or gold for my
   friends,
10 Only these Souvenirs of Democracy – In them – in
      all my songs – behind me leaving,
   To You, whoever you are, (bathing, leavening this leaf
      especially with my breath – pressing on it a moment
      with my own hands; –
   Here! feel how the pulse beats in my wrists! – how my
      heart's-blood is swelling, contracting!)
   I will You, in all, Myself, with promise to never desert you,
   To which I sign my name,

Walt Whitman

From My Last Years

From my last years, last thoughts I here bequeath,
Scatter'd and dropt, in seeds, and wafted to the West,
Through moisture of Ohio, prairie soil of Illinois – through
    Colorado, California air,
For Time to germinate fully.

In Former Songs

1
In former songs Pride have I sung, and Love, and
    passionate, joyful Life,
But here I twine the strands of Patriotism and Death.

And now, Life, Pride, Love, Patriotism and Death,
To you, O FREEDOM, purport of all!
(You that elude me most – refusing to be caught in songs
    of mine,)
I offer all to you.

2
'Tis not for nothing, Death,
I sound out you, and words of you, with daring tone –
    embodying you,
In my new Democratic chants – keeping you for a close,
10 For a last impregnable retreat – a citadel and tower,
For my last stand – my pealing, final cry.

The Beauty of the Ship

When, staunchly entering port,
After long ventures, hauling up, worn and old,
Batter'd by sea and wind, torn by many a fight,
With the original sails all gone, replaced, or mended,
I only saw, at last, the beauty of the Ship.

After an Interval

(NOV. 22, 1875, MIDNIGHT – SATURN
AND MARS IN CONJUNCTION)

After an interval, reading, here in the midnight,
With the great stars looking on – all the stars of Orion
    looking,
And the silent Pleiades – and the duo looking of Saturn and
    ruddy Mars;
Pondering, reading my own songs, after a long interval,
    (sorrow and death familiar now,)
Ere closing the book, what pride! what joy! to find them,
Standing so well the test of death and night!
And the duo of Saturn and Mars!

Two Rivulets

Two Rivulets side by side,
Two blended, parallel, strolling tides,
Companions, travelers, gossiping as they journey.

For the Eternal Ocean bound,
These ripples, passing surges, streams of Death and Life,
Object and Subject hurrying, whirling by,
The Real and Ideal,

Alternate ebb and flow the Days and Nights,
(Strands of a Trio twining, Present, Future, Past.)

10 In You, who'er you are, my book perusing;
In I myself – in all the World – these ripples flow,
All, all, toward the mystic Ocean tending.

(O yearnful waves! the kisses of your lips!
Your breast so broad, with open arms, O firm,
    expanded shore!)

Or, from That Sea of Time

1

Or, from that Sea of Time,
Spray, blown by the wind – a double windrow-drift of weeds
    and shells;
(O little shells, so curious-convolute! so limpid-cold and
    voiceless!
Yet will you not, to the tympans of temples held,
Murmurs and echoes still bring up – Eternity's music, faint
    and far,
Wafted inland, sent from Atlantica's rim – strains for the
    Soul of the Prairies,

Whisper'd reverberations – chords for the ear of the West,
    joyously sounding
Your tidings old, yet ever new and untranslatable;)
Infinitesimals out of my life, and many a life,
10 (For not my life and years alone I give – all, all I give;)
These thoughts and Songs – waifs from the deep – here,
    cast high and dry,
Wash'd on America's shores.

2

Currents of starting a Continent new,
Overtures sent to the solid out of the liquid,
Fusion of ocean and land – tender and pensive waves,
(Not safe and peaceful only – waves rous'd and ominous too,
Out of the depths, the storm's abysms – Who knows
    whence? Death's waves,
Raging over the vast, with many a broken spar and
    tatter'd sail.)

As in a Swoon

As in a swoon, one instant,
Another sun, ineffable, full-dazzles me,
And all the orbs I knew – and brighter, unknown orbs;
One instant of the future land, Heaven's land.

Lessons

There are who teach only the sweet lessons of peace and
    safety;
But I teach lessons of war and death to those I love,
That they readily meet invasions, when they come.

[Last Droplets]

Last droplets of and after spontaneous rain,
From many limpid distillations and past showers;
(Will they germinate anything? mere exhalations as they
    all are – the land's and sea's – America's;
Will they filter to any deep emotion? any heart and brain?)

Ship Ahoy!

In dreams I was a ship, and sail'd the boundless seas,
Sailing and ever sailing – all seas and into every port, or
    out upon the offing,
Saluting, cheerily hailing each mate, met or pass'd, little
    or big,
'Ship ahoy!' thro' trumpet or by voice – if nothing more,
    some friendly merry word at least,
For companionship and good will for ever to all and each.

For Queen Victoria's Birthday
(AN AMERICAN ARBUTUS BUNCH TO BE PUT IN
A LITTLE VASE ON THE ROYAL BREAKFAST TABLE,
MAY 24TH, 1890)

Lady, accept a birth-day thought – haply an idle gift
    and token,
Right from the scented soil's May-utterance here,
(Smelling of countless blessings, prayers, and old-time
    thanks,)[1]
A bunch of white and pink arbutus, silent, spicy, shy,
From Hudson's, Delaware's, or Potomac's woody banks.

1. NOTE: very little, as we Americans stand this day, with our sixty-five
or seventy millions of population, an immense surplus in the treasury,
and all that actual power or reserve power (land and sea) so dear to
nations – very little I say do we realize that curious crawling national
shudder when the 'Trent affair' promis'd to bring upon us a war with
Great Britain – follow'd unquestionably, as that war would have, by
recognition of the Southern Confederacy from all the leading European
nations. It is now certain that all this then inevitable train of calamity
hung on arrogant and peremptory phrases in the prepared and written
missive of the British Minister, to America, which the Queen (and
Prince Albert latent) positively and promptly cancell'd; and which her
firm attitude did alone actually erase and leave out, against all the
other official prestige and Court of St James's. On such minor and
personal incidents (so to call them,) often depend the great growths
and turns of civilization. This moment of a woman and a queen
surely swung the grandest oscillation of modern history's pendulum.
Many sayings and doings of that period, from foreign potentates and
powers, might well be dropt in oblivion by America – but never *this*,
if I could have my way.
w.w.

L of G

Thoughts, suggestions, aspirations, pictures,
Cities and farms – by day and night – book of peace and war,
Of platitudes and the commonplace.

For out-door health, the land and sea – for good will,
For America – for all the earth, all nations, the common
    people,
(Not of one nation only – not America only.)

In it each claim, ideal, line, by all lines, claims, ideals
    temper'd;
Each right and wish by other wishes, rights.

After the Argument

A group of little children with their ways and chatter
    flow in,
Like welcome, rippling water o'er my heated nerves and
    flesh.

For Us Two, Reader Dear

Simple, spontaneous, curious, two souls interchanging,
With the original testimony for us continued to the last.

APPENDIX 3
Early Poems

Our Future Lot

This breast which now alternate burns
   With flashing hope, and gloomy fear,
Where beats a heart that knows the hue
   Which aching bosoms wear;

This curious frame of human mold,
   Where craving wants unceasing play –
The troubled heart and wondrous form
   Must both alike decay.

The cold wet earth will close around
10   Dull senseless limbs, and ashy face,
But where, O Nature! where will be
   My mind's abiding place?

Will it ev'n live? For though its light
   Must shine till from the body torn;
Then, when the oil of life is spent,
   Still shall the taper burn?

O, powerless is this struggling brain
   To pierce the mighty mystery;
In dark, uncertain awe it waits,
20   The common doom – to die!

    *

Mortal! and can thy swelling soul
   Live with the thought that all its life
Is centered in this earthy cage
   Of care, and tears, and strife?

Not so; that sorrowing heart of thine
   Ere long will find a house of rest;
Thy form, re-purified, shall rise,
   In robes of beauty drest.

The flickering taper's glow shall change
30   To bright and starlike majesty,
Radiant with pure and piercing light
   From the Eternal's eye!

Young Grimes

When old Grimes died, he left a son –
    The graft of worthy stock;
In deed and word he shows himself
    A chip of the old block.

In youth, 'tis said, he liked not school –
    Of tasks he was no lover;
He wrote sums in a ciphering book,
    Which had a pasteboard cover.

Young Grimes ne'er went to see the girls
10   Before he was fourteen;
Nor smoked, nor swore, for that he knew
    Gave Mrs Grimes much pain.

He never was extravagant
    In pleasure, dress, or board;
His Sunday suit was of blue cloth,
    At six and eight a yard.

But still there is, to tell the truth,
    No stinginess in him;
And in July he wears an old
20   Straw hat with a broad brim.

No devotee in fashion's train
    Is good old Grimes's son;
He sports no cane – no whiskers wears,
    Nor lounges o'er the town.

He does not spend more than he earns
    In dissipation's round;
But shuns with care those dangerous rooms
    Where sin and vice abound.

It now is eight and twenty years
30   Since young Grimes saw the light;
And no house in the land can show
    A fairer, prouder sight.

For there his wife, prudent and chaste,
   His mother's age made sweet,
His children trained in virtue's path,
   The gazer's eye will meet.

Upon a hill, just off the road
   That winds the village side,
His farm house stands, within whose door
40   Ne'er entered Hate or Pride.

But Plenty and Benevolence
   And Happiness are there –
And underneath that lowly roof
   Content smiles calm and fair.

Reader, go view the cheerful scene –
   By it how poor must prove
The pomp, and tinsel, and parade,
   Which pleasure's followers love.

Leave the wide city's noisy din –
50   The busy haunts of men –
And here enjoy a tranquil life,
   Unvexed by guilt or pain.

Fame's Vanity

O, many a panting, noble heart
   Cherishes in its deep recess
Th' hope to win renown o'er earth
   From Glory's priz'd caress.

And some will reach that envied goal,
   And have their fame known far and wide;
And some will sink unnoted down
   In dark Oblivion's tide.

But I, who many a pleasant scheme
10   Do sometimes cull from Fancy's store,
With dreams, such as the youthful dream,
    Of grandeur, love, and power –

Shall I build up a lofty name,
    And seek to have the nations know
What conscious might dwells in the brain
    That throbs aneath this brow?

And have thick countless ranks of men
    Fix upon *me* their reverent gaze,
And listen to the deafening shouts,
20   To *me* that thousands raise?

Thou foolish soul! the very place
    That pride has made for folly's rest;
What thoughts with vanity all rife,
    Fill up this heaving breast!

Fame, O what happiness is lost
    In hot pursuit of thy false glare!
Thou, whose drunk votaries die to gain
    A puff of viewless air.

So, never let me more repine,
30   Though I live on obscure, unknown,
Though after death unsought may be
    My markless resting stone.

For mighty one and lowly wretch,
    Dull, idiot mind, or teeming sense
Must sleep on the same earthy couch,
    A hundred seasons hence.

My Departure

Not in a gorgeous hall of pride,
   Mid tears of grief and friendship's sigh,
Would I, when the last hour has come,
   Shake off this crumbling flesh and die.

My bed I would not care to have
   With rich and costly stuffs hung round;
Nor watched with an officious zeal,
   To keep away each jarring sound.

Amidst the thunder crash of war,
10   Where hovers Death's ensanguined cloud,
And bright swords flash, and banners fly,
   Above the sickening sight of blood.

Not there – not there, would I lay down
   To sleep with all the firm and brave;
For death in such a scene of strife,
   Is not the death that I do crave.

But when the time for my last look
   Upon this glorious earth should come,
I'd wish the season warm and mild,
20   The sun to shine, and flowers bloom.

Just ere the closing of the day,
   My dying couch I then would have
Borne out in the refreshing air,
   Where sweet shrubs grow and proud trees wave

The still repose would calm my mind,
   And lofty branches overhead,
Would throw around this grassy bank,
   A cooling and a lovely shade.

At distance through the opening trees,
30   A bay by misty vapours curled,
I'd gaze upon, and think the haven
   For which to leave this fleeting world.

To the wide winds I'd yield my soul
   And die there in that pleasant place,
Looking on water, sun, and hill,
   As on their Maker's very face.

I'd want no human being near;
   But at the setting of the sun,
I'd bid adieu to earth, and step
40   Down to the Unknown World – alone.

The Death of the Nature-Lover

Not in a gorgeous hall of pride
   Where tears fall thick, and loved ones sigh,
Wished he, when the dark hour approached
   To drop his veil of flesh, and die.

Amid the thundercrash of strife,
   Where hovers War's ensanguined cloud,
And bright swords flash and banners fly
   Above the wounds, and groans, and blood.

Not there – not there! Death's look he'd cast
10   Around a furious tiger's den.
Rather than in the monstrous sight
   Of the red butcheries of men.

Days speed: the time for that last look
   Upon this glorious earth has come:
The Power he served so well vouchsafes
   The sun to shine, the flowers to bloom.

Just ere the closing of the day,
   His fainting limbs he needs will have
Borne out into the fresh free air,
20   Where sweet shrubs grow, and proud trees wave.

At distance, o'er the pleasant fields,
    A bay by misty vapors curled,
He gazes on, and thinks the haven
    For which to leave a grosser world.

He sorrows not, but smiles content,
    Dying there in that fragrant place,
Gazing on blossom, field, and bay,
    As on their Maker's very face.

The cloud-arch bending overhead,
30   There, at the setting of the sun
He bids adieu to earth, and steps
    Down to the World Unknown.

The Inca's Daughter

Before the dark-brow'd sons of Spain,
    A captive Indian maiden stood;
Imprison'd where the moon before
    Her race as princes trod.

The rack had riven her frame that day –
    But not a sigh or murmur broke
Forth from her breast; calmly she stood,
    And sternly thus she spoke:

'The glory of Peru is gone;
10   Her proudest warriors in the fight –
Her armies, and her Inca's power
    Bend to the Spaniard's might.

And I – a Daughter of the Sun –
    Shall I ingloriously still live?
Shall a Peruvian monarch's child
    Become the white lord's slave?

No: I'd not meet my father's frown
  In the free spirit's place of rest,
Nor seem a stranger midst the bands
20   Whom Manitou has blest.'

Her snake-like eye, her cheek of fire,
  Glowed with intenser, deeper hue;
She smiled in scorn, and from her robe
  A poisoned arrow drew.

'Now, paleface see! the Indian girl
  Can teach thee how to bravely die:
Hail! spirits of my kindred slain,
  A sister ghost is nigh!'

Her hand was clenched and lifted high –
30   Each breath, and pulse, and limb was still'd;
An instant more the arrow fell:
  Thus died the Inca's child.

The Love That Is Hereafter

O, beauteous is the earth! and fair
The splendors of Creation are:
Nature's green robe, the shining sky,
The winds that through the tree-tops sigh,
  All speak a bounteous God.

The noble trees, the sweet young flowers,
The birds that sing in forest bowers,
The rivers grand that murmuring roll,
And all which joys or calms the soul
10   Are made by gracious might.

The flocks and droves happy and free,
The dwellers of the boundless sea,
Each living thing on air or land,
Created by our Master's hand,
  Is formed for joy and peace.

But man – weak, proud, and erring man,
Of truth ashamed, of folly vain –
Seems singled out to know no rest
And of all things that move, feels least
20   The sweets of happiness.

Yet he it is whose little life
Is passed in useless, vexing strife,
And all the glorious earth to him
Is rendered dull, and poor, and dim,
From hope unsatisfied.

He faints with grief – he toils through care –
And from the cradle to the bier
He wearily plods on – till Death
Cuts short his transient, panting breath,
30   And sends him to his sleep.

O, mighty powers of Destiny!
When from this coil of flesh I'm free –
When through my second life I rove,
Let me but find *one* heart to love,
As I would wish to love:

Let me but meet a single breast,
Where this tired soul its hope may rest,
In never-dying faith: ah, then,
That would be bliss all free from pain,
40   And sickness of the heart.

For vainly through this world below
We seek affection. Nought but wo
Is with our earthly journey wove;
And so the heart must look above,
Or die in dull despair.

We All Shall Rest at Last

On earth are many sights of woe,
  And many sounds of agony,
And many a sorrow-withered cheek,
  And many a pain-dulled eye.

The wretched weep, the poor complain,
  And luckless love pines on unknown,
And faintly from the midnight couch
  Sounds out the sick child's moan.

Each has his care: old age fears death;
10   The young man's ills are pride, desire,
And heart-sickness, and in his breast
  The heat of passion's fire.

All, all know grief; and at the close,
  All lie earth's spreading arms within,
The pure, the black-souled, proud and low,
  Virtue, despair, and sin.

O, foolish, then, with pain to shrink
  From the sure doom we each must meet.
Is earth so fair or heaven so dark?
20   Or life so passing sweet?

No: dread ye not the fearful hour;
  The coffin, and the pall's dark gloom;
For there's a calm to throbbing hearts,
  And rest, down in the tomb.

Then our long journey will be o'er,
  And throwing off this load of woes,
The pallid brow, the feebled limbs,
  Will sink in soft repose.

Not only this; for wise men say
30   That when we leave our land of care,
We float to a mysterious shore,
  Peaceful, and pure, and fair.

So, welcome, death; whene'er the time
  That the dread summons must be met,
I'll yield without one pang of awe,
  Or sigh, or vain regret;

But like unto a wearied child,
  That over field and wood all day
Has ranged and struggled, and at last,
40   Worn out with toil and play –

Goes up at evening to his home,
  And throws him, sleepy, tired, and sore,
Upon his bed, and rests him there,
  His pain and trouble o'er.

The Spanish Lady

On a low couch reclining,
  When slowly waned the day,
Wrapt in gentle slumber,
  A Spanish maiden lay.

O beauteous was that lady;
  And the splendour of the place
Matched well her form so graceful,
  And her sweet, angelic face.

But what doth she lonely,
10   Who ought in courts to reign?
For the form that there lies sleeping
  Owns the proudest name in Spain.

Tis the lovely Lady Inez.
  De Castro's daughter fair,
Who in the castle chamber,
  Slumbers so sweetly there.

O, better had she laid her
   Mid the couches of the dead;
O better had she slumbered
20   Where the poisonous snake lay hid.

For worse than deadly serpent,
   Or mouldering skeleton,
Are the fierce bloody hands of men,
   By hate and fear urged on.

O Lady Inez, pleasant
   Be the thoughts that now have birth
In thy visions; they are last of all
   That thou shalt dream on earth.

Now noiseless on its hinges
30   Opens the chamber door,
And one whose trade is blood and crime
   Steals slow across the floor.

High gleams the assassin's dagger;
   And by the road that it has riven,
The soul of that fair lady
   Has passed from earth to heaven.

The End of All

Behold around us pomp and pride;
   The rich, the lofty, and the gay,
Glitter before our dazzled eyes,
   Live out their brief but brilliant day;
Then when the hour for fame is o'er,
    Unheeded pass away.

The warrior builds a mighty name,
   The object of his hopes and fears,
That future times may see it where
10   Her tower aspiring glory rears.
Desist, O fool! Think what thou'lt be
    In a few fleeting years.

The statesman's sleepless plodding brain
   Schemes out a nation's destiny;
His is the voice that awes the crowd,
   And his the bold, commanding eye.
But transient is his high renown;
    He, like the rest, must die.

Beside his ponderous, age-worn book,
20   A student shades his weary brow;
He walks philosophy's dark path,
   A journey difficult and slow:
But vain is all that teeming mind,
    He, too, to earth must go.

And beauty, sweet, and all the fair
   That sail on fortune's sunniest wave,
The poor, with him of countless gold,
   Owner of all that mortals crave,
Alike are fated soon to lie
30   Down in the silent grave.

Why, then, O, insects of an hour!
   Why, then, with struggling toil, contend
For honors you so soon must yield,
   When Death shall his stern summons send?
For honor, glory, fortune, wit,
    This is, to all, the end.

Think not, when you attain your wish,
    Content will banish grief and care!
High though you stand, though round you thrown
40   The robes that rank and splendor wear,
A secret poison in the heart
      Will stick and rankle there.

In night go view the solemn stars,
    Ever in majesty the same;
Creation's worlds: how poor must seem
    The mightiest honors earth can name;
And, most of all, this silly strife
      After the bubble, fame!

The Columbian's Song

What a fair and happy place
    Is the one where Freedom lives,
And the knowledge that our arm is strong,
    A haughty bearing gives!
For each sun that gilds the east,
When at dawn it first doth rise,
      Sets at night,
      Red and bright,
On a people where the prize
10 Which millions in the battle fight
Have sought with hope forlorn,
      Grows brighter every hour,
      In strength, and grace, and power,
    And the sun this land doth leave
    Mightier at filmy eve,
Than when it first arose, in the morn.

Beat the sounding note of joy!
    Let it echo o'er the hills,
Till shore and forest hear the pride,
20   That a bondless bosom fills.
And on the plain where patriot sires

Rest underneath the sod,
Where the stern resolve for liberty
  Was writ in gushing blood,
    Freeman go,
    With upright brow,
And render thanks to God.

O, my soul is drunk with joy,
  And my inmost heart is glad,
30 To think my country's star will not
  Through endless ages fade,
That on its upward glorious course
  Our red eyed eagle leaps,
While with the ever moving winds,
  Our dawn-striped banner sweeps:
That here at length is found
  A wide extending shore,
Where Freedom's starry gleam,
  Shines with unvarying beam;
40   Not as it did of yore,
With flickering flash, when CAESAR fell,
Or haughty GESLER heard his knell,
  Or STUART rolled in gore.

Nor let our foes presume
  That this heart-prized union band,
Will e'er be served by the stroke
  Of a fraternal hand.
Though parties sometimes rage,
  And Faction rears its form.
50 Its jealous eye, its scheming brain,
  To revel in the storm:
Yet should a danger threaten,
  Or enemy draw nigh,
Then scattered to the winds of heaven,
  All civil strife would fly;
And north and south, and east and west,
  Would rally at the cry –

'Brethren arise! to battle come,
For Truth, for Freedom, and for Home,
60   And for our Fathers' Memory!'

The Punishment of Pride

Once on his star-gemmed, dazzling throne,
Sat an all bright and lofty One,
    Unto whom God had given
To be the mightiest Angel-Lord
    Within the range of Heaven;
With power of knowing things to come,
To judge o'er man, and speak his doom.

O, he was pure! the fleecy snow,
Falling through air to earth below,
10   Was not more undefiled:
Sinless he was as the wreathed smile
    On lip of sleeping child.
Haply, more like the snow was he,
Freezing – with all its purity.

Upon his forehead beamed a star,
Bright as the lamps of even are;
    And his pale robe was worn
About him with a look of pride,
    A high, majestic scorn,
20 Which showed he felt his glorious might,
His favor with the Lord of Light.

Years, thus he swayed the things of earth –
O'er human crime and human worth –
    Haughty, and high, and stern;
Nor ever, at sweet Mercy's call,
    His white neck would he turn;
But listening not to frailty's plea,
Launched forth each just yet stern decree.

At last, our Father who above
30 Sits throned with Might, and Truth, and Love,
     And knows our weakness blind,
Behind him – proud, and pitying not
     The errors of mankind;
And doomed him, for a punishment,
To be forth from his birth-place sent.

So down this angel from on high
Came from his sphere, to live and die
     As mortal men have done;
That he might know the tempting snares
40   Which lure each human son;
And dwell as all on earth have dwelt.
And feel the grief we all have felt.

Then he knew Guilt, while round him weaved
Their spells, pale Sickness, Love deceived,
     And Fear, and Hate, and Wrath;
And all the blighting ills of Fate
     Were cast athwart his path:
He stood upon the grave's dread brink,
And felt his soul with terror sink.

50 He learned why men to sin give way,
And how we live our passing day
     In indolence and crime;
But yet his eye with awe looked on,
     To see in all its prime
That godlike thing, the human mind,
A gem in black decay enshrined.

Long years in penance thus he spent,
Until the Mighty Parent sent
     His loveliest messenger –
60 Who came with step so noiselessly,
     And features passing fair;
Death was his name; the angel heard
The call, and swift to heaven he soared.

There in his former glory placed,
The star again his forehead graced;
   But never more that brow
Was lifted up in scorn of sin;
   His wings were folded now –
But not in pride: his port, though high,
70 No more spoke conscious majesty.

And O, what double light now shone
About that pure and heavenly one;
   For in the clouds which made
The veil around his seat of power,
   In silvery robes arrayed,
Hovered the seraph Charity,
And Pity with her melting eye.

Ambition

One day, an obscure youth, a wanderer,
Known but to few, lay musing with himself
About the chances of his future life.
In that youth's heart, there dwelt the coal Ambition,
Burning and glowing; and he asked himself,
'Shall I, in time to come, be great and famed?'
Now soon an answer wild and mystical
Seemed to sound forth from out the depths of air;
And to the gazer's eye appeared a shape
10 Like one as of a cloud – and thus it spoke:

'O, many a panting, noble heart
   Cherishes in its deep recess
The hope to win renown o'er earth
   From Glory's prized caress.

And some will win that envied goal,
   And have their deeds known far and wide;
And some – by far the most – will sink
   Down in oblivion's tide.

But *thou*, who visions bright dost cull
20   From the imagination's store,
With dreams, such as the youthful dream
   Of grandeur, love, and power,

Fanciest that thou shalt build a name
   And come to have the nations know
What conscious might dwells in the brain
   That throbs beneath that brow?

And see thick countless ranks of men
   Fix upon *thee* their reverent gaze –
And listen to the plaudits loud
30   To *thee* that thousands raise?

Weak, childish soul! the very place
   That pride has made for folly's rest;
What thoughts, with vanity all rife,
   Fill up thy heaving breast!

At night, go view the solemn stars
   Those wheeling worlds through time the same –
How puny seem the widest power,
   The proudest mortal name!

Think too, that all, lowly and rich,
40   Dull idiot mind and teeming sense,
Alike must sleep the endless sleep,
   A hundred seasons hence.

So, frail one, never more repine,
   Though thou livest on obscure, unknown;
Though after death unsought may be
   Thy markless resting stone.'

And as these accents dropped in the youth's ears,
He felt him sick at heart; for many a month
His fancy had amused and charmed itself
50   With lofty aspirations, visions fair
Of what he *might be*. And it pierced him sore
To have his airy castles thus dashed down.

The Death and Burial of McDonald Clarke
A PARODY

Not a sigh was heard, not a tear was shed,
   As away to the 'tombs' he was hurried,
No mother or friend held his dying head,
   Or wept when the poet was buried.

They buried him lonely; no friend stood near,
   (The scoffs of the multitude spurning,)
To weep o'er the poet's sacred bier;
   No bosom with anguish was burning.

No polish'd coffin enclosed his breast,
10   Nor in purple or linen they wound him,
As a stranger he died; he went to his rest
   With cold charity's shroud wrapt 'round him.

Few and cold were the prayers they said,
   Cold and dry was the cheek of sadness,
Not a tear of grief baptised his head,
   Nor of sympathy pardon'd his madness.

None thought, as they stood by his lowly bed,
   Of the griefs and pains that craz'd him;
None thought of the sorrow that turn'd his head,
20   Of the vileness of those who prais'd him.

Lightly they speak of his anguish and woe,
   And o'er his cold ashes upbraid him,
By whatever he was that was evil below,
   Unkindness and *cruelty* made him.

Ye hypocrites! stain not his grave with a tear,
   Nor blast the fresh planted willow
That weeps o'er his grave; for while he was there,
   Ye refused him a crumb and a pillow.

Darkly and sadly his spirit has fled,
30   But his name will long linger in story;
He needs not a stone to hallow his bed;
    He's in Heaven, encircled with glory.

Time to Come

O, Death! a black and pierceless pall
    Hangs round thee, and the future state;
No eye may see, no mind may grasp
    That mystery of Fate.

This brain, which now alternate throbs
    With swelling hope and gloomy fear;
This heart, with all the changing hues,
    That mortal passions bear –

This curious frame of human mould,
10   Where unrequited cravings play,
This brain, and heart, and wondrous form
    Must all alike decay.

The leaping blood will stop its flow;
    The hoarse death-struggle pass; the cheek
Lay bloomless, and the liquid tongue
    Will then forget to speak.

The grave will tame me; earth will close
    O'er cold dull limbs and ashy face;
But where, O, Nature, where shall be
20   The soul's abiding place?

Will it e'en live? for though its light
    Must shine till from the body torn;
Then, when the oil of life is spent,
    Still shall the taper burn?

O, powerless is this struggling brain
  To rend the mighty mystery;
In dark, uncertain awe it waits
  The common doom, to die.

The Play-Ground

When painfully athwart my brain
  Dark thoughts come crowding on,
And, sick of worldly hollowness,
  My heart feels sad or lone –

Then out upon the green I walk,
  Just ere the close of day,
And swift I ween the sight I view
  Clears all my gloom away.

For there I see young children –
10 The cheeriest thing on earth –
I see them play – I hear their tones
  Of loud and reckless mirth.

And many a clear and flute-like laugh
  Comes ringing through the air;
And many a roguish, flashing eye,
  And rich red cheek, are there.

O, lovely, happy children!
  I am with you in my soul;
I shout – I strike the ball with you –
20 With you I race and roll. –

Methinks white-winged angels,
  Floating unseen the while,
Hover around this village green,
  And pleasantly they smile.

O, angels! guard these children!
   Keep grief and guilt away:
From earthly harm – from evil thoughts
   O, shield them night and day!

Ode

TO BE SUNG ON FORT GREENE;
4TH OF JULY, 1846
TUNE *The Star Spangled Banner*

I

O, God of Columbia! O, Shield of the Free!
   More grateful to you than the fanes of old story,
Must the blood-bedewed soil, the red battle-ground, be
   Where our fore-fathers championed America's glory!

Then how priceless the worth of the sanctified earth,
We are standing on now. Lo! the slopes of its girth
Where the Martyrs were buried: Nor prayers, tears, or
     stones,
Mark their crumbled-in coffins, their white, holy bones!

2

Say! sons of Long-Island! in legend or song,
10   Keep ye aught of its record, that day dark and cheerless –
That cruel of days – when, hope weak, the foe strong,
   Was seen the Serene One – still faithful, still fearless,
Defending the worth, of the sanctified earth
We are standing on now, etc.

3

Ah, yes! be the answer. In memory still
   We have placed in our hearts, and embalmed there
     forever!
The battle, the prison-ship, martyrs and hill,
– O, may *it* be preserved till those hearts death shall sever!
For how priceless the worth, etc.

4

20 And shall not the years, as they sweep o'er and o'er
   Shall they not, even *here*, bring the children of ages –
To exult as their fathers exulted before,
   In the freedom achieved by our ancestral sages?
And the prayer rise to heaven, with pure gratitude given
And the sky by the thunder of cannon be riven?
Yea! yea! let the echo responsively roll
The echo that starts from the patriot's soul!

New Year's Day, 1848

A morning fair: A noontide dubious:
Then gathering clouds obscure the Sun:
Then rain in torrents falls, subsiding soon
Into a gentle dropping. By eve the sun
Sinks into a cloudless west; and a mild breeze
With pleasant motion stirs the atmosphere.
Next in the blue vault above do moon and stars
Vie in bright emulation to destroy the gloom of night.

Such was our New Year's Day, and eventide!
10 Was it not an index of each passing Year,
Within whose seasons circumstance and change
Ever with Hope and Happiness war?
One now superior: anon the other:
And as succeeds pleasure or pain or joy or sorrow,
Clouding the firmament of each heart,
Raindrops of melancholy dim the eyes,
To shortly dry, hiding the Past and Present
'Neath bright starry thoughts –
Suggestive of a Future aye serene.

20 Day of a coming year promising change,
Yet full of promises, we need but watch
And pray for guardianship to come
Over caprices and all foolish ways!
So shall bright sunshine in advancing days
And starry invitations lead to Heavenly praise.

The House of Friends
*And one shall say unto him, What are those wounds in
thy hands? Then he shall answer, Those with which I was
wounded in the house of my friends.*
Zachariah, xiii 6

If thou art balked, O Freedom,
The victory is not to thy manlier foes;
From the house of thy friends comes the death stab.

Vaunters of the Free,
Why do you strain your lungs off southward?
Why be going to Alabama?
Sweep first before your own door;
Stop this squalling and this scorn
Over the mote there in the distance;
10 Look well to your own eye, Massachusetts –
Yours, New-York and Pennsylvania;
– I would say yours too, Michigan,
But all the salve, all the surgery
Of the great wide world were powerless there.

Virginia, mother of greatness,
Blush not for being also mother of slaves.
You might have borne deeper slaves –
Doughfaces, Crawlers, Lice of Humanity –
Terrific screamers of Freedom,
20 Who roar and bawl, and get hot i' the face,
But, were they not incapable of august crime,
Would quench the hopes of ages for a drink –
Muck-worms, creeping flat on the ground,

A dollar dearer to them than Christ's blessing;
All loves, all hopes, less than the thought of gain;
In life walking in that as in a shroud:
Men whom the throes of heroes,
Great deeds at which the gods might stand appalled,
The shriek of a drowned world, the appeal of women,
30   The exulting laugh of untied empires,
Would touch them never in the heart,
But only in the pocket.

     Hot-headed Carolina,
Well may you curl your lip;
With all your bondsmen, bless the destiny
Which brings you no such breed as this.

     Arise, young North!
Our elder blood flows in the veins of cowards –
The gray-haired sneak, the blanched poltroon,
40   The feigned or real shiverer at tongues
That nursing babes need hardly cry the less for –
Are they to be our tokens always?
     Fight on, band braver than warriors,
Faithful and few as Spartans;
But fear not most the angriest, loudest malice –
Fear most the still and forked fang
That starts from the grass at your feet.

Resurgemus

Suddenly, out of its stale and drowsy air, the air of slaves,
Like lightning Europe le'pt forth,
Sombre, superb and terrible,
As Ahimoth, brother of Death.

God, 'twas delicious!
That brief, tight, glorious grip
Upon the throats of kings.

You liars paid to defile the People,
Mark you now:

10   Not for numberless agonies, murders, lusts,
For court thieving in its manifold mean forms,
Worming from his simplicity the poor man's wages;
For many a promise sworn by royal lips
And broken, and laughed at in the breaking;
Then, in their power, not for all these,
Did a blow fall in personal revenge,
Or a hair draggle in blood:
The People scorned the ferocity of kings.

But the sweetness of mercy brewed bitter destruction,
20   And frightened rulers come back:
Each comes in state, with his train,
Hangman, priest, and tax-gatherer,
Soldier, lawyer, and sycophant;
An appalling procession of locusts,
And the king struts grandly again.

Yet behind all, lo, a Shape
Vague as the night, draped interminably,
Head, front and form, in scarlet folds;
Whose face and eyes none may see,
30   Out of its robes only this,
The red robes, lifted by the arm,
One finger pointed high over the top,
Like the head of a snake appears.

Meanwhile, corpses lie in new-made graves,
Bloody corpses of young men;
The rope of the gibbet hangs heavily,
The bullets of tyrants are flying,
The creatures of power laugh aloud:
And all these things bear fruits, and they are good.

40   Those corpses of young men,
Those martyrs that hang from the gibbets,
Those hearts pierced by the grey lead,
Cold and motionless as they seem,

Live elsewhere with undying vitality;
They live in other young men, O, kings,
They live in brothers, again ready to defy you;
They were purified by death,
They were taught and exalted.

Not a grave of those slaughtered ones
50   But is growing its seed of freedom,
In its turn to bear seed,
Which the winds shall carry afar and resow,
And the rain nourish.

Not a disembodied spirit
Can the weapon of tyrants let loose,
But it shall stalk invisibly over the earth,
Whispering, counseling, cautioning.

Liberty, let others despair of thee,
But I will never despair of thee:
60   Is the house shut? Is the master away?
Nevertheless, be ready, be not weary of watching,
He will surely return; his messengers come anon.

The Mississippi at Midnight

How solemn! sweeping this dense black tide!
    No friendly lights i' the heaven o'er us;
A murky darkness on either side,
    And kindred darkness all before us!

Now, drawn near the shelving rim,
    Weird-like shadows suddenly rise;
Shapes of mist and phantoms dim
    Baffle the gazer's straining eyes.

River fiends, with malignant faces!
10   Wild and wide their arms are thrown,
As if to clutch in fatal embraces
    Him who sails their realms upon.

Then, by the trick of our own swift motion,
    Straight, tall giants, an army vast,
Rank by rank, like the waves of ocean,
    On the shore march stilly past.

How solemn! the river a trailing pall,
    Which takes, but never again gives back;
And moonless and starless the heavens' arch'd wall,
20   Responding an equal black!

Oh, tireless waters! like Life's quick dream,
    Onward and onward ever hurrying –
Like Death in this midnight hour you seem,
    Life in your chill drops greedily burying!

Song for Certain Congressmen

We are all docile Dough-Faces,
    They knead us with the fist,
They, the dashing southern lords,
    We labor as they list;
For them we speak – or hold our tongues,
    For them we turn and twist.

We join them in their howl against
    Free soil and 'abolition',
That firebrand – that assassin knife –
10   Which risk our land's condition,
And leave no peace of life to any
    Dough-Faced politician.

To put down 'agitation', now,
    We think the most judicious;
To damn all 'northern fanatics',
    Those 'traitors' black and vicious;
The 'reg'lar party usages'
    For us, and no 'new issues'.

Things have come to a pretty pass,
20   When a trifle small as this,
Moving and bartering nigger slaves,
   Can open an abyss,
With jaws a-gape, for 'the two great parties',
   A pretty thought, I wis!

Principle – freedom! – fiddlesticks!
   We know not where they're found.
Rights of the masses – progress! – bah!
   Words that tickle and sound;
But claiming to rule o'er 'practical men'
30   Is very different ground.

Beyond all such we know a term
   Charming to ears and eyes,
With it we'll stab young Freedom,
   And do it in disguise;
Speak soft, ye wily dough-faces –
   That term is 'compromise'.

And what if children, growing up,
   In future season read
The thing we do? and heart and tongue
40   Accurse us for the deed?
The future cannot touch us;
   The present gain we heed.

Then, all together, dough-faces!
   Let's stop the exciting clatter,
And pacify slave-breeding wrath
   By yielding all the matter;
For otherwise, as sure as guns,
   The union it will shatter.

Besides, to tell the honest truth
50   (For us an innovation,)
Keeping in with the slave power
        Is our personal salvation;
We've very little to expect
        From t' other part of the nation.

Besides it's plain at Washington
        Who likeliest wins the chase,
What earthly chance has 'free soil'
        For any good fat place?
While many a daw has feather'd his nest,
60   By his creamy and meek dough-face.

Take heart, then, sweet companions,
        Be steady, Scripture Dick!
Webster, Cooper, Walker,
        To your allegiance stick!
With Brooks, and Briggs and Phoenix,
        Stand up through thin and thick!

We do not ask a bold brave front;
        We never try that game;
'Twould bring the storm upon our heads,
70   A huge mad storm of shame;
Evade it, brothers – 'subterfuge'
        Will answer just the same.

Blood-Money
Guilty of the body and the blood of Christ

1

Of olden time, when it came to pass
That the beautiful god, Jesus, should finish his work on
        earth,
Then went Judas, and sold the divine youth,
And took pay for his body.

Curs'd was the deed, even before the sweat of the clutching
  hand grew dry;
And darkness frown'd upon the seller of a Son of God,
Where, as though earth lifted her breast to throw him
  from her, and heaven refused him,
He hung in the air, self-slaughter'd.

The cycles, with their long shadows, have stalk'd silently
  forward,
10 Since those ancient days – many a pouch enwrapping
  meanwhile
Its fee, like that paid for the son of Mary.

Again goes one, saying
What will ye give me, and I will deliver this man unto you?
And they make the covenant, and pay the pieces of silver.

2
Look forth, deliverer,
Look forth, first-born of the dead,
Over the tree-tops of Paradise;
See thyself in yet-continued bonds,
Toilsome and poor, thou bear'st man's form again,
20 Thou art reviled, scourged, put into prison,
Hunted from the arrogant equality of the rest;
With staves and swords throng the willing servants of
  authority,
Again they surround thee, mad with devilish spite;
Toward thee stretch the hands of a multitude, like vultures'
  talons,
The meanest spit in thy face, they smite thee with their
  palms;
Bruised, bloody, and pinion'd is thy body,
More sorrowful than death is thy soul.

Witness of anguish, brother of slaves,
Not with thy price closed the price of thine image:
30 And still Iscariot plies his trade.

665

Pictures

In a little house pictures I keep, ¶ many pictures
    hanging suspended – It is not a fixed house,
It is round – it is but a few inches from one side of it to the
    other side,
But behold! it has room enough – in it, hundreds and
    thousands, – all the varieties;
– Here! do you know this? This is cicerone himself;
And here, see you, my own States – and here the world
    itself, bowling rolling through the air;
And there, on the walls hanging, portraits of women and
    men, carefully kept,
This is the portrait of my dear mother – and this of my
    father – and these of my brothers and sisters;
This, (I name every thing as it comes,) This is a beautiful
    statute, long lost, dark buried, but never destroyed – now
    found by me, and restored to the light;
There five men, a group of sworn friends, stalwart, bearded,
    determined, work their way together through all the
    troubles and impediments of the world;
10 And that is a magical wondrous mirror – long it lay clouded,
    but the cloud has passed away,
It is now a clean and bright mirror – it will show you all you
    can conceive of, all you wish to behold;
And that is a picture intended for Death – it is very
    beautiful – (what else is so beautiful as Death?)
There is represented the Day, full of effulgence – full of
    seminal lust and love – full of action, life, strength,
    aspiration,
And there the Night, with mystic beauty, full of love also,
    and full of greater life – the Night, showing where the
    stars are;
There is a picture of Adam in Paradise – side by side with
    him Eve, (the Earth's bride and the Earth's bridegroom;)

There is an old Egyptian temple – and again, a Greek
    temple, of white marble;
There are Hebrew prophets chanting, rapt, extatic – and
    here is Homer;
Here is one singing canticles in an unknown tongue, before
    the Sanskrit was,
And here a Hindu sage, with his recitative in Sanskrit;
20   And here the divine Christ expounds eternal truth –
    expounds the Soul,
And here he appears en-route to Calvary, bearing the cross –
    See you, the blood and sweat streaming down his face,
    his neck;
And here, behold, a picture of once imperial Rome, full of
    palaces – full of masterful warriors;
And here, the questioner, the Athenian of the classical
    time – Socrates, in the market place,
(O divine tongue! I too grow silent under your elenchus,
O you with bare feet, and bulging belly! I saunter along,
    following you, and obediently listen;)
And here Athens itself, – it is a clear forenoon,
Young men, pupils, collect in the gardens of a favorite
    master, waiting for him.
Some, crowded in groups, listen to the harangues or
    arguments of the elder ones,
Elsewhere, single figures, undisturbed by the buzz around
    them, lean against pillars, or within recesses, meditating,
    or studying from manuscripts,
30   Here and there, couples or trios, young and old,
    clear-faced, and of perfect physique, walk with twined
    arms, in divine friendship, happy,
Till, beyond, the master appears advancing – his form shows
    above the crowd, a head taller than they,
His gait is erect, calm and dignified – his features are
    colossal – he is old, yet his forehead has no wrinkles,
Wisdom undisturbed, self-respect, fortitude unshaken, are
    in his expression, his personality;
Wait till he speaks – what God's voice is that, sounding
    from his mouth?

He places virtue and self-denial above all the rest,
He shows to what a glorious height the man may ascend,
He shows how independent one may be of fortune – how
    triumphant over fate;
– And here again, this picture tells a story of the Olympic
    games,
See you, the chariot races? See you, the boxers boxing,
    and the runners running?
40 See you, the poets off there reciting their poems and
    tragedies, to crowds of listeners?
– And here, (for I have all kinds,) here is Columbus setting
    sail from Spain on his voyage of discovery;
This again is a series after the great French revolution,
This is the taking of the Bastile, the prison – this is the
    execution of the king.
This is the queen on her way to the scaffold – those are
    guillotines;
But this opposite, (abruptly changing,) is a picture from the
    prison-ships of my own old city – Brooklyn city;
And now a merry recruiter passes, with fife and drum,
    seeking who will join his troop;
And there is an old European martyrdom – See you, the
    cracking fire – See the agonized contortions of the limbs,
    and the writhing of the lips! See the head thrown back;
And here is a picture of triumph – a General has returned,
    after a victory – the city turns out to meet him,
And here is a portrait of the English king, Charles the First,
    (are you a judge of physiognomy?)
50 And here is a funeral procession in the country,
A beloved daughter is carried in her coffin – there follow the
    parents and neighbors;
And here, see you – here walks the Boston truckman, by the
    side of his string-team – see the three horses, pacing
    stately, sagacious, one ahead of another;
– And this – whose picture is this?
Who is this, with rapid feet, curious, gay – going up and
    down Manahatta, through the streets, along the shores,

working his way through the crowds, observant and
singing?

And this head of melancholy Dante, poet of penalties – poet
of hell;

But this is a portrait of Shakespear, limner of feudal
European lords (here are my hands, my brothers – one for
each of you;)

– And there are wood-cutters, cutting down trees in my
north east woods – see you, the axe uplifted;

And that is a picture of a fish-market – see there the shad,
flat-fish, the large halibut, – there a pile of lobsters, and
there another of oysters;

Opposite, a drudge in the kitchen, working, tired – and there
again the laborer, in stained clothes, sour-smelling,
sweaty – and again black persons and criminals;

60   And there the frivolous person – and there a crazy
enthusiast – and there a young man lies sick of a fever,
and is soon to die;

This, again, is a Spanish bull-fight – see, the animal with
bent head, fiercely advancing;

And here, see you, a picture of a dream of despair, (– is it
unsatisfied love?)

Phantoms, countless, men and women, after death,
wandering;

And there are flowers and fruits – see the grapes, decked off
with vine-leaves;

But see this! – see where graceful and stately the young
queen-cow walks at the head of a large drove, leading
the rest;

And there are building materials – brick, lime, timber, paint,
glass, and iron, (so now you can build what you like;)

And this black portrait – this head, huge, frowning,
sorrowful – is Lucifer's portrait – the denied God's
portrait,

(But I do not deny him – though cast out and rebellious, he
is my God as much as any;)

And again the heads of three other Gods – the God Beauty,

the God Beneficence, and the God Universality, (they are
mine, also;)

70 And there an Arab caravan, halting – See you, the palm
trees, the camels, and the stretch of hot sand far away;

And there are my woods of Kanada, in winter, with ice
and snow,

And here my Oregon hunting-hut, See me emerging from
the door, bearing my rifle in my hand;

But there, see you, a reminiscence from over sea – a very old
Druid, walking the woods of Albion;

And there, singular, on ocean waves, downward, buoyant,
swift, over the waters, an occupied coffin floating;

And there, rude grave-mounds in California – and there a
path worn in the grass,

And there hang painted scenes from my Kansas life – and
there from what I saw in the Lake Superior region;

And here mechanics work in their shops, in towns – There
the carpenter shoves his jack-plane – there the
blacksmith stands by his anvil, leaning on his upright
hammer;

This is Chicago with railroad depots, with trains arriving
and departing – and, in their places, immense stores of
grain, meat, and lumber;

And here are my slave-gangs, South, at work upon the
roads, the women indifferently with the men – see, how
clumsy, hideous, black, pouting, grinning, sly, besotted,
sensual, shameless;

80 And this of a scene afar in the North, the arctic – those are
the corpses of lost explorers, (no chaplets of roses will ever
cap their icy graves – but I put a chaplet in this poem,
for you, you sturdy English heros;)

But here, now copious – see you, here, the Wonders of eld,
the famed Seven,

The Olympian statue this, and this the Artemesian tomb,

Pyramid this, Pharos this, and this the shrine of Diana,

These Babylon's gardens, and this Rhodes' high-lifted
marvel,

(But for all that, nigh at hand, see a wonder beyond any
    of them,
Namely yourself – the form and thoughts of a man,
A man! because all the world, and all the inventions of the
    world are but the food of the body and the soul of one
    man;)
And here, while ages have grown upon ages,
Pictures of youths and greybeards, Pagan, and Jew, and
    Christian,
90   Some retiring to caves – some in schools and piled libraries,
To pore with ceaseless fervor over the myth of the Infinite,
But ever recoiling, Pagan and Jew and Christian,
As from a haze, more dumb and thick than vapor above the
    hot sea;
– And here now, (for all varieties, I say, hang in this little
    house,)
A string of my Iroquois, aborigines – see you, where they
    march in single file, without noise, very cautious,
    through passages in the old woods;
O a husking-frolic in the West – see you, the large rude
    barn – see you, young and old, laughing and joking, as
    they husk the ears of corn;
And there in a city, a stormy political meeting – a
    torch-light procession – candidates avowing themselves
    to the people;
And here is the Lascar I noticed once in Asia – here he
    remains still, pouring money into the sea, as an offering to
    demons, for favor;
And there, in the midst of a group, a quell'd revolted slave,
    cowering,
100 See you, the hand-cuffs, the hopple, and the blood-stain'd
    cowhide;
And there hang, side by side, certain close comrades of
    mine – a Broadway stage-driver, a lumberman of Maine,
    and a deck-hand of a Mississippi steamboat;
And again the young man of Mannahatta, the celebrated
    rough,

(The one I love well – let others sing whom they may – him I
    sing for a thousand years!)
And there a historic piece – see you, where Thomas
    Jefferson of Virginia sits reading Rousseau, the Swiss,
    and compiling the Declaration of Independence, the
    American compact;
And there, tall and slender, stands Ralph Waldo Emerson, of
    New England, at the lecturer's desk lecturing,
And there is my Congress in session in the Capitol – there
    are my two Houses in session;
And here, behold two war-ships, saluting each other – behold
    the smoke, bulging, spreading in round clouds from the
    guns and sometimes hiding the ships;
And there, on the level banks of the James river in Virginia
    stand the mansions of the planters;
And here an old black man, stone-blind, with a placard on
    his hat, sits low at the corner of a street, begging,
    humming hymn-tunes nasally all day to himself and
    receiving small gifts;
110   And this, out at sea, is a signal-bell – see you, where it is
    built on a reef, and ever dolefully keeps tolling, to warn
    mariners;
And this picture shows what once happened in one of
    Napoleon's greatest battles,
(The tale was conveyed to me by an old French soldier,)
In the height of the roar and carnage of the battle, all of a
    sudden, from some unaccountable cause, the whole fury
    of the opposing armies subdued – there was a perfect
    calm,
It lasted almost a minute – not a gun was fired – all was
    petrified,
It was more solemn and awful than all the roar and
    slaughter;
– And here, (for still I name them as they come,) here are
    my timber-towers, guiding logs down a stream in the
    North;
And here a glimpse of my treeless llanos, where they skirt

the Colorado, and sweep for a thousand miles on either
   side of the Rocky Mountains;
And there, on the whaling ground, in the Pacific, is a sailor,
   perched at the top-mast head, on the look out,
(You can almost hear him crying out, *There-e-'s white water*,
   or *The-e-re's black skin* ;)

120 But here, (look you well,) see here the phallic choice of
   America, a full-sized man or woman – a natural,
   well-trained man or woman
(The phallic choice of America leaves the finesse of cities,
   and all the returns of commerce or agriculture, and the
   magnitude of geography, and achievements of literature
   and art, and all the shows of exterior victory, to enjoy the
   breeding of full-sized men, or one full-sized man or
   woman, unconquerable and simple;)
– For all those have I in a round house hanging – such
   pictures have I – and they are but little.
For wherever I have been, has afforded me superb pictures,
And whatever I have heard has given me perfect pictures,
And every hour of the day and night has given me copious
   pictures,
And every rod of land or sea affords me, as long as I live,
   inimitable pictures.

Song of Myself: *The Text from the First Edition of* Leaves of Grass (1855)

Song of Myself

I celebrate myself,
And what I assume you shall assume,
For every atom belonging to me as good belongs to you.

I loafe and invite my soul,
I lean and loafe at my ease . . . . observing a spear of summer
    grass.

Houses and rooms are full of perfumes . . . . the shelves are
    crowded with perfumes,
I breathe the fragrance myself, and know it and like it,
The distillation would intoxicate me also, but I shall not
    let it.

The atmosphere is not a perfume . . . . it has no taste of the
    distillation . . . . it is odorless,
It is for my mouth forever . . . . I am in love with it,
I will go to the bank by the wood and become undisguised
    and naked,
I am mad for it to be in contact with me.

The smoke of my own breath,
Echos, ripples, and buzzed whispers . . . . loveroot,
    silkthread, crotch and vine,
My respiration and inspiration . . . . the beating of my
    heart . . . . the passing of blood and air through my lungs,
The sniff of green leaves and dry leaves, and of the shore and
    darkcolored searocks, and of hay in the barn,
The sound of the belched words of my voice . . . . words
    loosed to the eddies of the wind,
A few light kisses . . . . a few embraces . . . . a reaching
    around of arms,
The play of shine and shade on the trees as the supple
    boughs wag,
The delight alone or in the rush of the streets, or along the
    fields and hillsides,

The feeling of health . . . . the full-noon trill . . . . the song of
    me rising from bed and meeting the sun.

Have you reckoned a thousand acres much? Have you
    reckoned the earth much?
Have you practiced so long to learn to read?
Have you felt so proud to get at the meaning of poems?

Stop this day and night with me and you shall possess the
    origin of all poems,
You shall possess the good of the earth and sun . . . . there are
    millions of suns left,
You shall no longer take things at second or third hand . . . .
    nor look through the eyes of the dead . . . . nor feed on the
    spectres in books,
You shall not look through my eyes either, nor take things
    from me,
You shall listen to all sides and filter them from yourself.

30   I have heard what the talkers were talking . . . . the talk of the
    beginning and the end,
But I do not talk of the beginning or the end.

There was never any more inception than there is now,
Nor any more youth or age than there is now;
And will never be any more perfection than there is now,
Nor any more heaven or hell than there is now.

Urge and urge and urge,
Always the procreant urge of the world.

Out of the dimness opposite equals advance . . . . Always
    substance and increase,
Always a knit of identity . . . . always distinction . . . . always
    a breed of life.

40   To elaborate is no avail . . . . Learned and unlearned feel
    that it is so.

Sure as the most certain sure . . . . plumb in the uprights,
    well entretied, braced in the beams,
Stout as a horse, affectionate, haughty, electrical,
I and this mystery here we stand.

Clear and sweet is my soul . . . . and clear and sweet is all
    that is not my soul.

Lack one lacks both . . . . and the unseen is proved by
    the seen,
Till that becomes unseen and receives proof in its turn.

Showing the best and dividing it from the worst, age
    vexes age,
Knowing the perfect fitness and equanimity of things, while
    they discuss I am silent, and go bathe and admire myself.

Welcome is every organ and attribute of me, and of any
    man hearty and clean,
50 Not an inch nor a particle of an inch is vile, and none shall be
    less familiar than the rest.

I am satisfied . . . . I see, dance, laugh, sing;
As God comes a loving bedfellow and sleeps at my side all
    night and close on the peep of the day,
And leaves for me baskets covered with white towels
    bulging the house with their plenty,
Shall I postpone my acceptation and realization and scream
    at my eyes,
That they turn from gazing after and down the road,
And forthwith cipher and show me to a cent,
Exactly the contents of one, and exactly the contents of two,
    and which is ahead?

Trippers and askers surround me,
People I meet . . . . the effect upon me of my early life . . . . of
    the ward and city I live in . . . . of the nation,
60 The latest news . . . . discoveries, inventions, societies . . . .
    authors old and new,
My dinner, dress, associates, looks, business, compliments,
    dues,

The real or fancied indifference of some man or woman I
    love,
The sickness of one of my folks – or of myself . . . . or
    ill-doing . . . . or loss or lack of money . . . . or depressions
    or exaltations,
They come to me days and nights and go from me again,
But they are not the Me myself.

Apart from the pulling and hauling stands what I am,
Stands amused, complacent, compassionating, idle, unitary,
Looks down, is erect, bends an arm on an impalpable
    certain rest,
Looks with its sidecurved head curious what will come next,
70 Both in and out of the game, and watching and wondering
    at it.
Backward I see in my own days where I sweated through fog
    with linguists and contenders,
I have no mocking or arguments . . . . I witness and wait.

I believe in you my soul . . . . the other I am must not abase
    itself to you,
And you must not be abased to the other.

Loafe with me on the grass . . . . loose the stop from your
    throat,
Not words, not music or rhyme I want . . . . not custom or
    lecture, not even the best,
Only the lull I like, the hum of your valved voice.

I mind how we lay in June, such a transparent summer
    morning;
You settled your head athwart my hips and gently turned
    over upon me,
80 And parted the shirt from my bosom-bone, and plunged
    your tongue to my barestript heart,
And reached till you felt my beard, and reached till you
    held my feet.

Swiftly arose and spread around me the peace and joy and
    knowledge that pass all the art and argument of the earth;

And I know that the hand of God is the elderhand of my
   own,
And I know that the spirit of God is the eldest brother of
   my own,
And that all the men ever born are also my brothers . . . . and
   the women my sisters and lovers,
And that a kelson of the creation is love;
And limitless are leaves stiff or drooping in the fields,
And brown ants in the little wells beneath them,
And mossy scabs of the wormfence, and heaped stones, and
   elder and mullen and pokeweed.

90   A child said, What is the grass? fetching it to me with full
         hands;
      How could I answer the child? . . . . I do not know what it
         is any more than he.

      I guess it must be the flag of my disposition, out of hopeful
         green stuff woven.

      Or I guess it is the handkerchief of the Lord,
      A scented gift and remembrancer designedly dropped,
      Bearing the owner's name someway in the corners, that we
         may see and remark, and say Whose?

      Or I guess the grass is itself a child . . . . the produced babe
         of the vegetation.

      Or I guess it is a uniform hieroglyphic,
      And it means, Sprouting alike in broad zones and narrow
         zones,
      Growing among black folks as among white,
100   Kanuck, Tuckahoe, Congressman, Cuff, I give them the
         same, I receive them the same.

      And now it seems to me the beautiful uncut hair of graves.

Tenderly will I use you curling grass,
It may be you transpire from the breasts of young men,
It may be if I had known them I would have loved them;
It may be you are from old people and from women, and
    from offspring taken soon out of their mothers' laps,
And here you are the mothers' laps.

This grass is very dark to be from the white heads of old
    mothers,
Darker than the colorless beards of old men,
Dark to come from under the faint red roofs of mouths.

110 O I perceive after all so many uttering tongues!
And I perceive they do not come from the roofs of mouths
    for nothing.

I wish I could translate the hints about the dead young men
    and women,
And the hints about old men and mothers, and the offspring
    soon out of their laps.

What do you think has become of the young and old men?
And what do you think has become of the women and
    children?

They are alive and well somewhere;
The smallest sprout shows there is really no death,
And if ever there was it led forward life, and does not wait
    at the end to arrest it,
And ceased the moment life appeared.

120 All goes onward and outward .... and nothing collapses,
And to die is different from what any one supposed, and
    luckier.

Has any one supposed it lucky to be born?
I hasten to inform him or her it is just as lucky to die,
    and I know it.

I pass death with the dying, and birth with the new-washed
   babe .... and am not contained between my hat and
   boots,
And peruse manifold objects, no two alike, and every one
   good,
The earth good, and the stars good, and their adjuncts
   all good.

I am not an earth nor an adjunct of an earth,
I am the mate and companion of people, all just as immortal
   and fathomless as myself;
They do not know how immortal, but I know.

130 Every kind for itself and its own .... for me mine male
   and female,
For me all that have been boys and that love women,
For me the man that is proud and feels how it stings to be
   slighted,
For me the sweetheart and the old maid .... for me mothers
   and the mothers of mothers,
For me lips that have smiled, eyes that have shed tears,
For me children and the begetters of children.

Who need be afraid of the merge?
Undrape .... you are not guilty to me, not stale nor
   discarded,
I see through the broadcloth and gingham whether or no,
And am around, tenacious, acquisitive, tireless .... and
   can never be shaken away.

140 The little one sleeps in its cradle,
I lift the gauze and look a long time, and silently brush away
   flies with my hand.

The youngster and the redfaced girl turn aside up the bushy
   hill,
I peeringly view them from the top.

The suicide sprawls on the bloody floor of the bedroom.
It is so .... I witnessed the corpse .... there the pistol
   had fallen.

The blab of the pave . . . . the tires of carts and sluff of
    bootsoles and talk of the promenaders,
The heavy omnibus, the driver with his interrogating
    thumb, the clank of the shod horses on the granite floor,
The carnival of sleighs, the clinking and shouting jokes and
    pelts of snowballs;
The hurrahs for popular favorites . . . . the fury of roused
    mobs,
150 The flap of the curtained litter – the sick man inside, borne
    to the hospital,
The meeting of enemies, the sudden oath, the blows and fall,
The excited crowd – the policeman with his star quickly
    working his passage to the centre of the crowd;
The impassive stones that receive and return so many
    echoes,
The souls moving along . . . . are they invisible while the
    least atom of the stones is visible?
What groans of overfed or half-starved who fall on the flags
    sunstruck or in fits,
What exclamations of women taken suddenly, who hurry
    home and give birth to babes,
What living and buried speech is always vibrating here . . . .
    what howls restrained by decorum,
Arrests of criminals, slights, adulterous offers made,
    acceptances, rejections with convex lips,
I mind them or the resonance of them . . . . I come again
    and again.

160 The big doors of the country-barn stand open and ready,
The dried grass of the harvest-time loads the slow-drawn
    wagon,
The clear light plays on the brown gray and green
    intertinged,
The armfuls are packed to the sagging mow:
I am there . . . . I help . . . . I came stretched atop of the load,
I felt its soft jolts . . . . one leg reclined on the other,

I jump from the crossbeams, and seize the clover and
    timothy,
And roll head over heels, and tangle my hair full of wisps.

Alone far in the wilds and mountains I hunt,
Wandering amazed at my own lightness and glee,
170 In the late afternoon choosing a safe spot to pass the night,
Kindling a fire and broiling the freshkilled game,
Soundly falling asleep on the gathered leaves, my dog and
    gun by my side.

The Yankee clipper is under her three skysails . . . . she cuts
    the sparkle and scud,
My eyes settle the land . . . . I bend at her prow or shout
    joyously from the deck.

The boatmen and clamdiggers arose early and stopped for
    me,
I tucked my trouser-ends in my boots and went and had a
    good time,
You should have been with us that day round the
    chowder-kettle.

I saw the marriage of the trapper in the open air in the
    far-west . . . . the bride was a red girl,
Her father and his friends sat near by crosslegged and
    dumbly smoking . . . . they had moccasins to their feet and
    large thick blankets hanging from their shoulders;
180 On a bank lounged the trapper . . . . he was dressed mostly
    in skins . . . . his luxuriant beard and curls protected
    his neck,
One hand rested on his rifle . . . . the other hand held firmly
    the wrist of the red girl,
She had long eyelashes . . . . her head was bare . . . . her
    coarse straight locks descended upon her voluptuous
    limbs and reached to her feet.

The runaway slave came to my house and stopped outside,
I heard his motions crackling the twigs of the woodpile,
Through the swung half-door of the kitchen I saw him
　　limpsey and weak,
And went where he sat on a log, and led him in and assured
　　him,
And brought water and filled a tub for his sweated body and
　　bruised feet,
And gave him a room that entered from my own, and gave
　　him some coarse clean clothes,
And remember perfectly well his revolving eyes and his
　　awkwardness,
190　And remember putting plasters on the galls of his neck
　　and ankles;
He staid with me a week before he was recuperated and
　　passed north,
I had him sit next me at table . . . . my firelock leaned in
　　the corner.

Twenty-eight young men bathe by the shore,
Twenty-eight young men, and all so friendly,
Twenty-eight years of womanly life, and all so lonesome.

She owns the fine house by the rise of the bank,
She hides handsome and richly drest aft the blinds of the
　　window.

Which of the young men does she like the best?
Ah the homeliest of them is beautiful to her.

200　Where are you off to, lady? for I see you,
You splash in the water there, yet stay stock still in your
　　room.

Dancing and laughing along the beach came the
　　twenty-ninth bather,
The rest did not see her, but she saw them and loved them.

The beards of the young men glistened with wet, it ran from
　　their long hair,
Little streams passed all over their bodies.

An unseen hand also passed over their bodies,
It descended tremblingly from their temples and ribs.

The young men float on their backs, their white bellies
    swell to the sun . . . . they do not ask who seizes fast
    to them,
They do not know who puffs and declines with pendant
    and bending arch,
210 They do not think whom they souse with spray.

The butcher-boy puts off his killing-clothes, or sharpens his
    knife at the stall in the market,
I loiter enjoying his repartee and his shuffle and breakdown.

Blacksmiths with grimed and hairy chests environ the anvil,
Each has his main-sledge . . . . they are all out . . . . there is a
    great heat in the fire.

From the cinder-strewed threshold I follow their
    movements,
The lithe sheer of their waists plays even with their massive
    arms,
Overhand the hammers roll – overhand so slow – overhand
    so sure,
They do not hasten, each man hits in his place.

The negro holds firmly the reins of his four horses . . . . the
    block swags underneath on its tied-over chain,
220 The negro that drives the huge dray of the stoneyard . . . .
    steady and tall he stands poised on one leg on the
    stringpiece,
His blue shirt exposes his ample neck and breast and
    loosens over his hipband,
His glance is calm and commanding . . . . he tosses the
    slouch of his hat away from his forehead,
The sun falls on his crispy hair and moustache . . . . falls on
    the black of his polish'd and perfect limbs.

I behold the picturesque giant and love him . . . . and I do
    not stop there,
I go with the team also.

In me the caresser of life wherever moving . . . . backward
    as well as forward slueing,
To niches aside and junior bending.

Oxen that rattle the yoke or halt in the shade, what is that
    you express in your eyes?
It seems to me more than all the print I have read in my life.

230 My tread scares the wood-drake and wood-duck on my
    distant and daylong ramble,
They rise together, they slowly circle around.
    . . . . I believe in those winged purposes,
And acknowledge the red yellow and white playing within
    me,
And consider the green and violet and the tufted crown
    intentional;
And do not call the tortoise unworthy because she is not
    something else,
And the mockingbird in the swamp never studied the gamut,
    yet trills pretty well to me,
And the look of the bay mare shames silliness out of me.

The wild gander leads his flock through the cool night,
Ya-honk! he says, and sounds it down to me like an
    invitation;
240 The pert may suppose it meaningless, but I listen closer,
I find its purpose and place up there toward the November
    sky.

The sharphoofed moose of the north, the cat on the housesill,
    the chickadee, the prairie-dog,
The litter of the grunting sow as they tug at her teats,
The brood of the turkeyhen, and she with her halfspread
    wings,
I see in them and myself the same old law.

The press of my foot to the earth springs a hundred
    affections,
They scorn the best I can do to relate them.

I am enamoured of growing outdoors,
Of men that live among cattle or taste of the ocean or woods,
250   Of the builders and steerers of ships, of the wielders of axes
     and mauls, of the drivers of horses,
I can eat and sleep with them week in and week out.

What is commonest and cheapest and nearest and easiest
    is Me,
Me going in for my chances, spending for vast returns,
Adorning myself to bestow myself on the first that will
    take me,
Not asking the sky to come down to my goodwill,
Scattering it freely forever.

The pure contralto sings in the organloft,
The carpenter dresses his plank .... the tongue of his
    foreplane whistles its wild ascending lisp,
The married and unmarried children ride home to their
    thanksgiving dinner,
260   The pilot seizes the king-pin, he heaves down with a
    strong arm,
The mate stands braced in the whaleboat, lance and
    harpoon are ready,
The duck-shooter walks by silent and cautious stretches,
The deacons are ordained with crossed hands at the altar,
The spinning-girl retreats and advances to the hum of the
    big wheel,
The farmer stops by the bars of a Sunday and looks at the
    oats and rye,
The lunatic is carried at last to the asylum a confirmed case,
He will never sleep any more as he did in the cot in his
    mother's bedroom;
The jour printer with gray head and gaunt jaws works at
    his case,
He turns his quid of tobacco, his eyes get blurred with the
    manuscript;
270   The malformed limbs are tied to the anatomist's table,
What is removed drops horribly in a pail;

The quadroon girl is sold at the stand .... the drunkard
    nods by the bar-room stove,
The machinist rolls up his sleeves .... the policeman travels
    his beat .... the gate-keeper marks who pass,
The young fellow drives the express-wagon .... I love him
    though I do not know him;
The half-breed straps on his light boots to compete in
    the race,
The western turkey-shooting draws old and young ....
    some lean on their rifles, some sit on logs,
Out from the crowd steps the marksman and takes his
    position and levels his piece;
The groups of newly-come immigrants cover the wharf
    or levee,
The woollypates hoe in the sugarfield, the overseer views
    them from his saddle;
280   The bugle calls in the ballroom, the gentlemen run for their
    partners, the dancers bow to each other;
The youth lies awake in the cedar-roofed garret and harks
    to the musical rain,
The Wolverine sets traps on the creek that helps fill the
    Huron,
The reformer ascends the platform, he spouts with his
    mouth and nose,
The company returns from its excursion, the darkey brings
    up the rear and bears the well-riddled target,
The squaw wrapt in her yellow-hemmed cloth is offering
    moccasins and beadbags for sale,
The connoisseur peers along the exhibition-gallery with
    halfshut eyes bent sideways,
The deckhands make fast the steamboat, the plank is thrown
    for the shoregoing passengers,
The young sister holds out the skein, the elder sister winds
    it off in a ball and stops now and then for the knots,
The one-year wife is recovering and happy, a week ago she
    bore her first child,
290   The cleanhaired Yankee girl works with her sewing-machine
    or in the factory or mill,

The nine months' gone is in the parturition chamber, her
    faintness and pains are advancing;
The pavingman leans on his twohanded rammer – the
    reporter's lead flies swiftly over the notebook – the
    signpainter is lettering with red and gold,
The canal-boy trots on the towpath – the book-keeper counts
    at his desk – the shoemaker waxes his thread,
The conductor beats time for the band and all the
    performers follow him,
The child is baptised – the convert is making the first
    professions,
The regatta is spread on the bay . . . . how the white sails
    sparkle!
The drover watches his drove, he sings out to them that
    would stray,
The pedlar sweats with his pack on his back – the purchaser
    higgles about the odd cent,
The camera and plate are prepared, the lady must sit for
    her daguerreotype,
300 The bride unrumples her white dress, the minutehand of the
    clock moves slowly,
The opium eater reclines with rigid head and just-opened
    lips,
The prostitute draggles her shawl, her bonnet bobs on her
    tipsy and pimpled neck,
The crowd laugh at her blackguard oaths, the men jeer and
    wink to each other,
(Miserable! I do not laugh at your oaths nor jeer you,)
The President holds a cabinet council, he is surrounded by
    the great secretaries,
On the piazza walk five friendly matrons with twined arms;
The crew of the fish-smack pack repeated layers of halibut
    in the hold,
The Missourian crosses the plains toting his wares and
    his cattle,
The fare-collector goes through the train – he gives notice
    by the jingling of loose change,

310   The floormen are laying the floor – the tinners are tinning
the roof – the masons are calling for mortar,

In single file each shouldering his hod pass onward the
laborers;

Seasons pursuing each other the indescribable crowd is
gathered . . . . it is the Fourth of July . . . . what salutes of
cannon and small arms!

Seasons pursuing each other the plougher ploughs and the
mower mows and the wintergrain falls in the ground;

Off on the lakes the pikefisher watches and waits by the hole
in the frozen surface,

The stumps stand thick round the clearing, the squatter
strikes deep with his axe,

The flatboatmen make fast toward dusk near the
cottonwood or pekantrees,

The coon-seekers go now through the regions of the Red
river, or through those drained by the Tennessee, or
through those of the Arkansas,

The torches shine in the dark that hangs on the
Chattahoochee or Altamahaw;

Patriarchs sit at supper with sons and grandsons and great
grandsons around them,

320   In walls of abodes, in canvass tents, rest hunters and
trappers after their day's sport.

The city sleeps and the country sleeps,

The living sleep for their time . . . . the dead sleep for their
time,

The old husband sleeps by his wife and the young husband
sleeps by his wife;

And these one and all tend inward to me, and I tend
outward to them,

And such as it is to be of these more or less I am.

I am of old and young, of the foolish as much as the wise,

Regardless of others, ever regardful of others,

Maternal as well as paternal, a child as well as a man,

Stuffed with the stuff that is coarse, and stuffed with the
stuff that is fine,

330   One of the great nation, the nation of many nations – the
      smallest the same and the largest the same,
  A southerner soon as a northerner, a planter nonchalant and
      hospitable,
  A Yankee bound my own way .... ready for trade .... my
      joints the limberest joints on earth and the sternest joints
      on earth,
  A Kentuckian walking the vale of the Elkhorn in my
      deerskin leggings,
  A boatman over the lakes or bays or along coasts .... a
      Hoosier, a Badger, a Buckeye,
  A Louisianian or Georgian, a poke-easy from sandhills and
      pines,
  At home on Canadian snowshoes or up in the bush, or with
      fishermen off Newfoundland,
  At home in the fleet of iceboats, sailing with the rest and
      tacking,
  At home on the hills of Vermont or in the woods of Maine
      or the Texan ranch,
  Comrade of Californians .... comrade of free
      northwesterners, loving their big proportions,

340   Comrade of raftsmen and coalmen – comrade of all who
      shake hands and welcome to drink and meat;
  A learner with the simplest, a teacher of the
      thoughtfulest,
  A novice beginning experient of myriads of seasons,
  Of every hue and trade and rank, of every caste and religion,
  Not merely of the New World but of Africa Europe or
      Asia .... a wandering savage,
  A farmer, mechanic, or artist .... a gentleman, sailor,
      lover or quaker,
  A prisoner, fancy-man, rowdy, lawyer, physician or priest.

  I resist anything better than my own diversity,
  And breathe the air and leave plenty after me,
  And am not stuck up, and am in my place.

350 The moth and the fisheggs are in their place,
The suns I see and the suns I cannot see are in their place,
The palpable is in its place and the impalpable is in its place.

These are the thoughts of all men in all ages and lands, they
are not original with me,
If they are not yours as much as mine they are nothing or
next to nothing,
If they do not enclose everything they are next to nothing,
If they are not the riddle and the untying of the riddle they
are nothing,
If they are not just as close as they are distant they are
nothing.

This is the grass that grows wherever the land is and the
water is,
This is the common air that bathes the globe.

360 This is the breath of laws and songs and behaviour,
This is the tasteless water of souls .... this is the true
sustenance,
It is for the illiterate .... it is for the judges of the supreme
court .... it is for the federal capitol and the state
capitols,
It is for the admirable communes of literary men and
composers and singers and lecturers and engineers and
savans,
It is for the endless races of working people and farmers and
seamen.

This is the trill of a thousand clear cornets and scream of the
octave flute and strike of triangles.

I play not a march for victors only .... I play great marches
for conquered and slain persons.

Have you heard that it was good to gain the day?
I also say it is good to fall .... battles are lost in the same
spirit in which they are won.

I sound triumphal drums for the dead . . . . I fling through
    my embouchures the loudest and gayest music to them,
370 Vivas to those who have failed and to those whose war-vessels
    sank in the sea, and those themselves who sank in the sea,
And to all generals that lost engagements, and all overcome
    heroes, the numberless unknown heroes equal to the
    greatest heroes known.

This is the meal pleasantly set . . . . this is the meat and drink
    for natural hunger,
It is for the wicked just the same as the righteous I
    make appointments with all,
I will not have a single person slighted or left away,
The keptwoman and sponger and thief are hereby invited
    . . . . the heavy-lipped slave is invited . . . . the venerealee
    is invited,
There shall be no difference between them and the rest.

This is the press of a bashful hand . . . . this is the float and
    odor of hair,
This is the touch of my lips to yours . . . . this is the
    murmur of yearning,
This is the far-off depth and height reflecting my own face,
380 This is the thoughtful merge of myself and the outlet again.

Do you guess I have some intricate purpose?
Will I have . . . . for the April rain has, and the mica on the
    side of a rock has.

Do you take it I would astonish?
Does the daylight astonish? or the early redstart
    twittering through the woods?
Do I astonish more than they?

This hour I tell things in confidence,
I might not tell everybody but I will tell you.

Who goes there! hankering, gross, mystical, nude?
How is it I extract strength from the beef I eat?

390 What is a man anyhow? What am I? and what are you?
     All I mark as my own you shall offset it with your own,
     Else it were time lost listening to me.

     I do not snivel that snivel the world over,
     That months are vacuums and the ground but wallow and
         filth,
     That life is a suck and a sell, and nothing remains at the end
         but threadbare crape and tears.

     Whimpering and truckling fold with powders for invalids
         .... conformity goes to the fourth-removed,
     I cock my hat as I please indoors or out.

     Shall I pray? Shall I venerate and be ceremonious?
     I have pried through the strata and analyzed to a hair,
400 And counselled with doctors and calculated close and found
         no sweeter fat than sticks to my own bones.

     In all people I see myself, none more and not one a
         barleycorn less,
     And the good or bad I say of myself I say of them.

     And I know I am solid and sound,
     To me the converging objects of the universe perpetually
         flow,
     All are written to me, and I must get what the writing
         means.

     And I know I am deathless,
     I know this orbit of mine cannot be swept by a carpenter's
         compass,
     I know I shall not pass like a child's carlacue cut with a
         burnt stick at night.

     I know I am august,
410 I do not trouble my spirit to vindicate itself or be
         understood,
     I see that the elementary laws never apologize,
     I reckon I behave no prouder than the level I plant my
         house by after all.

I exist as I am, that is enough,
If no other in the world be aware I sit content,
And if each and all be aware I sit content.

One world is aware, and by far the largest to me, and that
     is myself,
And whether I come to my own today or in ten thousand or
     ten million years,
I can cheerfully take it now, or with equal cheerfulness I
     can wait.

My foothold is tenoned and mortised in granite,
420 I laugh at what you call dissolution,
And I know the amplitude of time.

I am the poet of the body,
And I am the poet of the soul.

The pleasures of heaven are with me, and the pains of hell
     are with me,
The first I graft and increase upon myself .... the latter I
     translate into a new tongue.

I am the poet of the woman the same as the man,
And I say it is as great to be a woman as to be a man,
And I say there is nothing greater than the mother of men.

I chant a new chant of dilation or pride,
430 We have had ducking and deprecating about enough,
I show that size is only development.

Have you outstript the rest? Are you the President?
It is a trifle .... they will more than arrive there every one,
     and still pass on.

I am he that walks with the tender and growing night;
I call to the earth and sea half-held by the night.

Press close barebosomed night! Press close magnetic
     nourishing night!
Night of south winds! Night of the large few stars!
Still nodding night! Mad naked summer night!

Smile O voluptuous coolbreathed earth!
440   Earth of the slumbering and liquid trees!
Earth of departed sunset! Earth of the mountains
misty-topt!
Earth of the vitreous pour of the full moon just tinged
with blue!
Earth of shine and dark mottling the tide of the river!
Earth of the limpid gray of clouds brighter and clearer for
my sake!
Far-swooping elbowed earth! Rich apple-blossomed earth!
Smile, for your lover comes!

Prodigal! you have given me love! .... therefore I to you
give love!
O unspeakable passionate love!

Thruster holding me tight and that I hold tight!
450   We hurt each other as the bridegroom and the bride hurt
each other.

You sea! I resign myself to you also .... I guess what you
mean,
I behold from the beach your crooked inviting fingers,
I believe you refuse to go back without feeling of me;
We must have a turn together .... I undress .... hurry me
out of sight of the land,
Cushion me soft .... rock me in billowy drowse,
Dash me with amorous wet .... I can repay you.

Sea of stretched ground-swells!
Sea breathing broad and convulsive breaths!
Sea of the brine of life! Sea of unshovelled and
always-ready graves!
460   Howler and scooper of storms! Capricious and dainty sea!
I am integral with you .... I too am of one phase and of all
phases.

Partaker of influx and efflux .... extoler of hate and
conciliation,
Extoler of amies and those that sleep in each others' arms.

I am he attesting sympathy;
Shall I make my list of things in the house and skip the
    house that supports them?

I am the poet of commonsense and of the demonstrable
    and of immortality;
And am not the poet of goodness only . . . . I do not decline
    to be the poet of wickedness also.

Washes and razors for foofoos . . . . for me freckles and a
    bristling beard.

What blurt is it about virtue and about vice?
470   Evil propels me, and reform of evil propels me . . . . I stand
    indifferent,
My gait is no faultfinder's or rejector's gait,
I moisten the roots of all that has grown.

Did you fear some scrofula out of the unflagging
    pregnancy?
Did you guess the celestial laws are yet to be worked over
    and rectified?

I step up to say that what we do is right and what we affirm
    is right . . . . and some is only the ore of right,
Witnesses of us . . . . one side a balance and the antipodal
    side a balance,
Soft doctrine as steady help as stable doctrine,
Thoughts and deeds of the present our rouse and early start.

This minute that comes to me over the past decillions,
480   There is no better than it and now.

What behaved well in the past behaves well today is not
    such a wonder,
The wonder is always and always how there can be a mean
    man or an infidel.

Endless unfolding of words of ages!
And mine a word of the modern . . . . a word en masse.

A word of the faith that never balks,
One time as good as another time .... here or
    henceforward it is all the same to me.

A word of reality .... materialism first and last imbueing.

Hurrah for positive science! Long live exact demonstration!
Fetch stonecrop and mix it with cedar and branches of lilac;
490   This is the lexicographer or chemist .... this made a
    grammar of the old cartouches,
These mariners put the ship through dangerous unknown
    seas,
This is the geologist, and this works with the scalpel, and
    this is a mathematician.

Gentlemen I receive you, and attach and clasp hands with
    you,
The facts are useful and real .... they are not my dwelling
    .... I enter by them to an area of the dwelling.

I am less the reminder of property or qualities, and more the
    reminder of life,
And go on the square for my own sake and for others'
    sakes,

And make short account of neuters and geldings, and favor
    men and women fully equipped,
And beat the gong of revolt, and stop with fugitives and
    them that plot and conspire.

Walt Whitman, an American, one of the roughs, a kosmos,
500   Disorderly fleshy and sensual .... eating drinking and
    breeding,
No sentimentalist .... no stander above men and women
    or apart from them .... no more modest than immodest.

Unscrew the locks from the doors!
Unscrew the doors themselves from their jambs!

Whoever degrades another degrades me .... and
    whatever is done or said returns at last to me,
And whatever I do or say I also return.

Through me the afflatus surging and surging .... through
    me the current and index.

I speak the password primeval .... I give the sign of
    democracy;
By God! I will accept nothing which all cannot have their
    counterpart of on the same terms.

Through me many long dumb voices,
510   Voices of the interminable generations of slaves,
Voices of prostitutes and of deformed persons,
Voices of the diseased and despairing, and of thieves and
    dwarfs,
Voices of cycles of preparation and accretion,
And of the threads that connect the stars – and of wombs,
    and of the fatherstuff,
And of the rights of them the others are down upon,
Of the trivial and flat and foolish and despised,
Of fog in the air and beetles rolling balls of dung.

Through me forbidden voices,
Voices of sexes and lusts .... voices veiled, and I
    remove the veil,
520   Voices indecent by me clarified and transfigured.

I do not press my finger across my mouth,
I keep as delicate around the bowels as around the head
    and heart,
Copulation is no more rank to me than death is.

I believe in the flesh and the appetites,
Seeing hearing and feeling are miracles, and each part and
    tag of me is a miracle.

Divine am I inside and out, and I make holy whatever I
    touch or am touched from;
The scent of these arm-pits is aroma finer than prayer,
This head is more than churches or bibles or creeds.

If I worship any particular thing it shall be some of the
 spread of my body;
530 Translucent mould of me it shall be you,
Shaded ledges and rests, firm masculine coulter, it shall
 be you,
Whatever goes to the tilth of me it shall be you,
You my rich blood, your milky stream pale strippings of
 my life;
Breast that presses against other breasts it shall be you,
My brain it shall be your occult convolutions,
Root of washed sweet-flag, timorous pond-snipe, nest of
 guarded duplicate eggs, it shall be you,
Mixed tussled hay of head and beard and brawn it shall
 be you,
Trickling sap of maple, fibre of manly wheat, it shall be you;
Sun so generous it shall be you,
540 Vapors lighting and shading my face it shall be you,
You sweaty brooks and dews it shall be you,
Winds whose soft-tickling genitals rub against me it shall
 be you,
Broad muscular fields, branches of liveoak, loving lounger
 in my winding paths, it shall be you,
Hands I have taken, face I have kissed, mortal I have ever
 touched, it shall be you.

I dote on myself . . . . there is that lot of me, and all so
 luscious,
Each moment and whatever happens thrills me with joy.

I cannot tell how my ankles bend . . . . nor whence the cause
 of my faintest wish,
Nor the cause of the friendship I emit . . . . nor the cause of
 the friendship I take again.

To walk up my stoop is unaccountable .... I pause to
consider if it really be,
550   That I eat and drink is spectacle enough for the great
authors and schools,
A morning-glory at my window satisfies me more than the
metaphysics of books.

To behold the daybreak!
The little light fades the immense and diaphanous shadows,
The air tastes good to my palate.

Hefts of the moving world at innocent gambols, silently
rising, freshly exuding,
Scooting obliquely high and low.

Something I cannot see puts upward libidinous prongs,
Seas of bright juice suffuse heaven.

The earth by the sky staid with .... the daily close of their
junction,
560   The heaved challenge from the cast that moment over
my head,
The mocking taunt, See then whether you shall be master!

Dazzling and tremendous how quick the sunrise would kill
me,
If I could not now and always send sunrise out of me.

We also ascend dazzling and tremendous as the sun,
We found our own my soul in the calm and cool of the
daybreak.

My voice goes after what my eyes cannot reach,
With the twirl of my tongue I encompass worlds and
volumes of worlds.

Speech is the twin of my vision .... it is unequal to measure
itself.

It provokes me forever,
570   It says sarcastically, Walt, you understand enough .... why
don't you let it out then?

Come now I will not be tantalized . . . . you conceive too
      much of articulation.

Do you not know how the buds beneath are folded?
Waiting in gloom protected by frost,
The dirt receding before my prophetical screams,
I underlying causes to balance them at last,
My knowledge my live parts . . . . it keeping tally with the
      meaning of things,
Happiness . . . . which whoever hears me let him or her set
      out in search of this day.

My final merit I refuse you . . . . I refuse putting from me
      the best I am.

Encompass worlds but never try to encompass me,
580   I crowd your noisiest talk by looking toward you.

Writing and talk do not prove me,
I carry the plenum of proof and every thing else in my face,
With the hush of my lips I confound the topmost skeptic.

I think I will do nothing for a long time but listen,
And accrue what I hear into myself . . . . and let sounds
      contribute towards me.

I hear the bravuras of birds . . . . the bustle of growing
      wheat . . . . gossip of flames . . . . clack of sticks cooking
      my meals.

I hear the sound of the human voice . . . . a sound I love,
I hear all sounds as they are tuned to their uses . . . . sounds
      of the city and sounds out of the city . . . . sounds of the
      day and night;
Talkative young ones to those that like them . . . . the
      recitative of fish-pedlars and fruit-pedlars . . . . the loud
      laugh of workpeople at their meals,
590   The angry base of disjointed friendship . . . . the faint tones
      of the sick,
The judge with hands tight to the desk, his shaky lips
      pronouncing a death-sentence,

The heave'e'yo of stevedores unlading ships by the wharves
.... the refrain of the anchor-lifters;
The ring of alarm-bells .... the cry of fire .... the whirr of
swift-streaking engines and hose-carts with premonitory
tinkles and colored lights,
The steam-whistle .... the solid roll of the train of
approaching cars;
The slow-march played at night at the head of the
association,
They go to guard some corpse .... the flag-tops are draped
with black muslin.

I hear the violincello or man's heart's complaint,
And hear the keyed cornet or else the echo of sunset.

I hear the chorus .... it is a grand-opera .... this indeed
is music!

600 A tenor large and fresh as the creation fills me,
The orbic flex of his mouth is pouring and filling me full.

I hear the trained soprano .... she convulses me like the
climax of my love-grip;
The orchestra whirls me wider than Uranus flies,
It wrenches unnamable ardors from my breast,
It throbs me to gulps of the farthest down horror,
It sails me .... I dab with bare feet .... they are licked by
the indolent waves,
I am exposed .... cut by bitter and poisoned hail,
Steeped amid honeyed morphine .... my windpipe
squeezed in the fakes of death,
Let up again to feel the puzzle of puzzles,
610 And that we call Being.

To be in any form, what is that?
If nothing lay more developed the quahaug and its callous
shell were enough.

Mine is no callous shell,
I have instant conductors all over me whether I pass or
stop,
They seize every object and lead it harmlessly through me.

I merely stir, press, feel with my fingers, and am happy,
To touch my person to some one else's is about as much as
I can stand.

Is this then a touch? .... quivering me to a new identity,
Flames and ether making a rush for my veins,
620   Treacherous tip of me reaching and crowding to help them,
My flesh and blood playing out lightning, to strike what is
hardly different from myself,
On all sides prurient provokers stiffening my limbs,
Straining the udder of my heart for its withheld drip,
Behaving licentious toward me, taking no denial,
Depriving me of my best as for a purpose,
Unbuttoning my clothes and holding me by the bare waist,
Deluding my confusion with the calm of the sunlight and
pasture fields,
Immodestly sliding the fellow-senses away,
They bribed to swap off with touch, and go and graze at the
edges of me,
630   No consideration, no regard for my draining strength or
my anger,
Fetching the rest of the herd around to enjoy them awhile,
Then all uniting to stand on a headland and worry me.

The sentries desert every other part of me,
They have left me helpless to a red marauder,
They all come to the headland to witness and assist
against me.

I am given up by traitors;
I talk wildly .... I have lost my wits .... I and nobody else
am the greatest traitor,
I went myself first to the headland .... my own hands
carried me there.

You villain touch! what are you doing? .... my breath is
 tight in its throat;
640 Unclench your floodgates! you are too much for me.

Blind loving wrestling touch! Sheathed hooded
 sharptoothed touch!
Did it make you ache so leaving me?

Parting tracked by arriving .... perpetual payment of the
 perpetual loan,
Rich showering rain, and recompenser richer afterward.

Sprouts take and accumulate .... stand by the curb
 prolific and vital,
Landscapes projected masculine full-sized and golden.

All truths wait in all things,
They neither hasten their own delivery nor resist it,
They do not need the obstetric forceps of the surgeon,
650 The insignificant is as big to me as any,
What is less or more than a touch?

Logic and sermons never convince,
The damp of the night drives deeper into my soul.

Only what proves itself to every man and woman is so,
Only what nobody denies is so.

A minute and a drop of me settle my brain;
I believe the soggy clods shall become lovers and lamps,
And a compend of compends is the meat of a man or
 woman,
And a summit and flower there is the feeling they have for
 each other,
660 And they are to branch boundlessly out of that lesson until
 it becomes omnific,
And until every one shall delight us, and we them.

I believe a leaf of grass is no less than the journeywork
 of the stars,
And the pismire is equally perfect, and a grain of sand, and
 the egg of the wren,

And the tree-toad is a chef-d'ouvre for the highest,
And the running blackberry would adorn the parlors of
    heaven,
And the narrowest hinge in my hand puts to scorn all
    machinery,
And the cow crunching with depressed head surpasses any
    statue,
And a mouse is miracle enough to stagger sextillions of
    infidels,
And I could come every afternoon of my life to look at the
    farmer's girl boiling her iron tea-kettle and baking
    shortcake.

670   I find I incorporate gneiss and coal and long-threaded moss
    and fruits and grains and esculent roots,
And am stucco'd with quadrupeds and birds all over,
And have distanced what is behind me for good reasons,
And call any thing close again when I desire it.

In vain the speeding or shyness,
In vain the plutonic rocks send their old heat against my
    approach,
In vain the mastadon retreats beneath its own powdered
    bones,
In vain objects stand leagues off and assume manifold shapes,
In vain the ocean settling in hollows and the great monsters
    lying low,
In vain the buzzard houses herself with the sky,
680   In vain the snake slides through the creepers and logs,
In vain the elk takes to the inner passes of the woods,
In vain the razorbilled auk sails far north to Labrador,
I follow quickly . . . . I ascend to the nest in the fissure of
    the cliff.

I think I could turn and live awhile with the animals . . . .
    they are so placid and self-contained,
I stand and look at them sometimes half the day long.

They do not sweat and whine about their condition,
They do not lie awake in the dark and weep for their sins,
They do not make me sick discussing their duty to God,
Not one is dissatisfied .... not one is demented with the
    mania of owning things,
690 Not one kneels to another nor to his kind that lived
    thousands of years ago,
Not one is respectable or industrious over the whole earth.

So they show their relations to me and I accept them;
They bring me tokens of myself .... they evince them
    plainly in their possession.

I do not know where they got those tokens,
I must have passed that way untold times ago and
    negligently dropt them,
Myself moving forward then and now and forever,
Gathering and showing more always and with velocity,

Infinite and omnigenous and the like of these among them;
Not too exclusive toward the reachers of my
    remembrancers,
700 Picking out here one that shall be my amie,
Choosing to go with him on brotherly terms.

A gigantic beauty of a stallion, fresh and responsive to
    my caresses,
Head high in the forehead and wide between the ears,
Limbs glossy and supple, tail dusting the ground,
Eyes well apart and full of sparkling wickedness .... ears
    finely cut and flexibly moving.

His nostrils dilate .... my heels embrace him .... his well
    built limbs tremble with pleasure .... we speed around
    and return.

I but use you a moment and then I resign you stallion ....
    and do not need your paces, and outgallop them,
And myself as I stand or sit pass faster than you.

Swift wind! Space! My Soul! Now I know it is true what I
     guessed at;
710   What I guessed when I loafed on the grass,
     What I guessed while I lay alone in my bed .... and again
          as I walked the beach under the paling stars of the
          morning.

My ties and ballasts leave me .... I travel .... I sail .... my
     elbows rest in the sea-gaps,
I skirt the sierras .... my palms cover continents,
I am afoot with my vision.

By the city's quadrangular houses .... in log-huts, or
     camping with lumbermen,
Along the ruts of the turnpike .... along the dry gulch and
     rivulet bed,
Hoeing my onion-patch, and rows of carrots and parsnips
     .... crossing savannas .... trailing in forests,
Prospecting .... gold-digging .... girdling the trees of a
     new purchase,
Scorched ankle-deep by the hot sand .... hauling my boat
     down the shallow river;
720   Where the panther walks to and fro on a limb overhead ....
     where the buck turns furiously at the hunter,
Where the rattlesnake suns his flabby length on a rock ....
     where the otter is feeding on fish,
Where the alligator in his tough pimples sleeps by the bayou,
Where the black bear is searching for roots or honey ....
     where the beaver pats the mud with his paddle-tail;
Over the growing sugar .... over the cottonplant .... over
     the rice in its low moist field;
Over the sharp-peaked farmhouse with its scalloped scum
     and slender shoots from the gutters;
Over the western persimmon .... over the longleaved corn
     and the delicate blue-flowered flax;
Over the white and brown buckwheat, a hummer and a
     buzzer there with the rest,
Over the dusky green of the rye as it ripples and shades in
     the breeze;

Scaling mountains .... pulling myself cautiously up ....
holding on by low scragged limbs,

730 Walking the path worn in the grass and beat through the
leaves of the brush;

Where the quail is whistling betwixt the woods and the
wheatlot,

Where the bat flies in the July eve .... where the great
goldbug drops through the dark;

Where the flails keep time on the barn floor,

Where the brook puts out of the roots of the old tree and
flows to the meadow,

Where cattle stand and shake away flies with the tremulous
shuddering of their hides,

Where the cheese-cloth hangs in the kitchen, and andirons
straddle the hearth-slab, and cobwebs fall in festoons
from the rafters;

Where triphammers crash .... where the press is whirling
its cylinders;

Wherever the human heart beats with terrible throes out of
its ribs;

Where the pear-shaped balloon is floating aloft .... floating
in it myself and looking composedly down;

740 Where the life-car is drawn on the slipnoose .... where the
heat hatches pale-green eggs in the dented sand,

Where the she-whale swims with her calves and never
forsakes them,

Where the steamship trails hindways its long pennant of
smoke,

Where the ground-shark's fin cuts like a black chip out of
the water,

Where the half-burned brig is riding on unknown currents,

Where shells grow to her slimy deck, and the dead are
corrupting below;

Where the striped and starred flag is borne at the head of
the regiments;

Approaching Manhattan, up by the long-stretching
island,

Under Niagara, the cataract falling like a veil over my
 countenance;
Upon a door-step . . . . upon the horse-block of hard wood
 outside,
750 Upon the race-course, or enjoying pic-nics or jigs or a good
 game of base-ball,
At he-festivals with blackguard jibes and ironical license and
 bull-dances and drinking and laughter,
At the cider-mill, tasting the sweet of the brown squash . . . .
 sucking the juice through a straw,
At apple-pealings, wanting kisses for all the red fruit I find,
At musters and beach-parties and friendly bees and
 huskings and house-raisings;
Where the mockingbird sounds his delicious gurgles, and
 cackles and screams and weeps,
Where the hay-rick stands in the barnyard, and the
 dry-stalks are scattered, and the brood cow waits in
 the hovel,
Where the bull advances to do his masculine work, and the
 stud to the mare, and the cock is treading the hen,
Where the heifers browse, and the geese nip their food with
 short jerks;
Where the sundown shadows lengthen over the limitless
 and lonesome prairie,
760 Where the herds of buffalo make a crawling spread of the
 square miles far and near;
Where the hummingbird shimmers . . . . where the neck of
 the longlived swan is curving and winding;
Where the laughing-gull scoots by the slappy shore and
 laughs her near-human laugh;
Where beehives range on a gray bench in the garden
 half-hid by the high weeds;
Where the band-necked partridges roost in a ring on the
 ground with their heads out;
Where burial coaches enter the arched gates of a cemetery;
Where winter wolves bark amid wastes of snow and icicled
 trees;

Where the yellow-crowned heron comes to the edge of the
marsh at night and feeds upon small crabs;
Where the splash of swimmers and divers cools the warm
noon;
Where the katydid works her chromatic reed on the
walnut-tree over the well;
770 Through patches of citrons and cucumbers with
silver-wired leaves,
Through the salt-lick or orange glade . . . . or under
conical furs;
Through the gymnasium . . . . through the curtained
saloon . . . . through the office or public hall;
Pleased with the native and pleased with the foreign . . . .
pleased with the new and old,
Pleased with women, the homely as well as the handsome,
Pleased with the quakeress as she puts off her bonnet and
talks melodiously,
Pleased with the primitive tunes of the choir of the
whitewashed church,
Pleased with the earnest words of the sweating Methodist
preacher, or any preacher . . . . looking seriously at the
camp-meeting;
Looking in at the shop-windows in Broadway the whole
forenoon . . . . pressing the flesh of my nose to the thick
plate-glass,
Wandering the same afternoon with my face turned up to
the clouds;
780 My right and left arms round the sides of two friends and I
in the middle;
Coming home with the bearded and dark-cheeked bush-boy
. . . . riding behind him at the drape of the day;
Far from the settlements studying the print of animals' feet,
or the moccasin print;
By the cot in the hospital reaching lemonade to a feverish
patient,
By the coffined corpse when all is still, examining with a
candle;
Voyaging to every port to dicker and adventure;

Hurrying with the modern crowd, as eager and fickle as any,
Hot toward one I hate, ready in my madness to knife him;
Solitary at midnight in my back yard, my thoughts gone
     from me a long while,
Walking the old hills of Judea with the beautiful gentle god
     by my side;
790   Speeding through space .... speeding through heaven
     and the stars,
Speeding amid the seven satellites and the broad ring and
     the diameter of eighty thousand miles,
Speeding with tailed meteors .... throwing fire-balls like
     the rest,
Carrying the crescent child that carries its own full mother
     in its belly:
Storming enjoying planning loving cautioning,
Backing and filling, appearing and disappearing,
I tread day and night such roads,
I visit the orchards of God and look at the spheric product,
And look at quintillions ripened, and look at quintillions
     green.

I fly the flight of the fluid and swallowing soul,
800   My course runs below the soundings of plummets.

I help myself to material and immaterial,
No guard can shut me off, no law can prevent me.

I anchor my ship for a little while only,
My messengers continually cruise away or bring their
     returns to me.

I go hunting polar furs and the seal .... leaping chasms
     with a pike-pointed staff .... clinging to topples of
     brittle and blue.

I ascend to the foretruck .... I take my place late at night
     in the crow's nest .... we sail through the arctic
     sea .... it is plenty light enough,
Through the clear atmosphere I stretch around on the
     wonderful beauty,

The enormous masses of ice pass me and I pass them . . . .
the scenery is plain in all directions,
The white-topped mountains point up in the distance I
fling out my fancies toward them;
810 We are about approaching some great battlefield in which
we are soon to be engaged,
We pass the colossal outposts of the encampments . . . . we
pass with still feet and caution;
Or we are entering by the suburbs some vast and ruined
city . . . . the blocks and fallen architecture more than all
the living cities of the globe.

I am a free companion . . . . I bivouac by invading
watchfires.

I turn the bridegroom out of bed and stay with the bride
myself,
And tighten her all night to my thighs and lips.

My voice is the wife's voice, the screech by the rail of the
stairs,
They fetch my man's body up dripping and drowned.

I understand the large hearts of heroes,
The courage of present times and all times;
820 How the skipper saw the crowded and rudderless wreck of
the steamship, and death chasing it up and down the
storm,
How he knuckled tight and gave not back one inch, and was
faithful of days and faithful of nights,
And chalked in large letters on a board, Be of good cheer,
We will not desert you;
How he saved the drifting company at last,
How the lank loose-gowned women looked when boated
from the side of their prepared graves,
How the silent old-faced infants, and the lifted sick, and the
sharp-lipped unshaved men;
All this I swallow and it tastes good . . . . I like it well, and it
becomes mine,
I am the man . . . . I suffered . . . . I was there.

The disdain and calmness of martyrs,
The mother condemned for a witch and burnt with dry
    wood, and her children gazing on;
830 The hounded slave that flags in the race and leans by the
    fence, blowing and covered with sweat,
The twinges that sting like needles his legs and neck,
The murderous buckshot and the bullets,
All these I feel or am.

I am the hounded slave . . . . I wince at the bite of the dogs,
Hell and despair are upon me . . . . crack and again crack the
    marksmen,
I clutch the rails of the fence . . . . my gore dribs thinned
    with the ooze of my skin,
I fall on the weeds and stones,
The riders spur their unwilling horses and haul close,
They taunt my dizzy ears . . . . they beat me violently over
    the head with their whip-stocks.

840 Agonies are one of my changes of garments;
I do not ask the wounded person how he feels . . . . I myself
    become the wounded person,
My hurt turns livid upon me as I lean on a cane and observe.

I am the mashed fireman with breastbone broken . . . .
    tumbling walls buried me in their debris,
Heat and smoke I inspired . . . . I heard the yelling shouts of
    my comrades,
I heard the distant click of their picks and shovels;
They have cleared the beams away . . . . they tenderly lift
    me forth.

I lie in the night air in my red shirt . . . . the pervading hush
    is for my sake,
Painless after all I lie, exhausted but not so unhappy,
White and beautiful are the faces around me . . . . the heads
    are bared of their fire-caps,
850 The kneeling crowd fades with the light of the torches.

Distant and dead resuscitate,
They show as the dial or move as the hands of me .... and I
    am the clock myself.

I am an old artillerist, and tell of some fort's
    bombardment .... and am there again.

Again the reveille of drummers .... again the attacking
    cannon and mortars and howitzers,
Again the attacked send their cannon responsive.

I take part .... I see and hear the whole,
The cries and curses and roar .... the plaudits for well
    aimed shots,
The ambulanza slowly passing and trailing its red drip,
Workmen searching after damages and to make
    indispensible repairs,
860 The fall of grenades through the rent roof .... the
    fan-shaped explosion,
The whizz of limbs heads stone wood and iron high in the
    air.

Again gurgles the mouth of my dying general .... he
    furiously waves with his hand,
He gasps through the clot .... Mind not me ....
    mind .... the entrenchments.

I tell not the fall of Alamo .... not one escaped to tell the
    fall of Alamo,
The hundred and fifty are dumb yet at Alamo.

Hear now the tale of a jetblack sunrise,
Hear of the murder in cold blood of four hundred and twelve
    young men.

Retreating they had formed in a hollow square with their
    baggage for breastworks,
Nine hundred lives out of the surrounding enemy's nine
    times their number was the price they took in advance,
870 Their colonel was wounded and their ammunition gone,
They treated for an honorable capitulation, received

writing and seal, gave up their arms, and marched back
prisoners of war.

They were the glory of the race of rangers,
Matchless with a horse, a rifle, a song, a supper or a
courtship,
Large, turbulent, brave, handsome, generous, proud and
affectionate,
Bearded, sunburnt, dressed in the free costume of hunters,
Not a single one over thirty years of age.

The second Sunday morning they were brought out in
squads and massacred . . . . it was beautiful early summer,
The work commenced about five o'clock and was over
by eight.

None obeyed the command to kneel,
880   Some made a mad and helpless rush . . . . some stood stark
and straight,
A few fell at once, shot in the temple or heart . . . . the living
and dead lay together,
The maimed and mangled dug in the dirt . . . . the
new-comers saw them there;
Some half-killed attempted to crawl away,
These were dispatched with bayonets or battered with the
blunts of muskets;
A youth not seventeen years old seized his assassin till two
more came to release him,
The three were all torn, and covered with the boy's blood.

At eleven o'clock began the burning of the bodies;
And that is the tale of the murder of the four hundred
and twelve young men,
And that was a jetblack sunrise.

890   Did you read in the seabooks of the oldfashioned
frigate-fight?
Did you learn who won by the light of the moon and stars?

Our foe was no skulk in his ship, I tell you,
His was the English pluck, and there is no tougher or truer,
    and never was, and never will be;
Along the lowered eve he came, horribly raking us.

We closed with him . . . . the yards entangled . . . . the
    cannon touched,
My captain lashed fast with his own hands.

We had received some eighteen-pound shots under the
    water,
On our lower-gun-deck two large pieces had burst at the
    first fire, killing all around and blowing up overhead.

Ten o'clock at night, and the full moon shining and the
    leaks on the gain, and five feet of water reported,
900   The master-at-arms loosing the prisoners confined in the
    after-hold to give them a chance for themselves.

The transit to and from the magazine was now stopped by
    the sentinels,
They saw so many strange faces they did not know
    whom to trust.

Our frigate was afire . . . . the other asked if we demanded
    quarters? if our colors were struck and the fighting done?

I laughed content when I heard the voice of my little
    captain,
We have not struck, he composedly cried, We have just
    begun our part of the fighting.

Only three guns were in use,
One was directed by the captain himself against the
    enemy's mainmast,
Two well-served with grape and canister silenced his
    musketry and cleared his decks.

The tops alone seconded the fire of this little battery,
    especially the maintop,
910   They all held out bravely during the whole of the action.

Not a moment's cease,
The leaks gained fast on the pumps . . . . the fire eat
    toward the powder-magazine,
One of the pumps was shot away . . . . it was generally
    thought we were sinking.

Serene stood the little captain,
He was not hurried . . . . his voice was neither high nor
    low,
His eyes gave more light to us than our battle-lanterns.

Toward twelve at night, there in the beams of the moon
    they surrendered to us.

Stretched and still lay the midnight,
Two great hulls motionless on the breast of the darkness,
920 Our vessel riddled and slowly sinking . . . . preparations to
    pass to the one we had conquered,
The captain on the quarter deck coldly giving his orders
    through a countenance white as a sheet,
Near by the corpse of the child that served in the cabin,
The dead face of an old salt with long white hair and
    carefully curled whiskers,
The flames spite of all that could be done flickering aloft
    and below,
The husky voices of the two or three officers yet fit for duty,
Formless stacks of bodies and bodies by themselves . . . .
    dabs of flesh upon the masts and spars,
The cut of cordage and dangle of rigging . . . . the slight
    shock of the soothe of waves,
Black and impassive guns, and litter of powder-parcels,
    and the strong scent,
Delicate sniffs of the seabreeze . . . . smells of sedgy grass
    and fields by the shore . . . . death-messages given in
    charge to survivors,
930 The hiss of the surgeon's knife and the gnawing teeth of
    his saw,

The wheeze, the cluck, the swash of falling blood . . . . the
    short wild scream, the long dull tapering groan,
These so . . . . these irretrievable.

O Christ! My fit is mastering me!
What the rebel said gaily adjusting his throat to the
    rope-noose,
What the savage at the stump, his eye-sockets empty, his
    mouth spirting whoops of defiance,

What stills the traveler come to the vault at Mount Vernon,
What sobers the Brooklyn boy as he looks down the shores
    of the Wallabout and remembers the prison ships,
What burnt the gums of the redcoat at Saratoga when he
    surrendered his brigades,
These become mine and me every one, and they are
    but little,
940 I become as much more as I like.

I become any presence or truth of humanity here,
And see myself in prison shaped like another man,
And feel the dull unintermitted pain.

For me the keepers of convicts shoulder their carbines and
    keep watch,
It is I let out in the morning and barred at night.

Not a mutineer walks handcuffed to the jail, but I am
    handcuffed to him and walk by his side,
I am less the jolly one there, and more the silent one with
    sweat on my twitching lips.

Not a youngster is taken for larceny, but I go up too and am
    tried and sentenced.

Not a cholera patient lies at the last gasp, but I also lie at the
    last gasp,
950 My face is ash-colored, my sinews gnarl . . . . away from me
    people retreat.

Askers embody themselves in me, and I am embodied in
   them,
I project my hat and sit shamefaced and beg.

I rise extatic through all, and sweep with the true gravitation,
The whirling and whirling is elemental within me.

Somehow I have been stunned. Stand back!
Give me a little time beyond my cuffed head and
   slumbers and dreams and gaping,
I discover myself on a verge of the usual mistake.

That I could forget the mockers and insults!
That I could forget the trickling tears and the blows of the
   bludgeons and hammers!
960   That I could look with a separate look on my own
   crucifixion and bloody crowning!

I remember . . . . I resume the overstaid fraction,
The grave of rock multiplies what has been confided to
   it . . . . or to any graves,
The corpses rise . . . . the gashes heal . . . . the fastenings
   roll away.

I troop forth replenished with supreme power, one of an
   average unending procession,
We walk the roads of Ohio and Massachusetts and Virginia
   and Wisconsin and New York and New Orleans and
   Texas and Montreal and San Francisco and Charleston
   and Savannah and Mexico,
Inland and by the seacoast and boundary lines . . . . and we
   pass the boundary lines.

Our swift ordinances are on their way over the whole earth,
The blossoms we wear in our hats are the growth of two
   thousand years.

Eleves I salute you,
970 I see the approach of your numberless gangs . . . . I see you
    understand yourselves and me,
And know that they who have eyes are divine, and the blind
    and lame are equally divine,
And that my steps drag behind yours yet go before them,
And are aware how I am with you no more than I am
    with everybody.

The friendly and flowing savage . . . . Who is he?
Is he waiting for civilization or past it and mastering it?

Is he some southwesterner raised outdoors? Is he Canadian?
Is he from the Mississippi country? or from Iowa, Oregon
    or California? or from the mountains? or prairie life or
    bush-life? or from the sea?

Wherever he goes men and women accept and desire him,
They desire he should like them and touch them and speak
    to them and stay with them.

980 Behaviour lawless as snow-flakes . . . . words simple as
    grass . . . . uncombed head and laughter and naivete;
Slowstepping feet and the common features, and the
    common modes and emanations,
They descend in new forms from the tips of his fingers,
They are wafted with the odor of his body or breath . . . .
    they fly out of the glance of his eyes.

Flaunt of the sunshine I need not your bask . . . . lie over,
You light surfaces only . . . . I force the surfaces and the
    depths also.

Earth! you seem to look for something at my hands,
Say old topknot! what do you want?

Man or woman! I might tell how I like you, but cannot,
And might tell what it is in me and what it is in you,
    but cannot,
990 And might tell the pinings I have . . . . the pulse of my
    nights and days.

Behold I do not give lectures or a little charity,
What I give I give out of myself.

You there, impotent, loose in the knees, open your scarfed
    chops till I blow grit within you,
Spread your palms and lift the flaps of your pockets,
I am not to be denied . . . . I compel . . . . I have stores
    plenty and to spare,
And any thing I have I bestow.

I do not ask who you are . . . . that is not important to me,
You can do nothing and be nothing but what I will infold
    you.

To a drudge of the cottonfields or emptier of privies I
    lean . . . . on his right cheek I put the family kiss,
1000 And in my soul I swear I never will deny him.

On women fit for conception I start bigger and nimbler
    babes,
This day I am jetting the stuff of far more arrogant
    republics.

To any one dying . . . . thither I speed and twist the knob
    of the door,
Turn the bedclothes toward the foot of the bed,
Let the physician and the priest go home.

I seize the descending man . . . . I raise him with resistless
    will.

O despairer, here is my neck,
By God! you shall not go down! Hang your whole weight
    upon me.

I dilate you with tremendous breath . . . . I buoy you up;
1010 Every room of the house do I fill with an armed force . . . .
    lovers of me, bafflers of graves:

Sleep! I and they keep guard all night;
Not doubt, not decease shall dare to lay finger upon you,
I have embraced you, and henceforth possess you to myself,
And when you rise in the morning you will find what I tell
  you is so.

I am he bringing help for the sick as they pant on their
  backs,
And for strong upright men I bring yet more needed help.

I heard what was said of the universe,
Heard it and heard of several thousand years;
It is middling well as far as it goes .... but is that all?

1020 Magnifying and applying come I,
Outbidding at the start the old cautious hucksters,
The most they offer for mankind and eternity less than a
  spirt of my own seminal wet,
Taking myself the exact dimensions of Jehovah and laying
  them away,
Lithographing Kronos and Zeus his son, and Hercules his
  grandson,
Buying drafts of Osiris and Isis and Belus and Brahma and
  Adonai,
In my portfolio placing Manito loose, and Allah on a leaf,
  and the crucifix engraved,
With Odin, and the hideous-faced Mexitli, and all idols and
  images,
Honestly taking them all for what they are worth, and not a
  cent more,
Admitting they were alive and did the work of their day,
1030 Admitting they bore mites as for unfledged birds who have
  now to rise and fly and sing for themselves;
Accepting the rough deific sketches to fill out better in
  myself .... bestowing them freely on each man and
  woman I see.
Discovering as much or more in a framer framing a house,
Putting higher claims for him there with his rolled-up
  sleeves, driving the mallet and chisel;

Not objecting to special revelations . . . . considering a curl of
    smoke or a hair on the back of my hand as curious as
    any revelation;
Those ahold of fire-engines and hook-and-ladder ropes more
    to me than the gods of the antique wars,
Minding their voices peal through the crash of
    destruction,
Their brawny limbs passing safe over charred laths . . . .
    their white foreheads whole and unhurt out of the flames;
By the mechanic's wife with her babe at her nipple
    interceding for every person born;
Three scythes at harvest whizzing in a row from three lusty
    angels with shirts bagged out at their waists;
1040 The snag-toothed hostler with red hair redeeming sins past
    and to come,
Selling all he possesses and traveling on foot to fee lawyers
    for his brother and sit by him while he is tried for
    forgery:
What was strewn in the amplest strewing the square rod
    about me, and not filling the square rod then;
The bull and the bug never worshipped half enough,
Dung and dirt more admirable than was dreamed,
The supernatural of no account . . . . myself waiting my
    time to be one of the supremes,
The day getting ready for me when I shall do as much good
    as the best, and be as prodigious,
Guessing when I am it will not tickle me much to receive
    puffs out of pulpit or print;
By my life-lumps! becoming already a creator!
Putting myself here and now to the ambushed womb of
    the shadows!

1050 . . . . A call in the midst of the crowd,
My own voice, orotund sweeping and final.

Come my children,
Come my boys and girls, and my women and household
    and intimates,

Now the performer launches his nerve . . . . he has passed
his prelude on the reeds within.

Easily written loosefingered chords! I feel the thrum of
their climax and close.

My head evolves on my neck,
Music rolls, but not from the organ . . . . folks are around
me, but they are no household of mine.

Ever the hard and unsunk ground,
Ever the eaters and drinkers . . . . ever the upward and
downward sun . . . . ever the air and the ceaseless tides,
1060 Ever myself and my neighbors, refreshing and wicked and
real,
Ever the old inexplicable query . . . . ever that thorned
thumb – that breath of itches and thirsts,
Ever the vexer's hoot! hoot! till we find where the sly one
hides and bring him forth;
Ever love . . . . ever the sobbing liquid of life,
Ever the bandage under the chin . . . . ever the tressels of
death.

Here and there with dimes on the eyes walking,
To feed the greed of the belly the brains liberally spooning,
Tickets buying or taking or selling, but in to the feast never
once going;
Many sweating and ploughing and thrashing, and then the
chaff for payment receiving,
A few idly owning, and they the wheat continually
claiming.

1070 This is the city . . . . and I am one of the citizens;
Whatever interests the rest interests me . . . . politics,
churches, newspapers, schools,
Benevolent societies, improvements, banks, tariffs,
steamships, factories, markets,
Stocks and stores and real estate and personal estate.

They who piddle and patter here in collars and tailed
coats . . . . I am aware who they are . . . . and that they are
not worms or fleas,
I acknowledge the duplicates of myself under all the
scrape-lipped and pipe-legged concealments.

The weakest and shallowest is deathless with me,
What I do and say the same waits for them,
Every thought that flounders in me the same flounders
in them.

I know perfectly well my own egotism,
1080 And know my omniverous words, and cannot say any less,
And would fetch you whoever you are flush with myself.

My words are words of a questioning, and to indicate
reality;
This printed and bound book . . . . but the printer and the
printing-office boy?
The marriage estate and settlement . . . . but the body and
mind of the bridegroom? also those of the bride?
The panorama of the sea . . . . but the sea itself?
The well-taken photographs . . . . but your wife or friend
close and solid in your arms?
The fleet of ships of the line and all the modern
improvements . . . . but the craft and pluck of the
admiral?
The dishes and fare and furniture . . . . but the host and
hostess, and the look out of their eyes?
The sky up there . . . . yet here or next door or across the
way?
1090 The saints and sages in history . . . . but you yourself?
Sermons and creeds and theology . . . . but the human
brain, and what is called reason, and what is called love,
and what is called life?

I do not despise you priests;
My faith is the greatest of faiths and the least of faiths,
Enclosing all worship ancient and modern, and all between
ancient and modern,

Believing I shall come again upon the earth after
    five thousand years,
Waiting responses from oracles .... honoring the gods ....
    saluting the sun,
Making a fetish of the first rock or stump .... powowing
    with sticks in the circle of obis,
Helping the lama or brahmin as he trims the lamps of
    the idols,
Dancing yet through the streets in a phallic procession ....
    rapt and austere in the woods, a gymnosophist,
1100 Drinking mead from the skull-cup .... to shasta and vedas
    admirant .... minding the koran,
Walking the teokallis, spotted with gore from the stone and
    knife – beating the serpent-skin drum;
Accepting the gospels, accepting him that was crucified,
    knowing assuredly that he is divine,
To the mass kneeling – to the puritan's prayer rising –
    sitting patiently in a pew,
Ranting and frothing in my insane crisis – waiting
    dead-like till my spirit arouses me;
Looking forth on pavement and land, and outside of
    pavement and land,
Belonging to the winders of the circuit of circuits.

One of that centripetal and centrifugal gang,
I turn and talk like a man leaving charges before a journey.

Down-hearted doubters, dull and excluded,
1110 Frivolous sullen moping angry affected disheartened
    atheistical,
I know every one of you, and know the unspoken
    interrogatories,
By experience I know them.

How the flukes splash!
How they contort rapid as lightning, with spasms and
    spouts of blood!

Be at peace bloody flukes of doubters and sullen mopers,
I take my place among you as much as among any;
The past is the push of you and me and all precisely the
    same,
And the night is for you and me and all,
And what is yet untried and afterward is for you and me
    and all.

1120 I do not know what is untried and afterward,
But I know it is sure and alive and sufficient.

Each who passes is considered, and each who stops is
    considered, and not a single one can it fail.

It cannot fail the young man who died and was buried,
Nor the young woman who died and was put by his side,
Nor the little child that peeped in at the door and then drew
    back and was never seen again,
Nor the old man who has lived without purpose, and feels
    it with bitterness worse than gall,
Nor him in the poorhouse tubercled by rum and the bad
    disorder,
Nor the numberless slaughtered and wrecked .... nor the
    brutish koboo, called the ordure of humanity,
Nor the sacs merely floating with open mouths for food to
    slip in,
1130 Nor any thing in the earth, or down in the oldest graves of
    the earth,
Nor any thing in the myriads of spheres, nor one of the
    myriads of myriads that inhabit them,
Nor the present, nor the least wisp that is known.

It is time to explain myself .... let us stand up.

What is known I strip away .... I launch all men and
    women forward with me into the unknown.

The clock indicates the moment .... but what does
    eternity indicate?

Eternity lies in bottomless reservoirs .... its buckets are
    rising forever and ever,
They pour and they pour and they exhale away.

We have thus far exhausted trillions of winters and
    summers;
There are trillions ahead, and trillions ahead of them.

1140 Births have brought us richness and variety,
And other births will bring us richness and variety.

I do not call one greater and one smaller,
That which fills its period and place is equal to any.

Were mankind murderous or jealous upon you my brother
    or my sister?

I am sorry for you .... they are not murderous or jealous
    upon me;
All has been gentle with me .... I keep no account with
    lamentations;
What have I to do with lamentation?

I am an acme of things accomplished, and I an encloser
    of things to be.

My feet strike an apex of the apices of the stairs,
1150 On every step bunches of ages, and larger bunches between
    the steps,
All below duly traveled – and still I mount and mount.

Rise after rise bow the phantoms behind me,
Afar down I see the huge first Nothing, the vapor from the
    nostrils of death,
I know I was even there .... I waited unseen and always,
And slept while God carried me through the lethargic mist,
And took my time .... and took no hurt from the foetid
    carbon.

Long I was hugged close .... long and long.

Immense have been the preparations for me,
Faithful and friendly the arms that have helped me.

1160 Cycles ferried my cradle, rowing and rowing like cheerful
         boatmen;
     For room to me stars kept aside in their own rings,
     They sent influences to look after what was to hold me.

     Before I was born out of my mother generations guided me,
     My embryo has never been torpid . . . . nothing could
         overlay it;
     For it the nebula cohered to an orb . . . . the long slow strata
         piled to rest it on . . . . vast vegetables gave it sustenance,
     Monstrous sauroids transported it in their mouths and
         deposited it with care.

     All forces have been steadily employed to complete and
         delight me,
     Now I stand on this spot with my soul.

     Span of youth! Ever-pushed elasticity! Manhood balanced
         and florid and full!

1170 My lovers suffocate me!
     Crowding my lips, and thick in the pores of my skin,
     Jostling me through streets and public halls . . . . coming
         naked to me at night,
     Crying by day Ahoy from the rocks of the river . . . . swinging
         and chirping over my head,
     Calling my name from flowerbeds or vines or tangled
         underbrush,
     Or while I swim in the bath . . . . or drink from the pump
         at the corner . . . . or the curtain is down at the opera . . . .
         or I glimpse at a woman's face in the railroad car;
     Lighting on every moment of my life,
     Bussing my body with soft and balsamic busses,
     Noiselessly passing handfuls out of their hearts and giving
         them to be mine.

     Old age superbly rising! Ineffable grace of dying days!

1180 Every condition promulges not only itself . . . . it promulges
         what grows after and out of itself,
     And the dark hush promulges as much as any.

I open my scuttle at night and see the far-sprinkled systems,
And all I see, multiplied as high as I can cipher, edge but
    the rim of the farther systems.

Wider and wider they spread, expanding and always
    expanding,
Outward and outward and forever outward.

My sun has his sun, and round him obediently wheels,
He joins with his partners a group of superior circuit,
And greater sets follow, making specks of the greatest
    inside them.

There is no stoppage and never can be stoppage;
1190 If I and you and the worlds and all beneath or upon their
    surfaces, and all the palpable life, were this moment
    reduced back to a pallid float, it would not avail in the
    long run,
We should surely bring up again where we now stand,
And as surely go as much farther, and then farther and
    farther.

A few quadrillions of eras, a few octillions of cubic leagues,
    do not hazard the span, or make it impatient,
They are but parts . . . . any thing is but a part.

See ever so far . . . . there is limitless space outside of that,
Count ever so much . . . . there is limitless time around that.

Our rendezvous is fitly appointed . . . . God will be there
    and wait till we come.

I know I have the best of time and space – and that I was
    never measured, and never will be measured.

I tramp a perpetual journey,
1200 My signs are a rain-proof coat and good shoes and a staff
    cut from the woods;
No friend of mine takes his ease in my chair,
I have no chair, nor church nor philosophy;
I lead no man to a dinner-table or library or exchange,
But each man and each woman of you I lead upon a knoll,

My left hand hooks you round the waist,
My right hand points to landscapes of continents, and a
    plain public road.

Not I, not any one else can travel that road for you,
You must travel it for yourself.

It is not far . . . . it is within reach,
1210 Perhaps you have been on it since you were born, and did
    not know,
Perhaps it is every where on water and on land.

Shoulder your duds, and I will mine, and let us hasten forth;
Wonderful cities and free nations we shall fetch as we go.

If you tire, give me both burdens, and rest the chuff of your
    hand on my hip,
And in due time you shall repay the same service to me;
For after we start we never lie by again.

This day before dawn I ascended a hill and looked at the
    crowded heaven,
And I said to my spirit, When we become the enfolders of
    those orbs and the pleasure and knowledge of every thing
    in them, shall we be filled and satisfied then?
And my spirit said No, we level that lift to pass and continue
    beyond.

1220 You are also asking me questions, and I hear you;
I answer that I cannot answer . . . . you must find out for
    yourself.

Sit awhile wayfarer,
Here are biscuits to eat and here is milk to drink,
But as soon as you sleep and renew yourself in sweet
    clothes I will certainly kiss you with my goodbye kiss and
    open the gate for your egress hence.

Long enough have you dreamed contemptible dreams,
Now I wash the gum from your eyes,
You must habit yourself to the dazzle of the light and of every
    moment of your life.

Long have you timidly waded, holding a plank by the shore,
Now I will you to be a bold swimmer,
1230 To jump off in the midst of the sea, and rise again and nod
 to me and shout, and laughingly dash with your hair.

I am the teacher of athletes,
He that by me spreads a wider breast than my own proves
 the width of my own,
He most honors my style who learns under it to destroy the
 teacher.

The boy I love, the same becomes a man not through
 derived power but in his own right,
Wicked, rather than virtuous out of conformity or fear,
Fond of his sweetheart, relishing well his steak,
Unrequited love or a slight cutting him worse than a
 wound cuts,
First rate to ride, to fight, to hit the bull's eye, to sail a skiff,
 to sing a song or play on the banjo,
Preferring scars and faces pitted with smallpox over all
 latherers and those that keep out of the sun.

1240 I teach straying from me, yet who can stray from me?
I follow you whoever you are from the present hour;
My words itch at your ears till you understand them.

I do not say these things for a dollar, or to fill up the time
 while I wait for a boat;
It is you talking just as much as myself . . . . I act as the
 tongue of you,
It was tied in your mouth . . . . in mine it begins to be
 loosened.

I swear I will never mention love or death inside a house,
And I swear I never will translate myself at all, only to him
 or her who privately stays with me in the open air.

If you would understand me go to the heights or
    water-shore,
The nearest gnat is an explanation and a drop or the motion
    of waves a key,
1250 The maul the oar, and the handsaw second my words.

No shuttered room or school can commune with me,
But roughs and little children better than they.

The young mechanic is closest to me . . . . he knows me
    pretty well,
The woodman that takes his axe and jug with him shall take
    me with him all day,
The farmboy ploughing in the field feels good at the sound
    of my voice,
In vessels that sail my words must sail . . . . I go with
    fishermen and seamen, and love them,
My face rubs to the hunter's face when he lies down alone
    in his blanket,
The driver thinking of me does not mind the jolt of his
    wagon,
The young mother and old mother shall comprehend me,
1260 The girl and the wife rest the needle a moment and forget
    where they are,
They and all would resume what I have told them.

I have said that the soul is not more than the body,
And I have said that the body is not more than the soul,
And nothing, not God, is greater to one than one's-self is,
And whoever walks a furlong without sympathy walks to
    his own funeral, dressed in his shroud,
And I or you pocketless of a dime may purchase the pick of
    the earth,
And to glance with an eye or show a bean in its pod
    confounds the learning of all times,
And there is no trade or employment but the young man
    following it may become a hero,
And there is no object so soft but it makes a hub for the
    wheeled universe,

1270 And any man or woman shall stand cool and supercilious
    before a million universes.

And I call to mankind, Be not curious about God,
For I who am curious about each am not curious about God,
No array of terms can say how much I am at peace about
    God and about death.

I hear and behold God in every object, yet I understand
    God not in the least,
Nor do I understand who there can be more wonderful than
    myself.

Why should I wish to see God better than this day?
I see something of God each hour of the twenty-four, and
    each moment then,
In the faces of men and women I see God, and in my own
    face in the glass;
I find letters from God dropped in the street, and every one
    is signed by God's name,
1280 And I leave them where they are, for I know that others will
    punctually come forever and ever.

And as to you death, and you bitter hug of mortality . . . . it
    is idle to try to alarm me.

To his work without flinching the accoucheur comes,
I see the elderhand pressing receiving supporting,
I recline by the sills of the exquisite flexible doors . . . . and
    mark the outlet, and mark the relief and escape.

And as to you corpse I think you are good manure, but that
    does not offend me,
I smell the white roses sweet-scented and growing,
I reach to the leafy lips . . . . I reach to the polished breasts
    of melons.

And as to you life, I reckon you are the leavings of many
    deaths,
No doubt I have died myself ten thousand times before.

1290 I hear you whispering there O stars of heaven,
    O suns . . . . O grass of graves . . . . O perpetual transfers
      and promotions . . . . if you do not say anything how can I
      say anything?

Of the turbid pool that lies in the autumn forest,
Of the moon that descends the steeps of the soughing
    twilight,
Toss, sparkles of day and dusk . . . . toss on the black stems
    that decay in the muck,
Toss to the moaning gibberish of the dry limbs.

I ascend from the moon . . . . I ascend from the night,
And perceive of the ghastly glitter the sunbeams reflected,
And debouch to the steady and central from the offspring
    great or small.

There is that in me . . . . I do not know what it is . . . . but I
    know it is in me.

1300 Wrenched and sweaty . . . . calm and cool then my body
    becomes;
I sleep . . . . I sleep long.

I do not know it . . . . it is without name . . . . it is a word
    unsaid,
It is not in any dictionary or utterance or symbol.
Something it swings on more than the earth I swing on,
To it the creation is the friend whose embracing awakes me.

Perhaps I might tell more . . . . Outlines! I plead for my
    brothers and sisters.

Do you see O my brothers and sisters?
It is not chaos or death . . . . it is form and union and
    plan . . . . it is eternal life . . . . it is happiness.

The past and present wilt . . . . I have filled them and
    emptied them,
1310 And proceed to fill my next fold of the future.

Listener up there! Here you . . . . what have you to confide
  to me?
Look in my face while I snuff the sidle of evening,
Talk honestly, for no one else hears you, and I stay only a
  minute longer.

Do I contradict myself?
Very well then . . . . I contradict myself;
I am large . . . . I contain multitudes.

I concentrate toward them that are nigh . . . . I wait on the
  door-slab.

Who has done his day's work and will soonest be through
  with his supper?
Who wishes to walk with me?

1320 Will you speak before I am gone? Will you prove already
  too late?

The spotted hawk swoops by and accuses me . . . . he
  complains of my gab and my loitering.

I too am not a bit tamed . . . . I too am untranslatable,
I sound my barbaric yawp over the roofs of the world.

The last scud of day holds back for me,
It flings my likeness after the rest and true as any on the
  shadowed wilds,
It coaxes me to the vapor and the dusk.

I depart as air . . . . I shake my white locks at the runaway
  sun,
I effuse my flesh in eddies and drift it in lacy jags.

I bequeath myself to the dirt to grow from the grass I love,
1330 If you want me again look for me under your bootsoles.

You will hardly know who I am or what I mean,
But I shall be good health to you nevertheless,
And filter and fibre your blood.

Failing to fetch me me at first keep encouraged,
Missing me one place search another,
I stop some where waiting for you

APPENDIX 5
Prefaces

Leaves of Grass, 1855

America does not repel the past or what it has produced under its forms or amid other politics or the idea of castes or the old religions . . . . accepts the lesson with calmness . . . is not so impatient as has been supposed that the slough still sticks to opinions and manners and literature while the life which served its requirements has passed into the new life of the new forms . . . perceives that the corpse is slowly borne from the eating and sleeping rooms of the house . . . perceives that it waits a little while in the door . . . that it was fittest for its days . . . that its action has descended to the stalwart and wellshaped heir who approaches . . . and that he shall be fittest for his days.

The Americans of all nations at any time upon the earth have probably the fullest poetical nature. The United States themselves are essentially the greatest poem. In the history of the earth hitherto the largest and most stirring appear tame and orderly to their ampler largeness and stir. Here at last is something in the doings of man that corresponds with the broadcast doings of the day and night. Here is not merely a nation but a teeming nation of nations. Here is action untied from strings necessarily blind to particulars and details magnificently moving in vast masses. Here is the hospitality which forever indicates heroes . . . . Here are the roughs and beards and space and ruggedness and nonchalance that the soul loves. Here the performance disdaining the trivial unapproached in the tremendous audacity of its crowds and groupings and the push of its perspective spreads with crampless and flowing breadth and showers its prolific and splendid extravagance. One sees it must indeed own the riches of the summer and winter, and need never be bankrupt while corn grows from the ground or the orchards drop apples or the bays contain fish or men beget children upon women.

Other states indicate themselves in their deputies . . . . but the genius of the United States is not best or most in its executives or legislatures, nor in its ambassadors or authors or colleges or churches or parlors, nor even in its newspapers or inventors . . . but always most in the common people. Their manners speech dress friendships – the freshness and candor of their physiognomy

– the picturesque looseness of their carriage . . . their deathless attachment to freedom – their aversion to anything indecorous or soft or mean – the practical acknowledgment of the citizens of one state by the citizens of all other states – the fierceness of their roused resentment – their curiosity and welcome of novelty – their self-esteem and wonderful sympathy – their susceptibility to a slight – the air they have of persons who never knew how it felt to stand in the presence of superiors – the fluency of their speech – their delight in music, the sure symptom of manly tenderness and native elegance of soul . . . their good temper and openhandedness – the terrible significance of their elections – the President's taking off his hat to them not they to him – these too are unrhymed poetry. It awaits the gigantic and generous treatment worthy of it..

The largeness of nature or the nation were monstrous without a corresponding largeness and generosity of the spirit of the citizen. Not nature nor swarming states nor streets and steamships nor prosperous business nor farms nor capital nor learning may suffice for the ideal of man . . . nor suffice the poet. No reminiscences may suffice either. A live nation can always cut a deep mark and can have the best authority the cheapest . . . namely from its own soul. This is the sum of the profitable uses of individuals or states and of present action and grandeur and of the subjects of poets. – As if it were necessary to trot back generation after generation to the eastern records! As if the beauty and sacredness of the demonstrable must fall behind that of the mythical! As if men do not make their mark out of any times! As if the opening of the western continent by discovery and what has transpired since in North and South America were less than the small theatre of the antique or the aimless sleepwalking of the middle ages! The pride of the United States leaves the wealth and finesse of the cities and all returns of commerce and agriculture and all the magnitude of geography or shows of exterior victory to enjoy the breed of full-sized men or one fullsized man unconquerable and simple.

The American poets are to enclose old and new for America is the race of races. Of them a bard is to be commensurate with a people. To him the other continents arrive as contributions . . . he gives them reception for their sake and his own sake. His spirit responds to his country's spirit . . . . he incarnates its geography

and natural life and rivers and lakes. Mississippi with annual
freshets and changing chutes, Missouri and Columbia and Ohio
and Saint Lawrence with the falls and beautiful masculine Hudson,
do not embouchure where they spend themselves more than they
embouchure into him. The blue breadth over the inland sea of
Virginia and Maryland and the sea off Massachusetts and Maine
and over Manhattan bay and over Champlain and Erie and over
Ontario and Huron and Michigan and Superior, and over the
Texan and Mexican and Floridian and Cuban seas and over the
seas off California and Oregon, is not tallied by the blue breadth
of the waters below more than the breadth of above and below is
tallied by him. When the long Atlantic coast stretches longer and
the Pacific coast stretches longer he easily stretches with them
north or south. He spans between them also from east to west and
reflects what is between them. On him rise solid growths that offset
the growths of pine and cedar and hemlock and liveoak and locust
and chestnut and cypress and hickory and limetree and cotton-
wood and tuliptree and cactus and wildvine and tamarind and
persimmon . . . . and tangles as tangled as any canebrake or
swamp . . . . and forests coated with transparent ice and icicles
hanging from the boughs and crackling in the wind . . . . and sides
and peaks of mountains . . . . and pasturage sweet and free as
savannah or upland or prairie . . . . with flights and songs and
screams that answer those of the wildpigeon and highhold and
orchard-oriole and coot and surf-duck and redshouldered-hawk
and fish-hawk and white-ibis and indian-hen and cat-owl and
water-pheasant and qua-bird and pied-sheldrake and blackbird
and mockingbird and buzzard and condor and night-heron and
eagle. To him the hereditary countenance descends both mother's
and father's. To him enter the essences of the real things and past
and present events – of the enormous diversity of temperature and
agriculture and mines – the tribes of red aborigines – the weather-
beaten vessels entering new ports or making landings on rocky
coasts – the first settlements north or south – the rapid stature and
muscle – the haughty defiance of '76, and the war and peace and
formation of the constitution . . . . the union always surrounded by
blatherers and always calm and impregnable – the perpetual
coming of immigrants – the wharf-hem'd cities and superior

marine – the unsurveyed interior – the loghouses and clearings and wild animals and hunters and trappers . . . . the free commerce – the fisheries and whaling and gold-digging – the endless gestation of new states – the convening of Congress every December, the members duly coming up from all climates and the uttermost parts . . . . the noble character of the young mechanics and of all free American workmen and workwomen . . . . the general ardor and friendliness and enterprise – the perfect equality of the female with the male . . . . the large amativeness – the fluid movement of the population – the factories and mercantile life and laborsaving machinery – the Yankee swap – the New-York firemen and the target excursion – the southern plantation life – the character of the northeast and of the northwest and southwest – slavery and the tremulous spreading of hands to protect it, and the stern opposition to it which shall never cease till it ceases or the speaking of tongues and the moving of lips cease. For such the expression of the American poet is to be transcendant and new. It is to be indirect and not direct or descriptive or epic. Its quality goes through these to much more. Let the age and wars of other nations be chanted and their eras and characters be illustrated and that finish the verse. Not so the great psalm of the republic. Here the theme is creative and has vista. Here comes one among the wellbeloved stonecutters and plans with decision and science and sees the solid and beautiful forms of the future where there are now no solid forms.

Of all nations the United States with veins full of poetical stuff most need poets and will doubtless have the greatest and use them the greatest. Their Presidents shall not be their common referee so much as their poets shall. Of all mankind the great poet is the equable man. Not in him but off from him things are grotesque or eccentric or fail of their sanity. Nothing out of its place is good and nothing in its place is bad. He bestows on every object or quality its fit proportions neither more nor less. He is the arbiter of the diverse and he is the key. He is the equalizer of his age and land . . . . he supplies what wants supplying and checks what wants checking. If peace is the routine out of him speaks the spirit of peace, large, rich, thrifty, building vast and populous cities, encouraging agriculture and the arts and commerce – lighting the study of man, the soul, immortality – federal, state or municipal government, marriage, health, freetrade, intertravel by land and sea . . . . nothing too close, nothing too far off . . . the stars not too far off. In war he is the most deadly force of the war. Who recruits him recruits horse and foot . . . he fetches parks of artillery the best that engineer ever knew. If the time becomes slothful and heavy he knows how to arouse it . . . he can make every word he speaks draw blood. Whatever stagnates in the flat of custom or obedience or legislation he never stagnates. Obedience does not master him, he masters it. High up out of reach he stands turning a concentrated light . . . he turns the pivot with his finger . . . he baffles the swiftest runners as he stands and easily overtakes and envelops them. The time straying toward infidelity and confections and persiflage he withholds by his steady faith . . . he spreads out his dishes . . . he offers the sweet firmfibred meat that grows men and women. His brain is the ultimate brain. He is no arguer . . . he is judgment. He judges not as the judge judges but as the sun falling around a helpless thing. As he sees the farthest he has the most faith. His thoughts are the hymns of the praise of things. In the talk on the soul and eternity and God off of his equal plane he is silent. He sees eternity less like a play with a prologue and denouement . . . . he sees eternity in men and women . . . he does not see men and women as dreams or dots. Faith is the antiseptic of the soul . . . it pervades the common people and preserves them . . . they never give up believing and expecting and trusting. There is that indescribable freshness and unconsciousness about an illiterate person that humbles and mocks the power of the noblest expressive genius. The poet sees for a certainty how one not a great artist may be just as sacred and perfect as the greatest artist. . . . The power to destroy or remould is freely used by him but never the power of attack. What is past is past. If he does not expose superior models and prove himself by every step he takes he is not what is wanted. The presence of the greatest poet conquers . . . not parleying or struggling or any prepared attempts. Now he has passed that way see after him! there is not left any vestige of despair or misanthropy or cunning or exclusiveness or the ignominy of a nativity of color or delusion of hell or the necessity of hell . . . . . and no man thenceforward shall be degraded for ignorance or weakness or sin.

The greatest poet hardly knows pettiness or triviality. If he breathes into any thing that was before thought small it dilates with the grandeur and life of the universe. He is a seer . . . . he is individual . . . he is complete in himself . . . . the others are as good as he, only he sees it and they do not. He is not one of the chorus . . . . he does not stop for any regulation . . . he is the president of regulation. What the eyesight does to the rest he does to the rest. Who knows the curious mystery of the eyesight? The other senses corroborate themselves, but this is removed from any proof but its own and foreruns the identities of the spiritual world. A single glance of it mocks all the investigations of man and all the instruments and books of the earth and all reasoning. What is marvellous? what is unlikely? what is impossible or baseless or vague? after you have once just opened the space of a peachpit and given audience to far and near and to the sunset and had all things enter with electric swiftness softly and duly without confusion or jostling or jam.

The land and sea, the animals, fishes and birds, the sky of heaven and the orbs, the forests mountains and rivers, are not small themes . . . but folk expect of the poet to indicate more than the beauty and dignity which always attach to dumb real objects . . . . they expect him to indicate the path between reality and their souls. Men and women perceive the beauty well enough . . . . probably as well as he. The passionate tenacity of hunters, woodmen, early risers, cultivators of gardens and orchards and fields, the love of healthy women for the manly form, seafaring persons, drivers of horses, the passion for light and the open air, all is an old varied sign of the unfailing perception of beauty and of a residence of the poetic in outdoor people. They can never be assisted by poets to perceive . . . . some may but they never can. The poetic quality is not marshalled in rhyme or uniformity or abstract addresses to things nor in melancholy complaints or good precepts, but is the life of these and much else and is in the soul. The profit of rhyme is that it drops seeds of a sweeter and more luxuriant rhyme, and of uniformity that it conveys itself into its own roots in the ground out of sight. The rhyme and uniformity of perfect poems show the free growth of metrical laws and bud from them as unerringly and loosely as lilacs or roses on a bush, and take shapes as compact as the shapes of chestnuts and oranges and melons and pears, and shed the perfume impalpable to form. The fluency and ornaments of the finest poems or music or orations or recitations are not independent but dependent. All beauty comes from beautiful blood and a beautiful brain. If the greatnesses are in conjunction in a man or woman it is enough . . . . the fact will prevail through the universe . . . . but the gaggery and gilt of a million years will not prevail. Who troubles himself about his ornaments or fluency is lost. This is what you shall do: Love the earth and sun and the animals, despise riches, give alms to every one that asks, stand up for the stupid and crazy, devote your income and labor to others, hate tyrants, argue not concerning God, have patience and indulgence toward the people, take off your hat to nothing known or unknown or to any man or number of men, go freely with powerful uneducated persons and with the young and with the mothers of families, read these leaves in the open air every season of every year of your life, re-examine all you have been told at school or church or in any book, dismiss whatever insults your own soul, and your very flesh shall be a great poem and have the richest fluency not only in its words but in the silent lines of its lips and face and between the lashes of your eyes and in every motion and joint of your body. . . . The poet shall not spend his time in unneeded work. He shall know that the ground is always ready ploughed and manured . . . . others may not know it but he shall. He shall go directly to the creation. His trust shall master the trust of everything he touches . . . . and shall master all attachment.

The known universe has one complete lover and that is the greatest poet. He consumes an eternal passion and is indifferent which chance happens and which possible contingency of fortune or misfortune and persuades daily and hourly his delicious pay. What balks or breaks others is fuel for his burning progress to contact and amorous joy. Other proportions of the reception of pleasure dwindle to nothing to his proportions. All expected from heaven or from the highest he is rapport with in the sight of the daybreak or a scene of the winter woods or the presence of children playing or with his arm round the neck of a man or

woman. His love above all love has leisure and expanse . . . . he
leaves room ahead of himself. He is no irresolute or suspicious
lover . . . he is sure . . . he scorns intervals. His experience and the
showers and thrills are not for nothing. Nothing can jar him . . . .
suffering and darkness cannot – death and fear cannot. To him
complaint and jealousy and envy are corpses buried and rotten in
the earth . . . . he saw them buried. The sea is not surer of the
shore or the shore of the sea than he is of the fruition of his love
and of all perfection and beauty.

The fruition of beauty is no chance of hit or miss . . . it is in-
evitable as life . . . . it is exact and plumb as gravitation. From the
eyesight proceeds another eyesight and from the hearing proceeds
another hearing and from the voice proceeds another voice etern-
ally curious of the harmony of things with man. To these respond
perfections not only in the committees that were supposed to
stand for the rest but in the rest themselves just the same. These
understand the law of perfection in masses and floods . . . that its
finish is to each for itself and onward from itself . . . that it is
profuse and impartial . . . that there is not a minute of the light
or dark nor an acre of the earth or sea without it – nor any direc-
tion of the sky nor any trade or employment nor any turn of events.
This is the reason that about the proper expression of beauty there
is precision and balance . . . one part does not need to be thrust
above the other. The best singer is not the one who has the most
lithe and powerful organ . . . the pleasure of poems is not in them
that take the handsomest measure and similes and sound.

Without effort and without exposing in the least how it is done
the greatest poet brings the spirit of any or all events and passions
and scenes and persons some more and some less to bear on your
individual character as you hear or read. To do this well is to
compete with the laws that pursue and follow time. What is the
purpose must surely be there and the clue of it must be there . . . .
and the faintest indication is the indication of the best and then
becomes the clearest indication. Past and present and future are
not disjoined but joined. The greatest poet forms the consistence
of what is to be from what has been and is. He drags the dead out
of their coffins and stands them again on their feet . . . . he says to
the past, Rise and walk before me that I may realize you. He learns

the lesson . . . . he places himself where the future becomes present. The greatest poet does not only dazzle his rays over character and scenes and passions . . . he finally ascends and finishes all . . . he exhibits the pinnacles that no man can tell what they are for or what is beyond . . . . he glows a moment on the extremest verge. He is most wonderful in his last half-hidden smile or frown . . . by that flash of the moment of parting the one that sees it shall be encouraged or terrified afterward for many years. The greatest poet does not moralize or make applications of morals . . . he knows the soul. The soul has that measureless pride which consists in never acknowledging any lessons but its own. But it has sympathy as measureless as its pride and the one balances the other and neither can stretch too far while it stretches in company with the other. The inmost secrets of art sleep with the twain. The greatest poet has lain close betwixt both and they are vital in his style and thoughts.

The art of art, the glory of expression and the sunshine of the light of letters is simplicity. Nothing is better than simplicity . . . . nothing can make up for excess or for the lack of definiteness. To carry on the heave of impulse and pierce intellectual depths and give all subjects their articulations are powers neither common nor very uncommon. But to speak in literature with the perfect rectitude and insousiance of the movements of animals and the unimpeachableness of the sentiment of trees in the woods and grass by the roadside is the flawless triumph of art. If you have looked on him who has achieved it you have looked on one of the masters of the artists of all nations and times. You shall not contemplate the flight of the graygull over the bay or the mettlesome action of the blood horse or the tall leaning of sunflowers on their stalk or the appearance of the sun journeying through heaven or the appearance of the moon afterward with any more satisfaction than you shall contemplate him. The greatest poet has less a marked style and is more the channel of thoughts and things without increase or diminution, and is the free channel of himself. He swears to his art, I will not be meddlesome, I will not have in my writing any elegance or effect or originality to hang in the way between me and the rest like curtains. I will have nothing hang in the way, not the richest curtains. What I tell I tell precisely for what it is. Let who may exalt or startle or fascinate or sooth I will have purposes as health or heat or snow has and be as regardless of observation. What I experience or portray shall go from my composition without a shred of my composition. You shall stand by my side and look in the mirror with me.

The old red blood and stainless gentility of great poets will be proved by their unconstraint. A heroic person walks at his ease through and out of that custom or precedent or authority that suits him not. Of the traits of the brotherhood of writers savans musicians inventors and artists nothing is finer than silent defiance advancing from new free forms. In the need of poems philosophy politics mechanism science behaviour, the craft of art, an appropriate native grand-opera, shipcraft, or any craft, he is greatest forever and forever who contributes the greatest original practical example. The cleanest expression is that which finds no sphere worthy of itself and makes one.

The messages of great poets to each man and woman are, Come to us on equal terms, only then can you understand us, We are no better than you, What we enclose you enclose, What we enjoy you may enjoy. Did you suppose there could be only one Supreme? We affirm there can be unnumbered Supremes, and that one does not countervail another any more than one eyesight countervails another...and that men can be good or grand only of the consciousness of their supremacy within them. What do you think is the grandeur of storms and dismemberments and the deadliest battles and wrecks and the wildest fury of the elements and the power of the sea and the motion of nature and of the throes of human desires and dignity and hate and love? It is that something in the soul which says, Rage on, Whirl on, I tread master here and 'everywhere, Master of the spasms of the sky and of the shatter of the sea, Master of nature and passion and death, And of all terror and all pain.

The American bards shall be marked for generosity and affection and for encouraging competitors.... They shall be kosmos... without monopoly or secresy...glad to pass any thing to any one... hungry for equal night and day. They shall not be careful of riches and privilege . . . . they shall be riches and privilege . . . . they shall perceive who the most affluent man is. The most affluent man is he that confronts all the shows he sees by equivalents out of the stronger wealth of himself. The American bard shall delineate no class of persons nor one or two out of the strata of interests nor love most nor truth most nor the soul most nor the body most . . . . and not be for the eastern states more than the western or the northern states more than the southern.

Exact science and its practical movements are no checks on the greatest poets but always his encouragement and support. The outself and remembrance are there . . . . there the arms that lifted him first and brace him best . . . . there he returns after all his goings and comings. The sailor and traveler . . . the anatomist chemist astronomer geologist phrenologist spiritualist mathematician historian and lexicographer are not poets, but they are the lawgivers of poets and their construction underlies the structure of every perfect poem. No matter what rises or is uttered they sent the seed of the conception of it . . . of them and by them stand the visible proofs of souls . . . . . always of their fatherstuff must be begotten the sinewy races of bards. If there shall be love and content between the father and the son and if the greatness of the son is the exuding of the greatness of the father there shall be love between the poet and the man of demonstrable science. In the beauty of poems are the tuft and final applause of science.

Great is the faith of the flush of knowledge and of the investigation of the depth of qualities and things. Cleaving and circling here swells the soul of the poet yet is president of itself always. The depths are fathomless and therefore calm. The innocence and nakedness are resumed . . . they are neither modest nor immodest. The whole theory of the special and supernatural and all that was twined with it or educed out of it departs as a dream. What has ever happened . . . . what happens and whatever may or shall happen, the vital laws enclose all . . . . they are sufficient for any case and for all cases . . . none to be hurried or retarded . . . . any miracle of affairs or persons inadmissible in the vast clear scheme where every motion and every spear of grass and the frames and spirits of men and women and all that concerns them are unspeakably perfect miracles all referring to all and each distinct and in its place. It is also not consistent with the reality of the soul to admit that there is anything in the known universe more divine than men and women.

Men and women and the earth and all upon it are simply to be taken as they are, and the investigation of their past and present and future shall be unintermitted and shall be done with perfect candor. Upon this basis philosophy speculates ever looking toward the poet, ever regarding the eternal tendencies of all toward happiness never inconsistent with what is clear to the senses and to the soul. For the eternal tendencies of all toward happiness make the only point of sane philosophy. Whatever comprehends less than that . . . whatever is less than the laws of light and of astronomical motion . . . or less than the laws that follow the thief the liar the glutton and the drunkard through this life and doubtless afterward . . . . . . or less than vast stretches of time or the slow formation of density or the patient upheaving of strata – is of no account. Whatever would put God in a poem or system of philosophy as contending against some being or influence is also of no account. Sanity and ensemble characterize the great master . . . spoilt in one principle all is spoilt. The great master has nothing to do with miracles. He sees health for himself in being one of the mass . . . . he sees the hiatus in singular eminence. To the perfect shape comes common ground. To be under the general law is great for that is to correspond with it. The master knows that he is unspeakably great and that all are unspeakably great . . . . that nothing for instance is greater than to conceive children and bring them up well . . . . that to be is just as great as to perceive or tell.

In the make of the great masters the idea of political liberty is indispensable. Liberty takes the adherence of heroes wherever men and women exist . . . . but never takes any adherence or welcome from the rest more than from poets. They are the voice and exposition of liberty. They out of ages are worthy the grand idea . . . . to them it is confided and they must sustain it. Nothing has precedence of it and nothing can warp or degrade it. The attitude of great poets is to cheer up slaves and horrify despots. The turn of their necks, the sound of their feet, the motions of their wrists, are full of hazard to the one and hope to the other. Come nigh them awhile and though they neither speak or advise you shall learn the faithful American lesson. Liberty is poorly served by men whose good intent is quelled from one failure or two failures or any number of failures, or from the casual indifference or ingratitude of the people, or from the sharp show of the tushes of power, or the bringing to bear soldiers and cannon or any penal statutes. Liberty relies upon itself, invites no one, promises nothing, sits in calmness and light, is positive and composed, and knows no discouragement. The battle rages with many a loud alarm and frequent advance and retreat . . . . the enemy triumphs . . . . the prison, the handcuffs, the iron necklace and anklet, the scaffold, garrote and leadballs do their work . . . . the cause is asleep . . . . the strong throats are choked with their own blood . . . . the young men drop their eyelashes toward the ground when they pass each other . . . . and is liberty gone out of that place? No never. When liberty goes it is not the first to go nor the second or third to go . . . . it waits for all the rest to go. . . . it is the last. . . When the memories of the old martyrs are faded utterly away . . . . when the large names of patriots are laughed at in the public halls from the lips of the orators . . . . when the boys are no more christened after the same but christened after tyrants and traitors instead . . . . when the laws of the free are grudgingly permitted and laws for informers and bloodmoney are sweet to the taste of the people . . . . when I and you walk abroad upon the earth stung with compassion at the sight of numberless brothers answering our equal friendship and calling no man master – and when we are elated with noble joy at the sight of slaves . . . . when the soul retires in the cool communion of the night and surveys its experience and has much extasy over the word and deed that put back a helpless innocent person into the gripe of the gripers or into any cruel inferiority . . . . when those in all parts of these states who could easier realize the true American character but do not yet – when the swarms of cringers, suckers, doughfaces, lice of politics, planners of sly involutions for their own preferment to city offices or state legislatures or the judiciary or congress or the presidency, obtain a response of love and natural deference from the people whether they get the offices or no . . . . when it is better to be a bound booby and rogue in office at a high salary than the poorest free mechanic or farmer with his hat unmoved from his head and firm eyes and a candid and generous heart . . . . and when servility by town or state or the federal government or any oppression on a large scale or small scale can be tried on without its own punishment following duly after in exact proportion against the smallest chance of escape . . . . or rather when all life and all the souls of men and women are discharged from any part of the earth – then only shall the instinct of liberty be discharged from that part of the earth.

As the attributes of the poets of the kosmos concentre in the real body and soul and in the pleasure of things they possess the superiority of genuineness over all fiction and romance. As they emit themselves facts are showered over with light . . . . the daylight is lit with more volatile light . . . . also the deep between the setting and rising sun goes deeper many fold. Each precise object or condition or combination or process exhibits a beauty . . . . the multiplication table its – old age its – the carpenter's trade its – the grand-opera its . . . . the hugehulled cleanshaped New-York clipper at sea under steam or full sail gleams with unmatched beauty . . . . the American circles and large harmonies of government gleam with theirs . . . . and the commonest definite intentions and actions with theirs. The poets of the kosmos advance through all interpositions and coverings and turmoils and stratagems to first principles. They are of use . . . . they dissolve poverty from its need and riches from its conceit. You large proprietor they say shall not realize or perceive more than any one else. The owner of the library is not he who holds a legal title to it having bought and paid for it. Any one and every one is owner of the library who can read the same through all the varieties of tongues and subjects and styles, and in whom they enter with ease and take residence and force toward paternity and maternity, and make supple and powerful and rich and large. . . . These American states strong and healthy and accomplished shall receive no pleasure from violations of natural models and must not permit them. In paintings or mouldings or carvings in mineral or wood, or in the illustrations of books or newspapers, or in any comic or tragic prints, or in the patterns of woven stuffs or any thing to beautify rooms or furniture or costumes, or to put upon cornices or monuments or on the prows or sterns of ships, or to put anywhere before the human eye indoors or out, that which distorts honest shapes or which creates unearthly beings or places or contingencies is a nuisance and revolt. Of the human form especially it is so great it must never be made ridiculous. Of ornaments to a work nothing outre can be allowed .... but those ornaments can be allowed that conform to the perfect facts of the open air and that flow out of the nature of the work and come irrepressibly from it and are necessary to the completion of the work. Most works are most beautiful without ornament. ... Exaggerations will be revenged in human physiology. Clean and vigorous children are jetted and conceived only in those communities where the models of natural forms are public every day.... Great genius and the people of these states must never be demeaned to romances. As soon as histories are properly told there is no more need of romances.

The great poets are also to be known by the absence in them of tricks and by the justification of perfect personal candor. Then folks echo a new cheap joy and a divine voice leaping from their brains: How beautiful is candor! All faults may be forgiven of him who has perfect candor. Henceforth let no man of us lie, for we have seen that openness wins the inner and outer world and that there is no single exception, and that never since our earth gathered itself in a mass have deceit or subterfuge or prevarication attracted its smallest particle or the faintest tinge of a shade – and that through the enveloping wealth and rank of a state or the whole republic of states a sneak or sly person shall be discovered and despised . . . . and that the soul has never been once fooled and never can be fooled . . . . and thrift without the loving nod of the soul is only a foetid puff . . . . and there never grew up in any of the continents of the globe nor upon any planet or satellite or star, nor upon the asteroids, nor in any part of ethereal space, nor in the midst of density, nor under the fluid wet of the sea, nor in that condition which precedes the birth of babes, nor at any time during the changes of life, nor in that condition that follows what we term death, nor in any stretch of abeyance or action afterward of vitality, nor in any process of formation or reformation anywhere, a being whose instinct hated the truth.

Extreme caution or prudence, the soundest organic health, large hope and comparison and fondness for women and children, large alimentiveness and destructiveness and causality, with a perfect sense of the oneness of nature and the propriety of the same spirit applied to human affairs . . these are called up of the float of the brain of the world to be parts of the greatest poet from his birth out of his mother's womb and from her birth out of her mother's. Caution seldom goes far enough. It has been thought that the prudent citizen was the citizen who applied himself to solid gains and did well for himself and his family and completed a lawful life without debt or crime. The greatest poet sees and admits these economies as he sees the economies of food and sleep, but has higher notions of prudence than to think he gives much when he gives a few slight attentions at the latch of the gate. The premises of the prudence of life are not the hospitality of it or the ripeness and harvest of it. Beyond the independence of a little sum laid aside for burial-money, and of a few clapboards around and shingles overhead on a lot of American soil owned, and the easy dollars that supply the year's plain clothing and meals, the melancholy prudence of the abandonment of such a great being as a man is to the toss and pallor of years of moneymaking with all their scorching days and icy nights and all their stifling deceits and underhanded dodgings, or infinitessimals of parlors, or shameless stuffing while others starve . . . . and all the loss of the bloom and odor of the earth and of the flowers and atmosphere and of the sea and of the true taste of the women and men you pass or have to do with in youth or middle age, and the issuing sickness and desperate revolt at the close of a life without elevation of naivete, and the ghastly chatter of a death without serenity or majesty, is the great fraud upon modern civilization and forethought, blotching the surface and system which civilization undeniably drafts, and moistening with tears the immense features it spreads and spreads with such velocity before the reached kisses of the soul. . . . Still the right explanation remains to be made about prudence. The prudence of the mere wealth and respectability of the most esteemed life appears too faint for the eye to observe at all when little and large alike drop quietly aside at the thought of the prudence suitable for immortality. What is wisdom that fills the thinness of a year or seventy or eighty years to wisdom spaced out by ages and coming back at a certain time with strong reinforcements and rich presents and the clear faces of wedding-guests as

far as you can look in every direction running gaily toward you?
Only the soul is of itself . . . . all else has reference to what ensues.
All that a person does or thinks is of consequence. Not a move can
a man or woman make that affects him or her in a day or a month
or any part of the direct lifetime or the hour of death but the same
affects him or her onward afterward through the indirect lifetime.
The indirect is always as great and real as the direct. The spirit
receives from the body just as much as it gives to the body. Not
one name of word or deed . . . not of venereal sores or discolorations
. . . not the privacy of the onanist . . . not of the putrid veins of
gluttons or rumdrinkers . . . not peculation or cunning or betrayal
or murder . . . no serpentine poison of those that seduce women . . .
not the foolish yielding of women . . . not prostitution . . . not of any
depravity of young men . . . not of the attainment of gain by dis-
creditable means . . . not any nastiness of appetite . . . not any harsh-
ness of officers to men or judges to prisoners or fathers to sons or
sons to fathers or of husbands to wives or bosses to their boys . . .
not of greedy looks or malignant wishes . . . nor any of the wiles
practised by people upon themselves . . . ever is or ever can be
stamped on the programme but it is duly realized and returned,
and that returned in further performances . . . and they returned
again. Nor can the push of charity or personal force ever be any
thing else than the profoundest reason, whether it bring argu-
ments to hand or no. No specification is necessary . . . to add or
subtract or divide is in vain. Little or big, learned or unlearned,
white or black, legal or illegal, sick or well, from the first inspira-
tion down the windpipe to the last expiration out of it, all that a
male or female does that is vigorous and benevolent and clean is
so much sure profit to him or her in the unshakable order of the
universe and through the whole scope of it forever. If the savage
or felon is wise it is well . . . . if the greatest poet or savan is wise
it is simply the same . . . if the President or chief justice is wise it is
the same . . . if the young mechanic or farmer is wise it is no more
or less . . . if the prostitute is wise it is no more nor less. The
interest will come round . . . all will come round. All the best
actions of war and peace . . . all help given to relatives and strangers
and the poor and old and sorrowful and young children and
widows and the sick, and to all shunned persons . . . all furtherance

of fugitives and of the escape of slaves . . . all the self-denial that stood ready and aloof on wrecks and saw others take the seats of the boats . . . all offering of substance or life for the good old cause, or for a friend's sake or opinion's sake . . . all pains of enthusiasts scoffed at by their neighbors . . . all the vast sweet love and precious suffering of mothers . . . all honest men baffled in strifes recorded or unrecorded . . . . all the grandeur and good of the few ancient nations whose fragments of animals we inherit . . . and all the good of the hundreds of far mightier and more ancient nations unknown to us by name or date or location . . . . all that was ever manfully begun, whether it succeeded or no . . . . all that has at any time been well suggested out of the divine heart of man or by the divinity of his mouth or by the shaping of his great hands . . . and all that is well thought or done this day on any part of the surface of the globe . . . or on any of the wandering stars or fixed stars by those there as we are here . . . or that is henceforth to be well thought or done by you whoever you are, or by any one – these singly and wholly inured at their time and inure now and will inure always to the identities from which they sprung or shall spring. . . Did you guess any of them lived only its moment? The world does not so exist . . . no parts palpable or impalpable so exist . . . no result exists now without being from its long antecedent result, and that from its antecedent, and so backward without the farthest mentionable spot coming a bit nearer the beginning than any other spot. . . . Whatever satisfies the soul is truth. The prudence of the greatest poet answers at last the craving and glut of the soul, is not contemptuous of less ways of prudence if they conform to its ways, puts off nothing, permits no let-up for its own case or any case, has no particular sabbath or judgment-day, divides not the living from the dead or the righteous from the unrighteous, is satisfied with the present, matches every thought or act by its correlative, knows no possible forgiveness or deputed atonement. . . knows that the young man who composedly periled his life and lost it has done exceeding well for himself, while the man who has not periled his life and retains it to old age in riches and ease has perhaps achieved nothing for himself worth mentioning . . . and that only that person has no great prudence to learn who has learnt to prefer real longlived things, and favors body and soul the same, and perceives the indirect assuredly following the direct, and what evil or good he does leaping onward and waiting to meet him again – and who in his spirit in any emergency whatever neither hurries or avoids death.

The direct trial of him who would be the greatest poet is today. If he does not flood himself with the immediate age as with vast oceanic tides . . . and if he does not attract his own land body and soul to himself and hang on its neck with incomparable love and plunge his semitic muscle into its merits and demerits . . . and if he be not himself the age transfigured . . . and if to him is not opened the eternity which gives similitude to all periods and locations and processes and animate and inanimate forms, and which is the bond of time, and rises up from its inconceivable vagueness and infiniteness in the swimming shape of today, and is held by the ductile anchors of life, and makes the present spot the passage from what was to what shall be, and commits itself to the representation of this wave of an hour and this one of the sixty beautiful children of the wave – let him merge in the general run and wait his development. . . . Still the final test of poems or any character or work remains. The prescient poet projects himself centuries ahead and judges performer or performance after the changes of time. Does it live through them? Does it still hold on untired? Will the same style and the direction of genius to similar points be satisfactory now? Has no new discovery in science or arrival at superior planes of thought and judgment and behaviour fixed him or his so that either can be looked down upon? Have the marches of tens and hundreds and thousands of years made willing detours to the right hand and the left hand for his sake? Is he beloved long and long after he is buried? Does the young man think often of him? and the young woman think often of him? and do the middle-aged and the old think of him?

A great poem is for ages and ages in common and for all degrees and complexions and all departments and sects and for a woman as much as a man and a man as much as a woman. A great poem is no finish to a man or woman but rather a beginning. Has any one fancied he could sit at last under some due authority and rest satisfied with explanations and realize and be content and full? To no such terminus does the greatest poet bring . . . he brings neither cessation or sheltered fatness and ease. The touch of him tells in action. Whom he takes he takes with firm sure grasp into live regions previously unattained . . . thenceforward is no rest . . . they see the space and ineffable sheen that turn the old spots and lights into dead vacuums. The companion of him beholds the birth and progress of stars and learns one of the meanings. Now there shall be a man cohered out of tumult and chaos . . . the elder encourages the younger and shows him how . . . they two shall launch off fearlessly together till the new world fits an orbit for itself and looks unabashed on the lesser orbits of the stars and sweeps through the ceaseless rings and shall never be quiet again.

There will soon be no more priests. Their work is done. They may wait awhile . . . perhaps a generation or two . . . dropping off by degrees. A superior breed shall take their place . . . the gangs of kosmos and prophets en masse shall take their place. A new order shall arise and they shall be the priests of man, and every man shall be his own priest. The churches built under their umbrage shall be the churches of men and women. Through the divinity of themselves shall the kosmos and the new breed of poets be interpreters of men and women and of all events and things. They shall find their inspiration in real objects today, symptoms of the past and future . . . . They shall not deign to defend immortality or God or the perfection of things or liberty or the exquisite beauty and reality of the soul. They shall arise in America and be responded to from the remainder of the earth.

The English language befriends the grand American expression. . . . it is brawny enough and limber and full enough. On the tough stock of a race who through all change of circumstance was never without the idea of political liberty, which is the animus of all liberty, it has attracted the terms of daintier and gayer and subtler and more elegant tongues. It is the powerful language of resistance . . . it is the dialect of common sense. It is the speech of the proud and melancholy races and of all who aspire. It is the chosen tongue to express growth faith self-esteem freedom justice equality friendliness amplitude prudence decision and courage. It is the medium that shall well nigh express the inexpressible.

No great literature nor any like style of behaviour or oratory or social intercourse or household arrangements or public institutions or the treatment by bosses of employed people, nor executive detail or detail of the army or navy, nor spirit of legislation or courts or police or tuition or architecture or songs or amusements or the costumes of young men, can long elude the jealous and passionate instinct of American standards. Whether or no the sign appears from the mouths of the people, it throbs a live interrogation in every freeman's and freewoman's heart after that which passes by or this built to remain. Is it uniform with my country? Are its disposals without ignominous distinctions? Is it for the evergrowing communes of brothers and lovers, large, well-united, proud beyond the old models, generous beyond all models? Is it something grown fresh out of the fields or drawn from the sea for use to me today here? I know that what answers for me an American must answer for any individual or nation that serves for a part of my materials. Does this answer? or is it without reference to universal needs? or sprung of the needs of the less developed society of special ranks? or old needs of pleasure overlaid by modern science and forms? Does this acknowledge liberty with audible and absolute acknowledgement, and set slavery at nought for life and death? Will it help breed one goodshaped and well-hung man, and a woman to be his perfect and independent mate? Does it improve manners? Is it for the nursing of the young of the republic? Does it solve readily with the sweet milk of the nipples of the breasts of the mother of many children? Has it too the old ever-fresh forbearance and impartiality? Does it look with the same love on the last born and on those hardening toward stature, and on the errant, and on those who disdain all strength of assault outside of their own?

The poems distilled from other poems will probably pass away. The coward will surely pass away. The expectation of the vital and great can only be satisfied by the demeanor of the vital and great. The swarms of the polished deprecating and reflectors and the polite float off and leave no remembrance. America prepares with composure and goodwill for the visitors that have sent word. It is not intellect that is to be their warrant and welcome. The talented, the artist, the ingenious, the editor, the statesman, the erudite . . . . they are not unappreciated . . . . they fall in their place and do their work. The soul of the nation also does its work. No disguise can pass on it . . . no disguise can conceal from it. It rejects none, it permits all. Only toward as good as itself and toward the like of itself will it advance half-way. An individual is as superb as a nation when he has the qualities which make a superb nation. The soul of the largest and wealthiest and proudest nation may well go half-way to meet that of its poets. The signs are effectual. There is no fear of mistake. If the one is true the other is true. The proof of a poet is that his country absorbs him as affectionately as he has absorbed it.

Leaves of Grass, 1856
RALPH WALDO EMERSON TO WALT WHITMAN,
21 JULY 1855

Concord
Masstts

Dear Sir,
I am not blind to the worth of the wonderful gift of *Leaves of Grass*. I find it the most extraordinary piece of wit and wisdom that America has yet contributed. I am very happy in reading it, as great power makes us happy. It meets the demand I am always making of what seemed the sterile and stingy Nature, as if too much handiwork or too much lymph in the temperament were making our western wits fat and mean. I give you joy of your free and brave thought. I have great joy in it. I find incomparable things said incomparably well, as they must be. I find the courage of treatment, which so delights us, and which large perception only can inspire. I greet you at the beginning of a great career, which yet must have had a long foreground somewhere, for such a start. I rubbed my eyes a little to see if this sunbeam were no illusion; but the solid sense of the book is a sober certainty. It has the best merits, namely, of fortifying and encouraging.

I did not know until I, last night, saw the book advertised in a newspaper, that I could trust the name as real and available for a

post-office. I wish to see my benefactor, and have felt much like
striking my tasks, and visiting New York to pay you my respects.

R. W. Emerson

Mr Walter Whitman

WALT WHITMAN TO RALPH WALDO EMERSON

Brooklyn, August 1856

Here are thirty-two Poems, which I send you, dear Friend and
Master, not having found how I could satisfy myself with sending
any usual acknowledgment of your letter. The first edition, on
which you mailed me that till now unanswered letter, was twelve
poems – I printed a thousand copies, and they readily sold: these
thirty-two Poems I stereotype, to print several thousand copies of.
I much enjoy making poems. Other work I have set for myself to
do, to meet people and The States face to face, to confront them
with an American rude tongue; but the work of my life is making
poems. I keep on till I make a hundred, and then several hundred –
perhaps a thousand. The way is clear to me. A few years, and the
average annual call for my Poems is ten or twenty thousand
copies – more, quite likely. Why should I hurry or compromise?
In poems or in speeches I say the word or two that has got to be
said, adhere to the body, step with the countless common foot-
steps, and remind every man and woman of something.

Master, I am a man who has perfect faith. Master, we have not
come through centuries, caste, heroisms, fables, to halt in this land
today. Or I think it is to collect a ten-fold impetus that any halt is
made. As nature, inexorable, onward, resistless, impassive amid the
threats and screams of disputants, so America. Let all defer. Let
all attend respectfully the leisure of These States, their politics,
poems, literature, manners, and their free-handed modes of
training their own offspring. Their own comes, just matured,
certain, numerous and capable enough, with egotistical tongues,
with sinewed wrists, seizing openly what belongs to them. They
resume Personality, too long left out of mind. Their shadows are
projected in employments, in books, in the cities, in trade; their
feet are on the flights of the steps of the Capitol; they dilate, a
larger, brawnier, more candid, more democratic, lawless, positive

native to The States, sweet-bodied, completer, dauntless, flowing, masterful, beard-faced, new race of men.

Swiftly, on limitless foundations, the United States too are founding a literature. It is all as well done, in my opinion, as could be practicable. Each element here is in condition. Every day I go among the people of Manhattan Island, Brooklyn, and other cities, and among the young men, to discover the spirit of them, and to refresh myself. These are to be attended to; I am myself more drawn here than to those authors, publishers, importations, re-prints, and so forth. I pass coolly through those, understanding them perfectly well, and that they do the indispensable service, outside of men like me, which nothing else could do. In poems, the young men of The States shall be represented, for they out-rival the best of the rest of the earth.

The lists of ready-made literature which America inherits by the mighty inheritance of the English language – all the rich repertoire of traditions, poems, histories, metaphysics, plays, classics, trans-lations, have made, and still continue, magnificent preparations for that other plainly signified literature, to be our own, to be elec-tric, fresh, lusty, to express the full-sized body, male and female – to give the modern meanings of things, to grow up beautiful, lasting, commensurate with America, with all the passions of home, with the inimitable sympathies of having been boys and girls together, and of parents who were with our parents.

What else can happen [to] The States, even in their own despite? That huge English flow, so sweet, so undeniable, has done in-calculable good here, and is to be spoken of for its own sake with generous praise and with gratitude. Yet the price The States have had to lie under for the same has not been a small price. Payment prevails; a nation can never take the issues of the needs of other nations for nothing. America, grandest of lands in the theory of its politics, in popular reading, in hospitality, breadth, animal beauty, cities, ships, machines, money, credit, collapses quick as lightning at the repeated, admonishing, stern words, Where are any mental expressions from you, beyond what you have copied or stolen? Where the born throngs of poets, literats, orators, you promised? Will you but tag after other nations? They struggled long for their literature, painfully working their way, some with deficient languages, some with priest-craft, some in the endeavor just to live – yet achieved for their times, works, poems, perhaps the only solid consolation left to them through ages afterward of shame and decay. You are young, have the perfectest of dialects, a free press, a free government, the world forwarding its best to be with you. As justice has been strictly done to you, from this hour do strict justice to yourself. Strangle the singers who will not sing you loud and strong. Open the doors of The West. Call for new great masters to comprehend new arts, new perfections, new wants. Submit to the most robust bard till he remedy your barrenness. Then you will not need to adopt the heirs of others; you will have true heirs, begotten of yourself, blooded with your own blood.

With composure I see such propositions, seeing more and more every day of the answers that serve. Expressions do not yet serve, for sufficient reasons; but that is getting ready, beyond what the earth has hitherto known, to take home the expressions when they come, and to identify them with the populace of The States, which is the schooling cheaply procured by any outlay any number of years. Such schooling The States extract from the swarms of reprints, and from the current authors and editors. Such service and extract are done after enormous, reckless, free modes, characteristic of The States. Here are to be attained results never elsewhere thought possible; the modes are very grand too. The instincts of the American people are all perfect, and tend to make heroes. It is a rare thing in a man here to understand The States.

All current nourishments to literature serve. Of authors and editors I do not know how many there are in The States, but there are thousands, each one building his or her step to the stairs by which giants shall mount. Of the twenty-four modern mammoth two-double, three-double, and four-double cylinder presses now in the world, printing by steam, twenty-one of them are in These States. The twelve thousand large and small shops for dispensing books and newspapers – the same number of public libraries, any one of which has all the reading wanted to equip a man or woman for American reading – the three thousand different newspapers, the nutriment of the imperfect ones coming in just as usefully as any – the story papers, various, full of strong-flavored romances, widely circulated – the one-cent and two-cent journals – the political ones, no matter what side – the weeklies in the country – the sporting and pictorial papers – the monthly magazines, with plentiful imported feed – the sentimental novels, numberless copies of them – the low-priced flaring tales, adventures, biographies – all are prophetic; all waft rapidly on. I see that they swell wide, for reasons. I am not troubled at the movement of them, but greatly pleased. I see plying shuttles, the active ephemeral myriads of books also, faithfully weaving the garments of a generation of men, and a generation of women, they do not perceive or know. What a progress popular reading and writing has made in fifty years! What a progress fifty years hence! The time is at hand when inherent literature will be a main part of These States, as general and real as steam-power, iron, corn, beef, fish. First-rate American persons are to be supplied. Our perennial materials for fresh thoughts, histories, poems, music, orations, religions, recitations, amusements, will then not be disregarded, any more than our perennial fields, mines, rivers, seas. Certain things are established, and are immovable; in those things millions of years stand justified. The mothers and fathers of whom modern centuries have come, have not existed for nothing; they too had brains and hearts. Of course all literature, in all nations and years, will share marked attributes in common, as we all, of all ages, share the common human attributes. America is to be kept coarse and broad. What is to be done is to withdraw from precedents, and be directed to men and women – also to The States in their federalness; for the union of the parts of the body is not more necessary to their life than the union of These States is to their life.

A profound person can easily know more of the people than they know of themselves. Always waiting untold in the souls of the armies of common people, is stuff better than anything that can possibly appear in the leadership of the same. That gives final verdicts. In every department of These States, he who travels with a coterie, or with selected persons, or with imitators, or with infidels, or with the owners of slaves, or with that which is ashamed of the body of a man, or with that which is ashamed of the body of a woman, or with any thing less than the bravest and the openest, travels straight for the slopes of dissolution. The genius of all foreign literature is clipped and cut small, compared to our genius, and is essentially insulting to our usages, and to the organic compacts of These States. Old forms, old poems, majestic and proper in their own lands here in this land are exiles; the air here is very strong. Much that stands well and has a little enough place provided for it in the small scales of European kingdoms, empires, and the like, here stands haggard, dwarfed, ludicrous, or has no place little enough provided for it. Authorities, poems, models, laws, names, imported into America, are useful to America today to destroy them, and so move disencumbered to great works, great days.

Just so long, in our country or any country, as no revolutionists advance, and are backed by the people, sweeping off the swarms of routine representatives, officers in power, book-makers, teachers, ecclesiastics, politicians, just so long, I perceive, do they who are in power fairly represent that country, and remain of use, probably of very great use. To supersede them, when it is the pleasure of These States, full provision is made; and I say the time has arrived to use it with a strong hand. Here also the souls of the armies have not only overtaken the souls of the officers, but passed on, and left the souls of the officers behind out of sight many weeks' journey; and the souls of the armies now go *en masse* without officers. Here also formulas, glosses, blanks, minutiae, are choking the throats of the spokesmen to death. Those things most listened for, certainly those are the things least said. There is not a single History of the World. There is not one of America, or of the organic compacts of These States, or of Washington, or of Jefferson, nor of Language, nor any Dictionary of the English Language. There is no great author; every one has demeaned himself to some etiquette or some impotence. There is no manhood or life-power in poems; there are shoats and geldings more like. Or literature will be dressed up, a fine gentleman, distasteful to our instincts, foreign to our soil. Its neck bends right and left wherever it goes. Its costumes and jewelry prove how little it knows Nature. Its flesh is soft; it shows less and less of the indefinable hard something that is Nature. Where is any thing but the shaved Nature of synods and schools? Where is a savage and luxuriant man? Where is an overseer? In lives, in poems, in codes

of law, in Congress, in tuitions, theatres, conversations, argumenta-
tions, not a single head lifts itself clean out, with proof that it is
their master, and has subordinated them to itself, and is ready to
try their superiors. None believes in These States, boldly illus-
trating them in himself. Not a man faces round at the rest with
terrible negative voice, refusing all terms to be bought off from
his own eye-sight, or from the soul that he is, or from friendship,
or from the body that he is, or from the soil and sea. To creeds,
literature, art, the army, the navy, the executive, life is hardly
proposed, but the sick and dying are proposed to cure the sick
and dying. The churches are one vast lie; the people do not
believe them, and they do not believe themselves; the priests are
continually telling what they know well enough is not so, and
keeping back what they know is so. The spectacle is a pitiful one.
I think there can never be again upon the festive earth more bad-
disordered persons deliberately taking seats, as of late in These
States, at the heads of the public tables – such corpses' eyes for
judges – such a rascal and thief in the Presidency.

Up to the present, as helps best, the people, like a lot of large
boys, have no determined tastes, are quite unaware of the grandeur
of themselves, and of their destiny, and of their immense strides –
accept with voracity whatever is presented them in novels,
histories, newspapers, poems, schools, lectures, every thing.
Pretty soon, through these and other means, their development
makes the fibre that is capable of itself, and will assume determined
tastes. The young men will be clear what they want, and will have
it. They will follow none except him whose spirit leads them in
the like spirit with themselves. Any such man will be welcome as
the flowers of May. Others will be put out without ceremony. How
much is there anyhow, to the young men of These States, in a
parcel of helpless dandies, who can neither fight, work, shoot, ride,
run, command – some of them devout, some quite insane, some
castrated – all second-hand, or third, fourth, or fifth-hand –
waited upon by waiters, putting not this land first, but always
other lands first, talking of art, doing the most ridiculous things
for fear of being called ridiculous, smirking and skipping along,
continually taking off their hats – no one behaving, dressing,
writing, talking, loving, out of any natural and manly tastes of his

own, but each one looking cautiously to see how the rest behave, dress, write, talk, love – pressing the noses of dead books upon themselves and upon their country – favoring no poets, philosophs, literats here, but dog-like danglers at the heels of the poets, philosophs, literats, of enemies' lands – favoring mental expressions, models of gentlemen and ladies, social habitudes in These States, to grow up in sneaking defiance of the popular substratums of The States? Of course they and the likes of them can never justify the strong poems of America. Of course no feed of theirs is to stop and be made welcome to muscle the bodies, male and female, for Manhattan Island, Brooklyn, Boston, Worcester, Hartford, Portland, Montreal, Detroit, Buffalo, Cleveland, Milwaukee, St Louis, Indianapolis, Chicago, Cincinnati, Iowa City, Philadelphia, Baltimore, Raleigh, Savannah, Charleston, Mobile, New Orleans, Galveston, Brownsville, San Francisco, Havana, and a thousand equal cities, present and to come. Of course what they and the likes of them have been used for, draws toward its close, after which they will be discharged and not one of them will ever be heard of any more.

America, having duly conceived, bears out of herself offspring of her own to do the workmanship wanted. To freedom, to strength, to poems, to personal greatness, it is never permitted to rest, not a generation or part of a generation. To be ripe beyond further increase is to prepare to die. The architects of These States laid their foundations, and passed to further spheres. What they laid is a work done; as much more remains. Now are needed other architects, whose duty is not less difficult, but perhaps more difficult. Each age forever needs architects. America is not finished, perhaps never will be; now America is a divine true sketch. There are Thirty-Two States sketched – the population thirty millions. In a few years there will be Fifty States. Again in a few years there will be A Hundred States, the population hundreds of millions, the freshest and freest of men. Of course such men stand to nothing less than the freshest and freest expression.

Poets here, literats here, are to rest on organic different bases from other countries; not a class set apart, circling only in the circle of themselves, modest and pretty, desperately scratching for rhymes, pallid with white paper, shut off, aware of the old pictures and traditions of the race, but unaware of the actual race around them – not breeding in and in among each other till they all have the scrofula. Lands of ensemble, bards of ensemble! Walking freely out from the old traditions, as our politics has walked out, American poets and literats recognize nothing behind them superior to what is present with them – recognize with joy the sturdy living forms of the men and women of These States, the divinity of sex, the perfect eligibility of the female with the male, all The States, liberty and equality, real articles, the different trades, mechanics, the young fellows of Manhattan Island, customs, instincts, slang, Wisconsin, Georgia, the noble Southern heart, the hot blood, the spirit that will be nothing less than master, the filibuster spirit, the Western man, native-born perceptions, the eye for forms, the perfect models of made things, the wild smack of freedom, California, money, electric-telegraphs, free-trade, iron and the iron mines – recognize without demur those splendid resistless black poems, the steam-ships of the seaboard states, and those other resistless splendid poems, the locomotives, followed through the interior states by trains of rail-road cars.

A word remains to be said, as of one ever present, nor yet permitted to be acknowledged, discarded or made dumb by literature, and the results apparent. To the lack of an avowed, empowered, unabashed development of sex, (the only salvation for the same,) and to the fact of speakers and writers fraudently assuming as always dead what every one knows to be always alive, is attributable the remarkable non-personality and indistinctness of modern productions in books, art, talk; also that in the scanned lives of men and women most of them appear to have been for some time past of the neuter gender; and also the stinging fact that in orthodox society today, if the dresses were changed, the men might easily pass for women and the women for men.

Infidelism usurps most with foetid polite face; among the rest infidelism about sex. By silence or obedience the pens of savans, poets, historians, biographers, and the rest, have long connived at the filthy law, and books enslaved to it, that what makes the manhood of a man, that sex, womanhood, maternity, desires, lusty animations, organs, acts, are unmentionable and to be ashamed of, to be driven to skulk out of literature with whatever belongs to them. This filthy law has to be repealed – it stands in the way of great reforms. Of women just as much as men, it is the interest that there should not be infidelism about sex, but perfect faith. Women in These States approach the day of that organic equality with men, without which, I see, men cannot have organic equality among themselves. This empty dish, gallantry, will then be filled with something. This tepid wash, this diluted deferential love, as in songs, fictions, and so forth, is enough to make a man vomit; as to manly friendship, everywhere observed in The States, there is not the first breath of it to be observed in print. I say that the body of a man or woman, the main matter, is so far quite un-expressed in poems; but that the body is to be expressed, and sex is. Of bards for These States, if it come to a question, it is whether they shall celebrate in poems the eternal decency of the amativeness of Nature, the motherhood of all, or whether they shall be the bards of the fashionable delusion of the inherent nastiness of sex, and of the feeble and querulous modesty of deprivation. This is important in poems, because the whole of the other expressions of a nation are but flanges out of its great poems. To me henceforth, that theory of any thing, no matter what, stag-nates in its vitals, cowardly and rotten, while it cannot publicly accept, and publicly name, with specific words, the things on which all existence, all souls, all realization, all decency, all health, all that is worth being here for, all of woman and of man, all beauty, all purity, all sweetness, all friendship, all strength, all life, all immortality depend. The courageous soul, for a year or two to come, may be proved by faith in sex, and by disdaining con-cessions.

To poets and literats – to every woman and man, today or any day, the conditions of the present, needs, dangers, prejudices, and the like, are the perfect conditions on which we are here, and the conditions for wording the future with undissuadable words. These States, receivers of the stamina of past ages and lands, initiate the outlines of repayment a thousand fold. They fetch the American great masters, waited for by old worlds and new, who accept evil as well as good, ignorance as well as erudition, black as soon as white, foreign-born materials as well as home-born, reject none, force discrepancies into range, surround the whole, concentrate them on present periods and places, show the application to each and any one's body and soul, and show the true use of precedents. Always America will be agitated and turbulent. This day it is taking shape, not to be less so, but to be more so, stormily, capriciously, on native principles, with such vast proportions of parts! As for me, I love screaming, wrestling, boiling-hot days.

Of course, we shall have a national character, an identity. As it ought to be, and as soon as it ought to be, it will be. That, with much else, takes care of itself, is a result, and the cause of greater results. With Ohio, Illinois, Missouri, Oregon – with the states around the Mexican sea – with cheerfully welcomed immigrants from Europe, Asia, Africa – with Connecticut, Vermont, New Hampshire, Rhode Island – with all varied interests, facts, beliefs, parties, genesis – there is being fused a determined character, fit for the broadest use for the freewomen and freemen of The States, accomplished and to be accomplished, without any exception whatever – each indeed free, each idiomatic, as becomes live states and men, but each adhering to one enclosing general form of politics, manners, talk, personal style, as the plenteous varieties of the race adhere to one physical form. Such character is the brain and spine to all, including literature, including poems. Such character, strong, limber, just, open-mouthed, American-blooded, full of pride, full of ease, of passionate friendliness, is to stand compact upon that vast basis of the supremacy of Individuality – that new moral American continent without which, I see, the physical continent remained incomplete, may be a carcass, a bloat – that newer America, answering face to face with The States, with ever-satisfying and ever-unsurveyable seas and shores.

These shores you found. I say you have led The States there – have led Me there. I say that none has ever done, or ever can do, a greater deed for The States, than your deed. Others may line out the lines, build cities, work mines, break up farms; it is yours to have been the original true Captain who put to sea, intuitive, positive, rendering the first report, to be told less by any report, and more by the mariners of a thousand bays, in each tack of their arriving and departing, many years after you.

Receive, dear Master, these statements and assurances through me, for all the young men, and for an earnest that we know none before you, but the best following you; and that we demand to take your name into our keeping, and that we understand what you have indicated, and find the same indicated in ourselves, and that we will stick to it and enlarge upon it through These States.

Walt Whitman

As a Strong Bird on Pinions Free, 1872

The impetus and ideas urging me, for some years past, to an utterance, or attempt at utterance, of New World songs, and an epic of Democracy, having already had their published expression, as well as I can expect to give it, in *Leaves of Grass*, the present and any future pieces from me are really but the surplusage forming after that Volume, or the wake eddying behind it. I fulfilled in that an imperious conviction, and the commands of my nature as total and irresistible as those which make the sea flow, or the globe revolve. But of this Supplementary Volume, I confess I am not so certain. Having from early manhood abandoned the business pursuits and applications usual in my time and country, and obediently yielded myself up ever since to the impetus mentioned, and to the work of expressing those ideas, it may be that mere habit has got dominion of me, when there is no real need of saying anything further. . . . But what is life but an experiment? and mortality but an exercise? with reference to results beyond. And so shall my poems be. If incomplete here, and superfluous there, *n'importe* – the earnest trial and persistent exploration shall at least be mine, and other success failing, shall be success enough. I have been more anxious, anyhow, to suggest the songs of vital endeavor and manly evolution, and furnish something for races of outdoor athletes, than to make perfect rhymes, or reign in the parlors. I ventured from the beginning, my own way, taking chances – and would keep on venturing.

I will therefore not conceal from any persons, known or unknown to me, who take interest in the matter, that I have the ambition of devoting yet a few years to poetic composition. . . . The mighty present age! To absorb, and express in poetry, any thing of it – of its world – America – cities and States – the years, the events of our Nineteenth Century – the rapidity of movement – the violent contrasts, fluctuations of light and shade, of hope and fear – the entire revolution made by science in the poetic method – these great new underlying facts and new ideas rushing in and spreading everywhere; – Truly a mighty age! As if in some colossal drama, acted again like those of old, under the open sun, the Nations of our time, and all the characteristics of Civilization, seem hurrying, stalking across, flitting from wing to wing, gathering, closing up, toward some long-prepared, most tremendous denouement. Not to conclude the infinite scenas of the race's life and toil and happiness and sorrow, but haply that the boards be cleared from oldest, worst incumbrances, accumulations, and Man resume the eternal play anew, and under happier, freer auspices. . . . To me, the United States are important because, in this colossal drama, they are unquestionably designated for the leading parts, for many a century to come. In them History and Humanity seem to seek to culminate. Our broad areas are even now the busy theatre of plots, passions, interests, and suspended problems, compared to which the intrigues of the past of Europe, the wars of dynasties, the scope of kings and kingdoms, and even the development of peoples, as hitherto, exhibit scales of measurement comparatively narrow and trivial. And on these areas of ours, as on a stage, sooner or later, something like an *eclaircissement* of all the past civilization of Europe and Asia is probably to be evolved.

The leading parts. . . . Not to be acted, emulated here, by us again, that role till now foremost in History – Not to become a conqueror Nation, or to achieve the glory of mere military, or diplomatic, or commercial superiority – but to become the grand Producing Land of nobler Men and Women – of copious races, cheerful, healthy, tolerant, free – To become the most friendly Nation, (the United States indeed,) – the modern composite Nation, formed from all, with room for all, welcoming all immigrants – accepting the work of our own interior development, as the work fitly filling ages and ages to come; – the leading Nation of peace, but neither ignorant not incapable of being the leading Nation of war; – not the Man's Nation only, but the Woman's Nation – a land of splendid mothers, daughters, sisters, wives.

Our America to-day I consider in many respects as but indeed a vast seething mass of *materials*, ampler, better, (worse also,) than previously known – eligible to be used to carry toward its crowning stage, and build for good the great Ideal Nationality of the future, the Nation of the Body and the Soul.[1] – no limit here to land, help, opportunities, mines, products, demands, supplies, etc.; – with (I think) our political organization, National, State, and Municipal, permanently established, as far ahead as we can calculate – but, so far, no social, literary, religious, or esthetic organizations, consistent with our politics, or becoming to us – which organizations can only come, in time, through native schools or teachers of great Democratic Ideas, Religion – through Science, which now, like a new sunrise, ascending, begins to illuminate all – and through our own begotten Poets and Literatures. . . . (The moral of a late well-written book on Civilization seems to be that the only real foundation-walls and basis – and also *sine qua non* afterward – of true and full Civilization, is the eligibility and certainty of boundless products for feeding, clothing, sheltering every body – perennial fountains of physical and domestic comfort, with intercommunication, and with civil and ecclesiastical freedom – and that then the esthetic and mental business will take care of itself . . . Well, the United States have established this basis, and upon scales of extent, variety, vitality, and continuity, rivaling those of Nature; and have now to proceed to build an Edifice upon it. I say this Edifice is only to be fitly built by new Literatures, especially the poetic. I say a modern Image-making creation is indispensable to fuse and express modern Political and Scientific creations – and then the Trinity will be complete.)

When I commenced, years ago, elaborating the plan of my poems, and continued turning over that plan, and shifting it in my mind

1. The problems of the achievements of this crowning stage through future first-class National Singers, Orators, Artists, and others – of creating in literature an *imaginative* New World, the correspondent and counterpart of the current Scientific and Political New Worlds – and the perhaps distant, but still delightful prospect (for our children, if not in our own day), of delivering America, and, indeed, all Christian lands everywhere, from the thin, moribund and watery, but appallingly extensive nuisance of conventional poetry – by putting something really alive and substantial in its place – I have undertaken to grapple with, and argue, in *Democratic Vistas*.

through many years, (from the age of twenty-eight to thirty-five,) experimenting much, and writing and abandoning much, one deep purpose underlay the others, and has underlain it and its execution ever since – and that has been the Religious purpose. Amid many changes, and a formulation taking far different shape from what I at first supposed, this basic purpose has never been departed from in the composition of my verses. Not of course to exhibit itself in the old ways, as in writing hymns or psalms with an eye to the church-pew, or to express conventional pietism, or the sickly yearnings of devotees, but in new ways, and aiming at the widest sub-bases and inclusions of Humanity, and tallying the fresh air of sea and land. I will see, (said I to myself,) whether there is not, for my purposes as poet, a Religion, and a sound Religious germenancy in the average Human Race, at least in their modern development in the United States, and in the hardy common fiber and native yearnings and elements, deeper and larger, and affording more profitable returns, than all mere sects or churches – as boundless, joyous, and vital as Nature itself – A germenancy that has too long been unencouraged, unsung, almost unknown. . . . With Science, the Old Theology of the East, long in its dotage, begins evidently to die and disappear. But (to my mind) Science – and may be such will prove its principal service – as evidently prepares the way for One indescribably grander – Time's young but perfect offspring – the New Theology – heir of the West – lusty and loving, and wondrous beautiful. For America, and for to-day, just the same as any day, the supreme and final Science is the Science of God – what we call science being only its minister – as Democracy is or shall be also. And a poet of America (I said) must fill himself with such thoughts, and chant his best out of them. . . . And as those were the convictions and aims, for good or bad, of *Leaves of Grass*, they are no less the intention of this Volume. As there can be, in my opinion, no sane and complete Personality, nor any grand and electric Nationality, without the stock element of Religion imbuing all the other elements, (like heat in chemistry, invisible itself, but the life of all visible life,) so there can be no Poetry worthy the name without that element behind all. . . . The time has certainly come to begin to discharge the idea of Religion, in the United States, from mere ecclesiasticism, and from Sundays and churches and church-going, and assign it to that general position, chiefest, most indispensable, most exhilarating, to which the others are to be adjusted, inside of all human character, and education, and affairs. The people, especially the young men and women of America, must begin to learn that Religion, (like Poetry,) is something far, far different from what they supposed. It is, indeed, too important to the power and perpetuity of the New World to be consigned any longer to the churches, old or new, Catholic or Protestant – Saint this, or Saint that. . . . It must be consigned henceforth to Democracy *en masse*, and to Literature. It must enter into the Poems of the Nation. It must make the Nation.

The Four Years' War is over – and in the peaceful, strong, exciting, fresh occasions of To-day, and of the Future, that strange, sad war is hurrying even now to be forgotten. The camp, the drill, the lines of sentries, the prisons, the hospitals – (ah! the hospitals!) – all have passed away – all seem now like a dream. A new race, a young and lusty generation, already sweeps in with oceanic currents, obliterating the war, and all its scars, its mounded graves, and all its reminiscences of hatred, conflict, death. So let it be obliterated. I say the life of the present and the future makes undeniable demands upon us each and all, South, North, East, West. . . . To help put the United States (even if only in imagination) hand in hand, in one unbroken circle in a chant – To rouse them to the unprecedented grandeur of the part they are to play, and are even now playing – to the thought of their great Future, and the attitude conformed to it – especially their great Esthetic, Moral, Scientific future, (of which their vulgar material and political present is but as the preparatory tuning of instruments by an orchestra,) these, as hitherto, are still, for me, among my hopes, ambitions.

Leaves of Grass, already published, is, in its intentions, the song of a great composite *Democratic Individual*, male or female. And following on and amplifying the same purpose, I suppose I have in my mind to run through the chants of this Volume, (if ever completed,) the thread-voice, more or less audible, of an aggregated, inseparable, unprecedented, vast, composite, electric *Democratic Nationality*.

Purposing, then, to still fill out, from time to time through years to come, the following Volume, (unless prevented,) I conclude this Preface to the first instalment of it, penciled in the open air, on my fifty-third birthday, by wafting to you, dear Reader, whoever you are, (from amid the fresh scent of the grass, the pleasant coolness of the forenoon breeze, the lights and shades of tree-boughs silently dappling and playing around me, and the notes of the cat-bird for undertone and accompaniment,) my true good-will and love.

W.W.
Washington, DC, May 31, 1872

Preface, 1876

At the eleventh hour, under grave illness, I gather up the pieces of Prose and Poetry left over since publishing, a while since, my first and main volume, *Leaves of Grass* – pieces, here, some new, some old – nearly all of them (sombre as many are, making this almost Death's book) composed in by-gone atmosphere of perfect health – and, preceded by the freshest collection, the little *Two Rivulets*, and by this rambling Prefatory gossip,[1] now send them out, embodied in the present Melange, partly as my contribution and outpouring to celebrate, in some sort, the feature of the time, the first Centennial of our New World Nationality – and then as chyle and nutriment to that moral Indissoluble Union, equally representing All, and the mother of many coming Centennials.

And e'en for flush and proof of our America – for reminder, just as much, or more, in moods of towering pride and joy, I keep my special chants of Death and Immortality[2] to stamp the coloring-finish of all, present and past. For terminus and temperer to all,

1. This Preface is not only for the present collection, but, in a sort, for all my writings, both Volumes.
2. *Passage to India* – As in some ancient legend-play, to close the plot and the hero's career, there is a farewell gathering on ship's deck and on shore, a loosing of hawsers and ties, a spreading of sails to the wind – a starting out on

unknown seas, to fetch up no one knows whither – to return no more – And the curtain falls, and there is the end of it – So I have reserv'd that Poem, with its cluster, to finish and explain much that, without them, would not be explain'd, and to take leave and escape for good, from all that has preceded them. (Then probably *Passage to India*, and its cluster, are but freer vent and fuller expression of what, from the first, and so on throughout, more or less lurks in my writings, underneath every page, every line, everywhere.)

I am not sure but the last inclosing sublimation of Race or Poem is, What it thinks of Death. . . . After the rest has been comprehended and said, even the grandest – After those contributions to mightiest Nationality, or to sweetest Song, or to the best Personalism, male or female, have been glean'd from the rich and varied themes of tangible life, and have been fully accepted and sung, and the pervading fact of visible existence, with the duty it devolves, is rounded and apparently completed, it still remains to be really completed by suffusing through the whole and several, that other pervading invisible fact, so large a part, (is it not the largest part?), of life here, combining the rest, and furnishing, for Person or State, the only permanent and unitary meaning to all, even the meanest life, consistently with the dignity of the Universe, in Time. . . . As, from the eligibility to this thought, and the cheerful conquest of this fact, flash forth the first distinctive proofs of the Soul, so to me, (extending it only a little further), the ultimate Democratic purports, the ethereal and spiritual ones, are to concentrate here, and as fixed stars, radiate hence. For, in my opinion, it is no less than this idea of Immortality, above all other ideas, that is to enter into, and vivify, and give crowning religious stamp, to Democracy in the New World.

It was originally my intention, after chanting in *Leaves of Grass* the songs of the Body and Existence, to then compose a further, equally needed Volume, based on those convictions of perpetuity and conservation which, enveloping all precedents, make the unseen Soul absolutely at last. I meant, while in a sort continuing the theme of my first chants, to shift the slides, and exhibit the problem and paradox of the same ardent and fully appointed Personality entering the sphere of the resistless gravitation of Spiritual Law, and with cheerful face estimating Death, not at all as the cessation, but as somehow what I feel it must be, the entrance upon by far the greatest part of existence, and something that Life is at least as much for, as it is for itself.

But the full construction of such a work (even if I lay the foundation, or give impetus to it) is beyond my powers, and must remain for some bard in the future. The physical and the sensuous, in themselves or in their immediate continuations, retain holds upon me which I think are never entirely releas'd; and those holds I have not only not denied, but hardly wish'd to weaken.

Meanwhile, not entirely to give the go-by to my original plan, and far more to avoid a mark'd hiatus in it, than to entirely fulfil it, I end my books with thoughts, or radiations from thoughts, on Death, Immortality, and a free entrance into the Spiritual world. In those thoughts, in a sort, I make the first steps or studies toward the mighty theme, for the point of view necessitated by foregoing poems, and by Modern Science. In them I also seek to set the

they were originally written, and that shall be their office at the last.

For some reason – not explainable or definite to my own mind, yet secretly pleasing and satisfactory to it – I have not hesitated to embody in, and run through the Volume, two altogether distinct veins, or strata – Politics for one, and for the other, the pensive thought of Immortality. . . . Thus, too, the prose and poetic, the dual forms of the present book. The pictures from the Hospitals during the War, in *Memoranda*, I have also decided to include. Though they differ in character and composition from the rest of my pieces, yet I feel that they ought to go with them, and must

---

keystone to my Democracy's enduring arch. I re-collate them now, for the press, (much the same, I transcribe my *Memoranda* following, of gloomy times out of the War, and Hospitals) in order to partially occupy and off-set days of strange sickness, and the heaviest affliction and bereavement of my life; and I fondly please myself with the notion of leaving that cluster to you, O unknown Reader of the future, as 'something to remember me by,' more especially than all else. Written in former days of perfect health, little did I think the pieces had the purport that now, under present circumstances, opens to me.

(As I write these lines, May 31, 1875, it is again early summer – again my birthday – now my fifty-sixth. Amid the outside beauty and freshness, the sunlight and verdure of the delightful season, O how different the moral atmosphere amid which I now revise this Volume, from the jocund influence surrounding the growth and advent of *Leaves of Grass*. I occupy myself, arranging these pages for publication, still envelopt in thoughts of the death two years since of my dear Mother, the most perfect and magnetic character, the rarest combination of practical, moral and spiritual, and the least selfish, of all and any I have ever known – and by me O so much the most deeply loved – and also under the physical affliction of a tedious attack of paralysis, obstinately lingering and keeping its hold upon me, and quite suspending all bodily activity and comfort . . . I see now, much clearer than ever – perhaps these experiences were needed to show – how much my former poems, the bulk of them, are indeed the expression of health and strength, the sanest, joyfullest life.)

Under these influences, therefore, I still feel to keep *Passage to India* for last words even to this Centennial dithyramb. Not as, in antiquity, at highest festival of Egypt, the noisome skeleton of Death was also sent on exhibition to the revelers, for zest and shadow to the occasion's joy and light – but as the perfect marble statue of the normal Greeks at Elis, suggesting death in the form of a beautiful and perfect young man, with closed eyes, leaning on an inverted torch – emblem of rest and aspiration after action – of crown and point which all lives and poems should steadily have reference to, namely, the justified and noble termination of our identity, this grade of it, and outlet-preparation to another grade.

do so. . . . The present Volume, therefore, after its minor episodes, probably divides into these Two, at first sight far diverse, veins of topic and treatment. One will be found in the prose part of *Two Rivulets*, in *Democratic Vistas*, in the Preface to *As a Strong Bird*, and in the concluding Notes to *Memoranda* of the Hospitals. The other, wherein the all-enclosing thought and fact of Death is admitted, (not for itself so much as a powerful factor in the adjustments of Life,) in the realistic pictures of *Memoranda*, and the free speculations and ideal escapades of *Passage to India*.

Has not the time come, indeed, in the development of the New World, when its Politics should ascend into atmospheres and regions hitherto unknown – (far, far different from the miserable business that of late and current years passes under that name) – and take rank with Science, Philosophy and Art? . . . Three points, in especial, have become very dear to me, and all through I seek to make them again and again, in many forms and repetitions, as will be seen: 1. That the true growth-characteristics of the Democracy of the New World are henceforth to radiate in superior Literary, Artistic and Religious Expressions, far more than in its Republican forms, universal suffrage, and frequent elections, (though these are unspeakably important). . . . 2. That the vital political mission of The United States is, to practically solve and settle the problem of two sets of rights – the fusion, thorough compatibility and junction of individual State prerogatives, with the indispensable necessity of centrality and Oneness – the National Identity power – the sovereign Union, relentless, permanently comprising all, and over all, and in that never yielding an inch . . . then 3d. Do we not, amid a general malaria of Fogs and Vapors, our day, unmistakably see two Pillars of Promise, with grandest, indestructible indications – One, that the morbid facts of American politics and society everywhere are but passing incidents and flanges of our unbounded impetus of growth – weeds, annuals of the rank, rich soil – not central, enduring, perennial things? The Other, that all the hitherto experience of The States, their first Century, has been but preparation, adolescence – and that This Union is only now and henceforth (i.e. since the Secession war) to enter on its full Democratic career?

Of the whole, Poems and Prose, (not attending at all to chrono-
logical order, and with original dates and passing allusions in the
heat and impression of the hour, left shuffled in, and undisturb'd,)
the chants of *Leaves of Grass*, my former Volume, yet serve as the
indispensable deep soil, or basis, out of which, and out of which
only, could come the roots and stems more definitely indicated by
these later pages. (While that Volume radiates Physiology alone,
the present One, though of the like origin in the main, more palp-
ably doubtless shows the Pathology which was pretty sure to come
in time from the other.)

In that former and main Volume, composed in the flush of my
health and strength, from the age of 30 to 50 years, I dwelt on Birth
and Life, clothing my ideas in pictures, days, transactions of my
time, to give them positive place, identity – saturating them with
that vehemence of pride and audacity of freedom necessary to
loosen the mind of still-to-be-form'd America from the accumu-
lated folds, the superstitions, and all the long, tenacious and
stifling anti-democratic authorities of the Asiatic and European
past – my enclosing purport being to express, above all artificial
regulation and aid, the eternal Bodily Character of One's-Self.[1]

1. *Leaves of Grass* – Namely, a character, making most of common and
normal elements, to the superstructure of which not only the precious accumu-
lations of the learning and experiences of the Old World, and the settled social
and municipal necessities and current requirements, so long a-building, shall
still faithfully contribute, but which, at its foundations and carried up thence,
and receiving its impetus from the Democratic spirit, and accepting its gauge,
in all departments, from the Democratic formulas, shall again directly be
vitalized by the perennial influences of Nature at first hand, and the old heroic
stamina of Nature, the strong air of prairie and mountain, the dash of the briny
sea, the primary antiseptics – of the passions, in all their fullest heat and
potency, of courage, rankness, amativeness, and of immense pride. . . . Not to
lose at all, therefore, the benefits of artificial progress and civilization, but to
re-occupy for Western tenancy the oldest though ever-fresh fields, and reap
from them savage and sane nourishment indispensable to a hardy nation, and the
absence of which, threatening to become worse and worse, is the most serious
lack and defect to-day of our New World literature.

Not but what the brawn of *Leaves of Grass* is, I think, thoroughly spiritualized
everywhere, for final estimate, but, from the very subjects, the direct effect is a
sense of the Life, as it should be, of flesh and blood, and physical urge, and
animalism. . . . While there are other themes, and plenty of abstract thoughts
and poems in the Volume – While I have put in it (supplemented in the present

Work by my prose *Memoranda*,) passing and rapid but actual glimpses of the great struggle between the Nation and the Slavepower (1861–'65), as the fierce and bloody panorama of that contest unroll'd itself – While the whole Book, indeed, revolves around that Four Years' War, which, as I was in the midst of it, becomes, in *Drum-Taps*, pivotal to the rest entire – follow'd by *Marches now the War is Over* – and here and there, before and afterward, not a few episodes and speculations – *that* – namely, to make a type-portrait for living, active, worldly, healthy Personality, objective as well as subjective, joyful and potent, and modern and free, distinctively for the use of the United States, male and female, through the long future – has been, I say, my general object. (Probably, indeed, the whole of these varied songs, and all my writings, both Volumes, only ring changes in some sort, on the ejaculation, How vast, how eligible, how joyful, how real, is a Human Being, himself or herself.)

Though from no definite plan at the time, I see now that I have unconsciously sought by indirections at least as much as directions, to express the whirls and rapid growth and intensity of the United States, the prevailing tendency and events of the Nineteenth Century, and largely the spirit of the whole current World, my time; for I feel that I have partaken of that spirit, as I have been deeply interested in all those events, the closing of long-stretch'd eras and ages, and, illustrated in the history of the United States, the opening of larger ones. (The death of President Lincoln, for instance, fitly, historically closes, in the Civilization of Feudalism, many old influences – drops on them, suddenly, a vast, gloomy, as it were, separating curtain. The world's entire dramas afford none more indicative – none with folds more tragic, or more sombre or far spreading.)

Since I have been ill (1873–'74–'75), mostly without serious pain, and with plenty of time and frequent inclination to judge my poems (never composed with eye on the book-market, nor for fame, nor for any pecuniary profit), I have felt temporary depression more than once, for fear that in *Leaves of Grass* the *moral* parts were not sufficiently pronounc'd. But in my clearest and calmest moods I have realized that as those *Leaves*, all and several, surely prepare the way for, and necessitate Morals, and are adjusted to them, just the same as Nature does and is, they are what, consistently with my plan, they must and probably should be. . . . (In a certain sense, while the Moral is the purport and last intelligence of all Nature, there is absolutely nothing of the moral in the works, or laws, or shows of Nature. Those only lead inevitably to it – begin and necessitate it.)

Then I meant *Leaves of Grass*, as publish'd, to be the Poem of Identity, (of *Yours*, whoever you are, now reading these lines.) . . . For genius must realize that, precious as it may be, there is something far more precious, namely, simple Identity, One's-self. A man is not greatest as victor in war, nor inventor or explorer, nor even in science, or in his intellectual or artistic capacity, or exemplar in some vast benevolence. To the highest Democratic view, man is most acceptable in living well the average, practical life and lot which happens to him as ordinary farmer, sea-farer, mechanic, clerk, laborer, or driver – upon and from which position as a central basis or pedestal, while performing its labors, and his duties as citizen, son, husband, father and employed person, he preserves his physique, ascends, developing, radiating himself in other regions – and especially where and when, (greatest of all, and nobler than the proudest mere genius or magnate in any field), he fully realizes the Conscience, the Spiritual, the divine faculty, cultivated well, exemplified in all his deeds and words, through life, uncompromising to the end – a flight loftier than any of Homer's or Shakspere's – broader than all poems and bibles – namely, Nature's own, and in the midst of it, Yourself, your own Identity, body and soul. (All serves, helps – but in the centre of all, absorbing all, giving, for your purpose, the only meaning and vitality to all, master or mistress of all, under the law, stands Yourself.) . . . To sing the Song of that divine law of Identity, and of Yourself, consistently with the Divine Law of the Universal, is a main intention of these *Leaves*.

Something more may be added – for, while I am about it, I would make a full confession. I also sent out *Leaves of Grass* to arouse and set flowering in men's and women's hearts, young and old, (my present and future readers), endless streams of living, pulsating love and friendship, directly from them to myself, now and ever. To this terrible, irrepressible yearning (surely more or less down underneath in most human souls) – this never-satisfied appetite for sympathy, and this boundless offering of sympathy – this universal demo-cratic comradeship – this old, eternal, yet ever-new interchange of adhesive-ness, so fitly emblematic of America – I have given in that book, undisguisedly, declaredly, the openest expression. . . . Poetic literature has long been the formal and conventional tender of art and beauty merely, and of a narrow, constipated, special amativeness. I say, the subtlest, sweetest, surest tie between me and Him or Her, who, in the pages of *Calamus* and other pieces realizes me – though we never see each other or through ages and ages hence – must, in this way, be personal affection. And those – be they few, or be they many – are at any rate *my readers* in a sense that belongs not, and can never belong, to better, prouder poems.

Besides, important as they are in my purpose as emotional expressions for humanity, the special meaning of the *Calamus* cluster of *Leaves of Grass* (and more or less running through that book, and cropping out in *Drum-Taps*,) mainly resides in its Political significance. In my opinion it is by a fervent, accepted development of Comradeship, the beautiful and sane affection of man for man, latent in all the young fellows, North and South, East and West – it is by this, I say, and by what goes directly and indirectly along with it, that the United States of the future, (I cannot too often repeat) are to be most effectually welded together, intercalated, anneal'd into a Living Union.

Then, for enclosing clue of all, it is imperatively and ever to be borne in mind that *Leaves of Grass* entire is not to be construed as an intellectual or scholastic effort or Poem mainly, but more as a radical utterance out of the abysms of the Soul, the Emotions and the Physique – an utterance adjusted to, perhaps born of, Democracy and Modern Science, and in its very nature regardless of the old conventions, and under the great Laws, following only its own impulses.

The varieties and phases, (doubtless often paradoxical, contra-dictory,) of the two Volumes, of *Leaves*, and of these *Rivulets*, are ultimately to be considered as One in structure, and as mutually explanatory of each other – as the multiplex results, like a tree, of series of successive growths, (yet from one central or seed-purport) – there having been five or six such cumulative issues, editions, commencing back in 1855 and thence progressing through twenty years down to date, (1875–'76) – some things added or re-shaped from time to time, as they were found wanted, and other things represt. Of the former Book, more vehement, and perhaps pursuing a central idea with greater closeness – join'd with the present One, extremely varied in theme – I can only briefly reiterate here, that all my pieces, alternated through Both, are only of use and value, if any, as such an interpenetrating, composite, inseparable Unity.

Two of the pieces in this Volume were originally Public Recita-tions – the College Commencement Poem, *As a Strong Bird* – and then the *Song of the Exposition*, to identify these great Industrial gatherings, the majestic outgrowths of the Modern Spirit and Practice – and now fix'd upon, the grandest of them, for the Material event around which shall be concentrated and cele-brated, (as far as any one event can combine them,) the associa-tions and practical proofs of the Hundred Years' life of the Republic. The glory of Labor, and the bringing together not only representatives of all the trades and products, but, fraternally, of all the Workmen of all the Nations of the World, (for this is the Idea behind the Centennial at Philadelphia,) is, to me, so welcome and inspiring a theme, that I only wish I were a younger and a fresher man, to attempt the enduring Book, of poetic character, that ought to be written about it.

The arrangement in print of *Two Rivulets* – the indirectness of the name itself, (suggesting meanings, the start of other meanings, for the whole Volume) are but parts of the Venture which my poems entirely are. For really they have all been Experiments, under the urge of powerful, quite irresistible, perhaps wilful influences, (even escapades,) to see how such things will eventually turn out – and have been recited, as it were, by my Soul, to the special audience of Myself, far more than to the world's audience. Till now, by far the best part of the whole business is, that, these days, in leisure, in sickness and old age, my Spirit, by which they were written or permitted erewhile, does not go back on them, but still and in cabinet hours, fully, deliberately allows them.

Estimating the American Union as so far and for some time to come, in its yet formative condition, I therefore now bequeath Poems and Essays as nutriment and influences to help truly assimilate and harden, and especially to furnish something toward what The States most need of all, and which seems to me yet quite unsupplied in literature, namely, to show them, or begin to show them, Themselves distinctively, and what They are for. For though perhaps the main points of all ages and nations are points of resemblance, and, even while granting evolution, are sub-stantially the same, there are some vital things in which this Republic, as to its individualities, and as a compacted Nation, is to specially stand forth, and culminate modern humanity. And these are the very things it least morally and mentally knows – (though, curiously enough, it is at the same time faithfully acting upon them.)

I count with such absolute certainty on the Great Future of The United States – different from, though founded on, the past – that I have always invoked that Future, and surrounded myself with it, before or while singing my Songs. . . . (As ever, all tends to follow-ings – America, too, is a prophecy. What, even of the best and most successful, would be justified by itself alone? by the present, or the material ostent alone? Of men or States, few realize how much they live in the future. That, rising like pinnacles, gives its main significance to all You and I are doing to-day. Without it, there were little meaning in lands or poems – little purport in human lives. . . . All ages, all Nations and States, have been such prophe-cies. But where any former ones with prophecy so broad, so clear, as our times, our lands – as those of the West?)

Without being a Scientist, I have thoroughly adopted the con-clusions of the great Savans and Experimentalists of our time, and of the last hundred years, and they have interiorly tinged the chyle of all my verse, for purposes beyond. Following the Modern Spirit, the real Poems of the Present, ever solidifying and expand-ing into the Future, must vocalize the vastness and splendor and reality with which Scientism has invested Man and the Universe, (all that is called Creation,) and must henceforth launch Humanity into new orbits, consonant with that vastness, splendor, and reality, (unknown to the old poems,) like new systems of orbs, balanced upon themselves, revolving in limitless space, more subtle than the stars. Poetry, so largely hitherto and even at present wedded to children's tales, and to mere amorousness, upholstery and superficial rhyme, will have to accept, and, while not denying the Past, nor the Themes of the past, will be revivified by this tremendous innovation, the Kosmic Spirit, which must henceforth, in my opinion, be the background and underlying impetus, more or less visible, of all first-class Songs.

Only, (for me, at any rate, in all my Prose and Poetry,) joyfully accepting Modern Science, and loyally following it without the slightest hesitation, there remains ever recognized still a higher flight, a higher fact, the Eternal Soul of Man, (of all Else too,) the Spiritual, the Religious – which it is to be the greatest office of Scientism, in my opinion, and of future Poetry also, to free from fables, crudities and superstitions, and launch forth in renewed Faith and Scope a hundred fold. To me, the worlds of Religiousness, of the conception of the Divine, and of the Ideal, though mainly latent, are just as absolute in Humanity and the Universe as the world of Chemistry, or anything in the objective worlds. To me,

The prophet and the Bard,
Shall yet maintain themselves – in higher circles yet,
Shall mediate to the Modern, to Democracy – interpret yet to
    them,
God and Eidólons.

To me, the crown of Savantism is to be, that it surely opens the way for a more splendid Theology, and for ampler and diviner Songs. No year, or even century, will settle this. There is a phase of the Real, lurking behind the Real, which it is all for. There is also in the Intellect of man, in time, far in prospective recesses, a judgment, a last appellate court, which will settle it.

In certain parts, in these flights, or attempting to depict or suggest them, I have not been afraid of the charge of obscurity, in either of my Two Volumes – because human thought, poetry or melody, must leave dim escapes and outlets – must possess a certain fluid, aerial character, akin to space itself, obscure to those of little or no imagination, but indispensable to the highest purposes. Poetic style, when address'd to the Soul, is less definite form, outline, sculpture, and becomes vista, music, half-tints, and even less than half-tints. True, it may be architecture, but again it may be the forest wild-wood, or the best effects thereof, at twilight, the waving oaks and cedars in the wind, and the impalpable odor.

Finally, as I have lived in fresh lands, inchoate, and in a revolutionary age, future-founding, I have felt to identify the points of that age, these lands, in my recitatives, altogether in my own way. Thus my form has strictly grown from my purports and facts, and is the analogy of them. . . . Within my time the United States have emerg'd from nebulous vagueness and suspense, to full orbic, (though varied,) decision – have done the deeds and achiev'd the triumphs of half a score of centuries – and are henceforth to enter upon their real history – the way being now, (i.e. since the result of the Secession War,) clear'd of death-threatening impedimenta, and the free areas around and ahead of us assured and certain, which were not so before – (the past century being but preparations, trial-voyages and experiments of the Ship, before her starting out upon deep water.)

In estimating my Volumes, the world's current times and deeds, and their spirit, must be first profoundly estimated. Out of the Hundred Years just ending, (1776–1876,) with their genesis of inevitable wilful events, and new introductions, and many unprecedented things of war and peace, (to be realized better, perhaps only realized, at the remove of a Century hence) – Out of that stretch of time, and especially out of the immediately preceding Twenty-Five Years, (1850–'75,) with all their rapid changes, innovations, and audacious movements – and bearing their own inevitable wilful birth-marks – my Poems too have found genesis.
W. W.

APPENDIX 6
A Sketch

A Sketch

Upon the ocean's wave-worn shore
   I marked a solitary form,
Whose brooding look, and features wore
   The darkness of the coming storm!
And, from his lips, the sigh that broke,
   So long within his bosom nursed,
In deep and mournful accents spoke,
   Like troubled waves, that shining burst!

And as he gazed on earth and sea,
   Girt with the gathering night, his soul,
Wearied and life-worn, longed to flee,
   And rest within its final goal!
He thought of her whose love had beamed,
   The sunlight of his ripened years;
But now her gentle memory seemed
   To brim his eye with bitter tears!

'Oh! thou bless'd Spirit!' thus he sighed –
   Smile on me from thy realm of rest!
My dark and doubting spirit guide,
   By conflict torn, and grief oppressed!
Teach me, in every saddening care,
   To see the chastening hand of Heaven;
The Soul's high culture to prepare,
   Wisely and mercifully given!

'Could I this sacred solace share,
   'Twould still my struggling bosom's moan;
And the deep peacefulness of prayer,
   Might for thy heavy loss atone!
Earth, in its wreath of summer flowers,
   And all its varied scenes of joy,
Its festal halls and echoing bowers,
   No more my darkened thoughts employ.

'But here, the billow's heaving breast,
   And the low thunder's knelling tone,
Speak of the wearied soul's unrest,
   Its murmuring, and conflicts lone!
And yon sweet star, whose golden gleam,
   Pierces the tempest's gathering gloom,
In the rich radiance of its beam,
   Tells me of light beyond the tomb!'

Notes

ABBREVIATIONS

The following dates have been used to identify editions of
Leaves of Grass:

LG 1855	*Leaves of Grass*, 1st edn
LG 1856	*Leaves of Grass*, 2nd edn, containing 'Leaves-Droppings'
LG 1860	*Leaves of Grass*, 3rd edn
1865	*Drum-Taps*
1865 Sequel	*Sequel to Drum-Taps*
LG 1867	*Leaves of Grass*, 4th edn
1868	*Poems by Walt Whitman* (Rossetti)
LG 1871	*Leaves of Grass*, 5th edn
LG 1871 Second Issue	*Leaves of Grass* (5th edn, 2nd issue), including *Passage to India*
LG 1876	*Leaves of Grass*, 6th edn (two volumes)
LG 1881	*Leaves of Grass*, 7th edn
1888	*November Boughs*
1888 Complete	*Complete Poems and Prose of Walt Whitman*
LG 1889	*Leaves of Grass*, 8th edn
1891	*Good-Bye My Fancy*
LG 1892	*Leaves of Grass*, 9th edn
LG 1897	*Leaves of Grass*, 10th edn

Other abbreviations which have been used are:

Blodgett and Bradley	Harold Blodgett and Sculley Bradley (eds), *Reader's Comprehensive Edition of* Leaves of Grass, New York University Press, 1965.
CWW	*Collected Writings of Walt Whitman*, New York University Press, 1961 (continuing).
UPP	Emory Holloway (ed.), *Uncollected Prose and Poetry of Walt Whitman*, Doubleday, 1921.
Webster 1841	Noah Webster, *An American Dictionary of the English Language*, New Haven, Connecticut, 1841.

COME, SAID MY SOUL

First printed New York *Daily Graphic*, December 1874, and used as the title-page epigraph of *LG 1876*, *LG 1882*, *1888 Complete* and *LG 1892*.

Inscriptions

A group title for the original nine opening poems of *LG 1871*; increased in *LG 1881* to twenty-four poems, only one of which was new.

ONE'S-SELF I SING

This poem is a shorter version of the 'Inscription' to *LG 1867*, reprinted in *1888* as *Small the Theme of My Chant*.
title] *LG 1871*.

2 *En-Masse* OED: 'in a mass or body; bodily, all at once'. The first instance cited is 1802; in 1848 Mrs Gaskell writes: 'The things were lifted *en masse* to the drawer.'

AS I PONDER'D IN SILENCE

Appeared in *LG 1871*.

IN CABIN'D SHIPS AT SEA

Appeared in *LG 1871*.

TO FOREIGN LANDS

Transferred to *Inscriptions* in *LG 1881*.
title] *LG 1871*; To Other Lands *LG 1860*.

TO A HISTORIAN

Transferred to *Inscriptions* in *LG 1871*.
title] *LG 1867*; Chants Democratic, No. 10 *LG 1860*.

4 *habitan* properly 'habitant'. *Webster 1841* notes: 'Habitant n. (Fr. from *habitans*.) An inhabitant; a dweller; a resident; one who has a permanent abode in a place.' *Blodgett and Bradley* refer to the word as 'apparently the poet's coinage, perhaps derived from "habitant", a native of Canada (or Louisiana) of French descent'. OED notes: 'habitant 2 (pronounced abitan; pl. often as formerly in F. *habitans*). A native of Canada (also of Louisiana) of French descent; one of the race of original French colonists, chiefly small farmers or yeomen', and cites an example by Washington Irving in 1855: 'To ascertain the feelings of the *habitans*, or French yeomanry.' The sense of the passage, however, suggests that Whitman had in mind a native dweller and that he spelled the word as he pronounced it. See *Poem of Remembrances for a Girl or Boy of These States* 10 and *Salut Au Monde!* 132.

4 *Alleghanies* properly 'Alleghenies'.

TO THEE OLD CAUSE

Appeared in *LG 1871*.

EIDÓLONS

First printed New York *Tribune*, 19 February 1876; transferred to *Inscriptions* in *LG 1881*.

title] images, spectres, phantoms. OED cites instances by Carlyle, Scott, Poe, Mrs Browning and J. R. Lowell. Whitman told Traubel (H. Traubel (ed.), *With Walt Whitman in Camden*, III, 131): 'It is the custom everywhere to pronounce the word *ei*dolons: I always make it ei*dol*ons: this is right, too. I make considerable use of the word.'

15 *ateliers* workshops; artists' studios. OED cites Thackeray's use of the word in 1840.

21 *ostent* *Webster 1841*: '2. show, manifestation, token.'

22 *savan* *Webster 1841* defines a 'savant' as 'a man of learning'. OED notes that 'the misapprehension of the obs. Fr. spelling *savans* of the plural has given rise in Eng. to the incorrect form savan' and cites Chambers' *Encyclopedia* in 1864 as referring to Manzoni's mother as the 'gifted daughter of the great savan, the Marquis Beccaria'.

45 *Exalté* French: raised up, elevated.

FOR HIM I SING

Appeared in *LG 1871*.

WHEN I READ THE BOOK

Appeared in *LG 1867*; transferred to *Inscriptions* in *LG 1871*. Originally a poem of five lines: the first three as printed here and the last two as follows:

(As if any man really knew aught of my life;
As if you, O cunning Soul, did not keep your secret well!)

BEGINNING MY STUDIES

Appeared in *1865*; *LG 1867*; transferred to *Inscriptions* in *LG 1871*.

BEGINNERS

Appeared in *LG 1860*; transferred to *Inscriptions* in *LG 1881*.

3 *inure* *Webster 1841*: 'v. i. to serve to the use or benefit of; as, a gift of lands *inures* to the heirs of the grantee, or it *inures* to their benefit.'

TO THE STATES

title] *LG 1881*, in *Inscriptions*; Walt Whitman's Caution *LG 1860*, *as one of the Messenger Leaves poems, and LG 1871, LG 1876, as one of the Songs of Insurrection.*

ON JOURNEYS THROUGH THE STATES

Appeared in *LG 1860* but was dropped from *LG 1867*. Transferred to *Inscriptions* in *LG 1881*.
title] *LG 1871 Second Issue*; Chants Democratic, No. 17 *LG 1860*.
6 *effuse · Webster 1841*: 'to pour out as a fluid, to spill, to shed.'
8 *Kanada* Whitman's spelling.
11 *promulge Webster 1841*: 'to publish or teach.'

TO A CERTAIN CANTATRICE

Appeared in *LG 1860* as one of the *Messenger Leaves*; in *LG 1871*, *LG 1876* as one of the *Songs of Insurrection*; and transferred to *Inscriptions* in *LG 1881*.
title] 'Cantatrice' is glossed by OED: 'a female professional singer.' The first instance cited is 1866 *Daily Telegraph*: 'the rival cantatrice'. Whitman has in mind one Madame Marietta Alboni, who appeared in New York in the season 1852-3.

ME IMPERTURBE

Transferred to *Inscriptions* in *LG 1881*.
title] *LG 1867*; Chants Democratic, No. 18 *LG 1860*.
5 *Mannahatta* Algonquin Indian ·name for New York, meaning· 'large island'.

SAVANTISM

Appeared in *LG 1860*; transferred to *Inscriptions* in *LG 1881*. *Webster 1841* defines a 'savant' as 'a man of learning'. 'Savantism' seems to be Whitman's coinage.

THE SHIP STARTING

Appeared in *1865* and *LG 1867*; then as one of the 'Paumanok' group in *LG 1871* and *LG 1876*; transferred to *Inscriptions* in *LG 1881*.
2 *moonsails* a sail carried in light winds above a skysail.
3 *emulous waves* anxious to equal or excel each other.

I HEAR AMERICA SINGING

Transferred to *Inscriptions* in *LG 1881*.
title] *LG 1867*; Chants Democratic, No. 20 *LG 1860*.

WHAT PLACE IS BESIEGED?

Originally the last four lines of *Calamus, No. 31* in *LG 1860*; it became a separate poem with the present title in *LG 1867*; and was transferred to *Inscriptions* in *LG 1881*.

STILL THOUGH THE ONE I SING

Appeared in *LG 1871* as part of the group of *Songs of Insurrection*; present position in *LG 1881*.

SHUT NOT YOUR DOORS

Appeared in *1865* and *LG 1867*; transferred to *Inscriptions* in *LG 1881*. See *As They Draw to a Close*.

POETS TO COME

Appeared as part of *The Answerer* group in *LG 1871*; transferred to *Inscriptions* in *LG 1881*.
title] *LG 1867*; Chants Democratic, No. 14 *LG 1860*.

TO YOU

Appeared in *LG 1860* in the *Messenger Leaves* group; transferred to *Inscriptions* in *LG 1881*.

THOU READER

Appeared in *LG 1881*.

STARTING FROM PAUMANOK

Appeared in present position in *LG 1871*.
title] *LG 1867*; Proto-Leaf *LG 1860*; Premonition *MS*.

1–14 Starting . . . World] *LG 1860* has:

Free, fresh, savage,
Fluent, luxuriant, self-content, fond of persons and places,
Fond of fish-shape Paumanok, where I was born,
Fond of the sea – lusty-begotten and various,
Boy of the Mannahatta, the city of ships, my city,
Or raised inland, or of the south savannas,
Or full-breath'd on Californian air, or Texan or Cuban air,
Tallying, vocalizing all – resounding Niagara – resounding Missouri,
Or rude in my home in Kanuck woods,
Or wandering and hunting, my drink water, my diet meat,
Or withdrawn to muse and meditate in some deep recess,
Far from the clank of crowds, an interval passing, rapt and happy,
Stars, vapor, snow, the hills, rocks, the Fifth Month flowers, my amaze, my
  love,

Aware of the buffalo, the peace-herds, the bull, strong-breasted and hairy,
Aware of the mocking-bird of the wilds at daybreak,
Solitary, singing in the west, I strike up for a new world.

1 *Paumanok* the Indian name for Long Island means fish-shaped.
27 *debouch* *Webster 1841*: 'to issue or march out of a narrow place, or from defiles, as troops'. OED: 'to emerge from a narrower into a wider place or space'.
49 *conn'd* studied with care.
75 *comity* courteous understanding.
98 *Omnes!* Latin plural: 'all'; here meaning 'the whole'.
123 *camerado* cf. OED *camrado*: also *camerado*: 'the Spanish word was a collective feminine, of the same type as *ambuscade*, *cavalcade*, which, like *Company*, sense 4, was at length applied to a single person who is one's "company" or chamber-mate; in which sense also it was sometimes altered into the masculine form *camarado*.' The OED cites an example of 1636 by Healey: 'He beggeth more (victuail) of his Camerado's.'
134 *Melange* blending, mingling.
233 *dolce affettuoso* Italian musical direction, used here as a noun: sweet, affectionate comrade.
255 *in arriere* behind. See *One Old Feuillage* 48n.
257 *Kaw* a river in Kansas.

SONG OF MYSELF

Appeared untitled and unsectioned in *LG 1855* (see Appendix 4, p. 675).
title] *LG 1881*; Poem of Walt Whitman, an American *LG 1856*; Walt Whitman *LG 1860 and succeeding editions till LG 1881.*

4 *loafe* *Webster 1841* defines a *loafer* as 'an idle man who seeks his living by spunging or expedients'. OED cites use of the word as a verb in 1838; in 1852 Mrs Stowe in *Uncle Tom's Cabin* observed that 'Men talked, and loafed, and read and smoked'.
49 *entretied* a term from carpentry meaning cross-braced.
60–61 *As the hugging . . . plenty*] *LG 1855* read:

As God comes a loving bed-fellow and sleeps
  at my side all night and close on the peep of day,
And leaves for me baskets covered with white towels
  bulging the house with their plenty.

95 *kelson* a line of jointed timbers in a ship laid on the middle of the floor-timbers over the keel, fastened with long bolts and clinched.
109 *Kanuck . . . Cuff* A Kanuck is a French Canadian; a Tuckahoe is a tide-water Virginian, so named because he eats a fungus also known as 'Virginia truffle'; Cuff is a common name for a black man and derived from the African name of the weekday on which the man was born; in this case, Friday.
185 *I saw the marriage . . .* Whitman has in mind a painting by Alfred Jacob Miller called *The Trapper's Bride*.

218 *shuffle and break-down*   two kinds of popular minstrel dancing, one slow and sliding, the other fast.

226 *string-piece   Webster 1841*: 'a piece of timber in bridges'; used for shoring and construction.

243 *gamut   Webster 1841*: 'a scale on which notes in music are written or printed'; any recognized musical scale.

267 *king-pin*   an extended spoke of the pilot-wheel.

272 *on a First-day loafe*] of a Sunday *LG 1855*. Whitman adopted the use of Quaker terms for the days of the week in *LG 1860*.

275 *jour printer*   journeyman printer.

289 *Wolverine*   a man from the state of Michigan.

321 *Chattahooche or Altamahaw*   two Southern rivers, the first flows between Georgia and Alabama, and Georgia and Florida; the second is in the state of Georgia.

338 *Hoosier, Badger, Buckeye*   a man from either Indiana, Wisconsin, or Ohio.

396 *truckling fold with powders*   powdered medicine was formerly dispensed in folded paper packets.

408 *carlacue*   Whitman's spelling for 'carlicues or curlicues'; a fantastic curl or twist.

468 *scrofula*   tubercular growth.

486 *stonecrop*   a moss-like plant, used for healing.

487 *cartouches*   a tablet for inscription as well as a scroll-shaped ornament.

497 *Walt Whitman, a kosmos, of Manhattan the son*] Walt Whitman, an American, one of the roughs, a kosmos *LG 1855*.

505 *afflatus*   inspiration; a force from within.

530 *colter*   the blade attached to the beam of a plow used to cut the sward; here the phallus.

531 *tilth*   the depth to which tilling may be carried; here meaning 'to the root' of me.

580 *plenum*   fullness.

604 *Uranus*   The Greek personification of Heaven; the seventh planet.

608 *fakes   Webster 1841*: 'one of the circles or windings of a cable or hawser, as it lies in a coil; a single turn or coil.'

613 *quahaug*   an Atlantic coast clam.

661 *omnific*   all-creating.

664 *pismire*   an ant.

675 *plutonic rocks*   granite, solidified below the surface.

698 *omnigenous*   of all kinds.

727 *scallop'd scum and slender shoots*   the sediment on roofs and moss in wooden gutters.

741 *life-car*   a water-tight boat travelling on a rope from a wrecked vessel to the shore.

752 *bull-dances*   slang for Indian 'buffalo-dances'.

755 *musters*   an assembly; here in the sense of a party or ball.

806 *topples*   OED: '? a crest, tuft'; more commonly used as an intr. verb meaning 'to overhang threateningly'. OED quotes Tyndall, 1860: 'Masses of granite . . . toppling above the terminal face of the glacier.'

824   *the . . . wreck*   the wreck of the *San Francisco*, helpless at sea for twelve days, was reported in the New York *Weekly Tribune* on 21 January 1854.

840   *dribs*   to fall in drops; to go on little by little. OED notes that this form is apparently 'an onomatopoeic formation arising out of *Drip* or *Drop*, the modified consonant expressing a modification of the notion'.

865   *ambulanza*   Spanish: properly *ambulancia*, ambulance.

875   *the tale*   the episode referrred to is the massacre of the soldiers of Captain Fannin by the Mexicans after his surrender at Goliad, March 1836.

897   *Would you hear* . . .   Whitman's sources for this tale were his maternal grandmother and a letter of John Paul Jones to Benjamin Franklin printed in *Old South Leaflets* (Boston, n.d.).

974   *Eleves   Webster 1841:* 'pronounced *elevaí*: one brought up or protected by another.' OED: 'a pupil' and cites use of the word in English as early as 1736; in 1829 *Gentleman's Magazine:* 'Their Eleves should have . . . an excellent classical education.'

997   *scarf'd   Webster 1841:* 'joined; pieced'; here in the sense of 'sealed'.

1029–32 *Kronos . . . Mexitli* Kronos, a Titan, was the son of Uranus and Gaea and dethroned by his son, Zeus. Osiris was the Egyptian god of the underworld and Isis the Egyptian goddess of fertility. Belus was the legendary king of Assyria. Manito was the spirit of Nature in the mythology of the Algonquin Indians. Odin in Norse mythology is the supreme god as well as the god of war. Mexitli was the Aztec god of war.

1048   *The bull and the bug*   the bull was held sacred by the Egyptians and the scarabaeus or dung-beetle was the ikon of the sun god Khepera.

1069   *trestles   Webster 1841:* 'a moveable form for supporting anything'; in this case the supporting forms upon which a coffin rests.

1101   *circle of obis*   obeah or obi is a West African word referring to a kind of sorcery practised in Africa and the West Indies. It may refer to an amulet or charm used for magical purposes or, OED 3, 'one who practises obeah, a negro sorcerer or sorceress', an *obi-man*. Whitman's plural is not common.

1102   *llama*   properly 'lama', a Tibetan priest, and so spelled in *Webster 1841*. The OED notes, however, that the word is frequently misspelled 'llama' and cites an example by Swinhow – 'the majority of the llama temples were situated outside the wall' – in 1861.

1103   *gymnosophist*   a Hindu ascetic.

1104   *Shastas and Vedas . . . the Koran*   collections of Hindi scriptures; the *Koran* contains the the revelations to Mohammed.

1105   *teokallis*   Aztec temples.

1115   *flukes*   OED 2 pl.: 'The two parts which constitute the large triangular tail of the whale'; bloody because harpooned.

1129   *koboo*   native of Palembang, Sumatra.

1167   *sauroids*   the Sauria, prehistoric mammoth reptiles, were thought to carry their eggs in their mouths.

1217 *chuff* OED: 'swollen or puffed out with fat, chubby'; here the heel of the hand.

1242 *latherers* those who shave their faces smooth.

1290 *accoucheur Webster 1841*: 'a man who assists women in childbirth.'

1308 *debouch Webster 1841*: 'to issue or march out of a narrow place, or from defiles, as troops.'

1322 *snuff the sidle of evening* extinguish the unobtrusive glimmer of evening.

1334 *scud Webster 1841*: 'low thin cloud, or thin clouds driven by the wind.'

1346 *you. in LG 1855 there is no final punctuation.*

Children Of Adam

This was a group title for sixteen poems. In *LG 1860* there were fifteen poems entitled *Enfans d' Adam*; the present title was adopted in *LG 1867*. In *LG 1871* fourteen poems of the preceding edition were retained and two poems from *1865* were added.

TO THE GARDEN THE WORLD

title] *LG 1867*; Enfans d'Adam, No. 1 *LG 1860*.

FROM PENT-UP ACHING RIVERS

title] *LG 1867*; Enfans d'Adam, No. 2 *LG 1860*.

I SING THE BODY ELECTRIC

title] *LG 1867*; *untitled in LG 1855*; Poem of the Body *LG 1856*; Enfans d' Adam, No. 3 *LG 1860*.

53 *nimbus Webster 1841*: 'on ancient medals and monuments, a circle or disc of rays or light.'

96 (*For before the war . . .*) a line added in *LG 1881-2*.

138 *scapula* the shoulder-blade.

A WOMAN WAITS FOR ME

title] *LG 1867*; Poem of Procreation *LG 1856*; Enfans d'Adam, No. 4 *LG 1860*.

SPONTANEOUS ME

title] *LG 1867*; Bunch Poem *LG 1856*; Enfans d'Adam, No. 5 *LG 1860*.

23 *no-form'd stings* formless accusations.

24 *hubb'd* central.

ONE HOUR TO MADNESS AND JOY

title] *LG 1867*; Enfans d'Adam, No. 6 *LG 1860*.

OUT OF THE ROLLING OCEAN THE CROWD

This poem was first published in *1865* and it then appeared in *LG 1867*. It was transferred to *Children Of Adam* in *LG 1871*.

9 *rondure   Webster 1841*: 'a circle'; roundness. OED cites Symonds's *Sketches of Italy and Greece* (1874): 'Cherubs clustered in the rondure of rose-windows'. Whitman's sense is closer to 'wholeness', the completion suggested by a circular form.

AGES AND AGES RETURNING AT INTERVALS

title] *LG 1867*; Enfans d'Adam, No. 12 *LG 1860*.

WE TWO, HOW LONG WE WERE FOOL'D

title] *LG 1867*; Enfans d'Adam, No. 7 *LG 1860*; *original first line* – You and I – what the earth is, we are – *was dropped in LG 1867*.

O HYMEN! O HYMENEE!

Esther Shepherd in *Walt Whitman's Prose* (New York, 1938) suggests that Whitman took the title of this poem from a passage in George Sand's *The Countess of Rudolstadt* (1842–7). Properly 'hymen, hyménée', the masculine and feminine form of the French word for marriage, here it may be translated as 'O married man! O married woman!'.

I AM HE THAT ACHES WITH LOVE

title] *LG 1867*; Enfans d'Adam, No. 14 *LG 1860*.

NATIVE MOMENTS

title] *LG 1867*; Enfans d'Adam, No. 8 *LG 1860*.

ONCE I PASS'D THROUGH A POPULOUS CITY

The manuscript (*UPP*, II, 102) reveals that the original subject was a man:

Once I passed through a populous city, imprinting on my brain, for future use, its shows, architecture, customs and traditions

But now of all that city I remember only the man who wandered with me there, for love of me,

Day by day, and night by night, we were together.

All else has long been forgotten by me – I remember, I say, only one rude and ignorant man who, when I departed, long and long held me by the hand, with silent lips, sad and tremulous.

title] *LG 1867*; Enfans d'Adam, No. 9 *LG 1860*.

I HEARD YOU SOLEMN-SWEET PIPES OF THE ORGAN

First printed New York *Leader*, 12 October 1861, entitled *Little Bells Last Night*. It appeared in *LG 1867*; and was transferred to *Children Of Adam* in *LG 1871*.

FACING WEST FROM CALIFORNIA'S SHORES

title] *LG 1867*; Enfans d'Adam, No. 10 *LG 1860*.

AS ADAM EARLY IN THE MORNING

title] *LG 1867*; Enfans d'Adam, No. 15 *LG 1860*.

Calamus

This was a group title for thirty-nine poems; in *LG 1860* the group consisted of forty-five numbered poems. In *LG 1867* Whitman rejected three poems (*Who Is Now Reading This, I Thought That Knowledge Alone Would Suffice* and *Hours Continuing Long*); and in *LG 1871, Second Issue*, Whitman added one poem – *The Base of All Metaphysics* – and transferred four poems to *Passage to India*.

In a letter to Moncure D. Conway, 1 November 1867, *CWW, Correspondence*, I, 347, Whitman remarked: ' "Calamus" is a common word here. It is the very large and aromatic grass, or rush, growing about water-ponds in the valleys – (spears about three feet high – often called "sweet flag" – grows all over the Northern and Middle States – see Webster's Large Dictionary – Calamus – definition 2). The recherché or ethereal sense of the term, as used in my book, arises probably from the actual Calamus presenting the biggest and hardiest kind of spears of grass – and their fresh, aquatic, pungent bouquet.'

Whitman may have had in mind Webster's *fourth* definition of the word, but all of *Webster 1841* is worth having here:

1. 'the generic name of the Indian cane, called also Rotang. It is without branches, has a crown at the top, and is beset with spines.'
2. 'in antiquity, a pipe or fistula, a wind instrument, made of a reed or oaten stalk.'
3. 'a rush or reed, used anciently as a pen to write on parchment or papyrus.'
4. 'a sort of reed, or sweet-scented cane used by the Jews as a perfume. It is a knotty root, reddish without and white within, and filled with a spungy substance. It has an aromatic smell.'
5. 'the sweet-flag, called by Linnaeus, *acorus*.'

IN PATHS UNTRODDEN

title] *LG 1867*; Calamus, No. 1 *LG 1860*.

15 *Ninth-month in my forty-first year*   September 1859.

SCENTED HERBAGE OF MY BREAST

title] *LG 1867*; Calamus, No. 2 *LG 1860*.

WHOEVER YOU ARE HOLDING ME NOW IN HAND

title] *LG 1867*; Calamus, No. 3 *LG 1860*.

27 *conning* studying carefully.

FOR YOU O DEMOCRACY

In *1865* lines from the first twelve stanzas were used for *Over the Carnage Rose Prophetic a Voice*; the present poem, *LG 1867*, is based on the last three stanzas.

title] *LG 1881*; Calamus, No. 5 *LG 1860*; A Song *LG 1867*.

THESE I SINGING IN SPRING

title] *LG 1867*; Calamus, No. 4 *LG 1860*.

NOT HEAVING FROM MY RIBB'D BREAST ONLY

title] *LG 1867*; Calamus, No. 6 *LG 1860*.

OF THE TERRIBLE DOUBT OF APPEARANCES

title] *LG 1867*; Calamus, No. 7 *LG 1860*.

THE BASE OF ALL METAPHYSICS

First appeared in *LG 1871*.

RECORDERS AGES HENCE

title] *LG 1867*; Calamus, No. 10 *LG 1860*.

WHEN I HEARD AT THE CLOSE OF THE DAY

title] *LG 1867*; Calamus, No. 11 *LG 1860*.

ARE YOU THE NEW PERSON DRAWN TOWARD ME?

title] *LG 1867*; Calamus, No. 12 *LG 1860*.

9 *maya* in Hindu philosophy the term for deception – the physical and sensuous universe conceived as a tissue of appearances.

After line 9 *LG 1860* read:

O the next step may precipitate you!

O let some past deceived one hiss in your ears, how many have prest on the same as you are pressing now,

How many have fondly supposed what you are supposing now – only to be disappointed.

ROOTS AND LEAVES THEMSELVES ALONE

title] *LG 1867*; Calamus, No. 13 *LG 1860*.

NOT HEAT FLAMES UP AND CONSUMES

This was the first numbered poem in the original manuscript group of twelve, entitled *Calamus Leaves*.
title] *LG 1867*; Calamus, No. 14 *LG 1860*.

TRICKLE DROPS

title] *LG 1867*; Calamus No. 15 *LG 1860*.

CITY OF ORGIES

title] *LG 1867*; Calamus No. 18 *LG 1860*.

BEHOLD THIS SWARTHY FACE

title] *LG 1867*; Calamus No. 19 *LG 1860*.

I SAW IN LOUISIANA A LIVE-OAK GROWING

title] *LG 1867*; Calamus No. 20 *LG 1860*.

TO A STRANGER

title] *LG 1867*; Calamus No. 22 *LG 1860*.

THIS MOMENT YEARNING AND THOUGHTFUL

title] *LG 1867*; Calamus No. 23 *LG 1860*.

I HEAR IT WAS CHARGED AGAINST ME

title] *LG 1867*; Calamus No. 24 *LG 1860*.

THE PRAIRIE-GRASS DIVIDING

title] *LG 1867*; Calamus No. 25 *LG 1860*.

WHEN I PERUSE THE CONQUER'D FAME

title] *LG 1867*; Calamus No. 28 *LG 1860*.

WE TWO BOYS TOGETHER CLINGING

title] *LG 1867*; Calamus No. 26 *LG 1860*.

A PROMISE TO CALIFORNIA

title] *LG 1867*; Calamus No. 30 *LG 1860*.

HERE THE FRAILEST LEAVES OF ME

title] *LG 1867*; Calamus No. 44 *LG 1860*.

NO LABOR-SAVING MACHINE

title] *LG 1867*; Calamus No. 33 *LG 1860*.

A GLIMPSE

title] *LG 1867*; Calamus No. 29 *LG 1860*.
2 *unremark'd* unnoticed.

A LEAF FOR HAND IN HAND

title] *LG 1867*; Calamus No. 37 *LG 1860*.

EARTH, MY LIKENESS

title] *LG 1867*; Calamus No. 36 *LG 1860*.

I DREAM'D IN A DREAM

title] *LG 1867*; Calamus No. 34 *LG 1860*.

WHAT THINK YOU I TAKE MY PEN IN HAND?

title] *LG 1867*; Calamus No. 32 *LG 1860*.

TO THE EAST AND TO THE WEST

title] *LG 1867*; Calamus No. 35 *LG 1860*.

SOMETIMES WITH ONE I LOVE

title] *LG 1867*; Calamus No. 39 *LG 1860*.

TO A WESTERN BOY

title] *LG 1867*; Calamus No. 42 *LG 1860*.
1 *eleve* see *Song of Myself*, note to line 974.

FAST-ANCHOR'D ETERNAL O LOVE!

title] *LG 1867*; Calamus No. 38 *LG 1860*.

AMONG THE MULTITUDE

title] *LG 1867*; Calamus No. 41 *LG 1860*.

O YOU WHOM I OFTEN AND SILENTLY COME

title] *LG 1867*; Calamus No. 43 *LG 1860*.

THAT SHADOW MY LIKENESS

title] *LG 1867*; Calamus No. 40 *LG 1860*.

1 *chaffering   Webster 1841*: 'bargaining, buying'.

FULL OF LIFE NOW

title] *LG 1867*; Calamus No. 45 *LG 1860*.

SALUT AU MONDE!

title] *LG 1860*; Poem of Salutation *LG 1856*.

26 *rebeck*   a stringed instrument of the viol class.
34 *base   Webster, 1841*: 'the lowest or gravest part in music; improperly written *bass*'; OED notes that this spelling 'is the regular form up to the present century of the word now spelt "bass"'.
35 *Okotsk*   a Siberian seaport.
36 *slave-coffle*   slave caravan.
50 *Chian Shahs, Altays, Ghauts*   mountain ranges in China, Siberia and India.
51 *Elbruz, Kazbek, Bazardjusi*   mountain peaks in the Caucasus.
52 *Styrian Alps . . . Karnac Alps*   Austrian and Italian Alps.
53 *mount Hecla*   volcano in south-west Iceland.
54 *mountains of the Moon*   placed by Ptolemy in the African interior.
67 *cape of Storms*   Cape of Good Hope.
    cape Verde   westernmost point of Africa.
    Guardafui   north-east Somali, Africa.
    Bon   north-east Tunis, Africa.
    Bajadore   properly 'Cape Bojador', headland of Spanish West Africa on the Atlantic near the border of Saguia el Hamra and Rio de Oro.
68 *Dondra head*   southernmost cape of Ceylon.
    straits of Sunda   sea passage separating Sumatra and Java.
    cape Lopatka   southern extremity of Kamchatka.
71 *Scheld*   more commonly spelt 'Schelde' or 'Scheldt'; a river that rises in France.
74 *Obi*   an inlet of the Arctic Ocean.
    Lena   a river in Siberia.
86 *Amour*   properly 'Amur'; a river in east Asia.
87 *Guadalquiver*   a river in southern Spain.
92 *Saukara   Blodgett and Bradley* 141–2 suggest that this represents a misspelling of the Hindu male divinity 'Sankara', or Siva, in his aspect as healer.

The source of the Ganges river, according to Indian mythology, is Sankara's head, 'the high rim' of his curled brow.

93 *avatars* in Hindu mythology the descent of a deity to earth in the incarnation of a man or animal.

94 *sabians* according to the *Dictionary of Comparative Religion*, ed. S. G. F. Brandon (New York, 1970), 'they are most probably the *Mandaeans*, wrongly called Christians of St John, still found near the Euphrates and Tigris. . . . in Harran they were star-worshippers who called themselves Sabians . . . . they include famous learned men, notably astronomers.'

llamas properly 'lamas', Tibetan priests; for the spelling see note on line 1102 of *Song of Myself.*

muftis teachers of the law of Mohammad.

95 *Mona* an island between Britain and Ireland, once inhabited by Druids and supposed by some to be Anglesey and others to be the Isle of Man.

vervain *Webster 1841*: 'a plant; the popular name of some species of the genus Verbain.'

98 *Hercules* Roman deity identified with the Greek Heracles, son of Alcmene and Zeus. When the time came for him to serve Eurystheus he was assigned twelve tasks, each corresponding to the movement of the sun. He became a constellation in the Northern sky after being burned by the robes of Nessus.

99 *Bacchus* Greek and Roman god of fertility and wine, the son of Zeus and Semele. His rites were held at night and consisted in part of devouring animals; an Egyptian deity *Bacis* (great light) appears related to him.

100 *Kneph* Egyptian deity of primeval darkness; literally *breath* or *wind*. As David Goodale notes ('Some of Walt Whitman's Borrowings', *American Literature* (1938), 202–13) Whitman is indebted here to C. F. Volney's *Ruins* (Paris, 1791). In R. M. Bucke's *Notes and Fragments* (London, 1899) there is a notebook entitled 'Religions – Gods' (pp. 152–4) in which Whitman writes: 'Kneph – "existence" – a Theban god, a human figure dressed in dark blue holding in one hand a sceptre and a girdle, with a cap of feathers on his head (to express fugacity of thought).' Kneph is customarily represented with a man's body and the head of a ram.

101 *Hermes* Gertrude Jobes in the *Dictionary of Mythology* (New York, 1961) comments: 'The Egyptian god *Toth*, confounded by the Greeks with Hermes, was called Hermes Trismegistus. Toth is a moon god and instrument of the creator; the healer of the sun's eye.' Whitman took these lines almost directly from chapter 21, p. 183 of Volney's *Ruins* (see above), in the translation of 1796, New York, 'The Problem of Religious Contradictions'. In this chapter the unity of all religions is explored. In a passage in which the llama explains that Christian doctrine was known in the East 'upwards of a thousand years' there is a note which states: 'if, as is the case, the doctrine of Pythagoras and that of Orpheus are of Egyptian origin, that of Bedou goes back to the common source; and in reality the Egyptian priests recite that Hermes as he was dying said: "I have hitherto lived an exile from my country, to which I now return.

Weep not for me; I ascend to the celestial abode where each of you will follow in his turn: there God is: this life is only death." '

110 *Scandinavian warriors* R. M. Bucke in *Notes and Fragments* (London, 1899, 43) quotes the newspaper clipping found in one of Whitman's notebooks which provided the source for these lines: 'The old Scandanavian heroes, when they died, desired to have their funeral mounds raised high above them; their corpses close to the margin of the restless ocean, so that the spirit, when it grew weary of the narrow, quiet grave, might rise up through the mound and gaze forth over the vast expanse of tossing billows, and then become refreshed by a sense of immensity, liberty, action.'

113 *tumuli* plural of *tumulus*, an ancient sepulchral mound, a barrow. OED cites an example of 1863 by Tyell: 'Tumuli of the stone period'.

Kalmucks and Baskirs nomadic Mongolians.

119 *teff-wheat* an Abyssinian grain plant which yields a fine grade of white flour.

122 *Wacho* a Caddoan Indian tribesman from Texas.

125 *Samoiede* a member of a neo-Siberian tribe.

143 *Kruman* a Liberian tribesman.

145 *Khiva* a khanate in western Asia, now the USSR.

145 *Herat* a city in north-west Afghanistan.

Teheran capital of Iran.

Muscat capital of Oman, Arabia.

146 *Medina* city in Hejaz, Saudi Arabia.

171 *Styria* a province of south-east Austria.

173 *Weser* a river in Germany.

174 *Swabian* a native of Swabia, now a part of south-west Bavaria.

Wallachian a native of Wallachia, now a part of Romania.

178 *Bokh* Bokhara was formerly a khanate of central Asia.

186 *Bab-el-mandeb* a strait connecting the Red Sea with the Indian Ocean.

187 *lake Tiberias* the Sea of Galilee in Palestine.

199 *Hottentot Webster 1841*: 'a native of the southern extremity of Africa; a savage brutal man.'

202 *koboo* more commonly 'Kubu', a small, semi-nomadic group found in swampy areas near watercourses in south-east Sumatra, Indonesia.

203 *Kamtschatkan* a native of a peninsula in north-east Siberia.

206 *Bedowee* a nomadic Arabian tribesman.

207 *Nankin* properly 'Nanking', the former capital city of China.

Kaubul the capital of Afghanistan.

SONG OF THE OPEN ROAD

title] *LG 1867*; Poem of the Road *LG 1856*.

103 *seine Webster 1841*: 'a large net for catching fish'. Although spelled without a final e in *Webster 1841*, the OED cites examples with Whitman's spelling.

114 *Allons! French*: 'Let us go'.

130 *formules* Webster *1841*: '*Formula/Formule*: a prescribed form, a rule or model.'

153 *Habitués* OED: 'One who has the habit of going to or frequenting a place; a habitual visitor or resident.' OED cites an example of 1841 by O'Malley – 'a smile in which any habitué in the house would have read our fate.'

220 *Camerado* see *Starting from Paumanok* 123n.

CROSSING BROOKLYN FERRY

title] LG *1860*; Sun-Down Poem LG *1856*.

28 *Twelfth-month*] December LG *1856*.

126–32 *You have waited . . . the soul*] LG *1856* has:

We descend upon you and all things,
   we arrest you all,
We realize the soul only by you
   faithful solids and fluids
Through you color, form, location,
   sublimity, ideality,
Through you every proof, comparison,
   and all the suggestions and
   determinations of ourselves.

SONG OF THE ANSWERER

The complete poem with this title appeared in *LG 1881*. The first section of this poem was one of the twelve untitled poems of *LG 1855*; and in the editions which followed the title was often changed: *Poem of the Poet* (*LG 1856*); *Leaves of Grass, No. 3* (*LG 1860*); *Now List to my Morning Romanza* (*LG 1867*), a title taken from the added opening two lines. This title was retained until the second section was added in *LG 1881*. In *LG 1856* part two was entitled *Poem of the Singers and of the Words of Poems*; in *LG 1860 Leaves of Grass, No. 6*; and in *LG 1867 The Indications*.

1 *romanza* a short romance or song in verse or music; the OED cites several seventeenth-century English examples of the word meaning 'a romantic fancy'.

35 *Cudge* a common name for a black man, like Sambo, more often spelled Cudjo. In his essay on 'Slave Names in Colonial South Carolina' (*American Speech*, XXVII (1952), 102–7) Henig Cohen writes that as early as 1774 Edward Long noted that Jamaican Negroes 'called their children by the African day of the week on which they were born' and that *Cuffee* and *Cudjo* were 'perhaps the most widely used of the male "day" names, and Abba (Thursday) and Juba (Monday) of the female'. Cudjo is the word for Monday, Cuffee the word for Friday.

74 *phrenologist* one who studies the conformation of the human skull to determine mental faculties and traits of character.

OUR OLD FEUILLAGE

title] *LG 1881*; Chants Democratic, No. 4 *LG 1860*; American Feuillage *LG 1867*.

1   *feuillage   Webster 1841*: 'a bunch or row of leaves', used as a decorative motif. The OED suggests 'foliage' and cites a letter of Jarves to Pope in 1714: 'I . . . enclose the outline . . . that you may determine whether you would have it . . . reduced to make room for feuillage or laurel round the oval.' Here Whitman seems to use the word in the sense of 'scenery'.

In a letter to the editor of *Harper's Magazine* (7 January 1860) Whitman wrote that the theory behind this poem was to introduce a 'comprehensive collection of touches, locales, incidents, idiomatic scenes, from every section, South, West . . . the Mississippi Valley, etc., . . . as having a huge bouquet to collect, and quickly taking and binding in every characteristic subject that offers itself – making a compact, the-whole-surrounding, *National Poem*, after its sort, after my own style'. *Harper's* rejected the poem.

18   *sheldrake*   any duck of the old world genera *Tadorna* and *Casarca*.

27   *tylandria*   properly 'tillandsia'; *tillandsia usneoides* is also called long-beard, hanging moss, Florida moss or Spanish moss. It hangs from trees in long grey pendent tufts.

28   *Pedee*   a river in South Carolina.

48   *arriere   Webster 1841*: 'the last body of an army; now called *rear* . . .'; the OED notes that it is a 'modern French form of *arrear*, used in combinations, partly modern French, partly refashionings of Anglo-French or earlier English equivalents in *arrere, arrear*', e.g. *arriere* – supper, a late supper, and cites Whitman in 1881: 'An inferr'd arrière of such storms, such wrecks.' *In arriere* means 'in time past'.

    calumet   Webster 1841: 'a symbol or instrument of peace and war. The calumet of peace is used to seal or ratify contracts and alliances, to receive strangers kindly, and to travel with safety.'

49   *sachem   Webster 1841*: 'In America, a chief among some of the native Indian tribes.'

67   *sporades   Webster 1841* defines 'sporadic' as 'separate, scattered; whence certain isles of Greece were called "Sporades"'; here those stars not a part of any constellation.

70   *the Nueces, the Brazos, the Tombigbee*   the first two are rivers in Texas, the last is a river in eastern Mississippi and western Alabama.

A SONG OF JOYS

This poem, which first appeared in *LG 1860* as *Poem of Joys*, received its present title in *LG 1881*. The whole poem underwent extensive revision.

31   *once more*   after line 31 in *LG 1860* read:

O male and female!
O the presence of women! (I swear, nothing is more exquisite to me than the
    mere presence of women;)

O for the girl, my mate! O for happiness with my mate!

O the young man as I pass! O I am sick after the friendship of him who, I fear, is indifferent to me.

O the streets of cities!

The flitting faces – the expressions, eyes, feet, costumes! O I cannot tell how welcome they are to me;

O of men – of women toward me as I pass – The memory of only one look – the boy lingering and waiting.

44 *Fifth-month* Quaker designation of May.

130 *agonistic Webster 1841*: 'pertaining to prize-fighting, contests of strength, or athletic combats.' Webster defines *agonist* as 'one who contends for the prize in public games. Milton used *agonistes* in this sense, and so called his tragedy, from the similitude of Samson's exertions, in slaying the Philistines, to prize-fighting.'

SONG OF THE BROAD-AXE

title] *LG 1867*; Broad-Axe Poem *LG 1856*; Chants Democratic, No. 2 *LG 1860*.

34 *Ottawa* a river in Canada.

Willamette a river in Oregon.

79 *Mizra* 'Mizraim' is the Biblical name for Egypt.

80 *lictors* Roman officials who carried the fasces and made the path clear for the magistrates.

104 *chef d'oeuvres* French: masterpieces.

122 *unript Webster 1841*: 'ript – pp for ripped, torn open'; the waves are thus uninterrupted, unending.

156 *Albic* 'Albion' is an ancient name for England; Albic would seem to be Whitman's coinage.

194 *rounce* the handle of a hand press.

213 *hackmatack-roots for knees* the American larch tree or Tamarack is found in northern swamps; knees are pieces of timber naturally bent, and used to secure parts of a ship.

249 *The main shapes arise!* after this line in *LG 1856* read:

His shape arises!

Arrogant, masculine, naïve, rowdyish,

Laughter, weeper, worker, idler, citizen, countryman,

Saunterer of woods, stander upon hills, summer swimmer in rivers or by the sea,

Of pure American breed, of reckless health, his body perfect, free from taint from top to toe, free forever from headache and dyspepsia, clean-breathed,

Ample-limbed, a good feeder, weight a hundred and eighty pounds, full-blooded, six feet high, forty inches round the breast and back,

Countenance sun-burnt, bearded, calm, unrefined,

Reminder of animals, meeter of savage and gentleman on equal terms,

Attitudes lithe and erect, costume free, neck open, of slow movement on foot,

Passer of his right arm round the shoulders of his friends, companion of the
  street,
Persuader always of people to give him their sweetest touches, and never their
  meanest,
A Manhattanese bred, fond of Brooklyn, fond of Broadway, fond of the life of
  the wharves and the great ferries,
Enterer everywhere, welcomed everywhere, easily understood after all,
Never offering others, always offering himself, corroborating his phrenology,
Voluptuous, inhabitive, combative, conscientious, alimentive, intuitive,
  of copious friendship, sublimity, firmness, self-esteem, comparison,
  individuality, form, locality, eventuality,
Avowing by life, manners, work, to contribute illustrations of results of
  The States,
Teacher of the unquenchable creed, namely, egotism,
Inviter of others continually henceforth to try their strength against his.

SONG OF THE EXPOSITION

This poem was originally recited by Whitman for the Fortieth Annual Exhibi-
tion of the American Institute, New York, 7 September 1871, and prefaced
by the following note:

Struggling steadily to the front, not only in the spirit of Opinion, Govern-
ment, and the like, but, in due time, in the Artistic also, we see actual operative
LABOR and LABORERS, with Machinery, Inventions, Farms, Products, etc.,
pressing to place our time, over the whole civilized world. Holding these by
the hand, we see, or hope we see, THE MUSE (radiating, representing, under
its various expressions, as in every age and land, the healthiest, most heroic
Humanity, common to all, fusing all) entering the demesnes of the New World,
as twin and sister of our Democracy – at any rate we will so invite Her, here
and now – to permanently infuse in daily toils, and be infused by them.

Perhaps no clearer or more illustrative sign exists of the current adjustment
and tendency than those superb International Expositions of the World's
Products, Inventions and Industries, that, commencing in London under
Prince Albert, have since signalized all the principal Nations of our age, and
have been rife in the United States – culminating in this great Exposition at
Philadelphia, around which the American Centennial, and its thoughts and
associations, cluster – with vaster ones still in the future.

Ostensibly to inaugurate an Exposition of this kind – still more to outline
the establishment of a great *permanent* Cluster-Palace of Industry from an
imaginative and Democratic point of view – was the design of the following
poem; from such impulses it was first orally deliver'd.
title] LG *1876*; After All, Not to Create Only LG *1871 Second Issue.*

18 *Parnassus*   a mountain peak in Greece sacred to the Muses.
19 *Jaffa's gate*   a seaport in Israel.
  Mount Moriah   the Hill of Jerusalem; Solomon's temple was built on it.

38 *Castaly's fountain* a spring on Mount Parnassus sacred to Apollo and the Muses and hence a source of poetic inspiration.

41 *Calliope . . . Clio, Melpomene, Thalia* the muses of epic poetry, history, tragedy and comedy.

42 *Una* in Spenser's *Faerie Queene* I, Una symbolizes true religion.

Oriana Queen Elizabeth the first.

45 *Amadis* the hero of a fifteenth-century Spanish or Portuguese romance by Garcia de Montalvo. He became the flower of chivalry and achieved great feats of arms.

Tancred Norman leader of the First Crusade, died in 1112.

Charlemagne King of the Franks, 800–814.

Roland a hero of the Charlemagne cycle; legend made him a great defender of the Christians against the Saracens.

Oliver a friend of Roland's and one of Charlemagne's twelve peers.

46 *Palmerin* the hero of the sixteenth-century Portuguese romance *Palmerin of England*; *Palmerin* and *Amadis of Gaul* were exempted from the holocaust of romance by the curate and the barber in *Don Quixote*.

Usk a river in Wales and England mentioned in the Arthurian romances.

47 *Arthur* legendary King of Britain.

Merlin in Malory's *Morte d'Arthur* Merlin makes the Round Table for Arthur's father; in Tennyson's *Merlin and Vivien* (from the *Idylls*) Vivien seduces Merlin during a storm (her half-simulated fear sends her into his arms) and he tells her the spell by which she is enabled to imprison him in an oak tree.

Lancelot the knight closest to Arthur and most respected.

Galahad in Malory's *Morte d' Arthur* the son of Lancelot and Elaine; predestined by his purity to seek the Holy Grail.

53 *Tennyson* Whitman has in mind the *Idylls of the King*, a series of connected poems published by Tennyson beginning in 1842 and concluding in 1885.

61 *Columbia* Mathew's *Dictionary of Americanisms* (Chicago, 1951) notes that America was first referrred to as 'Columbia' in 1775; in 1846 the New York *Tribune* proposed 'that our country should take to herself the name of Columbia, in honor of the great discoverer of this continent'.

83 *palace* Whitman has in mind the great exhibition 'palaces' of the mid-nineteenth century, especially the American Crystal Palace for the 1853 World's Fair in New York.

84 *history's seven* the Seven Wonders of the Ancient World.

104 *Hoe press* named for the inventor of the rotary press, Richard Hoe; the press was displayed at the New York Exhibition.

112 *Alexandrian Pharos, gardens of Babylon* the lighthouse near Alexandria and the hanging gardens of Babylon were two of the Seven Wonders of the Ancient World.

113 *Olympia* another of the Wonders, a Greek temple containing an enormous statue of Zeus by Phidias.

137 *sane sisters* the nine muses. *Webster 1841* defines sane as 'sound healthy'; OED suggests 'free from delusive prejudices or fancies' and quotes Tennyson's *Enid* (1859), 'One of our noblest, our most valorous,/Sanest and most obedient'.

157 *longeve*   OED: 'long-lived'.

165 *rondure*   *Webster 1841*: 'a round, a circle'; OED cites Symonds, 1874, 'Cherubs clustered in the rondure of rose-windows'.

SONG OF THE REDWOOD-TREE

First printed *Harper's Magazine*, February 1874.
title] *LG 1881*; Centennial Songs, No. 2 *LG 1876*. Redwoods are the great Sequoia trees found in the California Coast Range.

3 *dryads*   *Webster 1841*: 'a deity or nymph of the woods'.
  hamadryads   *Webster 1841*: 'a wood-nymph, feigned to live and die with the tree to which it was attached'.

11 *Mendocino country*   a county on the California coast, north of San Francisco.

41 *Shasta*   a mountain peak in California.
  Nevadas   the Sierra Nevada mountain range is in Eastern California.

79 *Cascade range*   mountains in Oregon, Washington and British Columbia.
  Wahsatch   the Wasatch range is in northern Utah and south-east Idaho; Whitman's spelling is his own.

A SONG FOR OCCUPATIONS

This poem was revised extensively. Appeared untitled in *LG 1855*.
title] *LG 1881*; Poem of the Daily Work of the Workmen and Workwomen of these States *LG 1856*; Chants Democratic, No. 3 *LG 1860*; To Workingmen *LG 1867*; Carol of Occupations *LG 1871, LG 1876*.

56 *bon-mot*   *Webster 1841*: 'a jest, a witty repartee. The word is not anglicized, and may be pronounced *bong-mo*'.
  reconnoissance   *Webster 1841*: 'a reconnoitering; discovery'.
67 *savans*   see *Eidólons* 22. *Webster 1841* gives 'savans' as the plural of *savant*: 'a man of learning; in the plural, literary men'.
88 *exurge*   more frequently 'exsurge', to rise up, to start out.
105 *flaggers*   *Webster 1841*: 'flagged – laid with flat stones'; OED: 'one who flags or lays down flagstones', citing Whitman in 1868.
109 *loup-lump*   mass of iron in pasty form; the end of smelting.
111 *jib*   shield.

A SONG OF THE ROLLING EARTH

title] *LG 1881*; Poem of the Sayers of the Words of the Earth *LG 1856*; To the Sayers of Words *LG 1860, LG 1867*; Carol of Words *LG 1871, LG 1876*.

28 *Accouche! accouchez!* French: 'Accouchée! accouchez!', meaning 'You pregnant one! be delivered'.

44 *interminable sisters* the stars and planets; OED cites examples by Skelton and Shelley using 'interminable' in the sense of endless, boundless: 'O radiant Luminary of lyght interminable Celestial Father'; 'Will yon vast suns run on Interminably?'

45 *cotillons* Webster *1841*: 'cotillon – a brisk dance, performed by eight persons together'. OED notes that the more common spelling is 'cotillions' but gives *cotillon* as a second spelling.

YOUTH, DAY, OLD AGE AND NIGHT

Appeared in *LG 1881*; it consists of four lines (19–22) of the excluded *LG 1855* poem (untitled) which begins 'Great are the myths . . .'.

Birds of Passage

A group title for seven poems in *LG 1881*.

SONG OF THE UNIVERSAL

Appeared in *LG 1876* as one of the *Centennial Songs*; it was written for commencement at Tufts College, 17 June 1874, and was published in several newspapers on that date.

PIONEERS! O PIONEERS!

First published in *1865*; appeared in *LG 1867*; and in *LG 1871* and *LG 1876* as one of a group of poems entitled *Marches Now the War is Over*.

18 *debouch* cf. *Starting from Paumanok* 27.

TO YOU

title] *LG 1871*; Poem of You, Whoever You Are *LG 1856*; To You, Whoever You Are *LG 1860*; Leaves of Grass, No. 4 *LG 1867*.

44 *hopples* fetters.

45 *promulges* Webster *1841*: 'promulge – to teach, or publish', here meaning 'declares itself'.

FRANCE, THE 18TH YEAR OF THESE STATES

Appeared in *LG 1860*; and in *LG 1871* and *LG 1876* as one of the *Songs of Insurrection*. The French Revolutionary Tribunal took place in 1794.

6 *tumbrils* a farmer's dung cart; one of the kind used to carry condemned persons to the guillotine.

7 *battues* wholesale slaughters; OED cites an example from 1864: 'the great *battue* of St Bartholomew's Day'.

22 *chansonniers* French: song writers.

28 *ma femme* French : my woman; here 'Democracy'.

MYSELF AND MINE

title] *LG 1871 Second Issue*; Leaves of Grass, No. 10 *LG 1860*; Leaves of Grass, No. 2 *LG 1867*.

11 *promulge* *Webster 1841*: 'to publish or teach'.
25 *... indirections?* after this line in *LG 1860* read:

Let others deny the evil their enemies charge against them – but how can I the like?

Nothing ever has been, or ever can be, charged against me, half as bad as the evil I really am.

YEAR OF METEORS (1859–60)

Appeared in *1865* and *LG 1867*.

3 *19th Presidentiad* the 1860 Lincoln–Douglas contest.
4 *old man* John Brown (1800–1859) the Abolitionist, who was hanged on 2 December 1859.
11 *fair stripling* Edward, Prince of Wales, who visited New York in October 1860.
15 *Great Eastern* the British steamship which arrived in New York on 28 June 1860.

WITH ANTECEDENTS

First printed New York *Saturday Press*, 14 January 1860, entitled *You and Me and To-Day*.
title] *LG 1867*; Chants Democratic, No. 7 *LG 1860*.

5 *the Alb* an Englishman, a man of Albion, Whitman's coinage.
7 *the skald* an ancient Scandinavian poet; also sometimes used generally to mean a poet.

A BROADWAY PAGEANT

First printed New York *Times*, 27 June 1860, entitled *The Errand-Bearers*.
title] *LG 1867*; *in 1865 with a subtitle* (Reception Japanese Embassy, June 16, 1860).
1 *Niphon* now more commonly spelled 'Nippon', but most nineteenth-century gazetteers give *Niphon* as the preferred spelling for the empire of Japan.
5 *Libertad!* Spanish: 'Liberty!'
25 *Antipodes* the opposite point on the globe.
32 *cantabile* OED: 'a piece or passage of music in cantabile [flowing] style'. The OED cites an example of 1856: 'It expresses them admirably in its cantabile'.

44 *bonze, brahmin, and llama* a Japanese Buddhist monk; a Hindu priest; a Tibetan priest.
69 *eldest son* Edward VII, then Prince of Wales; see *Years of Meteors* (*1859–60*).

Sea-Drift

A group title for eleven poems in *LG 1881*; included are seven poems from *Sea-Shore Memories*, *LG 1871 Second Issue*, two new poems, and two poems transferred from *LG 1876*.

OUT OF THE CRADLE ENDLESSLY ROCKING

First printed New York *Saturday Press*, 24 December 1859, entitled *A Child's Reminiscence*.
title] *LG 1871*; A Word Out of the Sea *LG 1860*.

1–31 *Out . . . translating*] *in LG 1860 the first thirty-two lines read as follows:*
Out of the rocked cradle,
Out of the mocking-bird's throat, the musical shuttle,
Out of the boy's mother's womb, and from the nipples of her breasts,
Out of the Ninth Month midnight,
Over the sterile sands, and the fields beyond, where the child, leaving his bed, wandered alone, bare-headed, barefoot,
Down from the showered halo,
Up from the mystic play of shadows, twining and twisting as if they were alive,
Out from the patches of briers and blackberries,
From the memories of the bird that chanted to me,
From your memories, sad brother – from the fitful risings and fallings I heard,
From under that yellow half-moon, late-risen, and swollen as if with tears,
From those beginning notes of sickness and love, there in the transparent mist,
From the thousand responses of my heart, never to cease,
From the myriad thence-aroused words,
From the word stronger and more delicious than any,
From such, as now they start, the scene revisiting,
As a flock, twittering, rising, or overhead passing,
Borne hither – ere all eludes me, hurriedly,
A man – yet by these tears a little boy again,
Throwing myself on the sand, confronting the waves,
I, chanter of pains and joys, uniter of here and hereafter,
Taking all hints to use them – but swiftly leaping beyond them,
A reminiscence sing.

REMINISCENCE:

Once, Paumanok,
When the snows had melted, and the Fifth Month grass was growing,
Up this sea-shore, in some briers,
Two guests from Alabama – two together,
And their nest, and four light-green eggs, spotted with brown,
And every day the he-bird, to and fro, near at hand,
And every day the she-bird, crouched on her nest, silent, with bright eyes,
And every day I, a curious boy, never too close, never disturbing them,
Cautiously peering, absorbing, translating.

3 *Ninth-month* Quaker designation for September.
23 *Paumanok* Indian name (meaning 'fish-shaped') for Long Island, New York.
144] Bird! (then said the boy's Soul,) *LG 1860.*

AS I EBB'D WITH THE OCEAN OF LIFE

First printed *Atlantic Monthly*, April 1860, entitled *Bardic Symbols*. Appeared as part of the group called *Sea-Shore Memories* in *LG 1871 Second Issue* and *LG 1876*.
title] *LG 1881*; Leaves of Grass, No. 1 *LG 1860*; Elemental drifts *LG 1867* (*derived from opening lines, later dropped*: Elemental drifts!/O I wish I could impress others as you and the waves have just been impressing me).

35-7 *You oceans . . . and all*] *in LG 1860 read*:

You oceans both! you tangible land!
  Nature!
Be not too rough with me – I submit –
  I close with you,
These little shreds shall, indeed, stand for all.
59-60 (*See . . . rolling,*) James Russell Lowell, as editor of the *Atlantic Monthly*, refused to print these two lines.

TEARS

Appeared in *LG 1871 Second Issue* and *LG 1876* among *Sea-Shore Memories* with the present title.
title] *LG 1871 Second Issue, LG 1876*; Leaves of Grass, No. 2 *LG 1867*.

TO THE MAN-OF-WAR BIRD

First printed London *Athenaeum*, 1 April 1876, and pasted into some volumes of *LG 1876*. The poem is a near paraphrase of Jules Michelet's *The Bird* and Whitman acknowledged his indebtedness in the Philadelphia *Progress*, 16 November 1878.

ABOARD AT A SHIP'S HELM

title] *LG 1871 Second Issue in Sea-Shore Memories*); Leaves of Grass, No. 3
LG 1867.

ON THE BEACH AT NIGHT

Appeared in *LG 1871 Second Issue*, in the group *Sea-Shore Memories*.

10 *Pleiades* a group of stars in the constellation Taurus.

THE WORLD BELOW THE BRINE

title] *LG 1871 Second Issue (in Sea-Shore Memories)*; Leaves of Grass, No. 16
LG 1860; Leaves of Grass, No. 4 *LG 1867*.

5 *aliment* sustenance.

ON THE BEACH AT NIGHT ALONE

This poem was revived extensively for *LG 1867*.
title] *LG 1871 Second Issue*; Clef Poem *LG 1856*; Leaves of Grass, No. 12
LG 1860; Leaves of Grass, No. 1 *LG 1867*. The title in *LG 1856* means 'clue'
or 'key'. In this edition the poem read:

This night I am happy
As I watch the stars shining, I think a thought of the clef of the universe and
the future.

What can the future hold for me more than I have?
Do you suppose I wish to enjoy life in other spheres?

I say distinctly I comprehend no better sphere than this earth,
I comprehend no better life than the life of my body.

I do not know what follows the death of my body,
But I know well that whatever it is, it is best for me,
And I know well that what is really Me shall live just as much as before.

I am not uneasy but I shall have good housing to myself,
But this is my first – how can I like the rest any better?
Here I grew up – the studs and rafters are grown parts of me.

I am not uneasy but I am to be beloved by young and old men and to love
them the same,
I suppose the pink nipples of the breasts of women with whom I shall sleep
will taste the same to my lips,
But this is a nipple of a breast of my mother, always near and always divine to
me, her true child and son, (whatever comes.)

I suppose I am to be eligible to visit the stars, in my time,
I suppose I shall have myriads of new experiences – and that the experience
of this earth will prove only one out of myriads;
But I believe my body and my soul already indicate those experiences,

And I believe I shall find nothing in the stars more majestic and beautiful than
   I have already found on the earth,
And I believe that I have this night a clue through the universes,
I believe I have this night thought a thought of the clef of eternity.

A vast similitude interlocks all,
All spheres, grown, ungrown, small, large, suns, moons, planets, comets,
   asteroids.
All the substances of the same and all that is spiritual upon the same,
All distances of place however wide,
All distances of time, all inanimate forms,
All souls, all living bodies though they be in different worlds,
All gaseous, watery, vegetable, mineral processes, the fishes, the brutes,
All men and women – me also,
All nations, colors, barbarisms, civilizations, languages,
All identities that have existed on this globe, or any globe,
All lives and deaths all of the past, present, future,
This vast similitude spans them, and always has spanned,
   and shall forever span them.

SONG FOR ALL SEAS, ALL SHIPS

First printed New York *Daily Graphic*, 4 April 1873, entitled *Sea Captains
Young or Old*. The poem was written after the loss of two steamships in 1873,
the *Northfleet* and the *Atlantic*; more than eight hundred people were drowned.
title] *LG 1876*.

PATROLING BARNEGAT

First printed *American*, June 1880; then appeared in *LG 1881*. Barnegat Bay
is off the coast of Ocean county, New Jersey.

AFTER THE SEA-SHIP

First printed New York *Daily Graphic*, December 1874, entitled *In the Wake
Following*.
title] *LG 1876*.

By the Roadside

A group title for twenty-nine poems in *LG 1881*, three of which were newly
written. The first two are from *LG 1855*, sixteen from *LG 1860*, five from
1865, one from *LG 1867* and two from *LG 1871 Second Issue*.

A BOSTON BALLAD (1854)

Appeared in *LG 1855*. *Blodgett and Bradley* note that it was probably com-
posed in June 1854 on the arrest of the fugitive slave Anthony Burns in Boston

shortly before the passage of the Kansas-Nebraska bill affirming 'local option' on slavery.

title] *LG 1871*; Poem of Apparitions in Boston, the 78th Year of These States *LG 1856*; A Boston Ballad *LG 1860*; To Get Betimes in Boston Town *LG 1867*.

3 *Jonathan*   a New England rustic.

EUROPE, THE 72D AND 73D YEARS OF THESE STATES

First printed New York *Daily Tribune*, 21 June 1850, entitled *Resurgemus*. The poem was occasioned by the year of European revolutions, 1848. Appeared untitled in *LG 1855*.

title] *LG 1860*; Poem of the Dead Young Men of Europe, the 72d and 73d Years of These States *LG 1856*.

A HAND-MIRROR

Appeared in *LG 1860*.

GODS

Appeared in *LG 1871 Second Issue* with two opening lines later dropped: 'Thought of the Infinite – the All/Be thou my god'.

GERMS

title] *LG 1871*; Leaves of Grass, No. 19 *LG 1860*; Leaves of Grass, No. 2 *LG 1867*.

THOUGHTS

Appeared in *LG 1860* and *LG 1867* as the second of a group of poems called *Thoughts*; the present first line is from the fourth poem of that group and added to this poem in *LG 1871*. In *LG 1860* the poem began:

Of waters, forest, hills;
Of the earth at large, whispering through medium of me . . .

WHEN I HEARD THE LEARN'D ASTRONOMER

First published in *1865*; then appeared in *LG 1867*.

PERFECTIONS

Appeared in *LG 1860*.

O ME! O LIFE!

First published in *1865 Sequel*; then appeared in *LG 1867*.

TO A PRESIDENT

Appeared in *LG 1860* in the *Messenger Leaves* group. The American President referred to is James Buchanan, fifteenth President of the United States (1857–61). Whitman was openly disdainful of Buchanan and his tolerance of slavery. In an article written to support Freemont in 1856 (reprinted in *Walt Whitman's Workshop* (1964), 100–101) Whitman wrote:

Stript of padding and paint, who are Buchanan and Fillmore? What has this age to do with them? Two galvanized old men, close on the summons to depart this life, their early contemporaries long since gone, only they two left, relics and proofs of the little political bargains, chances, combinations, resentments of a past age, having nothing in common with this age, standing for the first crop of political graves and grave-stones planted in These States, but in no sort standing for the lusty young growth of the modern times of The States.

I SIT AND LOOK OUT

title] *LG 1871*; Leaves of Grass, No. 17 *LG 1860*; Leaves of Grass, No. 5 *LG 1867*.

TO RICH GIVERS

Appeared in *LG 1860*.

THE DALLIANCE OF THE EAGLES

First printed *Cope's Tobacco Plant*, November 1880; then appeared in *LG 1881*.

ROAMING IN THOUGHT

Appeared in *LG 1881*.

A FARM PICTURE

Appeared in *1865*; then *LG 1867*.

A CHILD'S AMAZE

Appeared in *1865*; then *LG 1867*.

THE RUNNER

Appeared in *LG 1867*.

BEAUTIFUL WOMEN

Appeared in *LG 1860* as a stanza from the poem *Debris*; then as a separate poem in *LG 1867*.
title] *LG 1871*; Picture *LG 1867*.

MOTHER AND BABE

Appeared in *1865*; then *LG 1867*.

THOUGHT

title] *LG 1871*; Thoughts, No. 7 *LG 1860*.

VISOR'D

Appeared in *LG 1860* as a stanza from the poem *Debris*; then as a separate poem, with the present title, in *LG 1867*.

THOUGHT

Appeared in *LG 1860* as the third and fourth lines of *Thoughts, No. 4*; then as a separate poem in *LG 1871 Second Issue*.

GLIDING O'ER ALL

Appeared as the epigraph on the title page of *Passage to India* in *LG 1871 Second Issue*.

HAST NEVER COME TO THEE AN HOUR

Appeared in *LG 1881*.

THOUGHT

Appeared in *LG 1860* as the second line of *Thoughts, No. 4*; then as a separate poem, with the present title, in *LG 1871 Second Issue*.

TO OLD AGE

Appeared in *LG 1860*.

LOCATIONS AND TIMES

This poem is a revision of four lines (133-6) of the *LG 1856 Sun-Down Poem*, later entitled *Crossing Brooklyn Ferry*.
title] *LG 1871 Second Issue*; Leaves of Grass, No. 23 *LG 1860*.

OFFERINGS

Appeared in *LG 1860* as the seventh stanza of *Debris*; then as a separate poem in *LG 1867*.
title] *LG 1871 Second Issue*; Picture *LG 1867*.

TO THE STATES

Appeared in *LG 1860*. Whitman in his 'Blue-Copy' (New York Public Library) notes that this poem was composed in the years from 1857-9; the Presidents referred to are Millard Fillmore, the thirteenth President of the United States (1850-53); Franklin Pierce, the fourteenth President (1853-7); and James Buchanan, the fifteenth President (1857-61). See Whitman's *To a President* (p. 299).
7 *lambent* flickering.

Drum-Taps

A group title for forty-three poems. *Drum-Taps* was published separately in 1865 and originally consisted of fifty-three poems; *Sequel to Drum-Taps*, including *When Lilacs Last in the Dooryard Bloom'd*, appeared in the autumn of the same year; it contained eighteen poems and was bound into the second issue of *Drum-Taps*. Both were incorporated into *LG 1867* as annexes and in *LG 1871* appeared in the main body of the text. The grouping which follows dates from *LG 1881*, twenty-nine of the original *Drum-Taps* poems being retained and nine of the *Sequel*.

FIRST O SONGS FOR A PRELUDE

Appeared in *1865*.
title] *LG 1881*; Drum-Taps *1865*, *LG 1867*.

EIGHTEEN SIXTY-ONE

Appeared in *1865*; then *LG 1867*.

BEAT! BEAT! DRUMS!

First printed *Harper's Weekly*, and New York *Leader*, 28 September 1861; then *1865* and *LG 1867*.

FROM PAUMANOK STARTING I FLY LIKE A BIRD

Appeared in *1865*; then *LG 1867*.

SONG OF THE BANNER AT DAYBREAK

Appeared in *1865* and *LG 1867*; in *LG 1871* and *LG 1876* it formed a part of a group called *Bathed in War's Perfume*.

RISE O DAYS FROM YOUR FATHOMLESS DEEPS

Appeared in *1865*; then *LG 1867*.

VIRGINIA – THE WEST

First published in *As a Strong Bird On Pinions Free*, 1872; then *LG 1876*.

CITY OF SHIPS

Appeared in *1865*; then *LG 1867*.

THE CENTENARIAN'S STORY

Appeared in *1865*; then *LG 1867*; composed before 1860. The story is based on the Battle of Long Island which occurred on 27 August 1776 and allowed for Washington's safe retreat across the East River.

39 *Declaration* the American Declaration of Independence was signed on 2 August 1776.
41 *General* George Washington.
56 *Gowanus' waters* Gowanus bay lies south-west of the battleground.

CAVALRY CROSSING A FORD

Appeared in *1865*; then *LG 1867*.

7 *guidon* *Webster 1841*: 'the flag or standard of a troop of cavalry'.

BIVOUAC ON A MOUNTAIN SIDE

Appeared in *1865*; then *LG 1867*.

AN ARMY CORPS ON THE MARCH

Appeared in *1865 Sequel*; then *LG 1867*.
title] *LG 1871*; An Army on the March *LG 1867*.

BY THE BIVOUAC'S FITFUL FLAME

Appeared in *1865*; then *LG 1867*.

COME UP FROM THE FIELDS FATHER

Appeared in *1865*; then *LG 1867*.

VIGIL STRANGE I KEPT ON THE FIELD ONE NIGHT

Appeared in *1865*; then *LG 1867*.

A MARCH IN THE RANKS HARD-PREST, AND THE ROAD UNKNOWN

Appeared in *1865*; then *LG 1867*.

A SIGHT IN CAMP IN THE DAYBREAK GRAY AND DIM

Appeared in *1865*; then *LG 1867*.

AS TOILSOME I WANDER'D VIRGINIA'S WOODS

Appeared in *1865*; then *LG 1867*.

NOT THE PILOT

Appeared in *LG 1860* as a part of the group *Debris*; then as a separate poem, with the present title, in *LG 1867*.

YEAR THAT TREMBLED AND REEL'D BENEATH ME

Appeared in *1865*; then *LG 1867*.

THE WOUND-DRESSER

First appeared in *1865*.
title] *LG 1881*; The Dresser *LG 1867*.

LONG, TOO LONG AMERICA

First appeared in *1865*.
title] *LG 1881*; Long, Too Long, O Land *LG 1867*.

GIVE ME THE SPLENDID SILENT SUN

Appeared in *1865*; then *LG 1867*.

24 *trottoirs* OED: 'a paved footway on each side of the street'; Mrs Trollope, in *Domestic Manners of Americans* (1832), comments that 'the trottoir paving, in most of the streets, is extremely good, being of large flag stones, very superior to the bricks of Philadelphia'.

DIRGE FOR TWO VETERANS

Appeared in *1865 Sequel*; then *LG 1867*.

OVER THE CARNAGE ROSE PROPHETIC A VOICE

Appeared in *LG 1860*, entitled *Calamus, No. 5*, with the exception of the first and last lines; included in its present form in *1865* and *LG 1867*.

I SAW OLD GENERAL AT BAY

Appeared in *1865*; then *LG 1867*.

THE ARTILLERYMAN'S VISION

First appeared in *1865*.
title] *LG 1871*; The Veteran's Vision *LG 1867*.

ETHIOPIA SALUTING THE COLORS

Appeared in *LG 1871* as a part of the group *Bathed in War's Perfume*.

NOT YOUTH PERTAINS TO ME

Appeared in *1865*; then *LG 1867*.

RACE OF VETERANS

Appeared in *1865 Sequel*; then *LG 1867*.

WORLD TAKE GOOD NOTICE

Appeared in *1865*; then *LG 1867*. In the *Century Magazine*, LIX (February 1911), 532, an earlier manuscript version now at Yale University reads as follows:

Rise, lurid stars

Rise, lurid stars, woolly white no more;
Change, angry cloth – weft of the silver stars no more;
Orbs blushing scarlet – thirty-four stars, red as flame,
On the blue bunting this day we sew.

World take good notice, silver stars have vanished;
Orbs now of scarlet – mortal coals, all aglow,
Dots of molten iron, wakeful and ominous,
On the blue bunting henceforth appear.

2   *ript   Webster 1841*: 'pp. for *ripped*, torn or cut off or out'.
    weft   Webster 1841: 'the woof; the threads that cross the warp'.
3   *thirty-eight*   Colorado, the thirty-eighth state, was admitted to the Union on 1 August 1876.

O TAN-FACED PRAIRIE-BOY

Appeared in *1865*; then *LG 1867*.

LOOK DOWN FAIR MOON

Appeared in *1865*; then *LG 1867*.

RECONCILIATION

Appeared in *1865 Sequel*; then *LG 1867*.

HOW SOLEMN AS ONE BY ONE

Appeared in *1865 Sequel*; then *LG 1867*.

AS I LAY WITH MY HEAD IN YOUR LAP CAMERADO

Appeared in *1865 Sequel*; then *LG 1867*. For a note on the word 'Camerado' see *Starting from Paumanok* 123n.

DELICATE CLUSTER

Appeared in *LG 1871* in the group *Bathed in War's Perfume*.
5 *cerulean* deep blue.

TO A CERTAIN CIVILIAN

First appeared in *1865*, then *LG 1867*.
title] *LG 1871 Second Issue*; Did You Ask Dulcet Rhymes from Me? *LG 1867*.

LO, VICTRESS ON THE PEAKS

Appeared in *1865 Sequel*; then *LG 1867*.

SPIRIT WHOSE WORK IS DONE

Appeared in *1865 Sequel*; then *LG 1867*.

ADIEU TO A SOLDIER

Appeared in *LG 1871* in the group *Marches Now the War is Over*.

TURN'O LIBERTAD

Appeared in *1865*; then *LG 1867*.

TO THE LEAVEN'D SOIL THEY TROD

Appeared in *1865 Sequel*; then *LG 1867*.

Memories of President Lincoln

A group title for four poems in *LG 1881*; in *LG 1871 Second Issue* this group
was entitled *President Lincoln's Burial Hymn*.

WHEN LILACS LAST IN THE DOORYARD BLOOM'D

Appeared in *1865 Sequel*; then *LG 1867*. The poem was composed in the weeks
following Lincoln's assassination on 14 April 1865. The funeral train left
Washington, DC, for Springfield, Illinois on 21 April, six days after Lincoln
died. Whitman's lecture on the 'Death of Abraham Lincoln' may be found in
Specimen Days and Collect (1882).

2 *great star* Venus.
135 *Come lovely* first italicized in *LG 1871 Second Issue*. *Death Carol*, a sub-
title for this italicized section, was dropped in *LG 1881*.

O CAPTAIN! MY CAPTAIN!

First printed New York *Saturday Press*, 4 November 1865; then *1865 Sequel*
and *LG 1867*.

HUSH'D BE THE CAMPS TO-DAY

Appeared in *1865*; then *LG 1867*. Lincoln was buried in Springfield, Illinois on 4 May 1865.

THIS DUST WAS ONCE THE MAN

Appeared in *LG 1871 Second Issue*.

BY BLUE ONTARIO'S SHORE

First appeared in *LG 1856*, when, as *Blodgett and Bradley* note, about one-fourth of its then 280 lines came from the *Preface* of *LG 1855*. In *LG 1867* it was part of the group called *Songs Before Parting*, and in *LG 1876* of the group *Marches Now the War is Over*.

title] *LG 1881*; Poem of the Many in One *LG 1856*; Chants Democratic, No. 1 *LG 1860*; As I Sat Alone by Blue Ontario's Shore *LG 1867*.

75 *embouchure* *Webster 1841*: '1. a mouth, or aperture, as of a river, cannon, etc. 2. the mouth-hole of a wind instrument of music'. The noun is used here as an adjective and parallels the construction in the line above: wars finding a voice in him, bays finding a mouth in him.

88 *Year One* the first year of American independence.

90 *blatherers* *Webster 1841*: *blatherer*: a 'noisy, blustering boaster'; OED notes that the American spelling – *blather* – is more common than the English *blether* and cities the *Richmond Inquirer* in 1865: 'All the eloquence and all the blather in the world will not alter the facts'.

99 *amativeness* OED: 'a word derived from phrenology meaning propensity to love, or sexual passions', citing Swinburne in 1869: 'The satyrs retain their natural amativeness'.

REVERSALS

Appeared in *LG 1856* as part of the *Poem of the Propositions of Nakedness*; this fifty-seven line poem was entitled *Chants Democratic, No. 5* in *LG 1860* and *Respondez* in *LG 1867*; it was dropped in *LG 1881* with the exception of these six lines with the present title and three lines which were saved to make the poem *Transpositions*.

Autumn Rivulets

A group title for thirty-eight poems in *LG 1881*, four of which are new.

AS CONSEQUENT, ETC.

Appeared in *LG 1881*; some of its lines, however, are from rejected poems of *LG 1876*.

22 *vasting* OED: 'v.trans. to lay waste, destroy.' M. M. Mathews in his *Dictionary of Americanisms* (Chicago, 1951) points out that the word *vastation*,

meaning 'purification by destruction of evil impulses', has special American overtones in the writings of Emerson and Howells, and later, William James.

THE RETURN OF THE HEROES

First printed *Galaxy*, September 1867, entitled *A Carol of Harvest for 1867*; then appeared in *LG 1871 Second Issue* and, with its present title, in *LG 1881*.

8 *parturient* *Webster 1841*: 'bringing forth or about to bring forth young'.

THERE WAS A CHILD WENT FORTH

Appeared untitled in *LG 1855*.
title] Poem of the Child That Went Forth, and Always Goes Forth, Forever and Forever *LG 1856*; Leaves of Grass, No. 9 *LG 1860*; Leaves of Grass, No. 1 *LG 1867*.

OLD IRELAND

First printed New York *Leader*, 2 November 1861; then appeared *1865* and *LG 1867*.

THE CITY DEAD-HOUSE

Appeared in *LG 1867*.

THIS COMPOST

title] *LG 1867*; Poem of Wonder at the Resurrection of the Wheat *LG 1856*; Leaves of Grass, No. 4 *LG 1860*.

TO A FOIL'D EUROPEAN REVOLUTIONAIRE

title] *LG 1871*; Liberty Poem for Asia, Europe, America, Australia, Cuba, and the Archipelagoes of the Sea *LG 1856*; To a Foiled Revolter or Revoltress *LG 1860*.

5 *tushes* teeth.
16 *garroté* Spanish method of capital punishment by strangulation; the apparatus for inflicting this punishment, a wooden stick which when turned tightens the rope. The accent is erroneous and first appeared in *1888 Complete*. It did not appear in the softbound issue of *LG 1891–2*, according to *Blodgett and Bradley*.

UNNAMED LANDS

Appeared in *LG 1860*.

SONG OF PRUDENCE

This poem is taken from the Preface to *LG 1855*.
title] *LG 1881*; Poem of the Last Explanation of Prudence *LG 1856*; Leaves of Grass, No. 5 *LG 1860*; Manhattan's Streets I Saunter'd, Pondering *LG 1867*.

THE SINGER IN THE PRISON

First printed Washington *Saturday Evening Visitor*, 25 December 1869; then appeared in *LG 1871 Second Issue*. The poem celebrates the visit of the singer Parepa-Rosa to Sing Sing Prison.

WARBLE FOR LILAC-TIME

First printed *Galaxy*, May 1870; then appeared *LG 1871 Second Issue*.

4 *hylas*   tree-toads; the piping frog.

OUTLINES FOR A TOMB

First printed *Galaxy*, January 1870, entitled *Brother of All, with Generous Hand*; then appeared in *LG 1871 Second Issue* and with its present title, *LG 1881*. George Peabody (1795–1869) founded the Peabody Anthropological Museums at Yale and Harvard Universities.

47 *Patapsco*   a Maryland river near Baltimore.

OUT FROM BEHIND THIS MASK

First printed New York *Tribune*, 19 February 1876; then appeared in *LG 1876* with the note 'To confront My Portrait, illustrating "the Wound-Dresser", in *Leaves of Grass*'. The wood-engraving of W. J. Linton was derived from a photograph by G. C. Potter taken in 1871.

13 *burin'd*   engraved.

VOCALISM

Appeared in *LG 1881*. The poem combines, however, two previously published poems: section one from *Chants Democratic, No. 12* in *LG 1860*; section two from *Leaves of Grass, No. 21* in *LG 1860*. In *LG 1871 Chants Democratic, No. 12* was known as *The Oratists*, and the poem *Leaves of Grass, No. 21* was entitled *Voices*.

TO HIM THAT WAS CRUCIFIED

Appeared in *LG 1860*.

YOU FELONS ON TRIAL IN COURTS

title] *LG 1867*; Leaves of Grass, No. 13 *LG 1860*.

LAWS FOR CREATIONS

title] *LG 1871*; Chants Democratic, No. 13 *LG 1860*; Leaves of Grass, No. 13 *LG 1867.*

TO A COMMON PROSTITUTE

Appeared in *LG 1860.*

I WAS LOOKING A LONG WHILE

title] *LG 1867*; Chants Democratic, No. 19 *LG 1860.*

THOUGHT

title] *LG 1871*; Thoughts, No. 3 *LG 1860.*

8 *sonnambules* sleepwalkers.

MIRACLES

title] *LG 1867*; Poem of Perfect Miracles *LG 1856*; Leaves of Grass, No. 8 *LG 1860.*

SPARKLES FROM THE WHEEL

Appeared in *LG 1871 Second Issue.*

TO A PUPIL

Appeared in *LG 1860.*

UNFOLDED OUT OF THE FOLDS

title] *LG 1871*; Poem of Women *LG 1856*; Leaves of Grass, No. 14 *LG 1860*; Leaves of Grass, No. 2 *LG 1867.*

WHAT AM I AFTER ALL

title] *LG 1871 Second Issue*; Leaves of Grass, No. 22 *LG 1860*; Leaves of Grass, No. 4 *LG 1867.*

KOSMOS

Appeared in *LG 1860.*

OTHERS MAY PRAISE WHAT THEY LIKE

Appeared in *1865*; then *LG 1867.*

WHO LEARNS MY LESSON COMPLETE?

Appeared untitled in *LG 1855*.
title] *LG 1871 Second Issue*; Lesson Poem *LG 1856*; Leaves of Grass, No. 11 *LG 1860*; Leaves of Grass, No. 3 *LG 1867*.

9 *quits and quits* equally.

TESTS

Appeared in *LG 1860*.

THE TORCH

Appeared in *1865*, then *LG 1867*.

O STAR OF FRANCE (1870–71)

First printed *Galaxy*, June 1871; included in *As a Strong Bird on Pinions Free* (1872) and *LG 1876*. The Franco-Prussian war concluded with the signing of the Treaty of Frankfort in 1871; in May of that year an insurrection by the Commune of Paris followed French ratification.

THE OX-TAMER

First printed New York *Daily Graphic*, December 1874; then *LG 1876*.

AN OLD MAN'S THOUGHT OF SCHOOL

First printed New York *Daily Graphic*, 3 November 1874; then *LG 1876*.

WANDERING AT MORN

First printed New York *Daily Graphic*, 15 March 1873, entitled *The Singing Thrush*; then *LG 1876*.

4 *evil times* 1873 was a year of financial depression.

ITALIAN MUSIC IN DAKOTA

Appeared in *LG 1881*.

9 *Sonnambula's innocent love* in Bellini's opera *La Sonnambula* the heroine, Amina, walks in her sleep into the room of a stranger and is accused of unfaithfulness.
    Norma's anguish in this Bellini opera the heroine's love makes it impossible for her to take revenge upon her unfaithful lover.
10 *Poliuto* an opera by Donizetti.

WITH ALL THY GIFTS

First printed New York *Daily Graphic*, 6 March 1873; then *LG 1876*.

MY PICTURE GALLERY

First printed in *American*, 30 October 1880; then *LG 1881*. See *Pictures* in Appendix 3, p. 665.

THE PRAIRIE STATES

First printed in manuscript facsimile in *Art Autograph*, May 1880; then *LG 1881*.

PROUD MUSIC OF THE STORM

First printed *Atlantic Monthly*, February 1869; then *LG 1871 Second Issue*.

22   *cantabile*   melodious and flowing sound; here referring to the harp's arpeggios as opposed to the flute's clear, single notes.

24   *Victoria!*   Queen of England (1837–1901). *Blodgett and Bradley* suggest that Whitman is referring to the Crimean War and the charge of the Light Brigade at Balaklava in 1854, or to the fact that while England remained neutral during the American Civil War it was openly sympathetic to the South.

31   *minnesingers*   medieval German lyric poets and musicians who sang of love and beauty.

48   *the Paradiso*   the concluding part of Dante's *Divina Commedia*.

52   *Tutti!*   Italian: all together; the conductor's command to the orchestra to play.

54   *strophe*   one of the alternating movements of the Greek choral dance.

77   *Norma*   the heroine of Bellini's opera of that name.

78   *Lucia*   the heroine of Donizetti's opera *Lucia di Lammermoor*. She is driven mad by marriage to a man who does not love her.

80   *Ernani*   the hero of Verdi's opera of that name; his suicide is the result of his unattainable love.

85   *trombone duo*   referring to a trombone duet in Bellini's *I Puritani*.

89   *Fernando*   the hero of Donizetti's opera *La Favorita*.

90   *Amina*   the heroine of *La Sonnambula*.

94   *Alboni*   Marietta Alboni was an opera singer much admired by Whitman.

97   *Meyerbeer*   Giacomo Meyerbeer (1791–1863) was the composer of *Les Huguenots* and other operas.

107   *Eleusis*   ancient Greek city.
      Ceres   Roman goddess of harvest.

110   *Corybantian*   a Corybant was one of the mythical attendants of the goddess Cybele; supposedly they accompanied her with wild dances and music as her torchlight processions wound through the mountains.

111   *flageolets*   small wooden instruments which make a shrill sound.

119   *the king*   an ancient Chinese instrument struck with a hammer.

120   *vina*   a Hindu zither-like instrument.

121   *bayaderes*   Indian dancing girls and singers.

124   *Eine . . . Gott*   German: 'A Mighty Fortress is our God'.

125   *Stabat Mater dolorosa*   Italian: 'she stood, the sorrowing Mother'.

Rossini's oratorio has as its subject the events of the Crucifixion, and takes its title from the posture of Mary before the Cross.

127 *Agnus Dei* or *Gloria in Excelsis* Latin: 'the Lamb of God'; 'Glory in the Highest'. Both are hymns sung during High Mass.

137 *The Creation* an oratorio by Franz Joseph Haydn.

PASSAGE TO INDIA

First published in 1871 as the title poem of a volume of seventy-five poems, twenty-three of which were new; this volume was bound as a supplement to *LG 1871 Second Issue*; the poem received its present position *LG 1881*.

4 *Seven* the seven wonders of the ancient world were: the Egyptian pyramids; the tomb of Halicarnassus; the temple of Artemis at Ephesus; the hanging gardens of Babylon; the Colossus of Rhodes; the statue of Zeus at Olympia; and the lighthouse at Alexandria.

5 *Suez* the Suez Canal was opened in 1869.

6 *railroad* the Union Pacific and the Central Pacific were joined in 1869.

7 *wires* the Atlantic cable was completed in 1866.

17 *Eclaircise* OED: to clear up. Newton in 1754 writes: 'till time shall accomplish and eclaircise all the particulars'.

44 *Empress Eugenie's leading the van* the wife of Napoleon III was one of the official party aboard *L'Aigle*, the steamship which lead the procession inaugurating the opening of the Suez Canal.

49–64 *I see over . . . Asia* Blodgett and Bradley point out that these lines follow the railroad route from Omaha to San Francisco.

65 *Genoese* Christopher Columbus.

76 *Vasco de Gama* da Gama, a Portuguese, was the first European to sail around Africa to India.

119 *doge of Venice* the doge, as chief magistrate, annually performed a ceremony celebrating the 'marriage' of the City of Venice to the Adriatic Sea.

137 *Tamerlane . . . Aurungzebe* Tamerlane (?1336–1405) conquered Turkey and Persia; Aurungzebe (1618–1707) was a warring Emperor of Hindustan.

139 *Marco Polo* a Venetian (1254–1324) who travelled to Cathay.

Batouta the Moor Batoutah was a fourteenth-century traveller in Egypt and China; only fragments of his diaries have been discovered.

156 *Palos* Spanish seaport from which Columbus sailed.

228 *Vedas* ancient Hindu scriptures.

240 *Sirius and Jupiter!* Sirius, or the Dog-Star, is the greatest star in the heavens; Jupiter is one of the largest and brightest planets.

PRAYER OF COLUMBUS

First printed *Harper's Magazine*, March 1874; then appeared in *LG 1876*.

22 *emprises* *Webster 1841*: 'emprise – an undertaking'.

THE SLEEPERS

Appeared untitled in *LG 1855*.

title] *LG 1871*; Night Poem *LG 1856*; Sleep Chasings *LG 1860*.

8 *ennuyés* those affected by ennui, weariness and boredom. OED cites a title by Mrs Jameson in 1826: *Diary of an Ennuyée*.

34 *douceurs Webster 1841*: 'douceur – a gift, a bribe'.

35 *Cache Webster 1841*: 'a hole in the ground for hiding and preserving provisions which it is inconvenient to carry . . .'.

40 *cunning* knowing.

59 *I fade away* after section 1, *LG 1855* read:

O hot-cheek'd and blushing! O foolish hectic!

O for pity's sake, no one must see me now! my clothes were stolen while I was abed,

Now I am thrust forth, where shall I run?

Pier that I saw dimly last night, when I look'd from the windows!

Pier out from the main, let me catch myself with you, and stay – I will chafe you,

I feel ashamed to go naked about the world.

I am curious to know where my feet stand and what this is flooding me, childhood or manhood – and the hunger that crosses the bridge between.

The cloth laps a first sweet eating and drinking,

Laps life-swelling yolks – laps ear of rose-corn, milky and just ripen'd;

The white teeth stay, and the boss-tooth advances in darkness,

And liquor is spill'd on lips and bosoms by touching glasses, and the best liquor afterward.

90 *defeat at Brooklyn* the Battle of Brooklyn Heights took place on 27 August 1776; the Americans were badly beaten and Washington retreated to the city of New York.

116 *again* after section 6, *LG 1855* read:

Now Lucifer was not dead – or if he was, I am his sorrowful terrible heir;

I have been wrong'd – I am oppress'd – I hate him that oppresses me,

I will either destroy him, or he shall release me.

Damn him! how he does defile me!

How he informs against my brother and sister, and takes pay for their blood!

How he laughs when I look down the bend, after the steamboat that carries away my woman!

Now the vast dusk bulk that is the whale's bulk, it seems mine;

Warily, sportman! though I lie so sleepy and sluggish, the tap of my flukes is death.

140 *erysipalite* a diseased person affected with inflammed skin.

141 *antipodes Webster 1841*: 'antipode – one who lives on the opposite side

of the globe, and, of course, those whose feet are directly opposite'. Here, those
whom we are all against.

TRANSPOSITIONS

This poem, which first appeared in *LG 1881*, was reconstructed from three
lines of a poem originally entitled *Poem of the Propositions of Nakedness* in *LG
1856*, *Chants Democratic, No. 5* in *LG 1860* and *Respondez* in *LG 1867*. See
Reversals, (p. 378).

TO THINK OF TIME

Appeared untitled in *LG 1855*.
title] *LG 1871*; Burial Poem *LG 1856*.

11 *accouchement* *Webster 1841*: 'delivery in childbirth'.
36 *posh* OED: 'the fragments produced by a smash; a soft, decayed, rotten
or pulpy mass; a state of slush; 2. *posh-ice*: ice broken into small fragments.'
OED cites an example of 1885: 'Forcing our way through a stream of posh'.
Whitman's use of the word seems early.
41 *whip* traditionally buried with the driver.
50 *hostler* *Webster 1841*: 'the person who has the care of horses at an inn'.

Whispers of Heavenly Death

A group title for thirteen poems first used in *LG 1871 Second Issue*; in *LG 1881*
five more poems were added; in the London *Broadway Magazine* for October
1868, five of these poems appeared with the present group title.

DAREST THOU NOW O SOUL

First printed London *Broadway Magazine*, October 1868; then *LG 1871
Second Issue*.

WHISPERS OF HEAVENLY DEATH

First printed London *Broadway Magazine*, October 1868; then *LG 1871
Second Issue*.

CHANTING THE SQUARE DEIFIC

Appeared in *1865 Sequel* and *LG 1867*. Regarding this poem, Whitman told
Horace Traubel (*With Walt Whitman in Camden*, I, 156):
'It would be hard to give the idea mathematical expression: the idea of spiritual
equity – the north, south, east, west of the constituted universe (even the soul
universe) – the four sides as sustaining the universe (the supernatural some-
thing): this is not the poem but the idea back of the poem or below the poem.'
3 *Jehovah* in Hebrew theology the Supreme Being.
4 *Brahm* Braham: Hindu spirit of the universe; the uncreated creator.
    Saturnius *Webster 1841*: Saturn 'in mythology, one of the oldest and

principle deities, the son of Coelus and Terra, (heaven and earth,) and the father of Jupiter. He answers to the Greek Χρονος, Chronus or Time.'

7 *Kronos* in Greek mythology a Titan identified with harvest; the Romans identified him with Saturn; because of the confusion of his name with Chronos, he came to be regarded as the god of time.

16 *Hermes* an Olympian god, herald and messenger.

Hercules son of Jupiter and Alcmene, celebrated for his strength.

29 *sudra* the lowest Hindu caste.

36 *Santa Spirita* the Holy Spirit. The more common Latin phrase is *Spiritus Sanctus* and in Italian, *Spirito Santo*. Whitman's phrase seems to be his own.

OF HIM I LOVE DAY AND NIGHT

title] *LG 1867*; Calamus, No. 17 *LG 1860*.

YET, YET, YE DOWNCAST HOURS

Appeared in *LG 1860* as sections five and six of *Debris*.

title] *LG 1871 Second Issue*; Despairing Cries *LG 1867*.

AS IF A PHANTOM CARESS'D ME

Appeared in *LG 1860* as the concluding stanza of *Debris*; and, with its present title, in *LG 1867*.

ASSURANCES

Appeared with its present title in *LG 1867* in the *Songs Before Parting* group.

title] *LG 1867*; Faith Poem *LG 1856*; Leaves of Grass, No. 7 *LG 1860*.

QUICKSAND YEARS

First appeared in *1865*.

title] *LG 1871 Second Issue*; in *1865* and *LG 1867* the first line appeared as the title.

THAT MUSIC ALWAYS ROUND ME

title] *LG 1867*; Calamus, No. 2 *LG 1860*.

6 *tutti* Italian; all together; usually a command to an orchestra to proceed to play in unison.

WHAT SHIP PUZZLED AT SEA

title] *LG 1881*; Calamus, No. 31 *LG 1860*; Here, Sailor *LG 1867*.

A NOISELESS PATIENT SPIDER

First printed London *Broadway Magazine*, October 1868; then *LG 1871
Second Issue*. The manuscript version of 1862-3 (*UPP*, II, 93) differs sig-
nificantly:

The Soul, reaching, throwing out for love,
As the spider, from some little promontory, throwing out filament after
  filament, tirelessly out of itself, that one at least may catch and form a link,
  a bridge, a connection
O I saw one passing alone, saying hardly a word – yet full of love I detected
  him, by certain signs
O eyes wishfully turning! O silent eyes!
For then I thought of you oer the world
O latent oceans, fathomless oceans of love!
O waiting oceans of love! yearning and fervid! and of you sweet souls perhaps
  in the future, delicious and long:
But Dead, unknown on the earth – ungiven, dark here, unspoken, never
  born:
You fathomless latent souls of love – you pent and unknown oceans of love!

O LIVING ALWAYS, ALWAYS DYING

title] *LG 1867*; Calamus, No. 27 *LG 1860*.

TO ONE SHORTLY TO DIE

Appeared in *LG 1860*.

NIGHT ON THE PRAIRIES

title] *LG 1871 Second Issue*; Leaves of Grass, No. 15 *LG 1860*; Leaves of
Grass, No. 3 *LG 1867*.

7 *resumé* OED glosses *résumé*: 'a summary, epitome'. In 1861 Pattison
writes 'Some of the papers are mere résumés of English books' and in 1804
in the *Edinburgh Review*: 'After a short resumé of his observations on coffee-
houses and prisons'. Whitman's use of the noun as an adjective is his own.

THOUGHT

title] *LG 1871 Second Issue*; Thoughts, No. 5 *LG 1860*.

4 *the President* a steamship lost between New York and Liverpool in 1841.
5 *Arctic* collided with the French vessel Vesta in 1854 with a loss of 350
persons.

THE LAST INVOCATION

First printed London *Broadway Magazine*, October 1868; then *LG 1871 Second Issue*.

3 *keep* the stronghold of a medieval castle.

AS I WATCH'D THE PLOUGHMAN PLOUGHING

Appeared in *LG 1871 Second Issue*.

PENSIVE AND FALTERING

First printed London *Broadway Magazine*, October 1868; then *LG 1871 Second Issue*.

THOU MOTHER WITH THY EQUAL BROOD

First published in 1872 as the title poem in a volume containing seven additional poems; this volume was bound as a supplement to *LG 1876, Two Rivulets*; the poem appeared in its present position *LG 1881*. It was delivered at Dartmouth College Commencement, 26 June 1872.

23 *Saguenay's black stream* a river in Quebec, Canada.
Huron the second largest of the Great Lakes.
51 *résumé* essence, summation. See note on *Night on the Prairies* 7.

A PAUMANOK PICTURE

This poem appeared as canto eight of *Salut au Monde!* in *LG 1856*. It appeared as a separate poem in *LG 1881*.

2 *moss-bonkers* the menhaden, an Atlantic coast fish commonly used for bait.
seine-ends a large fishing net, the ends of which are joined offshore.

From Noon to Starry Night

A group title for twenty-one poems in *LG 1881*, five of which were new.

THOU ORB ALOFT FULL-DAZZLING

First printed *American*, 4 June 1881, entitled 'A Summer Invocation'; then, with its present title, in *LG 1881*.

FACES

Appeared untitled in *LG 1855*.
title] *LG 1871*; Poem of Faces *LG 1856*; Leaf of Faces *LG 1860*; A Leaf of Faces *LG 1867*.

19 *wrig* *Webster 1841*: 'wrig – for wriggle, to move briskly'; OED: (now dialect) 'to move sinuously, or writhingly; to wriggle'.
23 *wabbling* toppling, uncertain.

25 *laudanum* formerly any of the various preparations of opium.
caoutchouc crude rubber.
29 *speculates* contemplates.
38 *Splay* cut open.
fores Traubel records in *With Walt Whitman in Camden*, IV, 243, that when Dr Bucke asked Whitman what he meant by this word he answered: 'the front, the snout, whatever'.

THE MYSTIC TRUMPETER

First printed *Kansas Magazine*, February 1872, and included in *As A Strong Bird on Pinions Free* the same year; then *LG 1876*.

19 *imbonded* fettered; a Whitman coinage.
36 *alembic Webster 1841*: 'a chemical vessel used in distillation; usually made of glass or copper.'

TO A LOCOMOTIVE IN WINTER

First printed New York *Daily Graphic*, 19 February 1876; *LG 1876*.

O MAGNET-SOUTH

First printed *Southern Literary Messenger*, 15 July 1860.
title] *LG 1881*; Longings for Home *LG 1860*.

5 *Roanoke . . . Sabine* all rivers of the deep South.
7 *Okeechobee* a lake in Florida.
11 *Pamlico sound* a channel in eastern North Carolina, separated from the Atlantic by narrow barrier beaches.
15 *freebooter* a pillager or member of a predatory band.

MANNAHATTA

Appeared in *LG 1860*. The Algonquin Indian name means 'large island'.

ALL IS TRUTH

title] *LG 1871*; Leaves of Grass, No. 18 *LG 1860*; Songs Before Parting, No. 1 *LG 1867*.

A RIDDLE SONG

First printed *Forney's Magazine*, Philadelphia, 17 April 1880; then *LG 1881*.

EXCELSIOR

title] *LG 1867*; Poem of the Heart of the Son of Manhattan Island *LG 1856*; Chants Democratic, No. 15 *LG 1860*.

AH POVERTIES, WINCINGS, AND SULKY RETREATS
Appeared in *1865*; then *LG 1867*.

THOUGHTS
title] *LG 1871*; Thought *LG 1860*.

MEDIUMS
title] *LG 1867*; Chants Democratic, No. 16 *LG 1860*.

WEAVE IN, MY HARDY LIFE
Appeared in *1865*; then *LG 1867*.

SPAIN, 1873-74
First printed New York *Daily Graphic*, 24 March 1873; then *LG 1876*. In December 1874 Don Alfonso was proclaimed King of Spain and the effort to establish a constitutional republic failed.

BY BROAD POTOMAC'S SHORE
First published in *As a Strong Bird on Pinions Free*, 1872; then *LG 1876*.

FROM FAR DAKOTA'S CAÑONS (JUNE 25, 1876)
First printed New York *Tribune*, 10 June 1876. It appeared as an intercalation in some editions of *LG 1876*, entitled *A Death Sonnet for Custer*; and, with its present title, in *LG 1881*.
8 *Custer* General George Armstrong Custer died at Little Big Horn in 1876.

OLD WAR-DREAMS
Appeared in *1865 Sequel* and *LG 1867*; then *LG 1871 Second Issue* as part of the *Ashes of Soldiers* group.
title] *LG 1881*; In Clouds Descending, in Midnight Sleep *1865 Sequel*, *LG 1867*; In Midnight Sleep *LG 1871 Second Issue*.

THICK-SPRINKLED BUNTING
title] *LG 1871*; Flag of Stars, Thick-Sprinkled Bunting *1865*, *LG 1867*.

WHAT BEST I SEE IN THEE
Appeared in *LG 1881*. General Ulysses S. Grant returned from a world tour in 1879.

SPIRIT THAT FORM'D THIS SCENE

First printed *Critic*, 10 September 1881; then *LG 1881*.

AS I WALK THESE BROAD MAJESTIC DAYS

title] *LG 1871*; Chants Democratic, No. 21 *LG 1860*; As I Walk Solitary, Unattended *LG 1867*.

A CLEAR MIDNIGHT

Appeared in *LG 1881*.

Songs of Parting

A group title for seventeen poems in *LG 1881*, two of which are new; *Songs Before Parting* is a group title of *LG 1867*; the present group title appeared in *LG 1871*.

AS THE TIME DRAWS NIGH

title] *LG 1871*; To My Soul *LG 1860*; As Nearing Departure *LG 1867*.

YEARS OF THE MODERN

Appeared in *1865* and *LG 1867*. Transferred to *Songs of Parting* in *LG 1871*. Holloway notes that lines 11–24 are taken from Whitman's unpublished political tract *The Eighteenth Presidency!* which dates from the campaign of 1856; the tract was published in C. J. Furness's *Walt Whitman's Workshop* (1928).
title] *LG 1871*; Years of the Unperformed *1865*, *LG 1867*.

ASHES OF SOLDIERS

Appeared in *1865*; then *LG 1867* and *LG 1871 Second Issue*, where it served as the title poem for a group of the same name.
title] *LG 1871 Second Issue*; Hymn of Dead Soldiers *1865*, *LG 1867*.

THOUGHTS

This was originally two separate poems: stanza one appeared in *LG 1860* as *Chants Democratic*, No. *9*; and stanza two as *Chants Democratic*, No. *11* in *LG 1860*; they were combined in *LG 1867* with the present title.

20 *Sitka* in the nineteenth century Sitka was a post village and capital of Alaska and, according to *Lippincott's Gazeteer*, 'one of the principal places in the territory, situated on the west coast of Baranoff Island'.

Aliaska sometimes written *Aliashka*, a peninsula of Alaska, 'extending some four-hundred and fifty miles into the Pacific, with an average breadth of twenty-five miles' (*Lippincott's Gazeteer*).

21 *feuillage* scenery. See *Our Old Feuillage*.

30 *Anahuacs* Anahuac is an Aztec name meaning 'near the water' and commonly refers to that part of the central plateau of Mexico which includes the valleys of the Pánuco and Lerma river systems. Whitman seems to be referring to the mountain ranges known as the 'Cordillera de Anahuac'.

SONG AT SUNSET

title] *LG 1867*; Chants Democratic, No. 8 *LG 1860*.

AS AT THY PORTALS ALSO DEATH

Appeared in *LG 1881*. The poem is an elegy to Whitman's mother, Louisa Van Velsor Whitman, who died 23 May 1873.

MY LEGACY

First published as an epigraph entitled *Souvenirs of Democracy* in *As a Strong Bird on Pinions Free*, 1872; then *LG 1876* and, with its present title, *LG 1881*.

PENSIVE ON HER DEAD GAZING

First appeared in *1865*.
title] *LG 1881*; *first line as title in 1865 and LG 1867*.

CAMPS OF GREEN

Appeared in *1865*; then *LG 1867* and *LG 1871 Second Issue* as part of the *Ashes to Soldiers* group.

THE SOBBING OF THE BELLS

First printed Boston *Daily Globe*, 27 September 1881; then *LG 1881*. Whitman was in Boston overseeing the publication of the 1881 edition when the news of President Garfield's death on 19 September was announced. Garfield had been shot on 2 July.

AS THEY DRAW TO A CLOSE

title] *LG 1881*; Thought *LG 1871 Second Issue*. Lines 7–10 are from the *LG 1871* poem *Shut Not Your Doors*, added to 'Inscriptions' in *LG 1881*.

JOY, SHIPMATE, JOY!

Appeared in *LG 1871 Second Issue*.

THE UNTOLD WANT

Appeared in *LG 1871 Second Issue*.

PORTALS

Appeared in *LG 1871 Second Issue*.

THESE CAROLS

Appeared in *LG 1871 Second Issue*.

NOW FINALÈ TO THE SHORE

Appeared in *LG 1871 Second Issue*, in a group with the same title.

1 *finalè* properly: finale. It appears without an accent in *LG 1871 Second Issue*. *Webster 1841*: 'the last performance in any act of an opera, or that which closes a concert'.

SO LONG!

Appeared in *LG 1860*.

22 *adhesiveness* OED: in phrenology 'the faculty of forming and maintaining attachments to persons'. The OED cites an example from Chambers's *Encyclopedia* in 1879: 'Adhesiveness is strongest and its organ largest in woman'.

67 *avataras* *Webster 1841*: 'avatar: a Hindoo word denoting incarnation, or descent of a deity in a visible form'.

First Annex: Sands at Seventy

In 1888 Whitman published a collection of poems and prose pieces entitled *November Boughs*. *Sands at Seventy* was the group title for the poems collected in this volume. These were appended as an annex in *1888 Complete* and *LG 1889*.

MANNAHATTA

First printed New York *Herald*, 22 February 1888; then *1888*, *1888 Complete* and *LG 1889*.

PAUMANOK

First printed New York *Herald*, 29 February 1888; then *1888*, *1888 Complete* and *LG 1889*.

FROM MONTAUK POINT

First printed New York *Herald*, 1 March 1888; then *1888*, *1888 Complete* and *LG 1889*. Montauk Point is a headland at the eastern end of Long Island, New York.

TO THOSE WHO'VE FAILED

First printed New York *Herald*, 27 January 1888; then *1888, 1888 Complete* and *LG 1889*.

A CAROL CLOSING SIXTY-NINE

First printed New York *Herald*, 21 May 1888; then *1888, 1888 Complete* and *LG 1889*.

THE BRAVEST SOLDIERS

First printed New York *Herald*, 18 March 1888; then *1888, 1888 Complete* and *LG 1889*.

A FONT OF TYPE

Appeared in *1888, 1888 Complete* and *LG 1889*.
3 *nonpareil . . . primer* names of printing type ranging from six to ten points.

AS I SIT WRITING HERE

First printed New York *Herald*, 14 May 1888; then *1888, 1888 Complete* and *LG 1889*.
2 *querilities* properly 'querulities', complaints.

MY CANARY BIRD

First printed New York *Herald*, 2 March 1888; then *1888, 1888 Complete* and *LG 1889*.

QUERIES TO MY SEVENTIETH YEAR

First published New York *Herald*, 2 May 1888; then *1888, 1888 Complete* and *LG 1889*.

THE WALLABOUT MARTYRS

First printed New York *Herald*, 16 March 1888; then *1888, 1888 Complete* and *LG 1889*. Wallabout Bay is the present site of the Brooklyn Navy Yard.

THE FIRST DANDELION

First printed New York *Herald*, 12 March 1888; then *1888, 1888 Complete* and *LG 1889*.

AMERICA

First printed New York *Herald*, 11 February 1888; then *1888, 1888 Complete* and *LG 1889*.

MEMORIES

Appeared in *1888*, *1888 Complete* and *LG 1889*.

TO-DAY AND THEE

First printed New York *Herald*, 23 April 1888; then *1888*, *1888 Complete* and *LG 1889*.

AFTER THE DAZZLE OF DAY

First printed New York *Herald*, 3 February 1888; then *1888*, *1888 Complete* and *LG 1889*.

ABRAHAM LINCOLN, BORN FEB. 12, 1809

First printed New York *Herald*, 12 February 1888; then *1888*, *1888 Complete* and *LG 1889*.

OUT OF MAY'S SHOWS SELECTED

First printed New York *Herald*, 10 May 1888: then *1888*, *1888 Complete* and *LG 1889*.

HALCYON DAYS

First printed New York *Herald*, 29 January 1888; then *1888*, *1888 Complete* and *LG 1889*.

Fancies at Navesink

A group title for eight poems first printed *Nineteenth Century*, August 1885; then *1888*, *1888 Complete* and *LG 1889*.

THE PILOT IN THE MIST

See *Fancies at Navesink n.*, above.

HAD I THE CHOICE

See *Fancies at Navesink n.*, above.

YOU TIDES WITH CEASELESS SWELL

See *Fancies at Navesink n.*, above.

4 *Sirius* the Dog Star, the brightest star.
    Capella a star of the first magnitude in Auriga.

LAST OF EBB, AND DAYLIGHT WANING

See *Fancies at Navesink n.*, above.

12 *debouché* more commonly a verb and without an accent. See *Starting from Paumanok* 27.

AND YET NOT YOU ALONE

See *Fancies at Navesink n.*, above.

PROUDLY THE FLOOD COMES IN

See *Fancies at Navesink n.*, above.

BY THAT LONG SCAN OF WAVES

See *Fancies at Navesink n.*, above.

THEN LAST OF ALL

See *Fancies at Navesink n.*, above.

ELECTION DAY, NOVEMBER, 1884

First printed Philadelphia *Press*, 26 October 1884; then *1888*, *1888 Complete* and *LG 1889*. The candidates involved were James Blaine and Grover Cleveland.

WITH HUSKY-HAUGHTY LIPS, O SEA!

First printed *Harper's Monthly*, March 1884; then *1888*, *1888 Complete* and *LG 1889*.

DEATH OF GENERAL GRANT

First printed *Harper's Weekly*, 16 May 1885; then *1888*, *1888 Complete* and *LG 1889*. The poem was published while Grant was still alive; he died on 23 July 1885.

RED JACKET (FROM ALOFT)

First printed Philadelphia *Press*, 10 October 1884; then *1888*, *1888 Complete* and *LG 1889*. Red Jacket was the grand sachem of the Iroquois.

8 *Ossian* a legendary Gaelic bard of the third century.

WASHINGTON'S MONUMENT, FEBRUARY, 1885

First printed Philadelphia *Press*, 22 February 1885, entitled *Ah, Not This Granite Dead and Cold*. It appeared, with its present title, in *1888*, *1888 Complete* and *LG 1889*.

OF THAT BLITHE THROAT OF THINE

First printed *Harper's Monthly*, January 1885; then *1888*, *1888 Complete* and *LG 1889*.

BROADWAY

First printed New York *Herald*, 10 April 1888; then *1888*, *1888 Complete* and *LG 1889*.

TO GET THE FINAL LILT OF SONGS

First printed New York *Herald*, 16 April 1888; then *1888*, *1888 Complete* and *LG 1889*.

OLD SALT KOSSABONE

First printed New York *Herald*, 25 February 1888; then *1888*, *1888 Complete* and *LG 1889*. Kossabone was Louisa Van Velsor Whitman's great-grandfather.

THE DEAD TENOR

First printed *Critic*, 8 November 1884; then *1888*, *1888 Complete* and *LG 1889*. The singer referred to is Pasquale Brignole.

8   *Fernando's . . . Gennaro's*   characters from operas by Donizetti and Verdi.

CONTINUITIES

First printed New York *Herald*, 20 March 1888; then *1888*, *1888 Complete* and *LG 1889*.

YONNONDIO

First printed *Critic*, 26 November 1887; then *1888*, *1888 Complete* and *LG 1889*.

LIFE

First printed New York *Herald*, 15 April 1888; then *1888*, *1888 Complete* and *LG 1889*.

'GOING SOMEWHERE'

First printed *Lippincott's Magazine*, November 1887; then *1888*, *1888 Complete* and *LG 1889*.

1   *science-friend*   Anne Gilchrist, who died in 1885; she came from England as an enthusiast of *Leaves of Grass* and wished to marry Whitman.

SMALL THE THEME OF MY CHANT

Appeared in *LG 1867* on the flyleaf; then *1888*, *1888 Complete* and *LG 1889*. See *One's Self I Sing* n.

TRUE CONQUERORS

First printed New York *Herald*, 15 February 1888; then *1888*, *1888 Complete* and *LG 1889*.

THE UNITED STATES TO OLD WORLD CRITICS

First printed New York *Herald*, 8 May 1888; then *1888*, *1888 Complete* and *LG 1889*.

THE CALMING THOUGHT OF ALL

First printed New York *Herald*, 27 May 1888; then *1888*, *1888 Complete* and *LG 1889*.

THANKS IN OLD AGE

First printed Philadelphia *Press*, 24 November 1887; then *1888*, *1888 Complete* and *LG 1889*.

LIFE AND DEATH

First printed New York *Herald*, 23 May 1888; then *1888*, *1888 Complete* and *LG 1889*.

THE VOICE OF THE RAIN

First printed *Outing*, August 1885; then *1888*, *1888 Complete* and *LG 1889*.

SOON SHALL THE WINTER'S FOIL BE HERE

First printed New York *Herald*, 21 February 1888; then *1888*, *1888 Complete* and *LG 1889*.

WHILE NOT THE PAST FORGETTING

Blodgett and Bradley note that the date of publication (30 May 1888) provided by Whitman has 'not been substantiated'. The poem appeared in *1888*, *1888 Complete* and *LG 1889*.

THE DYING VETERAN

First printed *McClure's Magazine*, June 1887; then *1888*, *1888 Complete* and *LG 1889*.

STRONGER LESSONS

Appeared in *LG 1860* as part of *Debris*; then as a separate poem, with the present title, in *LG 1867*. It was then dropped from further editions until *1888*; and appeared in *1888 Complete* and *LG 1889*.

A PRAIRIE SUNSET

First printed New York *Herald*, 9 March 1888; then *1888*, *1888 Complete* and *LG 1889*.

TWENTY YEARS

First printed New York *Magazine of Art*, July 1888; then *1888*, *1888 Complete* and *LG 1889*.

ORANGE BUDS BY MAIL FROM FLORIDA

First printed New York *Herald*, 19 March 1888; then *1888*, *1888 Complete* and *LG 1889*.

TWILIGHT

First printed *Century*, December 1887; then *1888*, *1888 Complete* and *LG 1889*.

3 *nirwana*   more commonly 'nirvana', but Whitman's spelling is acceptable; OED: 'in Buddhist theology the extinction of individual existence and absorption into the supreme spirit, or the extinction of all desires and passions and attainment of perfect beatitude'.

YOU LINGERING SPARSE LEAVES OF ME

First printed *Lippincott's Magazine*, November 1887; then *1888*, *1888 Complete* and *LG 1889*.

NOT MEAGRE, LATENT BOUGHS ALONE

First printed *Lippincott's Magazine*, November 1887; then *1888*, *1888 Complete* and *LG 1889*.

THE DEAD EMPEROR

First printed New York *Herald*, 10 March 1888; then *1888*, *1888 Complete* and *LG 1889*. Wilhelm I of Germany died in Berlin on 9 March.

AS THE GREEK'S SIGNAL FLAME

First printed New York *Herald*, 15 December 1887; then *1888*, *1888 Complete* and *LG 1889*.

THE DISMANTLED SHIP

First printed New York *Herald*, 23 February 1888; then *1888, 1888 Complete* and *LG 1889*.

NOW PRECEDENT SONGS, FAREWELL

Appeared in *1888, 1888 Complete* and *LG 1889*.

AN EVENING LULL

Appeared in *1888, 1888 Complete* and *LG 1889*.

OLD AGE'S LAMBENT PEAKS

First printed *Century*, September 1888; then *1888, 1888 Complete* and *LG 1889*.

AFTER THE SUPPER AND TALK

First printed *Lippincott's Magazine*, November 1887; then *1888, 1888 Complete* and *LG 1889*.

Second Annex: Good-Bye My Fancy

Like *November Boughs*, *Good-Bye My Fancy*, a miscellany, was published separately in 1891; it consisted of thirty-one poems annexed to *LG 1892*.

PREFACE NOTE TO SECOND ANNEX

Appeared in *1891* and *LG 1892*.

SAIL OUT FOR GOOD, EIDÓLON YACHT!

First printed *Lippincott's Magazine*, March 1891, with three other poems in a group entitled *Old Age Echoes*; then *1891* and *LG 1892*.

9 *eidólon* OED: 'image, spectre, phantom', citing examples by Carlyle, Scott, and Mrs Browning. Poe, in *Dreamland*, writes: 'Where an Eidolon, named Night,/On a black throne reigns upright'. See Whitman's comment on the word in *Eidólons*.

LINGERING LAST DROPS

Appeared in *1891* and *LG 1892*.

GOOD-BYE MY FANCY

Appeared in *1891* and *LG 1892*.

ON, ON THE SAME, YE JOCUND TWAIN!

Appeared in *1891* and *LG 1892*.

MY 71ST YEAR

First printed *Century*, November 1889; then *1891* and *LG 1892*.

APPARITIONS

Appeared in *1891* and *LG 1892*.

THE PALLID WREATH

First printed *Critic*, 10 January 1891; then *1891* and *LG 1892*.

AN ENDED DAY

Appeared in *1891* and *LG 1892*.

OLD AGE'S SHIP AND CRAFTY DEATH'S

First printed *Century*, February 1890; then *1891* and *LG 1892*.

TO THE PENDING YEAR

First printed *Critic*, 5 January 1889, entitled *To the Year 1889*; appeared with its present title in *1891* and *LG 1892*.

SHAKSPERE-BACON'S CIPHER

First printed *Cosmopolitan*, October 1887; then *1891* and *LG 1892*. Francis Bacon (1561-1626) is sometimes proposed as the true author of Shakespeare's plays.

LONG, LONG HENCE

Appeared in *1891* and *LG 1892*.

BRAVO, PARIS EXPOSITION!

First printed *Harper's Weekly*, 28 September 1889; then *1891* and *LG 1892*.

INTERPOLATION SOUNDS

First printed New York *Herald*, 12 August 1888; then *1891* and *LG 1892*.

TO THE SUN-SET BREEZE

First printed *Lippincott's Magazine*, December 1890; then *1891* and *LG 1892*.

OLD CHANTS

First printed New York *Truth*, 19 March 1891, then *1891* and *LG 1892*.

A CHRISTMAS GREETING

Appeared in *1891* and *LG 1892*.

8 *the Cross . . . the Crown* constellations in the Southern Hemisphere.

SOUNDS OF THE WINTER

First printed *Lippincott's Magazine*, March 1891; then *1891* and *LG 1892*.

A TWILIGHT SONG

First printed *Century*, May 1890; then *1891* and *LG 1892*.

WHEN THE FULL-GROWN POET CAME

First printed New York *Tribune*, 19 February 1876. In *LG 1876* it was pasted on blank end-pages, and then appeared as the final poem in the group *Bathed in War's Perfume* in the second issue of *LG 1876*. It was not included in *LG 1881*; it appeared in *1891* and *LG 1892*.

OSCEOLA

First printed *Munson's Illustrated World*, April 1890; then *1891* and *LG 1892*. Osceola died on 30 January 1838.

A VOICE FROM DEATH

First printed New York *World*, 7 June 1889; then *1891* and *LG 1892*. The Johnstown flood caused the death of more than two thousand persons.

A PERSIAN LESSON

Appeared in *1891* and *LG 1892*.

1 *sufi* OED: 'one of a sect of Mohammadan ascetic mystics who in later times embraced pantheistic views'; the 1875 edition of the *Encyclopaedia Britannica* observes that 'the Persian Sufis especially distinguished themselves by the practice of abstinence and solitary meditation'.

THE COMMONPLACE

First printed in manuscript facsimile in *Monson's Magazine*, March 1891; then *1891* and *LG 1892*.

'THE ROUNDED CATALOGUE DIVINE COMPLETE'

Appeared in *1891* and *LG 1892*.

MIRAGES

Appeared in *1891* and *LG 1892*.

L. OF G.'S PURPORT

Appeared in *1891* and *LG 1892*.

THE UNEXPRESS'D

First printed *Lippincott's Magazine*, March 1891, as a part of the group *Old Age Echoes*; then *1891* and *LG 1892*.

GRAND IS THE SEEN

Appeared in *1891* and *LG 1892*.

UNSEEN BUDS

Appeared in *1891* and *LG 1892*.

GOOD-BYE MY FANCY!

Appeared in *1891* and *LG 1892*.

A BACKWARD GLANCE O'ER TRAVEL'D ROADS

First published as the introduction to *1888*; then *LG 1892*.

Appendix I: Old Age Echoes

A group title for thirteen poems added to *LG 1897*.

AN EXECUTOR'S DIARY NOTE, 1891

Horace Traubel was Walt Whitman's executor; he is the author of *With Walt Whitman in Camden*, a record of his conversations with Whitman which first took place in 1888.

TO SOAR IN FREEDOM AND IN FULLNESS OF POWER

Appeared in *LG 1897*.

THEN SHALL PERCEIVE

Appeared in *LG 1897*.

THE FEW DROPS KNOWN

Appeared in *LG 1897*.

ONE THOUGHT EVER AT THE FORE

Appeared in *LG 1897*.

WHILE BEHIND ALL, FIRM AND ERECT

Appeared in *LG 1897*.

A KISS TO THE BRIDE

First printed New York *Daily Graphic*, 21 May 1874; then *LG 1897*.

NAY, TELL ME NOT TODAY THE PUBLISH'D SHAME

First printed New York *Daily Graphic*, 5 March 1873; then *LG 1897*. The events referred to surround the scandals of the Credit Mobilier and bribery accusations directed at Congressmen who favored passage of a bill to reorganize this company to finance the Union Pacific Railway and the 'Salary Grab' act which would greatly increase the salary of the President and other government officials.

SUPPLEMENT HOURS

Appeared in *LG 1897*.

OF MANY A SMUTCH'D DEED REMINISCENT

Appeared in *LG 1897*.

TO BE AT ALL

Appeared in *LG 1897*. As the subtitle indicates, however, the poem is a draft of the twenty-seventh section of *Song of Myself*, *LG 1855*.

DEATH'S VALLEY

First printed *Harper's New Monthly Magazine*, April 1892; then *LG 1897*. George Inness (1824–94) was one of the greatest American landscape painters in the nineteenth century. This particular picture, however, is not typical: a single figure in a mountainous valley looks toward a distant illuminated cross.

ON THE SAME PICTURE

Appeared in *LG 1897*, with the title supplied by Traubel.

A THOUGHT OF COLUMBUS

Printed as a manuscript facsimile in *Once a Week*, 9 July 1892; then *LG 1897*. According to Horace Traubel this is the last poem Whitman wrote and was given to Traubel on 16 March 1892.

Appendix 2: Poems Excluded from **Leaves of Grass**

GREAT ARE THE MYTHS

Appeared first untitled in *LG 1855* and finally in *LG* 1876. The text printed here is from *LG 1860*.
title] *LG 1867*; Poem of a Few Greatnesses *LG 1856*; Leaves of Grass, No. 2 *LG 1860*.

POEM OF REMEMBRANCES FOR A GIRL OR A BOY OF THESE STATES

Appeared in *LG 1856* with its present title; then *LG 1860* as a poem of forty-four lines, entitled *Chants Democratic, No. 6*, of which the first part is printed here. In *LG 1867* Whitman published the second half of this poem separately as *Leaves of Grass, No. 1*, retitled *Think of the Soul* in *LG 1871*.

10 *habitan* see *To a Historian* 4.

THINK OF THE SOUL

Appeared in *LG 1856* as the last nine stanzas of *Poem of Remembrances...*; and made its last appearance in *LG 1876*, the text being that printed here.
title] *LG 1871*; Leaves of Grass, No. 1 *LG 1867*.

RESPONDEZ!

Made its last appearance in *LG 1876*, the text being that printed here.
title] *LG 1867*; Poem of the Propositions of Nakedness *LG 1856*; Chants Democratic, No. 5 *LG 1860*.

[IN THE NEW GARDEN]

title] Enfans d'Adam, No. 11 *LG 1860*.

[WHO IS NOW READING THIS?]

title] Calamus, No. 16 *LG 1860*.

[I THOUGHT THAT KNOWLEDGE ALONE WOULD SUFFICE]

title] Calamus, No. 8 *LG 1860*.

[HOURS CONTINUING LONG]

title] Calamus, No. 9 *LG 1860*.

[SO FAR, AND SO FAR, AND ON TOWARD THE END]

title] Leaves of Grass, No. 20 *LG 1860*.

THOUGHTS–1: VISAGES

Appeared finally in *LG 1867*.
title] Thoughts, No. 1 *LG 1860*.

LEAFLETS

Appeared once only as a separate poem, in *LG 1867*. In *LG 1860* these two lines were ll. 4–5 of *Debris*.

THOUGHTS – 6: 'OF WHAT I WRITE'

Appeared in *LG 1860* as the sixth of a cluster of poems entitled *Thoughts*; made its last appearance in *LG 1876*, the text being that used here.

SAYS

Appeared in *LG 1860* with the present title and with the text used here; in *LG 1867* stanzas 1, 5, 7 and 8 were retained; retitled as *Suggestions* in *LG 1871*; and made its last appearance in *LG 1876*.

APOSTROPH

Appeared in *LG 1860* with the present title as the introductory poem to *Chants Democratic and Native American*; the last nineteen lines became *Leaves of Grass, No. 1* in *LG 1867*.

O SUN OF REAL PEACE

Appeared in *LG 1867*, entitled *Leaves of Grass, No. 1*, with the first line 'O hastening light!'; derived from *LG 1860*, *Apostroph*; got its present title in *LG 1871* and made its last appearance in *LG 1876*, the text being that used here.

TO YOU

Appeared in *LG 1860* in the *Messenger Leaves* group; made its last appearance in *LG 1876*, the text being that used here.

NOW LIFT ME CLOSE

Made its last appearance in *LG 1867*. First collected by *Blodgett and Bradley*, 1965.
title] Leaves of Grass, No. 24 *LG 1860*.

TO THE READER AT PARTING

Appeared in *LG 1871 Second Issue*, but derived from *Now Lift Me Close* in *LG 1860*; made its last appearance in *LG 1876*. First collected by *Blodgett and Bradley*, 1965.

DEBRIS

Made its first and only appearance in *LG 1860*. Seven passages, however, survive in *LG 1892*:

ll. 7–8   : cf. *Stronger Lessons*
ll. 10–18 : cf. *Yet, Yet, Ye Downcast Hours*
ll. 19–20 : cf. *Offerings*
ll. 21–4 : cf. *Visor'd*
ll. 33–4 : cf. *Beautiful Women*
ll. 52–6 : cf. *Not the Pilot*
ll. 57–60 : cf. *As if a Phantom Caress'd Me*

[STATES!]

Appeared in *LG 1860* as *Calamus, No. 5*, its first and only appearance. Passages from the poem survive, however, in *Over the Carnage Rose Prophetic a Voice* and *For You O Democracy*.

BATHED IN WAR'S PERFUME

Appeared in *1865* and *LG 1867*; then in *LG 1871* (with the second line added), as the title poem of a cluster of seven poems; made its last appearance in *LG 1876*.

SOLID, IRONICAL, ROLLING ORB

Appeared in *1865* and *LG 1867*; made its last appearance in *LG 1876*.

NOT MY ENEMIES EVER INVADE ME

Appeared in *1865 Sequel* and *LG 1867*.

THIS DAY, O SOUL

Appeared in *1865 Sequel* and *LG 1867*: made its last appearance in *LG 1876*.

ASHES OF SOLDIERS: EPIGRAPH

Appeared in *LG 1871 Second Issue*; made its final appearance in *LG 1876*.

ONE SONG, AMERICA, BEFORE I GO

Appeared in one of two prefatory poems in *As a Strong Bird on Pinions Free* (1872), a supplement to *LG 1876*. In *LG 1881* this poem was revised to form the opening section of *Thou Mother with Thy Equal Brood*.

SOUVENIRS OF DEMOCRACY

Appeared as the second prefatory poem of *As a Strong Bird on Pinions Free* (1872), a supplement to *LG 1876*. In *LG 1881* the poem was revised to become *My Legacy*.

FROM MY LAST YEARS

Made its first and only appearance in *LG 1876*.

IN FORMER SONGS

Made its first and only appearance in *LG 1876*.

THE BEAUTY OF THE SHIP

First printed New York *Daily Tribune*, 19 February 1876; then *LG 1876*, as an 'intercalation' pasted on the end-pages of some editions.

AFTER AN INTERVAL

First printed New York *Daily Tribune*, 19 February 1876; then *LG 1876*, its first and only appearance.

2–3 *Orion . . . Mars* Orion, the hunter, was slain by Artemis, and he is represented in the constellations as a hunter with belt and sword. The Pleiades were seven daughters of Atlas and Pleione, one of whom hid in shame for loving a mortal, and are represented in the constellation Taurus as a group of stars, six visible and one hidden. Saturn, in Roman mythology, is a god of seed-sowing and is the name for a planet next in magnitude to Jupiter. Mars is the Roman god of war and protector of fields as well as a planet conspicuous for its red light.

TWO RIVULETS

Made its first and only appearance in *LG 1876*; but ll. 10–12 appear in a revised form in *As Consequent* in *LG 1881*.

OR, FROM THAT SEA OF TIME

Made its first and only appearance in *LG 1876*; but then revised to become part of *As Consequent* in *LG 1881*.

2 *windrow-drift*] winrow-drift *LG 1876*.

AS IN A SWOON

Appeared in *LG 1876*; then *1891* and *Complete Prose Works* (1892).

LESSONS

Appeared in the volume *Passage to India* (1871), but did not appear in *LG 1871 Second Issue*.

[LAST DROPLETS]

Appeared as the conclusion to the second paragraph of the 'Preface Note' to *1891*, but did not appear in *LG 1892*.

SHIP AHOY!

First published in *1891*, and reprinted in *Complete Prose Works* (1892); it did not appear in *LG 1892*.

FOR QUEEN VICTORIA'S BIRTHDAY

First printed Philadelphia *Public Ledger*, 22 May 1890; it appeared in *1891* and was reprinted in *Complete Prose Works* (1892); it did not appear in *LG 1892*.

L OF G

First published in *1891* and reprinted in *Complete Prose Works* (1892); it did not appear in *LG 1892*.

AFTER THE ARGUMENT

First published in *1891* and reprinted in *Complete Prose Works* (1892); it did not appear in *LG 1892*.

FOR US TWO, READER DEAR

First published in *1891* and reprinted in *Complete Prose Works* (1892); it did not appear in *LG 1892*.

Appendix 3: Early Poems

OUR FUTURE LOT

First printed *Long Island Democrat*, 31 October 1838, and reprinted in *UPP*. It would seem to be Whitman's earliest known published poem. See *Time to Come*, p. 653.

YOUNG GRIMES

First printed *Long Island Democrat*, 1 January 1840. Thomas L. Brasher, editor of the New York University edition of *The Early Poems and the Fiction of Walt Whitman* (1963), notes that the poem is a direct imitation of Albert Gorton Greene's *Old Grimes*, a popular poem first published in 1822. Brasher reprints two stanzas for comparison; one of them reads:

He lived at peace with all mankind,
  In friendship he was true;
His coat had pocket-holes behind,
  His pantaloons were blue.

FAME'S VANITY

First printed *Long Island Democrat*, 23 October 1839, and reprinted in *UPP*.

MY DEPARTURE

First printed *Long Island Democrat*, 27 November 1839, and reprinted in *UPP*.

THE DEATH OF THE NATURE-LOVER

First printed *Brother Jonathan*, 11 March 1843, and reprinted in *UPP*. It is a later version of *My Departure*.

THE INCA'S DAUGHTER

First printed *Long Island Democrat*, 5 May 1840, and reprinted in *UPP*.

THE LOVE THAT IS HEREAFTER

First printed *Long Island Democrat*, 19 May 1840, and reprinted in *UPP*.

WE ALL SHALL REST AT LAST

First printed *Long Island Democrat*, 14 July 1840, and reprinted in *UPP*. Whitman revised this poem in 1841 when it appeared retitled as *Each Has His Grief* in New York *New World*, 20 November.

THE SPANISH LADY

First printed *Long Island Democrat*, 4 August 1840, and reprinted in *UPP*.

4 *A Spanish maiden lay* Inez de Castro (*c.* 1320–55) was murdered by King Alfonso after her marriage to a man who was not of the royal family.

THE END OF ALL

First printed *Long Island Democrat*, 22 September 1840, and reprinted in *UPP*. On 22 June 1841 Whitman revised and retitled this poem, calling it *The Winding-Up*.

13 *The statesman's* *UPP* notes that Daniel Webster was scheduled 'to deliver an address at Jamaica, Long Island, two days after the appearance of this poem'.

THE COLUMBIAN'S SONG

First printed *Long Island Democrat*, 27 October 1840, and reprinted in *UPP*.

THE PUNISHMENT OF PRIDE

First printed New York *New World*, 18 December 1841. The poem seems to have been composed in 1839 when Whitman was teaching at Little Bay Side, Long Island, and was referred to by one of Whitman's former students when interviewed by Traubel.

AMBITION

First printed *Brother Jonathan*, New York, 29 January 1842, and reprinted in *UPP*. The poem is an extensive revision of *Fame's Vanity*, reprinted on p. 635.

THE DEATH AND BURIAL OF MCDONALD CLARKE

First printed New York *Aurora*, 18 March 1842, and reprinted in J. J. Rubin and Charles H. Brown (eds), *Walt Whitman of the New York* Aurora (1950). The poem is an imitation of Charles Wolfe's *The Burial of Sir John Moore at Corunna*, first published in 1817. The final stanza can serve as an example:

Slowly and sadly we laid him down,
  From the field of his fame fresh and gory;
We carved not a line, and we raised not a stone,
  But we left him alone with his glory.

TIME TO COME

First printed New York *Aurora*, 9 April 1842, and reprinted in J. J. Rubin and Charles H. Brown (eds.), *Walt Whitman of the New York* Aurora (1950). The poem is a revision of *Our Future Lot*, reprinted on p. 633.

THE PLAY-GROUND

First printed *Brooklyn Daily Eagle*, 1 June 1846, and reprinted in *UPP*.

ODE

First printed *Brooklyn Daily Eagle*, 2 July 1846, and reprinted in *UPP*. Fort Greene was near Brooklyn. See *The Wallabout Martyrs*.

NEW YEAR'S DAY, 1848

First printed New York *Home Journal*, 30 March 1892, and reprinted in *UPP*.

865 NOTES FOR PP. 657–8

THE HOUSE OF FRIENDS

First printed New York *Tribune*, 14 June 1850; then *Collect* (1892), as *Wounded in the House of Friends*; and reprinted in *UPP*, the text being that reproduced here. Holloway notes that the editor of the *Advertizer*, Henry A. Lees, quoted parts of the poem to 'play Whitman off against the conservative Democrats. . . . He may have known the author's own reasons for the composition of this poem. Perhaps Whitman had in mind the turn of fortune which soon transferred the Freesoil paper which he had started (the *Freeman*) into a Hunker journal. But the poem itself seems to imply a somewhat broader view of the whole slavery situation' (p. 26).

RESURGEMUS

First printed New York *Daily Tribune*, 21 June 1850, and published untitled in *LG 1855*, the only poem in that volume to have been published previously. The *LG 1855* version is as follows:

Suddenly out of its stale and drowsy lair, the lair of slaves,
Like lightning Europe le'pt forth . . . . half startled at itself,
Its feet upon the ashes and the rags . . . . Its hands tight to the throats
    of kings.

O hope and faith! O aching close of lives! O many a sickened heart!
Turn back unto this day, and make yourselves afresh.

And you, paid to defile the People . . . . you liars mark:
Not for numberless agonies, murders, lusts,
For court thieving in its manifold mean forms,
Worming from his simplicity the poor man's wages;
10 For many a promise sworn by royal lips, and broken, and laughed at in
    the breaking,
Then in their power not for all these did the blows strike of personal
    revenge . . or the heads of the nobles fall;
The People scorned the ferocity of kings.

But the sweetness of mercy brewed bitter destruction, and the frightened
    rulers come back:
Each comes in state with his train . . . . hangman, priest and tax-gatherer
    . . . . soldier, lawyer, jailer and sycophant.

Yet behind all, lo, a Shape,
Vague as the night, draped interminably, head front and form in
    scarlet folds,
Whose face and eyes none may see,
Out of its robes only this . . . . the red robes, lifted by the arm,
One finger pointed high over the top, like the head of a snake appears.

20 Meanwhile corpses lie in new-made graves . . . . bloody corpses of
    young men:
The rope of the gibbet hangs heavily . . . . the bullets of princes are
    flying . . . . the creatures of power laugh aloud;
And all these things bear fruits . . . . and they are good.
Those corpses of young men,
Those martyrs that hang from the gibbets . . . those hearts pierced by
    the gray lead,
Cold and motionless as they seem . . . live elsewhere with unslaughter'd
    vitality.

They live in other young men, O kings,
They live in brothers, again ready to defy you:
They were purified by death . . . . they were taught and exalted.

Not a grave of the murdered for freedom but grows seed for freedom . . . .
    in its turn to bear seed,
30 Which the winds carry afar and re-sow, and the rains and the snows
    nourish.
Not a disembodied spirit can the weapons of tyrants let loose,
But it stalks invisibly over the earth.. whispering counseling cautioning.

Liberty let others despair of you . . . . I never despair of you.

Is the house shut? Is the master away?
Nevertheless be ready . . . . but not weary of watching,
He will soon return . . . . his messengers come anon.

title] Poem of the Dead Young Men of Europe, the 72d and 73d Years of
These States *LG 1856*; Europe, the 72d and 73d Years of These States
LG 1860.

1 *suddenly, out of . . . slaves* this line contains three typographical errors:
LG 1855 reads: 'Suddenly out of its stale and drowsy lair, the lair of slaves'.

THE MISSISSIPPI AT MIDNIGHT

First printed New Orleans *Crescent*, 6 March 1848, where Whitman was
employed as an editor; reprinted in R. M. Bucke (ed.), *Notes and Fragments*
(1899). In *Collect* (1892), the poem appeared revised as *Sailing the Mississippi
at Midnight*, with the text as follows:

Sailing the Mississippi at Midnight

Vast and starless, the pall of heaven
  Laps on the trailing pall below;
And forward, forward, in solemn darkness,
  As if to the sea of the lost we go.

Now drawn nigh the edge of the river,
  Weird-like creatures suddenly rise;
Shapes that fade, dissolving outlines
  Baffle the gazer's straining eyes.

Towering upward and bending forward,
  Wild and wide their arms are thrown,
Ready to pierce with forked fingers
  Him who touches their realm upon.

Tide of youth, thus thickly planted,
  While in the eddies onward you swim,
Thus on the shore stands a phantom army,
  Lining forever the channel's rim.

Steady, helmsman! you guide the immortal;
  Many a wreck is beneath you piled,
Many a brave yet unwary sailor
  Over these waters has been beguiled.

Nor is it the storm or the scowling midnight,
  Cold, or sickness, or fire's dismay –
Nor is it the reef, or treacherous quicksand,
  Will peril you most on your twisted way.

But when there comes a voluptuous languor,
  Soft the sunshine, silent the air,
Bewitching your craft with safety and sweetness,
  Then, young pilot of life, beware.

SONG FOR CERTAIN CONGRESSMEN

First printed New York *Evening Post*, 2 March 1850, signed *Paumanok*; it was
published in *Collect* (1892), as *Dough-Face Song*, where after the title Whitman
noted: 'Like Dough; soft; yielding to pressure; pale. – *Webster's Dictionary*'.
The poem protests the sentiment in Congress for an easy resolution to the
question of slavery.

56   *chase*] race *Collect* (*1892*).
71   *subterfuge*] compromise *Collect* (*1892*).

BLOOD-MONEY

First printed New York *Tribune Supplement*, 22 March 1850, and reprinted in
the *Evening Post*, 30 April. Whitman included the poem among his early poems
in *Collect* (1892), with some minor changes. The poem was occasioned by
Webster's speech in Congress on 7 March 1850 and his support of the Fugitive
Slave Law. The poem was signed *Paumanok*. Thomas L. Brasher tells us that
the date of the poem as it appears in *Collect*, 'April 1843', is wrong.

6 *a Son*] the like *Collect* (*1892*).
12 *Again*] And still *Collect* (*1892*).

PICTURES

First published in Emory Holloway's 'Whitman's Embryonic Verse', *Southwest Review*, X (July 1925), 28–40. The poem was written before 1855 in a notebook of some twenty-nine pages. Holloway edited an edition of the poem in *Pictures: An Unpublished Poem by Walt Whitman* (1928).

1   ¶ the paragraph symbol is Whitman's own.
4 *cicerone* a tourist's guide.
24 *elenchus* a syllogistic refutation; a disproof.
98 *Lascar* an East Indian native sailor.
117 *llanos* an extensive plain.

Appendix 4: Song of Myself

First published in *LG 1855*, untitled.

1334 the repetition of 'me' was corrected in *LG 1856*.
1336 punctuation was provided in *LG 1856*.

Appendix 5: Prefaces

LEAVES OF GRASS, 1855

This essay served without a title as the Preface to *LG 1855*.

EMERSON TO WHITMAN, AND WHITMAN'S LETTER TO EMERSON, 1856

Both Emerson's letter and Whitman's response were printed in *Leaves-Droppings*, an appendix to the second edition of *Leaves of Grass*, which also included selected reviews of *LG 1855*.

PREFACE, 1872

In addition to the Preface this 1872 volume contained seven poems, including the title poem *As a Strong Bird on Pinions Free* (*Thou Mother with Thy Equal Brood*).

PREFACE, 1876

This essay served as the Preface to volume 2, *Two Rivulets*, of the Centennial Edition of *Leaves of Grass*.

Appendix 6: A Sketch

This poem was first published in *The New World* on 10 December 1842, and was identified by Jerome Loving in 'A Newly Discovered Whitman Poem', *Walt Whitman Quarterly Review*, no. 11. Winter 1994.

Index of Titles

Index of First Lines

THE STORY OF PENGUIN CLASSICS

Before 1946 ... 'Classics' are mainly the domain of academics and students, without readable editions for everyone else. This all changes when a little-known classicist, E. V. Rieu, presents Penguin founder Allen Lane with the translation of Homer's *Odyssey* that he has been working on and reading to his wife Nelly in his spare time.

1946 *The Odyssey* becomes the first Penguin Classic published, and promptly sells three million copies. Suddenly, classic books are no longer for the privileged few.

1950s Rieu, now series editor, turns to professional writers for the best modern, readable translations, including Dorothy L. Sayers's *Inferno* and Robert Graves's *The Twelve Caesars*, which revives the salacious original.

1960s The Classics are given the distinctive black jackets that have remained a constant throughout the series's various looks. Rieu retires in 1964, hailing the Penguin Classics list as 'the greatest educative force of the 20th century'.

1970s A new generation of translators arrives to swell the Penguin Classics ranks, and the list grows to encompass more philosophy, religion, science, history and politics.

1980s The Penguin American Library joins the Classics stable, with titles such as *The Last of the Mohicans* safeguarded. Penguin Classics now offers the most comprehensive library of world literature available.

1990s The launch of Penguin Audiobooks brings the classics to a listening audience for the first time, and in 1999 the launch of the Penguin Classics website takes them online to a larger global readership than ever before.

The 21st Century Penguin Classics are rejacketed for the first time in nearly twenty years. This world famous series now consists of more than 1300 titles, making the widest range of the best books ever written available to millions – and constantly redefining the meaning of what makes a 'classic'.

The Odyssey continues ...

The best books ever written

PENGUIN 🐧 CLASSICS

SINCE 1946

Find out more at www.penguinclassics.com